CONTROLLING UNEMPLOYMENT INSURANCE COSTS

CONTROLLING UNEMPLOYMENT INSURANCE COSTS

The Employer's Comprehensive Guide to the UIC System

*By Gabe Donnadieu
and Robert A. Schuler*

Q

Quorum Books
Westport, Connecticut • London

HD
7096
U5
D57
1994

Notice: The information in this book is true and complete to the best of our knowledge. This book is intended only as an informative guide for those wishing to know more about unemployment insurance. It is not intended to replace, countermand, or conflict with the advice given to you by legal counsel. He or she knows your specific case history and the many other variables that challenge his or her judgment in handling your situation. The information in this book is general and is offered with no guarantees on the part of the authors or Quorum Books. The authors and publisher disclaim all liability in connection with use of or reliance on this book.

Library of Congress Cataloging-in-Publication Data

Donnadieu, Gabe.
   Controlling unemployment insurance costs : the employer's
comprehensive guide to the UIC system / by Gabe Donnadieu & Robert
A. Schuler.
        p.   cm.
   Includes bibliographical references and index.
   ISBN 0–89930–831–7 (alk. paper)
   1. Insurance, Unemployment–United States–States–Costs.
I. Schuler, Robert A. II. Title.
HD7096.U5D57 1994   93–42763
658.3'254–dc20

British Library Cataloguing in Publication Data is available.

Library of Congress Catalog Card Number: 93–42763
ISBN: 0–89930–831–7

First published in 1994

Quorum Books, 88 Post Road West, Westport, CT 06881
An imprint of Greenwood Publishing Group, Inc.

Printed in the United States of America

The paper used in this book complies with the
Permanent Paper Standard issued by the National
Information Standards Organization (Z39.48–1984).

10 9 8 7 6 5 4 3 2 1

Contents

Appendixes

Figures

Acknowledgments

We would like to take this opportunity to thank the many people who were instrumental in seeing this work to its completion.

Our deepest thanks to Mary Donnadieu, who suggested and encouraged the idea of the book. Without her creative insights and support, the book would not have been possible.

Special thanks to Judi Schuler, whose energy, editing, rewriting, and organizational skills made the book a coherent whole. Her stewardship and encouragement brought the project to fruition. Thanks, too, to Ian Schuler for his patience during this long process.

We would also like to express our thanks to Karel McGuire, who shared with us her many years of expertise as a local office UIC manager. Her knowledge and information helped us provide the reader with an accurate, unique inside look at the UIC system.

We are equally grateful to Administrative Laws Judges Cynthia Wicker and Carol Wilson of the Tucson, Arizona, Office of Appeals for their review of the UIC script. We are certain readers will find the script a valuable learning tool. Their critical remarks and encouragement are appreciated.

We also wish to thank Hugo Franco, Administrative Law Judge and Acting Chief of Arizona Appeals, for his portion of the manuscript review and critical remarks regarding the script material.

Finally, we would like to acknowledge the late Administrative Law Judge, Don Dunbar. During the writing of the book, we discovered he taught us a great deal about unemployment insurance. Although he was not an attorney, he was a tough, no-nonsense instructor who worked his way up through the UIC system the old-fashioned way. He valued honesty, hard work, respect for claimants and employers, and intellectual integrity. He instilled those values in those of us who worked with him. In many ways, this book is a tribute to him.

We are very pleased all those named were willing to share their time and knowledge with us on this project. As with all books, writing is only the visible part of the larger whole.

Introduction: The Unemployment Insurance Compensation Maze

Many employers represent themselves in unemployment insurance matters. This book is designed to guide you safely and successfully through the unemployment insurance maze. It contains the information and advice you need to prevent being victimized by the Unemployment Insurance Compensation (UIC) system.

This is not an academic examination or legal treatise about unemployment insurance, its agencies, or its programs. It is a practical, useful tool for employers in the competitive world of private and public business. The book takes you through the unemployment insurance system with a tough, uncompromising eye. If you are a large employer with professional representation, you can use the book to help you prepare information for your representative or attorney.

Information in this book will also make you a better witness if you are called to testify about unemployment insurance matters. If you are a professional unemployment insurance hearing representative or attorney, this information is also valuable because it helps you prepare and present your case with the most complete information available about the UIC system.

Skim through the book and read first any sections that interest you. As an employer, you know best what problems you face most often. Pay special attention to the sections that cover information on cases similar to those you have lost. Examine the strategies in these sections, then decide how they could have helped you at the time.

The book is organized so you can see how the system works and use it to your advantage. Use it as a handy reference source for preparing future cases. You have a powerful weapon in your hands—use it wisely and often.

WE'VE BOTH BEEN THERE

After working nearly twenty-five years with the unemployment insurance program, we have acquired special insights into the strengths and weaknesses of the program. We believe we know how each can be exploited.

Gabe Donnadieu

Author Gabe Donnadieu spent nearly fifteen years as a claims examiner, supervisor, investigator, and auditor for the Arizona unemployment insurance program. For two years, he was assigned to a special federal audit of the unemployment insurance program. During his tenure as a government employee, he was directly involved in issuing over 25,000 unemployment insurance decisions.

For the past eight years, Donnadieu has been on the other side of the fence. He has represented over 150 employers in more than 1,000 unemployment insurance hearings in Arizona, California, Utah, Nevada, Colorado, and New Mexico. Many of his clients are Fortune 500 companies; some are small or medium-size employers. He has obtained a favorable decision for clients in over 97 percent of his cases in an eight-year period.

Robert Schuler

Coauthor, attorney Robert Schuler, served as an administrative law judge for unemployment hearings for over four years. In this capacity, he made decisions at the initial appeal of a local office deputy's decision. His view of the system is unique because he had the opportunity to hear the reasons employers discharged employees and the reasons of employees for quitting their jobs. He observed firsthand the problems of employers who did not understand the regulations or correctly document their actions or evidence, which resulted in former employees collecting unemployment insurance.

Before accepting the position of administrative law judge, Schuler owned and operated a manufacturing firm and was in private practice. As an employer, he has experienced the same frustrations and problems you have in warning, disciplining, and discharging those who worked for him. His insights as a past employer are valuable.

Experience Counts

Our experience inside and outside the UIC has given us an insight into the system that few others have. As we analyzed hundreds of cases — what was done correctly or incorrectly, what should have been done differently, what was overlooked or ignored — a clear pattern of success began to emerge. Over the years, techniques and strategies have been tested; those that were ineffective were discarded. Strategies, tactics, and tricks of the trade that *did* work are included in this book. We have refined and honed successful techniques so the reader need not go through the same expensive, time-consuming process.

We wish we could sit down and pass along our hard-earned information, but that is impossible. So we did the next best thing — we pulled it all together into this book. We do not claim that our analysis is perfect or that our way of dealing with unemployment insurance is foolproof, but we know if you invest some time and effort in reading and applying these techniques and strategies, you will be pleased with the results.

Consider the alternative — wasting time, energy, and money trying to duplicate the information we have compiled and organized for you. It is easier to use the book. It gives you a significant advantage in limiting your unemployment insurance costs. We've done most of the work for you. We've seen most of the mistakes employers make. Even if you only give the book a quick once-over and pick out a few strategies to help you win *one* unemployment insurance case, you're money ahead. One lost unemployment case could cost you thousands of dollars.

After you read and digest these techniques and strategies, you'll see that they aren't difficult to master. When you win your own unemployment insurance cases, the time and money you've invested will be returned to you in the unemployment insurance taxes you save each year.

The Focus of the Book

This book is written for laypersons and for attorneys and paralegals who work with unemployment insurance. Certain compromises in legal language were necessary for the purposes of clarity and brevity. Where possible we have used language that is familiar to the general public rather than "legalese." Most employers attend unemployment insurance hearings without professional representation. They are capable of winning their own cases with some help in preparation and organization. This is the primary focus of the book.

We believe that attorneys and other legal professionals can also benefit from the information we provide. Although attorneys may be familiar with the law, they may be at a disadvantage when representing a client at a UIC hearing. For those lawyers who wish to use this book to help them gain insights into how the UIC system works, we believe the information we provide will supplement and complement their legal training and expertise.

We tell you what should happen in UIC cases and what often happens. We hesitate to say "always" because sometimes claims examiners and judges make mistakes. Sometimes they don't listen to the facts before them. Sometimes they misinterpret, misunderstand, or misapply the law. Occasionally they are misled by their own prejudices or opinions on how a case should be decided.

No amount of preparation or advice can prevent this from occurring. Fortunately, most claims examiners and administrative law judges are well trained and usually do a reasonable job of weighing facts and deciding cases. Irrational, "off-the-wall" decisions are rare, but they do occur. Our strategy and intention is to give you the tools you need to minimize the risk of incorrect UIC determinations.

1 ———————————————

Understanding the
Unemployment Insurance
Compensation Program

As an employer, the law requires you to pay into your state's Unemployment Insurance Compensation (UIC) program. Although you have no control over the fact you have to pay into the program, you *do* have a great deal of control over the amount you are required to pay. By controlling the charges to your account, you can control how much you must pay each calendar quarter. All it takes is knowledge of how the game is played and the strategies and techniques needed to put your knowledge to good use. This book provides all the information you'll need.

Many employers are overwhelmed by the unemployment insurance system; they feel powerless to do anything about it. If you're like many, you may believe you're going to lose the game. Consider the following questions:

- Have you discharged employees who constantly reported late to work or who didn't come to work and didn't bother to call in?
- Have you discharged employees who stole from your business or cost you time and money because of negligence, rudeness, incompetence, or loafing?
- Have you discharged employees for lying or using alcohol or drugs at work?
- Have you discharged employees who refused to follow simple instructions?
- Have you discharged employees who were insubordinate or who harassed other employees?

- Have you warned employees they were going to be discharged if they didn't shape up, only to have them ignore your warnings?
- Have you had employees quit their jobs then claim you discharged them?
- Have you called laid-off employees back to work, only to have them refuse so they could continue to collect unemployment insurance at your expense?
- Have you ever felt the unemployment insurance system was treating you like a criminal?
- Have you encountered rude, officious, unreasonable unemployment insurance employees who refused to listen to your side of the story but accepted the claimant's statements as gospel?
- Have you felt you were treated unfairly and were powerless to do anything about it?

If you answered yes to any of these questions, you're not alone. Nearly all employers must deal with the UIC system sooner or later. Many find the encounter unpleasant and frustrating. Some employers believe they are treated unfairly by a system that favors claimants. Many employers believe they must accept their role as victim of a government program beyond their control. Take heart—the unemployment insurance monster *can* be tamed and mastered!

DEALING WITH THE SYSTEM

Warning an employee about his or her behavior or performance at work is an unpleasant task. Discharging someone is a serious, painful, often undesirable course of action; it is also time consuming and expensive. No employer wants to lose the investment a business makes in its work force. Discharging an employee means you have to endure the difficulty of the discharge process, then go through the cost and effort of hiring a replacement.

Once an employee has been discharged, laid off, or quit a job, he or she is likely to become a claimant for unemployment insurance. When dealing with the UIC claims system, you may feel uncomfortable explaining your reason for letting someone go. In a dispute over a claim, which is frequently the case, you may be placed on the defensive. It often appears that the unemployment insurance system is on the claimant's side from the beginning. The process may even seem confrontational and adversarial—and the stakes are high. If you win, your UIC tax account is not charged. If you lose, there is almost always an increase in UIC tax charges.

If you've had to deal with your local UIC program, this book is for you. It is for any employer who believes unemployment insurance taxes are beyond his or her control and the system is too confusing, too complex, and too big to deal with. It is for all employers whose experience has led them to conclude they cannot win unemployment insurance cases.

Giving in to the UIC system is *not* a normal cost of doing business — neither is having undeserving former employees collect UI benefits you pay for. Dealing with the unemployment insurance system is complex, but it can be done. If you do it correctly, with techniques we provide you, it will take no more time than absolutely necessary, and that time will be well spent. You *can* control unemployment insurance tax costs.

This book is not designed to give unscrupulous or dishonest employers the tools to abuse or cheat the UIC system. It is written for honest, hard-working employers who want to make a sincere effort to understand unemployment insurance and who are willing to take charge of this aspect of their business. To accomplish this, you must be willing to invest your time and effort. As an employer, you can use a powerful tool — knowledge — to help you win. If you follow the instructions in this book, you'll acquire the knowledge you need to master unemployment insurance. Be confident and comfortable in your contacts with the program. Stop wasting energy as you learn how the unemployment insurance system works. Your new strategies will quickly begin to pay off.

A BRIEF HISTORY OF UNEMPLOYMENT INSURANCE

The unemployment insurance program was part of the 1933 Wagner-Pyser Social Security Act. Like most Depression-era legislation, it was designed to stabilize a faltering economy and restore political and economic confidence during a crisis. Although unemployment insurance became law at the federal level, the program is designed to be administered by the states. The UIC program is a payroll tax supported by public- and private-sector employers. Modeled on private insurance programs, trust funds were created to pay benefits to workers who were unemployed through no fault of their own. (In some states, an employer can elect to use a reimbursement plan. For further information, see page 12.) In its ideal form, unemployment insurance was to be self-supporting and impartially and competently administered through a series of state programs.

Although the UIC program is federally mandated, each state or jurisdiction makes its own rules and establishes levels of benefits as legislatures perceive the needs of their citizens. Employers can reduce their payrolls by laying people off and supporting them with unemployment insurance benefits to ensure a convenient, willing reserve labor force.

The UIC program provides a pool, or trust fund, of tax money for workers unemployed through no fault of their own. The fund is supported by imposing a payroll tax on employers. (Three states — Alaska, New Jersey and Pennsylvania — collect a small contribution from employees.) Benefits to eligible workers are withdrawn from trust funds, as needed. Employers pay into the program based on a variable percentage tax on their payroll. This percentage increases as former employees or claimants are paid benefits by the program. It is reduced if there are no claims or few claims against an employer's account. The program is not voluntary. Each state decides who pays into the trust funds, how much, the manner of payments, and when an employer will pay.

To reform and restore balance and reasonableness to the program as it is today would be a monumental task. However, it is possible for you to understand *how* the system works and how employers as a group can protect themselves from abuses of the system.

THE MODERN UIC SYSTEM

Today's UIC system is organized into 53 jurisdictions—the 50 states plus Puerto Rico, the American Virgin Islands, and the District of Columbia. Puerto Rico is an independent commonwealth. The American Virgin Islands is a territory of the United States. The District of Columbia is a special federal district. In the interests of brevity and clarity, when we use the word "state" in this book, it includes these special jurisdictions.

Each state is free to pass its own laws, develop its own administrative rules, select and apply its own precedent cases, and provide for its own appeals process. In general, all operating procedures are subject to approval by the U.S. Department of Labor. However, the federal government is not inclined to interfere with the autonomous authority of the states and other jurisdictions unless absolutely necessary. The state in which you do business is the principal rule-making and enforcement agency for the purposes of this book.

Some states give a great deal of weight to precedent decisions; others do not. All states recognize the binding nature of court decisions within their own boundaries and of UIC cases decided by the federal court system.

Although each state has developed different programs, similarities are much greater than differences. Nevertheless, the rules used in Maine or New Hampshire may be different from those used in California, Illinois, Alabama, or Texas.

At the end of many chapters is a list of questions for you to ask UIC agency officials in your state. This is the most efficient way to determine which rules apply to your program.

UIC ORGANIZATION

Unemployment insurance programs are organized like most large, private insurance companies. At the first administrative level are the local offices, where the claims process begins. Claims are taken and initial decisions are made as to who is eligible to receive benefits.

Local offices may be permanent or itinerant, depending on population. Each office has a manager and may have supervisors, claims takers, and claims examiners, depending on its size. Initial charges to your business tax account are based on first-level local office decisions. Determinations by local office personnel inform you when your account is subject to UIC tax charges. Normally actual charges are computed later, based on the experience rating of your account. (*Experience rating* is discussed on page 13.) An employer usually receives a telephone call and written contact from the local office following a claim's filing if the claim involves an issue of separation from work.

Like many government bureaucracies, the UIC system has various levels of management (see Figure 1.1). For administrative purposes, most local offices report to a second-level manager (titles may vary) at a regional or area level. People at this level listen to complaints regarding treatment received from those at the local office. A manager at this level usually has direct-line authority over a number of local offices and responds to written or verbal complaints, often with satisfactory results.

Managers at this regional level do not usually interfere in the claims and quasi-legal process of determining employer charges. They deal with specific complaints about rudeness, unfair treatment, or negligence encountered at local offices. They can place pressure on a local office to act professionally.

Developing a strong relationship with the person in charge at the regional or area level can save you time because you may receive claim notices from more than one local office. Regional managers are less likely to cover up mistakes or inappropriate treatment of employers, which is often encountered at the local office level. They are more responsive to an employer. Ask for the name and telephone number of the person at this management level. Don't hesitate to contact him or her as often as necessary.

All UIC programs have a state- or territorial-level office with support staff, technical staff, management specialists, and others the public rarely sees. In some cases, these offices are staffed by career employees under a civil-service system. The head of this office is a UIC administrator who oversees all state offices. In some states, the administrator is a career or civil-service employee; in others, he or she is a political appointee. It is important to find out who is in charge at this level in your area. These people are public servants; you pay their salaries. You're entitled to their time and assistance when you need it or want it.

All program administrators have direct-line authority that reaches from their offices down through the levels of management to the local offices. Enlisting their help in solving a problem with a local office or

Figure 1.1
UIC Organization Chart

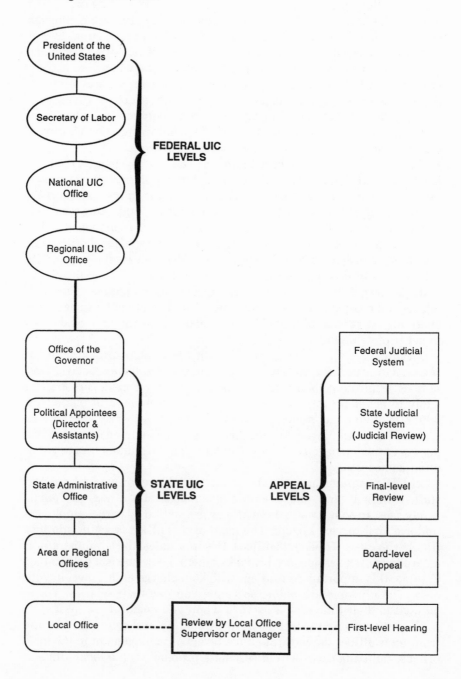

any other level of administration in the UIC program can be highly effective.

At the highest state level are political appointees and the governor. Political appointees may be called *directors* or *commissioners*, or they may have other titles, depending on the state. As political employees, they are temporary, but they are usually highly responsive to complaints that reach their level. Contact people at this management level when other levels of contact prove fruitless. In many states, state-level administrators are accountable to a commission or bureau run by political appointees who are appointed by the governor (a federal commission in Washington, D.C.).

At the end of this chapter we provide tips on how to make an effective complaint to any level of the UIC management program. Reading and using these techniques ensures the results you're looking for.

THE FEDERAL ARM OF THE SYSTEM

Although each of the 53 jurisdictions is autonomous, there is a federal bureaucracy. In practical terms, it's important to be aware that this federal bureaucracy exists only so you will have some idea of what you're up against.

The federal unemployment insurance system begins at the regional level (see Figure 1.1). There are nine regional offices in the United States providing administrative support for the states and territories within their areas of responsibility. These offices have no real authority over the offices within their regions. Their primary responsibilities are to advise on technical matters, such as compliance with federal regulations. They sometimes serve as research agencies for unemployment insurance offices in their regions.

It is a good idea to have the name and address of the regional administrator responsible for your state. If you want to make suggestions to him or her regarding changes in the UIC program or address complaints to this office, you'll have the information handy. These regional offices have little contact with the general public; any specific complaints you send them regarding the UIC system will be sent back to the state in which you do business. You will probably receive a polite letter from the regional administrator's office but little else. Complaints made to this management level may influence personnel at state-level offices to give your complaint or suggestion higher priority and greater credibility.

The nine federal regional offices report to the U.S. Department of Labor, through the undersecretaries and deputy secretaries of labor to the secretary of labor. The last office in the chain of command is the president of the United States.

The federal chain of command doesn't have much practical value for you as an employer. Communication at this level is far removed from the real world. If you write a letter to the president or the secretary of labor complaining about unfair, rude treatment from your local office, the complaint will be sent down the chain of command for appropriate response.

In our experience, complaints to higher federal levels are acknowledged; they may put some pressure on unemployment insurance offices to respond. Lower-level offices are aware that you know who their bosses are and that you'll take your complaints to higher levels. If you do send a complaint to this level, don't expect a quick response, and don't be too surprised if you encounter bureaucratic buck passing.

THE APPEAL PROCESS

Separate from, but parallel to, the UIC administrative structure is the UIC appeals organization (see Figure 1.1). Understanding the appeals organization and how the appeal process works is critical to containing your UIC tax costs. The appeals unit of the UIC program has the power to review and change local office decisions. It has the authority to charge employer accounts and pay or deny UIC benefits to claimants. Decisions are made by hearing officers, referees, examiners, or administrative law judges (ALJs). The titles may vary, but many states now use the ALJ title.

Appeals units hold hearings during which employers and claimants are questioned. Sworn testimony is used to affirm, reverse, modify, set aside, or remand local office decisions.

Following a determination or decision of a local office, either party (employer or claimant) has a legal right to appeal that initial finding. In some states, the initial local office determination of charges to the employer and eligibility of the claimant go through a formal review. The local office may then reconsider or change the determination. If no changes are made and a written request for appeal has been made, the determination is sent to the next level.

Many states hold only one appeal hearing following a local office decision. New testimony is usually not accepted after evidence is taken at this first hearing level. Once this hearing is closed, testimony is used to make higher-level decisions. All states review first-level appeals decisions and make additional, higher-level decisions. You must get all your evidence on the record before the first-level appeals hearing is closed— you may not get another opportunity.

Once a first-level appeal decision is made, either the claimant or the employer can file additional written appeals. In most states, higher-level boards have the power to uphold or change decisions. Once appeals to all UIC levels have been exhausted, they can be filed in the state and federal court systems, ultimately reaching the Supreme Court of the United States.

The right of an employer or claimant to appeal an unemployment insurance decision is fundamental to the UIC system. Ways to master the appeals process with simple, powerful techniques is described in the chapters that follow.

THE UIC SYSTEM – OUT OF BALANCE

Many employers believe the UIC system favors claimants; they are not far from wrong. While the laws and rules that govern the UIC system are essentially fair, application of these laws and rules is not. Below is a list of some of the major reasons the UIC system is out of balance.

- UIC decisions are made by human beings; humans aren't perfect.
- Claims examiners and ALJs are employees. They have a natural tendency to identify with claimants.
- Many UIC personnel have dealt with employers who are demanding, obnoxious, and unpleasant. They may take out their frustrations on you.
- At the local office level, UIC employees sit face to face with the claimant. The employer is only a voice on the telephone or a written response to a UIC inquiry. There is a strong tendency for UIC personnel to empathize with the actual person rather than someone they may never meet.
- Many UIC employees at the local office level and the appeals level believe employers are exploitive. We have encountered some ALJs who are so blindly prejudicial they find any way they can to rule in the claimant's favor and charge employer tax accounts.
- Many UIC employees have been poorly trained and are inadequately supervised or monitored.
- Some first-level UIC personnel believe employers have unlimited resources and should be forced to pay claimants who "need" UIC benefits. Many UIC employees seem to make decisions on what they *believe* should happen rather than on the facts and the law. The result has been skyrocketing UIC tax costs and payments to claimants who are not entitled to them.
- UIC employees may be overworked and make mistakes. There is a strong belief in bureaucracies that someone "down the line" will catch a mistake and correct it. The UIC program is a typical bureaucracy in this respect. Expecting UIC employees to correct and admit their errors is unrealistic. When it comes to protecting your tax account from unfair charges, you must assume the responsibility for catching and correcting errors.
- The UIC program is a revolving door, especially at the appeals level, where many employees are attorneys. Few lawyers spend their careers in the UIC

program. They usually consider their job a stepping stone to positions that pay better or are more prestigious. At the local office level, many states hire almost anyone willing to do the job, and there is constant turnover. Employees often learn their jobs only to be promoted or transferred. The result is a government program with a weak employee base.

Don't expect claimants or UIC employees to change. The only one who can change is you, the employer. Use the information and strategies in this book to learn effective ways of approaching UIC problems. Learn how to limit and reduce your UIC tax obligations legally and legitimately. If you don't look out for yourself, the system will remain out of balance, and you will never contain your UIC tax rates and charges. The case study below illustrates how an employer can believe he has all the data he needs to win a case and still lose.

A Case in Point

The Roadrunner Restaurant has a problem with one of its cooks, Bud. The manager suspects Bud has been selling and using marijuana and other drugs while at work. Although Bud has never been caught red-handed, both his behavior and rumors from other employees confirm the manager's suspicions. Several weeks before the separation from work, the manager and regional vice president call a meeting to talk to employees about drug use. During the meeting, they emphasize how serious they are about not having drugs or drug users on the premises. The meeting includes a 30-minute talk by two police officers who are drug-enforcement specialists.

The next day, Marlene, a waitress, approaches the manager. She complains Bud has been smoking marijuana in his car in the employee's parking lot. She says he tried to get her to buy "half a key" (kilo) from him. The manager consults with his regional and national corporate offices; the company decides to call in the police.

The Roadrunner Restaurant agrees to let the narcotics division place a surveillance team in the employee parking lot. On the third night of the stake out, two narcotics detectives see Bud come out the rear door of the restaurant and get into his car. They watch him light up what appears to be a homemade cigarette. After a few minutes, the narcotics officers approach the car and ask Bud to roll the window down. Bud obeys, and the officers smell marijuana smoke. The officers place Bud under arrest, search the car and find 3 kilos of marijuana. Bud admits to the officers he is a small-time dealer, and the marijuana is his. Other police officers arrive and take Bud away in handcuffs.

The police prevent the manager and assistant manager from involvement in the actual arrest. They stay in the restaurant during Bud's arrest and the search of his car. When the manager and assistant manager come out of the restaurant, Bud is being taken away in a police car. The police tell them the details of the arrest. Based on what the manager has been told by the police and what he has seen, he fires Bud that night. The police tell him and the assistant manager they will send the employer a written report of the incident within a week.

A few days later the investigation report from the police arrives. With the police report and what he knows, the manager believes everything is under control. Unfortunately, he is wrong. When Bud files his claim for unemployment insurance, his criminal case is still pending.

The restaurant manager gets a call from the UIC office. He tells his story to the claims examiner and expresses surprise that Bud is not in jail. The claims examiner asks for a copy of the police report. The manager sends the claims examiner a copy of the report, assuming he will win the case. To the claims examiner, Bud denies he made any admissions to the police. He denies the marijuana was his. He further denies being a dealer, smoking marijuana, and trying to sell marijuana to Marlene. He denies the narcotics found in the car were his.

The manager is certain the evidence is on his side. He is surprised and outraged when he receives the UIC decision stating that Bud is eligible for unemployment insurance and that the restaurant's UIC tax account will be charged for Bud's benefits.

The restaurant files an appeal to the claims examiner's determination. The case is reviewed by the local officer manager and sent to the appeals section. The employer contacts the police department and the prosecutor's office. Neither can attend the hearing because of pending criminal charges. The employer calls and asks the appeals office to subpoena the police officers, but his request is denied. The employer asks for a postponement, but they deny his request again. The manager, assistant manager, and Marlene appear for the employer at the appeal hearing. The employer believes the police report and Marlene's testimony will be enough to win the case.

At the hearing, the employer realizes he and the assistant manager really can't testify to much more than hearsay. They did not *see* Bud arrested. They did not *see* the marijuana. They did not *hear* Bud's admissions to the police. They did not smell marijuana smoke or see Bud smoking any illegal substance. Marlene can only testify that several days before the discharge Bud tried to sell her some marijuana. Her testimony is not specific to the night of the discharge, and Bud adamantly denies Marlene's testimony.

Under oath, Bud testifies he is innocent. The ALJ has no choice. She affirms the claims examiner's decision ruling for Bud, against the employer. Confused, bitter, and totally frustrated with the UIC system, the employer gives up and accepts the liability for the claim.

• Did the employer have a good case?
• Should the company be required to pay Bud's UIC benefits?
• Was Bud discharged for misconduct?
• Could the employer have won the case and protected the UIC tax account from charges?

The answer to all these questions is yes. Most employers lose UIC cases because they don't know the rules of the game, not because they have poor cases. By using the strategies and tips we provide, you will have the tools to avoid the mistakes made by the employer in this case. If you read and use the tips and strategies we give you, a case like this can be quickly and easily handled. You can do it—once you have the correct information and a good idea of how to use this information to get the desired results.

This story is a classic example of why employers feel animosity toward the unemployment insurance program. The employer *should* have won. They had an excellent case. Why did they lose? Because they did not know how to deal with the UIC system. They didn't know the rules of the game. They didn't understand how the process worked and how to use the system. We don't want you to be in that situation. We want you to be prepared and informed about the UIC decision-making process. We want you to win your UIC cases.

REIMBURSEMENT AND INSURED UIC ACCOUNTS

Important to your complete understanding of the UIC system is the way you are charged for unemployment benefits paid to former employees. Most states allow employers to pay taxes through an *insured* (tax-rated) account or a *reimbursement* account. An insured UIC account is similar to private home or auto insurance—you pay in advance, and money is placed into a trust fund for future use. A reimbursement account is a form of self-insurance. There is no experience rating or sliding index to determine UIC rates or UIC tax charges. Employers must reimburse (repay) the state for benefits paid to claimants on a dollar-for-dollar basis.

In most states, reimbursement accounts are available only to large nonprofit institutions, such as public universities; school districts; and local, state, or federal government agencies. In some cases, those covered by reimbursement accounts may opt for insured accounts. Most choose the reimbursement system because it is more cost effective.

The Experience Rating

If you select the insured account, the amount you pay is based on a percentage of your payroll, often called an *experience rating* (it may have a different name in your state). When charges are made against your UIC tax account, the rating increases. If you have no charges during a certain period of time (usually a calendar year), the rate is reduced. This "sliding scale" tax rate determines how much you pay in UIC taxes. Keeping this tax rate at a minimum is the key to containing UIC costs.

Types of Experience Ratings

There are four types of experience ratings currently in use for determining UIC tax charges. The experience-rating provisions of state tax laws vary greatly from state to state. In spite of these differences, all rating systems have certain common characteristics. They all take into account the relative experience of individual employers with tax charges and benefits paid to their former employees. All four rating plans are designed to ensure that a state's UIC trust fund remains solvent and able to cover adequately all payments of benefits.

Reserve-Ratio Formula. The most commonly used rating is called the *reserve-ratio formula*. This system—essentially cost accounting—is used in thirty-three states. Employers report their total payroll, the amount of UIC taxes paid, and the benefits paid to former employees (claimants). The actual UIC benefits are deducted from the contributions (taxes), and the resulting balance is divided into the payroll. States that currently use this system are Arizona, Arkansas, California, Colorado, District of Columbia, Georgia, Hawaii, Idaho, Indiana, Kansas, Kentucky, Louisiana, Maine, Massachusetts, Missouri, Montana, Nebraska, Nevada, New Hampshire, New Jersey, New Mexico, New York, North Carolina, North Dakota, Ohio, Puerto Rico, Rhode Island, South Carolina, South Dakota, Tennessee, Virgin Islands, West Virginia, and Wisconsin.

Benefit-Ratio Formula. This is the second most commonly used form of financing UIC benefits program. This formula uses benefits paid to claimants to determine the employer's experience rating. However, it excludes employer taxes or contributions from the formula. States that currently use this formula are Alabama, Connecticut, Florida, Illinois, Iowa, Maryland, Michigan, Minnesota, Mississippi, Oregon, Pennsylvania, Texas, Utah, Vermont, Virginia, Washington, and Wyoming.

Benefit-Wage Ratio Formula. This formula is currently used by Delaware and Oklahoma. This experience-rating formula does not take into account benefits paid to workers of individual employers, nor does it account for the length of time claimants collect benefits.

The plan fixes the employer tax rate on the basis of work separations that result in payment of UIC benefits to claimants. Only one separation per claimant is charged to any one employer in a given benefit year. The tax charge is made *after* the employee is paid benefits. In addition, this plan computes a statewide tax rate that is used to help determine the tax rate for individual employers.

Payroll-Variation Plan. This plan is currently used only in Alaska. The plan does not measure benefits to claimants or length of unemployment. It does examine relative decreases or increases in the employer's payroll each quarter. If payrolls remain fairly constant, the experience rating for that employer remains constant or decreases.

Should You Use the Reimbursement Plan or the Insured Payment Plan?

Check with your state UIC program to learn whether you qualify for the reimbursement program. Have them explain the reimbursement plan and the insured-payment plan to you. Find out which program(s) you qualify for and which will work best for your type of business.

Advantages and Disadvantages of an Insured Account

The greatest advantage of an insured (tax-rated) account is that you remain "non-charged" for the entire claim if you are exempted from UIC charges. Another advantage is the experience rating has a minimum and a maximum limit. New employers begin in a middle range— about 3 to 4 percent of their total payroll. Some states maintain this starting rate for up to two years. After that time, the rate may go up or down, depending on UIC benefit payments charged to the account.

The major disadvantage of the insured account is that you must pay into the UIC trust fund, even if no claims are filed against you. This is like paying home or car insurance premiums, even though your house never burns down or you never have an automobile accident. No matter how low your experience rating drops, it never reaches zero.

Advantages and Disadvantages of a Reimbursement Account

The principal advantage of a reimbursement account is that you pay no UIC taxes if no claims are filed against you or if a claim is filed against you and the claimant is denied benefits. However, if the claimant requalifies for benefits by returning to work then files a subsequent claim for which he or she is paid, you *will* have a UIC tax liability. Wages you reported during the claimant's base period are used to pay the claimant if he or she is eligible for future claims.

If the claimant draws benefits for *any* reason, you must reimburse the UIC trust fund in the amount of those payments. You do not have a sliding experience rating to protect you. You must repay the trust fund dollar for dollar.

Often the initial savings of a reimbursement account are offset by later charges. You have no control over the future eligibility of a claimant after you have won your UIC case. Even in cases where the claimant quits his or her job for what may be "compelling personal reasons" (for example, on medical advice where other work is not available), you are not free from charges. You will have to repay the trust fund for any benefits paid to the claimant.

Some employers prefer the reimbursement system because it requires no advance payments that may never be used. They would rather repay the trust fund only when they lose a UIC case. The reimbursement system offers less tax liability protection than an insured or tax-rated account.

Changing from Reimbursement to Insured Coverage

Many states allow an employer to change the type of UIC coverage once every 3 years. If the law in your state requires you to have UIC coverage for your employees, you must choose the insured or reimbursement plan (if you're eligible). Also check with your state to see how often they allow plan changes for UIC coverage.

Exceptions to Lowering UIC Tax Charges

There are always exceptions to government rules and regulations. Sometimes tax rates increase when a state's trust fund reserves run low. To increase the amount of money in the trust fund, states may increase the tax rates for *all* employers, regardless of how good their experience rating is.

Employers may be penalized even when no UIC benefits have been charged to their account for years. We suggest you lobby your state legislature for laws that pass increases on to the employer with high tax rates rather than increasing all employer UIC taxes.

TIPS ABOUT COMPLAINTS AND PERSISTENCE

You are a tax-paying employer, and you have every right to insist on the best the government can provide. You are entitled to competent information and courteous service from government employees. If you find it necessary to make requests or complaints about the UIC system, follow these guidelines.

- Don't rant and rave over the telephone. Wait until you are calm before making your call. Angry or irrational remarks reduce your credibility and may result in dismissal of your complaint, no matter how valid it is.
- Be precise with your complaint. Jot down the points you want to cover *before* you call. Stick to the relevant points of your complaint.
- Be prepared to talk to more than one person. It's unlikely the secretary or receptionist who answers the telephone can help you with your complaint.
- Be patient. UIC offices are busy places; they'll call you back. A supervisor or manager will probably handle your complaint; it takes time to research a matter.
- Be persistent. Don't let your complaint be ignored.

QUESTIONS TO ASK IN YOUR STATE

Although most administrative rules and laws are similar, there are some significant differences in the UIC organization and its fifty-three jurisdictions. Many of your questions can be answered by making a few phone calls. When you obtain information by telephone, write it down, along with the name and title of the person who gives you the information. Include the date, time, and telephone number. Make sure you speak with someone who has the knowledge and authority to give you the information you seek.

Begin with the local office in your area. Obtain the name, mailing address, and telephone number of the local office managers in your area and for all levels of supervision above the local office. Your local office should be able to provide this information.

Written pamphlets, booklets, and bulletins can be very helpful. Ask personnel at the local office if they have any written material for employers and claimants; knowing the information your former employee has received may prove helpful later. Written material may come from other places than the local claims office. If this is the case, ask the local office how you can get the information. Get the local UIC office staff to work for you. As a taxpayer, you are entitled to this service, but you must be persistent. A few well-placed telephone calls usually get you what you want. If you are not satisfied with the response, call the next person in the chain of command with your request. Make a complaint if you think it's appropriate. Polite, informed, forceful complaints almost always produce the desired results.

Here are some questions for you to ask UIC personnel in the state, commonwealth, or territory where you do business.

1. What is the UIC chain of command in my state? (Be sure you note the names, addresses, and telephone numbers for people at each level.)

2. Does the state use wage reporting (quarterly tax collection) or wage demand (a bill after the fact) for UIC tax collection?

3. Does the state offer reimbursement accounts (dollar-for-dollar replacement of UIC benefits paid from the trust fund)?

4. Can I elect to use reimbursement or other options to pay UIC taxes other than the one current in use? How do I make the change? How often can I make the change?

5. Can the local UIC program provide copies of all written materials for employers and claimants?

6. Are all base-period and last employers notified if a claim is filed against them?

7. What are the minimum and maximum rates for insured accounts?

8. Can sole-proprietor, partnership, and corporate employers represent themselves at UIC appeals hearings or must they have attorneys?

9. Does my state use UIC regulations, precedent cases, or state law in making claims decisions? Which carries the most weight in my state?

10. How many claims decision levels does my state have? What are they?

2

Common Myths and Misconceptions about Unemployment Insurance

There are probably more myths, misconceptions, and misinformation about unemployment insurance compensation than there are about any other state or federal program. Information in this chapter is intended to help you forget many myths you have heard and allow you to re-evaluate the misconceptions you have formed. Many misconceptions have been circulating for so long that they have become part of the lore and developed a false, but powerful, validity. We have also included some ideas that employers believe are wrong, and we explain why they are true.

Let's expose some of these fairy tales. Below are more than thirty of the most common myths and misconceptions about unemployment insurance compensation.

Myth 1: If someone quits, he or she cannot collect unemployment insurance

False. Not all quits disqualify a claimant from receiving UIC compensation. Many states allow an employee to collect unemployment insurance benefits if he or she quits for good cause or compelling personal reasons. Compelling reasons, which might be personal or medical, are defined in each state's UIC laws or regulations. Employers are usually not charged for benefits paid in this situation.

Some employees quit for good cause or reasons attributable to the employer, such as failure to pay wages; harassment; or discrimination based on age, race, or sex. These instances are uncommon and difficult for the claimant to prove. They occur when a claimant can show he or she was treated unfairly by the employer *and* attempted to adjust the grievance. This type of quit results in charges to your account. A more detailed description of the different types of quits is included in the following chapters.

Myth 2: If someone is fired, he or she can always collect unemployment insurance

False. If an employee is fired for work-related misconduct and the employer can prove it, the claimant will be denied benefits. Your account will not be charged. This is one way you can begin containing unemployment insurance costs.

Not all employees who are discharged are fired for misconduct. Sometimes employees do their best but are simply unable to meet your standards. They make too many costly errors or can't keep up with the pace. You reach the point where you must let them go. In these cases, there is no allegation of misconduct. The best advice we can give you is minimize your tax charges by discharging these employees as soon as possible.

Myth 3: If someone is laid off, he or she can collect unemployment insurance

This is generally true. Employers lay off employees to reduce payroll obligations. However, in some states if an employee quits before the effective date of the layoff, it may be considered a quit without good cause.

If an employee is laid off, he or she is eligible to collect benefits if all other legal standards of eligibility are met. (Legal standards of eligibility are discussed in more depth in Chapter 4.)

Myth 4: Unemployment insurance is for people who need it

False. One of the fundamental principles of UIC is that claimants must meet the legal standards of eligibility to collect benefits. Need is *not* a criterion for eligibility in any of the fifty-three jurisdictions. Some states pay claimants an extra dependent's allowance, but the claimant must first meet all other legal criteria to be eligible.

Myth 5: Employees have a right to unemployment insurance compensation because they paid into the program

False. Unemployment insurance compensation is a payroll tax imposed on employers; employers pay for the UIC program. In a very few states, claimants are required to make a nominal nonvoluntary contribution. Even in these rare situations, the program is primarily supported by employers.

Employees have no "right" to unemployment insurance compensation. If they are able to satisfy the legal requirements for benefits, they are potentially eligible. If they don't meet the legal requirements, they are not eligible.

Myth 6: Because employers pay for unemployment insurance compensation, the government should believe an employer's word over a claimant's

False. There is no legal or procedural advantage to being an employer in this system. Your word as an employer carries no more weight than a claimant's word. The *quality* of your testimony and evidence determines who is more credible and who will prevail in an unemployment insurance case. One major focus of this book is helping you maximize your credibility. Another is providing techniques so you can raise the quality of your case.

Do not expect special treatment or consideration from the unemployment insurance program because you are an employer. If you use the strategies that we give you, your case will be so compelling and so strong that the claims examiner or administrative law judge should rule in your favor. This is a legitimate advantage you will be able to use effectively.

Myth 7: If an employee is laid off then called back to work, he or she must return to work or lose unemployment insurance benefits

Generally this is true. Unemployment insurance is intended to provide workers with the financial means to seek other work. Benefits were designed to provide a stable work force for employers who have temporarily laid workers off with the expectation of recalling them within a reasonable period of time.

Some workers refuse to return to the employer who laid them off. If they refuse to return to work, they will be denied further benefits unless they show a good reason for not returning. A definite offer of better work might be the best reason for refusing to return to a former employer.

Other personal reasons, such as lack of transportation or domestic responsibilities (child care, illness in the family), might be good reasons for not returning to work, but the existence of such problems usually means a claimant is not attached to the active labor force. These claimants are usually denied continued benefits because of these problems.

Report any refusal to return to work to your local UIC office. Do this in writing. Include the reason for refusal, if you know it.

Myth 8: If you cheat on your unemployment insurance, you'll never get caught

False. The UIC system is becoming more sophisticated at catching cheaters. Claimants and employers should be aware that UIC fraud is usually a felony. Claimant scams, such as not reporting wages while collecting UIC benefits, can be easily caught by computerized cross checking. (Quarterly employer reports are cross run against previously paid claim weeks.)

Like the federal and state income tax systems, the UIC program randomly audits selected claims. For claimants caught cheating, penalties can be severe. Most UIC programs have extensive, well-trained fraud investigation units that act on tips UIC personnel receive regarding cheating. Many are successful in penalizing claimants.

Myth 9: If you're going to school, you can't collect unemployment insurance

False. Claimants who attend school part time (usually less than twelve college semester hours) and continue to look for full-time work may be eligible to receive benefits. Full-time school usually removes a claimant from the active labor force, although there are several exceptions to this rule.

Many former employees who are eligible for unemployment insurance immediately think of going back to school. If a former employee has returned to school, let the local unemployment authorities know. A letter is usually the best way. In most states, you can request that you be made an interested party to any decision regarding school or other eligibility issues.

Myth 10: If a claimant wins an appeal, the employer must hire him or her back

False. Rehire of a claimant is never the subject of an unemployment insurance claim or proceeding. The issue is not whether the claimant is going to return to work. The only issues are whether the claimant is qualified and eligible to receive payment of benefits and whether benefits will be charged to the employer. The UIC system has no power to decide whether or not a claimant returns to work.

The purpose of an unemployment insurance appeal is to decide whether a claimant is legally entitled to benefits. The UIC program is interested only in determining eligibility for benefits based on the law and regulations in each jurisdiction. However, a UIC determination of the reason for separation from employment may be binding in a wrongful discharge suit brought by the employee.

Myth 11: If you can talk employees into quitting, you can prove they quit and they will be unable to collect unemployment insurance

False. Quitting doesn't automatically mean claimants can't qualify for unemployment insurance. The *reason* they quit is important. If you talk employees into quitting, it depends on what you said to them. If you told them they were going to be fired if they did not quit and you gave them the opportunity to resign, for unemployment insurance purposes they were discharged. They had no choice but to quit. This is called a *forced resignation*. (The old term was "constructive discharge.")

No matter what you call it, if the employer is the moving party the separation is always classified as a discharge, not a quit. This means the employer has the burden of proving misconduct to avoid charges to the employer's tax account.

Myth 12: If an employee offers his resignation and you accept it, he or she has quit the job

Usually true. Most states consider a voluntary resignation by the employee to be a quit. Some states have a time limit rule that determines whether this type of resignation is a quit or a discharge. If the employee gives long-term notice (usually more than 15 days) and you accept the resignation too quickly, the separation can become a discharge. In most cases, the employee becomes eligible for benefits. This type of work separation is very upsetting to employers. Let's look at an example.

Bill, a long-term employee, tells you on the first of the month that he's quitting in 90 days because he wants to take a long fishing trip. The same day, someone who can easily fill Bill's position comes to you looking for work. You accept Bill's resignation and replace him the next day, 89 days before the date of his planned resignation.

The only reason you take this action is that you want to prevent the qualified new worker from going somewhere else. You are acting logically and in the best interests of your company and the new employee. Should you be penalized for Bill's UIC benefits, even though he's quitting anyway? Unfortunately, you will be. In many states, it is considered a discharge because you accepted his resignation too early and there was no subsequent misconduct on which to base the discharge. Tips on how to avoid this trap can be found in Chapter 3.

Myth 13: A letter of resignation proves an employee quit

False. A letter of resignation proves only that the employee gave the employer a letter of resignation. If an employee was given the option of turning in a letter of resignation or being fired, for UIC purposes the employee was discharged. The reason the letter was demanded determines why the discharge took place. The burden once again rests with the employer to show misconduct.

Myth 14: It's OK to wait until you find a replacement for an unsatisfactory employee before you actually discharge him or her

Usually false. Waiting an unreasonable amount of time to fire someone can neutralize any allegations of misconduct. Suspend the employee if you must obtain higher-level permission to fire him or her, while an investigation is being conducted before the discharge, or if there is another legitimate reason for not firing the employee as soon as possible. If you do not do this, you will be in the contradictory position of alleging the employee was acting with willful disregard of your interests while you continued to employ him or her. It does not help your case.

Some states discount any allegations of misconduct, no matter how serious or well proved, if an unreasonable time elapses between the misconduct and separation from work. Never wait to find a replacement for an employee before you fire him or her. This excuse could lose the case for you.

Myth 15: If an employee is out sick, you cannot fire him or her

In most cases, this is false. Unless you have some specific legal obligation (union contract; federal, state, or local law; guaranteed leave-of-absence policy), you have no obligation to employ someone because he or she is absent from work due to illness.

If an employee uses up his or her sick leave and you must find a replacement, for UIC purposes most states allow you to end the employer–employee relationship. In many states, this is considered a "quit for compelling personal reasons." The employee may become eligible for UIC benefits when he or she is able to work, but your tax account will not be charged.

This situation varies from state to state. If an employee is ill, call your UIC office and ask for an explanation of the rules. Some UIC offices refuse to make a prejudgment as to what will happen, but they are required to tell you the law and regulations.

Myth 16: If an employee takes a leave of absence without a guarantee of reinstatement, you are required to take him or her back

False. Unless you have a union agreement or federal or state laws and regulations that compel (or force) you to rehire an employee, you are not obligated to reinstate workers who take leaves of absence. There are several types of leaves; the two most common are

1. True leave of absence, paid or unpaid, assures an employee that he or she can return to the original position or a comparable position. Such leaves are established by laws like the federal Family and Medical Leave Act of 1993.
2. Preference for rehire is not a true leave of absence but a promise to rehire an employee over other job applicants.

Even on a true leave of absence, a number of situations can prevent an employee from being re-employed. Sometimes an employer has layoffs during leaves of absence. If an employee is laid off, the UIC system treats the separation as a regular layoff. If an employee files for benefits during a leave of absence, most states consider it a voluntary quit.

In rare cases, employees have been discharged for filing false medical-insurance reports or engaging in other actions contrary to the employer's interests. During a true leave of absence, the employer–employee relationship continues. In any other type of leave of absence, an employee can be laid off, quit, or be discharged—just as he or she could while at work.

Myth 17: Every employee is entitled to a leave of absence

Usually false. In most states, the employer is under no obligation to allow a leave of absence just because the employee wants one. However, under the federal Family and Medical Leave Act of 1993, employers must provide leaves of absence to employees under certain circumstances. Your state may have special laws in this regard; check before making any final decisions.

Myth 18: Once a UIC decision has been issued in your favor, you can stop worrying

False. Even if you receive a favorable decision at the first or even the second decision level, the claimant has the right to file additional appeals. Some local office decisions have been decided by the United States Supreme Court. (For example, *Thomas v. Review Board of the In-*

diana Employment Security Division, 450 U.S. 707; 101 S.Ct. 1425; 67 L.Ed. 2d 624 [1981].)

Never assume you have won a case and will never need to deal with it again. Assume a claimant will continue to appeal to the highest level possible. Plan to attend all UIC proceedings related to any appealed claim. Use the appeals process when you feel you were right and the UIC system was wrong. Review each decision, even if a decision is in your favor. We provide tips on protesting decisions in Chapter 7.

Myth 19: Unemployment insurance is a "vacation plan" for employees

False. The UIC program is designed to help claimants return to work as soon as possible. Benefits are designed to provide the claimant with the means to seek new employment. To continue to receive benefits, claimants must conduct a diligent work search each week they receive benefits. They cannot refuse suitable work. They must be *actively* available and *physically* able to seek and accept suitable work (part time and full time) at any point in the claim.

A claimant should be working hard to find a job while collecting benefits. The law requires this in all states, except under special circumstances, such as areas affected by massive layoffs or areas where no work is available because of natural disasters.

The system is far from perfect. In the real world, claimants go fishing, take pleasure cruises, or goof off while collecting UIC benefits. Claims examiners are often unable or unwilling to enforce rules that require a claimant to seek work while drawing benefits.

Employers have little control over the UIC process once a claimant becomes eligible for benefits. If you discover a claimant is using the UIC program as a vacation, report it to the local office. Demand an investigation. Claims examiners will take the appropriate legal and administrative actions. Decisions issued to disqualify claimants who abuse the UIC system by "taking vacations" can reduce and limit your UIC tax liability.

Myth 20: An employee who gets severance pay cannot file for unemployment insurance

False. In most states, severance pay has no effect on unemployment insurance. Only unused holiday or vacation pay is allocated as wages to the period after separation from work. Severance pay is considered a courtesy or "gift," not wages, even if required by union contract.

Unused sick pay is almost never considered a wage. If it is paid to an employee following separation, it has no effect on eligibility.

These rules vary considerably from state to state. It's wise to check with your local office for information on how this can affect any claim in your area.

Myth 21: An employer must always warn an employee before discharging him or her

False. In many separations it is wise to issue written or verbal warnings before an employee is discharged for misconduct. The following are examples of discharges that require some form of warning: tardiness, excessive absence from work, failure to follow instructions, or inability to do the job.

Some employee activities require *no* warning from an employer before dismissal. Types of misconduct that fall into this category include theft, assault, drug or alcohol use on the job, gross negligence, intentional destruction of company property, and intentional insubordination.

Myth 22: An employer cannot collect unemployment insurance

Usually true but not always. Claimants who are employed by a corporation may be eligible to collect benefits, even though they are corporate officers or owners of the business. In most states, employers who own unincorporated businesses are *not* eligible for UIC benefits. Rules vary from state to state, so check with your local UIC office for further information.

Myth 23: You cannot draw worker's compensation and unemployment insurance at the same time

Usually true. Those who apply for worker's compensation are stating they have been injured on the job. If they also claim they cannot continue working because of the injury, they are unable to work. Report the inability to work to the UIC office; request you be a party to any decisions regarding the employee's *ability* to work. Keep your worker's compensation insurance carrier advised of all decisions, including payment of UIC benefits to the "injured" employee. It can affect your worker's compensation premiums.

Although a worker may be unable to do his or her "usual" work, there may be other types of work he or she can do. For example, a machinist off work because of an allergic reaction to cutting oil may be able to do other types of work that do not expose him to cutting oil. If you have work available, offer it to the employee. If he or she refuses, notify the UIC office and your worker's compensation carrier.

If you do not have suitable work, the employee may be able to establish that there is other suitable work available, and he or she can meet the UIC requirement he or she is *able* to work. In this situation, notify your worker's compensation carrier because UIC benefits are considered wages for worker's compensation purposes in most states.

The same is true for long-term Social Security disability. To be eligible to collect UIC benefits, a claimant must be *able* and *available* for work. To collect Social Security disability benefits, a person must be *unable* to work. In some states, the industrial disability program is connected to unemployment insurance.

When an employee leaves a job as a result of a job-related injury, he or she may leave for a compelling personal reason. Claimants are not disqualified from collecting UIC benefits because of the separation from work. However, they cannot collect benefits until they are medically able to accept work.

Myth 24: Claimants who draw private retirement pensions and Social Security benefits cannot receive unemployment insurance at the same time

False. Those who are employed while drawing retirement or Social Security benefits then become unemployed are eligible to collect unemployment benefits only if they meet all other requirements. In every state, employer contributions to private pension funds and Social Security are deducted from the claimants' weekly unemployment benefits. If the total deductions do not equal or exceed the claimants' weekly UIC benefits, they *can* receive the difference as a weekly UIC payment.

Myth 25: Claimants who own their own businesses can collect unemployment insurance

True. Most states allow claimants to operate their own businesses, even if it is a full-time enterprise. The claimant must prove his or her commitment to the business does not interfere with return to the regular, active labor force. Claimants can promote and run their own businesses during hours that do not prevent them from seeking full-time work. They must report all earnings to UIC offices; earnings are deducted from the weekly benefit check. Most states require self-employed claimants to sign a sworn affidavit stating they will give up their part-time or full-time business to accept other suitable employment.

Myth 26: If you're pregnant, you can't collect UIC benefits

False. The fact a claimant is pregnant does *not* automatically mean she is ineligible for benefits. Pregnant claimants are required to establish their attachment to the active labor market by conducting an active work search and meeting the same eligibility standards as all other claimants. In addition, a pregnant claimant must provide her local UIC office with periodic medical statements from her doctor saying she can work.

Claims examiners usually require one medical form from the claimant in the first three months of pregnancy. In the second trimester, most UIC offices require medical proof of the claimant's condition once every thirty days. During the final trimester, the claimant is usually required to provide a medical statement every one or two weeks, depending on her scheduled report to the local office.

Although it rarely happens, some claimants can seek and accept work up to the date of delivery. If a doctor is willing to provide written medical evidence the claimant is physically able to work, she is eligible for unemployment insurance benefits.

Myth 27: If I buy a business, I get a fresh start. I am not responsible for past UIC tax problems

False. UIC tax liabilities, even pending cases, are the responsibility of the *current* owner of the business. UIC tax and related problems are like any other business debt or liability; they are part of the package. Even getting a new UIC tax account does not relieve the current owner of his UIC obligations.

Anyone buying a business should carefully examine the UIC tax situation, along with other assets and liabilities of the company. There is a positive side to this. A low tax rate, good employees, and an organized approach to UIC taxes can be a valuable asset when buying or selling a business.

Myth 28: All employees are covered by unemployment insurance

False. In most states, domestic workers in private households, casual laborers, and some part-time employees are exempt from UIC coverage. This means an employer is not required to pay UIC taxes for these employees. All states base their UIC rules of coverage on time worked, wages earned, or a combination of these. Your local UIC office can tell you whether you must cover workers in these categories.

Myth 29: Teachers and other school employees can collect unemployment insurance during the summer when they are not working

False. In most states, school employees who have a contract or a reasonable assurance of returning to work after normal breaks in the school year (spring and winter breaks, summer vacation, Christmas vacation) are not unemployed and are ineligible for UIC benefits.

Myth 30: It is a good idea to lay off good workers. They are more likely to find work and not file UIC claims

False. When workers are laid off, especially in bad economic times, their only source of income may be unemployment insurance compensation. Some good workers might hesitate to file a claim but may be forced to do so because they need money.

Myth 31: Dealing with unemployment insurance claims is not worth the trouble. It takes too much time and effort; it's easier and cheaper to let the claim be paid

False. If your techniques for dealing with UIC claims are good, it's possible to minimize the time and effort you must spend. Floundering through the system without any guidance is a waste of your time, resources, and money. We're here to help you avoid the inefficient approach.

It's almost always more expensive to ignore unemployment insurance claims. The system is set up to induce you to participate, even if you don't always win. Ignoring claims can become an expensive bad habit because UIC claims can cost thousands of dollars. While some claims must be paid, we don't want you to pay more than your fair share.

Trying to fight the UIC system and trying to fight claimants who abuse it aren't easy because the system generally favors employees. The rules and the decision-making process of the UIC program are complex, sometimes contradictory, and often incorrectly administered.

The inner workings of the UIC program are well concealed from the general public. People who run the program have been largely successful in covering up its mistakes and keeping employers on the defensive. There is no reason for this to continue. You can make saving UIC tax dollars simple and cost effective.

Myth 32: An employee-at-will, by contract or state law, is entitled to unemployment insurance benefits if employment is terminated for any reason

False. For unemployment insurance purposes, the fact the employment was "at will" does not affect a claimant's entitlement to UIC benefits. In each state, the decision about a claimant's entitlement to UIC benefits is based on the reason for the separation from employment and the state's UIC laws and regulations. Under the "employment-at-will" doctrine, the employment relationship can be terminated at any time—at will—by the employer or the employee, for cause or without cause. A person may be an employee-at-will under common law, state law, or a contract of employment setting forth that he or she is an employee-at-will.

An employee handbook or policy manual may create or modify an unwritten employee-at-will understanding. In some states, a "probationary period" does not mean employment was "at will" but rather that there was a contract of employment under which the employee could be discharged only for cause after completing the probation.

Some states have allowed employers to terminate employees-at-will for any reason. However, more states are imposing a requirement that employers treat employees "fairly" as part of the traditional employment-at-will relationship in allowing wrongful discharge suits to be brought by employees-at-will.

3

Documenting and Warning

There are three ways an employee can be separated from work. An employee can be *discharged* from work, he or she can *quit,* and he or she can be *laid off* due to a lack of work. In this chapter, we examine how to prepare to discharge an employee. (Chapter 4 covers discharging an employee, and Chapter 5 deals with quits and layoffs.) We advise you what to document and how to document it for each type of work separation. We also show you how to give and record warnings and other disciplinary actions in such a way that it will help you win your UIC cases.

WHO IS THE "MOVING PARTY"?

In all separations, either the employer or the employee *acts* to end the employment. The UIC system uses a *moving party standard* to determine if a work separation is a discharge, a quit, or a layoff; whoever acts to cause the separation bears the burden of proof. (See Chapter 8 for a detailed explanation of burden of proof.)

If the employer acts to end the work relationship, the *employer* is the moving party. If the employee ends the work relationship, the *employee* is the moving party. In discharges, the employer is the moving party because he or she makes the decision to terminate a worker's employment and acts upon that decision. In many cases, the employer may be forced by company rules or restricted by union or employment agreements, but the employer is *still* the moving party.

When a worker quits a job and files a UIC claim, the claimant bears the burden of proof and must establish that he or she had a good reason for leaving the job. If the claimant fails to meet the burden of proof in a quit, the employer will win the case.

If the employer is the moving party, it is almost always considered a discharge by the UIC claims office. However, sometimes there can be confusion about who is the moving party. Consider the case of Fred and the Bowman Tool Company.

A Case in Point

The Bowman Tool Company has decided that Fred is not keeping up with his work as a valve maker. He is trying his best, but he doesn't have the skills and aptitude to maintain the pace the employer needs. Fred's mistakes and slowness have cost the company thousands of dollars; things are not improving. Management makes a reluctant decision to give Fred notice and let him go. At this point, the employer is clearly the moving party.

Fred knows he's not keeping up, but he's trying his best. He hopes to improve, and he doesn't want to lose his job.

On Wednesday, a couple of weeks before the scheduled dismissal, a friend of Fred's, a secretary in the personnel department, tells him the discharge is coming. Fred's friend has no authority to tell him he's going to be discharged, but she tells him anyway. Fred talks to a couple of other workers the next day, and they confirm the rumor. Fred's feelings are hurt, and he is angry. He's trying hard, and he's ashamed he's going to be fired. Fred thinks it over for a day, then goes to personnel and quits because he doesn't want to be fired. He believes it's better for his employment record to quit rather than be fired.

In this situation, who is the moving party?

Even though the employer may have started the action that led to Fred's resignation (and would have been the moving party in a couple of weeks), Fred's actions and intentions have now made *him* the moving party. He quit in anticipation of a discharge. What could have been a discharge is now a quit. The burden of proof now shifts to Fred. He must show he had a good reason for quitting before his discharge or that there is some legitimate reason for quitting before he was discharged.

Although Bowman Tool Company was the moving party at the beginning of the incident, Fred became the moving party when he chose to quit before he was fired. If Fred cannot establish good cause for leaving his job, he will be disqualified from receiving UIC benefits, and the company's tax account will not be charged.

DOCUMENTING THE FACTS

Employers have many questions about what should be documented to win a case and support it if the case is appealed. This documentation is necessary to assure you have pulled together the *right* information to support your case.

- What does it mean to "document" information?
- What do I document?
- How do I document facts?
- Why do I need to document information?

We answer these questions for you because understanding documentation is one of the major keys to preparing a strong UIC case. However, before we deal with these important issues, let's discuss how reaching the wrong conclusion can sometimes guarantee that you will lose your UIC case.

Reaching Conclusions

When you document facts, it is normal for you to reach conclusions about events, motivations, and other circumstances about a situation. Reaching a conclusion in UIC cases is acceptable *only* if the conclusion is supported by fact. This is an extremely important concept to grasp. Conclusions based not on fact but on speculation or assumption are almost always invalid. Invalid conclusions are of little value to you in documenting and winning UIC cases.

You must be sure that when you reach a conclusion you have carefully reviewed *how* you arrived at the conclusion. Consider the following examples. The first case in point is a valid conclusion based on supportable fact. The second case in point is invalid, based on speculation and assumption.

One Case in Point

You are documenting the case of Betty, a sales executive who is about to be warned for insubordination. You have concluded she has been insubordinate and defiant to the point where her actions can no longer be tolerated. The belief that Betty has been insubordinate is a *conclusion*. To determine if it is a valid conclusion, ask yourself how and why you reached the conclusion.

What exactly did Betty do or fail to do?

How was she insubordinate?

Betty was assigned to pick up a prospective buyer at the airport. She was also instructed to take two packets of important documents to the recorder's office. At the last minute, Betty decides she doesn't want to go to the airport to pick up the prospective buyer. She tells the secretary she is going to the recorder's office with the documents and she doesn't want to go to the airport.

The secretary asks Betty to wait to see if it's possible for someone else to go to the airport. Betty refuses to wait and leaves. The secretary cannot find anyone in authority. In desperation, she calls the airport, but she cannot reach the customer.

A few hours later, Betty returns to the office. By now, you have received several irate telephone calls from your customer and rushed to the airport yourself to pick him up.

When you return, you ask Betty to step into your office and tell you what happened. She informs you she didn't feel like picking up the client at the airport because she doesn't feel it's part of her job. She says she no longer wants to be assigned this task, even though you and all the other salespeople customarily pick customers up.

This is a clear act of failing to follow a reasonable instruction. Betty's actions have potentially jeopardized your interests as an employer. If you document exactly what Betty did, you can easily and fairly reach the valid conclusion she was insubordinate. At that point, she should be warned her actions were unacceptable and that she could be dismissed from employment.

A Second Case in Point

Marvin is a delivery driver assigned to take a load of roofing material to a customer 30 miles away. The trip should take about two hours, counting unloading time.

Marvin leaves and doesn't return for more than four hours. When he drives into the yard, he appears disoriented and is having trouble keeping his balance. When the yard supervisor asks Marvin why he is late, Marvin answers in a slurred voice. He states he had an "emergency." The supervisor looks in the bed of the delivery truck and sees several empty beer cans. He immediately calls the manager, who looks in the truck. The beer cans were not there when Marvin left to deliver the load.

The manager is furious. He concludes Marvin has been drinking on the job while operating a company truck and fires Marvin on the spot. After all, Marvin was two hours late. His speech is slurred. He is having trouble keeping his balance, and he appears disoriented. What other conclusion could you reach?

After Marvin is fired, the UIC claims examiner calls and tells the employer Marvin is filing an unemployment insurance claim against him. The employer decides this is an open-and-shut case and does not bother to call the claims examiner back with any information.

The employer is shocked when the UIC local office rules in Marvin's favor and charges the employer's UIC tax account. At the appeals hearing, Marvin testifies he was late getting back because he stopped to rescue a couple from a wrecked car. He became dehydrated to the point that when the paramedics arrived, he was treated for heat exhaustion and kept for observation for an extra hour.

At the hearing, the paramedics and two police officers testify that there were several empty beer cans at the scene of the accident. The police officers remember taking the cans off the road and throwing them into the bed of Marvin's truck. In the excitement, they forgot to remove them. The paramedics indicate that they were concerned about Marvin because he was slightly disoriented and his speech was slurred but add that Marvin insisted on getting back to work because he was concerned about the employer and his truck.

In this situation, the employer jumped to conclusions about why Marvin was late returning to the yard. He didn't ask why Marvin was staggering or how the beer cans got into the back of the truck. In making these erroneous conclusions, the employer has lost his UIC case.

What Does It Mean to "Document" Information?

When you document facts or actions, you are recording them so they can be referred to and used later. Your documentation will be used to prove or support your UIC case before a claims examiner or an ALJ. It helps to think of documentation as a *foundation for answering questions.*

What Do I Document?

The quickest, most effective way to document facts is to ask yourself, then answer, the *what, where, when, why,* and *how* questions. If an employee was late to work, use the "when" question.

Q: When was the employee late?

A: June 3, 1992.

Q: When was the employee scheduled to report for work?

A: 7:00 A.M.

Q: When did the employee report to work?

A: 8:15 A.M.

How Do I Document?

Answering these questions provides a great deal of information and helps you gather together facts for UIC claims examiners or ALJs. You don't need to write the information down in the form of a question. Your actual documentation for an employee's file should be concise, clear and easy to follow. The example below covers all the pertinent facts quickly and effectively.

On 6/3/92, Joe Johnson was scheduled to work morning shift starting at 7:00 A.M. Johnson reported at 8:15 A.M. (1 hour, 15 minutes late). Observed by me and witnessed by shift supervisor, Bill Smith. Spoke with Johnson in my office at 8:30 A.M. Bill Smith also present. This was third time this quarter Johnson was late. Johnson said he overslept. I issued final written warning (see other warnings in file). This is second and last written warning. Told Johnson if he was late again this quarter without a good reason, he would be fired. Johnson said he understood and would try not to be late again.

In a few short lines, you have documented a great deal of useful information. You know *when* the employee was late and *how* late he was. You know *why* the employee said he was late. You know *who* witnessed the incident and *who* witnessed the subsequent warning. You know *when* and *where* the warning took place. You know *why* you gave the warning and *what* you told the employee. You know *when* the employee was previously warned, and you know *what* the next disciplinary step is if the employee is late again this quarter—all in one short paragraph!

Why Do I Need to Document Information?

Recollection grows stale very quickly. The key to successful documentation is to record facts and events as they occur or as soon after as possible. The sooner you note the facts of an event, the clearer, more credible your documentation will be.

In legal terms, documenting facts is sometimes called "commemorating or memorializing an event." This means you kept or made a written record of an event. When you make written notes of an event as it happens, or very shortly after, these notes are sometimes called "contemporaneous notes."

You must document events related to separations from work because such documentation is the only credible source you have for accurately recalling facts about past events. It does not need to be difficult or time consuming—good documentation is short and precise. As we work through this chapter, we show you how to document quickly and effectively.

DOCUMENTATION RULES

Documentation can make or break your case if a local office decision is appealed. It is essential to know the basics of preparing a good case. Here are some useful fundamental rules to use when documenting events leading to a separation from work.

Rule 1

Be as *exact* and *detailed* as possible when documenting facts surrounding any incident. Provide enough information so you will be able to recall the incident clearly when necessary—maybe months later.

Rule 2

Document facts as soon as possible. Don't wait any longer than absolutely necessary to *write* down what took place. Notes made when an incident occurs have substantial weight because events are fresh in your mind when you make the notes.

Rule 3

Always note the time an incident occurs; check your watch or a reliable clock. The time of an incident often has some bearing on the facts. Noting the time adds detail and credibility to your notes.

Rule 4

If you are going to quote someone, write *exactly* what he or she says and to whom. This is especially critical if profanity is the cause of separation from work. Or an employee may state his or her intentions (in the case of quitting a job). If an employee gives you a specific reason why he or she did something ("I was late because I overslept"), note what the employee *stated* as accurately as possible.

Rule 5

If there are witnesses to an important work-related incident, note the names of *all* individuals present. Have them write and sign a short statement to place in the worker's personnel file.

This is essential if a witness is no longer an employee when you later need his or her statement. A written statement taken when an incident occurs may be the only statement you can present to a claims examiner or ALJ. Statements from witnesses do not carry the same weight as actual testimony, but they are the next best thing and can be very powerful evidence. In the absence of a witness, these written notes can mean the difference between winning and losing your case.

Rule 6

You must clearly understand the work rules you are enforcing, and you must be able to communicate them to the employee. Make sure an employee *understands* why you are taking disciplinary action. If you cannot clearly tell the employee what the rules are, the rules may be unclear or the employee's understanding of them may be unclear. Clarify for an employee how his or her actions may lead to a separation from work. This provides an opportunity for the employee to correct what he or she is doing wrong.

Rule 7

When you warn or discharge an employee, have witnesses present. If you know an employee is planning to quit, have a witness present. It is possible that an employee who is quitting will later allege you discharged him or her. In such cases, the burden of proof shifts to you. You may be called upon to prove that the employee quit and is lying about being discharged. With a witness, you are on solid ground.

Rule 8

If no witness is present, use a tape recorder for a clear record of your exchanges with the employee. We suggest you tell the employee you are recording the conversation so there is no misunderstanding later. An inexpensive handheld tape recorder pays for itself many times over if it helps you win a UIC case you would have otherwise lost. If you are unable to use a tape recorder, make simple, clear notes of the meeting.

Rule 9

Notes are only *partial* documentation. Written statements from other witnesses; copies of warnings; and copies of other work-related documents, such as the employee handbook, time cards, and written instructions, are almost always necessary to support your written notes.

Rule 10

It is essential to get into the habit of documenting *all* work-related issues. This is a learned skill. The more you document, the faster, more efficient, and better you will become.

EMPLOYER POLICY

At first glance, you may not believe the policies established by the employer fit into the category of documentation, but they can. Your policies are necessary to maintain control over the business you are trying to conduct. In general, most policies are fair and necessary, but when it comes to UIC cases, the ALJ decides whether your work policies are reasonable and fair as they relate to separation from work.

The ALJ does not have the authority to review your policy in general, nor does he or she have the power to make you change or modify your policies. The limits of an ALJ's authority and responsibilities do not extend beyond making a decision with regard to UIC charges to your tax account. In addition to reviewing the fairness and reasonableness of your work rules and policies, the ALJ must also decide whether the rules were fairly *applied* in each UIC case.

Employer Policy as It Relates to Documentation

We suggest you inform employees about your work policies at every convenient opportunity. Informing an individual employee about a particular policy when the employee violates that policy is a necessity. But letting all employees know the rules of game and the consequences of ignoring or breaking them is equally important. Most employees follow the policies and rules most of the time—provided they know what they are.

Many employers use employee handbooks to advise their employees about work rules and policies. Writing a handbook that is clear and that covers all the bases can be a difficult task. We recommend a handbook for large- to medium-size employers. Smaller employers may find a one- or two-page sheet will do the job.

If you have a set of written rules and policies you expect employees to follow, make sure each employee signs a receipt that he or she has *received, read,* and *understood* the handbook or instructions. This is important documentation; a receipt for this information is like gold in UIC cases.

If you have meetings where specific policies are discussed or clarified verbally, have each employee sign a sheet with the date of the meeting. Make a note on the top of the sheet giving the general heading of the meeting. Later, make a few notes about what was discussed. Keep all this material in a separate file in case you need it later.

If you pass out any memos or written material at a meeting, attach copies to the attendance sheet. These attendance sheets have won many UIC cases that involved company policies and work rules. When employees dispute that they knew specific rules, you will have to prove they were given the information. Receipts and attendance sheets can be critical documentation for winning many of your UIC cases.

WARNINGS

Discharging an employee is usually a cumulative process. An employee may commit a single major act of misconduct (fighting, theft, destruction of company property, drug or alcohol use at work) that is grounds for immediate discharge. More often, the employee's actions occur over a period of time. During this time, you have opportunities to warn the employee.

There are two different kinds of warnings for UIC purposes—*written warnings* and *verbal warnings*. The rules for giving either are similar.

Purpose of a Warning

A warning to an employee is intended to be a *corrective* measure. It is a written or verbal notice advising an employee that his or her action or behavior is unacceptable. The purpose of warnings is to give an employee fair notice that continued action will result in further disciplinary action, including possible discharge from work.

By warning an employee, you are telling him or her exactly what you are unhappy about and placing emphasis on the importance of the warning itself. A warning *must* be a clear statement to an employee. In your warning, detail precisely what is wrong and what must be done to correct the situation. In some cases, an employee will take corrective action, and a discharge can be avoided. At other times, the employee will disregard any warning(s), and you will be forced to discharge him or her.

In some cases, warnings clarify rules or policies so misunderstandings between you and the employee can be resolved. Once the employee has been informed that his or her actions must change, the employee is obligated to make those adjustments or face additional disciplinary action, including discharge.

When Warning an Employee

When you warn an employee, ask yourself the following questions. They can help you decide whether you are fairly warning an employee.

- Have I exposed the employee to the rules and explained how they are enforced?
- Does the employee understand the rules of employment?
- Are the rules written or verbal?
- If rules were verbal, who gave them?
- How do I know the employee understands the rules?
- Is the acknowledgment written or verbal?
- If the acknowledgment was verbal, who was present as a witness?

How to Issue an Effective Warning

Whether you issue a verbal or a written warning, an effective warning includes the following four statements.

1. A statement of the problem(s) in direct, easily understood language.
2. A statement of what you want done to correct the problem.
3. A statement as to why you are giving the warning.
4. A statement of the consequences if the employee does not make the required corrections.

Figure 3.1 shows a completed warning form. We have covered all four areas in that warning. You might also want to look in Appendix A, where we provide blank sample warning forms. Copy them and use

Figure 3.1
A Completed Warning Form

General Warning Form

Date _____9. 30-97_____

Name of Employee _____RICHARD REDDRICK_____

Reason for warning: _____YOU WERE ABSENT FROM YOUR WORK STATION WITHOUT PERMISSION FROM APPROX. 8:45 A.M TO 11:30 A.M. THE TELEPHONES WERE NOT ANSWERED AND YOUR OTHER DUTIES WERE NEGLECTED._____

Employee's response: _____I HAVE NOTHING TO ADD._____

This is the _____2ND_____ warning for this offense. Failure to comply with this or any other warning may result in further disciplinary action or termination from employment.

By signing this form, I am not agreeing or disagreeing with the warning; I am merely acknowledging receipt of the warning.

I have read this form and understand its contents.

Employee signature _____Richard Reddrick_____ Date _____9. 30. 97_____

Witness signature _____Betty Rogers_____ Date _____9-30-97_____

Employer signature _____Bob Hugo_____ Date _____9/30/97_____ them as they are or use them as guides to create your own warning forms.

Precise, carefully planned warnings can be a valuable tool for three reasons.

- They *emphasize* to workers that you are serious about these problems.
- They provide employees the time and opportunity to correct their actions.
- They provide an excellent foundation for eventual discharge if the employee will not (or cannot) comply with your warnings.

There are many effective ways to issue warnings. Below are some guidelines you can use to help you issue effective, powerful warnings.

Make the Warning as Clear as Possible

Don't confuse an employee or diminish the impact of a warning by "beating around the bush." Think about *exactly* why you are issuing the warning, then tell the employee. Let the employee know what you expect of him or her in the future, and advise the employee you expect immediate corrective action. Advise the employee what will happen if he or she does not take the necessary steps to correct his or her actions.

Don't Issue Any Warning in Anger

It is more effective to approach the employee when you are calm and thinking clearly. You don't have to issue warnings the instant an employee does something unacceptable. If you're mad, take a few minutes or even a few hours to formulate exactly what you want to say and how you want to say it.

Have a Witness Present

Always have at least one witness present when you issue a warning. No matter how professional you are in issuing a warning, there is a certain amount of emotion involved in giving and receiving a warning. Sometimes employees feel threatened and react with anger. Having a witness present can diffuse the situation. We have found that employees are less likely to react in anger when two or more people are present during disciplinary action.

The primary purpose of having a witness present is to have some proof you warned an employee. It is common for an employee to deny he or she was ever warned, especially if the employee is eventually discharged. It is also becoming more common for employees to make accusations and allegations about what was said in warning sessions. These complaints may involve allegations of sexual or racial harassment. Having a witness present during *all* disciplinary actions can help prevent this problem. If an employee later accuses you of harassment or improper conduct, a witness will be able to verify that you acted properly.

Make a Record of the Warning

Always make a written or tape-recorded record of the warning, even if it is only a verbal warning. Any type of documentation helps support your case.

Never Threaten an Employee

Inform an employee that his or her actions might lead to eventual discharge, but don't go beyond that. Once you have issued a warning and told the employee of the consequences of ignoring the warning, leave it at that. You have taken care of your obligations; it's up to the employee to follow through. This approach helps the employee understand that he or she bears a real responsibility for what happens in the future.

Be Consistent

If you warn one employee for being tardy to work, warn *all* other employees who commit the same offense. Inconsistency sends a contradictory message to your employees. Inconsistent warning practices won't be taken seriously and won't persuade employees to take corrective action. Inconsistency can also result in your losing a UIC case.

Note an Employee's Reaction to a Warning

Often an employee who is being warned acknowledges that he or she *knew* the action was wrong. It is important to record it when an employee admits wrongdoing and awareness of that wrongdoing. If the warning doesn't change your employee's behavior, you have begun a solid case for work-related misconduct.

VERBAL WARNINGS

Not all situations call for written warnings; sometimes a verbal (spoken) warning is all that is necessary. Some companies give a verbal warning for minor offenses. Some companies use a system of *progressive* disciplinary warnings, usually beginning with a verbal warning and ending with a written warning.

For UIC purposes, verbal warnings are the weakest kind of warning you can give. However, many employers make it a policy to warn an employee verbally before any written warnings are issued or more punitive disciplinary action is taken. If you are going to issue a verbal warning, all the rules listed above apply.

When you issue a verbal warning, it's important to have a witness present. Once you have completed the warning procedure, make some written notes covering the warning. Your witness should do the same. Unless your company policy requires that the employee be shown the notes, it's enough just to put them in the employee's file. Any notes should include the following information.

- The time, date, and place of the warning.
- Who was present at the warning.
- Why the warning was issued.
- What was said during the warning. (We suggest you include what the employee said as well as what you said.)
- Include the witness's statement.

Below we've provided an example of a quick, highly effective warning.

Employer: Ron, could I see you in my office? I have a matter I need to discuss with you. *(The employee enters the office.)* Have a seat, please. Ron, this is Jack Carter. I asked him to be here because I have a serious matter to discuss with you. Ron, in the last two weeks you've been over 20 minutes late to work four times. Today you came in 25 minutes late. As you know, work starts promptly at 8:00 A.M. It's essential for our employees to be here on time so we can maintain our production schedule and serve our customers. This is a longstanding company policy, and we cannot continue to employ people who are unable to come to work on time. Can you tell me why you were late today?

Employee: Well, my car wouldn't start this morning. I don't remember coming in late any other time except today.

Employer: Ron, our records show you were late on three occasions before today. The purpose of this meeting is to tell you that tardiness to work is a serious matter. We always advise employees that being late to work can lead to discharge from employment here. We want you to understand that. We hope this won't happen again. If it does, we'll consider additional disciplinary action; we may have to discharge you. We just want to make sure you understand the rules, and you understand the importance of being to work on time.

Employee: OK, well, I'll try not to let it happen again.

Employer: Thank you, Ron. I sincerely hope you can correct this problem. We're happy with your work and hope you understand our position in this matter.

This is a good place to end the verbal warning. The warning only took a few minutes, and the employee was given a great deal of effective information. The employee was introduced to the witness and made aware the witness would be present during the warning. He was told his actions were unacceptable and would not be tolerated by the employer. The employee was not harassed or berated. At the end of the warning, the employee's dignity and self-esteem are intact, but the employer clearly made the point. All that remains is for the employer and the employer witness to make a few notes, put them in the employee's personnel file, and everybody can get back to work.

Tip. Be sure you don't have a *language barrier* when you issue a verbal warning to an employee. In today's labor force, many workers do not speak English as a first language; they may have only a minimal understanding of the language you are speaking.

Have a good translator available to help you make your warnings clearly understood. It helps establish that a *valid* warning was issued. If the warning is given in English or another language the employee does not fully understand, the warning cannot be considered valid for the purpose of misconduct at a later date.

If you use a translator to help you issue a warning, have the translator write a short memo to the file stating

- His or her name.
- Date of the warning translation.
- Short statement of what was translated.
- Short statement verifying the translation was done accurately.

WRITTEN WARNINGS

Written warnings usually follow verbal warnings. However, some employers use only written warnings for disciplinary action. We recommend you follow your standard company policy when it comes to issuing written warnings.

Written warnings are the most common, most effective means of informing an employee his or her actions are unacceptable and must change. Review the sample warning forms we include in Appendix A. In addition to following the general guidelines for issuing warnings, we provide some rules here that also apply.

Prepare the Written Warning

Have the written warning prepared *before* the meeting. This seems like an obvious suggestion, but employers often don't think of it. Trying to fill in a warning notice while the employee is watching detracts from the serious, professional atmosphere you want to establish.

Have a Witness Present

Always have at least one witness present when issuing a written warning. Even though you are planning to issue a written document, many things can happen. An employee can refuse to sign the warning and later deny that it was given. The fact that the warning is in writing does not protect you from the possibility that an employee will accuse you of sexual or racial discrimination or harassment, especially in discharge cases. A witness can help you avoid many possible problems.

Have the Employee Sign and Date the Warning Form

This action acknowledges that the employee received the written warning and becomes your "receipt" to show that it was issued. Always give the employee a copy of the written warning; you may be asked later whether you did so. Not giving the employee a copy of the warning may give the appearance that you are trying to conceal something.

If the employee refuses to sign the warning form, note it on the form. You and the witness sign and date the form. Refusal by the employee to sign the form does not alter the fact that a valid warning was issued to the employee.

Warnings Should Be Exact and Direct

A written warning can be short, but it should always include the following information:

- The time and date of the warning.
- Who was present when the employee received the warning.
- Specific details why the warning was issued.
- Space for the employee being warned to write a response. (No explanation or an admission of the infraction can be strong evidence at a UIC hearing.)
- Signatures and dates of all present parties (including the witness or witnesses).

Don't Soft-Pedal the Warning

If you don't treat the warning as a serious matter, you send a contradictory, weak message to the employee. You can be direct and forceful yet maintain a courteous, professional demeanor. There is no reason to apologize to an employee for a proper, legitimate warning notice. On the other hand, there is no reason to belittle or harass an employee when issuing a warning. Give the warning, and let it speak for itself.

Keep the Warning on a Professional Level

Your warning is a professional, job-related matter. You may like the employee or even have a close personal relationship with him or her. The warning is being issued from employer (or supervisor) to employee. It is the employee's relationship with the employer that is at issue, not your work or personal relationship with the employee.

Follow Up

If your warning procedure is progressive and begins with verbal warnings then moves to written warnings before discharge, stick to the policy. This provides a clear message to the employee that you are following, and will continue to follow, a consistent, progressive disciplinary procedure. The employee will understand you are serious about warnings—he or she must also be serious.

NOT ALL DISCHARGES REQUIRE WARNINGS

Not all situations require warnings prior to discharge. Sometimes employees do things that require *immediate* dismissal without any warning. For UIC purposes, the following are examples of actions by an employee that warrant immediate discharge from employment:

- Theft.
- Falsification of company records.
- Altercation with or assault of another employee or supervisor when the employee was clearly at fault.
- Use of illegal drugs while at work.
- Intoxication while on the job.
- Serious damage to the employer's property when the employee was clearly at fault.
- Acts of willful and gross insubordination.
- Use of abusive or profane language.
- Intentional, major violations of company rules.

When you discharge an employee for any of these reasons and you can prove it, you have an excellent chance of winning your case, even though no warnings were issued.

4

Discharging an Employee

A discharge from employment is the harshest, most drastic disciplinary action an employer can take—it is the severing of the employer–employee relationship. By definition, a *discharge* is an action taken by the employer, under the control of the employer, to terminate a worker's affiliation with a company or business.

Below are some questions to ask yourself before you discharge an employee. They help you determine whether your employee committed acts of misconduct and help you focus on the precise reason you are planning to discharge him or her. The questions will also help you maintain a fair, reasonable approach to the difficult task of discharging someone.

- Does the employee's discharge require a warning or warnings?
- Who issued the warnings?
- Who witnessed the warnings?
- Were the warnings verbal, written, or both?
- Did the employee acknowledge the warnings?
- Were the acknowledgments written or verbal?
- What documents do I need?
- Will witnesses and documents be available when I need them?
- Do my witnesses have *firsthand* knowledge of what the employee did or didn't do to cause the discharge?
- If I am a witness, am I basing my knowledge of events on firsthand experience or am I relying on what others have told me?

- Did the employee make any admissions?
- Did he or she deny the facts that led to the discharge?
- Were witnesses present when admissions were made?
- If no admissions were made, do I have enough facts to win my case?
- What was the final incident that motivated the discharge? (This "straw that broke the camel's back" is extremely important. The UIC program calls this the *precipitating incident*. It is usually the incident the claims examiners and ALJs are most interested in.)

DISCHARGES ARE DIFFICULT

No employer enjoys discharging an employee. It is expensive and time consuming, and most employers lose a substantial investment in training costs and time. In addition, as an employer you will need to go through the expense and trouble of finding a replacement for your employee.

There are many federal and state regulations regarding racial, sexual, and age discrimination. To protect yourself, be aware of these *before* you discharge anyone. However, even if you follow all the regulations, you may be subjected to a routine investigation by the Equal Employment Opportunity Commission (EEOC), the U.S. Department of Labor, or myriad state agencies that investigate discriminatory employment practices. Employees who are discharged often report employers to the Office of Safety and Health (OSHA). They may even file private lawsuits against an employer for "wrongful discharge."

All this aside, there are occasions when you *must* discharge someone. When an employee acts in a way that is contrary to your interest—when an employee's actions substantially affect an employer's business—that employee usually must be discharged. This is a punitive action by the employer; the UIC program views a discharge from employment as punishment. Discharging someone is the ultimate disciplinary action.

HOW THE UIC VIEWS DISCHARGES

Claims examiners and judges must determine whether an *additional* punitive action should be taken—should they deny the claimant UIC benefits? To justify denial of benefits, UIC personnel must be convinced the claimant committed an act of willful or intentional misconduct. Claims examiners and judges must be certain that a claimant's actions were avoidable and that the employer's interests were, or could have been, in serious jeopardy.

Tip. The sole purpose of the UIC claims system is to determine whether a former employee is legally eligible to receive UIC benefits and your account should be charged for them. The UIC program has no authority to force you to rehire an employee. It has no jurisdiction over safety rules, allegations of discrimination, or any other issue except unemployment insurance benefits. The questions UIC personnel ask *must* be related to the narrow issue of UIC benefits. The decisions they issue are restricted to UIC benefits and UIC tax charges.

Executive Discharges

An executive, like all other employees, may be discharged from a position. The fact an employee has executive status does not exempt him or her from becoming unemployed. However, the UIC does not distinguish between "executive" separations and other separations. These former employees are not treated any differently because of their former rank or status.

Many high-level managers or executives do not file for unemployment insurance for various reasons:

- Their pride prevents them from filing a claim and submitting themselves to the UIC process.
- They feel the monetary gain is not worth their time.
- They believe they will become re-employed within a short period of time.

However, if you are an employer, there will be times when a former executive *does* file a claim against your UIC tax account. Whether the claim is paid or not depends on the same criteria (the merits of the case) used to determine whether any other person is eligible for UIC benefits, not the status or position of the former employee. Executives who quit their jobs voluntarily must meet the same standard of proof as other claimants. When an executive is discharged, the employer bears the same burden of proof in establishing misconduct. See "Burden of Proof" in Chapter 8.

The UIC system is a great "leveler." Executives who apply for UIC benefits must stand in line, register for work, fill out claim forms, and face the same tribulations as any other claimant. Many executives opt not to file because the benefit amounts they would be entitled to receive are insignificant compared to their customary earnings. As shown in Appendix F, each state has a minimum and a maximum benefit award. The maximum award *cannot* be exceeded, regardless of previous earnings.

Be prepared to defend your company, whether the executive quit or was discharged. Executives are usually better educated and have access to more resources than average employees. They are more likely to retain legal counsel and fight for their benefits in more sophisticated ways than other employees.

Because of the potential for legal proceedings, be sure you follow all our suggestions about warnings and discharges very carefully. You may need all your documentation to protect and defend yourself in court in a wrongful-discharge suit or other legal action.

Sometimes employers and executives make agreements regarding whether the employer will contest the award of UIC benefits. However, the state is not bound by any agreement that may exist between the employer and employee. Generally benefit awards are based on the merits of the case.

Often when executives leave work they are allowed to resign rather than face actual termination. For UIC purposes, these separations are almost always adjudicated or determined to be *discharges*. Employers bear the burden of proof, even if the claimant submitted a letter of resignation. See the discussion of forced quits on pages 67–68.

WHY DISCHARGES ARE IMPORTANT TO YOU

From a UIC standpoint, you bear the burden of proof when you discharge an employee. (Burden of proof is discussed in detail in Chapter 8.) Because you are the moving party in a discharge, you must prove the employee was discharged for work-related misconduct. If you cannot show the employee committed an act or acts of misconduct, the employee will be granted UIC benefits, and your tax account will be charged.

For an employer to prove misconduct, the employee must have failed in his or her duties for reasons *within* his or her control. Gross negligence and major omissions and errors made by an employee are normally considered misconduct if the employee failed to use ordinary care to avoid the problems.

If you fail to establish misconduct in a discharge, you will pay higher UIC tax rates. When discharging an employee from work, *always* try to establish that the discharge was for misconduct. This is one way to keep your UIC tax charges to a minimum. If you fail to establish misconduct, you can expect your contribution to your UIC tax account to increase.

PREPARING FOR DISCHARGES FOR
REASONS OF MISCONDUCT

Discharges for misconduct are the hardest separations for employers to deal with, but there is no reason to be intimidated by them. By the end of this chapter, you will have the tools you need to begin dealing with misconduct-related discharges. We show you how to recognize employee misconduct, how to document it, and how to organize your records for winning UIC cases. With some effort and a little practice, these separations can be the simplest, most straightforward to handle. Your greatest advantage in a misconduct-related discharge is that you have a great deal of control over the discharge.

- You know *why* the employee is being discharged.
- You know *who* the witnesses are.
- You know *what* the employer policy is.
- You know *how* you were adversely affected by the employee's acts, either actually or potentially.

Although there are major responsibilities in proving misconduct, they are all within your control. You will present the facts to the UIC claims examiner or administrative law judge. This puts you on the offensive, which can be to your advantage.

HOW TO DISCHARGE AN EMPLOYEE

Every company has ways of handling the unpleasant business of discharging employees. Below are some strategies and suggestions that help you establish the existence of work-related misconduct for UIC purposes.

Step One

Identify the precipitating incident that motivated you to discharge the employee. In nearly all discharges, an employer reaches a final breaking point when dealing with an unsatisfactory employee. Pin down that incident.

Step Two

Decide whether the final incident is substantial enough to constitute misconduct by itself. If the final incident is one of a series of events, document all prior events. Be certain you have all warnings in hand.

Step Three

Make sure you have adequate witness support to proceed with the discharge. Don't rely on what someone may have told you about the employee's last act(s). For example, if Joe reported to work late after his final written warning, make sure Joe really *was* late. Check his time card, and check with his supervisor. Have the facts straight before you make a final decision.

Step Four

If you have witnesses to the final incident, talk to them *before* discharging an employee. Call the witnesses into your office and have them tell you firsthand what happened. If you are the main witness, make sure the other witnesses saw and heard what you saw and heard. Very often their stories and perceptions are different from yours. Determine whether their observations will corroborate (back up) your observation.

We strongly recommend that you take a short statement from each witness at this point. Statements can be handwritten or typed; they should contain the current date and a statement as to what the witnesses saw and heard. Each statement must be signed.

A statement helps clarify and focus what a witness has to contribute. It also commits the witness to the statement he or she has made and signed. If the witness later changes his or her story or refuses to testify to a claims examiner or administrative law judge, you can submit the witness's written statement. You can also use written statements to refresh a witness's memory.

Step Five

When you have gathered all the information, stop and think about what you are going to do. Review your actions. Have you been fair? Do you have all the information you need?

In some cases, you may have to consult a superior before going forward. If this is the case, now is the time. If you work for a company that has personnel experts or legal counsel, consult them. Discussing your decision with someone less involved can be very helpful. Use all the resources at your disposal.

Step Six

Call the employee into a private area, such as your office. Have at least one other management or supervisory person with you while you tell the employee exactly why he or she is there. Don't put your discussion on a personal level. Be certain you offer the employee an opportunity to explain his or her side of the story.

If the employee admits he or she was wrong, make note of the admission. If the employee offers any excuses that contain admissions, write them down. Take brief notes of important points that are admissions. Tape record the meeting if possible.

Remain courteous, and do not enter into an argument. If you have specific allegations and you give the employee an opportunity to refute or counter those allegations, he or she may decline to do so. This can be an admission. Note your question and the employee's lack of response. In some cases, no answer *is* an answer.

Tip. Often an employee becomes angry and frustrated in a termination interview. He or she may practically ask to be discharged, shouting, "Go ahead and fire me; you're going to do it anyway." If this occurs, make an accurate note of what the employee says. Have your witness(es) write a corroborative note. The employee's statement can be used later to demonstrate the employee *agrees* with the reason he or she is being terminated. Agreement of this kind is an excellent way to demonstrate work-related misconduct.

Step Seven

Close the interview. If you feel comfortable, tell the employee he or she is discharged. If you are not comfortable, wait until the end of the shift or the end of the working day.

CATEGORIES OF DISCHARGES FOR MISCONDUCT

Below is a discussion of the categories of discharges that normally occur. Each type of discharge includes a brief description and comments to help you deal with discharges as they relate to UIC benefits.

Discharges for Absence

Repeated absences is one of the most common reasons for letting an employee go. You have the right to expect employees to show up to work when scheduled; they have an obligation to do so. If they fail to report to work as scheduled, they can be discharged for misconduct.

To establish absence as misconduct, you must show the employee was aware of his or her obligation to report on a regular basis. You almost always need to demonstrate that the employee was warned (usually more than once) that future absences could result in termination of employment. You must also show that your absenteeism rule is reasonable and uniformly enforced.

The employee must show that his or her absences were unavoidable or beyond the employee's control. In part, the employee shares a portion of the burden of proof in this type of discharge, but the greatest portion of the burden remains with the employer.

Tardiness to Work

Tardiness is another common reason for separation from work. You cannot continue to employ workers who are tardy. As an employer, you have a right to expect employees to report to work as scheduled.

If an employee shows a pattern of tardiness, he or she should be warned. Tardiness can disrupt and delay the work of others. If you allow it to continue, it is unfair to other employees who report to work on time. Continued tardiness, especially after warnings, is work-related misconduct. Any employee who is continually late to work should be discharged.

To establish tardiness as misconduct for UIC purposes, you need to demonstrate that the employee was late to work or late returning from lunch or other breaks on a continual basis. This usually means more than two or three times. You will need to prove that you warned the employee and that you enforce your tardiness policy uniformly and fairly.

You must also show that all employees are subject to the same set of rules as the employee who was discharged. You will need to prove that the employee was advised or warned regarding his or her continual tardiness. If you can establish these elements, you will win your UIC case.

Protection from Potential Damage

All states have rules that protect employers from employee actions that may cause damage to the employer's property or business. If these acts are willful or intentional, work-related misconduct is the case. These employee acts include

- Agitation of coworkers against the employer.
- Excessive criticism of the employer that becomes detrimental or disruptive to the employer's business.
- Competing with the employer or aiding an employer's competitor.
- Intentional damage of employer's property.
- Mistreatment of the employer's customers or clients.
- General repeated negligence or carelessness that causes damage to the employer's equipment or property.

Any act by an employee that falls into these categories, especially on a continual basis, is usually considered misconduct.

To establish misconduct, you must demonstrate that the employee clearly engaged in one or more of these acts. You must have clear evidence to support your contentions and be able to prove the acts of the employee had the potential to damage, or actually did damage, your business. If you can do this, you will win your UIC case.

Dishonesty on the Part of the Employee

Dishonesty, theft, misappropriation, falsifying company records, misuse of employer property, and lying to the employer about past work history or education, if relevant to the job, are grounds for discharge from work. This type of misconduct does not usually require a warning before discharge.

Tip. To establish misconduct in these cases, you need only present evidence to show that the employee committed one or more of these acts. Some states require you to demonstrate that the employee's acts were potentially damaging to your business, but most UIC officials believe misconduct is self-evident in these cases. It is especially important to present clear, convincing evidence in these situations.

Insubordination

No employer is required to tolerate acts of insubordination by an employee. You have every right to expect that reasonable orders will be followed without challenge to the authority of superiors. If an employee is insolent, uses profanity, or threatens a superior, he or she commits an act of misconduct and should be terminated from employment.

Generally, acts by an employee in this category do not require repeated, or even single, warnings. If you have warned an employee regarding insubordination, then discharge the employee for not heeding the warning, you have a very strong case. If you discharge an employee for refusing to follow reasonable orders and instructions, you are still likely to win your UIC case.

Tip. To establish insubordination as misconduct, you must show that the employee committed one or more of these acts. You must also show that you did nothing to provoke the employee, especially in cases of refusal to follow orders or insolent behavior. If you issue instructions in a civil, reasonable manner and the employee reacts with insolent behavior, you have misconduct. If you approach the employee with threats, profanity, or other hostile behavior and the employee reacts with similar behavior, misconduct is difficult to establish.

Claims examiners and judges usually allow employees to *react* to hostility with their own hostility. If you are acting in good faith and the employee is not, and you can prove the employee was discharged for misconduct, you will win your case.

Intoxication and Use of Drugs

If an employee reports to work under the influence of alcohol or illegal drugs or uses alcohol or illegal drugs while on the job, he or she usually has committed misconduct. This can be a sensitive area because some employers support drug and alcohol rehabilitation programs and are reluctant to discharge employees.

In cases of drug and alcohol abuse, some states require proof that the employee was impaired or that your interests were in jeopardy by their use of drugs or alcohol. Our advice is to be very cautious in discharging an employee for work-related misconduct in this category. Consult an attorney when faced with this problem. See Appendix G.

Work Performance

In some cases, you will find it necessary to discharge an employee because his or her work performance is substandard. If an employee is loafing, neglecting his or her duties, working carelessly, not following instructions, or generally failing to act in a reasonable and diligent manner, you may have a case of work-related misconduct.

It is crucial in such cases to understand why an employee's work performance is not up to par. You may need to discharge an employee who is trying his or her best but cannot meet your standards. Such employees generally are not discharged for misconduct. Usually you must treat discharges as if you were laying the employee off. Because the employee will probably be eligible to collect UIC benefits and you will be charged for this discharge, let the employee go as soon as you are sure he or she cannot do the work. Cut your losses. The longer you keep the employee, the higher your UIC charges are likely to be.

Tip. To establish misconduct, you must prove the employee failed to meet your performance standards (or failed to perform his or her job) because of something within the *employee's control*. If you can show the employee was loafing or careless with regard to some specific duty or assignment, you can prove misconduct.

Try to demonstrate that the employee performed at a high or acceptable standard then stopped performing at that standard. This shows the employee was capable of doing the work but chose not to continue to do so. If you can show that an employee acted willfully or carelessly and that you warned the employee about work standards, you will have an excellent chance of winning your UIC case.

Unacceptable Behavior

Fighting with, threatening, or harassing other employees and using abusive or profane language fall into the category of "unacceptable behavior." These discharges are almost always considered misconduct.

Most employers have rules against this type of behavior by employees. In cases of fighting, it is important to be sure an employee was not merely acting in self-defense before he or she is discharged. When it is self-defense, an employee may be justified in fighting after being attacked.

If an employee starts a fight, he or she can be discharged for misconduct. Employees who escalate levels of violence or who respond to verbal threats or taunting with physical violence commit misconduct.

Fighting and physical altercations do not normally require warning before discharge.

Harassment has become a well-publicized issue in recent years. There was a time when employees who experienced harassment on the job just "had to take it." Sexual harassment, racial harassment and similar behavior, insults, even teasing, among employees was tolerated. Those days are over.

We suggest you warn an employee when you believe harassment has occurred. Often employees will stop the harassment once they are aware it is unacceptable to you and other employees.

If an employee refuses to change his behavior, he should be discharged. However, this is a very sensitive area. We suggest you proceed with great caution when approaching employees about harassment of others. It is important to investigate carefully and to get all the facts so any action you take will be reasonable and fair.

The same holds true for use of profanity in the workplace. Sometimes the use of casual profanity, obscenity, or foul (even abusive) language can be a sort of "norm." This use of profanity is not usually directed at anyone in particular and is not intended in a malicious way.

However, when profanity bothers other employees or could pose a problem for you and your customers, it should be dealt with. Issue warnings to all employees that profanity will not be tolerated, especially if you are changing the way things have been done in the past. Make sure you are clear in your warning; tell employees that what they did previously is no longer acceptable. Inform them that continued use of profanity or abusive language will result in termination from employment.

Tip. In cases of sexual or racial harassment, it is a good idea to interview the employee who was the subject of these acts. Have the victim fill out a short statement telling what took place (who, what, where, when) and why he or she was offended. Plan to have the victim available to testify if there is a UIC appeal hearing. This can be a very effective way to win your case.

Violation of Law

An employee who violates the law is presumed to jeopardize the employer and is usually discharged for misconduct. Examples of this discharge are illegal drug transactions while on the job and theft from the employer that results in the employee's *conviction*.

Be careful when discharging an employee for violations of public law. The investigation, allegations, arrest, charge and indictment, and arraignment of an employee do not mean the employee violated the law. In these cases, you must follow the rules of criminal law and adhere to the standard of presumption of innocence.

Until an employee either admits that he or she is guilty of violating the law or has been *convicted* of violating the law, it is extremely difficult to prove misconduct. We recommend you suspend an employee who is charged or arrested for violating the law, pending the outcome of a criminal charge. If you discharge the employee, you run the risk of being dragged into the criminal proceedings, especially if you have information related to the incident.

If you discharge the employee, you also risk the possibility of a wrongful-discharge lawsuit if you act before the criminal case is resolved. You could be sued for wrongful discharge if you discharge an employee who is later cleared of criminal charges. Be cautious in discharging someone under these conditions.

Tip. Seek the advice of an attorney who is an expert in labor and unemployment insurance law before you take any final action to discharge or suspend an employee under these circumstances.

You should also be aware that if you discharge an employee while criminal charges are pending, you will probably lose your UIC case because it is unlikely the criminal case will be resolved first. UIC agencies must presume the employee is innocent, and they nearly always rule in his or her favor. In addition, much (if not all) information related to the alleged violation may be unusable for UIC purposes while the criminal action is pending.

TIMING A DISCHARGE IS IMPORTANT

In discharging someone, timing is a critical consideration. Take time to get your facts straight, but don't wait too long. If an *unreasonable* time elapses between the event and the act to discharge an employee, you may be unable to establish a case for work-related misconduct. This is a technical matter in nearly all states; no matter how strong your misconduct case, you will lose because you failed to act *promptly*.

We strongly recommend you discharge any employees who have committed misconduct as soon as possible. When practical, do not let them even finish the shift they are on. This is especially important when fighting, assault, or theft is involved.

If you need time to conduct an investigation before discharging an employee, place the employee on *suspension* pending the outcome of the investigation. This shows you took action. Begin the suspension as soon as you can. Consider the following example of how waiting to discharge an employee can be harmful to an employer.

A Case in Point

Susan's Gift Shop has been in operation for ten years. During that time, Susan has hired many part-time cashiers. A month before Christmas, Susan and her husband Mike hire Ellen to help with the holiday rush. The second day, Susan and Mike notice that whenever Ellen works, the cash register is short $30 to $40. They begin to keep an eye on her.

Five days before Christmas, both Mike and Susan see Ellen take $40 out of the cash register and slip the money into her pocket. They immediately confront her, and she admits she needed the extra money to buy presents for her children. However, because of the Christmas rush, they do not fire her. Instead Mike and Susan give her a severe warning and threaten to file criminal charges if she steals from them again. Ellen swears she will not.

Ellen continues to work through the Christmas rush and even helps with the January inventory. Three weeks into January, Mike and Susan discharge Ellen for the attempted theft in December.

Ellen files a claim for unemployment insurance. Mike and Susan tell the claims examiner Ellen was fired for stealing. Ellen admits to the examiner she attempted to steal but was caught. The claims examiner asks Mike and Susan why they continued to employ Ellen after the attempted theft. They reply it would have been impossible to replace and train a new cashier during the Christmas season. Susan and Mike are astounded when they receive the Notice that Ellen is eligible for UIC benefits and that their tax account will be charged.

Did Susan and Mike have a good case for work-related misconduct? Yes. They caught their employee stealing red-handed, and they can both testify that Ellen was attempting to steal from the cash register. They both heard Ellen's admission that she was attempting to steal. Why did they lose? Because they did not act to discharge her within a reasonable amount of time.

Susan and Mike have no real reason for not discharging Ellen immediately. They waited to fire Ellen because they didn't want to train another employee during the Christmas rush. This is a reasonable thing to do from a business point of view, but it nullifies their UIC argument for misconduct.

Claims examiners and judges give almost no weight to actions taken for the employer's business convenience. It would have been inconvenient for Mike and Susan to discharge Ellen during the Christmas rush, but they could have done it. It would have been better to fire Ellen than to let her continue to handle money after she admitted to being a thief.

DISCHARGES FOR REASONS
NOT CONNECTED WITH MISCONDUCT

Not all discharges are for reasons of misconduct—sometimes employees are discharged when there is no case for misconduct. In most cases, an employer is charged for UIC benefits paid to employees discharged when no misconduct is present or alleged to be present. Here are some types of discharges not related to misconduct.

Employees Trying Their Best Who Cannot Meet Your Standards

Sometimes workers simply don't fit into your organization. Sometimes they lack the education, skills, speed, or potential to achieve the goals you expect. This can happen to an employee at any level—from mechanics at the local service station to corporate attorneys.

Employees with Medical Problems

Discharge of an employee with a medical problem who cannot be at work on a regular basis is another discharge for non-misconduct. This situation may be resolved if the employee has a curable problem. However, as an employer, you must put company goals first. You may ask yourself if the goals can be achieved while continuing to carry a worker who is constantly late or absent due to a physical or emotional condition.

Employees under medical treatment for alcohol or drug dependence may fall into this category. Require that the employee bring in a work-release form from his or her physician, listing either full duty or any restrictions (see Figure 4.1).

Employers with 25 or more employees (15 after July 1994) should not discharge any employee with a medical problem without first determining whether the discharge will be a violation of the Americans with Disabilities Act (ADA). The employee may fall into a protected class, and reasonable accommodations may need to be made. If the employee is in a protected class, consult a labor attorney about how to proceed.

Discharges for Absenteeism or Tardiness

If an employee can show he or she was discharged for absences *beyond* his or her control, the employee will normally be eligible for benefits.

This is a tough one for employers. You need reliable workers who report to work on time. Sometimes an employee has a legitimate reason for not coming to work regularly or not getting to work on time. There aren't many valid excuses an employee can offer, but sometimes pressing family emergencies or the employee's poor health can cause poor attendance or repeated tardiness.

In these situations, find out exactly what the employee's problem is. Insist that the employee provide specific information about the situation. If you believe the problem is genuine, find out how soon the em-

Figure 4.1
A Completed Work-Release Form

DEPARTMENT OF ECONOMIC SECURITY

REPORT OF ILLNESS OR PHYSICAL DISABILITY

(Español en el reverso)

CLAIMANT'S NAME _DICK REDDRICK_ SOC. SEC. NO. _000-14-1980_

PATIENT'S NAME _SAME AS ABOVE_ CLAIMANT'S PRIMARY OCCUPATION _JANITOR_

Is the claimant the patient? ☐Yes ☐No

STATEMENT OF AUTHORIZATION: I authorize you to release the information requested below to the Department of Economic Security with the understanding that it will be used to make a determination of eligibility for unemployment insurance benefits.

Signature _Dick Reddrick_ Date _10-6-7_

SECTION I TO BE COMPLETED BY PHYSICIAN

☒Mr.
☐Ms. _DICK REDDRICK_ has been most recently under my care

for _BROKEN ARM - FRACTURE OF_ from _9-5.7_ to _present_
(Nature of Illness) ULNA- _(Date)_ _(Date)_

IF THE CLAIMANT IS THE PATIENT, SECTION II MUST BE COMPLETED BY PHYSICIAN MAKING THE RECOMMENDATION OF CARE AND RELOCATION. IF NOT, PROCEED TO SECTION III.

SECTION II

1. In your opinion has the patient been able to work? ☒Yes ☐No
   If you answered no, please complete the following:

   a. The patient was unable to work full time as of _9-5.7_ 19_97_.
   b. The patient ☒was ☐will be able to work full-time as of _9.22-7_ 19___.
   c. Are there any work restrictions? *(lifting, driving, walking, etc.)*. Please list and specify: _NO HEAVY LIFTING - NO USE OF RIGHT ARM - NO DIFFICULT PHYSICAL LABOR._

2. In your opinion was it necessary for the patient to:

		Yes	No	Date Patient Advised
a.	Take time off from work for treatment and/or recovery?	☒	☐	9-5.7
b.	Change occupations?	☐	☒	
c.	Move to another area?	☐	☒	

COMPLETE ONLY IF APPLICABLE

3. Prenatal
   a. Expected date of birth _N/A_
   b. Patient should not work after_____

4. Postnatal
   a. Date of birth _____ 19___
   b. Patient can work full-time by_____ 19___

SECTION III

1. In your opinion, did the patient need full-time care during the period of treatment and/or recovery? ☐Yes ☒No

2. Was the claimant's presence necessary in providing care/treatment of the patient? ☐Yes ☒No
   Type of care _N/A._ Date needed _____

Return completed form to patient or mail to:

D.E.S. L.O. 101
2903 Broadway
Peoria, Kansas 65700

SIGNATURE OF PHYSICIAN _Judith Gordon, M.D._ DATE _10.7.7_
PHYSICIAN'S PRINTED NAME _JUDITH GORDON, MD_ PHONE _555.3434_
PHYSICIAN'S ADDRESS *(No., Street, City, State, ZIP)* _PEORIA, 2721 E. 9TH ST. KANSAS 64718_

ployee can resolve it. Tell the employee exactly what your concerns are regarding his or her poor attendance record. Be specific and direct. If you can come to a workable solution, it may be the best course to pursue.

To avoid ADA violations, check out the reason for the repeated tardiness or absence. If the employee is in a protected class, you may want to consult a labor attorney before you warn or discharge the employee.

WAYS TO MINIMIZE UIC CHARGES FOR NON-MISCONDUCT DISCHARGES

Here are some tips to help you avoid problems before hiring someone and to help you deal with an employee problem after it occurs. Following these procedures may help minimize UIC charges by showing you how to avoid hiring a person you will later have to discharge. Do everything possible to avoid hiring employees with poor work records.

Check Background

Check into a worker's background *before* hiring. Take extra time to conduct an interview designed to find out what kind of worker you are hiring. We are always surprised to find out how few employers ask for work references or check with previous employers *before* they hire someone. If a worker is hired because of his or her educational background, verify that the background information is accurate. This simple process can save you thousands of dollars and many problems.

Test Before Hiring

Use simple but relevant aptitude tests, or contact your state employment agencies to do any testing for you before hiring. For example, if you are hiring a typist, give a typing test or have your local state employment office conduct a test.

Check Letters of Recommendation

Don't take a letter of recommendation at face value. Call or write the employer to verify that the letter is authentic and accurate. It is very easy to fake a letter of recommendation or to alter a letter, especially if it is a photocopy.

Be wary of glowing letters of recommendation. Call the employer who issued the letter and ask the following questions:

- Can you tell me why this person is no longer working for you?
- If you had the chance, would you rehire this person?
- Is there anything I should know before I consider hiring this person?

Speak with someone in authority before accepting the recommendation of a former employer. An employee who has been discharged may arrange for a friend or former coworker to give a good recommendation.

Are Tools Needed?

Unless you supply all needed work tools, find out if a potential employee has the necessary tools. This is important when hiring skilled workers such as mechanics or carpenters.

Consider a Transfer

If you have other duties an employee might perform better, consider a transfer. Sometimes employees who are poorly suited for one job will be excellent in another position. Transfer prevents a discharge and may produce a happy, productive work relationship.

Cut Your Losses

If an employee is unable to meet your standards and you do not believe the situation is going to improve, cut your losses. Discharge the employee as soon as possible. This does not eliminate your UIC tax liability, but it *minimizes* the cost.

Tip. Some employees who cannot meet your standards may fall into special protected categories, such as physically handicapped, pregnant, or special minority status. Check federal and state laws and regulations *before* taking any action to find out if discharging this employee violates any special laws.

Document Inability to Perform Job

If your discharge is based solely on inability to perform the work, document *exactly* what work was done incorrectly, how it was incorrect, the correct method of performing the work, and the steps taken to instruct and help the employee meet your standards.

DISCHARGE OR QUIT?

Sometimes disputes arise as to whether an employee was discharged or quit. In this situation, the "moving party" standard applies (see Chapter 3). You are the moving party if you act to end a worker's employment.

In some cases, it may be unclear who is the moving party. Some states have rules about accepting resignations too far in advance. For example, if an employee tenders a resignation for 30 days in the future and you act immediately to terminate the employee or accept the resignation early, you may have "discharged" the employee without intending to do so. These cases are rare, but they do occur. We suggest you check with your local UIC office to determine the law in your state for accepting early resignations.

On the other hand, employees who leave a job because they think they are going to be discharged are usually deemed to have quit their jobs and will *not* be paid UIC benefits.

A common error employers make is believing that forced letters of resignation are quits. These types of separations are sometimes called "constructive quits" or "discharges in lieu of resignation."

Any time an employee is asked for a letter of resignation and would be discharged if he or she did not resign, the separation is considered a discharge for UIC purposes. Even a signed letter of resignation does not make a separation a quit. To be a quit, the employee must resign voluntarily. When an employer demands a letter of resignation, the employer is the moving party.

Even if you allow an employee to resign to protect his or her employment record when you in fact intended to discharge him or her, it is *still* considered a discharge.

5 _____

Quits and Layoffs

Often an employer is upset when a person who quits files a claim for UIC benefits. There is no way to prevent a worker from filing a UIC claim after separation from work. However, whether a worker is eligible for or entitled to benefits is another matter. To receive benefits, a worker must be separated from employment for a *non-disqualifying* reason.

When an employee leaves a job voluntarily, it is considered a quit. For UIC purposes, there are three reasons a person leaves employment voluntarily.

- Quit for good cause.
- Quit without good cause.
- Quit for compelling personal reasons.

In many quits, the employer will not be charged for UIC benefits. In some quits, UIC benefits *will* be charged against the employer's account.

Some discharges appear to be quits, and some quits appear to be discharges (see the discussion in Chapter 4). If separation is involuntary on the employee's part, it is generally considered a discharge. When the employee is the moving party and leaves voluntarily, the separation will generally be a quit. The employee bears the burden of proving he or she left for good cause (a valid reason according to UIC rules). In most states, volunteering for a layoff is no longer considered a quit. If an employer intends to lay workers off and asks for volunteers, anyone who chooses to leave is considered to be laid off for UIC purposes.

Executive Quits

An executive, like any other employee, may decide to leave his or her job voluntarily. However, the UIC does not treat an executive quit or resignation differently from any other quit. Executives are treated like all other unemployed claimants. An executive who applies for UIC benefits must stand in line, register for work, fill out claim forms, and face the same trials as every other claimant.

QUITS FOR GOOD CAUSE

There are a few situations that may *force* employees to quit their jobs. These acts are attributable to the employer. If the employer creates intolerable, illegal, or grossly unfair working conditions, employees may quit with *good cause*. These good-cause quits are charged to the employer and almost always result in an increase in UIC tax rates. Unfortunately, there are limited defenses against such tax charges.

You can avoid needless tax charges by not letting certain situations occur. Below are some examples of situations that can cause an employee to quit with good cause.

- Non-payment of wages.
- Legally substandard or hazardous working conditions.
- Harassment.
- Discriminatory job practices.
- Violations of law.

Non-Payment of Wages

Repeated non-payment of wages can constitute good cause for quitting. This includes not issuing paychecks, issuing paychecks on insufficient funds and asking employees to wait before cashing or depositing their paychecks. Isolated instances or bona fide mistakes are not grounds for quitting for good cause.

If an employer regularly fails to pay employees on a timely basis, they have grounds for quitting their jobs and may be eligible to collect UIC benefits. "Regularly" means more than once or twice, in most states. Often the term "regularly" is used because it is intentionally vague and allows the claims examiner or ALJ the discretion to determine what is fair or normal given all the facts of a case.

Also included in this category is paying wages that do not meet state or federal minimum-wage requirements. Benefits paid on any of these quits will be charged to the employer's UIC account.

Legally Substandard or Hazardous Working Conditions

In most states, workers who leave because working conditions are legally substandard (conditions violate state or federal regulations) quit with good cause. Employees bear the burden of proving that substandard conditions actually exist and that the employer has made no attempt to correct them. Generally an employee must prove that an independent investigation by an agency, such as OSHA, has determined the allegations are valid. The employee must usually demonstrate the employer made no attempt to correct the situation.

Harassment

For UIC purposes, the definition of harassment from *Black's Law Dictionary* is generally used. Harassment is defined as "words, gestures or actions that tend to annoy, alarm or physically or verbally abuse another person and serve no legitimate purpose." The situation must be more than merely unpleasant, and the employee must give the employer the opportunity to correct the problem. Examples of harassment include sexual advances (verbal or physical), racially abusive comments, and other forms of extreme verbal or physical abuse that create intolerable working conditions.

All forms of intimidation and unprovoked physical attacks fall into this category. Employers who fail to respond to allegations by employees that harassment is occurring run the risk of losing employees and may face additional legal action.

For UIC purposes, employees who claim harassment as the reason for quitting a job must present evidence to establish the situation actually existed. They must also show they made a reasonable attempt to resolve the problem before quitting.

Sometimes employees turn to independent state or federal agencies to conduct investigations and verify that harassment has occurred. The Equal Employment Opportunity Commission is one of the principle investigators of such complaints. Some states have their own agencies, including the state attorney general's office, that may conduct civil or criminal investigations regarding allegations of harassment. We strongly suggest you discourage harassment of any kind by employees in your written policies and by your actions. Tolerating harassment can lead to losing a UIC case.

Discriminatory Job Practices

This category is hard to pin down exactly because it can be very subjective. Generally any employee who quits because he or she is treated unfairly on a recurring basis may quit with good cause. "Good cause" in this category of quits includes unfair job assignments with regard to hours or amount of work, retaliatory action for past occurrences or other intentional acts by the employer that create an intolerable work situation.

Violation of Law

Generally, employees who quit because the employer requires them to violate the law at any level quit with good cause. One example of this type of problem is that of a truck driver being asked to drive more hours than allowed by the ICC and being told to falsify his or her records to hide the fact. Both requests are violations of the law.

Defending Quits for Good Cause

Although it is difficult to defend against a good-cause quit, it is not impossible. To establish a good-cause quit, a claimant must first show he or she attempted to *adjust* the grievance and show the attempt was futile. If your company has a written grievance procedure, you can present evidence that the claimant knew the procedure but did not follow it or complete it to allow you, the employer, to correct the situation. Even if you do not have a written procedure, at the hearing ask the claimant who he or she complained to or what was done to correct the situation. As an employer, you have the right to be told about unacceptable working conditions and given the chance to correct them.

If similar complaints have occurred in the past and you took no action or you let the situation recur, the claimant will be able to show an attempt to adjust the grievance would have been futile.

QUITS WITHOUT GOOD CAUSE

Most quits fall into the category of *quits without good cause*. In most states, it is difficult for claimants to establish good cause for quitting if they do not fall into the categories discussed earlier. Generally, quits without good cause fall into the following categories:

- Quitting to attend school.
- Quitting for personal reasons.
- Quitting to look for other work.
- Quitting because of reduction in wages or low wages.
- Quitting in anticipation of a discharge.

- Quitting because of unpleasant working conditions.
- Quitting because of incompatibility with a supervisor or coworker.

Quitting to Attend School

When an employee quits to attend school, unless it is an approved training program, he or she quits without good cause. If the employee quits to attend an approved training facility, the employer is usually not charged when benefits are paid.

Quitting for Personal Reasons

In most cases, quitting to attend to personal matters does not constitute good cause for quitting. If an employee must leave work because of some non-compelling personal reason, he or she may be eligible for benefits, but those benefits are not charged to you. "Compelling" personal reasons are those that meet the legal UIC definition for unavoidable reason. These reasons are so substantial that the employee has no other choice but to leave employment (see the discussion of quits for compelling personal reasons below). Check with your local UIC office if this occurs.

Quitting to Look for Other Work

Employees who quit to seek other work leave voluntarily and usually will not receive benefits. In most states, an exception to this is the situation in which an employee's hours have been reduced to part time and the employer schedules the employee to work so he or she cannot seek full-time work. The employee may be justified in quitting the part-time work to seek full-time employment.

Generally an employee is able to continue working part time while seeking full-time work. An employee who quits part-time work must demonstrate that the current employer's schedule made it impossible to seek full-time employment.

Quitting Because of Reduction in Wages or Low Wages

In many states, there is no implied agreement that an employer will not reduce wages. However, many jobs include union agreements that prohibit arbitrary reduction in wages. If an employer violates an expressed agreement, an employee's quit might be considered for good cause. When there is no agreement, a reduction in wages usually does not establish good cause for quitting.

Quitting in Anticipation of a Discharge

Generally, any employee who quits to avoid a discharge quits without good cause. Employees who believe they are going to be terminated and quit before the discharge also quit without good cause.

Quitting Because of Unpleasant Working Conditions

To establish good cause for quitting under these conditions, an employee must demonstrate an intolerable or genuinely dangerous situation existed. Working conditions that are merely difficult or unpleasant are generally not justification for quitting and will not be considered quits for good cause.

Quitting Because of Incompatibility with Supervisor or Coworker

An employee who quits because he or she doesn't get along with a supervisor or coworker does not quit for good cause. The employee *must* seek to resolve the problem through the proper channels.

QUITS FOR COMPELLING PERSONAL REASONS

Quits in this category are not usually charged to the employer. When an employee quits for a compelling personal reason, he or she leaves voluntarily for reasons beyond either the employer's or the employee's control. For UIC purposes, "compelling personal reasons" may include:

- Quitting to tend a sick relative.
- Quitting due to injury or illness of the employee.
- Quitting to move with a spouse or parent who is reassigned by the military or another employer. (Some states disallow this.)
- Quitting for compelling domestic circumstances.
- Quitting for conscientious objection (well-established personal or religious beliefs).

In situations where an employee quits for compelling personal reasons, if your UIC tax account is an insured account, you will not be charged. These quits are beyond your control and the employee's control. However, in most states, employees who quit for compelling personal reasons and are eligible for benefits pose a problem for reimbursement employers (see the discussion on reimbursement accounts in Chapter 1). Generally, there is no provision for exempting reimbursement employers from UIC taxes because they repay the UIC trust fund on a dollar-for-dollar basis for *all* benefits paid to claimants.

LAYOFFS

The UIC program treats a layoff as an action taken by an employer to reduce payroll costs; it is treated as a discharge for reasons other than misconduct. Employees who file UIC claims because they are laid off due to a lack of work are eligible to collect benefits in almost every case. Employer UIC tax accounts will be charged for the payment of those UIC benefits.

There *are* ways to limit your UIC costs if you have to lay employees off. Here are some ways to help limit the financial impact of a layoff.

If You Laid an Employee Off

Most states do not require that you return the Notice to Employer if you agree the claimant was laid off. If this is the case, keep the Notice in a file marked "Layoff Notices to Employer." You save the postage and handling charges, which can be $2.50 to $3.00 for each notice. When hundreds or thousands of workers are laid off, savings can mount up quickly. This is a relatively small saving, but it's a start.

Use Layoffs for Your Company's Benefit

Some employers try to get the most out of layoffs by keeping their best employees and laying off the least productive workers. This can be a useful strategy, but you must be careful not to violate union agreements or labor laws or other laws designed to protect specific groups of individuals.

Each layoff is going to cost you the same amount of money, so keep your best workers unless you are bound by agreements that *force* you to lay off on the basis of seniority or some other standard or federal or state law. Streamline and trim your work force during layoffs.

Keep Good Workers Part Time

Keep your most valuable workers busy on a part-time basis. Assign them to other duties rather than laying them off completely. These workers may be eligible for partial UIC claims; partial claims help limit your tax charges. Many states have special exemptions for employers who provide partial employment for workers during layoffs. Find out if your state has such a program.

Tip. The partial layoff strategy works especially well if you can reduce the amount paid to your workers but keep their weekly salaries high enough to equal or exceed the maximum UIC benefit in your state. By cutting hours, salaries, or hourly wage rates, you can substantially reduce your payroll costs and still not have valid UIC claims filed against you. For example, if your state's maximum weekly UIC benefit is $220 and you are paying a worker $350 a week, reduce your employee's salary to $220 per week. You save $130 in direct payroll costs. In addition to reducing your direct payroll costs, you also reduce the amount you must pay for Social Security, workers' compensation, and UIC taxes, which are based on a percentage of a worker's earnings.

If workers file UIC partial claims showing they are partially unemployed, they will not be eligible for benefits because they are earning too much money. If a worker quits because you have reduced his or her wages, that worker may be disqualified from receiving UIC benefits. Quitting for this reason is usually *not* considered good cause. Check with your local UIC office about local laws and regulations regarding quits due to wage, salary, or hour reductions. Either way, you win. You won't be charged for these UIC claims, even though they may be filed against your account.

6

The UIC Local Office Claims Process

You need specific strategies and tips to help you understand and deal with the local office claims process. Information in this chapter helps you organize your facts and shows you how to reduce the time you spend on UIC claims. An insider's look lets you see how a local UIC office operates, with a step-by-step description of how the claims process works. You will discover how claims examiners obtain and use information. We also reveal how personnel in local offices make decisions that can raise your UIC taxes. Specific strategies show you what to say and what to do at the right time when dealing with claims examiners.

This examination of the UIC local office and the process of filing a claim is something most employers never see. When you understand what you're up against, the timesaving strategies we provide will have real impact and meaning. Understanding how to use these strategies and techniques gives you the foundation and tools you need to master and win the UIC game.

AT THE LOCAL UIC OFFICE

The claims process can be your ally. Claimants entering an unemployment insurance office encounter an intimidating environment. The office is usually crowded and noisy. There are long lines and signs with confusing instructions. Children scream, papers litter the floor, and many unhappy people wait to take care of their business. This is good for *you*. Many would-be claimants never get past this first stage—they walk out of the office and go find a job.

Some claimants feel ashamed to file for UIC benefits. They believe they are applying for welfare or some other type of government hand-out. They feel embarrassed to admit to friends and relatives they must file for unemployment insurance benefits. In many cases, claimants already feel low self-esteem because they are out of work. Their self-image may suffer even more when they are exposed to the UIC claims process. The embarrassment of filing a claim keeps some former employees from filing for UIC benefits.

It would be great for you if the unpleasant experience of filing for unemployment insurance kept all former employees from filing for benefits. Unfortunately, you can't count on that strategy to contain your UIC tax costs. The fact is, most claimants file claims in spite of unpleasant conditions, and you must prepare your side of the case if you want to keep your UIC taxes under control.

Registering for Work

Once a claimant decides to brave the filing process, he or she is required to follow steps. All claimants must *register for work* unless they are members of a labor union or there are special exemptions due to poor labor-market conditions in the area. If jobs are available for which a claimant is qualified, a referral to that job or jobs is made. However, this *doesn't* mean the claims process stops.

Claimants have a legal right to file a UIC claim before they go on job interviews or accept job offers. To file claims, they must meet the legal standards of eligibility. These include

- Separated from work for non-disqualifying reason.
- Availability for work.
- Ability to work.
- Actively seeking full-time employment.
- Monetarily eligible (claimant has earned enough money to qualify for UIC benefits).
- If working part time, claimant must earn less than weekly UIC benefit.
- Willing to accept suitable full-time employment.

Some claimants find work through job referral and discontinue their UIC claims. This doesn't happen often, so do not count on this strategy to contain or lower your UIC taxes. If it does happen, you have saved some money. However, until a claimant is fully re-employed, he or she is entitled to continue filing.

Filling Out the Claim Forms

After a claimant registers for work, he or she is given a packet of claim forms to fill out. This packet usually includes the Initial Claim Form (Figure 6.1), an Availability Questionnaire (Figure 6.2), and other documents to determine if the claimant is available for work. The packet may also include a booklet or pamphlet explaining a claimant's rights and responsibilities while filing for benefits. In some states, claimants are required to watch a slide presentation or short movie about the UIC program. At this point, you are unaware the claimant is filing a UIC claim against you. You won't know a claim has been filed until you receive a written notice or a call from the UIC office requesting separation information.

Claims filing by former employees means job security for UIC employees. Local office jobs are based on the number of claims they process and adjudicate. It is in the interests of UIC employees to have as many claims as possible. While the claims filing process may be unpleasant, claimants are not discouraged by UIC personnel from filing them.

After the claimant fills out the forms in the UIC claim packet, paperwork is given to a claims examiner who reviews the forms and completes sections reserved for UIC information. The claims examiner reviews the initial claim form and the eligibility questionnaire to see if there are any issues on the claim. Major issues include

- Separation from work.
- Refusals of work.
- Labor union disputes.
- Availability for work (school attendance, transportation, child care, hours of employment).
- Ability to work (physical disability, pregnancy, illness).
- Part-time work.
- Pension (private or Social Security).
- Vacation, holiday, sick, or severance pay.

If the claims examiner detects any issue, the claimant is scheduled for an adjudication interview. This interview may take place immediately, or the claimant may be given a return appointment. At the adjudication interview, the claimant is interviewed on the issues, and the claimant's statement is taken.

If there are no issues on the claim, the claimant usually is scheduled to return in 1 to 2 weeks. The local office will try to issue the claimant a check as soon as possible. This is called a *first pay;* it is the first payable week in the claim series. For states that do not have a waiting week, the first payable week is the first week of unemployment—claimants can

Figure 6.1
A Completed Initial Claim Form

DEPARTMENT OF ECONOMIC SECURITY

INITIAL CLAIM FOR UNEMPLOYMENT INSURANCE

PRINT ONLY	DO NOT COMPLETE SHADED AREAS	SHADED AREA FOR OFFICIAL USE ONLY	27 SCREEN

1. SOCIAL SECURITY NUMBER 000-14-1980

28. EFFECTIVE DATE 0 9 2 8 9 7 **29. FILING DATE** 1 0 0 3 9 7

2. LAST NAME REDDRICK **FIRST NAME** RICHARD **MIDDLE INITIAL** NONE **30. LO** 101 **31. DEPUTY** 200 **32. TYPE** T

3. MAILING ADDRESS (No., Street, Apt. No., P.O. Box) 2555 E 1ST STREET APT. A-10 **33. FIPS** 04

CITY PEORIA, **STATE** KS **ZIP CODE** 65714

4. RESIDENCE ADDRESS (No., Street, Apt. No.) SAME AS ABOVE **CITY** — **STATE** — **ZIP CODE** —

5. OTHER NAME/SOC. SEC. NO. YOU USED IN LAST TWO (2) YEARS NONE **6. PHONE NO.** 555-1112 **7. BIRTHDATE** 1 1 2 5 5 5 **34. SEX** M

8. OCCUPATION JANITOR **35. ETH- NIC** 1 **36. DOT** 323.687 **37. DD** —

	Yes	No	*Additional deputy action required
9.	☒	•☐	Are you a citizen of the United States?
	☐	•☐	If not a citizen, were you legally authorized to work in the United States during the past 18 months. If Yes, Permit No. _____ .
10.	☐	☒	Are you handicapped as defined in Section 504 of the Rehabilitation Act of 1973?
11.	•☐	☒	Are you receiving or have you applied for a pension, annuity or retirement pay?
12.	•☐	☒	Have you received or will you receive vacation, holiday, or unused sick pay from your last employer?
13.	•☐	☒	Are you currently working and filing this claim to receive benefits under the Shared Work program?
14.	•☐	☒	Have you refused work or referral to work since becoming unemployed?
15.	•☐	☒	In the past 12 months have you filed an unemployment insurance claim in any state?
16.	•☐	☒	In the past 18 months have you worked in federal civilian service?
17.	•☐	☒	In the past 18 months have you worked in another state?
18.	•☐	☒	In the past 18 months have you been in military service?
19.	☐	☒	Are you required to make or do you owe court ordered child support payments?

38. ERI 4

20. LAST EMPLOYER YOU WORKED FOR BEFORE FILING THIS CLAIM (Regardless of State, Type of Work or Length of Job)
COMPANY NAME PRK JANITORIAL SERVICES

39 ER NUMBER 006 1112

MAILING ADDRESS (No., Street, P.O. Box) 1212 PARK ST. **CITY** PEORIA **STATE** KS **ZIP CODE** 65701

21. LAST DAY OF WORK BEFORE FILING THIS CLAIM Month 1 0 Day 0 3 Year 9 7 **40. NON-SEP ISSUE** 2 **41. SEND NOTICE** Y

	Yes	No	
22.	☐	☒	Have you worked at all since the LAST DAY OF WORK shown above?

42. BASE PERIOD ER #(s) (Additional B2 or F2 Screens) N

23. Why are you no longer working for your last employer? (Check (✓) the box which applies and write the reason in the space below)
- (40) ☐ I was laid off because of a lack of work or a reduction in force.
- (10) ☐ I quit my job because: _____
- (20) ☒ I was discharged because: BROKE MY ARM
- (45) ☐ I am still working part-time.
- (30) ☐ My employer and a union(s) are involved in a labor dispute. If this box is checked, deputy will complete LD-003.

24. PRIVACY ACT INFORMATION AND CLAIM CERTIFICATION (READ, BUT DO NOT SIGN UNTIL TOLD TO DO SO)

A. PRIVACY ACT INFORMATION

The Privacy Act of 1974 requires that you be furnished this statement because you are being asked to furnish your Social Security Account Number on the claim forms given to you. Your Social Security Number is solicited under the authority of the Internal Revenue Code of 1954 (26 U.S.C. 85, 6011(a), 6050B, and 6109(a)). Disclosure of your Social Security Number for this purpose is MANDATORY, and must be entered on the forms you submit to claim unemployment insurance. Your Social Security Number will be used to report your unemployment insurance to the Internal Revenue Service as income that is potentially taxable; it will also be used as a record index for processing your claim, for statistical purposes, and to verify your eligibility for unemployment insurance and other public assistance benefits. Should you decline to disclose your Social Security Number your claim for unemployment insurance will not be processed.

B. CERTIFICATION

I register for work and make application for unemployment insurance. I certify that I am not working or that I am on a part-time or reduced earnings basis. I am not seeking insurance under another state or federal unemployment insurance system. I have not applied for and I am not receiving a subsistence allowance for vocational rehabilitation training or a war orphans' educational assistance allowance from the Veterans' Administration. I further certify that the statements made hereon for the purpose of obtaining unemployment insurance under the Employment Security Law are true and correct to the best of my knowledge and belief. I KNOW THAT THE LAW PROVIDES PENALTIES FOR FALSE STATEMENTS IN CONNECTION WITH THIS CLAIM.

25. CLAIMANT SIGNATURE Richard Reddrick **26. DEPUTY SURNAME** Carol McGuire

Figure 6.2
A Completed Eligibility Review Questionnaire

DEPARTMENT OF ECONOMIC SECURITY
ELIGIBILITY REVIEW QUESTIONNAIRE

ESTE FORMULARIO ESTA
DISPONIBLE EN ESPAÑOL

Please complete this form and report IN PERSON on the date and time scheduled.

CLAIMANT'S NAME: *DICK REDDRICK*

SOC. SEC. NO.: *000-14-1980*

1. INDICATE THE KIND(S) OF WORK YOU ARE TRYING TO FIND AND LENGTH OF EXPERIENCE IN EACH

JANITOR — YRS. MOS. *18 YRS* | *BEEKEEPER 20 YRS* — YRS. MOS. | YRS. MOS.

2. INDICATE THE KIND OF WORK YOU DID FOR YOUR LAST FULL-TIME EMPLOYER: *JANITOR*
RATE OF PAY: $ *6.00* ☐HR. ☐WK. ☐MO.
LENGTH OF EMPLOY-MENT: *5* Yrs. *0* Mos.

3. LOWEST RATE OF PAY YOU ARE NOW WILLING TO ACCEPT FOR A NEW JOB
$ *6.00* per ☒Hr. ☐Wk. ☐Mo.

4. INDICATE THE SHIFT(S) YOU ARE WILLING AND ABLE TO WORK
☒Day Shift ☒Afternoon Shift ☒Night Shift

5. INDICATE (✓) THE DAYS YOU ARE WILLING AND ABLE TO WORK
☒Sun. ☒Mon. ☒Tue. ☒Wed. ☒Thur. ☒Fri. ☒Sat.

6. INDICATE THE NUMBER OF MILES YOU ARE WILLING AND ABLE TO TRAVEL TO WORK *20*

7. INDICATE (✓) THE MEANS OF TRANSPORTATION YOU NOW USE
☒Own Car ☒Bus ☐Walk ☐Bicycle ☐Other *(Specify)*:

Yes No
8. ☐ ☒ Do you have children or anyone else requiring care while you work? If yes:
INDIVIDUAL'S NAME AND ADDRESS *(No., Street, City, State, ZIP)* WHO WILL PROVIDE CARE

9. ☐ ☒ Do you have a definite date to return to work with a previous employer? If yes:
DATE — EMPLOYER'S NAME AND ADDRESS *(No., Street, City, State, ZIP)*

10. ☐ ☐ Are you pregnant? If yes:
☒N/A — EXPECTED DATE OF BIRTH

11.a. ☐ ☒ Do you obtain work only through a hiring hall of a Union? If yes:
b. ☐ ☐ Are you on the out-of-work list? If yes:
MOST RECENT DATE SIGNED ONTO THE LIST | UNION NAME | LOCAL NUMBER

12. ☐ ☒ Do you need a special license to do your work, e.g. chauffeur, barber, nurse, real estate, etc.? If yes:
DATE YOUR LICENSE EXPIRES | TYPE OF LICENSE

13. ☒ ☒ Are you or have you been in the past 12 months in business of any kind, or a corporate officer? If yes:
PLEASE EXPLAIN *PT BEEKEEPER*

14. ☐ ☒ Are you working on a commission basis? If yes:
PLEASE EXPLAIN

15. ☒ ☐ Are you doing any odd jobs, working part-time, or working full-time? If yes:
PLEASE EXPLAIN *PT BEEKEEPER - 10 HRS PER WEEK*

16.a. ☐ ☒ Are you attending a school? If yes:
NAME OF SCHOOL | DAYS/HOURS OF ATTENDANCE

b. ☐ ☒ Are you planning to attend school or have you attended school in the past six months? If yes:
NAME OF SCHOOL | DAYS/HOURS/DATES OF ATTENDANCE

17. ☐ ☒ Are you receiving/applied for Social Security, Retirement, or any other type of pension/annuity? If yes:
NAME/TYPE | AMOUNT ☐WK. ☐MO.

18. ☒ ☐ Do you have a physical condition or handicap which would limit your ability to work full-time now? If yes:
PLEASE EXPLAIN *BROKEN ARM*

19. ☒ ☐ Is there any reason you could not accept full-time work now? If yes:
PLEASE EXPLAIN *SEEING DR. FOR BROKEN ARM*

CERTIFICATION: I have answered these questions for the purpose of obtaining Unemployment Insurance, knowing that the law provides penalties for making false statements. I understand that I am to review this form for each week I claim benefits and if the information which I have provided changes, I must report in-person to my local Unemployment Insurance office immediately.

CLAIMANT'S SIGNATURE: *Dick Reddrick*
DATE: *10-6.7* ᵅ
DEPUTY SIGNATURE: *Carol Mc Guire*
DATE: *10/6/97*

81

Figure 6.3
A Completed Separation Questionnaire

DEPARTMENT OF ECONOMIC SECURITY

UNEMPLOYMENT INSURANCE — SEPARATION QUESTIONNAIRE

MAILING DATE	CLAIMANT NAME		SSN
	DICK REDDRICK		000-14-1980

EMPLOYER NAME	EMPLOYER PHONE NO.	LAST DAY WORKED
PRK JANITORIAL SERV.	555-3300	10-3-7

☒ This is your last employer of record and we need a statement from you to determine your eligibility for benefits.*
☐ This is NOT your last employer and the information you furnish will not affect the payment of benefits.

*SPECIAL NOTE: If this questionnaire was mailed to you, please respond within seven (7) days from the above mailing date.

If this questionnaire was given to you at the unemployment insurance (U.I.) office, please return the form as directed by the U.I. representative. Any determination concerning your eligibility will be based on information available at the time the determination is written.

If you should return to work before your scheduled report date, please complete the form and return it to your local office.

PLEASE ANSWER THE FOLLOWING QUESTIONS ABOUT THE EMPLOYER NAMED ABOVE.

TYPE OF WORK	HOURS PER DAY	HOURS PER WEEK	RATE OF PAY
JANITOR	8	40	$6.00 PH

LENGTH OF TIME ON THE JOB	SUPERVISOR NAME	TITLE
5 YRS	BOB HUGO	SUPERVISOR

DESCRIBE WHAT HAPPENED THAT CAUSED YOU TO BE OUT OF A JOB. BE SPECIFIC (If you need additional space, please use a blank sheet.)

I BROKE MY ARM. THEN THE BOSS STARTED TO GET MAD AND THEY STARTED TO PICK ON ME. THEY TOLD ME THEY WERE GOING TO FIRE ME AND THEY DID.

HAVE YOU WORKED SINCE LEAVING THIS EMPLOYER?	☐ YES ☒ NO	IF YES, COMPLETE BELOW.

EMPLOYER NAME	ADDRESS
—	

DATE BEGAN	RATE OF PAY
—	$ per

I certify that the answers to the above questions are correct to the best of my knowledge and belief. I am aware that the law provides penalties for false statements made knowingly in connection with a claim.

CLAIMANT SIGNATURE	DATE
Dick Reddrick	10-6-97

Español en el reverso

collect benefits almost immediately. For states that use a waiting week, the first pay is the first payable week *after* the waiting week.

When the claimant returns to the local office, many states give him or her a second series of forms. Claimants are instructed to mail in claims rather than report in person to the UIC office. After all issues have been covered by the local office, eligible claimants are scheduled to return from time to time for short interviews to make sure they are actively seeking work.

The Claimant's Adjudication Interview

An adjudication interview is required if a claimant's separation from work involves a quit or a discharge. Some local offices schedule claimants to return for an interview as soon as the initial claim is filed. In most cases, the claimant returns in 1 to 2 weeks, depending on the local office schedule. Most local offices schedule interviews according to the last four digits of a claimant's Social Security number. For example, claimants with SSA numbers from 0001 through 2999 might report on Monday, those with SSA numbers 3000 through 4999 report on Tuesday, and so on. By using this system, a local office maintains some control over traffic flow.

If a claimant indicates he or she was discharged or quit, a written statement must be completed that describes why the separation took place. This is called the *separation questionnaire* (see Figure 6.3); it is the claimant's written statement of record. The form asks for the following information:

- Employer's name.
- Employer's telephone number.
- Last day of work or date of separation.
- Rate of pay at time of separation.
- Work schedule.
- Name of immediate supervisor.
- Narrative statement telling why separation occurred.

The separation questionnaire is extremely important; other than the initial claim form, this is usually the first time the claimant makes a written statement about why he or she is no longer working. This written statement becomes part of the record used to issue a decision on the pending claim. That decision affects the claimant's eligibility for benefits and affects the charges to your tax account.

After the claims examiner reviews the claimant's written statement, he or she asks the claimant some questions regarding the separation from work. The examiner makes notes on a separate document, called

Figure 6.4
A Completed Eligibility Investigation Report

DEPARTMENT OF ECONOMIC SECURITY
ELIGIBILITY INVESTIGATION RECORD

☐C1	☐C2	☐C4		C5			
SOCIAL SECURITY NUMBER		**CLAIMANT NAME CHECK**	**ER NUMBER**				
000-14-1980		Reddrick	0061112				
ISSUE CODE	**ISSUE ID (C2)**	**DEPUTY ID**	**PGM**	**ER NAME AND ADDRESS**			
1	40	200	06	PRK Janitorial Services			
ISSUE STATUS	**RESOLUTION CODE**	**COUNT**	**UNTIMELI-NESS**				
R	S	A	01	1212 Park Street			
(RE)DETERMINATION DATE		**REDETERMINATION REASON (C2)**					
10/17/97		Sep.					
DISQUALIFICATION START		**DISQUALIFICATION END**					
9/28/97		00000					
STATEMENT 1	**STATEMENT 2**	**ER CHARGE STATEMENT**	**C5**	**CITY**		**STATE**	**ZIP**
2023	2024	5	2	Peoria		KS	65700
				CHARGE	**PGM**	**START**	**END**
☐Free Form Text.							
C9 Release Date _____ Ltr#_____							

I certify I obtained the following information from the parties named. Signature _Carol M ⸺_

FINDINGS OF FACT

Basis for Adjudication:_____ Separation from work

ER Protest: ☐Not Applicable   ☐Received Timely   ☐Received Untimely   ☐Not Received

Claimant Statement *(Date)*: _____ 10/6/97 _____

CLT: See UB 185 (sep from work questionnaire)

ER st: 10/6/97 Telecon 555-3300-Betty Rogers Will have ER call back ASAP.

10/10/97 Telecon Bob Hugo states. Claimant was discharged on 10/3/97. Clt was not discharged because he had a broken arm. Clt. suffered a broken arm 9/5/97. Clt. was unable to work as a janitor. Employer reassigned Clt. to other FT duties in the office. Clt. was to answer the phone and do some light filing. Clt. agreed to the assignment and returned to work on 9/22/97. On 9/26/97, Clt. was verbally warned for leaving his work station for 3 hours without permission. Warning witnessed by Bob Hugo (supervisor) and Betty Rogers (secretary). Clt. was given written warning for loafing and leaving work area for 4 hours on 9/30/97. Clt. was told any further infractions would lead to discharge. On 10/3/97 Clt. reported to work at 8a.m. Clt. disappeared from his work station at about 8:45a.m. until 11:30a.m. Absence was witnessed by Bob Hugo Betty Rogers and Hank Glade (foreman). Clt. was discharged at noon by Bob Hugo. At time of discharge, Clt. offered no explanation for leaving work station.

Clt. rebuttal: 10/10/97 Telecon. Clt. admits he received two warnings—one written and one verbal. Denies leaving work area for more than a few minutes on 10/3/97. Clt. did not protest first two warnings. States he was out of his work area on 10/3/97 because he wentto the restroom and took his regular break.

K.A.C. See R-5-3-5100.
R.C. See Determination.

the *Eligibility Investigation Report* (see Figure 6.4), on the claimant's statement.

If the initial evidence indicates the separation is a "quit," the UIC claims examiner asks the claimant a series of questions to determine exactly why the claimant left the job. If it appears the claimant was discharged, the examiner takes a short statement from the claimant. The examiner then contacts the employer by telephone to determine why the employer discharged the claimant.

YOUR FIRST TELEPHONE CONTACT
FROM THE UIC OFFICE

The initial telephone call from the UIC office is often your first notification that a former employee is filing a claim against you. Sometimes you receive a written *Notice to Employer* (see Figure 6.5) first, but usually the telephone call is the first notification, especially if the claimant was discharged or quit.

Do *not* respond to questions from the claims examiner in this initial telephone contact. You must take time to organize your facts and thoughts about what you're going to say. Any information you provide to a claims examiner becomes a permanent part of the UIC record. The examiner takes notes about what you say. In some cases, the conversation is tape recorded. Information becomes part of the official UIC record and helps determine whether you *win* or *lose* the case.

When the examiner calls, tell him or her (or have someone in the office advise the examiner) you will return their call with the separation information. This gives you time to prepare your statement. Later in this section we provide tips on how to organize and present your response.

Before making your return call to the examiner, you need to have some information available. You need to know

1. The name of the claims examiner.
2. The address and telephone number of the local UIC claims office where the claimant is filing.
3. The name and Social Security number of the claimant. (On some occasions, there are mix-ups with incorrect identifications.)
4. The claimant's reason for separation, with as much detail as possible.

   Getting this last information may be tricky; some claims examiners try not to give it out. You may have to insist on knowing what the claimant stated—tell the claims examiner you cannot provide adequate rebuttal if you don't know what the claimant said. Appeal to the fairness of the examiner. Tell the examiner, "I'll be calling you back with the information on the claimant's separation from work. I think it's only fair that I know what the claimant has told you, don't you?"

   If you can't get the information this way, ask the claims examiner to give you the information when you call back. Striking this kind of a quid pro quo deal

Figure 6.5
A Completed Notice to Employer

Department of Economic Security

Notice to Employer

To protest: *Complete, sign and return this form within 10 working days of the date of this notice.*

```
          L.O. #101
   L      Department of Economic Security
          2903 Broadway
   O      Peoria, Kansas   65700
```

```
          PRK Janitorial Services
   E      1212 Park Street
          Peoria, Kansas   65701
   R
```

Name: Richard Reddrick   Date: 10/6/97
SSN: 000-14-1980   ER Number: 0061112
BYB: 9/28/98   Charge Control Date: 9/28/97

Our records show the last day of work as: ___10/3/97_____

The claimant has stated the reason for separation was:

☐ Voluntary quit   ☐ Working part-time
☒ Discharge   ☐ Labor dispute
☐ Lack of work/R.I.F.

If you are the last employer, did you or will you pay severance, vacation, holiday or sick pay on or after termination:

☐ Yes   ☒ No

If YES, date of payment _____ Gross amount _____

Hrs. paid _____ Rate of pay _____ /per _____

Enter details of separation or other eligibility information on back of this form. Protest must be signed to be valid.

```
Company Name                          Date
    PRK Janitorial Services               10/9/97
Telephone
    555-3300
Print name & title

    Bob Hugo, Supervisor
Signature
    Bob Hugo
```

can be effective. In most states, you have a legal right to this information.

If an appeal to fairness doesn't work, in a pleasant way insist on your legal right to know what the claimant has alleged. Although it is not essential for you to know what the claimant has told the claims examiner, it's information worth having. It will help you provide rebuttal to what the claimant has said.

5. The date a decision is due out.

Ask the claims examiner when his or her decision is due out. All adjudications (except those past the last due-out date) are subject to deadlines. (Don't ask the adjudicator when he or she *wants* you to call back with information. Claims examiners always want the information as soon as possible.) Politely assure them you will call back as soon as possible; don't forget to call back.

It's an excellent idea to tell the claims examiner you will do everything you can to help him or her meet the deadline. Deadlines are extremely important to the UIC program, the local office, and individual examiners. Offering to assist a claims examiner helps forge a positive personal bond and begins to offset the empathy an examiner may have developed for a claimant.

6. The *effective date* of the claim.

Ask the claims examiner for the effective date of the claim. All claims are backdated to the Sunday of the week in which a claim is filed, unless there is special backdating of the claim. Backdating occurs for specific reasons—for example, when a local office cannot provide a permanent filing facility or when a claimant reported late the previous week and was given an appointment to come back, with a guarantee of backdating. Separation decisions are due out *21 days* from the effective date of the claim. Because most UIC employees do not work on Saturdays, the deadline is Friday, 20 days after the effective date.

Let's look at an example. The effective date of a claim is October 1. The technical due-out date for the decision is midnight, Saturday, October 21. In practical terms, the claims examiner wants to issue the decision by the close of business on Friday, October 20. You might receive a call from the claims examiner on October 10 or October 11. The latest you can provide your statement is October 20.

Delaying Your Response

When you receive the first call from the UIC office, the claimant may be sitting at the claims examiner's desk. A natural alliance has already been formed. It's the two of them talking to a faceless employer, employer's secretary, or some other voice over the telephone.

In this situation, you're at a disadvantage. If you provide any information, the claimant will have an opportunity to rebut it. He or she will get in the last word—often after you have hung up the telephone. You can avoid this by telling the claims examiner you will call back. The advantages of this strategy are twofold:

- You will have additional time to organize and present your case.
- You will have the claims examiner alone; the claimant will be gone.

Organizing Your Response

If you have used the strategies and tips provided in Chapter 3, your case is well organized. You should be able to pull out the claimant's file and review his or her record quickly and easily. There is no need to read the claims examiner the entire record over the telephone, but you must give the UIC office relevant information.

In this encounter, there are three major rules of engagement:

- Be brief.
- Be concise.
- Be polite.

Be Brief. The satisfaction is in winning the case, not in the amount of time you take to explain "everything" to the claims examiner. You don't want to spend any more of your valuable time on UIC matters than is absolutely necessary.

Be Concise. Stick to the point; don't bring up irrelevant grievances that don't bear on the claimant's separation from work. Don't argue with the UIC employee. Present your case and answer the questions posed by the claims examiner.

Be Polite. Everyone wants to be treated with respect and professional courtesy. Call the claims examiner Mr. or Ms., and contact the UIC office promptly (within a few days). If you call at the last minute, apologize for the delay. Many claims examiners are influenced by an employer's demeanor. If it's a close case, courtesy may mean the difference between winning and losing. If someone is going to be obnoxious or threatening to the claims examiner, let it be the claimant. Be firm and assertive, not abusive.

Returning the Claims Examiner's Call

You must be thoroughly prepared before you call the local office with separation information on your former employee's claim. This contact and the return of the Notice to Employer are the first two critical steps in containing your UIC tax charges. You may not have received the written UIC Notice to Employer when you call the claims examiner; it is not essential to have the Notice before you call back. It *is* essential for you to have the facts. Don't call the UIC office with information on why you fired the claimant for misconduct then write "laid off" on the Notice.

Speak directly with the claims examiner who interviewed the claimant then called you. This claims examiner is responsible for issuing the actual decision. He or she knows about the case and has already developed a professional connection with the claim.

If you cannot reach this examiner directly, leave a message to have him or her call you back. If you leave your information with someone else (a clerk, another examiner, a supervisor), the message may be garbled in transmission. The person taking messages for the absent examiner usually jots down a few notes and leaves them on the claims examiner's desk. This person isn't familiar with your former employee's case and is busy with his or her own cases and duties. In such circumstance, the claims examiner won't take the time to call you back and will issue a decision based on inaccurate and incomplete messages.

It is vital for you to *speak directly* with the examiner who will issue the decision. This is the only effective way you can counter what the claimant has said. It is the only way you can be sure the examiner is receiving accurate information. The claims examiner may have questions for you, especially in the case of a difficult or complex separation from work. The most powerful, convincing way to present your case is to give a short, fact-filled narrative of what happened.

Presenting Your Case Step by Step

When you reach the claims examiner handling your case, inform him or her you are calling back with the requested information. Here is how a good interview might sound.

Claims Examiner: Hello, Westside Unemployment Insurance. May I help you?

Employer: This is Mike Adams from Walnut Industries. I'm calling back with regard to the John Carter case. I'd like to speak with Carol Simpson please.

Claims Examiner: This is Carol Simpson. How can I help you?

Employer: Ms. Simpson, I'm glad I was able to reach you. My secretary received a call from you regarding John Carter, one of our former employees. I got the information several days ago, and I've been trying to reach you. In fact, I called yesterday and the day before, but you weren't available.

Claims Examiner: I know you called back, Mr. Adams, I have a couple of messages on my desk. I've been out ill and was planning to call you back as soon as I could.

Employer: If you have some questions regarding the reason John Carter was let go, I'll be glad to answer them. But first, I'd like to tell you what happened.

John was discharged on August twenty-fifth for not coming to work and not calling in. Our company has a strictly enforced policy that we negotiated with John's labor union. The policy is in writing, and John read the policy when he was hired two years ago. He signed a receipt showing he read on the policy on August 11, 19—. I have the original receipt right here in front of me—yes, there's John signature and the date.

This isn't the first time this has happened. On February fourth, about six months ago, John was absent from work and didn't call in all day. When he showed up two days later, I called him into the office and gave him a written warning. I had John sign the warning, and I had Alice Smart, our personnel director who was also present at the warning, sign the document. We thought the warning would solve the problem, but I guess it didn't.

On June fourteenth, John was scheduled to be at work at his usual time, 8:00 A.M. He didn't show up all day and again didn't call in. He was out only one day. I called John into the office again as soon as he came in; the meeting started about 8:05. Alice Smart was there too. I asked John what happened. He said he had to take a sick relative to the doctor and just forgot to call. I asked him if he remembered the previous warning. He said "No," so I showed it to him. He said, "OK, I guess that's right."

Alice and I explained we were going to issue one final warning. We told John this was his last warning, and if he didn't show up for work and didn't call in again, we'd have to fire him. John said he understood and was sorry. He assured us it wouldn't happen again. On August twenty-fourth, he was absent for three days with no call. When he came into work, he acted as if nothing had happened. Alice and I called John into the office at about 8:10 A.M. We asked him what happened; he said he was out of town and his car broke down. It took him three days to get the car fixed and get back. I asked him why he didn't call, and he just said, "I guess I forgot again."

At that point, I told him I was letting him go. I told him he had ignored the warnings; he should have called to let us know what was going on.

Claims Examiner: Thank you for the information, Mr. Adams. I do have a few questions I'd like to ask you.

Employer: Sure, Ms. Simpson. I'll be glad to tell you what I know.

The claims examiner may want more details about the claimant's job, his rate of pay, hours of employment, and the days of the week he usually worked. Have all this information in front of you; you'll be able to answer these types of questions easily.

The claims examiner should be pleased with the information she now has. As you were talking, she was making notes on the Eligibility Investigation Record (not word for word) of what you said, writing down relevant facts. In some cases, a tape recording is made. If your conversation is tape recorded, the examiner will tell you so and ask if you have any objection.

By presenting your side of the story in a concise, easy-to-follow format, you have made great progress toward winning your case. If your information is *precise, clear,* and *detailed,* you will almost always convince the claims examiner that your story is credible. He or she will be pleased that you were polite, researched the case in depth, and had your facts straight.

The claims examiner will probably want to ask you questions regarding company policy. She may want to know if calling in is required in all absences. She may ask you if the absence caused the discharge or was it the fact the claimant did not show up and did not call in that motivated you to discharge him. She may ask you how early employees are supposed to call in and who takes the calls. She may ask you to provide copies of the written policy, a copy of the receipt John signed when he read the policy, and copies of the two written warnings. The examiner may want to talk to the personnel director to verify your statements about her involvement.

There is *no way* to anticipate exactly what a claims examiner will ask you. Some new claims examiners ask irrelevant or awkward questions. They may be uncertain of what they want or where their questions are leading. Sometimes questions are awkwardly phrased or hard to follow. Don't worry about this. If your notes are organized and you have the employee file, you should be able to answer any question from any UIC claims examiner with confidence and authority. You can control the interview by supplying precise information.

Claims examiners ask questions to help them fill in the blanks so they have the facts they need to support a decision on the UIC claim. They want to have enough facts to make a decision, either for the employer or for the claimant. You also want the examiner to have enough facts so he or she is *compelled* to make a decision in your favor with no charge to your UIC tax account. The next case study demonstrates how a case can go awry, even when it may seem you hold all the cards.

A Case in Point

Alice, a room cleaner and maid at a local hotel, quit her job and filed a claim for UIC benefits. In the adjudication interview, she told the claims examiner she quit because of the way she was treated by her supervisor, Rose. Alice stated Rose was against her from the beginning. She alleged Rose called her "bad names" and often yelled at her, using profanity. Alice said Rose constantly criticized her work and on two occasions denied her a raise. Alice says the day she quit, Rose threw a plastic wastebasket at her and hit her in the back.

Alice said she complained to Rose's supervisor, but nothing was ever done. She said she even complained about Rose hitting her with the wastebasket, but the supervisor said he could do nothing. Rose says there were no witnesses to the wastebasket incident.

Alice's story doesn't seem credible to the claims examiner. Alice is unable to recall many details—when she talked to Rose's supervisor or exactly when Rose threw the wastebasket at her.

The claims examiner has only Alice's word these incidents took place, so he calls the employers for their side of the story. The assistant manager of the hotel says she will look into the matter and call back. She believes Rose would never treat anyone badly. She gives no other details, but says she will talk to Rose before she calls back. No one from the hotel calls the claims examiner back by the due date of the decision, and the Notice to Employer is not returned.

With no other choice at hand, the claims examiner rules that Alice quit her job for good cause. The weight of the evidence was in her favor because the employers failed to counter any of Alice's charges. Because they did not return the Notice to protest the claim, they are no longer an interested party, and they are not entitled to a written determination on the outcome of the case. Without the written determination, they cannot file an appeal.

About a month later, the assistant manager calls the claims examiner. She says she's sorry she didn't call back, but she was called away because her father died suddenly. She still has the Notice to Employer sitting on her desk. She asks the claims examiner if he made a decision and if she can still return the Notice. The claims examiner informs the assistant manager that although she can send the Notice to Employer to the local office it will no longer entitle the hotel a written decision on Alice's claim. The claims examiner also tells her he ruled in Alice's favor and that the employer will be charged for payment of benefits.

The assistant manager becomes furious. She tells the claims examiner Alice's story is a lie. She says Rose denied the story. Two other employees were witnesses; it was Alice, not Rose, who threw the wastebasket. They also verify that Alice used profanity constantly and that Rose felt the use of profanity violated her religious beliefs. The employees state that when Alice quit she said, "I'm going to lie to get my unemployment insurance." Alice also tried to get the other two employees to lie for her, but they refused.

After listening to all this, the claims examiner explains again to the assistant manager that he had no choice but to rule in Alice's favor. No Notice to Employer was returned to protest the claim, so the hotel has lost its legal standing as an interested party.

Returning the Notice to Employer and returning telephone calls are critical. It doesn't matter if it's a discharge or a quit. Without rebuttal from the employer, claimants almost *always* win unemployment insurance claims. You can't afford to let uncontested allegations remain on the record, even when a claimant quits.

Closing the Interview

A good way to close a telephone interview is to thank the claims examiner for his or her time. If you feel he or she has been courteous, say so. Leave the lines of communication open. The examiner may want to recontact the claimant (usually by telephone) and obtain rebuttal information (to find out what the claimant has to say). It's been our experience that this rarely happens at the local office level. Most UIC claims examiners are so busy that if your story is clear and credible, he or she will not waste time calling the claimant for clarification or rebuttal information.

Claims examiners hate to have their decisions reversed at the appeal level. If the examiner is convinced that you are basically right, have credible witnesses, and will present a strong case if he or she rules in your favor, you will almost always win your local office case.

Local office claims examiners have supervisors who evaluate them to ensure that decisions are *supported by evidence.* If the information and evidence you give them is strong and clear, it is easier to issue a decision supported by those facts and that evidence. If you give a claims examiner enough clear evidence, he or she should rule in your favor.

SUBMITTING WRITTEN DOCUMENTS

Although most information you give a claims examiner is provided over the telephone, there are times when you must supplement statements with written documentation. In this section, we provide you with tips on when and how to use written documents to strengthen your UIC case.

The documents you need to win UIC cases depend on the reason the claimant was separated from work. In the case of a quit, the two most valuable documents are the *employee's letter of resignation* (or any other signed or written proof showing why the claimant left) and *written statements from witnesses* showing the claimant voluntarily left his or her employment. Obtaining these documents is discussed in Chapter 3.

Documents that prove the claimant quit are important when the claimant is alleging he or she was discharged. Written evidence showing that the claimant told you one thing but is now telling the claims examiner another is crucial. If you submit written documents showing the claimant is lying, you greatly increase your chances of winning a UIC case.

If you discharged the claimant, sending the UIC examiner copies of documents may be the key to winning your case. Some of the important documents to consider using in discharge cases are

- Time cards (either signed or unsigned) in cases of tardiness or absence from work.
- Written customer complaints in cases of discharge for rudeness or inattention to clients.
- Forged or altered documents in cases of forgery or dishonesty.
- All relevant written warnings when warnings show misconduct.
- Police reports and traffic tickets when negligence or damage to vehicles is involved.

- Court documents showing convictions when employees are discharged for violation of law (drugs, alcohol, theft).

- Private investigative reports showing employee misconduct.

- Documents showing suspension of licenses when an employee lost a license required to do his or her job.

- All other written documentation that will help the claims examiner clearly understand your side of the case.

What Documents Will You Need?

It is impossible to anticipate or predict exactly which documents you will need in any particular case. Our rule of thumb is to discuss the matter with the claims examiner and find out exactly which documents will best meet the needs of each case. Claims examiners don't want to wait for or handle additional paperwork, but you can insist that your documents be made part of the record.

When you submit written documentation, be concise. Send in *only* documents that relate directly to the *reason* the claimant was discharged or quit. If you have any doubt as to what is relevant, it is better to submit too much rather than too little. There may be times when the claims examiner is not sure what he or she needs or wants. There may also be times when the claims examiner is simply uncooperative and refuses to tell you what documents are important to the case. If you are uncertain about what to submit, send more than is needed.

Do *not* send original documents to a claims examiner unless it is absolutely necessary. A legible photocopy is usually enough to prove misconduct or a quit without good cause and win your case at the local office level.

A claims examiner is authorized to accept photocopies in local office cases. If you give up your original documents, anything can happen; they can be lost or misplaced. Original documents can be critical to your case at higher levels. Give them up only under very special circumstances. We suggest you talk to the local office manager if original documents are requested; obtain a receipt for any originals you submit to a UIC office for a pending case. (At higher levels it may be necessary to provide original documents. We discuss this in more detail in Chapter 8.)

Submitting Documents

The best way to send documents to a local office claims examiner is regular first-class mail. Send any documents directly to the claims examiner who will issue a decision on the case or to the attention of the local office manager. Tell the claims examiner over the telephone what you're sending in. If you can get the documents together quickly, send them to the examiner along with the signed and dated Notice to Employer.

If it will take a few days to gather together and copy the documents, mail the Notice to Employer first. *Don't* wait to send in the Notice while you're organizing or copying documents. The Notice to Employer ensures your status as an interested party to the claim and protects your future appeal rights. The telephone interview with the claims examiner allows you to explain your side of the story; submission of documents helps you build a stronger case.

If you submit documents by first-class mail, call the claims examiner a few days later and verify that they arrived. Make sure they are being made part of the record. If the examiner tells you the documents did not arrive, send duplicate copies immediately and tell the examiner you are doing so. This may seem like extra work, but copying and mailing a few essential documents can be done in a few minutes, and winning a UIC case can save you thousands of dollars. Think of it as inexpensive insurance.

If you are short on time or have doubts about first-class mail, send your documents by registered, certified, or special overnight mail. The post office also provides an inexpensive certificate of mailing that gives you an independent record of the date and address of your mailing. The certificate of mailing is filled out by a postal employee and stamped and dated. As an official document of the U.S. Postal Service, it is certain proof you mailed your information to the UIC office.

You can also use local couriers, Federal Express, or UPS. Many UIC offices have fax machines and accept copies of documents submitted electronically. Transmitted copies must be readable when they arrive at the UIC office. If you send a fax, call the UIC office to make sure it was received in usable condition.

There are some documents you almost never need. You usually won't need a claimant's termination report, job application, income-tax forms, or warnings unrelated to the separation.

RESPONDING TO THE WRITTEN NOTICE TO EMPLOYER

The UIC office will send you a written Notice to Employer. Returning this notice in a timely manner is *vital* to protecting your legal rights under UIC rules. If you fail to respond within appropriate time limits, you may jeopardize your rights and pay otherwise avoidable UIC taxes.

The Notice to Employer is one of the *most important* documents in protecting your UIC account. If the claimant was fired or quit his or her job, it's crucial that you fill out the Notice to Employer and return it to the UIC office within the legal time limits. The time limit should be clearly stated on the Notice.

Returning the Notice to Employer entitles you to a written decision from the local UIC office. This Notice to Employer is the first major step in protecting your appeal rights. If you fail to return it in a proper and timely manner, you may lose *all* the rights you were entitled to. If the claimant is found eligible for benefits and you did not return the protest, you may lose any rights of appeal.

The claims process requires *you*, as the employer, to take the responsibility for requesting relief from UIC tax charges. If you don't return the Notice to Employer, the UIC system *assumes* you don't want to protest charges to your account. On that basis, they will *not* exempt you from charges, even though you may have a good reason for not being charged.

A Case in Point

Betty's Cafe receives a Notice to Employer telling her a former employee is filing a claim for unemployment insurance. Betty reads the Notice but knows she isn't the last employer—the Cloverleaf Truck Stop hired her former employee three months after he left Betty's. Betty knows her employee quit to look for other work. She assumes the Notice is a mistake, so she throws it away.

When Betty gets her UIC benefit-charge statement, she notices a charge to her account for almost $2,300. Angry and frustrated, Betty calls the local UIC office. They inform her that if she had returned the Notice to Employer, her account would not have been charged. Betty asks if she can still return the Notice and have the $2,300 charge removed. The claims examiner tells her she can return the Notice, but it will be considered late and the charge will remain. The UIC office representative informs her she can file an appeal to the charge.

In this case, Betty was not the last employer, but the claimant's base period was computed on wages from Betty's Cafe. The last employer laid the claimant off and may be subject to charges if the wages paid fall into the claimant's base period and the claimant is filing an active UIC claim. (For further information on base-period wages, see page 103.)

At this point, Betty is the only employer immediately subject to UIC tax charges. To avoid problems, she only had to fill out the Notice to Employer and write "voluntary quit, personal reasons," sign it, date it, and return it to the UIC address on the form.

If Betty had returned the Notice on time, the claims examiner would have asked the claimant why he quit. If the claimant agreed it was to seek other work, Betty might have avoided charges against her tax account. By not returning the Notice, Betty forces the UIC system to charge her account. Her simple oversight cost her business several thousand dollars.

As this example demonstrates, it is critical to *read, complete, sign, date,* and *return* all Notices to Employer if the claimant was discharged or quit. It doesn't matter if you are the last employer or a base-period employer. Failure to return a Notice almost always results in charges to your UIC tax account.

If a claimant was laid off, you don't need to return the Notice unless it is required in your state. You will be charged for all layoffs. If your state does not require you return the Notice to Employer when someone is laid off, save yourself time and postage. Stick it in the claimant's file and forget it.

Returning the Notice to Employer as the Last Employer

If you are the last employer and the claimant worked only for a few days, return the Notice to Employer. Many employers who fail to return the Notices are surprised when they receive charges to their tax accounts at the end of the quarter. Current last employers can become base-period employers in the future. Some states send out second Notices, but many do not. Our advice is to return *all Notices,* whether you are a last employer or a base-period employer. You can never go wrong by returning every Notice (except in cases of layoffs).

Don't take a chance. Return each Notice in every discharge and quit; it's important to your case. Below are some effective tips to help ensure that you return the Notice to Employer in the correct form and manner. Be sure each Notice from the UIC contains

- Date of Notice.
- Address of local office.
- Claimant's name and Social Security number.
- Date of the separation from work or last day of work.
- Claimant's reason for separation from work.
- Instructions on what to do with the Notice.
- Instructions on time limits for returning the Notice.

Read the Notice carefully; often it is the only one you will receive. It serves as official notification that a claim has been filed against your account. Once you have looked at the Notice, take these steps.

Incorrect Information

Sometimes a Notice to Employer will contain incorrect information. If information on a Notice is invalid or incorrect, circle it and write the correct information in the spaces provided.

Reason for Separation

Write down why the claimant was separated from work. For quits, write "voluntary quit, personal reasons." For discharges write "discharged, misconduct." These general statements are acceptable in most states. If your state requires specific written information on the Notice, comply with the law.

You save time by using general statements. You can always add to the information later by sending documents to support your case. The claims examiner relies on information given in the telephone interview. Information on the Notice itself is not usually essential to your case. However, getting the signed Notice back to the local office on time *is* essential.

Sign and Date Notice

Most states do not consider unsigned protests valid. Some states return Notices for signatures—several do not. If a Notice is invalid, it cannot be used to protect your rights of appeal.

Mail Notice before Deadline

Mail the Notice in time to meet the deadline; sending in a completed Notice late is one of the worst things you can do. States have very short time periods in which to return a Notice—most allow 10 to 15 days. Some states give employers only five days from the date of the Notice. If the Notice is going to an out-of-state address, it may have to be mailed back to the UIC office almost immediately after it arrives. Most UIC offices accept a Notice as timely if the *postmark* on the return envelope falls within the deadline period. A few want it back in their possession within the time period allowed by law (see the questions at the end of this chapter).

Instruct people in your organization you are expecting a Notice, and let them know the importance of returning it within the legal time period. Put your return Notice in the mail as soon as possible. Designate reliable people to this important job, and have reliable backup personnel in case the designated person goes on vacation or is out ill. Failure to handle a Notice correctly can result in the loss of many thousands of dollars.

Keep Records of Returned Notices

Keep a record of all Notices you return. Most UIC Notices provide a duplicate copy for you to keep. If yours has no attached duplicate, make a copy. On your copy, note the date it was mailed to the UIC office. This date is more important than the date the Notice was signed.

Returning Notice after Deadline

If you return a Notice after the deadline, you will *almost always* lose your protest rights. By returning the Notice late, you have given the UIC a record of your error. In most cases, *no* reason is acceptable when asking the UIC to excuse your mistake. Even death in the family or death of a company president doesn't buy extra time. Some late Notices have been accepted as valid in cases of natural disasters or major destruction of company property and records, but this is extremely rare and occurs only in the most extraordinary cases.

If you do not mail the late Notice, the UIC office will have no clear proof of what happened. Some employers have beaten the system by swearing they returned a Notice on time. If it never arrived at the UIC office, this is not the employer's fault. Some employers have successfully claimed that they never received a Notice because they would have returned it on time. We are not suggesting you do this. It's easier to stay on top of the situation and to use the techniques described above so your Notices *are* returned on time.

Verifying That Your Notice Arrived at the UIC Office

It is difficult to prove that the UIC office received your Notice. There is no way to prove you returned a Notice if it was sent by regular first-class mail. However, there several things you can do.

1. Call the local office several days after you return the Notice. Verify that it arrived.
2. If the Notice did not arrive, inform the claims examiner you want to protest the claim and you will return a duplicate Notice.
3. Note the time and date of your call and the name of the UIC employee you speak with.
4. Make a photocopy of your copy of the Notice and mail it the same day.
5. If you don't have a copy, type or write a Notice, and return it to the local office. Before you do this, ask the claims examiner what to include in this Notice to make it valid. You should include

   - Claimant's name.
   - Claimant's Social Security number.
   - Last day claimant worked.
   - Employer's business name.
   - Employer's UIC tax number.
   - Reason for separation.
   - Signature and date to make it a valid protest.

Withdrawing Written Notices

You may want to withdraw a Notice to Employer after it has been submitted to the local office. If you returned a Notice containing incorrect information, you can correct the information or withdraw the Notice completely. A written Notice is part of the official UIC record.

To withdraw a Notice, inform the local UIC office in writing of your desire to withdraw it. Photocopy your copy of the Notice and write on it, "We wish to withdraw our protest to the claim." If you want to correct information on the original Notice, follow the same procedure. If there isn't enough room on the Notice to include all the information, attach a short note or letter to the photocopy. All corrections and withdrawals must be made in writing.

GAMES CLAIMANTS PLAY AND
HOW TO COUNTER THEM

Many claimants are experts at manipulating the UIC claims systems and UIC claims examiners. Experienced claimants seem to know more about the UIC program than some claims examiners. A book for claimants, *How to Collect Unemployment Benefits* (1983), was written by former claimant Raymond Arvutis. The book provides tips on how to collect unemployment insurance. Arvutis, a self-described "seasoned veteran of the unemployment insurance maze," boasts he exhausted (totally collected) benefits on seven different occasions since 1966. We're uncertain how Arvutis managed to work long enough to establish and exhaust seven claims from 1966 to 1983, but we'll take him at his word.

Arvutis is the type of claimant an employer must be wary of. Such claimants have learned how to manipulate, and sometimes cheat, the UIC system. They take advantage of it every chance they get. They exploit the UIC program and drive tax costs to excessive, unfair levels. There is no reason Arvutis and others of his kind should continue to collect money undeservedly.

Claimants often do and say some outrageous things to collect unemployment insurance benefits. If a claimant has been discharged from a job, he or she is usually angry with the employer. Filing a claim is a way of fighting back. The adjudication interview is often the first time and place a claimant can tell the story to a government official. Many claimants believe a claims examiner has the power to get them reinstated or that the claims examiners can deal with aspects of their grievances beyond the scope of the UIC claim. We dispelled this myth in Chapter 2.

Many claimants persist in believing a claims examiner is empowered to resolve various matters, such as allegations of sexual, racial, or age discrimination; non-payment of wage disputes; or disputes over safety and working conditions. Even claimants who quit their jobs believe this, especially when separation involves hard feelings and unresolved conflicts.

Many claimants try to persuade a claims examiner that their separation from work was the employer's fault. In discharges, claimants may tell the examiner the employer had some personal reason for firing them. Claimants rarely admit any responsibility for being discharged. Some claimants falsify their reason for separation. The two most common false contentions claimants make are

- They were fired for trying to organize a union.
- The employer wanted sexual favors and they refused to comply.

Don't let false information deter you. You'll have an opportunity to set the record straight when you speak to the claims examiner. You can't control what a claimant tells the claims examiner—you can only contradict the information or rebut it. It's your job to present your side of the story and let the examiner decide who is telling the truth.

The claimant usually makes the first statement regarding separations from work at the local office level. (At appeal hearings, the administrative law judge decides who goes first.) Below are various tactics claimants use to try to qualify for benefits.

Bringing Children Along

A claimant brings along his or her children, hoping the claims examiner will see the claimant "needs" the UIC benefits because he or she has a family to support.

Countermeasure. There's not much you can do about this tactic. It usually works *against* claimants because unemployment benefits are not based on need. If you're lucky, the claimant's children will irritate the claims examiner to the point where he or she will ask the claimant to leave the office. Lack of child care may also call the claimant's child care arrangements into question.

Falsifying Medical Statements

When an employee leaves his or her job for alleged health reasons, he or she is required to obtain a statement from a licensed medical practitioner. Most states provide claimants with medical questionnaires (see sample in Appendix C), which are designed to help the UIC office obtain specific information used to write a decision on the pending claim.

It is the claimant's responsibility to return the form to the claims examiner. Many doctors will put something on the form to help a claimant receive benefits. Often the doctor does not understand the purpose of the form. Once the form is complete, it is usually returned to the claimant. After that, anything can happen.

Sometimes a form is altered by the claimant so information is consistent with the reason for separation from work. In some instances, a claimant will alter the date of the illness or injury so it appears he or she was injured or under the doctor's care earlier than the actual date. The most common alteration is a change from *no* to *yes* on the question of whether the doctor recommended the claimant leave work.

When an employee is discharged for absenteeism or tardiness, medical statements are often used to determine whether the absence was due to a legitimate medical problem. Often a claimant will state that he or she was absent and under a doctor's care. Medical questionnaires are used to determine if this claim is true and if the dates of the absences match the dates of medical treatment.

In addition to lying to health-care providers and altering legitimate medical UIC questionnaires, claimants sometimes fill out medical statements themselves. In metropolitan areas where there may be thousands of medical authorities, it is impossible to verify whether a form is actually completed by the person whose name appears on it. Claimants sometimes have spouses, relatives, or friends complete their medical forms. The document is then returned to the claims examiner as authentic.

Countermeasure 1. This is a difficult type of fraud for you to offset or even discover because you normally have no opportunity to see medical forms a local office uses in making first-level decisions. If you believe a claimant has submitted a falsified medical form, contact the claims examiner or local office manager.

Request that the claims examiner verify the form by calling the doctor who signed the form, or request that the examiner mail a second form to the doctor. The second form should be returned directly to the UIC local office rather than the claimant. This second statement can be compared with the first to see if information matches.

Countermeasure 2. At your business, establish a definite leave-of-absence policy. (It doesn't have to be paid leave.) Employees who try to quit for false medical reasons will have to explore your leave-of-absence policy before they quit. This also gives you an opportunity to get a medical statement from the employee before he or she leaves. You and the claims examiner can compare the medical statement with any future medical statements from a claimant.

In most states, your UIC tax account is not charged if a claimant leaves for medical reasons beyond your control. If the claimant quits because of substandard or dangerous working conditions that caused the medical condition, you must protect yourself from UIC liability (see Chapter 5).

PROTESTING A CHARGE

Don't wait until you receive your tax bill after the end of the calendar quarter to protest a charge. If you see a charge to your tax account, you *can* protest it, but you will have to convince the UIC office that you sent the original Notice back on time.

If you have a record of the date you received the original Notice and the date you sent it back, the odds that your protest will be accepted as timely are much greater. If you are unable to tell the UIC office when you received or returned the original Notice, it is unlikely you will be allowed a second protest.

A Notice to Employer is generated (usually by computer) after a claim is filed in a local office. A Notice is sent to an employer at the UIC address of record. When the Notice is sent out, the claimant is sent a wage statement advising him or her what the monetary claim is. This is not a statement telling the claimant he or she is eligible for benefits. The statement tells the claimant only how much can be received in benefits *if* the claimant meets the legal standards of eligibility.

ARE YOU A BASE-PERIOD EMPLOYER?

When an unemployment claim is filed, the last employer and all other employers in the base period are notified. The UIC program is required by state and federal regulations to issue a Notice to Employer to inform officially *all* base-period employers a claim has been filed against their accounts.

All UIC claims are computed on a period of time before the claim is filed. Most states use wages earned in the *first four of the last five completed* calendar quarters. The quarter in which the claim is filed is not used as part of the base period. The quarter immediately before the quarter in which the claim is filed, called the *lag* quarter, was often excluded from the base period to allow the UIC program time to complete the tax-collecting process. Many states have now eliminated the lag quarter because computerization allows for wage records to be updated almost immediately.

The four quarters (or year) immediately *before* the lag quarter are used to establish and compute a UIC claim. *All* employers in this base period who reported wages may be charged for a portion of the UIC benefits based on the amount of time worked and the wages earned. Notices are sent out to each employer. If you are one of these employers and you do not return a Notice, you are *automatically* charged. You must request relief from charges by UIC programs that collect taxes each quarter (in wage-reporting states).

Three states—Michigan, New York, and Massachusetts—are called *wage-request* or *wage-demand* states. These states send employers a tax bill after a claim is filed and benefits begin. The base period in these states is defined as the 52 weeks (1 year) before the week of the claim. All base-period employers and the last employer receive Notices advising them they are potentially liable for UIC tax charges.

ACTIONS TO TAKE TO ENSURE FAVORABLE DECISIONS

Use the following list to determine if you have taken all the necessary steps to ensure you receive a favorable decision from the claims examiner.

1. Sign, date, and return the Notice to Employer within the stated time limit. Mail the Notice to the correct address.
2. Delay your telephone response to the claims examiner.
3. Organize your response to the claims examiner. Before you call back, be sure you have the first and last dates of employment, the claimant's rate of pay, a short description of job duties, the supervisor's name, and the chain of command.
4. Prepare a short, detailed statement explaining why the claimant was separated from employment.
5. Call the claims examiner and present your statement.
6. Ask the claims examiner if written documentation is needed; if it is, find out how to submit it.
7. Gather all relevant documentation, and mail legible *copies* to the local UIC office.
8. Verify that all written documentation and the Notice to Employer arrived at the local UIC office.

MAKING EFFECTIVE COMPLAINTS

As you learn to deal with the UIC system, there will be times when you feel you must complain about an individual claims examiner or the service you received from a local office. You have every right to make complaints, and you should expect satisfactory results. You are complaining as a taxpayer and employer. These maxims help you keep your perspective while making your complaint.

The purpose of your complaint is corrective—you want something done about the problems you have encountered. You also want to make your complaints effectively and efficiently. Expending minimum time and effort with maximum results is the goal.

Should you make a written complaint or should you call the UIC office? It depends on the situation and what you want to accomplish. If you have made verbal complaints and found they were unanswered, it is time for a written complaint. If the situation you are trying to correct is serious enough, a written complaint is probably more appropriate. Whether the complaint is made by telephone, in person, or by letter, the following rules apply.

Be Sure of Your Facts

Be sure of your facts before you complain. If your complaint involves a claims examiner or a claims decision, gather all the facts before writing or calling in the complaint. We suggest you make a list of the sequence of events leading up to the complaint. Put your list of complaints in chronological order, starting with the date and description of the first contact with the UIC office. End with the most recent incident. When you make your complaint in chronological order, it is more credible and easier to follow. This method also helps you focus on the specific problem and will keep you organized if your complaint is verbal.

Be Specific about Complaints

Be specific when making your complaint. Don't cover more than the necessary facts, but be sure you cover all the facts that support your case.

Don't Make a Complaint When You're Angry

When you are angry, your complaint is more likely to be irrational and disjointed. Wait until you have calmed down before making any complaint. Write down your thoughts for later use.

QUESTIONS TO ASK IN YOUR STATE

1. If I am called by the local office on a pending claim, can I submit written documentation?
2. What is the procedure for submitting the material?
3. How do local offices advise or inform employers about the outcome of a case?
4. Are written decisions made in all cases?
5. Am I required to return the Notice to Employer in all situations?
6. Will I receive any written decision from the local UIC office even if I do not return the Notice to Employer?
7. If I return the Notice to Employer but still receive a quarterly tax charge, what are my protest rights?
8. What is the time limit for returning the Notice to Employer?
9. How do I exercise my protest rights?
10. What is the correct way to inform the UIC office if I change my business or mailing address?

QUICK REVIEW

1. The Notice to Employer is a critical document. It must be signed and returned within specific time limits.

2. Failure to return Notices on time usually results in loss of your protest rights. In such a case, if the UIC office rules against you, it is not required to give you formal notice; you lose your right to appeal any decisions.

3. Recovering protest rights is extremely difficult.

4. Failure to return the Notice to Employer almost always results in extra UIC taxes.

5. Fill out any Notice to Employer as soon as possible.
   - For *discharges* enter "Discharged, misconduct."
   - For *quits* enter "Quit, personal reasons."

6. Keep a record of the date you receive the Notice and the date you return it. Return Notices as soon as possible.

7. Be careful about what you say to claims examiners. They take notes or record conversations when you talk to them. A decision on whether your UIC tax account is charged depends largely on what you say.

8. Organize written and verbal responses before you call the claims examiner. Condense and concentrate your story.

9. Be polite, informed, and professional when speaking with claims examiners. This approach almost always influences them. It may mean the difference between winning and losing a case.

10. If you have a problem with a claims examiner, make your complaint in a professional manner to a manager or supervisor who can do something about it. You want results.

11. You cannot change the facts. Good cases are set up *before the employee is separated from work*. Well-organized cases, properly presented to local office claims examiners, are often won by the employer.

7

After the Local Office Decision

Once you have provided a claims examiner with all the written and verbal evidence you have, you must wait for a written decision. During the waiting period, there are a few things you can do to help ease your mind.

CHECK THE "EFFECTIVE DATE"

We suggest you call and ask the claims examiner when the decision is due out. Also ask what the effective date of the claim is. In most states, this date is a Sunday because claims generally become effective on the Sunday of the week in which the claim is filed.

For example, if a claim is filed on Thursday, March 6, the effective date of the claim is actually Sunday, March 2. All separation issues related to the claim are due out 21 days from the *effective date*. Because the twenty-first day falls on a weekend, the claims examiner has only until Friday, March 21, to issue a decision. This is three weeks from the effective date of the claim. You should receive a written decision early the week *after* the deadline, or, in this example, the week of March 24.

If you do not receive a decision by the middle of the fourth week, call the local claims office immediately. Ask the claims examiner the following questions.

- Was a written decision issued? If not, why not?
- What was the date of the decision?
- What was the result of the decision?

Figure 7.1
A Completed UIC Determination of Deputy

DEPARTMENT OF ECONOMIC SECURITY
Unemployment Insurance Program
DETERMINATION OF DEPUTY

Soc. Sec. No.   000-14-1980
Claimant   Richard Reddrick
Employer No. 0061112
Employer   PRK Janitorial Services

PRK Janitorial Services   Date   10/17/97
1212 Park Street   Deputy No. 200
Peoria, Kansas 65701

NOTICE TO CLAIMANT

You were discharged for repeated unauthorized absences from work and
neglecting your assigned duties. Evidence establishes you were warned
regarding leaving your job without permission and falsifying attendance
records. Your actions were a willful disregard of the employer's interests.

You are disqualified from receipt of benefits until you return to work and
earn five times your weekly benefit amount.

Discharge from employment, K.R.S. 23-775,   K.A.C. R5-3-51500.

NOTICE TO EMPLOYER

Your experience rating will not be charged.

NOTICE TO ALL INTERESTED PARTIES - APPEAL RIGHTS
This determination becomes final unless a written appeal is filed in person or by mail 15 calendar days after the mailing date shown
at the top of this determination. If the last day of the appeal period falls on a Saturday, Sunday or holiday, the appeal period will
be extended to the next working day. Please see reverse for further information.

ESTE DOCUMENTO AFECTA SU ELEGIBILIDAD PARA SEGURO DE DESEMPLEO. SI USTED NO LEE INGLES, COM-
UNIQUESE CON SU OFICINA LOCAL O BUSQUE QUIEN LE TRADUZCA.

- Am I going to be charged UIC benefits as result of the decision?
- May I have another copy of the decision?

Tip. In most states, no formal decision is issued if the claimant is found eligible for UIC benefits *and* the employer fails to return the protest or Notice to Employer within specific time limits. If you have followed our advice on returning the Notice to Employer, this should not be a problem. (This is another case that demonstrates the importance of returning the Notice to Employer on time.)

Because you have taken careful steps to provide the claims examiner with compelling, persuasive information to prove your case, you should receive a favorable decision in the mail. When you receive the decision, *read it carefully.* If you have any questions or doubts about the contents of the decision, call the claims examiner immediately.

In most cases, the decision is self-explanatory. Below is a discussion of the major points of information to check on the decision you receive. We provide a sample copy of a typical UIC local office decision in Figure 7.1.

DOES THE DECISION CHARGE YOUR UIC ACCOUNT?

If the decision shows you will *not* be charged for the claimant's UIC claim, you have a favorable decision; you have accomplished your primary goal.

In virtually all states, denial of benefits means the employer will *not* receive a tax charge for the claimant's benefits. In some states, a claimant is eligible for UIC benefits, but the employer will not be charged for the benefits. This is the reason checking to see if your account is being charged is so important.

A FAVORABLE DECISION

If the decision is favorable to you, there is nothing more to do at this point. If you are certain your UIC tax account will not be charged, you need take no further action.

We suggest you file a favorable decision with the other information related to this UIC claim for future reference because this is *not* the end of the process. If the claimant is disqualified from receiving benefits, he or she has the right to appeal. (You have the same right if your account is charged and you disagree with the UIC decision.)

If the claimant exercises his or her right to appeal, you will be required to prepare to attend a UIC hearing. We provide detailed information on preparing for an appeal hearing in Chapter 8.

You may want to call the UIC office to determine if an appeal by the

claimant has been filed. We suggest you do this only if you have encountered problems receiving notice of appeals or if you have had other
problems with the UIC local office. If the claimant files an appeal, you
will receive notice of it. (See Chapter 6 for additional information.)

AN UNFAVORABLE DECISION

By definition, an *unfavorable decision* is one you, the employer, disagree with. Usually you disagree with a UIC decision because your tax
account will be charged for the claimant's unemployment benefits. If
you receive an unfavorable decision, take the steps listed below as soon
as you receive the claim determination.

Read the Decision Carefully

The fact that the claimant is granted UIC benefits does *not* always
mean your account will be charged. In some cases, the claimant will
receive benefits but you are exempt from tax charges. Many states do
not charge employers when claimants quit for medical reasons, compelling personal reasons, or other reasons beyond the control of the
employer.

If you agree the claimant should receive benefits or don't care whether
the claimant is paid benefits as long as you aren't charged for them, you
do not need to take any further action unless specifically directed to do
so by the decision.

Read the Body of the Decision

Discover why the claims office is *disqualifying* the claimant or finding
the claimant *eligible*. Most states issue a narrative decision advising the
employer and claimant of the outcome of the claim. Make sure this narrative statement matches the decision regarding your UIC tax account.
For example, a decision might read

You are disqualified from receipt of benefits until you return to work and earn
five times your weekly benefit amount. You were discharged for theft and falsification of company records. The weight of credible evidence establishes that
you acted in a willful disregard of the employer's interest.

This statement tells the claimant he is denied unemployment insurance benefits. The decision should also indicate that the employer's
UIC account and experience rating will not be subject to tax charges.

In another example, a decision might read, "Evidence establishes that
you quit work because your doctor advised you to seek other employ-

ment. You have provided evidence to show you were compelled to leave your employment."

This decision tells the claimant he will be eligible for UIC benefits. It should indicate that the employer's account will not be subject to UIC tax charges.

In a third example, "You were discharged because the employer alleges you were negligent in the operation of company vehicles. You have denied the allegations. The evidence shows you were discharged for reasons other than misconduct."

This statement tells the claimant he is eligible for unemployment insurance benefits. The decision indicates the employer's UIC tax account *will* be charged for benefits.

Tip. The following phrases are red flags. If you see *any* of them in a decision, read the entire decision very carefully.

- "Other than misconduct."
- "The evidence does not support the employer's contention or allegation."
- "The employer has not presented evidence to support the allegation."

These phrases almost always mean the claimant is eligible for benefits and that your UIC tax account will be charged. These are the decisions you want to appeal.

What Is the Appeal Period?

Appeal periods vary from state to state. A *period of appeal,* usually 10 to 30 days following the issue or mailing date of the decision, should be clearly indicated on the decision. Sometimes this information can be confusing or misleading. It is essential that you determine when the appeal period begins and ends. This is especially true if you receive a decision showing a charge to your UIC account.

IF YOU DISAGREE WITH A DECISION, FILE AN APPEAL

If you disagree with any determination or decision issued to you at any level in the UIC process, you should file an appeal. Appeals are the only way to ensure you will be given a second chance to present your case.

When you file an appeal, it must be filed in *writing.* This is done by writing a letter stating you wish to appeal the decision. As with any letter, it must be signed and dated. Your appeal letter must also contain the claimant's name and Social Security number. It should also contain specific details about why you are appealing. The letter of appeal must be mailed and postmarked within the legal time limits for appealing in

Figure 7.2
A Letter of Appeal

Lender's Auto Repair

August 12, 1997

Office of Appeals
1603 W. Brownson Blvd.
Wellerton, New York 10136

Re: <u>Allen Johnson</u>
<u>SS# 000-38-0750</u>

Dear Sir or Madam;

Please accept this letter as a timely appeal to the claims
examiner's determination of August 1, 1997. We disagree with the
claims examiner's determination and request a reconsidered
determination or a hearing.

It is our contention that the claimant <u>was discharged for</u>
<u>work-related misconduct on June 17, 1997</u>. On <u>June 17, 1997</u>, the
claimant <u>attempted to remove an electronically calibrated torque</u>
<u>wrench from the employer's premises by concealing the item in his</u>
<u>lunch box. The incident took place at approximately 10:30a.m. and</u>
<u>was observed by the shop foreman and the service manager. The value</u>
<u>of the torque wrench was approximately $250. Company policy allows</u>
<u>employees to borrow tools after they obtain written permission from</u>
<u>two supervisors. The claimant failed to follow this procedure. When</u>
<u>confronted by the shop foreman and service manager, the claimant</u>
<u>acknowledged he was aware of the company policy. He also admitted</u>
<u>that he put the tool in his lunch box without obtaining the required</u>
<u>permission.</u>

We maintain the claimant willfully acted in an intentional disregard
of the employer's interests. We further maintain that his act(s)
constitute work-related misconduct. Accordingly, we request that the
claimant be disqualified from receiving benefits and that our
experience rating (UIC tax account) not be charged. If you need any
additional documentary evidence or statements from our witnesses,
please let us know.

If you do not reconsider your determination, please process this
letter as a formal appeal and inform us of the time and date of
hearing.

Thank you for your assistance in this matter.

Sincerely,

Martin Court, Owner

806 Pantano Highway   Wellerton, New York 10134   212-555-1285

your state. Figure 7.2 is an example of an appeal letter. Underlined portions indicate information you will supply for your own letter. It will help you format your appeal so you cover all the bases.

Read the appeals instructions on all decisions you receive. If you have *any* questions, immediately call your local UIC office or the appeals board in your state. Filing an appeal is the *only* way you can protect your legal right to a new hearing.

Take special notice of the appeal period or the time limit for filing an appeal. Like the Notice to Employer discussed earlier, appeals are covered by time limits that are strictly enforced at all levels of the UIC claims process. It is absolutely essential to file an appeal within the time limits set by your state.

This is a good time to remind you that UIC agencies do *not* accept many excuses for taking late or untimely action on appeals.

File Appeals in a Timely Manner

File all appeals to UIC decisions on a timely basis, even if you need to use a form letter (see sample in Figure 7.2). Most states do not require a detailed explanation of why you want to appeal. The only general requirement is you file a *written* appeal within the *specified time limit.*

If you are unsure whether to file an appeal, we strongly recommend you file one. You have the option of withdrawing the appeal or simply not appearing at the hearing if you decide not to pursue it. If you are unable to get all the information you need for the appeal, file to meet the statutory time requirements. You can always add to the initial appeal if you gather additional information.

Tip. All states require that appeals and requests for reconsideration be made in writing. Do not take a claims examiner's word that a decision will be reconsidered or an appeal will be processed on the basis of verbal communication. Follow any telephone conversations with your written appeal.

If you fail to meet a specific appeal deadline, you can automatically lose your right to file an appeal on the merits of your UIC case. All states take late appeals and hold separate hearings about why an appeal from the employer or the claimant was late. There are very few acceptable excuses for filing a late appeal, especially in the case of an employer.

Some Acceptable Excuses

Although an employer may believe that many excuses are valid, the UIC program accepts very few. Two reasons that have been accepted are

1. Natural disasters, such as hurricanes, floods, or other conditions, under which regular mail was known to have been disrupted.

2. Natural or unnatural disasters when an employer was directly affected, such as fires in which records were damaged or destroyed.

Unacceptable Excuses

Many excuses that you believe should be valid are unacceptable in the eyes of the UIC. These unacceptable excuses include unavailability of the person who handles your UIC claims because of illness, vacation, or other personal reasons. UIC claims offices believe an employer has an obligation to assign UIC claim responsibilities to another employee or supervisor if the person usually responsible for UIC claims is out of the office for any reason.

There are few acceptable or valid excuses when it comes to UIC time limits. We've previously stated this is true for returning the Notice to Employer; it's also true for filing appeals.

RECONSIDERED DECISIONS AND DETERMINATIONS

Most states have provisions under which a determination issued by the local UIC office or, in some cases, a higher-level decision can be reconsidered. If you or the claimant requests a review of any decision, the UIC claims office is required to examine the facts to see if the right decision was made.

If those in the UIC claims office believe the decision was incorrect, they may have the legal authority to issue a new decision. Usually this occurs only when significant new evidence is presented or when an error was made in interpreting the facts or the law.

Most of the time, the reconsideration is denied; the request is processed as an appeal. This means the case is "kicked upstairs" or sent to a higher level of jurisdiction.

If your state has a request for reconsidered determination, you can request it. This is usually a waste of time because even if you get a reconsidered determination the claimant can appeal. You will be required to attend a hearing anyway.

We suggest you file your appeal. If the state has a legal provision for reconsidering determinations and wants to use the provision, let it do so. If the claimant does not appeal, you win your case automatically. If the claimant appeals, you still have a good chance of winning at a higher-level hearing.

WHEN NOT TO APPEAL

When you receive a determination or decision from a local UIC claims office, review it quickly but carefully. If it is a decision that states a former employee is eligible for UIC benefits and you will be charged for those benefits, you have the option of letting the decision stand or filing an appeal. If you agree with the decision and do not want to pursue it further, you need take no further action. Once the time period for filing an appeal lapses, you lose your appeal rights, and the determination or decision becomes final.

If you are sure the claimant is entitled to benefits, let the determination stand. If you have any doubt, file an appeal. You can always change your mind later. We always prefer the safer course of action—file the appeal unless you are sure you do not want to pursue the matter.

WITHDRAWING AN APPEAL

After you file an appeal, you may change your mind. If this occurs, you can withdraw the appeal or choose not to appear at the next level in the appeals process. We know of no state that penalizes employers for withdrawing or electing not to attend further hearings.

Check with your state to find out how to withdraw an appeal. Usually you need only send a short signed letter indicating you intend to withdraw your original appeal. In some states, you can call your local UIC office or an appeals judge and withdraw by recorded telephone conversation. Using the written format is usually quicker and more efficient. Figure 7.3 is a sample appeal withdrawal letter.

AFTER AN APPEAL IS FILED

After filing an appeal, you will receive written notice from the local claims office that your appeal has been received and processed. The local claims office will send you a copy of the document used to complete the process (see Figure 7.4). This document is usually *not* the actual Notice of Hearing—it only acknowledges that your letter of appeal was received and processed.

The document you receive from the local claims office will indicate when your letter of appeal was received and when the envelope containing the appeal was postmarked. The document should also show a processing date and an annotation referring to your letter of appeal, such as "see letter of appeal."

If you do not receive this document within four or five days after mailing your original letter of appeal, call the local claims office to make sure your letter was received. If there is any delay in processing, find out why. Note the date and time you call and the name of the person you speak with.

It is usually unnecessary to call the local claims office. The process moves smoothly, and you will have the receipt document in your pos-

Figure 7.3
A Letter of Withdrawal from an Appeal Hearing

<u>Susan's Gift Shop</u>

3321 Wayside Blvd.
Salt Lake City, Utah 84009
801-555-3409

May 8, 1996

Office of Appeals
45768 W. Parklake Drive
Salt Lake City, Utah   84001

                        Re: <u>Ellen Roth</u>
                             <u>SS# 000-45-2387</u>
                             <u>Appeal #95729</u>

Dear Sir;

Please accept this letter as a formal notice of withdrawal from
the appeal hearing scheduled for <u>at 2:30p.m. on May 20, 1996,</u>
<u>with Administrative Law Judge Allen Hart</u>.

Thank you for your assistance in this matter.

                        Sincerely,

                        Michael Ian Gordon

                        Michael Ian Gordon,
                        President

Note: In some states, you may be required to give a reason for withdrawal; in others you
are not required to do so.

---

session quickly. File the document with other paperwork related to this
pending UIC case. The paperwork should also contain a copy of your
original letter of appeal.

   Tip. Never send anything to any UIC claims office without making a
copy; file all copies with other related paperwork. Keep all paperwork
you receive from the UIC claims office in the same file. This may sound
like a basic reminder, but it can be a lifesaver if anything goes wrong.

   There are times when you may not receive a return document following your letter of appeal. This can happen for a number of reasons.
Some of the more common reasons follow.

Figure 7.4

A Completed Request for Reconsideration/Appeal

DEPARTMENT OF ECONOMIC SECURITY

REQUEST FOR RECONSIDERATION/APPEAL

Este documento afecta su elegibilidad para Seguro por Desempleo. Si usted no lee inglés, comuníquese con su oficina local o busque quien le traduzca. La audiencia se conducirá en inglés.

In the Matter of the Claim of:

Name and Address of Appellant

Fender's Auto Repair
806 Pantano Hwy.
Wellerton, New York 10134

CLAIMANT'S NAME
Allen Johnson
SOC. SEC. NO.
000 - 38 - 0750
EMPLOYER'S NAME
Fender's Auto Repair

☒ I disagree with the Determination of Deputy dated _____8-1-97_____, involving the issue of

___Separation from Work___, and allege it is in error for the following reasons:

___See attached Letter___

☐ I also disagree with the Determination of Overpayment dated _____N/A_____ created by the above Determination of Deputy.

If request is not timely state reason _____N/A_____

APPELLANT'S SIGNATURE
See Signature on Attached Letter   DATE   8-12-97

NOTICE TO CLAIMANT

If your Request for Reconsideration is denied, and you are still unemployed and wish to claim benefits, you should continue to file claims pending disposition of your appeal.

COMPLETED BY DEPARTMENT REPRESENTATIVE

REQUEST FILED:

☐ In person on _____ *(Date)*

☒ By mail postmarked on ___8- 12 - 97___ *(Date)* *(envelope attached)*

Received at ___L.O. 81___ *(Local Office No.)* on ___8-14-97___ *(Date)*

Does the claimant speak English? ☒ Yes ☐ No ☐ Information not available

If no, what language does the claimant speak? ___N/A___

NOTICE TO APPELLANT REGARDING RECONSIDERATION

☐ Your request has been reviewed and a reconsidered Determination of Deputy will be issued.

☐ Your request for reconsideration has been denied on *(date)* _____ and this action will be forwarded to the Office of Appeals. The specific date and location for your appeal hearing will be provided in a separate communication. The hearing will be conducted in English.

BY *(Department Representative)*	APPROVED *(UI Manager)*	RESOLUTION CODE	ISSUE ID
Bob Jones	Sue Jordon	3	B

Reason 1

The local claims office is in the process of issuing a new determination favorable to you. They have received your letter of appeal and are trying to obtain a rebuttal or response from the claimant.

Solution. None required; this process takes care of itself. If the local office is in the process of issuing a different determination, you will receive a copy, and the claimant may become the appellant (the person who has appeal rights).

Reason 2

Your appeal has been lost in the mail or was never received by the local claims office.

Solution. A telephone call will determine if your appeal letter was received. If it was not received, make a copy and send it to the local office immediately. You are still required to meet the deadline or time limit for appeals set by law.

Tip. If you are sending your appeal in at the last minute (something we strongly advise you *not* to do), use certified mail or registered mail, with a return receipt requested. This ensures a record from the U.S. Postal Service showing when the original letter was sent. UIC claims offices treat U.S. postal records as sacred scrolls. A record from the postal service is beyond question as far as a local UIC office is concerned.

Reason 3

Your appeal was received by the local office but was lost or left unprocessed because of an error.

Solution. Usually this is not a problem because it does not happen very often. However, if you do not receive a notice that your appeal letter was received, call after five days to ask about the status of your appeal.

UIC offices are generally busy places. They can also be poorly organized, with undertrained claims examiners and clerks, claims examiners who quit or are fired, claims examiners who are out sick, or dishonest claims examiners who destroy documents rather than processing them. Any of these possibilities can result in problems processing your appeal and other paperwork. If you follow the steps we have outlined above, potential problems can be averted and minimized.

DEALING WITH IRATE FORMER EMPLOYEES

Sometimes after a claimant is disqualified from receiving UIC benefits, he or she may contact you to question your actions, complain to you, try to persuade you to call the UIC office on his or her behalf, or even to threaten or plead with you. This may occur when a claimant is eligible for UIC benefits and you file an appeal. We suggest you minimize your contact with the former employee at this point. You are under no legal obligation to discuss the matter any further.

Many claimants, and sometimes their attorneys, believe unemployment insurance is a benefit to which a former employee is automatically entitled. These people may believe the employer controls or determines who receives UIC benefits. If someone contacts you about a UIC claim, we suggest you explain to the claimant or his attorney that the question of eligibility for benefits rests with the UIC system. Advise the caller that as the employer you do *not* make any decisions regarding claimant eligibility.

At this point the matter is effectively out of your hands. Telling the claimant this is accurate and truthful on your part.

QUESTIONS TO ASK AT YOUR LOCAL OFFICE

1. How does the appeals program in this jurisdiction work?
2. After a local office determination or decision is made, what is the next step in the process?
3. What is the time limit for each level of the appeals process?
4. What is the title of the head of the appeals section? What are his or her name, address, and telephone number?
5. To whom do those in the appeals office report?
6. How many levels of appeal are there?
7. What are appeals judges called? Are they required to be lawyers? If not, what are their qualifications?
8. Must I attend hearings, or is it optional?
9. Does the appeals program have written material on the appeals process to send me?
10. Does the local office use administrative rules and precedent cases to make decisions? Which carries more weight or is more likely to be used in making appeal-level UIC decisions?
11. Do local offices in my jurisdiction use telephone calls to help resolve UIC disputes, or do they use only written notices?
12. What are the steps in the appeals process?
13. Does the appeals office allow me to appear by telephone, or must I appear at a hearing in person?

8 _____

Preparing for the Appeal Hearing

Whether you won or lost at the local UIC office level, there is a good chance that you will need to appear at an unemployment insurance appeal hearing. If you lost at the first level, you will be the *appellant* (the party who files the appeal). If the claimant lost at the first level, he or she will be the appellant. In either case, there is no procedural advantage to being the appellant. The party best prepared to present evidence has the major advantage.

Not all claimants who lose at the local office level file appeals. Sometimes a claimant finds another job or chooses not to appeal for a variety of reasons. However, you can't count on a claimant not filing an appeal if he or she is denied benefits.

Assume that *every* claimant who is denied benefits will appeal; every claimant has the legal right to do so. This means you must prepare to attend all UIC appeal hearings. If you have followed our advice, preparing for the hearing should be relatively simple—you have already done most of the work.

Occasionally a claimant withdraws his or her appeal or fails to attend the appeal hearing. If the claimant is the appellant and fails to show up at the hearing, you are likely to win your UIC hearing automatically. This is called *winning by default.*

If *you* are the appellant and the claimant does not appear, the hearing will still be opened for taking testimony and other evidence. The ALJ will hold the hearing with only you and your witnesses present. This is usually an ideal situation. Although the claimant will not be there to rebut or contradict the evidence you present, you must still prove your case. You should always organize and present your case as if the claimant is present. Do not become overconfident or complacent simply because the claimant doesn't appear at the hearing.

After attending thousands of hearings, we firmly believe that *thorough preparation is the key* to winning your UIC appeal hearing. We cannot emphasize this strongly enough. Presentation of your case is important, but preparation before the hearing is absolutely essential—it is where hearings are won or lost.

BURDEN OF PROOF

A fundamental concept of unemployment insurance is "burden of proof." It is a method used to help decide who bears the principle responsibility for proving a case. You don't have to be a lawyer to understand and use it.

In unemployment insurance, burden of proof falls upon the employer. As the employer, you must convince the claims examiner or administrative law judge that a majority of the credible evidence supports your case. In most discharges, the claimant bears little or no burden of proof. To win, the claimant needs only to provide persuasive, credible rebuttal. In many cases, this means just denying an employer's allegations.

When an employee quits, the opposite applies; the claimant bears the burden of proof. He or she must establish a good legal reason for leaving the job, or benefits will be denied.

It is helpful to think of burden of proof in terms of percentages. By the end of an unemployment insurance case, you must have at least 51 percent of the credible evidence on your side. If you do, you win the case and avoid increases in your tax liability. If the evidence is 50–50 or evenly balanced and the case is a discharge, you will probably lose. Conversely, a claimant usually loses in 50–50 cases when he or she quits.

Merely having the evidence is not enough to meet the burden of proof. You must present your evidence in a credible way. The claims examiner and the judge consider only the evidence actually presented to them that is made part of the official record of the hearing. If you don't present the evidence or if information is not made part of the record, the judge cannot use it in reaching a decision. It is as if it never existed. It is crucial for you to prepare and to know how to present your case in the strongest terms possible. The following two cases in point illustrate how and why.

One Case in Point

A mechanic from Lender's Auto Repair has been stealing tools and supplies from the service garage. On Wednesday, the shop foreman sees the mechanic slip an expensive torque wrench into his lunch box.

He reports this to the service manager and the general manager.

Just before quitting time, the shop foreman and the service manager both confront the employee and ask him to open his lunch box. Reluctantly, the employee complies. Caught red-handed, the employee admits to the two supervisors he put the wrench in his lunch box. He explains he intended to return the wrench in a week or so, after he finished working on his car at home. (The company allows employees to borrow tools, but they must fill out a request form, and the form must be approved and signed by the foreman or service manager.) After a meeting with the general manager, the employee is fired.

At the unemployment insurance appeal hearing, the claimant states he was unfairly fired. He testifies under oath he never put the torque wrench in his lunch box. He states that other employees were "out to get him" and planted the wrench in his lunch box. He swears he didn't know he had the wrench, and that he would never steal from the employer. He further denies he admitted putting the wrench in his lunch box.

The foreman, service manager, and general manager testify for the employer. The foreman and service manager tell what they saw and heard. The foreman testifies he saw the claimant put the wrench in his lunch box. Both the service manager and the foreman testify the claimant admitted he put the wrench in the lunch box.

The general manager also wants to testify. He knows all about the discharge because he *heard* the whole story from the foreman and the service manager before he approved the discharge. The administrative law judge thanks the general manager for his appearance but politely denies his request. The general manager's testimony would be hearsay, and two eyewitnesses are present.

In spite of the testimony of the foreman and the service manager, the claimant insists he did nothing wrong. He maintains he was "framed."

Who wins this hearing? If you said the employer, you were right. The employer was able to meet the burden of proof. The testimony of the two employer witnesses corroborated the fact the claimant put the wrench in his lunch box. He also admitted doing it in the presence of two witnesses. The claimant can deny that fact until he is blue in the face, but his previous admission will be the employer's most potent and convincing testimony. Even if the claimant's testimony is sincere and credible, the evidence weighs in the employer's favor.

A Second Case in Point

Suppose the employer had *not* sent the shop foreman and the service manager to the appeals hearing. Instead, the general manager and the personnel director decide to go because they believe it is their job to attend these hearings. They carefully prepare their testimony, make extensive notes, and interview other employees who state they have seen the claimant put tools in his lunch box on other occasions. The general manager and personnel director go to the hearing on the scheduled day.

At the hearing, the claimant steadfastly maintains all the employer allegations are false. The claimant testifies he was framed and discharged because the employer did not believe him.

Who do you think will win? If you said the claimant, you're right. No matter how sincere, courteous, and credible the general manager and personnel director are, they can give only *hearsay* testimony. The claimant can easily rebut their allegations by making a simple denial. The administrative law judge must rule in the claimant's favor, even if the claimant is not totally believable. Although the employer had a good case and credible witnesses, the correct witnesses did not attend the hearing. In most states, you don't get a second chance to present those witnesses.

Suppose the general manager, the personnel director, and the service manager had attended the hearing. The general manager and the personnel director weren't eyewitnesses to the attempted theft or later admission; only the service manager was. The general manager and personnel director can only present hearsay testimony—that leaves the employer with only one eyewitness.

The service manager saw the wrench in the claimant's lunch box and heard the claimant's admission, but he is only one witness. The foreman is the only other witness who heard the claimant's original admission (confession). He is the only one who saw the claimant put the wrench in the lunch box. The foreman's testimony is crucial to the case. Without him, the employer cannot back up the service manager's testimony.

The ALJ is left with only the service manager's eyewitness testimony about the claimant's alleged admission. The claimant has denied everything. The two additional employer witnesses can add nothing more than hearsay.

The case would probably end in a 50–50 balance. The employer cannot present more than one eyewitness account against the claimant's denials. The claims examiner or judge is compelled to rule against the employer; the case is considered a discharge without misconduct. That means an undeserving claimant will collect benefits, and the employer faces a UIC tax charge.

In this case, it is essential to present the testimony of the *two* witnesses who can give firsthand testimony. Without this competent testimony, the employer will lose. You can hope the claimant will tell the truth, but you should not depend on it.

OATHS

Taking an oath before an appeals hearing is a serious matter. There can be severe penalties for not telling the truth once the oath is taken.

Knowingly making false statements of a material fact or facts in most states is considered perjury and may be a felony. In addition, some states may further penalize employers for making false statements by assessing additional UIC tax charges.

Taking the oath does not *guarantee* that a witness will tell the truth. An oath does not compel the claimant to make true statements. The oath is only a tool. It gives the state a means to punish witnesses who lie, but it is not an iron-clad guarantee against lying.

CREDIBILITY

In all legal and quasi-legal cases, establishing and maintaining credibility is essential. It often means the difference between winning a case and losing it. Credibility does not mean looking someone in the eye, or being well dressed, sincere, articulate, or even courteous—that's *demeanor*. Demeanor is important, but it won't win or lose a case by itself.

Credible testimony is clear, concise, detailed, and consistent. The more details and facts you can present, the more credible your testimony will be. Testimony that can be independently corroborated by other witnesses or documents is the most credible you can present. The testimony must also be relevant to the case.

The judge may not be able to discern who is telling the truth—even though that is the judge's role. A judge must decide who bears the burden of proof, weigh the quality of the *credible* evidence, and decide which side has best met the burden of proof.

The party that meets the burden of proof (in discharges, it's you, the employer) will win the case. It is that simple. We believe understanding the concept of burden of proof and credibility will help you understand how evidence must be collected, organized, and presented to win your UIC cases.

BEGIN PREPARING YOUR CASE

When you are the appellant, begin preparing your case as soon as you file your letter of appeal. The more time you have, the better. We provide step-by-step instructions on how to get ready for your hearing and how to avoid overpreparing and wasting time preparing for the wrong things.

When the claimant is the appellant, you have less time to prepare because you will not know about the hearing until you receive notice that a hearing has been scheduled. In many states, the Notice of Hearing is sent out no more than ten days before the hearing. You might receive it with fewer than ten days to prepare. Make the Notice of Hearing part of your former employee's file, and take it with you to the appeal hearing.

Notice of Hearing and Copy of UIC File

As soon as you receive notice of the appeal hearing, read it carefully. Note the time, date, and place of the hearing. Find out what the issue of the hearing is; contact the Office of Appeals and request a copy of the *complete* UIC file. The original file will be used at the hearing. In some states, a complete copy of the UIC file is attached to the Notice of Hearing. In other states, you may be able to have the copy mailed to you. Some states require you to pick it up in person.

Carefully review the file as soon as you receive it. Pay special attention to the claimant's written statement—this may be the first time you've had a chance to see what your former employee stated. Review the deputy's fact-finding notes. These indicate what the claimant told the claims examiner about the separation. A discussion of these and other documents in the file, with comments as to their relative importance, begins on page 138.

It is wise to assume that every UIC case will end up at an appeals hearing. The information we provide is based on this assumption, so we help you prepare accordingly.

Upon receiving notification of an appeals hearing, review the file you have been building with regard to this individual claimant. This helps you prepare mentally for what lies ahead.

WHAT TO EXPECT AT AN APPEAL HEARING

Although a hearing is an "informal" administrative hearing, it is only *informal* in a relative sense. It is less formal than a court of law in that

- Strict rules of evidence do not apply.
- There is some informality and latitude with regard to the order of questioning.
- Photocopies rather than original documents are admitted as evidence.

However, the hearing is more formal than simply talking to a UIC claims examiner at the local office. In all but a few states, UIC hearing officers are now administrative law judges. In most states, they are trained lawyers or laypeople with extensive legal backgrounds.

Begin preparing for your hearing by gathering together all the evidence you have. Much of it will be presented at the hearing. In all but the most extraordinary circumstances, ALJs consider only testimony and evidence you and the claimant present at the hearing. Documents or witnesses not presented at the hearing are generally not considered. It is *crucial* that everything you wish to present to the ALJ be well organized ahead of time.

DOCUMENTS NEEDED FOR A HEARING

You can never have too many documents at a hearing. Taking documents doesn't mean you need them to win your case or even that the ALJ will want to see them or admit all of them to the record of the hearing. You will not be expected to submit a claimant's entire personnel file, but it is wise to bring it along in case it contains something relevant to your case.

With a little practice and guidance from the information we provide, you will be able to pick out and organize quickly and efficiently relevant documents for your appeal hearing.

PREPARING FOR A HEARING INVOLVING QUITS

If the local office has determined separation from work is a quit, nearly all states use this as a starting point, no matter what the facts of the case might later show. This is called *presumptive evidence of separation* and is used only initially to determine which party bears the burden of proof. During the hearing, if it becomes apparent that the presumed quit is really a discharge, the burden shifts from the claimant to the employer. These cases are relatively rare, but they do occur. Usually a case that starts out as a quit (or a discharge) stays a quit (or a discharge).

If you are positive that the claimant quit, there are certain documents you should take to the hearing. Below is a discussion of these important documents.

Claimant's Initial Work Application

This document, while not critical, will show the claimant's date of hire, rate of pay, and previous work history. This can be important background information at the hearing.

Correspondence between You and Claimant before Separation from Work

Place special emphasis on any correspondence related to your attempts to work with the employee to resolve any work-related grievances. This includes written warnings, copies of statements by the employee or witnesses, doctor's excuses, and any other written documentation that falls into this category.

Complete Copy of Written Company Policy
Regarding Grievance Procedures

This is important because most employees quit their jobs because of some perceived "grievance" or problem they experience on the job. Few employees bother to exhaust or even follow the normal grievance procedures. If you can demonstrate you have a reasonable grievance procedure and that the employee knew of it and had access to the procedure but failed to use the grievance system, you will generally win your case.

Paperwork Related to EEOC, OSHA, or Any
Government Investigations

You cannot stop claimants from filing complaints with myriad government agencies involved in policing the workplace. Usually these complaints have no merit, and an investigation proves it. There is no shame in being investigated; you probably cannot prevent it.

If the investigation establishes that you were in the right, bring the written report to the hearing. If the investigation shows you were wrong but took corrective action, this also can work in your favor. If you were investigated, found to be in the wrong, and took no corrective action, you may have a problem. However, the claimant must still demonstrate that he exhausted all possible avenues to correct the situation and that your actions created a situation that left him no alternative but to leave the job.

In many quits, minority claimants allege they were discriminated against. With female claimants, you may hear allegations of sexual harassment or abuse as a reason for quitting. No matter how untrue these charges are to you, they may be valid in the mind of the claimant. You may be obliged to sit in a hearing and listen to a long list of allegations, some of which you are hearing for the first time. Our advice is to be patient. This is common. A claimant fighting for benefits may make incredible claims, especially if he or she feels the case is not going well.

In the hearing, listen carefully. Take notes. We tell you how to use these notes in Chapter 10. You must realize you cannot prepare for *everything* the claimant will say at this point, but being as well prepared as possible will help you feel more confident in your ability to win.

Relevant Payroll Records if Claimant Quit Because of
Late Payment of Wages

Most states will rule against an employer who repeatedly pays employees late or pays employees with checks drawn on insufficient funds.

However, an isolated instance of late payment does *not* usually constitute good cause for the claimant to quit his or her job.

What You and Your Witnesses Should Know

Before the hearing, gather together this information about your former employee (now the claimant) for you and your witnesses. It is important for each of you to know

1. Date of hire.
2. Date of separation.
3. Last day of work (actual date).
4. Brief description of job duties.
5. Rate of pay.
6. Hours of work per week.
7. Hours of work per day.
8. Chain of command.
9. Reason for separation.
10. Any pertinent information in employee handbook.
11. When employee handbook was issued to claimant.
12. If separation involved working conditions or rate of pay, be prepared to give the ALJ an idea of what the prevailing standard is in your city or labor market.
13. How the employer was adversely affected by the claimant.

WITNESSES

Collecting witnesses for discharges and quits can be one of the most crucial prehearing preparatory steps you take. We cannot emphasize strongly enough or frequently enough that UIC cases are won or lost in the preparation of the case. Below are some suggestions for selecting which witnesses should attend the UIC hearing.

Witnesses with Firsthand Knowledge

The most important witness or witnesses are those who can testify from *firsthand* information or knowledge. A witness does not have to be a manager or supervisor. *What* a witness knows and can tell the UIC judge is more important than who he or she is or what position he or she holds in the company.

Many employers make the fatal mistake of sending personnel managers or company vice presidents to unemployment insurance hearings. One company insisted that the company president always be present to testify. Testimony by these witnesses is often worthless because the best they can do is interview the people who have *direct* or *firsthand* knowledge of what happened to cause the separation from work. This does not help you; you need witnesses who know from their own experience what actually transpired.

Be Sure the Witness Is Willing to Testify

Make sure the witness is willing to attend the hearing and to give testimony. This may sound pretty basic and simple, but employees may be reluctant to testify in a quit or discharge because they feel like they are "tattling" or "ratting" on other employees.

Sometimes employees are nervous or afraid to appear as witnesses because they lack sophistication and familiarity with the legal system. They may feel they do not want to get involved in "court business." They may even fear legal proceedings because of past unpleasant experiences as witnesses or defendants. They may also fear retaliation from the employee after testifying. There are ways to deal with this type of reluctance.

One approach to this resistance is to explain to the witnesses that they are being asked to appear at the hearing only to *tell the truth*. No one is asking them to take sides, even though they will be appearing as employer witnesses. Explain that their only obligation is to appear and answer questions about what they heard, saw, or know about the claimant's separation from work. Tell them it is not up to you as the employer to make decisions about unemployment insurance. That responsibility lies with the UIC program and the ALJ.

You can also tell the witness you are not taking sides either. Although you may feel the employer is correct, the judge will decide who wins or loses the UIC case.

Do not attempt to coerce an employee into appearing for you as a witness. This is a mistake some employers make. If you threaten a witness in any way (such as hinting at loss of employment) or offer anything in return for testimony, the consequences could be serious. If a witness admits in a hearing that he or she was forced to testify, the testimony will have seriously diminished value, and there may be other legal consequences to the employer. The same is likely to be true if you promise a witness something in return for testimony. The consequences are not worth it. Employees appearing under these conditions rarely make good witnesses. Getting caught, even once, can seriously damage your credibility for future cases.

Interview Witnesses before the Hearing

Take some time to interview your witnesses *before* presenting them. Never assume that employees have clear recollections of past events.

If you followed our advice in Chapter 3, you asked each employee to write out a brief statement as to what happened *at the time* the incident related to the quit or discharge took place. You also added your short statement to the file. The power and value of these statements now becomes apparent.

The few minutes you and the witness(es) took to make the contemporaneous statements now save you hours trying to recall exactly what happened. Witnesses will be able to help you review the record and fix their testimony clearly in their minds. It is even a good idea to provide the witnesses with copies of their original statements at this point. Let them take a few minutes to refresh their memories.

Tip. If any of your witnesses needs an interpreter, the UIC office will supply one. Contact the UIC Office of Appeals in writing to indicate that an interpreter is needed. Include in your letter the case number and the date and time the hearing is scheduled. Include the name of the ALJ, if you have it. Be sure to tell them what language your witness speaks.

Tell Witnesses What to Expect

Take a few minutes to explain to the witness what they are in for and what they are likely to face.

Testimony Will Be under Oath. Your witnesses will appear before an ALJ and give testimony under oath. If they knowingly give false testimony, they may be committing perjury and subject themselves to the penalties for doing so. Perjury is a serious crime. It far outweighs any possible benefit you or your witness can achieve by lying under oath.

Hearings Are Mostly Question and Answer. Usually your witness only *answers* questions. Some states allow witnesses to make short narrative statements telling the judge, in their own words, what happened. Because the rules of evidence in administrative hearings are more relaxed than they are in regular court proceedings, many judges are comfortable with a certain amount of narrative testimony. Often a judge will say, "Just tell me what happened in your own words." This is a wonderful opportunity for the witness to state what he or she saw and heard.

Tip. There is a downside to narrative testimony. Sometimes witnesses give confusing, irrelevant, misleading, or incorrect testimony because they are not responding to specific questions. Often they ramble on about the issues not involved in the hearing. We suggest you have your witnesses keep their testimony as short and as much to the point as possible. Give times, dates, and facts in the order they occurred. Have them restrict their narrative testimony to the shortest answers possible.

Do not ask your witnesses to offer opinions or draw conclusions. The less they say, the better it could be for you. If a witness does not cover a point, it's the judge's responsibility and your responsibility to ask additional questions to cover those points. It's better to give incomplete answers than to say too much. Incomplete answers can be added to and amended; long, rambling answers cannot be withdrawn.

Let Witnesses Know You May Ask Questions

In many states, the employer or his representative may ask questions, if allowed by the presiding hearing officer or judge. Take a few minutes to go over the major questions you plan to ask the witness. This is a good time to ask witnesses if they have any questions they believe *should* be asked. Often witnesses think of questions that have not occurred to you. Witnesses can be a valuable source of information. Including them in the processes also makes them feel more comfortable and confident; a comfortable, confident witness is almost always a good witness.

Witnesses Can Be Cross-Examined

Tell your witnesses they will not have the luxury of testifying only to you. Most states allow the other party to cross-examine or question the testimony of witnesses. In addition, the judge may ask some very probing questions designed to get at the facts and test the truth of witness testimony. Advise them to listen to the complete question *before* answering. If they don't understand a question, tell them to ask for it to be repeated.

Advise your witnesses that cross-examination can sometimes appear to be very hostile. Many witnesses feel uncomfortable, angry, demeaned, belittled, humiliated, belligerent, and defensive when they are cross-examined. It is very important for witnesses to try not to become hostile or argumentative. Explain before the hearing that, as witnesses, they are not there to confront or put the claimant down. They are not there to argue or besmirch the claimant's reputation.

If a witness is asked to recall details of a general statement, it is because the judge needs additional information for the record. If the claimant asks an angry or hostile question, advise the witness to answer the question in a civil manner. Stick to the point and give a simple factual response. Let's examine the following example.

Witness: I think I remember seeing the claimant at the drinking fountain before coffee break.

Judge: What time was that, do you recall?

Witness: I think it was about 10.

Judge: Was that 10 A.M. or 10 P.M., sir?

Witness: I think it was 10 A.M.

Judge: Do you think, or do you know what time it was?

This type of questioning is designed to clarify the record and test the witness's recollection of events. To many witnesses, this type of questioning may be aggravating or insulting. Sometimes the tone of voice used by the interrogator can cause witnesses to get angry or become intimidated. Our advice is to warn your witnesses *before* the hearing that some questions may be difficult to answer because of the way they are asked. We give you additional practice material to help you and your witnesses practice questions and answers in the next chapter.

SUBPOENAS

You may find it necessary to compel a witness to appear and testify. If a witness crucial to your case refuses to appear or you cannot control the appearance of a witness, most states will issue an administrative subpoena compelling the witness to appear. This can be a difficult and awkward situation, especially if an employer witness must be compelled to appear.

Most states allow you or the claimant to request subpoenas to produce *witnesses* or *documents* for use at UIC hearings. Usually the local office does not have this power, but the Office of Appeals may. Subpoenas are seldom used in UIC hearings, but they can be useful tools in some instances. Here are some tips on using subpoenas for UIC hearings.

1. Have a clear idea about the exact procedure for requesting a subpoena in your state. In most cases, you fill out a special subpoena request form and submit it to the Office of Appeals. The judge reviews the request and determines if a subpoena should be issued. In some states, the subpoena is mailed, delivered, or served by the Office of Appeals or one of their process servers. In some states, serving a subpoena is the employer's responsibility.

2. Carefully read the instructions for your state's subpoena request. If you have any questions, ask the clerk or ALJ for assistance. Insist on an answer if you do not understand something. Failure to follow the instructions may result in the denial of your subpoena request.

3. Have a clear idea about *why* you need the subpoena. In most cases, you must demonstrate why you are requesting the subpoena. You will usually be expected to provide some "offer of proof" to establish that the witnesses or documents you want are relevant and essential to your case. You may also be

required to show why the information cannot be obtained without using a subpoena. Providing this information can be very convincing. The more information you have, the more chance you will have to persuade the judge to issue the subpoena.

4. If you are requesting a subpoena for a witness, be certain you can show why this witness is essential to your case and why you cannot prove your case without the witness. You must provide specific information about how and where the witness can be contacted. This means address, telephone number, place of employment, and hours of employment. Without this information, the subpoena may be denied, or it may not be served in time for the witness to attend the hearing.

If a Subpoena Request Is Denied

Sometimes you will not be able to persuade the Office of Appeals to issue a subpoena to compel a witness(es) to attend or to produce specific documents. If this happens, take the following steps.

First, find out who issued the refusal. Find out if you have formal appeal rights to require the subpoena be issued. If you do not have formal appeal rights, bring the matter to the highest authority in the Office of Appeals. Each appeals office has someone in charge. If you are unsuccessful, take your request to the highest level you can within the UIC administration or the appeals system. Going to one or two higher levels with your request for a subpoena often works well.

Second, if you are still unsuccessful in obtaining a necessary subpoena, bring the matter of the denial up *at the hearing, on the record.* There is nothing wrong with indicating to the ALJ that a pending appeal request was denied. The request and the denial will usually be part of the hearing file already, but it is important to state the facts on the record.

Third, after you have noted the matter of the subpoena request on the record, *renew* or repeat your request for the judge to issue the subpoena after the hearing has started. We recommend that you make the first request during the opening or introductory remarks (see sample hearing script in Appendix E). It is not improper in most states to follow this procedure.

Point out to the ALJ, for the record, you were denied your request for a subpoena. Tell the ALJ you believe the witness or documents you request are essential to proving your case. Say, "I request the hearing be continued until the subpoena request is honored and the requested subpoenas are issued."

If the judge refuses to continue or to postpone the hearing, ask that the final decision be delayed until the judge issues the subpoena. This tactic forces the judge to consider your request for a subpoena, even though the hearing may continue. The judge may also consider keeping the "receipt of evidence" open until the subpoena is issued.

Fourth, when you reach the point in the hearing where you need the testimony or documents you were denied because the judge failed to issue the subpoena, bring the matter up again. Renew your request for the subpoena. Point out to the judge exactly why the witness or document is important at this point in the hearing by making an offer of proof. Ask again that the hearing be continued until the subpoena is issued to produce the witness or document. Be *firm* but *courteous.*

Finally, if the judge refuses to issue a subpoena by the end of the hearing, state your request one last time to the judge (and for the record). Before closing statements, make sure you make a final plea for the needed subpoena. Ask that the hearing be continued until the witness or document is produced.

Tip. If the judge refuses your final requests, all the requests and denials are *preserved* for the record. If you lose the case, you have established good grounds for an appeal. If you are not in agreement with the judge on the matter of subpoenas, it is essential to place the judge in the position of granting your request or denying the request on the record. This way, any review of the hearing by a higher authority will show what you wanted and what you were granted or denied.

Receiving a Subpoena

In some cases, the claimant will request and be granted the right to subpoena witnesses and documents from you. You will not know about the request in advance; you will learn of it when you receive the subpoena. Administrative subpoenas usually arrive by certified mail. In some states, a subpoena may actually be served by a process server, contracted for by the UIC agency or paid for by the claimant. In any case, don't panic. A subpoena is a tool designed to obtain information — nothing more.

In many cases, the witnesses or documents the claimant is subpoenaing are the witnesses and documents you plan to take to the hearing anyway. Claimants often feel they can "prove" their cases by requesting witnesses and documents that will prove damaging to them, but they obtain subpoenas anyway.

Tip. If you are planning to produce witnesses or documents for the hearing that have been subpoenaed, call the ALJ before the hearing. Let him him or her know you will produce the subpoenaed information voluntarily.

Take subpoenas seriously. When they are issued, it means the ALJ believes the information is important to the hearing. Carefully review all documents you are required to submit. When possible, interview all witnesses subpoenaed by the claimant. You will almost always discover the documents and witnesses will provide information and testimony helpful to you.

If You Can't Comply with a Subpoena

If you receive a subpoena and cannot produce the documents listed, contact the ALJ by telephone or in writing before the hearing and explain why you can't provide the material. At the hearing, you will probably be required to provide a statement and answer questions on the record regarding the subpoenaed documents. You may be asked to verify whether the documents existed, what the documents contained, and why you are unable to provide them for the hearing.

Do not be alarmed if you cannot produce subpoenaed documents for a hearing. As long as you make a good-faith effort to comply with the subpoena, the judge will probably give you extra time to produce documents. If the documents no longer exist or cannot be retrieved, the judge may have to proceed without them. The only time you are likely to have a problem is if you *refuse* to produce documents, without a valid reason for your refusal. In some states, this may lead to further legal action, including a contempt citation.

A subpoena is often issued to compel the attendance of a witness. In most cases, the witnesses will be current employees. Administrative subpoenas are usually mailed to witnesses at your place of business, but they may also be delivered to the employee at home. Interview every employee before he or she attends the hearing. Explain what a subpoena is and why he or she is being required to attend. Often these are witnesses you planned to take anyway.

If a witness is someone you did not plan on taking to the hearing, find out what he or she knows about the separation. Ask the employee what he or she plans to say. Never deny anyone permission to attend a hearing or try to tell a witness what to say. Under no circumstances should you try to coerce or offer anyone anything in return for testimony. Doing so could mean serious legal problems for you.

PREPARING DOCUMENTS FOR THE UIC HEARING

Witnesses are an important, if sometimes unpredictable, element in preparing and presenting your UIC case. Somewhat more predictable are the documents you should prepare for the UIC hearing.

Don't overload the ALJ with documents. They are usually unimpressed with irrelevant, extraneous documents. Each document you submit must be marked by the ALJ or one of the clerks. The ALJ must ask the claimant if he or she has any objection to the admission of each document, one at a time. This can become a time-consuming, time-wasting process for both you and the judge.

Too many documents usually means an irritated judge; nobody wants that. Resist the temptation to present the claimant's entire personnel file. Take it with you if it makes you feel more comfortable, but don't overpresent the documentary portion of your case.

Claimant's Written Termination Form

This document will identify the claimant's beginning and ending dates of employment. It is unlikely that it will be necessary to submit this document.

Any Written Warnings

Bring any written warnings that were issued before termination, especially in the case of a discharge. These can often be the pivotal documents in your case. They are discussed in detail in Chapters 3 and 4.

All Supporting Documents

It may be important to bring supporting documents, such as time cards and written instructions directed to the claimant or other workers, that were part of your decision to discharge the claimant.

Document Checklist

If you have followed our suggestions up to this point, you will have a well-kept, usable file to turn to. Now is the time to check the file and make sure you have the documents listed below.

1. Claimant's written termination report, if your company issues written reports.
2. Letter of resignation, if claimant quit.
3. Copies of written warnings, if claimant was discharged.
4. All notes related to termination interview, whether claimant was discharged or quit.
5. Statements from witnesses.
6. Documents related to written or verbal warnings, such as time cards, time reports, or anything related to claimant's misconduct (falsified reports, falsified expense reports).

Original Documents or Photocopies?

In most states, you are not required to submit original documents; photocopies are acceptable. We suggest you take original documents to the hearing with you, but don't submit them unless the judge requires it or you need to submit originals to win the case. If you have original documents with you, the ALJ may want to inspect the documents if they differ from the copies in any way or if there is some question about whether the copies are authentic or accurate. Make three copies—one for your use, one for the ALJ, and one for the claimant.

If you have several documents, an excellent way to organize them is in chronological order, beginning with the most recent documents and working backward to the oldest. If you have more than three or four documents, use a colored stick-pad to label the right side of each document with a short remark describing it. This prevents fumbling through a pile of papers during the hearing.

Once you have organized the witnesses and documents, most of your work is done. Each state has slightly different procedures regarding attendance. It is important to read all written instructions you receive from your state's Office of Appeals. If you have any questions, call the Office of Appeals and have your questions answered before the hearing. One of the biggest mistakes employers make is to wait until the hearing to ask questions. In many cases, this is too late; it can result in your losing a case.

DOCUMENTS IN THE APPEAL FILE

The UIC file from the Office of Appeals allows you to review the documents in the claimant's file—many documents will be new to you. Having these documents to review *before* the hearing helps you prepare your case more strongly.

Not all documents in a UIC file have the same importance. Below is a discussion of documents you are likely to see in a UIC file. We have included comments on the relative importance of each and the amount of time you should spend on it.

Exhibit 1: Initial Claim Form

The first document in the file is usually the initial claim for benefits. This is probably the first time you have seen it. It was filed by the claimant at the local UIC office and sent to the Office of Appeals as a technical part of the record. Quickly review the "reason for separation box" because it usually includes a short statement by the claimant. Do not spend more than a few seconds on this document.

Exhibit 2: Notice to Employer

This is usually the Notice to Employer you received when the claimant first applied for UIC benefits—signed, dated, and returned to the local UIC office. It is in the appeal file for technical reasons. You've seen this document before. Make sure it is the document you signed, but don't spend more than a few seconds here.

Exhibit 3: Wage Statement

Most states include a statement of the claimant's wages as part of the appeal file. This shows wages earned with one or more employers in the base period. If you are a base-period employer, your company name and UIC account number will appear on this document. Don't spend more than a few seconds reviewing this exhibit. It is there only for technical reasons.

Exhibit 4: Claimant's Statement of Reason for Separation

This is usually the claimant's statement of why he or she was separated from employment. It is probably the first time you have seen this document. It was taken at the local UIC office and sent to the Office of Appeals for inclusion in the record.

This is an important document. It is a written record of the reason the claimant gave for being fired or quitting his or her job. Take some time to review the document. If the claimant made any admissions or false statements, you can use this in your case once the document has been formally admitted as evidence. (The admission of this and other documents occurs after the hearing is convened.) Spending some time on this statement now can be very helpful at the hearing.

Take some time to review what the claimant stated. Was the claimant truthful in making his or her statement? If not, pick out places where the claimant's statement is at odds with your facts.

Does the claimant make any specific statements you would like to question him or her about in the hearing? If so, write down your questions, and ask them when you are given the chance to cross-examine the claimant. If you are not comfortable asking the claimant questions, write them down and ask the judge to ask them for you.

Consider the following example. It demonstrates how going over this statement can point up some very interesting differences in facts.

The claimant's statement as to why he was separated from work reads: "I was let go because the employer just didn't like me. My supervisor also said I was trying to start a union and take over the business. I never had any trouble until this one supervisor, Bill Nelson, started working there. He was always out to get me, and I guess he did."

As you review the claimant's statement, you realize your facts are completely different. As you check your notes, you discover the actual reasons the claimant was discharged.

The employee was tardy to work three times during the last month of his employment. Before that, he was late eleven other times over a 3-month period.

The employee was verbally warned on two occasions (March fifth and March seventh). He was given a written warning on April eighth for excessive tardiness. On May eighth, the employee was given a final written warning for excessive tardiness. The warnings were issued by Bill Nelson, who has been with the company ten years.

On May eighth, following the final written warning, the employee threatened Bill Nelson. Three witnesses besides Bill were present. The witnesses were me, Bob Martin, and shop foreman Josh Miller. The employee said, "Well, I guess you SOBs are really out to get me this time. If you don't back off, I'm going to kick the s—— out of someone." I warned the employee we would not tolerate threats on the job. He just shook his head and walked away. The warning and the incident took place about 11 A.M.

At 2 P.M., Bill Nelson and I asked the employee to help two other workers unload a truckload of furniture, which was part of his normal duties. He refused to help unload the truck. He said, "You've been giving me crap all day long. You can both go to hell. Now leave me alone before I really kick some butt." The employee continued swearing and refused to unload the truck. Bill Nelson and I went into my office, where we discussed the case for 20 to 30 minutes. At about 4 P.M., I called the employee into my office. Bill Nelson and Josh Miller were also present. I told the employee he was being discharged for insubordination and for excessive tardiness. He looked at me and said, "I know I screwed up. Well, I never liked this job much anyway."

Exhibit 5: Report of Claims Examiner's Investigation

This is often a fact-finding report filled out by the claims examiner at the local UIC office. The typed or handwritten document is usually in note form. These are notes the claims examiner made when the claimant was interviewed at the local UIC office.

The document usually indicates (in summary form) what you or your company representative told the claims examiner when he or she spoke with you by telephone. Take a few minutes to read this document. Make sure what you said was recorded by the claims examiner in an accurate manner. It will not be a word-for-word record, but the statement should be an accurate "representation" of what you said.

Take a few minutes to review the notes of what the claimant said to the claims examiner. A claimant may have admitted to the claims examiner the very points that will prove your case. In the hearing, the claimant may tell a different story. Make yourself aware of what the claimant told the claims examiner.

TELEPHONE HEARINGS

As soon as you receive the Notice of Hearing, check to see if you are scheduled to appear in person or by telephone. In most states, you have the option of appearing either way. You may be expected to call the Office of Appeals to make arrangements to change the way you are going to appear. If you are scheduled to appear by telephone and plan to do so, you need to take no further action unless instructed to do so on the Notice.

Most states allow the claimant, the employer, or any witnesses for either side to give testimony by telephone rather than in person. Testimony given over the telephone is treated and weighed in exactly the same way as if the witness appeared in person. Many states schedule hearings by telephone when the parties are more than a reasonable traveling distance from the Office of Appeals. It is important to read the Notice of Hearing to determine whether you are scheduled to appear in person or by telephone.

In nearly all states, you may appear in person even if the Notice of Hearing indicates you are scheduled to testify by telephone. If you decide to appear in person when you are scheduled to appear by telephone, we suggest you call the Office of Appeals to let them know you plan to appear in person.

If you or any of your witnesses cannot attend a hearing on the date and time scheduled, you may request your testimony be taken by telephone. Call the Office of Appeals as soon as you know you need to have a telephone hearing, if the hearing was originally scheduled to be an in-person hearing. Explain to the ALJ or clerk why you wish to appear by telephone. In some states, this request is automatically granted; in others, it is not.

Calling Instructions

Below is a list of questions you should ask the ALJ or other personnel at the Office of Appeals regarding telephone hearings.

- What time do I call in? (Many states require you call in 15 to 20 minutes before the hearing so there is enough time to hook the parties up by the scheduled starting time.)
- With whom do I speak or whom do I ask for?
- What number do I call? (The telephone hearing number may be different from the regular telephone number.)
- What do I do if there is a technical problem on the line and I can't get through?
- What do I do if I get disconnected?
- Do I call collect, or must I pay for the call? (Most states have you call collect.)
- If I am disconnected, will someone call me back?
- What if no one calls me back?
- How long should I wait to make a second call?
- How many people can be hooked up on my end?

- Can I have witnesses in more than one location participate in the hearing? (Some states can hook together up to ninety-nine witnesses for a single hearing. Others allow parties to have witnesses at only one location.)
- Are there any other instructions I should have before the hearing?

Submitting Documents at Telephone Hearings

An important point to remember about telephone hearings is that you will not be there to submit documents or examine documents offered by the claimant. It is essential for you to send your documents to the ALJ in enough time so the Office of Appeals personnel can send copies to the claimant.

In some states, you are allowed to mail documents directly to the claimant and to the Office of Appeals. However, if a claimant does not check the mail, he or she may not have copies of the documents you mailed. The ALJ will delay the hearing or take the time to read the documents to the claimant over the telephone. This wastes your valuable time.

Unless instructed otherwise by the ALJ, send your documents to the Office of Appeals and request that they send copies to the claimant. The responsibility for getting the documents to the claimants then rests with the judge.

You must also have copies of any documents the claimant submits. If the claimant submits documents, be sure you receive copies before the hearing. Carefully review these documents before the hearing. The more review time you have before the hearing, the better your preparation will be.

Examine the claimant's documents carefully. If you have objections to any of the documents being used in the hearing, note your objections. Take some time to review your objections to see if they have any real foundation. If the documents the claimant submits have no bearing on the outcome of the hearing, don't waste time preparing objections. Only relevant documents have any legal weight at the hearing. If these documents are admitted, you can ask the claimant to provide a foundation for admitting them.

Starting Times

Telephone hearings rarely start on time. Judges frequently encounter technical problems calling the parties back and making sure they are all connected by telephone. This does not mean that you should call in late. Call in at least 15 minutes before the hearing is scheduled to start.

Often you will get a busy signal when calling an Office of Appeals. If you're calling collect (as you do in most states) because of distance, have the operator keep trying. It's also a good idea to ask the operator for her operator ID number or name. That way you have some proof that you have been calling if you can't get through and the hearing starts without you.

Once you are connected to the Office of Appeals, the secretary or receptionist will note your name, the time of your call, your telephone number, and the hearing you are scheduled for. Someone will call you back for the hearing.

Ask the receptionist for her name. There have been cases in which the Office of Appeals made an error and did not call someone back. The only proof you called may be the fact you have the name of the person you spoke with when you made your initial call.

After you exchange information, the receptionist will instruct you to hang up. Someone will usually call you back within 15 to 30 minutes after the *scheduled* starting time of the hearing.

Be patient; sometimes the wait is longer, which can be frustrating and inconvenient. Often you are tying up other employees who are scheduled to appear as witnesses. Unfortunately, there's not much you can do to speed things up.

Regardless of the instructions you received, call the Office of Appeals back if you fail to hear from them in 30 minutes. Again, note the time and the name of the person you speak with. Remind them the hearing was scheduled for a specific time, and tell them how long you have been waiting. If the hearing started without you, inform the receptionist you wish to be connected immediately with the ALJ assigned to the case.

What to Have Ready for Telephone Hearings

Even though you are not appearing in person for the hearing, there are materials you need to have ready before the hearing starts. Below is a list of items to have ready *before* you call in for a telephone hearing.

Your Complete File. Have available the complete file related to the UIC hearing. It should contain all the documents preceding the separation from work. It should include a copy of the state's UIC file and the Notice of Hearing.

Pens and Tablets. Have several writing pads and pens or pencils available for note taking and passing notes to witnesses, if necessary.

Witnesses. Have all your witnesses ready *before* you call in. ALJs dislike having to wait for you to get a witness during a telephone hearing. Use a good speaker-phone when the witnesses are all with you in one room. This allows everyone on your end to hear clearly what is going on.

If witnesses are going to testify from their own offices or some other location, be sure you have their telephone numbers when you call in. They must be available to take the judge's call when he or she calls back to start the hearing.

Tip. We recommend all the witnesses be in the same room with you when possible. This allows you to pass notes back and forth and communicate with each other as you listen to the claimant's testimony.

Refreshments and Beverages. Have refreshments available to help keep you and your witnesses fresh and alert during the hearing. If you have a long wait before the ALJ starts the hearing and a long, drawn-out proceeding, fatigue may become a factor.

Coffee, soft drinks, water, trail mix, and other high-energy snacks sometimes mean the difference between winning and losing long, difficult hearings. If you need breaks to use the bathroom or to recover from fatigue, don't hesitate to ask the ALJ. Ask on the record.

In most cases, ALJs are required to grant short breaks or recesses during long hearings. If you or your witnesses have some special physical or medical problem that requires frequent breaks, tell the judge when the hearing begins. There should be no problem in accommodating the special needs of all the parties to a hearing.

Once the Hearing Begins

Once the telephone hearing is open, you must be sure you can hear and understand all the parties on the line. This includes the claimant, claimant witnesses (if any), and the ALJ. If you have any trouble hearing what anyone is saying, tell the ALJ immediately. The judge does not know what you are or are not hearing.

If there is a problem, it is up to the judge to fix it. If there is trouble on the line, the judge may ask you to hang up so the Office of Appeals can call you back and reconnect you. If that doesn't solve the problem, the ALJ must make other arrangements or postpone the hearing until the technical difficulties can be corrected.

It is fundamental for all parties to be able to hear clearly during UIC telephone hearings. Sometimes you have to insist on that right. If you do so forcefully and courteously, the judge has no choice but to comply.

Listen carefully to all instructions given by the ALJ and the testimony from the claimant's side. If you don't understand even the smallest part of the instructions or testimony, ask for clarification.

POSTPONEMENTS

Postponement is a dirty word to most ALJs working in the UIC system. They hate granting postponements because a postponement is an inconvenience to them and usually makes it difficult for them to issue timely decisions. However, if you *do* need extra time, don't hesitate to request a postponement "on the record," which means after the hearing is officially opened and the tape recorder is on.

Some states allow you to make a request for a postponement by telephone before the hearing. Some states require that you make the request in writing. Others require that you appear by telephone or in person to request the postponement. It is important to find out the procedure in your state. Some states are very liberal in granting at least one postponement for either party. Others are much stricter; they may grant postponements *only* for extreme cases, such as medical emergencies. This is known as *good cause.*

We strongly suggest that you not abuse the right to a postponement in your state. Save the right for situations when it is really necessary, then invoke the postponement rule. One good argument for a postponement is to emphasize to the ALJ or clerk that your case will be jeopardized if the postponement is not granted. You can tell the ALJ that while you understand his or her need to issue timely decisions, the principal interest or issue should be one of holding a fair and just hearing. If you compare the ALJ's convenience or the mandated need to issue timely decisions against the larger issue of justice, the latter should win.

If a Postponement Is Denied

Sometimes you will find an ALJ or clerk who will not grant a postponement for any reason, no matter how valid the cause or need. In most states, you can take the issue directly to a supervising ALJ or a chief judge for a ruling. In cases where a postponement is essential to your case, don't take no for an answer without exhausting all your options.

If a postponement is denied and you must attend the hearing without adequate preparation, witnesses, or documents, bring the issue up as soon as you are on the record in the hearing. Tell the ALJ that for the record you are *renewing* your request for a postponement. Get as much detail on the record as you can. If you lose the hearing, your objection to going forward will be on the record. On appeal, you may be granted a new hearing with additional time to prepare.

QUESTIONS TO ASK IN YOUR STATE

1. How many days before the hearing is my state required to send out the notice of the appeal hearing?
2. Does my state allow a witness to make a narrative statement or is the hearing all questions and answers?
3. Does the judge conduct the entire hearing or does he or she allow the parties to question each other and their own witnesses?
4. Does my state grant at least one postponement for any reason, or is a hearing postponed only in emergencies or for good cause?
5. Can I get a copy of the appeal file by mail, or must I appear in person to request it?

CHECKLIST FOR PREPARING FOR APPEAL HEARINGS

1. Verify the time, date, and place of the hearing. Make sure you know the physical location of the Office of Appeals. Take the Notice of Hearing with you.

2. Take pads, pens, and pencils with you to the hearing.

3. Have copies of all necessary documents with you when you go to the hearing, such as the employee handbook, time cards, written warnings, record of verbal warnings, witness statements, and notes of any action taken with regard to the claimant.

4. Take all pertinent original documents with you, in case the judge wants to examine them and compare them with your copies.

5. Take your copy of the state UIC file that you requested before the hearing.

6. Bring any subpoena requests or unserved subpoenas with you.

7. If you plan to submit tape-recorded or videotaped evidence, take a tape recorder or video equipment with you so the judge can examine the evidence.

8. Snack foods and refreshments may be welcomed at long hearings. They help you keep your energy level up so you can focus on the issues of the hearing.

9. Make sure you have the telephone numbers of any witnesses who are unable to appear in person.

Twenty-Five Ways to Win Your UIC Appeal Hearing

1. File your appeal on time.
2. Prepare to defend yourself if you file late.
3. Prepare your case before the hearing.
4. Be knowledgeable about the issues.
5. Prepare your case even if you are not the appellant.
6. Examine the Notice of Hearing.
7. Request a postponement if you need it.
8. Subpoena witnesses who won't otherwise attend.
9. Allow adequate time for subpoenas to be processed and served.
10. Prepare your witnesses for the hearing.
11. Prepare your general questions and strategy before the hearing.
12. Prepare your documents before the hearing.
13. Get to the hearing on time.
14. Present all the testimony you have when it is necessary.
15. Keep focused on the issues of the hearing.
16. Avoid leading the witness in testimony.
17. Avoid trying to change your witness's testimony.
18. Clarify technical terms for the judge.

19. Avoid asking questions unless you know the answer.
20. Keep focused, but prepare to be interrupted by the judge or claimant.
21. Ask relevant questions when cross-examining a witness or the claimant.
22. Resist fighting every point the claimant makes.
23. Present every case on its own merit.
24. Prepare a brief but comprehensive closing argument.
25. Get all the important points on the record.

9

The Day of the Appeal Hearing

Once the day of the UIC hearing finally arrives and it is nearly time to leave for the Office of Appeals, it is natural to feel some anxiety and apprehension. Attending a hearing is stressful, and there is always uncertainty about what will occur. Even professionals who have attended thousands of hearings get a few butterflies as the time of the hearing draws near.

It is important to remember you are going to the hearing with excellent preparation. Your preparation is superior to that of the claimant if you have taken the advice we provide in this book. Even if the claimant has an attorney or other legal representation, you are ready to present and *win* your case.

In some cases, emergencies completely beyond your control interfere with your attendance at a hearing or the attendance of a witness. Illness, accidents, and other compelling personal circumstances fall into this category. If this occurs, call the Office of Appeals *immediately*. Advise them of the problem, and request a postponement.

If you believe you can attend the hearing later in the day, offer to appear as soon as you can. If not, request a postponement to another day and time. If you speak with a clerk, receptionist, or ALJ, note the person's name and what he or she said to you.

In some states, the ALJ may want to proceed with the hearing, regardless of the emergency. He or she may request that you or your witnesses appear by telephone, so be prepared to go forward with the hearing, even under emergency circumstances.

A LAST-MINUTE CHECK

Below is a list of things to go over before you leave for the hearing. It will help you pull everything together so you are as prepared as you possibly can be.

Pens and Paper

Take several pens, a couple of sharp pencils, and a few tablets for note taking during the claimant's testimony. You may also want to communicate with your witnesses when they aren't testifying. Whispering is sometimes allowed, but written notes are less disruptive.

Snack Foods for Breaks

It is a good idea to take some snack foods to eat during breaks. You might also want to bring a soft drink or coffee or tea in a thermos. Eating and drinking are not normally allowed in hearings. During long hearings, the ALJ usually allows short breaks to go the bathroom and to get a drink of water. If you're feeling tired because of the stress or the length of the hearing, use a break to refresh yourself and your witnesses. It may provide you with a crucial edge.

Double Check Your Paperwork

Make sure you have everything you intend to take to the hearing. It can be devastating to discover at the hearing you have left important documents at your office.

Check on Witnesses

Be sure all your witnesses are ready to go. Make sure they know *exactly* where the hearing office is. Draw them a map if they have doubts about how to get to the Office of Appeals. Give them the telephone number in case they get lost or have an emergency on the way. We suggest that witnesses stay together and travel to the hearing together when possible. If this isn't possible, give everyone clear directions on how to get there and instructions on what to do in case of an emergency.

ARRIVING AT THE HEARING

If you have never attended an unemployment insurance hearing, this may be your first face-to-face contact with the UIC system. Until now, you have been communicating by telephone or in writing with the UIC office.

An Office of Appeals is different from a local unemployment insurance office. Most UIC offices of appeals have a reception area, which is often quiet. Fewer people come here because claims are not being filed at this office. People are not waiting in long lines to find out about their checks. Because hearings are scheduled by time and date, you and the claimant have a scheduled hearing time.

Even though you may be nervous about appearing at this hearing, there are some things you can do to help yourself. Below are some etiquette rules and smart ideas we suggest you follow.

Don't Be Late

Be 20 to 30 minutes early. This gives you a chance to review the state's hearing file and to have copies of documents made before the hearing starts. You can also locate the bathrooms and get settled before going into the hearing.

Be Polite

Administrative law judges and their staffs may be overworked and somewhat frazzled. A little common sense and courtesy goes a long way in making your interactions with them pleasant and helpful.

Read Posted Instructions

Read all written instructions posted in the reception or waiting area. If you have any questions at that point, ask the receptionist or clerk. In most cases, members of the staff are happy to answer your questions and assist you in any way they can.

Locate Bathrooms and Snack Areas

Locate the bathrooms, soda machines, and snack areas before the hearing. This can help you save time on breaks during long hearings.

Ask If There Is a Private Consulting Area

Find out if you can use a private conference room for consulting with your witnesses before the hearing and during any breaks or recesses.

Check on Special Equipment

If you need special equipment for your evidence, such as a tape recorder or a videocassette recorder or player, be sure they are available for your use. It is wise to call a few days before the hearing to let personnel at the Office of Appeals know you need this equipment. That usually gives them enough time to locate it for you.

Were Subpoenas Issued?

If you requested subpoenas for witnesses who were unwilling to attend the hearing, check to see if they were issued and served.

Ask about the Telephone Policy

Ask if the office has a private phone you can use to call your office in the event you need additional documents or witnesses.

Relax before the Hearing

Take a few moments to relax before the hearing. If your witnesses appear to be extremely tense or nervous, talk to them. Keep them as calm as possible. A little bit of anxiety and nervousness is usually good; too much can be a problem. Nervousness can be contagious. It can be transmitted to your witnesses and to the ALJ. It is important for you to project an image of confidence and calm. The best way to ensure this attitude is good preparation for the hearing.

Don't Overdress

Wear comfortable clothing. If you are accustomed to wearing a suit or coat and tie, wear them. If you usually dress in less formal work clothes, wear those. The same holds true for witnesses. You will not be judged by how you look at the hearing. The judge will be impressed by courteous, respectful demeanor and by the quality of your testimony. The most important point of the hearing is concise, detailed, precise, truthful testimony.

GET YOUR COPY OF THE FILE

In all states, you have a right to see the complete UIC file *before* the hearing. You also have a right to photocopies of the file (on request) before the hearing starts—you should already have your photocopy of the entire UIC file. As we state in Chapter 6, request by mail or in person a complete photocopy of the file *before* the UIC hearing. You can usually do this as soon as you receive the Notice of Hearing.

You should already have your copy—check it. Be sure yours is the same as the ALJ's original file; new documents may have been added to the original file. Request copies of any documents you do not have.

In some states, you can get the file by mail, but we have found it is usually better to get it in person. This way you can quickly check the original file with the UIC file you've been keeping. Make sure the appeals file contains the same documents you sent to the local UIC office. A clerk may fail to copy the back of an important original, and you may end up missing part of the file.

WHAT IF A HEARING DOESN'T START ON TIME?

Wait patiently. Despite the fact that UIC hearings are scheduled to start at specific times, sometimes they don't. There are several reasons the start of a hearing is delayed. Often the ALJ runs late with another hearing that goes on longer than anticipated. Some Offices of Appeals assign another judge who has become available because of a canceled or postponed hearing.

In some instances, you and your witnesses (and the claimant) will have no choice but to wait. Waiting when you've been on time for a scheduled hearing is a waste of valuable time.

If the hearing has not started by 20 minutes after the scheduled hearing time, ask the clerk or receptionist to find out what the delay is and when the judge plans to start the hearing. This is a safe place to be assertive without being rude. Wait another 10 minutes. Do not be afraid to ask again after that time. Remind the clerk that you were on time and ask for an explanation. If you are kept waiting more than an hour, ask to talk to the office manager or the lead ALJ about transferring the case to another ALJ or granting a continuance.

YOUR RIGHTS AS AN EMPLOYER

You have certain rights, which must be protected, as you enter a UIC appeals hearing. Below is a short discussion of your rights as an employer, regardless of who happens to be the appellant.

Courtesy

You have the right to be treated with courtesy. An appeal hearing is structured so you must answer questions, but these questions must be asked in a courteous, polite manner. No one has the right to abuse you or your witnesses. Just be sure you extend the same courtesy to the ALJ, the claimant, and any claimant witnesses.

Promptness

You have the right to expect a hearing to begin promptly. If there is a delay, you have the right to be notified, if possible, to save you time away from your work. If that cannot be done, you have the right to have your hearing begin as soon as possible or you can request a continuance or change of ALJ.

Telephone Calls

If you need to make a telephone call to your business for the purposes of checking on routine commitments or if you have urgent personal business, ask the receptionist or ALJ to use the telephone. Before the hearing begins, make a courteous request to make a phone call. During the course of an extra long hearing, tell the ALJ you need to use the phone if this is necessary. In most cases, you will find them accommodating.

Answers to Your Questions

You have the right to complete and understandable answers to any questions about the hearing. You have the right to understand the procedures of the hearing and to know exactly what is happening or going to happen. If you ask a question and you do not understand the answer, be sure you have the ALJ clarify the information to your satisfaction. Be courteous but persistent until you are satisfied that you understand the answer to your question.

10

The First-Level Appeal Hearing

The administrative law judge or one of the clerks will announce to the parties that the hearing is ready to begin. You will then be asked to follow the ALJ or clerk into a hearing room.

In most states, the hearing room is somewhat informal—more like a conference room than a courtroom. The ALJ generally does not wear a black judicial robe. The bench is not set above the rest of the hearing room. There is usually no bailiff. In most cases, there is no formal witness box or witness area.

You will probably find a table with chairs on each side. The ALJ generally sits at the head of the table, often behind a desk that contains the judge's files, a telephone, and a tape-recording device.

Tip. When you sit down, have your primary witness sit as close to the judge as possible. This allows his or her testimony to be heard and recorded with a minimum amount of voice energy. If your witness has a soft voice that is hard to hear, make sure he or she is seated as close to the judge and the recorder as possible.

Only one witness at a time can testify, so seat yourself next to your primary witness. If you are the primary witness, sit as close to the judge as you can. This puts you in the seat nearest the recorder and the ALJ. When you call additional witnesses, have them switch seats with the first witness. The claimant usually sits opposite you, across the table.

In some states, the ALJ determines the seating arrangement. If the ALJ allows you to choose, take every advantage, but try not to be too aggressive or insistent about where you sit.

As soon as you sit down, get out your files, notepads, and pens with a minimum of fuss and noise. Sit quietly and wait for the judge to open the hearing formally. Read the sample script of an appeal hearing included in Appendix E. It gives you an opportunity to find out what a typical hearing is like.

THE HEARING IS OPENED

The ALJ normally opens a hearing by introducing himself or herself and welcoming the parties to the hearing. The parties are introduced, and the judge usually asks for the names and the spellings of those who plan to participate in the hearing as witnesses or representatives or both.

The judge advises the parties that the hearing is being recorded so an accurate record of the testimony can be made. The judge advises the parties not to interrupt each other; only one party can speak at a time. If there is an overlap or interruption, the tape recording will be garbled. This can result in having to redo a hearing, which is a waste of everyone's time. Avoid this when possible.

Addressing the ALJ

Addressing the ALJ can be a touchy matter; it varies from state to state and judge to judge. Some judges insist on being called "judge" or "your honor." Others are much less formal and may prefer to be called Mr., Mrs., or Ms. We have found it is best to ask. If you have a choice, we suggest "judge" or "your honor." (As stated earlier, in some states this person is called a "referee," "examiner," "administrative hearing officer" or identified by some other title. To avoid problems, check to see what title is used in your state.)

Being respectful is not being submissive or condescending. The ALJ will respond to you with the same courtesy by calling you Mr., Ms., Miss, Mrs., or by a professional title (such as doctor), depending on what is appropriate.

TESTIMONY IS TAKEN UNDER OATH

The judge will advise the parties that testimony is taken under oath. Most states advise witnesses that there are penalties for perjury. In some states, the judge may also advise the employer and the claimant that there are additional monetary penalties for knowingly making false statements under oath.

The judge administers the oath or affirmation to the witnesses who plan to testify. Some judges swear in all witnesses at the beginning of the hearing to save time. Other ALJs swear in the witnesses as they are called to give testimony.

Excluding Witnesses

Most states allow either party to ask that witnesses other than the claimant and employer (or its representative) be excluded from the hearing room except to testify. When the claimant brings witnesses, ask that all witnesses be excluded. The judge will then exclude *all* witnesses, including yours. If the claimant does not bring any witnesses, you do not need to ask to have witnesses excluded.

There is a purpose in excluding witnesses. If you have reviewed your witnesses' testimony with them, they will know what to say. However, if the claimant has not prepared his or her witnesses, they may make contradictory statements about the claimant's case. This is to your advantage.

The judge may exclude witnesses from the hearing room on his or her own motion. Be sure your witnesses are prepared for this possibility. The ALJ will instruct the witnesses to be seated in the waiting room until they are called to testify. The ALJ will also instruct the witnesses not to discuss the case while they are waiting to be called.

IDENTIFYING THE DOCUMENTS

In almost all states, judges identify the documents that will be used for the hearing. Documents are usually numbered as exhibits to keep them in numerical order, beginning with number 1. Related documents may be lettered, such as 2A, 2B, and 2C.

Follow the judge as he or she goes through the documents; be sure your file matches the judge's file, and mark your documents with the same number the ALJ uses. If you become lost or confused during the process, ask the judge to clarify any misunderstanding before the hearing begins. Any new documents introduced by you or the claimant will also be numbered.

DOCUMENTS ARE ADMITTED

Once documents are identified, they must be officially admitted for use in the hearing. The ALJ will ask the employer and the claimant if either party has any legal objection to admitting the documents to the hearing.

A *legal objection* may mean you object to the *contents* of the document or to the way it has been used thus far in the UIC process. If you believe a document is irrelevant or not authentic (forged, altered, or misrepresented in any way), this is the time to make an objection.

If you simply disagree with what the document *says*, object to it for the record, so the ALJ knows you do not agree with it. You will have opportunities to rebut or counter the document later in the hearing. If you have no legal objection, answer the ALJ, "No objection, judge," or "The employer has no objection."

JUDGE EXPLAINS HOW HEARING WILL PROCEED

After documents are taken care of and witnesses are sworn in, the judge may take a few minutes to explain how the hearing will proceed. In discharges, employer witnesses usually testify first. In some states, the appellant goes first. For the most part, the hearing is a question-and-answer proceeding. The ALJ usually questions the witnesses first by direct examination and cross-examination using the documents in the UIC file, then each party has a chance to ask the other side questions.

The party who called the witness is allowed to ask questions by direct examination. Direct examination is asking the witness non-leading questions—a non-leading question seeks information without instructing or leading the witness in his or her answer. After each witness finishes testifying for the party who called him or her, he or she will be subject to cross-examination by the opposing party.

When all the witnesses for one party have testified and been cross-examined, then the other party presents his or her witnesses. They are questioned first by the ALJ, then by the person who called them (by direct examination), then by the other party (by cross-examination).

After all testimony has been taken and all questions have been asked and answered, each party may be allowed to make a closing statement. After these closing statements, the ALJ will close the hearing.

If the claimant quit, the claimant and claimant witnesses usually go first. If you have any questions about the order of testimony or any other procedural matters, the judge usually gives you an opportunity to ask them. In most states, you have the right to question or cross-examine the claimant after he or she testifies. You will also have the right to give your own testimony when you and your witnesses testify—*that* is the time to contradict or counter the claimant's testimony.

SUBMITTING NEW DOCUMENTS

In most states, the ALJ asks the parties if either party has any new documents to be submitted. In some states, the ALJ wants all documents submitted before the hearing for his or her review. These documents will be marked (numbered) and put in the file before the hearing begins. You will be asked if you have any objection to these documents being considered in reaching a decision in your UIC case.

Generally you will not object to admission of routine documents. If you have very specific objections because new documents have been falsified or altered, now is the time to make an objection. This is called *making an objection*. (We provide more information on objections later in this chapter.)

In virtually all states, you and the claimant are allowed to submit *new* documents relevant to your UIC case. New documents are generally those not already in the appeal file; these are documents you take to the hearing with you.

Getting new documents into the record is usually a routine matter. Most states take any documents you have before the hearing and attach them to the file. They are usually stamped with the time and date received. Some states and some judges require a reason (foundation) for their submission. In that case, the judge usually asks for documents *after* the hearing has been formally opened. Be prepared to explain how and why each document you plan to submit is relevant to the case.

Tip. In your preparation to attend the hearing, you will have selected documents you believe are relevant and crucial to your case. If you are unsure about submitting a document, take it to the hearing anyway. Use the *overkill technique* described later in this chapter. Submit all documents you believe may help your case. If the ALJ believes the documents you submit are not relevant to the hearing, they will be excluded (not admitted).

It is better to err on the side of caution and submit too many documents than fail to submit a crucial document that could mean the difference between winning and losing a case. However, do not overload the judge with *every* document in your file. As you follow the advice in this book and attend some hearings, you will be surprised at how expert you will become at selecting and presenting documents.

A judge may refuse to accept a document you believe is essential to your case. If this happens, make a strong objection, on the record, to the exclusion of that document. Use a statement such as this: "Judge, we believe this document is crucial to our case. Without it, we cannot establish our case, and the record of the hearing may be incomplete."

If You Do Not Attend in Person

In most states you can submit documents and send a letter outlining your position rather than attend a hearing in person. We discourage this practice mainly because you have a minimal opportunity to present your case. When possible, attend in person. If it is impossible for you to attend a hearing, provide the ALJ with the documents you would have submitted in person. You still may have a chance to win your case.

If you are not attending the hearing in person, send documents to the Office of Appeals as soon as possible. Call before the hearing date to make sure the documents were received. If documents are not available by the time the hearing is scheduled, it is highly unlikely they will be made part of the record or used during the hearing. The judge is unable to consider missing documents—it is as though they did not exist.

Admitting Documents after a Hearing Is Closed

Under exceptional circumstances, documents can be admitted after a hearing is closed. If the documents are not available because of theft, natural disasters, or documented administrative inability to retrieve or produce them, a judge may make an exception, but exceptions are rare.

Do not count on being granted an exception. Make sure all relevant documents are ready at the time of the hearing. If your state allows for postponements or continuances of hearings and you need the time to obtain your documents, ask for a postponement or a continuance until you can get the documents you need.

In some cases, when there is a valid reason for a document not being at the hearing, the judge may continue the hearing. Testimony will be taken at the initial hearing, and the hearing will be reconvened at a later date *only* for the purpose of accepting missing documents. Generally, no testimony at all or only testimony related to the document will be taken at the reconvened hearing.

MAKING MOTIONS

Most motions in UIC cases are made by the ALJ. Listen carefully to any motion the judge makes and respond appropriately. In some instances, you might be asked to "make a motion" that the documents you submitted be marked and entered as exhibits. If that happens, do not let it throw you. Just respond to the judge by saying, "I so move, judge," or "I make a motion the document I just handed you be made an exhibit in this hearing."

In most cases, the judge will make the motion for you. If you feel uncomfortable putting your request in the form of a motion, simply state your *request*, and let the judge assist you from there.

STIPULATIONS

In some UIC cases, the ALJ may ask one of the parties to stipulate or agree to certain facts that do not appear to be in dispute. For example, the claimant may not dispute the fact he or she was absent from work for a third time. Rather than go through each absence, the judge may ask the employer and the claimant to stipulate to the fact the claimant was late on two previous occasions and the third time. This saves everyone time. If you are certain of the facts and you are certain those facts will *not* harm your case, agree to stipulations the judge recommends or requests.

Be cautious. Do not be talked into stipulating or conceding any facts unless you have determined that you are making a factual stipulation. Do not agree to stipulate facts you may disagree with. Never stipulate to facts just to please the judge or to be cooperative. Once you have stipulated to facts for the record, you have entered into an agreement from which it is very difficult to withdraw without damaging your credibility and perhaps your UIC case.

You must be very careful with stipulations when the claimant is represented by Legal Aid or by a private attorney. *Fully understand* every stipulation you are asked to make in those cases. There is nothing wrong with refusing to stipulate to facts. Simply inform the ALJ you cannot agree to facts you feel may be in *dispute.*

RECESSES

A *recess* is a short break in a UIC hearing. Either party may request a short recess to take care of personal business, go to the bathroom, or get a snack.

Using Recesses to Your Advantage

Once the hearing starts, most ALJs try to complete it without taking a break, but sometimes that is impossible. If your hearing is longer than an hour and you or your witnesses start to feel tired, ask the judge for a short break or recess. You may need to use the restroom, or your witnesses may need water, a beverage, or a snack. Sometimes you may have pressing business that must be taken care of.

ALJs are usually accommodating. If you need a break to be at your best, ask for it. It is almost impossible for a judge to refuse a request to use the restroom. If you or any of your witnesses has a special medical problem, either temporary or permanent, that requires more frequent breaks, inform the ALJ that you may need extra breaks or recesses.

In some cases, you may need to consult your witness; most states allow breaks for this reason. Usually the judge allows a break to consult a witness when the claimant is being questioned. An ALJ is less likely to allow you a break to speak with your witness in the middle of the witness's testimony, but you can always ask.

If you plan to introduce a witness to present rebuttal testimony, it is a good idea to take a break *before* that witness begins to answer questions. Often you can assure yourself that he or she understands what is going on in the hearing. Double check what your witness is going to say; once he or she begins to testify, it is usually too late to consult.

During recesses, take a look at your witnesses. If they seem tired or stressed, reassure them. Attending hearings can be an exhausting experience. The stress and intensity of a hearing sometimes use up energy at a surprisingly fast rate.

If witnesses are hungry or tired, give them time to rest; refreshments can do wonders. This is the reason we suggested finding the soda machine, coffee machine, and water fountain before the hearing starts. Now is the time to use them. Snack foods can also be extremely valuable in reviving witnesses.

CONTINUANCES

Under certain conditions, a UIC hearing may be *continued*. A continuation is similar to a recess; it is not a postponement. The hearing actually begins but must be extended or carried over to another day and time because the case cannot be completed in one hearing session. Most ALJs grant continuances only when it is absolutely necessary and usually with great reluctance.

Before a judge continues a hearing, he or she must have a good reason for doing so. The ALJ will normally consult you and the claimant to determine if both parties can agree on the time and date of return. In some cases, a case may be continued after a long morning session to the afternoon of the same day, if everyone agrees to return and the judge has time to hear the case. It is more likely that a hearing will be continued a few days or even a few weeks in the future.

Many states try to limit a hearing to one hour. Some states allow each side to present only one witness. If this applies in your state and you have additional witnesses who plan to attend, inform the hearing office before the hearing so additional time can be set aside.

Tip. You have the right to take as much time as you need to present your witnesses, testimony, and documents and to put on your best case. On the other hand, UIC judges may hear as many as six to eight cases a day; this leaves little time for extra-long cases. If you organize and present your case concisely and efficiently, you save your time and the judge's. However, do not cut short a good defense and lose a case because you are reluctant to take too much time. Complex cases may take longer to present. Take as much time as you need.

OBJECTIONS

There are very few justifiable reasons for interrupting a hearing. However, in some cases, interruptions are unavoidable. This can happen when you object to a question or a claimant's answer.

Making objections during a hearing can be awkward and difficult, especially if you have never done it before. You may be appearing as a witness, as well as the person representing the employer. This can make the task even harder.

There are ways to pose objections effectively. Below we offer some suggestions on how and when to make objections.

Have a Valid Reason for Raising Objections

Do not raise an objection simply because you disagree with a claimant's testimony or a claimant witness's testimony. You will have an opportunity to rebut the claimant's testimony when you give evidence.

However, if the claimant begins to speculate, surmise, suppose, or draw unsupported conclusions about the facts of the case, you can object. Even though most states allow hearsay testimony at appeal hearings, you might object to hearsay testimony by the claimant or claimant witnesses.

The most likely time for you to object occurs when the claimant is given the opportunity to ask questions of you and your witnesses. In almost all cases, claimants begin to testify or to argue at this point rather than ask questions. You have the right to object to the claimant testifying or arguing rather than asking questions.

If the claimant does ask a question, the question may be irrelevant to the issues of the hearing. If the question asked by the claimant is clearly irrelevant, make an objection. This may be difficult to do if you are the witness and the claimant is asking the questions. However, if you handle the situation courteously, it can be done. It can also be beneficial to your case.

If the claimant asks a rambling question or one that requires multiple answers, object or tell the judge that you do not understand the question or do not know how to answer it. This forces the claimant to rephrase the question or forces the judge to intervene and pose the question in a better way.

Making an Objection

How you state an objection is extremely important. By definition, an *objection is an interruption.* It may be a necessary and proper interruption, but it is still disruptive and intrusive. How you make an objection is nearly as important as the contents of the objection itself. Below are some examples of how to make an effective objection.

Excuse me, Judge. I'd like to make an objection at this time. The claimant is testifying, not asking a question.

Judge, excuse me. I object to the line of questioning the claimant is taking. Those questions are not relevant to the issue of why he was discharged (quit).

Judge, excuse me, but I object to that question. I don't believe it's relevant to why the claimant was discharged (quit).

Judge, I'm sorry to interrupt, but I object to that question. It is irrelevant hearsay and has nothing to do with the claimant's separation from work.

Practice using the actual words—if necessary, write them down and take the phrases with you to the hearing. With a little practice, you can become very competent at making proper objections in the correct way.

If Your Objection Is Overruled

If your objection is overruled, the objection and ruling by the judge are part of the record and can be used if you need to make further appeals. Do not get upset, and do not lose your concentration if the judge overrules your objection. You must accept the fact the judge is not going to sustain (rule in your favor) on all your objections. Sometimes the ALJ will overrule an objection because he or she is not sure where the line of questioning might lead. The judge may wish to pursue an apparently irrelevant line of questioning to explore or determine whether the questioning will become useful (probative). The judge may overrule your objection to an irrelevant line of questioning only to discover you were correct. He or she will then stop that line of questioning.

Tip. In most states, judges do not have the time or energy to pursue irrelevant or improper lines of questioning. You can usually depend on the ALJ to keep the questions narrowly focused on the issues of the hearing. We suggest you object only if questions or answers are blatantly and clearly improper or irrelevant.

Improper Questions

Objections are usually made in response to questions, not answers. The judge will prevent you and the claimant from asking improper questions. Object when questions are not properly asked by the claimant. (You probably will not need to object to questions asked by the judge.) Be aware of two types of improper questions that should not be allowed by the judge—compound questions and irrelevant questions.

Compound Questions. Compound questions require more than one answer. They are usually poorly worded, rambling, and overly complex. An example of a compound question is, "What happened when you told me not to move those boxes; didn't you tell me it wasn't my job and the forklift was out of order, and it wouldn't be fixed for several days? That's what I heard you say, and there were others present, too."

Irrelevant Questions. Claimants often feel a hearing is the place to air all the grievances they had against an employer. Much of the testimony and some of the questions the claimant may want to ask have nothing to do which the reason for separation from work. Irrelevant questions— those that have no probative value to the hearing—should not be allowed by the ALJ. Object to them when the claimant asks them.

PRESERVING THE RECORD

It is important to make your points and to state on the record what you want and need for *all* matters related to any UIC proceeding. This is especially important in recorded hearings. At the local office level, you are not in a formal hearing, and no tape recordings of conversations with the claims examiner are made. However, there is still a "record"—it is just not mechanically or electronically taken.

At a UIC hearing, the tape recorder is almost always running when testimony is being taken and procedural matters are being attended to. It is essential that all your requests, motions, or objections be made for the record. This is called "preserving the record." If it is not on the *formal record* of the hearing, it might as well not have happened.

You have every legal and administrative right to present all evidence relevant to your case. If the ALJ agrees with your requests, there is usually no problem. If the ALJ disagrees, make sure you get a formal denial on the record of any matter you believe is important. Remain courteous, but assert your rights. Do not assume the judge is always right. ALJs are human and sometimes make mistakes in denying a request. It is essential to have all denials and rulings on the record.

Offer of Proof

If the ALJ refuses to allow testimony you believe is essential to your case, ask to make an *offer of proof.* An offer of proof is a brief statement of what the testimony would be so the ALJ can reconsider whether to allow the testimony.

Doing this preserves, in the record, what the testimony would have been. This can be crucial to a higher-level appeal. Do not be afraid to ask to make an offer of proof. Keep your statement short; state the name of the witness who will give the testimony and provide a short summary of what he or she would testify to.

Importance of Preserving the Record

If you lose the case and the record clearly shows you were denied some essential right or information, you have an excellent chance to force a remand of the decision. If the ALJ does not take note of the evidence you have presented, you stand a good chance of winning a higher-level hearing or of being granted a new hearing.

TESTIMONY IN THE HEARING

The most important part of the hearing process is about to begin. At this point, all the preliminary matters and business have been taken care of. The witnesses have been sworn in, and all the parties have been issued instructions. The file has been marked, and documents have been entered. The judge has a responsibility to develop a clear record by asking questions and obtaining answers. The questioning is about to begin.

In most states, the appeal hearing is a "finder and trier of facts." Similar to a regular court trial, this hearing is where nearly all the action is. Testimony is taken, and documents are submitted that comprise the record used to reach the decision regarding your tax rating and the claimant's benefits.

Even though all states provide for an extensive appeals process beyond the first-level appeal hearing, the *record* almost always remains the same. Higher-level appeals are essentially *review procedures*. With rare exceptions, they do not involve taking new testimony or admitting new documents. This is the reason it is crucial for you to prepare thoroughly for an appeal hearing. It may be the only chance you have to win your case. The record at the first-level appeals hearing is nearly always the only record for the entire case.

After the Opening Questions and Answers

Once the routine or "easy" questions are on the record, the judge moves to the questions that bear directly on the issues of the case (see the sample script in Appendix E as you read through this information). Many judges allow witnesses to testify in a narrative style. This means the judge does not start with direct, closed-ended questions that can be answered yes, no, or with a short answer. The judge may ask an open-ended question, such as, "Mr. Harrison, can you tell me why you discharged Mr. Arnold on August twenty-third?"

This provides you the opportunity to tell your side of the story. The judge probably won't let you go on too long before he or she begins to ask additional questions, so be prepared to be interrupted as you begin to fill in the details of the story.

If you have used the methods we described for organizing your case, you should have little trouble using the same material to testify in a narrative style. Fill in as many facts and details as you can. *Efficiency, brevity, clarity,* and *winning the case* are your goals.

Begin with the Last Event First

Most ALJs begin with the final event that caused the discharge, also called the *precipitating incident,* and work back in time. Organize your employee file the same way.

Do not worry about providing more than a loose framework the ALJ can use to ask more specific questions. You are not required to add all the details at this point—just get the ball rolling.

The claimant will not be allowed to ask you questions or interrupt until you have completed your testimony. You will have the same right to ask the claimant questions when he or she has finished testifying.

USING YOUR CLAIMANT FILE

You will see the payoff of keeping a comprehensive, up-to-date file on the claimant when you start answering questions at the hearing. The time and effort you invested provides these useful, positive benefits:

1. You have remained in touch with the case and should have an excellent grasp of the facts.

2. You are well organized and able to find the facts you need quickly and easily.

3. If others must attend the hearing on your behalf or give testimony, they will be able to use the file effectively.

TESTIFYING WITH MAXIMUM IMPACT

The testimony you give as to why the claimant was discharged or quit his or her job is the *crucial element* in winning your UIC appeal hearing. While courtesy, demeanor, and organization are important, you must still win on the merits of the case. Bad cases cannot be won, no matter how well organized or courteous the employer may be. But good cases *can* be lost because of a lack of organization and poor presentation.

Listen carefully to each question, and respond as *directly* and *briefly* as possible. Answer *only* the question you are asked; *never* volunteer any extra information. If the judge wants and needs additional information, he or she will ask further questions.

During the course of the hearing, there will be plenty of time and many opportunities for you to tell the judge everything you feel is relevant. While answering questions, stick to important points. This is not the time to say everything you want. It takes discipline and practice to answer only the question that is asked, but with a little work and patience, you can do it effectively and persuasively.

It is essential to establish your credibility as soon as you begin to answer questions. In virtually all UIC cases, the ALJ begins the questioning. Below are some common rules to follow.

Listen Carefully to the Complete Question

Do not begin to answer a question *before* you hear the entire question, and do not answer a question unless you are certain you understand it. There's nothing wrong with taking extra time to make sure you understand what you are being asked.

Tip. If you have any doubts about the question, ask to have it repeated. Say, "I'm sorry, could you please repeat the question?" This is very important at telephone hearings where quality sound reproduction may be lacking. Consider the following question.

Q: If the incident of October first hadn't taken place, would the claimant have been discharged?

This type of question can be confusing, but it is often asked at hearings. The questioner is trying to determine if the incident of October first was the precipitating incident—the final incident that caused the claimant's discharge. If it was, the answer would be no; but it is easy to become confused and answer incorrectly, especially if you are under pressure. We urge you to have questions like these clarified unless you are absolutely certain what they mean.

In some cases, questioners (especially on cross-examination) ask a question with a negative "spin." This can be very tricky. Study the following three examples. The italicized word or words in each question demonstrates the negative aspect.

Q: If Mr. Jones testified he was nowhere near the soda machine when it was vandalized, he *wouldn't* be lying would he?

Or the question might be phrased:

Q: If the claimant testified he *wasn't* anywhere near the soda machine when it was vandalized, he would be telling the truth, wouldn't he?

Or

Q: If the claimant testified (or has testified) he was *not* near the soda machine when it was vandalized, you are in *no* position to dispute his testimony, are you?

These are proper but misleading questions, and they can be confusing unless you listen carefully. In the first question, the questioner is trying to get you to say the claimant was nowhere near the soda machine. By agreeing with the questioner, you are helping establish the claimant was not near the soda machine. If you fired the claimant for vandalizing the soda machine and you were attempting to tell the judge he *was* near the machine, you would be stating the opposite.

The same holds true for the second question. The questioner is asking you if you agree the claimant is being truthful when he states (or might state) he was not close to the soda machine. If you agree by saying yes when you mean to say no, it might jeopardize your UIC case.

In the third question, you are being asked to agree that you cannot dispute or contradict what the claimant has said or is going to say. By agreeing, you have stated on the record that you cannot dispute what the claimant says with regard to being near the soda machine.

Ask for clarification unless you are certain you understand the question. These examples show how easy it is to say something incorrectly.

If you are confused or have any doubt about the question(s) you or your witnesses are asked, tell the questioner you do not understand. Ask to have the question repeated or rephrased. If you still are unclear, ask the judge or questioner *exactly* what the question means. For example, if you were confused by the first question, you might ask for clarification, as shown below.

A: I'm not sure what you mean. Could you repeat the question?

Or

A: I'm not sure what you mean. If you mean was Mr. Jones near the vandalized soda machine, yes he was.

Or

A: I'm not sure what you are asking me. Are you asking me if I know whether or not Mr. Jones was near the vandalized soda machine?

Do Not Rush to Tell Your Side

Do not rush into telling your whole side of the story while being questioned. You will have plenty of time and the opportunity to get the entire story told as the hearing progresses.

You will be given an opportunity to give narrative testimony at several points during the hearing. Many ALJs will ask you if there is anything additional you want to add before a hearing is concluded. This is the time to add any points you may not have covered during the questioning by the judge.

Give Relevant Detail

Give as much *relevant* detail as you can when you answer a question. Use specific times and dates when you can; use A.M. and P.M. if you are testifying about times. Provide the year as well if there could be confusion about dates.

Do Not Be Afraid to Say "I Don't Know"

In all likelihood, you will be asked questions you cannot answer. The most dangerous thing you can do is try to make up an answer. If you do not know the answer to the question, say so. If you know who does know the answer, tell the ALJ, "Judge, I'm sorry; I don't have that information. I believe the claimant (or one of your witnesses) can answer that question." If you don't know who might have the information, don't try to guess. Simply answer by saying, "I'm sorry, I don't know."

Be Careful of the Phrases You Use

Stay away from phrases that make you sound uncertain and equivocal. Avoid the following phrases when possible.

To the best of my knowledge . . .

I guess . . .

I think . . .

I believe . . .

I suppose so . . .

I assume . . .

Using these phrases can annoy the judge and reduce your credibility as a witness. With a little practice, you should be able to eliminate them from your answers.

Tip. If you *must* use the phrases given above, you may be asked by the questioner whether you "know" or are "guessing" at the answer. Do not let this break your concentration. You are not being harassed. The questioner is trying to clarify the record to determine what you are stating as fact and what you are speculating or concluding. Let's look at the following example.

Q: What time did you see the claimant leave the work area?

A: I guess it was about 10:30.

Q: Are you guessing, or do you know what time it was?

The second question is testing whether you are making a statement of fact or speculating. A better answer would be:

A: It was approximately 10:30 A.M.

Be Careful with Conclusions and Opinions

Stay away from conclusions and opinions unless the question requires you to state them. Conclusions and opinions usually begin with "I think" or "I believe." When you use these phrases in an answer, it appears that you are drawing a conclusion, speculating, or offering an opinion. The following example demonstrates how this can happen.

Q: Did you give the claimant a copy of the work rules?

A: I think so. He must have gotten one. We give all employees one when they start work.

Q: Do you know for a fact this claimant received a copy of the work rules?

A: I'm sure he did.

Q: But you don't know for a fact that he did, do you?

A: No, I don't.

Q: Your assumption the claimant received a copy of the work rules is based on what usually happens when employees are hired, isn't that a fact?

A: Yes, I guess it is.

It would have been much more powerful and effective to state the following in response to the first question.

A: Yes. The claimant was given a copy of the work rules the day he started. He signed a receipt for the rules. We have a copy of the receipt right here.

If You Do Make a Mistake

If you make an error in answering a question or making a statement for the record, correct it *immediately*. There is nothing wrong with making a mistake. You are not expected to be perfect.

Explain to the ALJ why you made the mistake and why you wish to correct, clarify, or modify your testimony. Some witnesses feel their credibility is challenged when they change their testimony. In some instances, this may be true. However, it is better to correct the record than let a major point in the hearing go uncorrected and be misunderstood, which could result in losing your UIC case.

THE CLAIMANT'S TESTIMONY

One of the most frustrating things you will have to do is sit quietly while the claimant testifies about why he or she was discharged or quit. Often you will be surprised at what the claimant says or believes to be true. Your immediate impulse is to interrupt the testimony, especially if the claimant is lying or distorting the truth. A claimant's testimony will not necessarily be accepted as *fact* or *truth*. You will have ample opportunity to counter with your own testimony.

Keep Track of the Claimant's Testimony

Now is the time to use the notepads and pens or pencils you brought to the hearing. Carefully take notes of what the claimant says, especially on points you feel he or she is distorting. Make notes on the exact points you want to *dispute* in the claimant's testimony and on points you wish to *contradict*.

Do not try to counter *every* statement or point the claimant makes. This adds to your confusion and needlessly prolongs the hearing. It may also obscure your major points. Use these notes to form your questions to cross-examine the claimant.

Apply the following rules as you listen to the claimant's testimony. These are especially important when the claimant quit.

Listen to the Questions *and* Answers

When the claimant (and any claimant witness) gives evidence, it is essential for you to *pay close attention* to what is said. Listen carefully to the questions the ALJ asks, and listen just as carefully to the answers given by the claimant or claimant witnesses. Do not try to keep all the points in your head. Jot down important points to refer to later.

An excellent method of keeping track of questions is to draw a line down the middle of your pad. Note what the claimant says on the left side. Jot down your comments on the right side. This technique takes a little practice, but it soon pays off. If any testimony from the claimant raises questions you want to focus on during your testimony, note them quickly.

Do not try to write down everything. Summarize and use short sentences; leave out unnecessary words. Put stars or checks by important comments you want to address later.

Do Not Get Upset

Allowing yourself to get upset because of the claimant's testimony is a dangerous luxury. When you become upset, you stop thinking clearly. Listen carefully to *exactly* what the claimant says. If you disagree, make a note. You will have plenty of time to counter what the claimant says with your own testimony. You will also have an opportunity to question the claimant or ask the judge to question the claimant on *everything* he or she says while under oath.

Do Not Interrupt the Claimant

Interrupt the claimant's testimony *only* if you have a specific objection to the ALJ's question or the claimant's answer. You have every right to interrupt *if* you have a legitimate legal objection. Claimants often damage their cases when they testify, so we suggest you let the claimant testify without interruption, other than legal objections.

Listen carefully—the key to winning your case is often *brought up by the claimant.* You cannot hurt yourself by listening, but you can hurt yourself by talking when you should not. Confine your interruptions strictly to legal objections.

Let the Judge Interrupt the Claimant

Often a claimant brings up points as he or she testifies that prompt questions from the ALJ. Listen carefully to the judge's questions and the claimant's answers. The judge often pursues matters that help you. When this happens, graciously accept the gift by keeping quiet.

Judges often like to resolve matters on their own. When they are in the process of helping you win your case, keep quiet. They are more likely to give their own questions and the answers they receive more weight than they give a question from someone else.

QUESTIONING THE CLAIMANT AND CLAIMANT WITNESSES

You must be cautious when questioning the claimant or any claimant witnesses. The answers they give can be unexpected and may seriously damage your case. Unless you are trained in cross-examination techniques, let the judge handle the questions in this category. If you feel comfortable asking the claimant or claimant witnesses questions, you will find some tips later in the chapter.

When the ALJ is through questioning a witness, he or she will ask you if you have any questions. Asking questions takes training and practice. Unless you are experienced at asking questions, have legal training, or attend hearings often, ask the judge for assistance.

If you feel the ALJ has not asked all the questions you believe should be asked, you have two alternatives.

You can request the judge to ask some additional questions. In most states, you will have to ask the judge to cover specific areas of testimony, or you may have to request specific questions. This can be difficult because you are asking the judge to do something extra; it may be something he or she believes has already been covered.

You can also ask the questions yourself. We want to caution you that asking questions in an effective way takes a great deal of practice and thought. However, if this is the only way to proceed, there are some techniques you can use.

Nearly any statement can be turned into a question by adding a few key phrases. Some of those phrases include the following questions:

Isn't that a fact?

That's correct, isn't it?

You're not disputing that, are you?

It's also true, isn't it . . .

You recall that, don't you?

State a fact and ask the claimant to agree with you. Below are some examples.

I issued you a written warning on September tenth; that's true isn't it?

You told me in our April third meeting you had fixed your car and would report to work on time. You recall that, don't you?

We had a meeting on August sixth at which all employees were told to limit their breaks to 15 minutes. You're not disputing that, are you?

I told you and all the other employees in our January second safety meeting that anyone caught speeding in a company vehicle would be terminated, didn't I?

You can use different combinations to change a statement into a proper question. Practice a few on your own. We strongly recommend you prepare these types of questions several days in advance of the hearing. Continue to prepare until you a comfortable with asking these questions at a hearing.

We also want to caution you that you should know the answer to these questions *before* you ask them. If the claimant does not give you the answer you are looking for, you must be able to prove your point by other means—your own testimony, the testimony of other witnesses, or documentary evidence you bring to the hearing.

Leading Questions

Leading questions can be used in cross-examination of the claimant and his or her witnesses. These questions are almost always statements put in the form of a question that instruct or suggest to the witness how to answer, put words into his or her mouth, but usually can be answered yes or no. Below are some examples of typical leading questions.

Q: So your policy regarding absences is not in writing, isn't that correct?

A: Yes.

Q: Employees have to rely on verbal instructions to determine what your work rules are, don't they?

A: Well, yes.

Q: The last time you had a meeting regarding work rules was over two years ago, isn't that a fact?

A: I don't remember when the last meeting was.

These are all statements phrased as questions. You can see the witness has little choice but to answer yes or no, with little explanation. The witness is being "led" to agree with the questioner because the leading questions are well constructed.

Sometimes leading questions are mixed with more direct questions or questions that call for a narrative response. Below is an example:

Q: You received a copy of the rules regarding discounting merchandise, isn't that correct?

A: Yes, I think so.

Q: In fact, you signed Exhibit 11 on October third, showing you received and read a copy of all the employer's work rules, didn't you?

A: Yes, I think so.

Q: You don't deny the signature on Exhibit 11 is yours, do you?

A: No.

Q: When Ms. Harrison testified that she held numerous meetings at which the merchandise discount policy was discussed in detail, she was telling the truth wasn't she?

A: Yes, she was telling the truth.

Q: In fact, the last meeting in which the merchandise policy was discussed was one week before you were discharged, that's also correct isn't it?

A: I don't know when the last meeting was.

Q: If Ms. Harrision testified the last meeting was exactly one week before you were discharged, you wouldn't be in a position to dispute her testimony, would you?

A: No, I guess not.

Q: In that last meeting of January fourth, Ms. Harrison cautioned you and all other employees that giving merchandise discounts without permission could lead to a discharge from employment, correct?

A: Yes, I guess so.

Q: You were at the meeting of January fourth, weren't you?

A: Yes.

Q: You were there for the entire meeting, correct?

A: Yes.

Q: Yet on January the eighth, you gave a 25 percent discount to a customer without asking permission, isn't that a fact?

A: Yes.

Q: You knew the 25 percent discount had to be authorized by a manager, didn't you?

A: Yes.

Q: You also knew that violating the rule could lead to your dismissal from work, didn't you?

A: Yes.

Q: Why did you violate the company rule that required you to obtain permission from a manager before you discounted the merchandise?

A: Well, there was no manager around, so I thought I could get permission later, then there'd be no problem. The customer was a friend of mine who bought a lot of jewelry in the store. If the discount was canceled, he would have paid the extra 25 percent or I would have made in up out of my own pocket. Anyway, even with the discount, the store still made a profit.

This is a good example of cross-examination in which the claimant is basically compelled to agree with what the questioner asks. The questioner makes statements of fact and "invites" the witness to agree. The witness cannot disagree without lying or contradicting himself or herself.

Once all or most of the facts have been established in the above example, the questioner asks the claimant to explain her actions. You can see the explanation is really an admission or confession. The claimant is providing a motive for her actions in the course of offering an explanation. This type of evidence is extremely useful in winning a UIC case.

Questions to Ask the Claimant's Witnesses

Here are some questions you may want to ask a witness appearing for the claimant. Rely on the ALJ to ask most of these questions; ask these questions *only* if the judge fails to ask them.

"What is your relationship to the claimant?" This question helps you establish, on the record, whether the witness is a friend, relative, or acquaintance of the claimant. If it is a close relationship, such as a spouse, the testimony may carry less weight than testimony of a disinterested party.

"Did the claimant ask you to come here and testify today, or are you appearing on your own?" The answer to this question is usually the same. "I was asked to be here by Mr. Smith (the claimant)." It's important to find out *what* motivated the witness to appear.

"How do you know what occurred?" This question is designed to test exactly how the witness came by the evidence he or she has. Does the witness know the information firsthand or was it told to him or her by the claimant?

Dangers of Cross-Examination

The greatest danger of cross-examination is getting an *unwanted* or *unexpected* answer on the record. A hearing is an interrogation—not the kind with hot lights and instruments of torture—a question-and-answer proceeding where questions (interrogatory statements) are used as a primary way to gather facts. A question is an interrogatory statement designed to test specific knowledge about a person or an event. That's all a question is—a test. Sometimes a question can evoke the opposite answer to the one you want. The following is a case in point.

Q: Why didn't you call in to say you were going to be late, Ms. Carter?

A: I did call in. I called in at 7:00 A.M. and spoke with Bob Rubin, my supervisor. I called two hours before my shift started because I knew it was very important to let someone know I was going to be absent. I told Mr. Rubin my mother was in the hospital for an emergency. Mr. Rubin said it was OK for me to be absent.

If you asked that question, the answer could deal your case a crippling blow. The questioner obviously did not know what answer the claimant was going to give. If he knew the answer, he never should have asked the question.

In most hearings, the judge does most of the questioning, using direct and cross-examination techniques when questioning each witness.

This is the fastest, most efficient way for the judge to obtain information. Most of the time, the judge will cover your questions for the claimant and your witnesses. Your job is to listen carefully and make sure all the questions and evidence you want on the record are covered by the judge. This saves you time and effort. You should bring up additional questions *only* if the judge overlooks some area you feel is important.

Your Role as Employer

You may attend a hearing both as a witness and as the person responsible for keeping track of the employer's case, presenting documents, making a closing statement, and generally representing the employer. Generally the judge will question all witnesses, including you, if you also appear as a witness.

Prepare yourself to testify the same way you prepare any other witness. It is essential to determine whether you have any firsthand evidence or are appearing only as the employer's representative. In many cases, you may be an organizer and a witness. Our advice is to determine your role and prepare accordingly.

Twelve Commandments of Cross-Examination

1. Be brief and to the point.
2. Use short questions and plain words.
3. Always ask leading questions.
4. Ask questions that need only a yes or no answer when possible.
5. Ask only those questions you know the answers to.
6. Be prepared to ask additional questions if you don't get a truthful answer.
7. Listen carefully to every answer.
8. Don't quarrel or argue with any witness.
9. Never permit a witness to repeat direct testimony.
10. When possible, save your best questions for last.
11. Limit the amount of explanation you permit a witness to give.
12. When you get the impulse to stop, it is a good time to stop.

Discrediting a Witness

There is nothing wrong with "discrediting" the claimant or claimant witness's testimony. In a legal context, *discrediting* does not mean you attack the witness personally. By discrediting a witness, you offer evidence to counter or rebut what the witness says. If statements are false, you have no choice but to present testimony to discredit what the witness states.

Important Questions the Judge Should Ask

It is important for the judge to ask questions that provide basic information for the record. Here are questions that *should* be asked at every hearing. Some apply to quits, others to discharges. Whatever the reason for separation, be sure the right questions are covered in every hearing.

1. What were the first and last days of work?
2. What was the claimant's rate of pay?
3. What was the date of the separation?
4. Why did the claimant quit?
5. Before the claimant quit, did he or she explore all reasonable alternatives or file any grievances?
6. On the day the claimant quit, why did he or she quit that day?
7. Could the claimant have taken his or her grievance to a higher authority in an attempt to resolve the grievance?
8. What was the employer's supervisory chain of command?
9. Who discharged the claimant?
10. Why was the claimant discharged?
11. What explanation does the claimant offer for his or her behavior or acts that led to the discharge?
12. If the claimant was discharged for violating company rules, what rules were violated?
13. Was the claimant aware of the rules?
14. Are the employer's rules fairly and uniformly enforced?

QUESTIONS FOR YOUR WITNESSES

Usually the judge will conduct a thorough examination of employer witnesses. The ALJ's examination may also include questions for you, if you plan to give evidence. We have included examples of questions asked and answers given in a typical hearing in Appendix E. Read the entire script and the comments that follow. We believe you will find it a valuable learning tool.

Occasionally the judge does not ask your witnesses all the necessary questions. You will have to ask questions to win your case. Below are some examples of useful questions, with a short explanation of how and when to use them.

"Then What Happened?"

This is a good question, especially for the employer's witnesses. It also works well with the claimant or claimant witnesses. Use the question when you need extra time to think of additional questions or you want to give your witness a chance to make a longer response. It often works well with witnesses who are nervous or those who have a hard time with a structured question-and-answer format.

"Can You Tell Us What You Saw?"

This question is similar to the previous question. It implies that the witness was present when something happened that the witness observed. It allows the witness to give a narrative response to what he or she observed.

"Were You There When the Incident Took Place?" or "Where Were You When That Took Place?"

These questions imply the witness was present and saw something that he or she can testify to. It places the witness at the scene of the event, which establishes that the witness observed what occurred.

"How Can You Recall Exactly What Took Place?"

This question allows the claimant to explain to the judge how he or she can recollect the facts of the case. It is an excellent time for the witness to bring up the matter of notes, especially if a period of time has passed since the incident occurred. If the incident was particularly graphic or memorable, the witness can testify he or she recalls it because the circumstances were so unusual.

"Can You Explain . . . ?"

Asking this question helps a witness clarify answers he or she has already given. It allows a witness the opportunity to explain in greater detail the circumstances that surround an event. Here is an example of a "can you explain . . . ?" question series:

Q: Why was the claimant discharged?

A: Because he violated our company policy.

Q: Can you explain how the claimant violated company policy?

A: The claimant was absent from work without notice twice within a six-month period. Our company policy states that an employee may be discharged for this infraction. The claimant was aware of the policy because it is in our handbook, and I discussed it with him.

If in Doubt, Overkill

Give as much testimony as you feel is necessary to win your case. Don't assume that making most of your major points is enough to win the case.

It is always better to have too much testimony than too little. If you do not get your statement onto the record, the information is of no value. You may feel as though you are overdoing it by giving extra testimony, but that is not always the case. Do not go on for hours, but say what needs to be said to win your case. In most cases, the judge will stop you if you are overdoing it.

QUESTIONING HOSTILE OR EVASIVE WITNESSES

You can question your own witnesses only by direct examination. When questioning your witnesses, you cannot ask leading questions unless the witness is hostile or prejudiced against you or becomes evasive.

A hostile witness is someone hostile toward you or prejudiced against you whom you need to call to support your case. You may have just reprimanded or fired that witness, or he may be reluctant to testify. When a witness is hostile or evasive, ask the ALJ to consider the witness a hostile witness. You will be allowed to cross-examine the witness as if he or she was called by the claimant.

Usually the judge questions any witness who appears for either party. Listen to the ALJ's questions carefully. Most ALJs are good at cross-examining witnesses. They are trained to do it, and they spend years practicing the art of asking questions.

In most instances, the judge asks all the questions for you. However, the judge may not ask all the questions *you* want answered. This is the time to establish that a witness you called is hostile so you can cross-examine him or her. (You can always cross-examine the claimant and claimant witnesses.)

Argumentative and Angry Witnesses

Occasionally the claimant's witnesses *will* be hostile, in the non-legal sense. They will respond to both your questions and the judge's questions with anger. They may yell, scowl, or be confrontational.

If this happens, don't let it bother you. (The judge should control the hearing; he or she has the responsibility and authority to do so.) Ask your questions calmly and professionally. If the witness responds with anger or threats, turn to the ALJ for help.

Never argue with a witness. Ask the judge to "instruct the witness to answer." If the witness gives a vague or nonresponsive answer, ask the same question again. Ask it a third time if necessary. The ALJ will get the point. Ask the ALJ to instruct the witness to answer the question.

If the witness still refuses or gets angry, ask the judge to put the question to the claimant. In some cases, the judge can alter the wording and get an answer. Sometimes just having another person ask the question cools off the situation.

You have the right to a direct, civil answer to your questions, and so does the judge. By remaining calm, you provide an excellent contrast to an angry, confrontational witness. This approach may help your case.

IMPORTANT TESTIMONY IN QUITS

Listening to the claimant's testimony is important in quits. Claimants commonly express many more reasons for quitting than they probably gave as an employee. Often they express grievances that were never called to your attention before they quit.

It is not unusual for a claimant to present accusatory, inflammatory, and inaccurate testimony. Resist the temptation to respond to every point. Choose the most important points, and present rebuttal when you testify. Take notes to help you remember which points to cover in your testimony and in your questions to the claimant.

Questions to Cover in Quits

Quits tend to follow a general pattern in most UIC cases. Usually the judge will cover the issue thoroughly when he or she questions the claimant, but do not depend on the judge to do everything correctly all the time. Here are some standard questions the claimant should answer in a hearing dealing with quits.

Why did you quit on (the date of separation)?

This question can be useful in getting the claimant to testify exactly why he or she decided to leave the job. Often the deciding factor will be trivial or petty. This can help your case because the claimant often has no valid or clear reason for quitting other than that he or she was "just fed up." On the other hand, the claimant may have a very specific reason for quitting on a particular day. The answer to this question may damage the claimant's case.

What did you do to resolve your grievances before you quit?

The answer to this question is often the most important answer a claimant will provide in the entire hearing. UIC regulations almost always require that employees attempt to resolve work-related problems before they quit. Failure to do so often constitutes "leaving without good cause."

DEALING WITH THE UNEXPECTED

Sometimes events are beyond anyone's control. Tape recorders malfunction. Air conditioners fail. Chairs break. Sometimes a funny event helps break the serious mood of the hearing. ALJs often react with apologetic humor as a way of relieving tension. It is best to enjoy a humorous situation; a little humor can be good for everyone.

Emotions at a hearing can run very high. It is not unusual for claimants to become agitated and frustrated during a hearing. Sometimes questions can be probing and confrontational. Claimants frequently respond by yelling, threatening, or even swearing during a hearing. In rare cases, physical altercations or threats of violence have occurred. The judge will take control of the situation and warn participants that outbursts, threats, and other inappropriate demonstrations will not be tolerated.

In addition to anger, claimants sometimes cry. Do not let this throw you. Stay calm, and do not get involved. Let the ALJ handle it; most ALJs can handle these situations quite well.

An ALJ usually controls a hearing very well and heads off trouble before it gets out of hand. A judge does not want to lose control of a hearing. In some cases, the judge will call for a recess or continue a hearing until a later date to allow emotions to cool down.

Do not let emotional outbursts break your concentration. Never allow yourself to be drawn into responding with out-of-control behavior of your own.

REBUTTAL TESTIMONY

In some instances, you will have no questions for the claimant or his or her witnesses. Often all the questions you have were asked by the judge. Never feel *obligated* to ask questions if the ALJ has thoroughly covered the issue and asked all the relevant questions. Asking questions that cover the same ground as the ALJ wastes time and can irritate the judge. If the ALJ has done a good job, move on.

If you do not have questions but you disagree with the claimant's testimony, you must provide *rebuttal* testimony. Rebuttal is defined as "providing testimony that contradicts, clarifies or conflicts with testimony from the claimant and/or claimant witnesses."

Rebuttal is extremely important in helping you win your case. You must listen carefully to the claimant's testimony so you can accurately and persuasively rebut it if necessary. Use your notes to help you. Often rebuttal testimony is the most powerful, effective way to discredit a claimant's evidence. The following is an excellent example.

ALJ (to claimant): Was anyone else present when Mr. Nelson spoke with you in his office about leaving your work station without permission?

Claimant: No.

ALJ: I have no further questions for you at this point. Mr. Nelson, do you have any questions for the claimant?

You could ask the claimant the following question:

Nelson: Bill (the claimant), do you recall that Roberta Clark, the personnel manager, was in my office when you told us you left your work station without permission?

Claimant: No, I don't remember that.

The claimant has given the same answer. Rather than get into an argument with the claimant, make your statement later in rebuttal testimony.

ALJ: Mr. Nelson, do you recall meeting with the claimant to discuss his leaving his work station?

Nelson: Yes, judge, I do.

ALJ: Was there anyone else present besides yourself?

Nelson: Yes, judge, Roberta Clark, our personnel manager was in the office with me. It's our policy to have two management employees present during any disciplinary investigation.

ALJ: What did the claimant say, with regard to leaving his work station?

Nelson: He said he left his work station for about half an hour. He admitted he did not ask permission or tell anyone where he was going. He knew he was required to ask the shift foreman for permission if he was going to be gone for any length of time. Bill said he just wasn't thinking about getting permission.

ALJ: We'll take Ms. Clark's testimony in a few minutes. Do you have anything else you wish to say, Mr. Nelson?

Nelson: I'd just like to state that the claimant admitted he left his work station without permission. As I've testified, he had been warned previously about not leaving the assembly line without permission. Doing so can cause a serious interruption to the quality control of the medical monitoring devices we make for diabetic patients who are undergoing dialysis and other procedures.

One good way to rebut claimant testimony is to use the following statement as often as possible. It helps to *directly* counter any points or statements the claimant may have made. This technique helps focus your countertestimony on specific statements the claimant makes.

In his testimony the claimant says _____ ,
but what really happened was _____ .

Use Detail in Rebuttal Statements

When rebutting a statement made by the claimant, use as much detail as possible. Generalities are not effective. For example, don't say:

The claimant was not telling the truth when he said he did not receive any warnings. He wasn't telling the truth when he said he never talked back to his supervisor. He did both plenty of times.

Effective rebuttal would be:

The claimant says he never received any warnings, but our records show he was warned three times before the discharge. We've provided written copies of the warnings and copies of the notes of the verbal warnings. In addition, the claimant was warned twice about refusing to follow the instructions of his supervisor on November 26. We've also included copies of those written warnings, judge. The copies include the dates and times of the warnings.

CLOSING STATEMENTS

A *closing statement* is a summing up of evidence and the points to support your case. It has been said a closing statement (sometimes called a closing argument) is an "exercise in persuasion." In UIC hearings, closing statements don't usually win or lose cases by themselves. The judge usually has legal training, and you are not arguing before a jury of laypeople, so don't depend on the closing statement alone. However, a good closing summary of your position can never hurt.

Preparing for Closing Statements

Forming a good closing statement involves two types of preparation.

1. Preparation *before* the hearing.
2. Preparation *during* the hearing.

Preparation before the hearing is extremely important. Before you attend the hearing, write down the main points of your case—the ones you plan to prove. As testimony is offered, note which points are being made and supported. When you make your closing statement, include these points in a clear, concise way.

Part of your closing statement will almost always include points brought up during the hearing. You must be alert during the hearing to incorporate these points in your closing statement. Some examples of the points likely to be developed in the hearing are discussed below.

Surprise admissions or acknowledgments by the claimant. Sometimes claimants admit things you don't expect. You might hear statements such as these:

Well, I guess I just forgot to set my alarm clock, and that's why I was late for work.

No I didn't tell anyone I wanted a raise. I just quit.

Yeah, I took the money from the cash register, but the employer wasn't paying me much, so I thought it was OK.

These admissions are very valuable. The ALJ will probably remember major admissions, but it bolsters your case immensely when you include them as a reminder in your closing statement.

Expected answers that prove your case and damage the claimant's. These answers can be useful to you if they prove your case. Be alert for them. Some examples include:

Yes, I told the claims examiner I swore at my supervisor, but he was really pushing me that day. I said it under my breath so he wouldn't hear me.

Yes, I refused to type those letters. I wasn't getting paid enough to do all that work.

These statements damage a claimant's case because they are acknowledgments or admissions of acts that are clearly misconduct. The claimant is now attempting to "explain" why the acts took place. By including claimant statements in your closing statement, you ensure the acts are clearly and sharply defined.

Incorporating Points in Your Closing Statement

When you incorporate points from the hearing in your closing statement, you must be aware of many things. Here are some important points to make in a closing statement if they fit into your case.

Point out *what* the claimant admitted or acknowledged in his or her testimony. For example, if the claimant admitted he did not set his alarm clock and that was the reason he was late to work, say in your closing statement:

In his own testimony, the claimant admitted he did not set his alarm clock. He was previously warned that tardiness to work was a violation of company policy and that he could be discharged for repeated offenses.

Point out what you and you witnesses have shown.

In our testimony, both Mr. Hardy (the shift foreman) and I spoke with the claimant. He admitted to both of us that he stole $30 from the cash register.

Point out what the claimant failed to do.

Judge, the claimant stated she made no attempt to resolve her grievance or discuss her work-related problems with anyone, including me, before she quit.

The claimant did not show up for work three days in a row. In addition, she didn't call us to let us know when she would be in.

Point out what your documentary evidence establishes.

We have provided copies of time cards, signed by the claimant and his supervisor, that clearly show the claimant was more than 20 minutes late eight times in the past two months. We have provided copies of written warnings to show the claimant knew he would be discharged if he continued to report late to work.

Show how the claimant's actions adversely affected you and your business interests.

Point out that you were fair and that you treat all your employees equally when it comes to work-related disciplinary measures.

Prove you tried everything to keep the claimant as an employee. This includes warnings you hoped would lead the claimant to correct his or her behavior. In the case of quits, emphasize what you could have done or what you did to accommodate the claimant. If the claimant demanded the impossible, point that out.

Be brief. A good rule of thumb is keep your closing statement to about two minutes. Three minutes is the outside limit.

The Golden Rules of Closing Statements

Be specific. Don't ramble. Stay with the important issues.
Stick to the evidence. Don't try to make up points not supported by

testimony and documentary evidence offered during the hearing. Follow the points you made in the hearing.

Be brief. There are no extra points for long closing statements.

If you are not prepared to make a closing statement or do not feel comfortable making one, waive it. In most states, closing statements are not required. It is better not to make a closing statement than to make a poor one.

Sample Closing Statement

Here is a sample of a good closing statement. This case involves a discharge for misconduct. The claimant was fighting with another employee.

Judge, in this case, we've shown the claimant was discharged for work-related misconduct. We believe the testimony and the documentary evidence in this case support the employer's position. In our testimony, Mr. Hardy, the claimant's immediate supervisor, and Bob Carter, another employee, testified the claimant pushed Mr. Hardy after Mr. Hardy told the claimant to return to work. Both witnesses testified Mr. Hardy asked the claimant to return to work in a reasonable manner. Mr. Hardy did not raise his voice or abuse the claimant in any way. Mr. Hardy has testified to this, and Bob Carter, a witness who was present during the incident, verifies Mr. Hardy's side of the story.

The claimant does not deny he was in a fight. He does not deny shoving Mr. Hardy with enough force to almost knock Mr. Hardy off his feet. In fact, the claimant shoved Mr. Hardy twice with both hands. The claimant's only defense is he maintains Mr. Hardy "provoked" him. We believe Mr. Hardy did not provoke the claimant in any way. On the contrary, Mr. Hardy was merely giving the claimant reasonable instructions in his capacity as the claimant's supervisor. The claimant may not have liked or agreed with what Mr. Hardy said to him, but that is not provocation and it does not excuse what the claimant did to Mr. Hardy.

Judge, our company has a clear company policy against fighting of any kind. We also have a rule against insubordination. We are very careful to enforce these rules uniformly. Any employee who did what the claimant did would also have been fired. We've fired employees in the past for insubordination and fighting, and we'll do it in the future when someone acts the way the claimant did. If we allowed this behavior in the workplace, employees would fear other employees. Supervisors would not be able to give instructions without fear of being physically attacked. This claimant's acts endangered other employees. We simply cannot conduct our business in an orderly manner with employees who act the way the claimant did.

We believe if you carefully review the evidence you heard here today, you'll agree the claimant was discharged for work-related misconduct. We do not believe our UIC tax account should be charged in this case. Accordingly, we ask you to affirm (or reverse) the claims examiner's determination and find in our favor. Thank you, judge.

This is a good closing statement. It is concise. It highlights the major points of the case, with special emphasis on the seriousness of the claimant's acts. It points out how the claimant's actions adversely affected other employees and the employer's business interests. It points out and emphasizes the claimant's admissions. It contrasts the claimant's improper, abusive acts to the rational actions of the employer. The closing statement points out there was a witness to the incident and his testimony was given. It also points out the claimant's later admission to two witnesses.

11 ————————————————

Beyond the Appeal Hearing

At the end of the hearing, the ALJ will inform the parties that a written decision will be issued as soon as possible. Judges do not usually specify exactly when decisions will be issued because they may not be sure themselves.

In most offices of appeals, ALJs are too busy to issue decisions immediately. Usually decisions are written on Fridays, with hearings scheduled Mondays through Thursdays (excluding holidays). ALJs usually dictate their decisions on tape after reviewing their notes and the written files of the hearings. They may also review specific parts of the tape recordings of hearings to help them write their decisions.

After a decision is dictated, it is usually turned over to the clerical staff for typing. A draft of the decision is returned to the ALJ for final review. The ALJ reviews the draft and makes necessary corrections before the corrected version goes back to the clerical staff for final typing.

After the final copy is prepared, it may be returned to the ALJ for approval or it may be reviewed by the presiding administrative law judge, chief judge, lead referee, or some other person in higher authority than the ALJ. Once the decision has gone through its last review process, copies are mailed to the interested parties—the employer and the claimant. The party who loses has the option of filing further appeals. Figure 11.1 is a sample of an appeal decision.

If you followed our advice and did a thorough job preparing for and attending the hearing, chances are you will have no need to file additional appeals. The claimant will lose the hearing and will have the op-

Figure 11.1
A Sample Appeal Decision

Department of Economic Security
Office of Appeals
207 W. Anderson Lane
Capital City, Texas   78466

DECISION OF APPEALS TRIBUNAL

Appeal No. T79403
Date of Mailing: June 7, 1996

Janet Smith   Good Eats Cafeteria
6100 N. Ridgeway Way   100 Adams Road
Azuma, Texas   78031   Azuma, Texas   78302
                                     Employer Account No. 051648

Issues:

Discharge from Employment (Section 48-0111)
Chargeability of Benefits (Section 46-0508)

Case History:
Effective Date of Claim: 3/17/96   Issue code: B
Date of Separation: 12/30/95
Date of Local Office Determination: 3/15/96
Appellant: Claimant
Date of Hearing: 5/23/96
Appearances: Claimant, three employer witnesses

Findings of Fact:

The claimant was employed as a table cleaner and bus person by a
private contract food service provider company for approximately 8 months
prior to being discharged for alleged work-related misconduct on December
30, 1995. The employer has a contract with the AJAX Airplane Company,
where the claimant worked.

The claimant was discharged for failing to perform her work to the
standards set by the employer. As part of her regular duties, the
claimant was responsible for clearing, cleaning and restocking 12 tables
between 9:00a.m. and 11:15a.m., so the cafeteria could open for lunch on
time. The claimant had established her ability to clean the tables
routinely in 5 to 10 minutes each during the previous 8 months, except on
September 3, 1995, October 10, 1995, and November 12, 1995, when she was
given written warnings for not cleaning tables on time. The claimant had
been given verbal warnings on May 8 and May 20, 1995, for not cleaning
the tables on time.

On December 30, 1995, at about 10:40a.m., the supervisor discovered
only two of the 12 tables were cleared, cleaned and restocked; the others
hadn't even been cleaned. Although the claimant started the work at
9:00a.m., she had not asked for any assistance to clean the tables nor
had she reported any problem or emergency to her supervisor or the
manager about not being able to clean more than two tables by 10:40a.m.

The supervisor reported this to the manager, who investigated and
found the claimant in the kitchen drinking coffee with one of the cooks.
When asked why she was drinking the coffee, the claimant said she was
taking a break. The claimant had taken a scheduled break at 8:00a.m. with
other employees, and was not scheduled for another break until 2:00p.m.
When asked why only two tables had been cleaned, the claimant first said
she didn't have time to do the rest and would get to them as soon as she
could. In a later conversation, she said was tired, but not ill, and had
been working too hard. During the second conversation, the claimant
started arguing with the manager, finally saying, "If you're going to
fire me, then get the damn thing over with," and she was discharged.

192

The claimant contends she was taking the break at 10:40a.m. because she only took a 10-minute break at 8:00a.m. and was owed 5 more minutes. She offered no explanation for cleaning only two tables from 9:00a.m. to 10:40a.m. nor any explanation as to why, after returning to the cafeteria with the manager and supervisor, she was able to clean only two tables while they cleaned four tables each.

Reasoning and Conclusion of Law:

The claimant has contested a determination of claims examiner that held the claimant was discharged for work-related misconduct. The issue before this Unemployment Insurance Tribunal involves Sections 23-41 and 23-42 of the Employment Security Law of Texas.

(The next section in a UIC decision normally includes boilerplate quotes and inclusions from the pertinent sections of state law. We do not include them here because they are the reprints of what is contained in the statutes of each particular state. Following quotations of law are usually a few paragraphs in which the ALJ summarizes the evidence and explains how he or she reached the decision for the employer or claimant. In most states, ALJs attempt to walk the line between issuing a decision that is too legalistic and one that is oversimplified. Because these quasi-legal decisions are for the general public, they tend to be written in easily understood, straightforward language. The following is an example of the wording in a typical decision.)

In this case, the evidence establishes the claimant did not complete or make a reasonable effort to complete her job duties to clean, clear and restock 12 tables between 9:00a.m. and 11:15a.m., on December 30, 1995, after receiving prior verbal and written warnings. She had completed these duties in a timely manner over an 8-month period, except on five occasions when she was given warnings. The claimant was aware of her duties and did not request assistance to complete her duties in a timely manner on December 30. As noted, the employer previously warned the claimant verbally and in writing that her failure to complete her assigned duties on time could lead to her dismissal from work.

Although the claimant maintains she did not complete her assigned duties in the time allotted because she did not have time to do them, she offered no explanation for not having the time, except to say she was tired and had been working too hard. The claimant offered no credible excuse or reason for not completing her duties in a timely manner.

The Tribunal finds the claimant's work assignment was not unreasonable, and she could have completed her duties if she had shown reasonable care and diligence in carrying out those duties. The claimant did not make a good faith effort to complete her assigned duties despite the warnings issued to her by the employer. Accordingly, the Tribunal concludes the claimant's actions were a willful disregard of the employer's interests and the claimant was discharged for work-related misconduct.

Decision:

1. The determination of claims examiner is affirmed. The claimant is disqualified from receipt of benefits from 12/24/95 until re-employed with earnings of no less than five times the claimant's weekly benefit amount.

2. The employer experience rating (UIC tax account) shall not be charged for any benefits claimed in this case or for subsequent benefits paid to the claimant on requalification for benefits.

M.G. Vondrak
Administrative Law Judge

(The ALJ's decision is normally followed by a distribution list for the decision, which includes the employer, the claimant, any attorneys or representatives, the UIC local office, the benefit payment control unit and tax-control unit. In most states, the decision will be followed by several pages explaining further appeal rights and procedures for each party.)

tion of continuing to appeal. No one can guarantee the outcome of a hearing, no matter how well you present your case. No employer wins all cases at the first level. You should win most of them, but you must always be ready to carry your case to the next level if it becomes necessary. The information that follows will help you prepare for higher-level appeals.

ADMINISTRATIVE TIME LIMITS

UIC appeals offices are mandated to meet certain time limits or deadlines set by the Department of Labor. There is a rough way to gauge when you should receive your written first-level appeals decision. While each state is responsible for setting up its own system for meeting these deadlines, all states are mandated to meet Department of Labor guidelines as a result of the Java decision.

30-Day Deadline

Department of Labor guidelines require 60 percent of the decisions be completed and mailed within 30 days of the date of filing the appeal. In most states, this means the majority of the decisions are issued on or before the 30-day limit expires.

Look at your UIC file, and find the Notice of Appeal that was originally processed at the local UIC office. You may see your letter of appeal or the claimant's appeal in the file. In most states, you will also find a document filled out by the local UIC office with a specific date showing when the appeal was processed. Most states begin the 30-day count from that date.

ALJs make a genuine effort to get their decisions mailed out within the 30-day limit. Individual ALJs and offices of appeals are rated in great part by their ability to meet these deadlines. They *are* important.

60-Day Deadline

The second "due out date" is 60 days from the date the appeal was processed at the local UIC office. The Department of Labor requires that 80 percent of all decisions must be completed within this 60-day limit. Some states allow the Office of Appeals to begin the 30-day and all subsequent deadlines from the date the appeal is actually received at the Office of Appeals. The ALJ will try to meet the 60-day deadline if the 30-day deadline is missed.

Note: Most states have deadlines and goals in addition to the federally mandated guidelines.

WHAT TO DO IF YOU RECEIVE NO DECISION

If you do not receive a decision by the end of the 30-day period, call the Office of Appeals and ask about the status of the case. Note the date and time of your call and the name of the person you speak with.

In some states, appeals office personnel are instructed *not* to give information over the telephone when a written decision is pending. This is done so you and the claimant will receive the decision by mail at about the same time. If the clerk or judge tells you the decision was mailed out in the last several days, wait for it to arrive. Do not insist on telephone information at this point.

If the decision was mailed out more than five days before your call, insist that they provide you with as much information as possible. If the clerk answering the telephone is not authorized to give out information, ask to speak to an ALJ, the presiding judge, or the head of the appeals office. If necessary, work your way up the chain of command until you get what you need.

If the decision has already been sent out and you have not received your copy, find out the date the decision was issued and the date it was mailed. Ask the clerk or judge if the ruling was in your favor. If it was, you need not take any further action other than to ask for a copy of the decision. If the appeal decision was in the claimant's favor, there are some steps to take.

Immediately Request a Copy of the Decision

You must immediately request a copy of the decision. If you and the Office of Appeals have fax machines, ask that they send you a copy by fax. Otherwise, request that a copy be mailed to you by the close of business that day.

Find Out the Appeal Period

Ask the clerk or judge when the appeal period is up. In most states, you have 30 days to file a second-level appeal. Your state may allow less time—find out what the second-level appeal time limit is in your state. In many states, you can protect your appeal rights by sending a letter to the next appeal level indicating that you disagree with the appeal decision.

Note: Be sure to follow instructions for further appeals. These are included with the decision.

Once you file an initial appeal, most states allow you additional time to obtain a complete transcript of the hearing and prepare a more detailed, precise written appeal. It is essential to determine the second-level appeal procedure in your state.

WHAT TO DO WHEN YOU RECEIVE THE DECISION

When you receive the appeal decision, examine it immediately. Note the date on the decision and the date the decision was mailed. Make sure the decision has your correct mailing address (sometimes mail is delivered even when the address is not correct). If the address is incorrect, make a note to call the Office of Appeals.

Check to see if the decision is in your favor. Read the wording carefully. If the decision is in your favor, make certain it contains a notation that your UIC tax account (or experience rating) will *not* be charged.

Read the Decision Carefully

Be careful not to misunderstand what the decision says. If the claims examiner originally ruled in your favor and the appeal decision *affirms* the local office decision, you won. If the claims examiner originally ruled in your favor and the appeals decision *reverses* or *sets aside* the local office decision, you lost the hearing.

If the local office claims examiner originally ruled against you and charged your UIC tax account, the appeal decision must *reverse* or *set aside* the claims examiner's decision for you to win. This can be confusing to employers who have had limited exposure to the UIC system. If you have any questions about what the appeal decision says or what it means, call the Office of Appeals immediately and request a full explanation.

WHAT TO DO IF YOU WIN

If the appeal decision is in your favor, you do not need to take any immediate action. Put the decision in the claimant's file. The ball is now in the claimant's court.

If the appeal decision went against the claimant, regardless of what happened at the local office, you win and the claimant loses. However, the claimant has the right to file a further appeal.

In most states, second- and third-level appeals (appeals beyond the first-level hearing) do not require actual participation of the parties. Usually higher-level appeals are *review* bodies. If you or the claimant files an appeal beyond the first level, the agency or body responsible for higher-level decisions reviews the entire record, including testimony taken at the first-level hearing.

Most states allow you to respond with a written brief or a letter to set forth a factual, legal argument in support of the decision, even if you won the first-level hearing and are not the appellant. Unless you feel you won without covering some major point, we recommend you not respond to a claimant appeal. It is highly unlikely your response will make any difference to the outcome of a higher-level appeal. Save your time and energy by letting the burden rest with the claimant.

WHAT TO DO IF YOU LOSE

We hope you won't have to face this issue very often. If you have followed the strategies and advice in the book, you can expect to win most of your first-level hearings, but nobody wins them all. Occasionally you will receive an unfavorable appeal decision. If that happens, don't panic. The game isn't over yet.

A well-thought-out, carefully presented second-level appeal has a good chance of succeeding. Claimants often lose higher-level appeals because they don't know how the system works; they have no idea how to win second- or third-level appeals. Below are some steps to take so you *can* win higher-level appeals.

Review the Decision Carefully

Don't worry if the decision "appears" to be supported by the evidence. When an ALJ writes a first-level appeal decision, he or she quotes the evidence that best supports the decision itself.

ALJs often do not quote evidence that doesn't support the decision. If evidence is not noted in the decision, this does not mean it is not part of the record. This is why *creating and preserving the record* is so important. The complete record will contain *all* the testimony and documentary evidence, even the evidence the ALJ may have chosen not to reference or quote in the decision.

Determine the Time Limits for Appeal

Determine exactly how much time you have for your second-level appeal and what the appeal procedure is. Written instructions for higher-level appeals should be included with the written decision. If they are not, call the Office of Appeals immediately and request a copy. After you receive them, read the instructions carefully.

If you are close to the end of the appeal period and discover you have lost, call the Office of Appeals and inform them you intend to file an appeal. To send a letter of appeal, you will need the case number, the name of the ALJ who issued the decision, and the address of the agency that handles second-level appeals. Immediately prepare a written appeal (see Figure 11.2, pp. 200–201). Take it to the post office, and have it postmarked the same day as your telephone call.

Order a Transcript

Order a transcript and a *complete copy* of the UIC file. Most states provide you with a complete written transcript of the hearing and a copy of all documents that were made part of the record. You already have a copy of the documents in your own claimant file. Obtain a copy of the official hearing file to make sure it matches the documents you kept for your own file.

Getting a copy of the transcript is essential. When you file your higher-level appeal, you must be able to reference exactly what was said during the hearing. The only way to do this is to examine the actual hearing transcript.

Tip. Most states allow 30 days for higher-level appeals; some may offer longer time periods. In addition, many states allow extensions on filing a final appeal if you submit the written letter of appeal on time and request a copy of the transcript.

Getting the transcript may take several weeks or longer. This gives you extra time, even though you don't have the transcript in hand. You can do little without the transcript, so many states allow you sufficient time to prepare your appeal *after* they complete the transcript and send it to you. In some states, it may be necessary to request an extension on the original appeal period. If your state allows extensions, take advantage of them when you need the extra time.

Some states provide only a copy of the tape recording of the hearing. If this is the case in your state, be sure you can understand the tapes of the hearing. If you can't, let the Office of Appeals know immediately. Request better tapes. Tell them you cannot prepare your appeal without an audible copy of the tape. In most states, there is a small charge or fee for transcripts or copies of recorded tapes.

Examine the Transcript

As soon as the transcript arrives, examine it carefully. If you have never seen a written transcript of a UIC hearing, you may be surprised by what you receive. In most states, transcripts are word for word (verbatim); the transcript is not edited or "sanitized." All the pauses, hesitations, and stumbles are included. Don't let that bother you.

In addition, the transcript will probably be numbered on each page and on each line. These numbers are very important; we show you how to use them to help you file your appeal. Following is a short sample of an actual transcript.

1 Q *(ALJ)*: Mr. Jackson, uh . . . state your name for the record.

2 A *(Mr. Jackson)*: Uh, my name is Bob . . . Bob Jackson.

3 Q: What is your position with the employer, the last employer

4 of record in this case?

5 A: Uh, well, I'm . . . I guess I was the claimant's supervisor.

6 Q: . . . Uh, at the time of the, uh, separation from work?

7 A: Uh-huh.

8 Q: Is that a "yes?"

9 A: Uh . . . yes.

This is not an exaggeration. It takes a great deal of practice to eliminate unnecessary words from your speech. Fortunately, these mannerisms of speech are not important. The *content* of the testimony during the hearing is important, not how it was said.

Scan the Transcript before You Read It Thoroughly

Scan the transcript the first time you read it. Get a sense of how the hearing looks on paper as opposed to how it appeared when you and the claimant were actually there in person.

When you read the transcript a second time, pick out your strongest points and the claimant's admissions and mistakes. Once you have identified the parts that will help you file your appeal, use the sample letter in Figure 11.2, pp. 200–201 as a guide to writing a letter that includes your own information.

WRITING A HIGHER-LEVEL APPEAL

Writing a second-level appeal is different from writing a letter of appeal for a local office decision. A second-level appeal letter does more than protect your appeal rights and ensure that your case is reviewed. In most states, the letter of appeal is the only chance you have to *state your side of the case.*

In nearly all states, the first-level appeal is your only opportunity to offer testimony and documentary evidence. A higher-level appeal is essentially a *review* process; *new* evidence is not usually taken. Because the higher-level body reviews only the record of hearing and your letter of appeal, your letter is your only chance to get your points across.

Here are some tips on writing a powerful, effective appeal letter. Use them to help you create your own letters.

Figure 11.2
A Sample Letter of a Second-Level Appeal

Lender's Auto Repair

November 1, 1997

Office of Appeals
1603 W. Brownson Blvd.
Wellerton, New York   10136

Re: <u>Allen Johnson</u>
<u>SS# 000-38-0750</u>

Dear Sir or Madam,

The employer's contention is that the credible and probative evidence of record supports our argument that the claimant was discharged for work-related misconduct. We maintain that the decision of the Tribunal in Case #853206 is in error for the following reasons:

1. The claimant was found to have company property concealed in his lunch box on June 17, 1997, against company rules, which require written permission to borrow tools. Exhibit A.

2. This fact was established by Mr. Harold Johnson, the shop foreman, in his testimony of record. Mr. Johnson was an eyewitness to the claimant's attempt to remove company property without permission. Page 11, Line 5, through Page 14, line 26.

3. Mr. Johnson's testimony was corroborated by a second supervisor, Bill Carter, the service manager. Mr. Johnson credibly testified he was called over to the claimant's work area by Harold Johnson. Mr. Carter observed the $250 electronic torque wrench in the claimant's lunch box, as did Mr. Johnson. Page 16, Line 2, through Page 23, Line 11.

4. The claimant admitted in his testimony he knowingly placed the torque wrench in his lunch box without permission. Page 26, Lines 3 through 17. He further admitted to putting the torque wrench in the lunch box when he was confronted by Mr. Johnson and Mr. Carter. Page 28, Lines 11 through 26.

5. In answer to the judge's question, the claimant denied he was aware of company rules regarding borrowing tools. However, the claimant admitted he was aware of the rules and procedure for borrowing tools. Page 30, Lines 6 through 11, and Page 31, Lines 2 through 21. The claimant admitted he had read the company rules and had borrowed shop tools on two previous occasions. He had obtained permission to borrow those tools, using the company procedure. Page 33, Lines 2 through 24, and on page 34, Lines 1

Figure 11.2 (continued)

Page 2

through 11. The claimant also acknowledged he knew taking tools without permission was a violation of company rules and grounds for possible discharge. Page 35, Lines 6 through 14. This establishes the claimant knew it was wrong to remove a company tool without permission.

6. The undisputed testimony shows the employer uniformly enforces all company rules and would discharge any employee who violated a company policy, as did the claimant. Our company rule is reasonable, and is fairly and consistently applied. It is one way we attempt to control the theft or misappropriation of valuable company property that is in the hands of employees at nearly all times during the work day.

7. Our interests were adversely affected by the claimant's actions, and the claimant was aware his actions were wrong.

We respectfully request you carefully review the entire record of the hearing, including the testimony and documentary evidence presented. We are convinced the weight of credible and probative evidence supports our position. Accordingly, we request you reverse (or set aside) the decision rendered by the Administrative Law Judge and find for the employer. Please advise us of your decision as soon as possible.

                              Sincerely,

                              Martin Court

                              Martin Court, Owner

Form a Basis for Your Appeal

It is essential to form a clear idea *why* you disagree with the first-level decision. Be as specific as possible. If you believe you proved your case to the administrative law judge at the first level but the ALJ disregarded your evidence, point out what evidence was ignored or omitted. If you think the first-level ALJ misinterpreted the UIC rules or the law, indicate in your letter of appeal where and how the ALJ erred or failed to apply the rules correctly.

Read the Transcript Thoroughly

Read the transcript thoroughly to find specific testimony that supports your side of the case or to find testimony that weakens the claimant's case. Look for mistakes, errors, or admissions of wrongdoing by the claimant. Look for instances in which the claimant failed to deny important allegations of misconduct or the claimant's credibility is questionable. Quote these in your letter; use specific page numbers and line numbers.

Have a Strong Closing Statement

Include in your letter a strong closing statement to convince the review ALJs they should reverse the first-level judge and rule in your favor. Your points must be significant enough and your arguments strong enough to convince the reviewing body to "disturb" the findings of the first-level ALJ. To help you in this task, we've included a sample higher-level appeal letter in Figure 11.2. This is an effective, concise letter of appeal for the following reasons:

- In the introduction, it clearly states the employer's position.
- It provides specific details about how the employer believes the ALJ erred.
- It calls attention to the strong points on the record that favor the employer.
- It points out specifically where the claimant admitted he knowingly acted against company policy. Note the citations to the transcript and exhibits always follow the sentence making reference to them. This draws the reviewing authority to these pages and lines or exhibits. The review board members usually will not go looking for them without these references.
- It reminds the ALJ at the higher level that the employer's rules are reasonable and uniformly enforced.
- It points out how the employer was adversely affected by the claimant's actions.
- It closes with a courteous request for a favorable decision.

If the record supports the contentions set forth in this letter, it is likely you would win your UIC case on appeal.

You should receive confirmation that your letter of appeal was received and processed by the Office of Appeals. If you do not receive a receipt within 5 to 7 days, call the Office of Appeals, and ask if the letter arrived. Note the time and date of your call and the name of the person you spoke with. Ask for the Office of Appeals to issue you a written receipt as soon as possible.

SUBMITTING NEW EVIDENCE AFTER A FIRST-LEVEL HEARING

In most cases, you will *not* be able to submit new evidence after the first-level hearing is closed. In many states, higher-level appeals are handled by review bodies that review the record of the original hearing but normally do not take new evidence.

A higher-level hearing is not a new hearing (hearing de novo). The proper form for submitting evidence in most states is the first-level hearing, which is the reason we place such emphasis and importance on presenting your original case and building and preserving a clear, strong record at the first-level hearing.

However, there are always exceptions to any rule. In nearly all states, you *may* be able to have new evidence admitted to a second-level appeals board or commission. Requests for admitting new evidence are usually made in writing to the appeals board or commission. In your request to submit new evidence, it is necessary to include a summary of the evidence showing why it is relevant or vital to your case. Only a few reasons are considered valid.

First, you may show that the evidence you are submitting was not available at the time of the first-level hearing. The higher-level board or commission will take into account the reason the evidence was not presented earlier. You must demonstrate some valid reason for not presenting this evidence at the first-level hearing. Some acceptable reasons include the following:

- These statements are from witnesses who were unable to testify because of serious illness. Include a short written summary of the witnesses' testimony and an explanation regarding the nature of the illness.
- The witness or document was not available because of natural disasters.
- The witnesses or documents could not be located or retrieved in time for the first hearing. This explanation could cover documents that were lost or destroyed for reasons beyond your control.

Second, the ALJ at the first-level hearing failed to allow you to admit documents or testimony. If this is your reason, you must show on the record of the first hearing that you made every reasonable attempt to make the testimony or documents part of the record of hearing, and that the judge erred in refusing your request.

In all cases in which you are attempting to add new evidence on the record, you must demonstrate a valid reason why the evidence is relevant and vital to your case. You must also provide a valid reason as to why the evidence was not presented at the first hearing or to the local office.

What Might Happen?

There are several possible outcomes when you submit new evidence. These include the following:

1. A higher-level appeals board or commission will refuse to take any new evidence. You usually receive a letter or notice from the appeals board informing you the evidence will not be admitted.
2. The appeals board will admit the new evidence but allow the claimant an opportunity to respond.
3. The appeals board will remand (send back) the case with the new evidence to the first-level judge with instructions to reopen it or, in some instances, to hold the hearing again.

We strongly suggest you submit any evidence you have at the first-level hearing. It is usually difficult to get new evidence admitted after the first-level hearing has concluded.

A MORE FORMAL APPEAL

In some cases, an employer, especially an employer represented by an attorney, may decide to file a letter of appeal in the form of a formal brief. The content of the appeal is essentially the same. Higher-level UIC boards and commissions are not usually impressed with the *way* an appeal is structured or written. They are more interested in what the appeal says than in its appearance.

A good appeal can carry you only so far—the actual hearing record is the most important evidence. If the evidence to support your case is in the record, the appeal is a tool to help you point out your position. If the record does not clearly support your side of the case, the most carefully crafted appeal will not win your case by itself. This is why preserving the record is so important to winning your UIC case.

LIMITS OF SELF-REPRESENTATION

In most UIC cases, you will be able to represent yourself successfully by using the information, tips, suggestions, and advice we provide in this book. By applying the information you have acquired over time and by practicing the techniques and strategies we have shown you, you can become very successful in UIC matters.

However, there are limits to self-representation. In some situations, the help of a qualified attorney or professional representative can be very beneficial.

Claimant Has Qualified Legal Counsel

If the claimant is represented by an experienced, well-qualified attorney or paralegal, it is a good idea to seek legal counsel. Contact a professional in the field of labor law or unemployment insurance representation. A lawyer who has little or no training representing clients at administrative hearings is less likely to do a good job than a professional who specializes in the field.

Your Case Is Unusually Complex

If you have a unusually complex case or one you believe might lead to additional legal action, such as a wrongful discharge or discrimination suit, we suggest you contact a professional who represents clients at

UIC hearings on a regular basis. You can be very helpful in preparing the case—from your notes, materials, documents, witnesses, and other information—but a legal professional may be needed to win.

If You Lose Your Appeal

You may lose your UIC case within the administrative appeals system. If this happens and you want to pursue the case into the higher courts, you should contact a qualified attorney or legal professional.

THE SECOND-LEVEL APPEAL

In all but a few states, the first-level appeal decision is final unless an interested party files a further appeal. Nearly all states provide for a second-level appeal within the UI administrative system. In Nebraska, Hawaii, and the Virgin Islands, however, appeals beyond the first level go directly to the state courts for judicial review. The other states have second-level review bodies with the authority to uphold a first-level decision, reverse it, modify it, or remand it for additional adjudication.

Thirty-four states have a second-level review authority called *a board of review, a board of appeals,* or *an appeals board.* The remaining nineteen states have a commission or commissioner responsible for second-level decisions. They are all called by different titles. For example, in Missouri the second-level appeal authority is the Labor and Industrial Relations Commission. In Wisconsin, those duties are fulfilled by the Labor and Industry Review Commission. Idaho uses the Industrial Accident Board part time as their equivalent of a UIC appeals board. In Kentucky, the commissioner of economic security and two associates comprise the UIC commission, which serves as the appeals board.

All second-level bodies have at least three members. In Colorado, Louisiana, Michigan, New Hampshire, and New York, boards have five members. In California, the board has seven members. Members of the boards represent employers, employees, organized labor, and the general public. Members are appointed by the governor, the head of the Economic Security Agency, or the UIC advisory commission, depending on the state.

In some states, if work separations involve a labor dispute with recognized unions and a strike occurs, appeals bypass the first-level decision process and go directly to the appeals board. In other states, labor dispute cases are handled the same way other UIC cases are handled, with an ALJ specially trained in labor dispute adjudication.

The sample appeal we provide and the advice we give should help you prepare a powerful, effective second-level appeal. If you lose a second-level appeal and still believe you have a good case, we encourage you to continue the process. We recommend you consult a qualified attorney or other legal professional before you file for judicial review. In many states, you cannot represent yourself at the judicial review level.

In several states, once you petition for judicial review, the appeals board reviews its own decision one last time before the matter is turned over to the courts.

HELPING YOUR ATTORNEY PREPARE A COURT APPEAL

You can use the information in this book to help you organize your facts for your legal counsel. The time and effort you have taken to learn the techniques and strategies presented in the book can pay off, even when you do not represent yourself.

This book also provides information that can help an attorney who is unfamiliar with UIC administrative proceedings. The more information you and your counsel have, the more quickly and easily you will win UIC cases at every procedural level.

Going to Court

After a case passes through the UIC administrative system, if one of the parties is not satisfied with the last decision, the case can go to court. All states provide for judicial review, which means the case enters the regular court system.

Here is a list of the 53 states and the courts that take jurisdiction after the UIC administrative process has been exhausted.

State	Court of Appeals
Alabama	Circuit Court
Alaska	Superior Court
Arizona	Court of Appeals
Arkansas	Court of Appeals
California	Superior Court
Colorado	Court of Appeals
Connecticut	Superior Court
Delaware	Superior Court
District of Columbia	District of Columbia Court of Appeals
Florida	District Court of Appeals
Georgia	Superior Court
Hawaii	Circuit Court
Idaho	Supreme Court

State	Court of Appeals
Illinois	Circuit Court
Indiana	Appellate Court
Iowa	District Court
Kansas	District Court
Kentucky	Circuit Court
Louisiana	District Court
Maine	Superior Court
Maryland	Circuit Court of county, or Superior Court of Baltimore
Massachusetts	District Court
Michigan	Circuit Court
Minnesota	Court of Appeals
Mississippi	Circuit Court
Missouri	Circuit Court
Montana	District Court
Nebraska	District Court
Nevada	District Court
New Hampshire	Supreme Court
New Jersey	Superior Court, Appellate Division
New Mexico	District Court
New York	Supreme Court, Appellate Division, Third Department
North Carolina	Superior Court
North Dakota	District Court
Ohio	Court of Common Pleadings
Oklahoma	District Court
Oregon	Circuit Court
Pennsylvania	Commonwealth Court
Puerto Rico	Superior Court
Rhode Island	Superior Court of Providence or Bristol, or Superior Court in county in which claimant resides
South Carolina	Court of Common Pleadings
South Dakota	Circuit Court
Tennessee	Chancery Court
Texas	County Court
Utah	Supreme Court
Vermont	Supreme Court
Virginia	Circuit Court
Virgin Islands	District Court of the Virgin Islands

State	Court of Appeals
Washington	Superior Court
West Virginia	Circuit Court of Kanawha County
Wisconsin	Circuit Court of Dane County
Wyoming	District Court of Natrona County or District Court of county in which claimant resides

SUMMARY

In this book we have provided you with a comprehensive look at the UIC system from the local office level to the highest administrative level. We have described how the UIC system is organized and how it actually works in determining your UIC tax charges. We have provided you with tips, strategies, and techniques to help you control and minimize the amount of UIC tax you pay. We have given you questions to ask your state UIC office to assist you in preparing and winning your UIC cases and keeping your UIC tax charges to a minimum. We have given you advice on how to present your side of a case to a UIC office, and we have shown you how to win UIC appeals hearings.

We have provided you with the kind of advice we would provide our own clients on a one-to-one basis. Our sincere desire is to give you the most complete information and the very best tools we have to offer to help you understand and successfully overcome the obstacles of the UIC system.

This book was designed to give you every advantage legally allowed. No advice is perfect. No amount of advice can ensure you will never lose a UIC case. No one can anticipate every possible scenario or situation that might arise as you deal with the UIC system. What we have given you is information and knowledge in an organized, comprehensive form. We believe it is a practical tool of great power and substance that can give you an extraordinary advantage in dealing with UIC matters when used correctly.

We are confident that with a little patience and practice you will begin to feel comfortable dealing with all types of UIC problems. We wish you the best of luck and success in your quest to master the UIC system and control the tax costs of the program.

A

Sample Warning Forms and Other Useful Forms

This appendix covers various forms you may want to use for warning employees, terminating employees, and suspending employees.

Figure A.1
General Warning Form

General Warning Form

Date _____

Name of Employee _____

Reason for warning: _____
_____
_____
_____
_____
_____
_____
_____

Employee's response: _____
_____
_____
_____
_____
_____
_____
_____

This is the _____ warning for this offense. Failure to comply with this or any other warning may result in further disciplinary action or termination from employment.

By signing this form, I am not agreeing or disagreeing with the warning; I am merely acknowledging receipt of the warning.

I have read this form and understand its contents.

Employee signature _____ Date _____

Witness signature _____ Date _____

Employer signature_____ Date _____

Figure A.2
Suggested Wording for Various Warnings

Suggested Wording for Various Warnings

Suggested wording for Tardiness:

"On _____ you were tardy _____ minutes (hours). Tardiness is a violation of company policy."

Suggested wording for Absenteeism:

"On _____ you were absent from work without a valid excuse. This is your _____ absence in _____ days. Excessive unexcused absences are a violation of company policy."

Suggested wording for Poor Work Performance (quality):

"On _____ your work performance was substandard. The quality-control department rejected _____ out of _____ parts that you completed. It is your responsibility to produce parts that meet our quality-control standards."

Suggested wording for Poor Work Performance (quantity):

"On _____ your work performance was substandard. You were assigned _____ parts to be completed, at a predetermined level of quality. Our investigation shows the quality of these parts was substandard. It is your responsibility to produce parts that meet our quality-control standards."

Suggested wording for Neglect of Clients and/or Customers:

"On _____ we received a customer complaint regarding your interaction with him/her. The client/customer stated that you_____

_____
This behavior is considered unacceptable and against company policy."

Suggested wording for Accidents:

"On _____ you were involved in an accident with a company vehicle. You were cited for the accident, and our investigation shows you were at fault."

Suggested wording for Negligent Behavior:

"On _____ your negligent behavior led to the damage of _____
You failed to _____

_____
_____
This is in violation of company policy."

211

Figure A.3
Termination Form

Termination Form

Date ______________________________

Name of Employee ____

Reason for termination: ____
____
____
____
____
____
____

Employee's response: ____
____
____
____
____
____
____

Employee signature ______________________________ Date ______________

Witness signature ______________________________ Date ______________

Employer signature______________________________ Date ______________

Figure A.4
Suspension Form

Suspension Form

Date _____

Name of Employee _____

Reason for suspension: _____
_____
_____
_____
_____
_____
_____
_____

Employee's response: _____
_____
_____
_____
_____
_____
_____

By signing this form, I am not agreeing or disagreeing with the warning; I am merely acknowledging receipt of the warning.

I have read this form and understand its contents.

Employee signature _____ Date _____

Witness signature _____ Date _____

Employer signature_____ Date _____

Figure A.5
Request for Medical Information

Request for Medical Information

Date _____

Name of Employee _____

You were absent from _____ **to** _____

We require the following information from your physician:

Name of physician or care provider: _____
_____
_____

Date(s) of treatment: _____
_____
_____

Nature of illness or injury: _____
_____
_____
_____

Date of release to return to work: _____

Physician-recommended restrictions or limitations: _____
_____
_____

Special instructions to patient (if applicable): _____
_____
_____
_____

Physician's signature _____*Date* _____

Address _____
_____

Telephone number _____

To employee: Information on this form is subject to verification.

B

Important Checklists

This appendix contains a variety of checklists you may need to use as you work your way through an unemployment case. Use each one as it applies to your situation.

PREPARING FOR APPEAL HEARINGS

1. Verify the time, date, and place of the hearing.
2. Make sure you know the physical location of the appeals office.
3. Take the Notice of Hearing with you.
4. Take pads, pens, and pencils to the hearing.
5. Have copies of all necessary documents with you when you go to the hearing.
6. Take all pertinent *original* documents with you.
7. Take your copy of the state UIC file you requested before the hearing.
8. Bring any subpoena requests or unserved subpoenas with you.
9. Take a tape recorder or video equipment if you plan to submit tape-recorded or videotaped evidence.
10. Take some snack foods and refreshments, or have change to buy them from a vending machine.
11. Have the telephone numbers of any witnesses who are unable to appear in person.

WHAT TO COVER WHEN WARNING AN EMPLOYEE

1. Have I exposed the employee to the rules and explained how they are enforced?
2. Does the employee understand the rules of employment?
3. Are the rules written or verbal?
4. If rules were verbal, who gave them?
5. How do I know the employee understands the rules?
6. Does the employee understand the consequences of violating the rules?
7. Was acknowledgment of rules written or verbal?
8. If acknowledgment was verbal, who was present as a witness?
9. If the rules are written, do I have a signed and dated receipt from the employee showing he or she received and read the rules?
10. Are the warnings and rules fairly and consistently applied to all employees?

CHECKLIST BEFORE DISCHARGE

1. Does the employee's discharge require warnings?
2. Who issued the warnings?
3. Who witnessed the warnings?
4. Were the warnings verbal, written, or both?
5. Did the employee acknowledge the warnings?
6. Were the acknowledgments written or verbal?
7. What documents do I need?
8. Will witnesses or documents be available when I need them?
9. Do my witnesses have *firsthand* knowledge of what the employee did or didn't do to cause the discharge?
10. If I am a witness, am I basing my knowledge of events on firsthand experience, or am I relying on what others have told me?
11. Did the employee make any admissions?
12. Did he or she deny the facts that led to the discharge?
13. Were witnesses present when admissions were made?
14. If no admissions were made, do I have enough facts to win my case?
15. What was the final incident that motivated the discharge?
16. Did the employee offer an explanation or reason for his or her actions or behavior?

ACTIONS TO TAKE TO ENSURE FAVORABLE DECISIONS

1. Sign, date, and return the Notice to Employer within the stated time limit.
2. Mail the Notice to the correct address.
3. Delay your telephone response to the claims examiner until you have all your facts organized and are ready to call back.
4. Organize your response to the claims examiner—know first and last dates of employment, claimant's rate of pay, short description of job duties, supervisor's name, and chain of command.
5. Prepare a short detailed statement explaining why claimant was separated from employment.
6. Call the claims examiner and present your statement.
7. Ask the claims examiner if written documentation is needed; if it is, find out how to submit it.
8. Gather all relevant documentation, and mail *copies* to the local UIC office.
9. Verify that all written documentation and the Notice to Employer arrived at the local UIC office.

WHAT YOU AND YOUR WITNESSES SHOULD KNOW
FOR AN APPEAL HEARING

1. Claimant's date of hire.
2. Claimant's date of separation.
3. Claimant's last day of work (actual date).
4. Brief description of claimant's job duties.
5. Claimant's rate of pay.
6. Claimant's hours of work per week.
7. Claimant's hours of work per day.
8. Chain of command.
9. Reason for separation.
10. Any pertinent information in employee handbook.
11. Date employee handbook was issued to employee.
12. Date employee signed or acknowledged receipt of the rules or handbook.
13. If separation involved working conditions or rate of pay, be prepared to give the ALJ an idea of the prevailing standard in your city or labor market.
14. How the employer was adversely affected by the claimant.

DOCUMENTS FOR THE APPEAL HEARING

1. Claimant's written termination report, if your company issues written reports.
2. Letter of resignation, if claimant quit.
3. Copies of written warnings, if claimant was discharged.
4. All notes related to termination interview, whether claimant was discharged or quit.
5. Statements from witnesses.
6. Documents related to written or verbal warnings, such as time cards, time reports, or anything related to claimant's misconduct (falsified reports, falsified expense reports).

DOCUMENTS IN THE UIC FILE

1. Initial claim form.
2. Notice to Employer.
3. Wage statement.
4. Claimant's statement of reason for separation.
5. Report of claims examiner's investigation.
6. Determination or decision of claims examiner.
7. Notice of Appeal.
8. Claimant or employer documentation.
9. Notice of Hearing.

CALLING INSTRUCTIONS FOR TELEPHONE HEARINGS

1. What time to call in.
2. Name of person to speak with or ask for.
3. The telephone number at the hearing office.
4. Procedures to follow if there are technical problems on the line, such as a disconnection or a poor connection.
5. How call is billed if it is long distance.
6. Number of people who can be hooked together (teleconferencing).
7. Any other special instructions.

C

Sample Forms Used during the Claims and Appeals Process

This appendix contains samples of forms commonly used in various stages of an unemployment claim—from the first form a claimant files to a sample notice of hearing.

Figure C.1
Initial Claim Form

DEPARTMENT OF ECONOMIC SECURITY

INITIAL CLAIM FOR UNEMPLOYMENT INSURANCE

PRINT ONLY DO NOT COMPLETE SHADED AREAS	SHADED AREA FOR OFFICIAL USE ONLY	27. SCREEN

1. SOCIAL SECURITY NUMBER	28. EFFECTIVE DATE	29. FILING DATE

2. LAST NAME	FIRST NAME	MIDDLE INITIAL	30. LO	31. DEPUTY	32. TYPE T

3. MAILING ADDRESS (No., Street, Apt. No., P.O. Box)			33. FIPS
CITY		STATE	ZIP CODE

4. RESIDENCE ADDRESS (No., Street, Apt. No.)	CITY	STATE	ZIP CODE

5. OTHER NAME/SOC. SEC. NO. YOU USED IN LAST TWO (2) YEARS	6. PHONE NO.	7. BIRTHDATE	34. SEX

8. OCCUPATION	35. ETH-NIC	36. DOT	37. DD

Yes   No   *Additional deputy action required

9. ☐ *☐ Are you a citizen of the United States?
☐ *☐ If not a citizen, were you legally authorized to work in the United States during the past 18 months. If Yes, Permit No. _____
10. ☐ ☐ Are you handicapped as defined in Section 504 of the Rehabilitation Act of 1973?
11. *☐ ☐ Are you receiving or have you applied for a pension, annuity or retirement pay?
12. *☐ ☐ Have you received or will you receive vacation, holiday, or unused sick pay from your last employer?
13. *☐ ☐ Are you currently working and filing this claim to receive benefits under the Shared Work program?
14. *☐ ☐ Have you refused work or referral to work since becoming unemployed?
15. *☐ ☐ In the past 12 months have you filed an unemployment insurance claim in any state?
16. *☐ ☐ In the past 18 months have you worked in federal civilian service?
17. *☐ ☐ In the past 18 months have you worked in another state?
18. *☐ ☐ In the past 18 months have you been in military service?
19. ☐ ☐ Are you required to make or do you owe court ordered child support payments?

38. ERI

39. ER NUMBER

20. LAST EMPLOYER YOU WORKED FOR BEFORE FILING THIS CLAIM (Regardless of State, Type of Work or Length of Job)
COMPANY NAME

MAILING ADDRESS (No., Street, P.O. Box)	CITY	STATE	ZIP CODE

21. LAST DAY OF WORK BEFORE FILING THIS CLAIM Month Day Year	40. NON-SEP ISSUE	41. SEND NOTICE

42. BASE PERIOD ER #(s) (Additional B2 or F2 Screens)

Yes   No

22. ☐ ☐ Have you worked at all since the LAST DAY OF WORK shown above?

23. Why are you no longer working for your last employer? (Check (✓) the box which applies and write the reason in the space below)

(40) ☐ I was laid off because of a lack of work or a reduction in force.
(10) ☐ I quit my job because: _____
(20) ☐ I was discharged because: _____
(45) ☐ I am still working part-time.
(30) ☐ My employer and a union(s) are involved in a labor dispute. If this box is checked, deputy will complete LD-003.

24. PRIVACY ACT INFORMATION AND CLAIM CERTIFICATION (READ, BUT DO NOT SIGN UNTIL TOLD TO DO SO)

A. PRIVACY ACT INFORMATION
The Privacy Act of 1974 requires that you be furnished this statement because you are being asked to furnish your Social Security Account Number on the claim forms given to you. Your Social Security Number is solicited under the authority of the Internal Revenue Code of 1954 (26 U.S.C. 85, 6011(a), 6050B, and 6109(a)). Disclosure of your Social Security Number for this purpose is MANDATORY, and must be entered on the forms you submit to claim unemployment insurance. Your Social Security Number will be used to report your unemployment insurance to the Internal Revenue Service as income that is potentially taxable; it will also be used as a record index for processing your claim, for statistical purposes, and to verify your eligibility for unemployment insurance and other public assistance benefits. Should you decline to disclose your Social Security Number your claim for unemployment insurance will not be processed.

B. CERTIFICATION
I register for work and make application for unemployment insurance. I certify that I am not working or that I am on a part-time or reduced earnings basis. I am not seeking insurance under another state or federal unemployment insurance system. I have not applied for and I am not receiving a subsistence allowance for vocational rehabilitation training or a war orphans' educational assistance allowance from the Veterans' Administration. I further certify that the statements made hereon for the purpose of obtaining unemployment insurance under the Employment Security Law are true and correct to the best of my knowledge and belief. I KNOW THAT THE LAW PROVIDES PENALTIES FOR FALSE STATEMENTS IN CONNECTION WITH THIS CLAIM.

25. CLAIMANT SIGNATURE	26. DEPUTY SURNAME

220

Figure C.2
Eligibility Review Questionnaire

DEPARTMENT OF ECONOMIC SECURITY
ELIGIBILITY REVIEW QUESTIONNAIRE

ESTE FORMULARIO ESTA DISPONIBLE EN ESPAÑOL

Please complete this form and report IN PERSON on the date and time scheduled.

CLAIMANT'S NAME	SOC. SEC. NO.

1. INDICATE THE KIND(S) OF WORK YOU ARE TRYING TO FIND AND LENGTH OF EXPERIENCE IN EACH

YRS. MOS.	YRS. MOS.	YRS. MOS.

2. INDICATE THE KIND OF WORK YOU DID FOR YOUR LAST FULL-TIME EMPLOYER | RATE OF PAY | ☐HR. ☐WK. ☐MO. | LENGTH OF EMPLOYMENT Yrs. Mos.

$

3. LOWEST RATE OF PAY YOU ARE NOW WILLING TO ACCEPT FOR A NEW JOB
$ _____ per ☐Hr. ☐Wk. ☐Mo.

4. INDICATE THE SHIFT(S) YOU ARE WILLING AND ABLE TO WORK
☐Day Shift   ☐Afternoon Shift   ☐Night Shift

5. INDICATE (✓) THE DAYS YOU ARE WILLING AND ABLE TO WORK
☐Sun. ☐Mon. ☐Tue. ☐Wed. ☐Thur. ☐Fri. ☐Sat.

6. INDICATE THE NUMBER OF MILES YOU ARE WILLING AND ABLE TO TRAVEL TO WORK

7. INDICATE (✓) THE MEANS OF TRANSPORTATION YOU NOW USE
☐Own Car ☐Bus ☐Walk ☐Bicycle ☐Other *(Specify)*:

Yes No

8. ☐ ☐ Do you have children or anyone else requiring care while you work? If yes:
INDIVIDUAL'S NAME AND ADDRESS *(No., Street, City, State, ZIP)* WHO WILL PROVIDE CARE

9. ☐ ☐ Do you have a definite date to return to work with a previous employer? If yes:
DATE | EMPLOYER'S NAME AND ADDRESS *(No., Street, City, State, ZIP)*

10. ☐ ☐ Are you pregnant? If yes:
☐N/A EXPECTED DATE OF BIRTH

11.a. ☐ ☐ Do you obtain work only through a hiring hall of a Union? If yes:
b. ☐ ☐ Are you on the out-of-work list? If yes:
MOST RECENT DATE SIGNED ONTO THE LIST | UNION NAME | LOCAL NUMBER

12. ☐ ☐ Do you need a special license to do your work, e.g. chauffeur, barber, nurse, real estate, etc.? If yes:
DATE YOUR LICENSE EXPIRES | TYPE OF LICENSE

13. ☐ ☐ Are you or have you been in the past 12 months in business of any kind, or a corporate officer? If yes:
PLEASE EXPLAIN

14. ☐ ☐ Are you working on a commission basis? If yes:
PLEASE EXPLAIN

15. ☐ ☐ Are you doing any odd jobs, working part-time, or working full-time? If yes:
PLEASE EXPLAIN

16.a. ☐ ☐ Are you attending a school? If yes:
NAME OF SCHOOL | DAYS/HOURS OF ATTENDANCE

b. ☐ ☐ Are you planning to attend school or have you attended school in the past six months? If yes:
NAME OF SCHOOL | DAYS/HOURS/DATES OF ATTENDANCE

17. ☐ ☐ Are you receiving/applied for Social Security, Retirement, or any other type of pension/annuity? If yes:
NAME/TYPE | AMOUNT | ☐WK. ☐MO.

18. ☐ ☐ Do you have a physical condition or handicap which would limit your ability to work full-time now? If yes:
PLEASE EXPLAIN

19. ☐ ☐ Is there any reason you could not accept full-time work now? If yes:
PLEASE EXPLAIN

CERTIFICATION: I have answered these questions for the purpose of obtaining Unemployment Insurance, knowing that the law provides penalties for making false statements. I understand that I am to review this form for each week I claim benefits and if the information which I have provided changes, I must report in-person to my local Unemployment Insurance office immediately.

CLAIMANT'S SIGNATURE	DATE	DEPUTY'S SIGNATURE	DATE

Figure C.3
Claimant Report of Work Search

DEPARTMENT OF ECONOMIC SECURITY

Page _____

WORKSEARCH LOG from (date) _____ to next visit
(WORKSEARCH LISTED IS SUBJECT TO PERIODIC VERIFICATION)

CLAIMANT'S NAME | | | | | | SOC. SEC. NO.

DATE	COMPANY NAME	ADDRESS (No. Street. City, State)	PHONE NO.	NAME OF PERSON CONTACTED	(✓ one col.) IN PERSON TELEPHONE	TYPE OF WORK SOUGHT	FILED APPL.	RESULTS OTHER (Specify)

CERTIFICATION

I have answered these questions for the purpose of obtaining Unemployment Insurance, knowing that the law provides penalties for making false statements.

CLAIMANT'S SIGNATURE _____ DATE _____

DEPUTY'S SIGNATURE _____ DATE _____

Figure C.4
Illness or Disability Report Form

DEPARTMENT OF ECONOMIC SECURITY

REPORT OF ILLNESS OR PHYSICAL DISABILITY
(Español en el reverso)

CLAIMANT'S NAME	SOC. SEC. NO.
PATIENT'S NAME	CLAIMANT'S PRIMARY OCCUPATION

Is the claimant the patient? ☐Yes ☐No

STATEMENT OF AUTHORIZATION: I authorize you to release the information requested below to the Department of Economic Security with the understanding that it will be used to make a determination of eligibility for unemployment insurance benefits.

Signature _____ Date _____

SECTION I	TO BE COMPLETED BY PHYSICIAN

☐Mr.
☐Ms. _____ has been most recently under my care

for _____ from _____ to _____
      (Nature of Illness)   *(Date)*   *(Date)*

IF THE CLAIMANT IS THE PATIENT, SECTION II MUST BE COMPLETED BY PHYSICIAN MAKING THE RECOMMENDATIONS OF CARE AND RELOCATION. IF NOT, PROCEED TO SECTION III.

SECTION II

1. In your opinion has the patient been able to work? ☐Yes ☐No
    If you answered no, please complete the following:

    a. The patient was unable to work full time as of _____ 19 _____ .
    b. The patient ☐was ☐will be able to work full-time as of _____ 19 _____ .
    c. Are there any work restrictions? *(lifting, driving, walking, etc.).* Please list and specify: _____

2. In your opinion was it necessary for the patient to:

		Yes	No	Date Patient Advised
a.	Take time off from work for treatment and/or recovery?	☐	☐	_____
b.	Change occupations?	☐	☐	_____
c.	Move to another area?	☐	☐	_____

    COMPLETE ONLY IF APPLICABLE

3. Prenatal   4. Postnatal
    a. Expected date of birth _____   a. Date of birth _____ 19 _____
    b. Patient should not work after_____   b. Patient can work full-time by_____ 19 _____

SECTION III

1. In your opinion, did the patient need full-time care during the period of treatment and/or recovery? ☐Yes ☐No

2. Was the claimant's presence necessary in providing care/treatment of the patient? ☐Yes ☐No
    Type of care _____ Date needed _____

Return completed form to patient or mail to:

SIGNATURE OF PHYSICIAN	DATE
PHYSICIAN'S PRINTED NAME	PHONE
PHYSICIAN'S ADDRESS *(No., Street, City, State, ZIP)*	

Figure C.5
Notice to Employer

Department of Economic Security

Notice to Employer

To protest: *Complete, sign and return this form within 10 working days of the date of this notice.*

```
+--+-------------------------------------+
|L |                                     |
|O |                                     |
+--+-------------------------------------+

+--+-------------------------------------+
|E |                                     |
|R |                                     |
+--+-------------------------------------+
```

Name:	Date:
SSN:	ER Number:
BYB:	Charge Control Date:

Our records show the last day of work as: _____

The claimant has stated the reason for separation was:

☐ Voluntary quit   ☐ Working part-time
☐ Discharge   ☐ Labor dispute
☐ Lack of work/R.I.F.

If you are the last employer, did you or will you pay severance, vacation, holiday or sick pay on or after termination:

☐ Yes   ☐ No

If YES, date of payment _____ Gross amount _____

Hrs. paid _____ Rate of pay _____ /per _____

Enter details of separation or other eligibility information on back of this form. Protest must be signed to be valid.

Company Name	Date
Telephone	
Print name & title	
Signature	

Figure C.6
Eligibility Investigation Record

DEPARTMENT OF ECONOMIC SECURITY
ELIGIBILITY INVESTIGATION RECORD

□C1	□C2	□C4		C5		
SOCIAL SECURITY NUMBER		CLAIMANT NAME CHECK	ER NUMBER			
ISSUE CODE	ISSUE ID (C2)	DEPUTY ID	PGM	ER NAME AND ADDRESS		
ISSUE STATUS	RESOLUTION CODE	COUNT	UNTIMELI-NESS			
(RE)DETERMINATION DATE		REDETERMINATION REASON (C2)				
DISQUALIFICATION START		DISQUALIFICATION END				
STATEMENT 1	STATEMENT 2	ER CHARGE STATEMENT	C5	CITY	STATE	ZIP

□Free Form Text.
C9 Release Date _____ Ltr#_____

	CHARGE	PGM	START	END

I certify I obtained the following information from the parties named. Signature_____

FINDINGS OF FACT

Basis for Adjudication:_____

ER Protest: □Not Applicable   □Received Timely   □Received Untimely   □Not Received

Claimant Statement *(Date)*: _____

225

Figure C.7
Determination of Deputy

DEPARTMENT OF ECONOMIC SECURITY
Unemployment Insurance Program
DETERMINATION OF DEPUTY

Soc. Sec. No.
Claimant
Employer No.
Employer

⌐   ⌐ Date
Deputy No.

└   ┘

NOTICE TO CLAIMANT

NOTICE TO EMPLOYER

NOTICE TO ALL INTERESTED PARTIES - APPEAL RIGHTS
This determination becomes final unless a written appeal is filed in person or by mail 15 calendar days after the mailing date shown at the top of this determination. If the last day of the appeal period falls on a Saturday, Sunday or holiday, the appeal period will be extended to the next working day. Please see reverse for further information.

ESTE DOCUMENTO AFECTA SU ELEGIBILIDAD PARA SEGURO DE DESEMPLEO. SI USTED NO LEE INGLES, COMUNIQUESE CON SU OFICINA LOCAL O BUSQUE QUIEN LE TRADUZCA.

Figure C.8
Witness Statement Form

DEPARTMENT OF ECONOMIC SECURITY

STATE OF _____)
                          ss
County of _____)

AFFIDAVIT of _____
                                  (Issue)

Taken at _____ M.
                        (Time of Day)

At _____
                        (Location)

_____

I, _____ , Social Security No. _____

being first duly sworn, say: I freely and voluntarily give this affidavit to _____
who is known to me as an employee of the DEPARTMENT OF ECONOMIC SECURITY. I have not been threatened or
abused in any way. I have not been promised anything for giving this statement.

_____

_____

_____

_____

_____

_____

_____

_____

_____

_____

_____

_____

_____

_____

_____

_____

_____

_____

_____

I have read the foregoing affidavit and it is true and correct to the best of my knowledge and belief.

Signature _____ Witness Signature _____

Subscribed and sworn to before me this _____ day of

_____ , 19_____   Page No. _____ of a

_____   _____ page affidavit
Department Representative

227

Figure C.9
Separation Questionnaire

DEPARTMENT OF ECONOMIC SECURITY

UNEMPLOYMENT INSURANCE — SEPARATION QUESTIONNAIRE

MAILING DATE	CLAIMANT NAME		SSN

EMPLOYER NAME	EMPLOYER PHONE NO.	LAST DAY WORKED

☐ This is your last employer of record and we need a statement from you to determine your eligibility for benefits.*
☐ This is NOT your last employer and the information you furnish will not affect the payment of benefits.

SPECIAL NOTE: *If this questionnaire was mailed to you, please respond within seven (7) days from the above mailing date.*

If this questionnaire was given to you at the unemployment insurance (U.I.) office, please return the form as directed by the U.I. representative. Any determination concerning your eligibility will be based on information available at the time the determination is written.

If you should return to work before your scheduled report date, please complete the form and return it to your local office.

PLEASE ANSWER THE FOLLOWING QUESTIONS ABOUT THE EMPLOYER NAMED ABOVE.

TYPE OF WORK	HOURS PER DAY	HOURS PER WEEK	RATE OF PAY

LENGTH OF TIME ON THE JOB	SUPERVISOR NAME	TITLE

DESCRIBE WHAT HAPPENED THAT CAUSED YOU TO BE OUT OF A JOB. BE SPECIFIC *(If you need additional space, please use a blank sheet.)*

_____

_____

_____

_____

_____

_____

_____

_____

_____

_____

_____

_____

HAVE YOU WORKED SINCE LEAVING THIS EMPLOYER?	☐ YES	☐ NO	IF YES, COMPLETE BELOW.

EMPLOYER NAME	ADDRESS

DATE BEGAN	RATE OF PAY
	$ per

I certify that the answers to the above questions are correct to the best of my knowledge and belief. I am aware that the law provides penalties for false statements made knowingly in connection with a claim.

CLAIMANT SIGNATURE	DATE

Español en el reverso

228

Figure C.10
Work Search Plan of Action Affidavit

DEPARTMENT OF ECONOMIC SECURITY

WORK SEARCH PLAN OF ACTION AFFIDAVIT

Name _____ SSN _____

The State requires that an individual filing a claim for Unemployment Insurance benefits must be actively seeking work for each week benefits are claimed. To meet the active work search requirement, you are required to comply with the following work search plan each week you file for benefits.

1. ☐   Register with Job Service. Renew this registration by _____ .

2. ☐   Register, apply and continue checking with:

     a. ☐ union hiring hall *(I am a union member in good*   d. ☐ placement offices of schools, colleges,
       standing.)   universities
     b. ☐ company employment *(hiring)* offices   e. ☐ former employer
     c. ☐ placement office of professional organization

3. ☐   Make weekly personal contacts with employers who may reasonably be expected to have suitable job openings and record these contacts on the Work Search Log, UB-101-A.

4. ☐   Submit resumes to prospective employers and attach a copy of the cover letter to the Work Search Log, UB-101-A.

5. ☐   Answer "want ads" in an attempt to arrange interviews and attach a copy of the cover letter to the Work Search Log, UB-101-A.

6. ☐   Check the telephone book and use the telephone to obtain job leads and make appointments for job interviews.

7. ☐   Apply for and/or take examinations for city, county, state or federal jobs. Specify government unit(s) and exam(s) to be taken:

_____

8. ☐   Since I have been unemployed for at least _____ weeks, I will expand my search for work to include other than my type of work or occupation.

9. ☐   Take the following action considered an effective means of seeking work.

_____

_____

DEPUTY COMMENTS *(Explain instructions or advice given regarding potential barriers to eligibility):*

_____

_____

_____

Date of next interview _____

I agree to search for work in accordance with the Work Search Plan of Action Affidavit above. I understand that I must report and record my work search contacts on the Work Search Log, UB-101-A, and that the contacts I report are subject to verification. I understand that if I do not seek work in the manner described above or in a manner equally acceptable to the Department I may not be eligible for Unemployment Insurance benefits.

_____   _____   _____   _____
Claimant's Signature   Date   Deputy's Signature   Date

            | ESTE FORMULARIO ESTA DISPONIBLE EN ESPAÑOL |

229

Figure C.11
Sample Appeal Decision

Department of Economic Security
Office of Appeals
207 W. Anderson Lane
Capital City, Texas   78466

DECISION OF APPEALS TRIBUNAL

Appeal No. T79403
Date of Mailing: June 7, 1996

Janet Smith   Good Eats Cafeteria
6100 N. Ridgeway Way   100 Adams Road
Azuma, Texas   78031   Azuma, Texas   78302
                                     Employer Account No. 051648

Issues:

Discharge from Employment (Section 48-0111)
Chargeability of Benefits (Section 46-0508)

Case History:
Effective Date of Claim: 3/17/96   Issue code: B
Date of Separation: 12/30/95
Date of Local Office Determination: 3/15/96
Appellant: Claimant
Date of Hearing: 5/23/96
Appearances: Claimant, three employer witnesses

Findings of Fact:

The claimant was employed as a table cleaner and bus person by a
private contract food service provider company for approximately 8 months
prior to being discharge for alleged work-related misconduct on December
30, 1995. The employer has a contract with the AJAX Airplane Company,
where the claimant worked.

The claimant was discharged for failing to perform her work to the
standards set by the employer. As part of her regular duties, the
claimant was responsible for clearing, cleaning and restocking 12 tables
between 9:00a.m. and 11:15a.m., so the cafeteria could open for lunch on
time. The claimant had established her ability to clean the tables
routinely in 5 to 10 minutes each during the previous 8 months, except on
September 3, 1995, October 10, 1995, and November 12, 1995, when she was
given written warnings for not cleaning tables on time. The claimant had
been given verbal warnings on May 8 and May 20, 1995, for not cleaning
the tables on time.

On December 30, 1995, at about 10:40a.m., the supervisor discovered
only two of the 12 tables were cleared, cleaned and restocked; the others
hadn't even been cleaned. Although the claimant started the work at
9:00a.m., she had not asked for any assistance to clean the tables nor
had she reported any problem or emergency to her supervisor or the
manager about not being able to clean more than two tables by 10:40a.m.

The supervisor reported this to the manager, who investigated and
found the claimant in the kitchen drinking coffee with one of the cooks.
When asked why she was drinking the coffee, the claimant said she was
taking a break. The claimant had taken a scheduled break at 8:00a.m. with
other employees, and was not scheduled for another break until 2:00p.m.
When asked why only two tables had been cleaned, the claimant first said
she didn't have time to do the rest and would get to them as soon as she
could. In a later conversation, she said was tired, but not ill, and had
been working too hard. During the second conversation, the claimant
started arguing with the manager, finally saying, "If you're going to
fire me, then get the damn thing over with," and she was discharged.

230

The claimant contends she was taking the break at 10:40a.m. because she only took a 10-minute break at 8:00a.m. and was owed 5 more minutes. She offered no explanation for cleaning only two tables from 9:00a.m. to 10:40a.m. nor any explanation as to why, after returning to the cafeteria with the manager and supervisor, she was able to clean only two tables while they cleaned four tables each.

Reasoning and Conclusion of Law:

The claimant has contested a determination of claims examiner that held the claimant was discharged for work-related misconduct. The issue before this Unemployment Insurance Tribunal involves Sections 23-41 and 23-42 of the Employment Security Law of Texas.

(The next section in a UIC decision normally includes boilerplate quotes and inclusions from the pertinent sections of state law. We do not include them here because they are the reprints of what is contained in the statutes of each particular state. Following quotations of law are usually a few paragraphs in which the ALJ summarizes the evidence and explains how he or she reached the decision for the employer or claimant. In most states, ALJs attempt to walk the line between issuing a decision that is too legalistic and one that is oversimplified. Because these quasi-legal decisions are for the general public, they tend to be written in easily understood, straightforward language. The following is an example of the wording in a typical decision.)

In this case, the evidence establishes the claimant did not complete or make a reasonable effort to complete her job duties to clean, clear and restock 12 tables between 9:00a.m. and 11:15a.m., on December 30, 1995, after receiving prior verbal and written warnings. She had completed these duties in a timely manner over an 8-month period, except on five occasions when she was given warnings. The claimant was aware of her duties and did not request assistance to complete her duties in a timely manner on December 30. As noted, the employer previously warned the claimant verbally and in writing that her failure to complete her assigned duties on time could lead to her dismissal from work.

Although the claimant maintains she did not complete her assigned duties in the time allotted because she did not have time to do them, she offered no explanation for not having the time, except to say she was tired and had been working too hard. The claimant offered no credible excuse or reason for not completing her duties in a timely manner.

The Tribunal finds the claimant's work assignment was not unreasonable, and she could have completed her duties if she had shown reasonable care and diligence in carrying out those duties. The claimant did not make a good faith effort to complete her assigned duties despite the warnings issued to her by the employer. Accordingly, the Tribunal concludes the claimant's actions were a willful disregard of the employer's interests and the claimant was discharged for work-related misconduct.

Decision:

1. The determination of claims examiner is affirmed. The claimant is disqualified from receipt of benefits from 12/24/95 until re-employed with earnings of no less than five times the claimant's weekly benefit amount.

2. The employer experience rating (UIC tax account) shall not be charged for any benefits claimed in this case or for subsequent benefits paid to the claimant on requalification for benefits.

M.G. Vondrak
Administrative Law Judge

(The ALJ's decision is normally followed by a distribution list for the decision, which includes the employer, the claimant, any attorneys or representatives, the UIC local office, the benefit payment control unit and tax-control unit. In most states, the decision will be followed by several pages explaining further appeal rights and procedures for each party.)

Figure C.12
Request for Reconsideration/Appeal

DEPARTMENT OF ECONOMIC SECURITY

REQUEST FOR RECONSIDERATION/APPEAL

Este documento afecta su elegibilidad para Seguro por Desempleo. Si usted no lee inglés, comuníquese con su oficina local o busque quien le traduzca. La audiencia se conducirá en inglés.

In the Matter of the Claim of:

Name and Address of Appellant

| CLAIMANT'S NAME |
| SOC. SEC. NO. |
| EMPLOYER'S NAME |

☐I disagree with the Determination of Deputy dated _____, involving the issue of

_____, and allege it is in error for the following reasons:

_____

_____

☐I also disagree with the Determination of Overpayment dated _____ created by the above Determination of Deputy.

If request is not timely state reason _____

_____

| APPELLANT'S SIGNATURE | DATE |

NOTICE TO CLAIMANT
If your Request for Reconsideration is denied, and you are still unemployed and wish to claim benefits, you should continue to file claims pending disposition of your appeal.

COMPLETED BY DEPARTMENT REPRESENTATIVE

REQUEST FILED:

☐In person on _____
(Date)

☐By mail postmarked on _____ *(envelope attached)*
(Date)

Received at _____ on _____
(Local Office No.) *(Date)*

Does the claimant speak English? ☐Yes ☐No ☐Information not available

If no, what language does the claimant speak? _____

NOTICE TO APPELLANT REGARDING RECONSIDERATION

☐Your request has been reviewed and a reconsidered Determination of Deputy will be issued.

☐Your request for reconsideration has been denied on *(date)* _____ and this action will be forwarded to the Office of Appeals. The specific date and location for your appeal hearing will be provided in a separate communication. The hearing will be conducted in English.

| BY *(Department Representative)* | APPROVED *(UI Manager)* | RESOLUTION CODE | ISSUE ID |

D

Additional Sample Letters

This appendix contains additional sample letters for you to study and adapt for your own use in dealing with the Office of Appeals. In each of these sample letters, we have <u>underlined</u> the parts of the letter you will need to change for your particular case. Use these samples to help you compose your own letters.

A *letter of appeal* is provided as Figure 7.2 (see p. 112). This is a fairly comprehensive letter because you must include a great deal of information about the circumstances of the separation and your company policies.

Figure D.1 is a *letter requesting a postponement.* Although it is a short letter, there are quite a few details you will need to fill in about your particular case.

A *letter of withdrawal* from an appeal hearing is provided as Figure 7.3 (see p. 116). It is a short letter, but you do need to fill in a few details.

Figure D.2 is a *letter requesting a change of judge.* Although you must provide some information, a great deal is not required.

A letter of *second-level appeal* is provided in Figure 11.2 (see pp. 200–201).

Figure D.1
Letter Requesting a Postponement

Betty's Cafe
34501 Parish Pike
Wannette, California 90021
213-555-5748

December 14, 1998

Office of Appeals
4503 W. Johnson Highway
Wannette, California 92023

                          Re: Herman Hansen
                               SS #000-34-7564
                               Hearing #73982057

Dear Sir or Madam;

Please accept this letter as a formal request for a postponement of
the hearing scheduled for 10:30a.m., December 21, 1998, with Judge
Ethel Marana.

We are unable to attend because (give your reason) our key witness
was called out of town due to a serious family illness. The witness
is unavailable to testify by telephone.

In accordance with (section of UIC rules and/or law in your state)
Section 18-481 of the California Revised Statutes and Section 11-146
of the UIC Administrative Code, we request you postpone the
scheduled hearing. Please inform us of the time and date set for the
new hearing.

Thank you for your assistance in this matter.

                          Sincerely,

                          Elizabeth Bastion

                          Elizabeth Bastion, Owner

Figure D.2
Letter Requesting a Change of Judge

Bowman Tool Company
1816 Yavapai Street
Turner, New Mexico 86710
505-555-7839

November 25, 1999

Office of Appeals
2845 Indian School Road
Albuquerque, New Mexico   86001

Re: Fred Lewis
     SS# 000-23-1379
     Appeal #16837934

Dear Sir or Madam;

Please accept this letter as a formal request for a change of
Administrative Law Judge, in accordance with Section 17-790.1 of the
New Mexico Revised Statutes, and Section R7-143 of the New Mexico
UIC Administrative Code (section of UIC rules and/or law of your
state).

The currently assigned ALJ is Judge Dick Simmons. Please inform us
of the change in administrative law judge for the hearing scheduled
for December 8, 1999 at 9:30a.m. If there are any changes in the
time and date of hearing, please inform us as soon as possible.

Thank you for your assistance in this matter.

Sincerely,

Lester Bowman, President

E

Sample Script

The following is a sample script from a typical unemployment insurance hearing. It is a powerful and valuable learning tool because it provides you the opportunity to attend an appeal hearing without leaving your office. Some employers may want to use the script to conduct mock hearings with their employees playing the hearing participants. In this hearing, the appellant (the one appealing the decision) is the former employee. The employer is defending the decision of the claims examiner to deny the claimant benefits.

You will find reference numbers included in the script. These numbers refer to detailed comments about what is happening in the hearing and how you can use this information to prepare for your own hearings. We have made these notes to point out ordinary occurrences in a hearing and important admissions or responses by witnesses. We believe that by reading this additional information, you will be more fully prepared to participate in your own appeals hearing.

ALJ (starts tape recorder): The hearing in Appeal No. T79403, a case arising out of the unemployment insurance program, is open on May 23, 1996, at 10:30 A.M. My name is M. G. Vondrak, and I am the administrative law judge assigned to hear this case and render a decision. The claimant for benefits, Janet Smith, is here in person. The last employer was determined to be the Good Eats Cafeteria. Appearing as witnesses for the last employer are Roberta Brown, cafeteria manager, and Al Green, supervisor. The purpose of this hearing is to consider the employee's appeal from a deputy's determination dated March 15, 1996, which found the claimant was not entitled to unemployment insurance benefits because of her discharge from employment.

The basis for the determination reads as follows: "You were discharged from work because you neglected your job duties and did not follow instructions. The employer presented sufficient evidence to support their case.

You are disqualified from receiving benefits until you return to work and earn five times your weekly benefit amount." The claimant filed a timely appeal from that determination by letter, postmarked March 19, 1996.

Parties to this hearing have the right to appear and testify, have witnesses testify on their behalf, and present other evidence relevant to the issue of the case. In your testimony, you may challenge any statement made in a document admitted into evidence or by another party's witness. You have the right to cross-examine opposing witnesses on the testimony they have given, which is the right to ask questions of the other party's witnesses. Parties also have the right to make closing statements.

Because this is an administrative hearing, the formal rules of evidence do not apply strictly. I will consider any information normally accepted by reasonable and prudent individuals in the conduct of business. However, I can only consider the evidence presented to me in this hearing in deciding this case. For the purposes of creating a record, these proceedings are being tape recorded. I have tested the recording device, and it is in working order.[1]

All testimony in the case is taken under oath. Any witness who knowingly makes a false statement while under oath may be subject to prosecution for perjury and may be subject to additional penalties, as provided by the laws of this state. Do each of you understand these instructions? *(ALJ asks each party to answer for the record.)*

I will now swear in the witnesses. Janet Smith, Al Green, and Roberta Brown, please raise your right hands for the oath: Do you solemnly swear or affirm under penalties of perjury that testimony you give in this hearing will be the truth? Ms. Smith? Mr. Green? Ms. Brown?[2]

Smith: I do.

Green: I do.

Brown: I do.

ALJ: Let the record show the witnesses have answered in the affirmative and have been duly sworn.

Prior to the hearing, I established that the parties had an opportunity to review the documents in the case file. I will now identify those documents into the record as they have been marked for identification.

Exhibit 1 is the claimant's new claim for benefits filed with the department on March 20, 1996.

Exhibit 2 is the claimant's wage statement, dated March 28, 1996.

Exhibit 3 is the Notice to Employer issued February 28, 1996.

Exhibit 4 is the Separation Questionnaire, apparently filled out and signed by the claimant on March 5, 1996.

Exhibit 5 is the Eligibility Investigation Record of claims examiner Johnson completed March 14, 1996.

Exhibits 6A and 6B are the Determination of Claims Examiner dated March 15, 1996. 6A is the claimant's copy; 6B is the copy mailed to the employer.

Exhibit 7A is the claimant's letter of appeal dated March 24, 1996, signed by Janet Smith.

Exhibit 7B is the envelope that contained exhibit 7A from the claimant, postmarked March 25, 1996.

Exhibit 8 is the Notice of Hearing in this matter, mailed to the parties by certified mail to their respective addresses of record on April 20, 1996.

The record from which I will make my decision will consist of documents admitted into evidence and all testimony presented at this hearing.

Ms. Brown and Mr. Green, do you have any objections to my considering any of the documents I have just described as part of the evidence in this case?[3]

Brown: No, Your Honor.

Green: No, Your Honor.

ALJ: Ms. Smith, do you have any objections to my considering any of the documents I have just described as part of the evidence in this case?

Smith: Yeah, because they fired me without any reason.

ALJ: No, Ms. Smith. My question is a procedural one. Each party has the right to present evidence—documents and testimony. You will have an opportunity later in this hearing to testify regarding your separation from employment. Right now, I want to know if you have any legal objections or feel I should not take into consideration any of the documents that are marked in the case file.

Smith: Yeah, the one that says I'm not eligible something. That's not true.

ALJ: Ms. Smith, that is Exhibit 5, the claims examiner's notes and record. Because that is a department record of this case, your objection is overruled but is noted for the record. Do you have any other objections?

Smith: No, I guess not.

ALJ: I will now have the persons present make their appearances for the record. Ms. Smith, please state your name and current business mailing address. Mr. Green, would you please state your name and job title? Ms. Brown, would you please state your name and job title? *(Each witness gives his or her full name and business address.)*

ALJ: Before we begin taking testimony, I will explain the order of testimony in today's hearing. Because the claims examiner determined the separation to be a discharge, I will take the testimony of the employer witnesses first. After each witness has testified, Ms. Smith you will have an opportunity to ask any questions you have. If you have no questions, I will take your testimony regarding the separation. The employer will in turn have the right to cross-examine you on your testimony.[4]

Does anyone have any questions regarding this procedure or any other instructions I've covered in the preliminary remarks? If there are no questions, I will now take the testimony of Ms. Brown.

I have reviewed the case file prior to the hearing. Ms. Brown, you are the cafeteria manager, is that correct?

Brown: Yes.

ALJ: How long have you been with the Good Eats Cafeteria?

Brown: Ten years.

ALJ: For the record, what type of business is the employer in?

Brown: We are a contract cafeteria for AJAX Airplane Company; we have an on-site facility there.

ALJ: Do you know the claimant, Ms. Smith?

Brown: Yes.

ALJ: How do you know her?

Brown: She was a former employee of the Good Eats Cafeteria.

ALJ: What was Ms. Smith's job title?

Brown: Cafeteria worker.

ALJ: What was her rate of pay?

Brown: Well, she was hired at $5 an hour.

ALJ: At the end of employment what was the rate of pay?

Brown: It was still $5 an hour, Judge.

ALJ: How long was Ms. Smith employed by the Good Eats Cafeteria?

Brown: It was about 8 months. She started work on April 3rd and was discharged on December 30th.

ALJ: Ms. Smith has indicated on documents submitted to the Department that her last day at work was December 30, 1995, a Friday. Is that the last day Ms. Smith actually last performed work for the employer?

Brown: Yes, that's the day we discharged her, Judge.

ALJ: Did Ms. Smith perform any work that day?

Brown: Yes, she did. She worked for about 6 hours—from 6 A.M. to noon.

ALJ: Who actually discharged the claimant, Ms. Brown?

Brown: I did, Your Honor.⁵

ALJ: What did you tell Ms. Smith when you discharged her?

Brown: That we had to let her go because she was not following policy.

ALJ: Did anything happen on December 30 that caused you to fire Ms. Smith?⁶

Brown: As indicated in the file, Judge, Ms. Smith was fired because she didn't clean the tables in the cafeteria, which was her specific job assignment.

ALJ: What did she fail to do on December 30?

Brown: Ms. Smith was responsible for cleaning tables in our cafeteria. We open for business at 6 A.M., and we stop serving at 9:00 A.M. We then have to clean up the area by 11:30 A.M. to open again for lunch at noon. Ms. Smith was supposed to clear the tables and clean them thoroughly with our commercial disinfectant. She was also required to make sure the napkin dispensers were full and to be sure each table was fully stocked with sugar, salt, and artificial sweetener. If these items were low, Ms. Smith was to refill or restock them.[7]

ALJ: What time did Ms. Smith usually start her clean-up duties?

Brown: She was scheduled to start at 9:00 A.M., as soon as we finish breakfast and close the cafeteria.

ALJ: Did Ms. Smith start her work on time on December 30th?

Brown: I don't know, Judge.

ALJ: Did Ms. Smith report to work on time?

Brown: Yes, Judge. She reported to work at 6:00 A.M.[8]

ALJ: How do you know?

Brown: By her time card.

ALJ: When did you first notice the tables assigned to the claimant hadn't been cleaned?

Brown: At about 10:30 A.M., Your Honor.

ALJ: How did you find out?

Brown: Mr. Green, the shift supervisor, came into my office and told me Ms. Smith had only finished cleaning two of her twelve tables.

ALJ: What did you do then?

Brown: I left my office with Mr. Green and went directly to the cafeteria.

ALJ: Did you observe Ms. Smith's work area?

Brown: Yes, Judge, I did.

ALJ: What time was that again, Ms. Brown?

Brown (looks at her notes): At about 10:40.

ALJ: What was the condition of Ms. Smith's work area?[9]

Brown: Only two of the twelve tables were cleaned. Ms. Smith's supply cart was at table number 3, but the table had not been cleaned.

ALJ: Did you speak to the claimant at that point?

Brown: No. I looked for her but she wasn't in her work area. Mr. Green and I began looking for Ms. Smith. We found her in the kitchen drinking a cup of coffee with one of the cooks.

ALJ: Did you speak to her at that time, Ms. Brown?

Brown: Yes, Your Honor.

ALJ: Who started the conversation?[10]

Brown: I did.

ALJ: Can you recall what you said?

Brown: I asked Ms. Smith why she was in the kitchen drinking coffee.

ALJ: Did she respond?

Brown: Yes, Your Honor, she did.

ALJ: What did she say?

Brown: She said she was taking a break.

Smith (interrupting): James was gonna do them, the tables and . . . he was supposed to help me out.

ALJ: Ms. Smith, please do not interrupt the testimony. If you have a legal objection, you may state one for the record, and I will make my ruling. Otherwise, you must wait until I take your testimony in the order I have already mentioned.[11]

Smith: But . . .

ALJ: Excuse me, Ms. Smith, I will not argue with you. Both parties have procedural due process rights in this hearing. One of those rights is the right to present evidence. After the party has had the opportunity to present that evidence, then the other party has the right to cross-examine. When you testify, you will be allowed to testify fully without interruption by the employer. Now, we will continue. Ms. Brown, what was Ms. Smith supposed to do on December 30 regarding the tables you mentioned?

Brown: She was supposed to clean them after cleaning the salad bar. It was part of her job. We instructed her many times on how and when to clean the tables.

ALJ: What did you do when you determined the tables had not been cleaned?

Brown: I talked to her about it. I pointed out to her that ten of the twelve tables assigned to her were not clean. I asked her why they weren't done.

ALJ: What time did you have this conversation with the claimant?

Brown: At about 10:45 A.M.

ALJ: What was Ms. Smith's answer to your question?

Brown: She said . . .

Smith (interrupting): They're not telling the truth. . . . This is all lies.

ALJ: Ms. Smith, I cannot allow you to interrupt; your remarks are going unnoticed at this time. If you continue to interrupt the proceedings, then we will not continue the hearing but will reconvene at such time as all parties agree to adhere to the simple procedural rules in effect. Now, Ms. Smith, may we continue with the hearing?

Smith: I'm sorry. This is all very upsetting.

ALJ: I understand, but the only way I can take all of the parties' evidence is in an orderly way. Let's continue then. Ms. Brown, what did Ms. Smith say when you asked her why she hadn't cleaned the tables?

Brown: She said she didn't have time. She said she would get to them as soon as she could.

ALJ: Did you say anything else to her?

Brown: Yes. I asked her when she planned to clean the tables. I told her the tables had to be cleaned by 11:30 A.M. so we could open for lunch at noon.

ALJ: Can you describe exactly what the claimant had to do to clean the tables satisfactorily?

Brown: Yes, Judge. Her job was to clear each table of all dishes and silverware or utensils. She was then supposed to spray each table with a commercial cleaner and wipe it clean.

ALJ: In her earlier testimony, Ms. Smith testified that another worker named James was supposed to assist her. Can you tell me who James is?[12]

Brown: Yes, Judge. James Wells is another worker who was present on December 30th.

ALJ: Was James also assigned to clean tables?

Brown: No, James was supposed to clean the floors. He had no responsibilities for cleaning tables.[13]

ALJ: Was James ever assigned to help Ms. Smith clean tables?

Brown: Sometimes Mr. Green or I would reassign James to help clean tables, but only in emergencies.

ALJ: Are you and Mr. Green the only ones who have the authority to change assignments?

Brown: Yes. That's correct.

ALJ: Did you change James' assignment and ask him to help Ms. Smith on December 30?

Brown: No, Judge.

ALJ: Did Mr. Green reassign James on December 30?

Brown: Not that I know of.

ALJ: If Ms. Smith had required assistance on December 30, how would she have gone about making a request?

Brown: She could have asked either Mr. Green or me.

ALJ: Have you ever assigned Ms. Smith extra help in the past, Ms. Brown?[14]

Brown: Yes, we have.

ALJ: How many times, do you recall?

Brown: I would estimate two or three times since she began working here.

ALJ: Have you ever had other employees who had extra workers assigned to help them?

Brown: Yes, Judge. If there is an emergency and Mr. Green or I can see that a worker needs help, we take immediate steps to provide that help. If no one else is available, Mr. Green or myself often pitch in and provide our workers with assistance. When a worker needs help and asks for it, we make every effort to assist that worker if the need is legitimate.[15]

ALJ: Did you consider Ms. Smith's need for help on December 30 a "legitimate" need?

Brown: No, we did not.

ALJ: Why not?

Brown: First of all, Ms. Smith made no request for assistance to Mr. Green or to me. Secondly, she only had twelve tables to clean in two hours. There was no emergency situation. It only takes about five to ten minutes to clear, clean, and restock a table. Ms. Smith started work at 9:00 A.M. If she worked at a normal pace, she could have been finished by 11 A.M. at the latest.

ALJ: What would constitute an "emergency situation"?[16]

Brown: An emergency could occur when a worker does not show up and the other workers have to clear extra tables. Another example would be a worker who arrives late and needs help to clear his or her assigned tables. We would provide assistance in those cases. Often Mr. Green and I have had to pitch in and provide the help ourselves.

ALJ: If Ms. Smith had made a legitimate request for assistance on December 30, could you have provided her with help?

Brown: Yes, Judge, certainly. We would have made every attempt to do so. It's very important for the tables to be cleaned for lunch.

ALJ: Before December 30, had Ms. Smith ever been warned about her work performance, especially with regard to cleaning tables?

Brown: Yes.

ALJ: When was Ms. Smith last warned about her work performance prior to the incident on December 30th?[17]

Brown (referring to her notes): She was warned on November 12. We have copies of the warning right here Judge *(witness hands two photocopies of the warning form to the judge).*

ALJ: Ms. Brown, do you wish to offer this into evidence and have it made part of the record?

Brown: Yes, Your Honor.

ALJ: Thank you, Ms. Brown. For the record, I've been handed two photocopies of an employer document titled "Warning Form." The document is dated November 12, 1995. The document contains a handwritten notation indicating the claimant was warned about not cleaning cafeteria tables on November 11, 1995. The form appears to be signed by Ms. Smith, the claimant, on November 12, 1995. The document also appears to be signed by Ms. Brown and Mr. Green for the employer. I'm going to mark this document as Exhibit 9.

Ms. Smith, here's a copy for you. Please take a few minutes to read the document. *(After a few minutes)* Ms. Smith, have you had time to read Exhibit 9?

Smith: Yes, I read it.

ALJ: Have you ever seen Exhibit 9 before, Ms. Smith?

Smith: No, I never saw it until just now. I don't ever remember seeing this paper before.

ALJ: That appears to be your signature and the signatures of Ms. Brown and Mr. Green, wouldn't you agree?

Smith: Yeah, now I remember. They said something about being warned. They were always picking on me about something. They never treated me right or gave me a chance to explain.

ALJ: Do you recall signing Exhibit 9 on or about November 12, 1995, Ms. Smith?

Smith: Yeah, I signed it. I thought they'd fire me if I didn't sign.

ALJ: Did Ms. Brown or Mr. Green coerce you or threaten you if you didn't sign Exhibit 9?

Smith: Coerce? I don't understand. I signed it because I had to . . . or they'd fire me.

ALJ: Did they tell you you'd be fired if you didn't sign Exhibit 9, Ms. Smith?

Smith: Well, they didn't say so . . . not in so many words, but they seemed like they would.

ALJ: Ms. Brown, when you issued Ms. Smith this warning, dated November 12, 1995, did you threaten to fire her if she did not sign it?

Brown: No, Your Honor. Ms. Smith was given the option of signing or not.[18] When we issue written warnings, our procedure is to discuss the form and discuss the reason they are getting the warning. If the employee refuses to sign it or doesn't want to sign it, we simply note that he or she does not wish to sign. The manager or supervisor issuing the warning initials where the employee would have signed, then the manager signs and dates the warning form themselves. In this case, Ms. Smith signed the form on her own.

ALJ: Did Ms. Smith say anything when she signed Exhibit 9?

Brown: She said she was sorry about not cleaning the tables. She said it wouldn't happen again.

ALJ: Does the form have a place for comments?

Brown: Yes, Judge.

ALJ: *(Judge takes judicial notice that the comment section was not filled out.)* Thank you, Ms. Brown. Ms. Smith, do you have any objection to my admitting Exhibit 9 and making it part of the record?

Smith: Yeah. I don't think it's fair to bring this up now. I mean, that was in November, and I was fired in December. Now it's almost March.

ALJ: Do you have any other objections, Ms. Smith, to admitting Exhibit 9?[19]

Smith: No.

ALJ: Ms. Smith, I am going to overrule your objection to entering Exhibit 9. The document is relevant to the issue before me. The document appears to be genuine. Ms. Smith states she saw and signed the document on November 12, 1995. Your objection is noted for the record, Ms. Smith. Exhibit 9 is entered and will be part of the record in this case.

Brown: Thank you, Judge.

ALJ: Does the employer have any other documents it wishes to offer in evidence in its case? If so, let's take care of all that now.

Brown: Yes, Your Honor. We issued her written warnings on October 10 and September 3. Here are copies of the warnings.

ALJ: Do these warnings also involve failure to clean tables?

Brown: Yes, Judge, they do.

ALJ: I've been handed two copies of written warnings. The first is dated October 10, 1995, and the second is dated September 3, 1995. Both documents appear to be warnings issued to the claimant, and they are similar to Exhibit 9. They appear to be signed by the claimant and signed by Ms. Brown and Mr. Green. I'm going to mark the warning dated October 10, 1995, as Exhibit 10 and the warning dated September 3, 1995, as Exhibit 11. *(ALJ hands exhibits to claimant)* Please read the documents carefully, Ms. Smith. *(after a few minutes)* Have you had an opportunity to read Exhibits 10 and 11, Ms. Smith?

Smith: Yes.

ALJ: Ms. Smith, is that your signature on Exhibit 10 and Exhibit 11?

Smith: Yes . . . I guess so.

ALJ: Have you ever seen Exhibits 10 and 11 before?

Smith: Uh . . . yes.

ALJ: Were Exhibits 10 and 11 warnings issued to you on October 10 and September 3?

Smith: I think so. They were always warning me about something.

ALJ: Is that a "yes," Ms. Smith?

Smith: Yes.

ALJ: Did you receive copies of these two warnings at the time they were issued, Ms. Smith?

Smith: They gave me copies, yes.

ALJ: Do you have any objections to making Exhibits 10 and 11 part of the record?

Smith: No.

ALJ: Ms. Brown, do you have any objections to making Exhibits 10 and 11 part of the record?

Smith: No, Your Honor, I don't.

ALJ: Ms. Brown, are there any other written documents you wish to submit?

Brown: No, Judge. Not at this time.[20]

ALJ: Ms. Brown, did Ms. Smith receive any other warnings, verbal or written, other than these documents?

Brown: Yes. We warned Ms. Smith verbally about not cleaning tables on May 8 and May 20.

ALJ: Who is "we?"

Brown: Mr. Green and myself. We told her that if she didn't clean the tables along with her other duties, she could be fired. We made notes about the verbal warnings and put them in Ms. Smith's personnel file.

ALJ: Did you give Ms. Smith a copy of your notations?

Brown: No, Judge, we only give employees copies of written warnings.

ALJ: Thank you, Ms. Brown. I don't have any other questions at this time. Ms. Smith, do you have any questions?

Smith: Well, what he said about telling me about getting fired, that's not true. I tried to clean the tables, but they fired me first. It wasn't fair.[21]

Brown: Judge, I'm going to have to object. Ms. Smith is testifying, not asking a question.

ALJ: I agree, Ms. Brown. Ms. Smith, that is not a question. Your right to cross-examine is your right to ask *questions* in the same way I have asked the witness questions. When you're done with your questions, or if you have no questions, then I will take all of your testimony, but not before. Now, do you have any questions for Ms. Brown?

Smith: Yeah. I want to ask why I was fired before I had time to do anything about the tables because I didn't see . . .

ALJ: Ms. Smith, I'm going to interrupt you. This is the time for you to ask Ms. Brown questions related to her testimony. If you want to ask a question, I'll assist you. However, this is not the time for you to testify. That will come later. *(ALJ asks questions for claimant)* Ms. Brown, I believe Ms. Smith's question was related to allowing her time to clean the tables. Is that correct, Ms. Smith?

Smith: Yes, that's what I wanted to know.

ALJ: Ms. Brown, did the employer allow the claimant adequate time to complete her assigned duties?

Brown: Yes, we believe we did, Judge.

ALJ: Ms. Smith, do you have any further questions?

Smith: No, I guess not.

ALJ: I will now take Mr. Green's testimony. Mr. Green, Ms. Brown has stated you were present when Ms. Smith was told she was being discharged. Is that correct?

Green: Yes.

ALJ: Did you and Ms. Brown talk about Ms. Smith before you both talked to her?

Green: Yes, I talked to Ms. Brown about Ms. Smith in her office. It was about 10:30 A.M. on December 30th.

ALJ: Before this, had you seen the tables?

Green: Yes.

ALJ: Can you describe what you saw?

Green: Yes, only two of the twelve tables assigned to Ms. Smith had been cleaned. The others still contained napkins, empty pop cans, food crumbs, and other material that needed cleaning. Some of the napkin holders needed to be refilled, too.

ALJ: What time was that?

Green: Around 10:30, Judge.

ALJ: Did you say anything to the claimant at that time?

Green: No.

ALJ: Why not?[22]

Green: I wanted to talk to the manager, Ms. Brown, to let her know what was going on and to see what I should do.

ALJ: Did you do so?

Green: Yes. I did.

ALJ: What time was that?

Green: About 10:40 A.M., Your Honor.

ALJ: Who started the conversation?

Green: I did.

ALJ: What did you say to Ms. Brown?

Green: I told her I had just come from the cafeteria and Janet (Ms. Smith) had only cleaned two tables. I said I was concerned because it was after 10:30, and we had to open for lunch in less than 90 minutes.

ALJ: Did you have this conversation with Ms. Brown in her office?

Green: Yes.

ALJ: What, if anything, did Ms. Brown say?[23]

Green: She was concerned too. She said Janet had received a couple of written warnings before this. Ms. Brown was real worried about the tables not getting cleaned on time.

ALJ: What happened next?

Green: Ms. Brown and I left the office and went down to the cafeteria.

ALJ: How long did it take you and Ms. Brown to arrive at the cafeteria?

Green: Oh, a few minutes—I guess about two minutes.

ALJ: How far is the cafeteria from Ms. Brown's office?

Green: I don't know exactly. It's in the same building as the cafeteria. About 100 yards, I'd guess. It's a pretty large building.

ALJ: So you arrived at the cafeteria about 10:45 or so, is that correct?

Green (looks at his notes): I wrote down it was about 10:50.

ALJ: Mr. Green, you are looking at what appears to be some handwritten notes before you answered my questions. Can you testify without using your notes?[24]

Green: Most of the time I can, but I can't remember all the times. A lot of things happened that day.

ALJ: By that day, do you mean December 30?

Green: Yes.

ALJ: When did you make the notes you are using to testify from, Mr. Green?

Green: They were made on the day we fired Ms. Smith. I made them on December 30, when Ms. Brown asked me to write down what happened.

ALJ: How long after Ms. Smith was dismissed did you make the notes?

Green: I made them right after she was let go. It took me about ten or fifteen minutes to write it all down.

ALJ: Before I allow you to continue to consult your notes or read from them during testimony, I'd like to inspect them. Do you have any objection to that, sir?

Green: No, Judge *(witness hands the notes to the judge).*

ALJ (after a few minutes): All right. For the record, I'm going to take judicial notice that I've read Mr. Green's notes related to the claimant's separation from work. The notes appear to have been made at the time of the separation, and Mr. Green has testified he cannot recall certain details of the separation without these notes. I will not enter the notes and make them part of the record at this time, but I will allow you to consult your notes if you need them to assist you in answering any questions. Now, Mr. Green, what did you see when you entered the cafeteria?

Green: Everyone was working. Ms. Smith had cleaned only two tables. Things in her work area looked just about the same as when I went to Ms. Brown's office.

ALJ: By "her," do you mean Ms. Smith?

Green: Yes, Ms. Smith.

ALJ: When you left to go to Ms. Brown's office, was Ms. Smith in her work area?

Green: No.

ALJ: When you returned to the cafeteria with Ms. Brown, the claimant was still not in her work area, is that correct?

Green: Yes, that's right.

ALJ: What happened next?[25]

Green: Ms. Brown talked to Janet in the kitchen, just the way Ms. Brown described it. Then Ms. Brown said she would talk with Janet after we all finished cleaning the tables. Ms. Brown and I cleaned four each, while Janet only cleaned two. After we finished, I told Janet to come to Ms. Brown's office with me. When we got to the office, Ms. Brown again asked Janet why she only finished two tables by 10:30, then took a second break. Janet said she was tired and needed a break. Ms. Brown asked if she was ill or seeing a doctor. Janet said no, but she was working too hard. Then Ms. Brown asked her why she only cleaned two tables while we, I mean me and Ms. Brown, cleaned four each. Janet said, "Well, I thought you could get them done. Is that my fault too?" Janet said we'd been picking on her and were out to get her. She said, "If you're going to fire me, then get the damn thing over with." Ms. Brown said she was fired for not doing her work properly.

ALJ: With regard to breaks, was Ms. Smith entitled to a break such as the one she took at about 10:30 A.M. on the 30th?

Green: No. We take a break at 8:00 A.M. and 2:00 P.M.

ALJ: Do you know if Ms. Smith got any breaks, other than the one at 10:30 A.M.?

Green: Yes. She took her normal break with the other employees at 8:00 A.M.

ALJ: How do you know this?[26]

Green: Because I saw her take the break. Also Ms. Brown asked her about the break when we were in the office, and Ms. Smith said she took a break at about 8:00 A.M.

ALJ: Thank you, Mr. Green. I don't have more questions for you at this time. Ms. Smith, any questions?

Smith: Yes. I only took a short break at 8:00 A.M. I was entitled to a fifteen-minute break, and I only took a ten-minute break. They owed me five minutes.

ALJ: Ms. Smith, that is not a question. I'm going to assist you in asking questions. You'll be given an opportunity to testify regarding the break and other matters when it's your turn to give evidence. Do you want to know if Mr. Green was aware that you only took ten minutes instead of fifteen on your 8:00 A.M. break?

Smith: Yes.

ALJ: Mr. Green, is it a fact that Ms. Smith only took ten minutes on her 8:00 break on December 30?

Green: No. She took at least fifteen minutes.

ALJ: How do you know that, sir?

Green: Because I was in the cafeteria area. All the employees, except maybe one or two, took a break at 8:00. They all had their break together, and they all came back together.

ALJ: Was Ms. Smith in the group of employees?

Green: Yes, she was.

ALJ: Mr. Green, are employees entitled to fifteen-minute breaks?

Green: Yes. Our rules allow a fifteen-minute morning break at 8:00 A.M. and a fifteen-minute afternoon break at 2:00 P.M., when we close the cafeteria after lunch. If an employee has to take additional time, they must get permission from Ms. Brown or me.

ALJ: How would Ms. Smith or any other employee be aware of the break schedule?[27]

Green: The break schedule is posted on the bulletin board for the 6:00 A.M. to 4:00 P.M. shift. We also remind employees about the break schedule at our weekly meetings.

ALJ: Thank you. Ms. Smith does that answer any questions you had about the break?

Smith: Yeah . . . yes.

ALJ: Do you have any additional questions for Mr. Green before we begin taking your testimony?

Smith: No. But . . . they aren't telling the truth. I took a ten-minute . . .

Brown: Objection, Your Honor.

ALJ: Ms. Smith, you'll have ample opportunity to testify regarding the matter of the break taking. For now, I'd like you to respond to the questions I have for you. Can we proceed with that now?

Smith: OK . . . yes.

ALJ: Ms. Smith, would you state your full name for the record?

Smith: My name in Janet Lorraine Smith.

ALJ: Is your Social Security number 000–12–9874?

Smith: Yes.

ALJ: Do you currently live at 1000 W. Riverside Drive, as shown on your initial claim form, Exhibit 1? *(ALJ also confirms state and ZIP code.)*

Smith: Yes.

ALJ: Is that where you wish the decision in this case to be mailed?

Smith: Yes.

ALJ: According to Exhibit 1, your initial claim for benefits, you indicated your last day of work was January 30. Two employer witnesses have testified your last day of work was December 30. Do you wish to modify your testimony at this point?

Smith: Yeah . . . I mean yes, it was December 30.

ALJ: Is it also correct that you started work April 3?

Smith: Yes, sometime at the beginning of April.

ALJ: Did you start at $5 per hour?

Smith: Yes.

ALJ: And were you making $5 per hour at the time of separation from work?

Smith: Yeah. I never got a raise. Yes, that's right.

ALJ: Did you normally work 10 hours a day, from 6:00 A.M. to 4:00 P.M.?

Smith: Yes.

ALJ: How many days a week did you work?

Smith: Four days a week—Tuesday through Friday. I was off Saturday through Monday.

ALJ: Thank you, Ms. Smith. Can you briefly describe your job duties?

Smith: I was assigned to clean up tables. Like Ms. Brown said, I had to clean ten tables. I had to do other stuff, too, like help clean up in the kitchen and serve at the salad bar. Then I had to clear those tables after lunch.

ALJ: Did you report to work as scheduled at 6:00 A.M. on December 30?

Smith: Yes.

ALJ: What did you do when you first got to work?

Smith: Well, I put on my uniform, then I cleaned up in the kitchen for about two hours. I helped the cook prepare some salad bar stuff, and I loaded up my cart.

ALJ: Is this the cart you used when you cleared and restocked the tables?

Smith: That's the one.

ALJ: Is that a yes?[28]

Smith: Yes.

ALJ: What did you do after you prepared your cart?

Smith: I guess that's when I went on break.

ALJ: Did you go on break with other employees?

Smith: Yes. I went with some of the other girls.

ALJ: Is 8:00 A.M. the time you normally go on break?

Smith: Yes.

ALJ: Is it a fact the break policy is also posted on a bulletin board?

Smith: Yeah, it could be. I don't read the bulletin board usually.

ALJ: Mr. Green has testified the break schedule and policy are posted on a bulletin board in the employee area. If you don't read the bulletin board, you would not be in a position to say if the policy is there or not, correct?[29]

Smith: Well . . . no.

ALJ: You would not be in a position to contradict Mr. Green's testimony regarding the posting of the break schedule, true?

Smith: That's true.

ALJ: Did Ms. Brown and Mr. Smith also conduct weekly meetings in which the break policy was discussed, along with other work-related matters?

Smith: Yeah. They were always getting on us for something. Sometimes about breaks. Sometimes about other stuff.

ALJ: Is that a yes, Ms. Smith?

Smith: Yes.

ALJ: During the time you worked for the employer, were you always assigned twelve tables to clear and restock?

Smith: Yes.

ALJ: How long did it usually take you to clean those twelve tables?

Smith: Usually about ten minutes each, depending on how dirty they were.

ALJ: Let's see—twelve tables at about ten minutes a table is 120 minutes or two hours. Would you agree, Ms. Smith?

Smith: Yes, I guess that's about right.

ALJ: Were there ever times when you where able to finish cleaning the twelve tables in less than two hours?

Smith: Well, no. It usually took about two hours.

ALJ: Was 9:00 A.M. your usual starting time for cleaning the tables?

Smith: Yes.

ALJ: On December 30, did you start cleaning the tables at 9:00 A.M.?

Smith: Yes.

ALJ: Is it true that by 10:30 A.M. you had only cleaned two tables?

Smith: I don't know how many tables I'd cleaned by then.

ALJ: Is it true you took a break sometime around 10:30 A.M. on December 30?

Smith: I took a break. I don't know what time it was.

ALJ: Did you take more than one break on that day, Ms. Smith?

Smith: Yeah. I told you; I took a break at 8:00 but it was only ten minutes. They owed me five minutes, so I took what they owed me.

ALJ: You took another break at about 10:30, is that correct?

Smith: I took a break. I didn't look at any clock.

ALJ: Where did you take your break?

Smith: Where I always do, in the kitchen.

ALJ: Do you recall Ms. Brown and Mr. Green coming into the kitchen when you were on your break?

Smith: Yeah. They came in.

ALJ: How long had you been in the kitchen when Ms. Brown and Mr. Green came into the kitchen?

Smith: I don't know. I didn't have a watch.

ALJ: How did you intend to keep track of your five-minute break, Ms. Smith?

Smith: Well, I can tell when five minutes is up.

ALJ: Is it your testimony that you thought you could estimate the time of your break without a watch or clock?

Smith: Yes.

ALJ: Is there a clock in the kitchen area?

Smith: Not that I know of.

ALJ: Mr. Green has testified that after he and Ms. Brown found you in the kitchen, there was a conversation between you and Ms. Brown, true?

Smith: I think so.

ALJ: Did Ms. Brown ask you what you were doing in the kitchen?

Smith: I believe so.

ALJ: In response to Ms. Brown's question, did you say, "I'm taking a break"?

Smith: I probably did.

ALJ: Was anything else said either by you, Ms. Brown, or Mr. Green that you can recall?

Smith: I don't remember.

ALJ: Did you leave the kitchen and return to the cafeteria with Ms. Brown and Mr. Smith?

Smith: Yes, we all left together.

ALJ: When you returned to your work area, were there still ten of twelve tables left to be cleaned?

Smith: Yeah, I think so.

ALJ: Did you begin working at that point?

Smith: Yes.

ALJ: Do you recall what time it was when you started working?

Smith: No. I don't know.

ALJ: Did you and Ms. Brown and Ms. Smith start cleaning the tables in your work area?

Smith: Yes.

ALJ: According to Mr. Green's testimony, the three of you worked for about an hour. Is that correct?

Smith: Yes. I think so.

ALJ: During that period of time, did you clean two tables?

Smith: Well, I don't know. We finished all the tables in time.

ALJ: Is it also a fact that Ms. Brown and Mr. Green cleaned four tables each in the time it took you to clean two tables?

Smith: I don't know how many tables they cleaned. I was busy doing my own work.

ALJ: I don't have any more questions for you at this point; thank you for your testimony Ms. Smith. Ms. Brown, do you have any questions for Ms. Smith?

Brown: No, Your Honor.[30]

ALJ: Ms. Brown do you wish to present James Wells as a witness?

Brown: Yes, Judge.

ALJ: Very well. I understand Mr. Wells is standing by and can be reached by telephone. I'll call him now. *(ALJ calls James Wells and connects him to the speaker phone and recording device in the hearing room.)*

　　Mr. Wells, this is Judge Vondrak at the Office of Appeals. We are in an unemployment insurance hearing for Janet Smith, a claimant for benefits. Ms. Smith is present with me. Also present are Roberta Brown and Al Green. Can you hear me clearly?

Wells: Yes.

ALJ: If you are unable to hear me or any party at the hearing, please let me know immediately. If we are disconnected for any reason, hang up the telephone on your end, and I will call you back. For the purpose of creating a record, we are recording this telephone conversation. Please speak clearly, and do not interrupt when someone else is speaking. The recording device can only pick up one voice at a time. Do you understand these instructions, Mr. Wells?

Wells: Yes, I do.

ALJ: Mr. Wells, all testimony given at this hearing is required to be given under oath or affirmation. I will caution you that knowingly making a false statement while under oath may subject you to penalties for perjury. *(ALJ administers oath)* Would you please state your full name for the record?

Wells: James Wells.

ALJ: Are you employed by the Good Eats Cafeteria?

Wells: Yes, I'm a janitor. I've worked there about three years.

ALJ: Do you know the claimant in this case, Janet Smith?

Wells: Yes, she was a table cleaner, and I worked with her.

ALJ: Were you present at work on December 30?

Wells: Yes.

ALJ: Did Ms. Smith approach you and ask you to help her clean the tables that day?

Wells: Yes.

ALJ: What time was that?

Wells: It was about 10:00 or 10:30 in the morning.

ALJ: What was your response to her request?

Wells: I told her I had my own work to do. I told her she would have to check with Mr. Green or the manager before I could help her. We had to have permission to do something different.

ALJ: By "something different" do you mean alter your job assignment?

Wells: Yes.

ALJ: Do you know if Ms. Smith requested permission for you to help her?

Wells: I don't know. She never came back, and Mr. Green didn't say anything to me.

ALJ: What happened next?

Wells: She worked for a while, then she went on break.

ALJ: What did you do?

Wells: I just stayed working.

ALJ: Thank you for your testimony, Mr. Wells. I don't have any further questions at this time. Ms. Smith, do you have any questions of this witness?

Smith: Yeah, when I asked you to help me, you said you'd try to give me a hand if you had time. And then . . .

ALJ: Ms. Smith, you are testifying, not asking a question. I believe you are attempting to ask Mr. Wells whether he offered to help you. He has already answered that question, but I will ask it again. Mr. Wells, did you offer to help Ms. Smith complete her job duties if you had time?

Wells: No, I told her I couldn't do it without permission.

ALJ: Any other questions, Ms. Smith?

Smith: No.

ALJ: Thank you, Mr. Wells. Is there any other testimony you'd like to offer at this time, Ms. Smith?

Smith: Yeah, I thought James was going to help me, so that's why I took my break and they owed me five minutes anyway.

ALJ: Anything further from either the employer or the claimant?[31]

Brown: No.

Green: No.

Smith: No.

Wells: No.

ALJ: Hearing nothing further, I will now close the evidentiary portion of this hearing. Both parties in this case now have the right to make a short closing statement. A closing statement is not evidence; it is a summary of your position. In your statement, you may tell me why you believe you should prevail in this matter. Because this is a discharge, I will allow the claimant to make the first closing statement and the employer may make the last statement. Ms. Smith, do you have anything you'd like to say as a closing statement?

Smith: Yes, I think it was real unfair to fire me. I tried to do my job, but sometimes I needed help. I didn't want to file for unemployment insurance, but I got fired and I haven't found a job. I need the money. I think they should give me a job or give me benefits. That's all I have to say.

ALJ: Thank you Ms. Smith. Does the employer wish to make a closing statement?

Brown: Yes, Judge. The employer in this case believes that Ms. Smith was discharged for work-related misconduct. We have presented testimony and evidence to show that she was negligent in completing her assigned job duties on December 30. From 9:00 A.M. to 10:30 A.M., Ms. Smith cleaned only two of the twelve tables assigned to her. As she said, it only takes about ten minutes to clean a table. When she wasn't finished, she tried to get James Wells to help her. She didn't get permission for James to change his assignment, and he followed proper procedure by refusing to do her work for her. Ms. Smith then went on an unauthorized break. Following this break, Ms. Smith only cleaned two additional tables in the next forty minutes.

The claimant had received two written warnings and two verbal warnings regarding her failure to clean tables. We believe the claimant knew her work responsibilities and she knew the break policy. It is our contention the claimant's actions disregarded our interests. We do not believe our unemployment insurance tax account should be charged in this case. We ask that you affirm the claims examiner's determination. Thank you.[32]

ALJ: Thank you. I will consider the evidence presented this morning, both the documents admitted into evidence and all the testimony. I will take the matter under advisement and issue a written decision in accordance with the employment security laws. If the decision is not in your favor, there will be further appeal rights included. In any event, the decision will be mailed to the parties by certified mail to your respective addresses of record in the same way the Notice of Hearing was sent.

Ms. Smith, if you are still filing claims for benefits, continue filing your weekly claims as you have been instructed by your local office. Any questions on this procedure? There being nothing further, this hearing is closed.

NOTES

1. This is usually the end of the ALJ's remarks and instructions to the parties as to how the hearing will proceed. The judge explains the rights of the witnesses with regard to questioning each other and the rights of each party. The ALJ also states the "formal rules" of evidence do not apply. This means the rules adhered

to in a court of law will not be strictly used—photocopies of documents may be admitted instead of originals, and witnesses may make narrative statements instead of statements that are narrowly responsive to questions. In addition, hearsay may be considered if it is the type of hearsay people rely on in their everyday business affairs.

The ALJ also issues instructions to the parties that *only* evidence presented at the hearing and made part of the record will be considered in reaching the UIC appeals decision. This is a self-restricting statement. The judge is cautioning the parties to present their evidence at this forum. If the evidence is not presented and made part of the record of the hearing, it is of no use to the judge.

2. The judge cautions all witnesses that taking the oath is a serious matter. There can be severe penalties for not telling the truth once the oath is taken. Knowingly making false statements of a material fact in most states is considered perjury and may be a felony. In addition, some states may further penalize employers for making false statements by assessing additional UIC tax charges.

The oath does not *guarantee* a witness will tell the truth. Don't count on taking an oath to compel the claimant to do so. The oath is only a tool. It provides the state a means of punishing witnesses who lie, but it does not keep someone from lying.

3. This is the end of identifying and marking documents. Most of the documents will be in the case file and will be marked. Follow along carefully; make sure your file matches the ALJ's original file. If there are any discrepancies or changes, mark your file to match the ALJ's file. If the judge is going too fast for you, ask him or her to repeat the numbers of the exhibits. If new documents are to be marked, they will be identified at this point. Documents submitted during the course of the hearing will be marked as they are introduced.

4. The ALJ issues instructions as to the order of testimony. In some states, the appellant is always questioned first. In other states, the employer goes first in discharges and the claimant goes first in quits. Some ALJs may take all employer testimony together, while some prefer to take the testimony of corroborative witnesses last. This is a time-saving technique. In the event a claimant agrees or admits to the statements of the first employer witness, additional employer testimony may be unnecessary.

Stay flexible. The order of testimony often varies dramatically from state to state, from appeals office to appeals office, and from judge to judge. If you and your witnesses are prepared to testify, the order should make little difference in the outcome of your case.

5. This is end of the preliminary questioning. The judge has asked basic questions to determine background material as to the claimant's rate of pay, length of employment, date of discharge, and actual last day of work. This information is usually provided by the lead employer witness. The claimant will also be asked the same questions to see if there is agreement on these issues.

It is important to have this information readily available for the judge. Having it ready makes for a smooth hearing and a good first impression. From here, the ALJ will begin to ask *substantive* questions regarding the actual facts of the separation from work.

6. The judge asks this question to determine if there was a "precipitating incident." As is discussed in Chapter 4, most ALJs like to begin with this incident

then work their way back in time. Providing as much detail about this last incident is extremely important in building your case.

7. The judge asks this question to determine *precisely* what the claimant's job duties were. It is important to add as much detail as you can at this point. Later, you will be able to tell the judge how the claimant failed to perform specific duties. This is a major building block in the foundation for establishing misconduct.

8. This question "sets the scene" for the ALJ and for the record. The ALJ is building a mental picture of how the incident began that led to the claimant's dismissal. In addition, the record now shows the claimant reported on time and cannot use tardiness as an excuse for not completing her assigned duties.

9. This is an open-ended question. The witness is prepared and gives a complete, detailed answer. This type of question allows a witness to give a *narrative* response. The more detail, the better. The judge will usually stop you if you go on too long.

10. This is more scene setting. The ALJ asks the question to help fill in the mental picture of how the conversation started and who started it. This is a common question when you or your witnesses are testifying about conversations held with the claimant leading up to the separation from work.

11. This is a common problem in hearings—interruptions by the claimant. Don't let them bother you or break your concentration. If you are testifying, remember the question or remember where you were in your answer. The ALJ may have to spend some time admonishing (instructing) the other side not to interrupt. Normally, the ALJ will repeat the question that was asked before the interruption. If he or she doesn't, simply ask the judge to please repeat the last question before you go on with your answer.

12. The ALJ asks this question to determine exactly who "James" is and whether or not his testimony is likely to be relevant to the hearing. The judge wants to avoid any testimony that will be needlessly repetitive or cumulative. If a witness's testimony corroborates (backs up) another witness's testimony, or if the witness can offer new or additional testimony, the ALJ will be obligated to take testimony from that witness.

13. This is a short, very critical question. The ALJ asks it to determine whether James had any obligation or duty to help the claimant. The answer is strong and direct; it helps the employer's case immensely.

14. This question is designed to establish whether the employer customarily reassigns workers to help others with specific duties. The ALJ wants to know if the claimant was being treated unfairly or if the employer has a history or implied obligation to assign help to the claimant.

15. This is an excellent answer by the witness. It explains that under special conditions the employer would help Ms. Smith, but the incident of December 30 was not a special or emergency condition.

16. This is a continuation of note 15. The ALJ asks the witnesses to define the conditions under which the employer would reassign an employee to help another worker. The witness gives an excellent, comprehensive answer and goes on to tell the ALJ the exact procedure for requesting assistance. The witness also does a good job in emphasizing that the claimant failed to follow

the procedure. Therefore, the employer had no obligation to assign Ms. Smith any help.

17. This question is very important. The ALJ asks the witness if there were any prior warnings, especially warnings regarding an incident similar to the incident of December 30 (the precipitating incident). This is the time to introduce copies of the actual warnings. Originals should be available for inspection.

It is a good idea to make an extra copy for the claimant. The ALJ will appreciate this, and it makes the hearing go faster. In some states, you may have to submit the warnings to the ALJ before the hearing starts. Either way, make sure any warnings are made part of the record.

18. The judge asks if Exhibit 9, which is being considered for inclusion in the record, was obtained under any kind of duress or coercion. If the document was forced, it may not be admitted. Even if it is admitted, it does not carry the same weight as a warning the claimant signed voluntarily.

19. The ALJ asks Ms. Smith if there are any *other* objections to admitting Exhibit 9. Judges usually want to hear all the objections, valid or not, before they rule on whether to admit a document. In this case, the claimant's objection is without merit and is overruled, but the objection is noted for the record.

20. Brown's answer, "No, Judge. Not at this time." is an excellent answer because she does not give up the employer's right to submit additional documents later in the hearing. Use this "qualifier" to *reserve* your right to submit documents, ask questions, or give testimony at a later point in the hearing.

21. At this point, the claimant is becoming argumentative and not asking questions. This frequently happens when claimants are given the opportunity to ask questions.

After listening to the testimony of an opposing witness, the claimant may want to counter that testimony. The judge should not allow this to occur. The ALJ properly tells the claimant she will have a chance to testify later then formulates the question and pursues a line of inquiry for the claimant.

If this happens to you, don't be alarmed. The judge is not taking the claimant's side. He or she is merely assisting the claimant in keeping the hearing moving. Keep your concentration. Listen to the question as it is posed by the ALJ, then answer the question as directly as you can. If the ALJ asks follow-up questions for the claimant, continue to answer them.

Tip. If the claimant asks a long, rambling, compound question that is impossible to understand or answer, ask for the question to be *repeated*. This usually forces the person to shorten the question because he or she cannot remember a long diatribe. Simply say, "I'm sorry, I don't understand the question. Could you please repeat it?" Often the ALJ will intervene and break it down to several proper, understandable questions.

22. The judge uses the "why" question here to find out exactly why something did or did not happen. It is commonly used and is important in determining the motive and intent of the parties. The "why" question is important for you to consider in all your dealings with employees and claimants.

Tip. Be careful how you answer "why" questions. As with all questions, take an extra moment or two to think about your answer. Ask yourself what your real motive or purpose was for doing or not doing something related to the separation from work. You should not feel that you are obliged to defend your position. The "why" question is merely probing or clarifying the reason something did or did not take place.

23. The ALJ is asking this question to determine if Ms. Brown said anything. The question is asked in this way so the judge will not appear to lead a witness into saying Ms. Brown said something if she did not. The questioner must first determine if something was said. If Ms. Brown made a statement (which she did), then the witness will be asked to recollect what was said. If the witness recalls that nothing was said, that in itself is an answer. Do not be intimidated or bothered by this type of question; it is commonly used. The ALJ is trying to test the recollection of the witness; this is part of the judge's job.

24. The judge questions the witness about having to refer to notes before he answers questions. Some judges can be very strict about requiring witnesses to testify from memory or recollection of events, with minimal use of notes.

Do not let this bother you. You are not expected to recall all the information, especially when it comes to specific times and dates. If you need to refer to notes or other information in your file, do so. Take as much time as you need to answer *correctly*.

Reviewing the file before the hearing helps prepare you to answer most questions, but if you are confused or uncertain, use the written information to help you recall details. If the judge asks you whether you can testify without notes, answer as Mr. Green did.

The judge may want to inspect the notes and may ask you questions about the origin or source of the notes. He or she may also want to know why and when the notes were made. These questions are important for the record.

25. This question provides another opportunity for the witness to give narrative testimony. The witness has his facts prepared and gives an excellent answer.

26. The ALJ asks a typical "how" question to determine whether the witness is assuming or speculating about what he knows. This question is *not* a challenge to the witness personally or to the *truth* of the witness's statement. The ALJ must determine for the record how the witness knows what he is testifying about.

If the witness merely heard that the claimant took a break with other employees, it would be *hearsay evidence*. Hearsay is usually admissible evidence in UIC hearings, but it cannot be given the same weight as eyewitness or firsthand knowledge. If the witness knew of the break because he thought the claimant probably took her break with all of the other employees, the witness would be *assuming* he knew about the break—again, probably admissible testimony, but not as strong as firsthand knowledge.

In our case, the witness has formed his answer from firsthand information. He knows the claimant took her break because he *saw* her take it.

27. The ALJ asks how Ms. Smith (or any other employee) is informed about the break schedule. This is a very good question. It is crucial for employees to be clearly and fairly informed about the rules of employment. If the employee knows the rules of the game but *chooses* to ignore them, that employee has acted *willfully* and *intentionally*, and you have a much stronger case for showing misconduct.

28. The ALJ asks the witness to clarify her answer. By stating "that's the one,"

the claimant has not answered the question. It is a question that requires a yes, no, or "I don't know" answer. The ALJ must create a clear record when possible. Requiring a claimant or an employer witness to answer yes or no is not harassment. It is a method of clarifying an answer.

29. In this question, the ALJ is cross-examining the claimant to some degree. To clarify the record, the ALJ is asking the claimant if she read the bulletin board. If she didn't, how can she possibly know what instructions regarding breaks were posted there?

The ALJ has taken testimony from the employer witness who stated the instructions were posted. The employer witness has testified as to what the break instructions were. If the claimant has no knowledge of the break policy, she cannot credibly contradict the testimony of Mr. Green.

This is a basic question intended to test exactly what a witness really knows and what he or she is "competent" or logically able to give evidence about.

30. At this point, the ALJ has done an excellent job of asking questions. There is no reason for the employer to ask anything further. The judge has been very accommodating and fair and is now in the process of calling a third employer witness by telephone. The hearing has been long. Save your energy for listening to your last witness and for presenting a short, powerful closing statement.

31. This is the last opportunity for the employer to add anything to the record. If you have any documents, questions, or additional testimony, now is the time to enter it into the record. Later will be too late. Don't go over testimony you have previously given; that is not what the ALJ is asking for. He or she is giving you one last opportunity to *add* to your case, not to repeat what has already been said. You will have a chance to summarize in your closing statement.

32. This is a good closing statement. It summarizes all the important points. It does not ramble, and it is not too long. We recommend a closing statement not exceed two minutes when possible. Long closing statements bore the judge and waste time. End your statement with a short thank you to the ALJ. It never hurts.

F

UIC Benefits by Jurisdiction

This appendix contains a list of the weekly benefits a claimant can receive. The list includes the minimum and maximum amounts allowed by law as of 1992, the most current figures to date.

Figure F.1
Minimum and Maximum Weekly Benefit Amounts for Each State*

	Minimum WBA†	Maximum WBA†
Alabama	$22	$150
Alaska	$44-68	$212-284
Arizona	$40	$175
Arkansas	$41	$230
California	$40	$230
Colorado	$25	$239
Connecticut	$15-22	$288-388
Delaware	$20	$245
District of Columbia	$13	$335
Florida	$10	$225
Georgia	$37	$185
Hawaii	$5	$306
Idaho	$44	$215
Illinois	$51	$214-279
Indiana	$50	$116-171
Iowa	$29-35	$194-238
Kansas	$57	$231
Kentucky	$22	$209
Louisiana	$10	$181
Maine	$35-52	$198-297
Maryland	$25-33	$223
Massachusetts	$14-21	$296-444
Michigan	$60	$283
Minnesota	$38	$265
Mississippi	$30	$165
Missouri	$45	$175
Montana	$50	$201
Nebraska	$20	$154
Nevada	$16	$211
New Hampshire	$34	$179
New Jersey	$66	$308
New Mexico	$37	$185
New York	$40	$280
North Carolina	$22	$258
North Dakota	$43	$206
Ohio	$42	$211-294
Oklahoma	$16	$212
Oregon	$60	$259
Pennsylvania	$35-40	$304-312
Puerto Rico	$7	$120
Rhode Island	$41-51	$285-356
South Carolina	$20	$186
South Dakota	$28	$154
Tennessee	$30	$170
Texas	$38	$231
Utah	$14	$230

Figure F.1 (continued)

	Minimum WBA†	Maximum WBA†
Vermont	$26	$192
Virginia	$65	$208
Virgin Islands	$32	$191
Washington	$64	$258
West Virginia	$24	$263
Wisconsin	$43	$230
Wyoming	$38	$200

*These figures are based on Department of Labor figures last revised in January 1992.
†WBA—*Weekly Benefit Amount*. Ranges for minimum and maximum WBAs reflect dependents' allowance and/or disability payments.

G _____

Drug Testing: What Every Employer Should Know

Testing employees for the use of illegal drugs has become a major problem for many employers committed to a "drug-free" work place. Regular, periodic, or random drug testing of employees has become routine, as has discharging employees who test positive for commonly found illegal drugs such as marijuana and cocaine.

If you use a drug-screening or drug-testing procedure or plan to begin using one, you will probably be obliged to discharge any employee who tests positive. In some cases, an employee may quit rather than take a drug test. Some employees may refuse to submit to drug testing and challenge you to take action against them.

This book focuses on winning unemployment insurance cases. In that context, and with that limitation in mind, we provide you with our best advice on how drug testing can be used to win UIC cases.

Legal Drug Usage

Not all drugs are illegal. At one time or another, employees will probably report to work who are using legal prescription medications and over-the-counter preparations for a variety of ills. These drugs may range from aspirin to narcotic pain killers or antidepressant medication. The effects of these drugs may or may not be apparent while the employee is performing his or her work. Many employees feel it is an invasion of privacy for an employer to require that they reveal when they are using medications on the job or what those medications are.

Under special circumstances, some employers require employees to disclose all medication usage. This is especially true in occupations involving the use of potentially dangerous machinery, chemicals, or hazardous equipment that could pose a danger to the employee or others.

The reality of the modern work place requires an employer give the matter of drug testing some thought. Each employer, myriad work situations, and every state pose different scenarios and different problems. We think it is wise and cost effective to consult a qualified attorney or personnel specialist who can help you evaluate your needs with regard to drug policies for your business.

Use and Abuse of Legal Drugs

The fact that an employee has a prescription for a drug or is using an over-the-counter product at work does not mean the employee is home free. Employees are obligated to use prescription and nonprescription drugs according to instructions from a physician or medical professional. If the medication is non-prescription, the employee should follow instructions provided by the pharmaceutical company. Failure to do so may constitute drug abuse and may be considered work-related misconduct.

Use of Illegal Drugs

In most cases, use of illegal drugs at work or reporting to work under the influence of illegal drugs is work-related misconduct. In some cases, merely testing positive for illegal drugs can be work-related misconduct if certain conditions are met.

To establish that an employee was *discharged for misconduct,* you must be able to build a very strong UIC case.

You must show that all employees were informed of the drug-testing procedure and knew the consequences of testing positive on a drug test.

You must show that the test is fairly administered. Your test cannot single out any individual or group of employees for testing. Most employers test all employees, usually on a random, unannounced basis.

In some cases, you may have a good reason for suspecting that an individual is using drugs at work. In cases where there is strong, convincing evidence that a particular individual or group of individuals should be tested, you might single out the individual or group for testing. This is a touchy situation; we recommend that you consult law enforcement authorities or legal counsel.

You must be prepared to establish that the test is well constructed and properly administered. Almost all employers use independent laboratories and testing facilities to conduct their drug tests. Often they are the same companies that conduct pre-employment drug screening. Our recommendation is to hire a reputable drug-testing company to conduct your testing.

For UIC purposes, you must be ready to present a *written report* from the drug company to the local office claims examiner and at any appeal hearing.

You must be prepared to have at least one witness from the drug-testing firm explain the testing procedure, including how the sample (urine, blood, or breath) was obtained. The witness should also be prepared to explain the chain of custody the sample went through to reach the lab.

The *chain of custody* is important to establish that drug-test results are from the sample given by the employee. Most drug-testing firms take urine samples from employees under the supervision of a laboratory employee. Each sample is then sealed in a specimen container for shipment to the lab, which may be in another city. Samples are usually numbered rather than identified by name for confidentiality. Each sealed sample is usually placed in a second container, which is also sealed. Some companies then seal the double container in a shipping package. When the package arrives at the laboratory, a receipt is signed for it and at least two employees open it. They may even sign a document verifying that the seals were intact on arrival.

The next step is to open the sealed containers and divide each sample into two or more subsamples for a "double-blind" or "multiple-blind" test. This means that more than one technician will test each sample without knowing the results of any other technician. This is to minimize the possibility of error or fraud.

The testing firm then writes a report showing what substances they tested for and whether the employee tested positive or negative. If the test was positive, the amount of substance detected should be clearly stated. The document should be signed by a qualified technician or technicians. Some labs require the head of the testing facility, usually an M.D. or Ph.D., to sign the form.

Tip. It is important to have at least one technician and the person who evaluated the findings and signed the lab report available to testify at a UIC hearing. The local UIC office will probably accept the written report and supporting documentation and your information, but the ALJ at the first-level hearing usually wants to question lab personnel directly. This can usually be done by telephone.

Check with representatives of the Office of Appeals *before* the hearing to make certain they will call the lab. You will be responsible for making arrangements and requesting a subpoena to have lab personnel available to testify. It is a good idea to talk to them before the hearing and make sure they understand what you want them to do. To ensure that you are able to obtain witnesses from the lab, you may want to include a provision in your contract that lab witnesses will be available for UIC hearings and other legal proceedings.

You must be prepared to explain to the local office claims examiner and the ALJ how the employee's use of an illegal substance *actually* or *potentially* affected your interests as an employer. In most states, the fact that you have a policy against testing positive on a legitimate drug test is, by itself, not enough to establish misconduct. Judges are wary when it comes to drug testing because of constitutionally protected privacy issues. We suggest using a few of the following arguments to strengthen your case if an employee tests positive.

- The claimant was impaired and could have caused an injury to himself or to others.
- The claimant could have been a danger to others and could have damaged expensive machinery.

If there was evidence that the employee was impaired in any way or acted in an unusual manner, present witnesses to verify that fact. In many cases, employees show no visible signs when they are under the influence of illegal drugs. Sometimes a drug test will be positive for drugs taken days or even weeks earlier. The employee may not actually be impaired when he or she tests positive.

If the claimant did not work around hazardous machinery or equipment, you cannot make a valid argument on this point. However, there are some other points you can make.

- The claimant knew the company rules about testing positive for drugs. The employee violated company rules by using or exposing himself or herself to illegal drugs.
- Drug use creates potential for substandard performance.
- It would be unfair and perhaps impossible to enforce the drug testing rule if some employees were discharged while others are allowed to remain on the job.

Refusal to Take a Drug Test

In some cases, an employee refuses to submit to a drug test. Be sure you have proof that random or specific drug testing was explained to the employee at the time of hire or at the time you began testing.

We strongly urge you to obtain, in writing, the employee's permission and agreement to submit to drug testing. Do this at the time of hire. On the written notice, include a notation that any employee who refuses to submit to drug testing willfully violates a company policy and is subject to immediate disciplinary action up to and including discharge. By following this strategy, you can show the employee intentionally violated a reasonable and uniformly applied company policy by refusing to take the drug test.

Glossary

Able to work. In UIC terms, a claimant's physical or mental ability to work in his normal occupation or at a job for which he is trained and has a reasonable possibility of finding work. Claimants unable to work are generally ineligible for UIC benefits even if the reason for separation from employment qualifies them for benefits.

Adjudication interview. Interview of claimant at local UIC office, designed to gather facts to determine whether claimant is eligible for UIC benefits.

Administrative hearing officer. See *Administrative law judge.*

Administrative law judge (ALJ). Term used by six states to designate individuals who hold first-level appeal hearings. Administrative law judges may also sit on higher-level appeals boards and issue higher-level administrative decisions. They are called by various terms—*referees, examiners, administrative hearing officers,* or *hearing officers.*

Affirmation. When a witness declines to use the word *swear* for religious reasons, the person agrees (affirms) that he or she will tell the truth.

ALJ. See *Administrative law judge.*

Appeals office. First-level appeals office that conducts hearings and renders decisions; it is the next level above the local UIC office. In some cases, term may designate higher-level appeals offices, but those are usually called the *appeals board* or *appeals commission.*

Appellant. Party who has and exercises the legal right to file an appeal; this can change as an appeal works its way through the system. In some states, the UIC office or another state agency may become an appellant. Except in rare cases, the appellant must be an "interested party" to a case and adversely affected by a UIC decision.

Approved training. Training approved by the UIC that allows claimants to attend school (vocational or academic) while collecting benefits. Benefits are charged to an employer's UIC tax account like normal UIC claims. When approved for training, claimants are not usually required to seek or accept work until training or schooling is completed.

Availability for work. Refers to UIC requirement that claimants qualified to receive benefits be *actively* seeking and ready to accept suitable employment. Claimants not actively available for work are generally ineligible for UIC benefits, unless exempted from seeking work by eligibility for approved training.

Base period. Time period during which wage credits for UIC claims are established. Some states use the first four of the last five completed calendar quarters to establish base period. Others use 52 weeks preceding the week in which a UIC claim is opened.

Base-period employer. Employer who appears in a claimant's base period. In most states, you will receive a Notice to Employer when you are the last employer or a base-period employer. Also see *Notice to Employer.*

Brief. Formal document filed with the UIC system to indicate employer or claimant disagrees with a decision and intends to file a higher-level appeal. Also a legal document prepared by a party to serve as the basis for a legal argument in an appeal to an appellate court. Also see *Letter of appeal.*

Burden of proof. Legal term meaning the duty of a party to prove or establish a fact(s) in support of their case. For UIC purposes, burden of proof is carried by the claimant in quits and by the employer in discharges.

Claim. See *Initial claim.*

Claimant's statement. For the purposes of this book, refers to written statement taken from or submitted to the local office claims examiner by the claimant in discharges and quits. In contrast to testimony, claimant's statements are generally not taken or given under oath. Also see *Statement.*

Claims examiner. Local office UIC employee who processes unemployment insurance claims, conducts interview with claimants and employers, and issues quasi-judicial written determinations or decisions involving separations from work, tax charges to employer accounts, and other situations involving UIC benefits. Claims examiners may also be called *adjustment deputies* or *adjudicators.*

Closing statement or argument. Term relating to the optional closing remarks allowed, but not required, at a UIC hearing. Usually a summation or statement of position. It is not evidence. It is designed to persuade the ALJ to rule in favor of the party making it.

Combined wage claim. UIC claim that combines wages transferred from one or more states to generate a valid UIC claim.

Compelling personal reason. Extreme reason that forces an employee to take action for reasons beyond his or her control. For example, an employee may quit a job because of health problems that could endanger his life or permanently damage his health if he does not leave a job after making reasonable attempts to resolve the situation.

Competent testimony. Testimony and evidence that can be accepted and used at a UIC hearing. Usually refers to firsthand or eyewitness testimony or hearsay testimony a witness could reasonably rely on, considering the circumstances. May also refer to expert testimony.

Constructive quit. Refers to an employer "allowing" an employee to resign from a job instead of being fired. For UIC purposes, this type of separation is considered a discharge. Also called a *forced resignation*.

Contemporaneous notes or documentation. Notes made when or shortly after an incident occurs, when events are clearest in note maker's mind. The more contemporaneous the notes, the higher their degree of credibility is likely to be.

Continuance. Break in a UIC hearing; usually longer in duration than a recess. Sometimes continuances mean the parties are unable to complete the hearing by the end of the UIC work day and must return to finish at a later date.

Contradictory testimony. Testimony that disputes or rebuts testimony previously given by another witness.

Credible evidence. Evidence that is consistent and detailed and has a high degree of believability.

Cross-examination. Portion of the hearing in which a party questions the other party's witnesses on the evidence they have given. Leading questions are allowed. Purpose is to test credibility and accuracy of opposing party's evidence or to set foundation for your own witnesses. Also see *Leading question*.

Decision. Written ruling holding for the employer or for the claimant.

Defaulted hearing. Hearing at which *appellant* fails to appear in person, by telephone, or in writing. The ALJ defaults the appellant, ruling in favor of the other party.

Demeanor. Outward behavior or conduct of participants, including dress, responsiveness or evasiveness in answering questions, facial expressions, uncalled for comments or gestures, or anything else that may affect the credibility of a witness.

Direct examination. See *Examination, direct.*

Discharge. Separation from work for misconduct or reasons other than misconduct (but not a layoff) in which the employer is the moving party. Employer bears the burden of proof in establishing misconduct.

Documents. Written evidence submitted at hearings to establish or support points. May include personnel records, warnings, notes, time cards, attendance logs, and other written materials. Contrasts to testimony given orally.

Effective date of claim. Beginning date of a claim, no matter which day of the week the claim is filed. In most states, the effective date of a claim is Sunday of the week the claim is filed.

Eligibility questionnaire. Series of written questions given to claimants at the local office level. Answers help UIC claims examiner determine whether a claimant is eligible to receive benefits.

Employer notice. See *Notice to Employer.*

Equipoise. Case in which the weight of evidence is divided equally (50%–50%). When the employer bears the burden of proof and the case is in equipoise, the employer cannot meet the burden of proof. If the case is a quit and the case is in equipoise, the claimant cannot meet the burden of proof. The party that cannot meet the burden of proof in a UIC case loses. Also see *Burden of proof* and *Preponderance of evidence*.

Evidence. Body of collected facts, including testimony and documents, used to make UIC decisions.

Evidentiary portion of hearing. Portion of the hearing in which testimony is taken and supportive documents are submitted. Contrasts with portions of UIC proceeding in which explanatory and introductory remarks are made, procedural matters are settled, and closing statements are made for the record.

Examination, cross. See *Cross-examination*.

Examination, direct. Portion of the hearing in which a party questions his or her own witnesses by asking nonleading questions. Questions should be restricted to what, where, how, why, and when. Contrasts with cross-examination, in which witnesses can be led by questions and asked to agree or disagree.

Examiner. See *Administrative law judge*.

Experience rating. Rating that determines percentage employer will pay into UIC tax account. Takes into account UIC claims charged to the employer and UIC claims that exempt the employer from tax charges.

Eyewitness testimony. Testimony from a witness who actually observed what occurred. Sometimes called *firsthand knowledge*.

Forced resignation. See *Constructive quit*.

Foundation. Testimony to establish that a witness has sufficient knowledge to answer other, later questions. An example of a question to establish foundation might be, "Did you hear the conversation?" Also background information that establishes facts, such as the existence of a written company policy.

Good cause. Valid reason for an act or acts.

Harassment. Words, gestures, or actions that tend to annoy, alarm, or physically or verbally abuse another person and serve no legitimate purpose.

Hearing. Quasi-legal proceeding in which claimant and employer have an opportunity to present their UIC case before an administrative law judge. Testimony is given under oath, documents may be submitted, and parties may cross-examine each other. After considering all the evidence, the ALJ will issue a written decision that can be appealed by the losing party.

Hearing de novo. Legal (Latin) term for "new hearing." In most states, first-level UIC hearings are *de novo*.

Hearing officer. See *Administrative law judge*.

Hearsay testimony. Testimony from a witness at the hearing based on what he or she heard from another person rather than what he or she personally heard, saw, or experienced. An employer should object to testimony that is meant to establish the truth of what the witness testifying was told by another person who is not being called as a witness. A statement or admission by a *claimant* is not hearsay. Contrasts with firsthand or eyewitness testimony.

Hostile witness. Witness who shows hostility or prejudice to the party who calls him or her as a witness. A hostile witness can be cross-examined by the party who calls him or her.

Initial claim. First claim filed in the claim series or benefit year.

Insured account. UIC tax account that uses an experience rating and quarterly accounting. Account can have an experience rating raised or lowered on the basis of the number of claims charged against it.

Interested party. Party affected by the outcome of a UIC decision. In most cases, interested parties include the claimant, whose benefits are at issue, and the employer, whose tax account may be charged. In some states, the UIC system as a state agency may also be an interested party to UIC decisions.

Interrogatory proceeding. Proceeding in which information and evidence are obtained by asking questions (interrogatory statements test knowledge). Most UIC local office adjudications and all first-level UIC hearings are interrogatory proceedings.

Interstate claim. UIC benefits claim filed against a state other than the state where the claimant is currently residing.

Investigative report. Fact-finding report filed by local office claims examiner, usually notes or summations of what claimant and employer said to the claims examiner. Although considered hearsay, it may contain admissions by the claimant. Because it is filled out by a third party who is theoretically neutral, it is admissible in most UIC hearings.

Judicial notice. Statement made by the judge based on common knowledge or reference information, entered into the record at the UIC hearing, that is considered evidence. For example, the judge may take judicial notice that July 1 was a Friday of the year in question.

Lag quarter. Most recently completed quarter, in states that use the first four of the last five completed calendar quarters to make up the base period. Lag quarter is not usually used to compute benefits for a UIC claim.

Layoff. Separation from employment due to lack of work. Contrasts to separation from work that involves a discharge for misconduct or a quit.

Leading question. Question that instructs or suggests to the witness how to answer. Questions are designed to encourage a witness to agree with the questioner. Also see *Cross-examination.*

Legal objection. Proper objection based on law; made for the record in a UIC hearing.

Letter of appeal. Letter from an interested party (almost always the claimant or the employer) to the appropriate UIC office indicating the party disagrees with the current decision and wants to have the matter heard by a higher-level authority. Also see *Brief.*

Making an objection. See *Objection.*

Misconduct. Willful, intentional (sometimes wanton) acts that are adverse to the business interests of employer. Results in employee's termination from employment. Misconduct can also include omissions or acts of negligence that could have been avoided by exercise of reasonable care and diligence on the part of an employee.

Motion. Request or application to the judge that certain actions be taken or made part of the record. Also an expression of the interested parties that the judge take certain actions in a hearing. For example, the employer may make a motion that time cards be marked and entered as exhibits for the record at a UIC hearing.

Moving party. Party with the power and control to cause the separation from work. When a claimant quits voluntarily, he or she is the moving party. When an employer discharges an employee, the employer is the moving party.

Narrative statements. Open-ended testimony or statements made in response to a question. Statements are not restricted to yes or no answers and may be longer and more involved. Narrative statements are usually allowed at administrative UIC hearings.

New claim. See *Initial claim.*

Notice of appeal. Document showing claimant, employer, or some other legally interested party has filed an appeal to a UIC decision.

Notice of hearing. Formal notice that a UIC hearing has been scheduled for a specific time and date.

Notice to Employer. Written document informing an employer that a UIC claim has been filed by a former employee.

Objection. Verbal protest to challenge or oppose admission of documents or testimony presented by the other party (sometimes the judge) in a UIC hearing or other proceeding.

Offer of proof. Statement offered to establish that a document or testimony is relevant to the issues of a UIC hearing. The ALJ may require the party to explain or show how documents and testimony they intend to enter into the record of hearing are pertinent or why they should be allowed.

Office of appeals. See *Appeals office.*

Postponement. Delay or change in the time and date of a UIC hearing or decision; rescheduling a UIC hearing at the request of one or both parties.

Precipitating incident. Final incident that causes an employer to discharge the claimant or that causes the claimant to quit his or her job.

Preponderance of credible evidence. Greater weight of evidence; favors one party over the other, as evidence is presented in UIC proceedings. Applies to evidence presented from the local office through the highest level of appeal.

Presumptive evidence of separation. Initial evidence used to determine whether a separation is a discharge or a quit. ALJs usually adopt the decision of the local UIC as presumptive evidence, although the judge may find the local office claims examiner was incorrect in deciding the nature of the separation from work.

Probative value. Documents, testimony, and other facts that can establish or prove a position and assist in making decisions in UIC cases.

Quit. Separation from work in which claimant terminates employment voluntarily or is compelled to leave by his or her circumstances.

Recess. Short break in a UIC hearing. Either party may request a short recess to take care of personal business, go to the bathroom, or get a snack. Contrasts with *Continuance.*

Reconsidered determination. Nearly all states provide local UIC offices with the opportunity to reconsider determinations before a local office decision is sent to the first-appeal level. In some states, only decisions that have gone through the reconsideration or review process may be sent to an appeals hearing conducted by an ALJ.

Referee. See *Administrative law judge.*

Reimbursement account. UIC tax accounts available to large nonprofit organizations and educational institutions (school districts, colleges, universities) and government bodies (city governments, county governments, state agencies, federal agencies). Employers reimburse state UIC trust funds on a dollar-for-dollar basis for benefits drawn by former employees. In contrast to insured accounts, reimbursement accounts have no experience rating.

Rules of evidence. General rules that bind UIC local offices and appeals offices regarding admission of testimony and documents. These rules are usually less formal than those used in court proceedings. For example, hearsay testimony is admitted in most states if no eyewitnesses were present. Most states admit photocopied documents rather than original documents for the record.

Statement. Answers to questions given by witness under oath or affirmation before an ALJ.

Stipulations. Facts to which both parties agree. In UIC cases, stipulations are usually made before the judge and entered into the record verbally.

Subpoena. Document issued by appeals office to compel attendance of a witness or production of documents for a UIC hearing or higher-level appeal.

Testimony. Statements given or answers made by a witness under oath or affirmation before an ALJ.

UIC. Unemployment Insurance Compensation. Used interchangeably with *unemployment insurance* and *UI.*

UIC regulations. Set of rules based on laws each state has adopted to control its UIC program. UIC regulations are more specific and more detailed than general rules of law. In some states, these rules may be part of a larger, comprehensive administrative law code.

Weekly benefit amount (WBA). Amount of money claimant is entitled to receive each week.

Bibliography

Arizona Department of Economic Security, *Income Maintenance Manual—Unemployment Insurance Rules and Regulations*, Articles 13–18; Rules R6–3–1301 through R6–3–1812 (1984).

Arizona Revised Statutes, Annotated, Sec. 23–601 through Sec. 23–799; Sec. 12–911; Sec. 41–195 through 41–1994 (1993).

Black, Henry Campbell, *Black's Law Dictionary*, 6th ed., St. Paul: West Publishing Co., 1990.

California Administrative Code and Supplement, Title 22, Sec. 5000–5168 (1990).

Index-Digest of Appeals Board Decisions, July 1989–June 1992.

Department of Economic Security v. Magma Copper Company, 119 Arizona 477, 581 P. 2d 711.

Gardiner v. Arizona Department of Economic Security, 127 AZ 603, 623 P. 2d 033 (App. 1980).

New Mexico Appeals Bureau, *Hearing Information and Instructions for Appeals Hearings*, 1989.

New Mexico Unemployment Insurance Regulations, Sec. 51–1–1 through 51–1–4 (1989).

U.S. Department of Labor. Employment and Training Division. Unemployment Insurance Services. *Comparison of State Unemployment Insurance Laws*. Washington, D.C.: The Bureau, revised January 1992.

Index

ABOUT THE AUTHORS

GABE DONNADIEU represents employers in unemployment insurance compensation matters. Before establishing his own firm, he was a claims examiner, supervisor, investigator, and auditor for the Arizona Unemployment Insurance Program.

ROBERT A. SCHULER, an attorney, served as an administrative law judge for unemployment hearings and has also owned and operated a manufacturing company. He is currently a senior defense attorney for the Arizona State Compensation Fund.

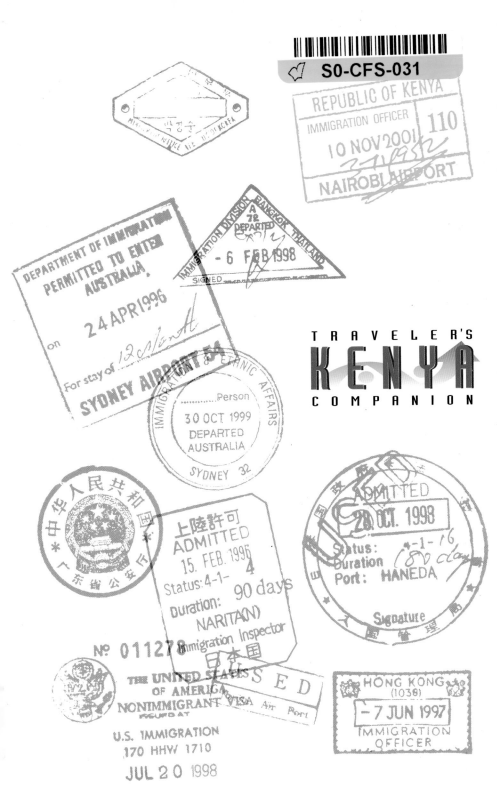

The 2002–2003 Traveler's Companions
ARGENTINA • AUSTRALIA • BALI • CALIFORNIA • CANADA • CHILE• CHINA • COSTA RICA •
CUBA • EASTERN CANADA • ECUADOR • FLORIDA • HAWAII • HONG KONG • INDIA •
INDONESIA • JAPAN • KENYA • MALAYSIA & SINGAPORE • MEDITERRANEAN FRANCE •
MEXICO • NEPAL • NEW ENGLAND • NEW ZEALAND • PERU • PHILIPPINES • PORTUGAL •
RUSSIA • SOUTH AFRICA • SOUTHERN ENGLAND • SPAIN • THAILAND • TURKEY •
VENEZUELA • VIETNAM, LAOS AND CAMBODIA • WESTERN CANADA

Traveler's KENYA Companion

First published 1998
Second Edition 2002
The Globe Pequot Press
246 Goose Lane, PO Box 480
Guilford, CT 06437 USA
www.globe-pequot.com

© 2002 by The Globe Pequot Press, Guilford CT, USA

ISBN: 0-7627-1009-8

Distributed in the European Union by
World Leisure Marketing Ltd, Unit 11
Newmarket Court, Newmarket Drive,
Derby, DE24 8NW, United Kingdom
www.map-guides.com

Created, edited and produced by
Allan Amsel Publishing, 53, rue Beaudouin
27700 Les Andelys, France.
E-mail: AAmsel@aol.com
Editor in Chief: Allan Amsel
Editor: Anne Trager
Picture editor and book designer: Roberto Rossi
Original design concept: Hon Bing-wah
Based on an original text by Peggy Bond and Michael Bond

Printed by Samwha Printing Co. Ltd., Seoul, South Korea

TRAVELER'S
KENYA
COMPANION

by Jack Barker

photographs by Storm Stanley

Second Edition

The
Globe
Pequot
Press

GUILFORD
CONNECTICUT

Contents

T R A V E L E R ' S
KENYA
C O M P A N I O N

SUDAN

Lokichokio
A1

Kakuma
A1

Lodwar

Lorugumo
Lokiriama

Loiya
Lokitanyala
Lokicha

U G A N D A

So
Nati
A1

Sigor

Wagagai
Mount Elgon
National Park
A1   Kitale
C45

Tororo   Webuye
A104
Bungoma   A1
Eldoret
Bumala   Kakamega
C30   Shikondi C39 A104
Ebusongo   B1
Maseno   C36
Nabkoi
Usengi   Akala   Kisumu   Sorget
Asembo   B1   B1
Kendu Bay   C19   A1   Kericho
Lake   Homa Bay   Sondu   Ke
Victoria   Ruma   Oyugis   Er
National
Karungu   Park   Bomet
Kisii   Gorgor
Uriri   Kilkoris   Lemek
A1   C13
Nyarombo   Lolgorien
Nyabikaye   Masai
Tarime   Ntimaru   Mara   Baki
National
Reserve
C

Serengeti
National Park

T A N Z A N I A

LEGEND

Populations
- ◉ **NAIROBI** Capital
- ○ Machakos Cities
- ○ Salama Towns

Transportation
- ═66═ Expressway
- ─── Highways
- ═══ Provincial Roads
- ⋯⋯ Secondary Roads
- ┿┿┿ Railways

Physical Features
- National Parks
- Regional Boundaries
- Lakes & Rivers
- ▲ Mountains & Volcanoes
- 800 m
- ✈ Airports

0   40   80   120   160 km
0   20   40   60   80   100 miles

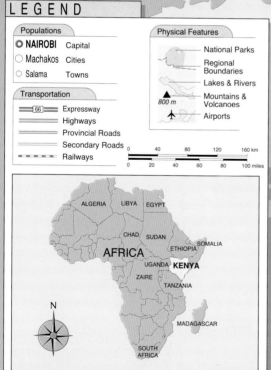

ALGERIA   LIBYA   EGYPT

CHAD   SUDAN
ETHIOPIA   SOMALIA
AFRICA
UGANDA   **KENYA**
ZAIRE
TANZANIA

MADAGASCAR

N

SOUTH
AFRICA

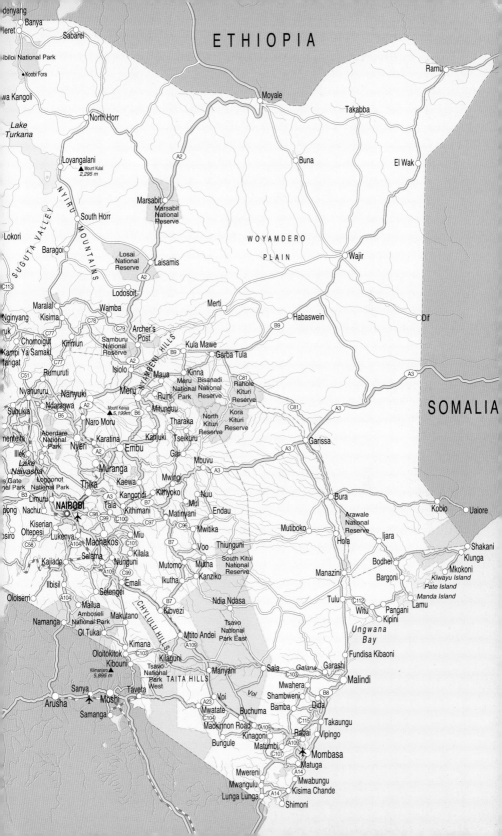

TOP SPOTS

Ride the Lunatic Line

Until the last century Kenya's capital was Mombasa, and Nairobi was just a swamp. What opened up the country's interior was the "Lunatic Line," the railway track laid across the country even before the colonial forces had explored the interior and well before there were any settlers to actually use the railway. In 1896 the first stretches were completed, and for the next three years the track made laborious progress through forest and swamp, across river and mountain. Twenty-eight workers were eaten by lions and countless more died of disease; laborers imported from India were to permanently change the demography of Kenya. By the time the track reached Nairobi, in 1899, sheer exhaustion might have dictated a permanent settlement;

while the railway tracked on to the shores of Lake Victoria and would eventually split off to reach Uganda, the city that is now capital of Kenya took shape.

Nairobi's Railway Museum, on Station Road but best reached by taxi, tells this story, completing the picture with the first trains and carriages to travel the continent.

If the museum experience isn't enough, the railway line itself still provides one of the great train journeys of the world. While road traffic founders in the washed-out surface of the route to the coast, the train runs from Nairobi to Mombasa, every night, in a white-gloved atmosphere of ultimate luxury. For 12 hours — admittedly, sometimes it takes longer — it makes stately progress along the meter-gauge track, passing through Tsavo and down to the steaming flatlands of the coast. Three-course meals prelude nights spent rocked to sleep by the unhurried motion of the ancient train, turned-back linen sheets recreating a golden age of colonial luxury. Dining is on crisp white tablecloths using crockery left over from the colonial era. Sometimes it seems as though the cuisine dates from the same period. Don't expect haute: hope for wholesome.

In first-class compartments just two passengers share a cabin fitted with

OPPOSITE: The Kenya Railway, once nicknamed the Lunatic Express, winds up and down near-vertical Rift Valley escarpments TOP and dashes straight across the flat Tsavo plains BOTTOM. The locomotive used in *Out of Africa* is on display at the Nairobi Railway Museum ABOVE.

washbowl and served by an attentive drinks waiter: families on the move can link two cabins together. Second-class travel puts four to a cabin but is also perfectly acceptable. Third — crammed wooden seats with chickens in the aisles — might be cheap but is not recommended for overnight journeys. And in Kenya almost all rail trips take place at night. First-class tickets cost Ksh3,000 per person and include all meals. The perfectly adequate second-class fares are Ksh2,100 per person. Third-class travel does not include food, a reserved seat, or even a seat of any kind, but only costs Ksh300.

The journey from Nairobi to Kampala in Uganda is significantly longer and crosses one of the few international

borders still with neither electricity nor telephone: the journey takes 24 hours and although the same luxuries are available on board, many travelers find this is just too slow a way of completing a journey that takes eight hours by *matatu*, the packed local minibuses, and one by air. The track east of Nairobi is sometimes washed out and the service doesn't always take passengers.

Reservations are essential for traveling first or second class: reserve the day before, although two or three days in advance is safer, to secure a berth. Without a reservation you'll end up traveling on the benches in third. Reservations can be made in person at Nairobi Station ℂ (02) 221211, one and a half kilometers (one mile) from the city center on Station Road, or at Mombasa Station ℂ (011) 312221, on Haile Selassie Avenue. Reservations are apparently taken by telephone, or perhaps easiest through a travel agent such as Let's Go Travel ℂ (02) 447151 or (02) 441030 FAX (02) 447270 or (02) 441690 E-MAIL info@letsgosafari.com WEB SITE www.letsgosafari.com, Box 60342, Nairobi.

Meet the Past

The prehistory of man is written in the stones of the Rift Valley, and for anyone interested in the birth of mankind, Kenya has archaeological sites and sights galore.

Much of the pioneering excavation that mapped out man's early years was performed by Louis and Mary Leakey. The Rift Valley, which stretches from Ethiopia in the north to Mozambique far to the south, passes down through the length of Kenya, and cradles many of the country's most spectacular lakes. The Leakeys discovered that although the Rift Valley was one of the world's oldest geological structures, comparatively recent volcanic activity had entombed a treasure-house of prehistoric remains and fossils, only now being laid bare by the actions of wind and rain. In many cases, the fossils literally lie on the earth's

surface, just waiting to be picked up and identified.

Some of the Leakeys' most important discoveries were made in Olduvai Gorge in northern Tanzania. However there are plenty of important sites in Kenya, often discovered even more recently and still not fully researched even now. One of the world's densest collections of surface fossils is found in the north of the country, at the Koobi Fora fossil site in Siboloi National Park on the shores of Lake Turkana. Here the combination of lake-floor mud and volcanic eruptions 90,000 years ago has preserved countless animals in pristine fossil form. Just kick away at the ground and every few inches you'll find something.

Recent discoveries of human remains thought to be up to six million years old have thrown the spotlight on the Lake Baringo area and the Tugen Hills. Other sites of interest include Hyrax Hill near Nakuru, a three-hour drive north of Nairobi, home to some of Kenya's earliest inhabitants and still bearing clear traces of their waterside camp and final tomb.

Even closer to Nairobi to the south, within range for a long day-trip or an overnight camping visit, is Olorgasailie,

which is threaded with catwalks, pathways and informative signs, and was inhabited by human beings half a million years ago. Countless hand-axes and animal remains have been uncovered at this site, but so far no human remains have been found. Archaeologists continue their painstaking search.

For the subsequent 500 millennia, pastoral Kenyans trod lightly on the earth and left little trace of their tranquil way of life. Exceptions to this include the coast, where Swahili settlers left stone mosques and villages. Perhaps the best of these are Gedi Ruins at Watamu. This almost complete Swahili village dates back to the fourteenth century, bigger and better than Jumba la Mtwana near Mombasa. Gateway to Kenya's colonial past, Mombasa's most atmospheric sight is Fort Jesus, symbol of the quite justified paranoia of the first years of colonial occupation, and finally stormed by Omani forces from the Middle East.

OPPOSITE: A million-and-a-half-year-old skull TOP of *Homo erectus* is displayed at the archaeological site of Koobi Fora on the shores of Lake Turkana. Fort Jesus, Portugal's toehold BOTTOM on the coast of East Africa. ABOVE: The Chuka dancers of the Meru area.

But sometimes it seems the past is still there, an integral part of everyday life. Sail-powered wooden dhows trade up and down the coast, while inland, wandering spear-carrying tribesmen track across vast plains. In Africa the far past is a timeless part of the present.

Take to the Skies

In the cool morning half-light, the roar of the burners heated the air and drove color into the billowing folds of the balloon's spreading canopy. Soon it rose, half-willing and wobbling, into the still air and caught the first rays of the sun on it's upper crescent. Gradually the basket lost weight on the ground and, trembling, strained against the ropes, before smoothly and silently taking to the air.

As the yellow light of dawn lit up the tips of low brush, the balloon glided over the steep banks of the Mara River and out over the open savannah. Peaceful herds of grazing game — wildebeest and zebra, gangling giraffes and purposeful, padding lions — could be seen in the grass far below. A blast on the burner and a family of elephants scattered, suddenly scared,

trumpeting and kicking dust-trails far below. In silence we glided on, over the endless plains of the Masai Mara, sheltered by the distant shades of the mountains of the Rift Valley. Binoculars brought the ground up close as the sun warmed the morning air and bled color into the tranquil scene. Whether dropping low for a closer view or drifting high for Africa's full panorama, the views were magical and the experience serene.

With all ballooning, things start moving quickly when it is time to land. As we dropped towards the ground we were suddenly aware that the gentle breeze, imperceptible at height, was moving us along quite quickly. With a few crisp commands in a broad American accent, our pilot settled us into brace positions on low benches and told us to hold tight to sturdy internal ropes. Striking the ground we turned on our side and dragged for a while as the basket flexed on stones and rocks, until finally we came to a halt. As the balloon collapsed onto the plain we scrambled gratefully clear and in a few minutes we were sipping at the day's first glass of bubbly while a lavish cooked breakfast was being prepared.

the Masai Mara would require two flights or several days on the road, the Hilton runs ballooning safaris from Salt Lick Lodge in the Taita Hills, which is much more convenient and even a few dollars cheaper. Their reservations department in Nairobi ((02) 334000 FAX (02) 339462 can take reservations — although they don't always realize this immediately.

Try Out a Treetop Lodge

About midnight, a shape moved slowly in from the forest beyond the lights. At first, it seemed a shadow, but it moved with the authority of the great cats, lethal but extraordinarily beautiful, tan-golden and huge. It was a young lioness, her body glimmering in the lights as she lithely picked her way through grass and brush upwind toward an unsuspecting bushbuck. She reached the last clump of brush that could shield her, the bushbucks only 20 m (60 ft) away, and crouched to wait, only her pointed ears visible above the bush.

Kenya led the way in bringing the night-time game to a wider audience with Treetops Lodge, famous as where Princess Elizabeth was staying when she learned she'd become Queen of England. These days Treetops is nowhere near any trees, as deforestation has taken its toll, but, along with The Ark, still offers overnight game-viewing over their own floodlit waterholes. Although it might seem a bit artificial, the animals are thoroughly habituated, and this can provide some of the most exciting game-viewing experiences in the country.

At The Ark, which is located in the mist forests, you enter along a 100-m-long (330-ft) catwalk and the gate closes behind you, remaining so until your departure the next morning. The order of the day and night? Quiet voices inside and whispers only on the open balconies

Kenya's climate is ideally suited to ballooning, at least in the timeless savannas of the Masai Mara. Unlike Europe, where fickle weather often means flights have to be canceled at short notice, in the Masai Mara mornings are almost invariably calm and cool, perfect for raising these fragile airships. And there is no better way to appreciate the full beauty of the African bush than from the still platform of a viewing basket, suspended high over the heads of some of the world's most exotic animals.

Ballooning in Kenya isn't cheap. It costs about US$380 per person for seats in a 12- or 18-seater basket, although this might be less expensive if reserved in advance through an overseas operator. Three companies offer ballooning in the Masai Mara. Adventures Aloft ((02) 221439 FAX (02) 332170, Box 40683, Nairobi, runs flights from Fig Tree Camp; Balloon Safaris Ltd. ((02) 502850 FAX (02) 501424, Box 43747, Nairobi, takes off from Keekerok Lodge; and Mara Balloon Safaris Ltd. ((02) 331871 FAX (02) 217416, Box 48217, Nairobi, flies from Governors Camp.

Although ballooning has been tried in other areas, it has never been quite as successful. In Samburu, thorns ripped the canopies to pieces and the only place to land the balloon safely turned out to be in the river, which irritated passengers, hippos and crocodiles. For travelers based on the coast, for whom

OPPOSITE AND FOLLOWING PAGES: A balloon safari provides breathtaking panoramas on a grand scale. ABOVE: Walkways bring the Gura Falls into view in the Aberdares.

and catwalk. Any variety of animals are likely to be grazing, drinking at the pool or eating at the salt lick on your arrival, and sightings are listed in vast ledgers that record the waterhole's status over the years. Buffaloes, giant forest hogs and the resident pair of Egyptian geese greeted us. The hotel's 30 years of statistics show a 50 percent chance of sighting a lion, 88 percent for an elephant, 40 percent for a rhinoceros (probably lower now), 20 percent for a leopard (baited), and two percent for the rare bongo. Buffaloes, baboons, bushbucks, and cute bushbabies are almost guaranteed.

About 6:30 PM, the staff feed the birds along the catwalk. It is a colorful sight — yellows, bright greens, red, orange, and iridescent blue. Thanks to Mike Clifton, our on-duty naturalist, we learned to spot golden-winged and eastern double-collard sunbirds, African rock martins, the pesky speckled mousebirds, and several varieties of weavers, montane warblers, streaky seedeaters, yellow-vented bulbuls, and olive thrush. He identified many more, far too many to remember them all.

Spotted and black genet cats, which are actually in the weasel family, usually chase the birds, and mongooses arrive to pick up the scraps that fall to the ground. At nightfall, cuddly and quite brazen bushbabies arrive to stay until the early morning hours, keeping those who remain awake company. They may try to follow you indoors, tug on your clothes, or sit beside you on a bench. After dark, activity picks up at the salt lick and floodlights are turned on. During the night we were there buffaloes were constantly present. We were also visited by a bull elephant, by forest hogs who were chased away by the buffaloes, by a spotted hyena who just waltzed through, by a white-tipped mongoose and by the 50 or so bushbucks who were continually harassed by the lioness.

Buffaloes drove the bushbucks nearer the lioness. One, a young female, ended up less than 10 m (30 ft) from the feline. Still the lioness waited patiently, knowing the bushbuck's leaping agility and speed. The wind changed, carrying the lion's scent; several bushbuck barked an alarm call, and the herd nervously sidled away, peering toward the darkness.

For the next two hours, the lioness lay motionless as the bushbucks edged nearer and scampered away, hungry for the grass but suspicious. Finally, she made a dash at one and missed, and they all bounded into the forest. Until nearly 4 AM, we could hear their sharp barks as she stalked them down the mountainside.

Experience a Camel Safari

The gentle pace of a strolling camel provides one of the best ways to experience Kenya's wildlife and spectacular landscapes, and no animal could be better suited to a long journey through the bush. First, ships of the desert are very strong, and a single camel can carry a load that will keep the average hiker living in luxury. They don't need to spend most of their days eating and drinking, and can keep going as long — or rather longer — than their human keepers. And finally, they form a comfortable steed — with a refreshingly high viewpoint. Ride sidesaddle for maximum comfort.

A camel's long range can take riders far from roads and civilization, and generally a camel safari will only be slightly more expensive than the equivalent lodge-based trip, with comforts varying according to your exact requirements. Simple safaris get close to nature with fly-camps and meals around the flames of a campfire. Vehicle assistance is needed if you want to arrive each evening to a pre-erected luxury camp with East African walk-in tents and en-suite bucket showers.

Yet another advantage of a camel safari is the real chance to get to know the local people. Most camel handlers are Samburu warriors (*morans*) and know the land. It's always useful to have a *moran*

OPPOSITE: Three zebras TOP watch as camels BOTTOM drink.

along, partly because they don't get lost but also because lions are scared of these braided men in red. *Morans* also act as guides, knowing most of the people along the way, including children too small to acknowledge, busy attending to father's cattle, young warriors striding through the bush looking for something to kill, or elderly women, leaning on sticks, tracing lonely tracks across vast spreading plains.

On my first day out on a camel safari, I met a newly circumcised brave, dressed in black, plastered with ash and with a dead bird tied round his head. At night, after putting up my complex and cumbersome tent, my Samburu *moran*, called Tched, simply rolled up his ochered braid of hair, folded himself flat on his back, pulled his red blanket up over his eyes, and went immediately to sleep, straight as a pole.

There are specialist companies that offer camel safaris, almost invariably in the arid north of the country. Probably the cheapest of the established operators is Yare Safaris Ltd. (/FAX (02) 214099

E-MAIL yare@africaonline.co.ke, Box 63006, Nairobi, based two kilometers (slightly over a mile) south of Maralal on the Nyahururu–Nairobi Road, with prices starting at around US$500 per person for seven days; longer trips are possible. More upmarket operators include Desert Rose Camel Safaris ((02) 228936 FAX (02) 212160, Box 44801, Nairobi, which operates eight-day safaris around the Lake Turkana area from their beautiful lodge in the northern Rift Valley, and Simon Evans, who runs safaris around the Ewaso Ngiro River in Samburu district: make reservations with Let's Go Travel ((02) 447151 or (02) 441030 FAX (02) 447270 or (02) 441690 E-MAIL info@letsgosafari.com WEB SITE www.letsgosafari.com, Box 60342, Nairobi. More casual safari experiences can also be undertaken at any small town in the north: the cheapest safari experience I've ever been offered was a US$10-a-day proposition from an unemployed Turkana graduate trailing three borrowed donkeys around the village of Baragoi, north of Maralal.

Ride the Rapids

One man has done more than any other to open up inland Kenya to the world of whitewater rafting, and that is Mark Savage, who — between taking expeditions scaling the peaks of Kenya's mountains — has run his zodiacs along the lengths of every navigable river in Kenya, and a few that aren't.

Regular clients include the British Army, for whom he trains instructors, but trips are usually tailored to the requirements of his clients, from first-timers to experienced rafters. One-day trips take place on the Tana River, starting from Nairobi. One option starts with three kilometers (two miles) of class II and III whitewater, followed by six kilometers (four miles) of calm scenic river (paddling) before completing the day with an exhilarating six kilometers (four miles) of fast class IV and V rapids.

Alternatively, a quieter day has been tailored to the requirements of ornithologists: a scenic, bird-filled float of three to four hours over eight kilometers (five miles) of river within easy reach of Nairobi. At least 100 species of bird have been regularly spotted by the guides on this stretch of the Tana, who are fully trained to identify fast-flitting rarities. Another one-day trip runs the length of the Muthoya North River for a distance of 22 km (nearly 14 miles) and a drop of over 450 m (1,450 ft). The water is not very big — the river is narrow and low-volume — but technically very difficult; lunch and drinks are carried on board the zodiac inflatables, so everybody prays that it won't capsize, at least until the afternoon.

For whitewater enthusiasts, or anyone wanting a different "take" on Kenya, longer trips are also available. The Athi River is raftable from near Nairobi all the way to the coast — a distance of 450 km (280 miles) that takes 21 days, and can be

OPPOSITE LEFT: Samburu *morans* are great camel handlers. RIGHT: Lions in Samburu National Reserve establish a licking order. BELOW: Brownwater rafting on the Ewaso Ngiro River.

combined with walking and caving in the Chyulu Hills. However it's the first 80-km (50-mile) stretch of the Athi River that is most popular: three days combining medium-grade whitewater with the sights and sounds of a scenic stretch of the river. Much of the time the launches run along the borders of Tsavo East, and wildlife abounds: bushbucks, giraffes, buffaloes and elephants are frequently seen, while crocodiles and prolific bird life are constant companions.

Talk to Mark Savage though and it's clear he has one particular favorite: the three-day trip rafting the Ewaso Ngiro River. This starts west of Barsalinga with a roller-coaster 35 km (22 miles) over almost continuous rapids. Extensions to this trip can continue east for a further 100 km (62 miles), through Samburu National Reserve and up to Chandler's Falls in Shaba National Reserve. All along the way game abounds: even lions have been spotted during rushed glances from the bucking platform of the paddling zodiac. For safety reasons, two boats are the minimum to run this route, with four people on each, but often Mark Savage is able to combine two or more groups to make this experience possible for smaller groups.

The lower age limit for whitewater rafting is 14, with parental consent, but there's no upper limit: it depends on individual health and fitness. Old 40-year-olds have found it hard, while a 72-year-old grandmother new to the sport was a complete convert and booked again. Full safety equipment, including lifejackets and crash helmets, are supplied and must be worn. Camp is on scenic points along the river, with two-person dome tents, airbeds and sleeping bags provided. Perishables are carried in a freezer trailer, along with soft drinks and beer, and while lunch is cold and casual, dinner has five courses, all cooked over a wood fire. May, June, July and November, December, and January are the best months, as rafting is dependent on water levels, but there can be too much water for some routes. In any case, rafting trips run year-round on one river

or another. Rates start at US$95 for a full day's rafting from Nairobi, including meals, beer and transport. Contact Savage Wilderness Safaris Ltd. (/FAX (02) 521590 WEB SITE www.kilimanjaro.com, Thigiri Road, Box 44827, Nairobi.

Game Fishing

Suddenly the twin caterpillar engines cut and the tubby boat wallowed to a halt. In the silence, the racing of the reel, letting line out into the ocean, was loud. One of the rods was taut and trembling. We had a bite. The air filled with shouts and activity. A crewman pushed me towards the rod, the 36-kg (80-lb) line

spinning out from the Shimano reel. While I pulled at the rod to strike the fish, two deckhands feverishly reeled in a kilometer of line from the other eight rods, clearing the way for me to play the fish. My rod, friction reel whirring out line, jumped and fought my arms as I was ushered into the "fighting seat," a racked wooden chair built out of rough-cut planks and sturdy metal fitments. It looked rather like an early dentist's homemade treatment chair.

A sailfish, blue and glittering graceful, broke the surface of the ocean 275 m (900 ft) behind our slackening boat with a sun-glinting splash. In a desperate attempt to break free of the one-inch hook, it had flipped into the air to try to void its stomach. The fish was getting tired. I started to haul in, taking the strain by pumping the rod, reeling in as I dipped the tense, bowed tip.

The sailfish crescented above the surface again, sail flashing lower and tired, and I kept reeling in. In the final moments the silver-sided form could be seen weaving exhausted below the stern of the boat, and then deckhands were pulling at the line, maneuvering the sailfish into position so they could grab its bony bill with thick protective gloves, remove the hook from its mouth and insert a tag. It wasn't a record-breaker —

Lake Victoria's Nile perch can take some landing. It can be useful to have some local help.

about 35 kg (77 lbs) — but it was my first game fish, and a lot taller than me. As my moment of glory faded, the deckhand took over an even more important job: sluicing water through the exhausted fish, waving its bony snout in the warm oxygenated surface layers to get the fish's powerful tail muscles working again. Once revived, it was pushed free and I watched the silvery-blue shape snake off at a tangent to the safety of the deep.

Most of Kenya's better operators have caught up with environmental considerations, and now feature the tag-and-release program, where instead of being killed and weighed the fish are fitted with a small identifying tag and released back into the wild. Game fishing, though, will never be a sport for the softhearted. The trauma of being towed around the ocean on the end of a hook will always prove fatal to some fish. On the day I was fishing, one of the three sailfish caught had been hooked in the gills and had no chance of survival. Meanwhile a 16-kg (35-lb) wahoo was destined for the pot. Swordfish, famous fighters now being caught at night in Kenya by boats trailing diving-light lures, often die of exhaustion in their struggle.

But you don't have to catch a big game fish to experience the thrill of fishing. And the best outing I had was where I caught least. "In America they'd laugh at you for going fishing in a boat like this," Ken Adcock, son of Mombasa fishing legend James Adcock, told me as we set off in a seven-meter (20-ft) canoe built from mango wood in a timeless, narrow, deep design. Rolling on the swell a couple of miles offshore, we powered after horizon specks of flocked feeding birds, slowing to approach as they dive-bombed, speckling the water with white splashes as they hunted bite-sized shoals of fry. Below the water would be the ocean carnivores: tuna and snapper, chased in turn perhaps by sailfish and shark. Stressed by their position halfway up a food chain, any of these fish might be panicked into mistaking our lures for an exotic snack.

Each shoal would drop away as our boat shadowed close. So there was only time for one cast, maybe two, before the fish moved to the deep and birds wheeled off to another bit of ocean. Standing insecure on the rocking canoe we flicked our rods to send crazy-colored rubber squid across the water, winding in, frantic and fast, the hooks skimming and splashing across the choppy waves. A bite: my line went tight and I started to reel in. My red rubber octopus had caught a myopic dorado. Three kilos (seven pounds) only, but this time, I felt, caught with skill. And anyone who seriously considers tagging and releasing a dorado has never really worked up a decent appetite.

Fishermen in Kenya are spoiled for choice. Bad times for offshore fishing are May, June and (in the north) July, when rough sea conditions mean the boats can't clear the fringing reef and many operators close their doors. Even at this time of year there's still fly-fishing in the rivers streaming off Mount Kenya, especially for browns and rainbows in the Burguret and Nanyuki rivers; you can rent fly tackle at the Naro Moru River Lodge. For lake fishing, upmarket lodges at Mfangano and Rusinga islands in Lake Victoria offer full equipment to hunt down Nile Perch. And you can always go native. Local boats might lack sophisticated tackle, but plenty of Kenyans live off the waters of lakes Turkana, Naivasha and Baringo. It's a great way to settle in to the Kenyan pace: just make sure the boat you rent isn't likely to sink.

Brush up Your Birding

Few countries are as rewarding as Kenya for bird watching. And one of the best places to settle down with binoculars is at Lake Baringo. Flat waters, dotted with floating cabbage, are home to countless species, including Humprick's hornbill.

A Goliath heron feeds on a shoreline in Nairobi National Park.

On my last visit, I caught sight of a group of colorful Madagascan bee-eaters. Hyrax clamber round the Baringo Cliffs while kingfishers dip into the waters of the lake. Boats paddle carefully in shallow waters, a constant haunt of hidden hippos, who seem to get annoyed at the beat of engines. Resident ornithologist at Lake Baringo Lodge (reservations through Block Hotels ((02) 535412-4 FAX (02) 545954 WEB SITE www.blockhotels.com), Stephen Heparsa-Laach, told me not to be concerned. "The hippos at Naivasha are far more aggressive."

A pity and a worry. Naivasha might not be as quiet and remote as Baringo, but the bird life is just as prolific, as at all the flamingo-pinked lakes that glow blue along the floor of the Rift Valley. And Kenya has plenty of different habitats, from swamp to desert to coastal wetland regions. The enthusiastic birder will find different species on the hot humid coast, on the open savannas, in the inland forest and swamps and around tall mountain peaks. Whether predator or prey, all Kenya's birds share exceptional beauty and aerial grace.

For the determinedly red-blooded, there's one further sport these birds can provide. In the Galana River area, just outside the borders of Tsavo East National Park, you can make reservations for vacations with Hemingways ((0122) 32624 FAX (0122) 32256 WEB SITE www.hemingways.com, Box 267, Watamu, and go out to their tented camp. In the bright light of dawn, you can walk out from your luxury camp into the bush, admire the thrilling sound of these beautiful birds' morning song, wonder at the flash of their feathers, lift your rented gun, and blast them from the sky.

Specific bird-watching specialist companies include Bateleur Safaris ((02) 227048 FAX (02) 891007, Mezzanine Floor, Hilton Building, Mama Ngina Street, Box 42562, Nairobi, and the rather more expensive East African Ornithological Safaris ((02) 331191 or (02) 222075 FAX (02) 330698 or (02) 216528 E-MAIL eaos @africaonline.co.ke WEB SITE www.savannah camps.com, P.O.Box 48019, Eleventh Floor, Fedha Towers, Standard Street, Nairobi. Birders arriving in Nairobi might want to call Nature (previously the East Africa Natural History Society) ((02) 749957 or (02) 741049, Box 4486, who operate bird walks at 8:45 AM every Wednesday, meeting at the National Museum.

Meet the Animals

It's all very well seeing Kenya's game, but sometimes it's tempting to make contact that much closer. There are a couple of opportunities to get close to Kenya's wildlife. In Nairobi's Giraffe Sanctuary ((02) 891658 endangered Rothschild's giraffes lean over to extend long gray tongues to slurp up afternoon tea: cattle nuts, held out on flat palms. Travel north to Nanyuki and Laikipia, where Sweetwaters camp is home to a tame rhinoceros. Once orphaned by poachers, he now thinks he's a pet, trundling around after guests like a big — very big — dog; he likes having his stomach tickled. Book Sweetwaters through Lonhro ((02) 216940 FAX (02) 216796, Box 58581, Nairobi (US$205 per double, full board): it's just about close enough for an overnight visit. At a more modest outlay of time and money, Nairobi's Maasai Ostrich Farm ((0150) 22505/6 lets you get close to these ungainly birds, and on Sunday afternoons you can

ride them. If the ride gives you an appetite, you can always tuck into an ostrich steak at the Carnivore Restaurant ((02) 602993, around the corner on Langata Road.

Race to Victory

My camel lay like a large desert iceberg, legs concertinaed in the dust. "Hello, Charlie," I said and wondered if I should pat him on the head. Languidly Charlie turned around and gave me a camel's gaze of indifferent contempt, chewing slowly. I wondered if he'd spit. Or maybe bite. Irritated by some small bite he shook his head violently and I jumped back.

Then Tched, the camel handler, pulled on the ropes attaching the loose bundle of sticks and foam rubber laughingly called a saddle. Charlie brayed in irritation, giving me a grandstand view of enough teeth to scalp a hairdresser and an insider's shot of his latest meal. "Don't annoy him," I advised Tched, who smiled shyly. He was an ochered Samburu warrior who hardly spoke Swahili let alone English. He planted his foot against Charlie's flank, pulled harder, and this time I was sure I could

OPPOSITE: An elephant meets an olive baboon at Amboseli National Park. ABOVE: Saddling up for the Camel Derby. FOLLOWING PAGES: Feeding time for orphan rhinos.

hear some serious irritation in Charlie's anguished bray. Tched stood back, indicating I should climb on. It was time to race.

I had signed up to ride in the Camel Derby at Maralal in northern Kenya, which takes place every year in July. Originally started to educate the locals about the environmental advantages of camels in this harsh land, it is nothing like the competitive Middle Eastern races with professional 11-year-old jockeys and pedigree steeds. In Maralal, the name of the game is endurance and anyone can play. I had entered the 10-km (six-mile) amateur category. The night before, I'd ridden a camel for the first time.

Reluctantly I scrambled aboard and began a slow lurching ascent. Against a background of shouted orders and flicking switches, Charlie unfolded long joints, heaving up at the front, and then high at the back. I was tipped forward in my seat, perched insecurely looking down on an audience of Samburu tribesmen who scattered clear in case I fell off on them. More shouts and a final heave: Charlie straightened his front legs and my seat flattened out, leaving me two and a half meters (eight feet) in the air. It seemed much more and the ground a long way down.

For a minute Charlie appeared to be reconsidering his original decision to stand, until Tched applied a stick and we

lurched off. With a certain ungainly grace, Charlie strolled up to the starting line before a thousand spectators: groups of tribesmen looked on from under shady trees while women and children, festooned in beads, hung onto the fences that kept spectators and racers apart.

Fewer than half the racers in the amateur race were foreigners; they included a 10-year-old boy, an American woman in her seventies, an Australian television journalist and a couple of overlanders.

A brief countdown was lost in the background noise and the race was underway. One camel set off in the wrong direction, and a few others, including Charlie, showed no particular urge to go anywhere, but in a minute or two we all thundered down the track between cheering (or were they laughing?) spectators.

We raced along the dirt road from Yare Safari Camp, down and through the town of Maralal, a Wild West scene of clapboard houses and shady verandahs, and back. Charlie was clearly aware he was in for a long haul and shambled off at a gentle trot.

Camel psychology is still a closed book to me. Camels only need food or drink every few days, and Charlie showed none of a horse's enthusiasm for the road home. I muttered endearments, encouragement, and threats, but he didn't seem to speak English. I watched the camel in front, shuffling along on feet the size of dinner plates, running like two tired knock-kneed men jammed into a pantomime suit. It was getting further away. I looked over my shoulder. The competition was falling back too. Psychology was cast to the wind as the race became a battle of wills, my acacia whip flailing against his tough hide, my voice wearing hoarse with continual threats and entreaties which fell on large, indifferent ears. I kept him trotting — barely.

Fifty minutes after I'd started, Charlie lolloped over the finishing line, to rapturous applause from the crowd whose enthusiasm didn't seem to have been diminished by 11 camels before me. Charlie sank to the ground and I tottered about on rubber legs, while occasional bursts of applause indicated the arrival of another racer. The 10-year-old boy had come third and I thought I'd done quite well to finish. Out of 25 starters, 19 made it across the finishing line. Despite the fact no riders wore protective helmets — Kenya, after all, is a land of adventure — there had been no casualties.

The Camel Derby brings together half the country's tourist industry in a convivial, off-duty mood. A tented town makes the camp look rather like a luxury refugee camp, humming with life and a great place to make contacts.

In the aftermath on Monday, the overland trucks threaded off in various directions and the tents were dismantled, packed and dispatched to Nairobi and beyond. Once more birdsong could be heard in the Safari Camp and herds of zebra grazed closer. A small group of travelers set off on a camel trek lasting days or maybe weeks. For another year the Camel Derby was over.

Maralal is 350 km (217 miles) north of Nairobi, the road paved for much of the way. Allow five hours by fast car, or a day by *matatu*, changing at Nyahururu. To get the dates of the next Camel Derby, call Yare Safaris Ltd. (/FAX (2) 214099 E-MAIL travelkenya@iconnect.co.ke, Box 63006, Nairobi.

Track the Migration of the Wildebeest

Every year, by some mass instinct, the Masai Mara sets the scene for one of nature's greatest wonders: the migration of the wildebeest. On some unspoken signal, many millions of these animals, broad-shouldered and slim-hipped, crowned with powerful horns, start off on a long and hazardous trek between Kenya's Masai Mara and Tanzania's adjoining Serengeti Plains. In endless lines they flood through the bush, trailed by lions, following instincts that have driven their movements since time immemorial.

Although at any time of year the Masai Mara is one of the only places in Africa to see the dense herds of game that once covered Africa before the arrival of man, concentrations build up to inconceivable levels when the annual migration happens. The exact timing depends on the weather, but every year, sometime between July and September, over a million wildebeest and hundreds of thousands of zebras arc through the Masai Mara National Reserve in uncountable crowds on their circuit around the plains of the Serengeti, following the rains in search of fresh pastures. Some predators trail, others lie in wait. The wildebeest add up to nine million kilos (20 million pounds) of meat to the park's predators through their long trek. Perhaps the best place to watch the drama of this natural wonder is on the banks of the Mara River, as nervous animals rush in a panicked crossing of the crocodile-filled waters. At this time of year all the Mara's predators are fat and contented, while the wildebeest mow down the lush wet-season growth of long savannah grass.

The Masai Mara is best reached by air from Nairobi, although if traveling on a budget there are plenty of operators who arrange transportation by road. Contact Let's Go Travel ((02) 447151 or (02) 441030

OPPOSITE: The start line LEFT and trouble at the finish RIGHT.

FAX (02) 447270 or (02) 441690 E-MAIL info @letsgosafari.com WEB SITE www.letsgo safari.com, Box 60342, Nairobi, or choose any of the operators listed in TAKING A TOUR, page 76, to arrange your visit. See THE MASAI MARA, page 145, for details on the Mara camps and lodges.

Rave It Up at Lake Turkana

I stared at the sunset. On either side, red, but the center was dyed a brilliant jade. It was the Jade Sea, Lake Turkana, reflected in the sky. I'd never seen anything like it. I'd been dragged from the high-street restaurant where a sign painted on the wall said, "We give you the best service no matter how long it takes" and out on the street. But my new friends had no interest in waiting for service, however good, nor in looking at the sky.

"Come on. We'll miss the film." My companions were impatient. "It's *Demetrius the Greek.*" By way of encouragement they recited whole scenes from memory, filled me in on the plot. They pulled me away from the sunset. "How tall are you?"

The Catholic mission has the television. Every Sunday they fire up the generator, plug in the video, and point the screen out through a doorway. A sea of 150 little faces, cross-legged, gazed up into the cathode glare: adolescents, strictly ranked by height, had a more distant view, and I worked out why I'd been asked my height as I squinted at the dated colors of a very old movie. Gasps followed every blow, giggles every kiss. Well, not so much followed. Often a voice from the crowd would beat the actor to their lines, and everyone knew each twist of the simple plot. Heroic Christians wow dissolute Romans. Then Chartlon Heston froze as the video broke down. The audience, chattering excitedly, didn't seem disappointed or surprised. Without hanging around in the hope of any repair they flooded out of the mission compound and split into countless paths that traced the stony ground, home to their clustered *manyattas* — reed or mud dwellings.

Soon the sounds of chanting echoed across the desolate landscape from clusters of round Turkana huts. There wasn't much moon, but the stars gave plenty of light. I followed faint trails, silver threading through the piled boulders of a barren land, and I discovered the locals don't mind spectators. In circles they chanted out traditional songs, while the men danced, pogo-ing across a charmed circle of spectators, in competitive groups or taking huge solo leaps, men singing and bare-breasted women helping the chorus. Shyly the women clapped and assisted, subordinate but interested, especially in the highest jumpers. I asked a spectator to translate the lyrics, expecting tales of romance and love. Far from it. All the

songs were about cattle, cows with large humps, bulls with nice horns.

Which was rather sad. In the desolate rocky wasteland that was home to these Turkana, the land isn't rich enough to support many animals. A few goats were the limit of most people's wealth and the constant complaint amongst young men is that the cost of a new bride is far beyond their means. But dancing the night away costs nothing, and until Turkana girls get married they're free to flirt as much as they like. I slipped away at about 10 PM. Early. From all directions the sound of private parties continued well into the night.

This scene was at Loyangalani on the shores of Lake Turkana, a stiff 12-hour drive or charter flight north of Nairobi.

However, through much of rural Kenya every weekend is a celebration. Where there's electricity there are concerts of local music and thumping discos held by overloaded speakers. And beyond the reach of mains power, where a white face is a novelty, the people are invariably pleased to welcome visitors to far more elemental festivities, the very different traditional dances of very traditional societies. One thing that can blunt this natural welcome though is a photographic camera or video. With such cultures it is easy to give offense, and the easiest way to do so is to take a picture.

Crossing time for wildebeest on their annual migration in the Masai Mara.

YOUR CHOICE

Most visitors will spend the better part of their visit in Kenya's national parks. The **Masai Mara** is, without doubt, the best of all in terms of the sheer numbers of animals seen. Joined across the unfenced border with Tanzania's Serengeti National Park, it has unbeatable concentrations of plains game, trailed by plenty of predators. It provides some of the best game viewing at all times of the year (especially during the wildebeest migration see TRACK THE MIGRATION OF THE WILDEBEEST, page 31 in TOP SPOTS) and also has some of the best lodges, maintained by a constant stream of visitors. This park is usually put at the end of any tour of Kenya to makes sure the safari ends on a high note.

Well-served by flights from Nairobi, **Amboseli** is a small park set around a swamp, with the brooding mass of snow-capped Mount Kilimanjaro providing a dramatic backdrop (when clear of cloud). In the dry seasons (from July to September and January to April) huge herds of elephants can be found around the central swamp, and the plains can be atmospheric as they are tracked by whirlwinds kicking up the dust in baby tornados. Since most of the trees have died (either because of salinity in the soil or from being pushed over by ellies) it is sometimes just a little bit desolate.

The Great Outdoors

For many visitors, Kenya *is* the great outdoors. Sun-baked bush stretches as far as the eye can see, mountains glow blue on the far horizon. Exotic animals graze on thorny bushes, predators wait to pounce … and that's the problem. Hungry wild animals keep many visitors to Kenya confined to their four-wheel drives, nervously watching the drama of the bush through the safe hatch in the roof of their vehicle. Unlike some other African countries, walking is not permitted in most of Kenya's national parks for the simple reason that there's too much game; the outdoor experience will generally be spent peering out of the viewing panel cut into the roofs of most safari vehicles.

OPPOSITE: Shaba National Reserve is one of Kenya's least visited. ABOVE: Normally placid, this elephant is starting to get twitchy.

Tsavo was the prime game area before the Masai Mara appeared on the international scene. It is by far Kenya's largest park, and is divided into two parts by the main Nairobi/Mombasa Road. **Tsavo West** is to the south of the road, running up to the slopes of Mount Kilimanjaro across the border in Tanzania. It is one of the most accessible and rewarding of the national parks, with a varied landscape on volcanic soils, and a good amount of wildlife. The animals here are fairly shy but the game-viewing experience is all the more rewarding for it. **Tsavo East** is to the north of the main road, and is even larger: however, much of the park, once closed to visitors while poachers decimated the elephant population, is now restricted to small groups on expensive walking safaris. The southern section, however, has a sprinkling of very worthwhile lodges and some good game-viewing. It is relatively accessible from Mombasa, and so is popular with visitors to the coast.

While these are the major parks, there are a number of smaller parks which can be even more rewarding, and can ideally be combined as part of any safari. Top amongst the "minor" parks is **Samburu**, north of Mount Kenya, where the arid landscape is a dramatic backdrop to game of all kinds, and you know where to find it: the game will be near the water. Traveling to Samburu, visitors will have passed the remote mountainous landscape of the **Aberdare National Park**, where the breeding populations of rhino and elephant can, in the lush growth, be a bit hard to see, and the peaks of **Mount Kenya National Park**, a varied and spectacular landscape, are only really accessible to experienced hikers and mountaineers.

The main road to Nakuru links three more national parks. **Longonot** and **Hell's Gate** national parks protect a dramatic volcanic landscape south of Lake Naivasha, better for hiking than game-viewing, while **Nakuru National**

Looking out over the Leno Valley from the Tot Escarpment.

Park surrounds the waters of flamingo-pinked Lake Nakuru in a park-like environment dense with game — you won't want to step out of your car here.

Other national parks well worth a visit include **Meru National Park**, off-limits for many years thanks to bandits and poachers but now reopening to a select few, and, far to the north by the shores of Lake Turkana, the arid fossil-strewn desert of **Sibiloi National Park**. And finally the most accessible of them all: **Nairobi National Park**, where the full range of plains game – and predators – live a wild life in hearing distance of the humming sound of the city's traffic.

From the coast, most visitors in search of wildlife come inland to Tsavo National Park, or to the small but beautiful **Shimba Hills National Reserve**, a fenced stronghold of the sable antelope and a full range of predators. There are marine national parks here too: guarding the coast off **Wasini** to the south, **Watamu** and **Malindi** to the north, and **Kiwayu** near the border with Somalia.

Alongside the national parks, there are a number of natural reserves. Practically, most regulations, entry fees and hours are the same: the difference is that natural reserves are policed and controlled by local councils rather than by the centralized Kenya Wildlife Service. For a private, generally more expensive and less regulated wildlife experience, there are a number of private reserves owned

and operated by individuals or groups of farmers; there are also community ranches, owned, but not always run, by local pastoral tribes with ancestral rights over the land. These are listed in the relevant sections of the touring chapters in this book.

Outside the protected areas, Kenya has plenty of fine hiking country, where there might not be too much wildlife, but at least you can escape from your vehicle and explore the countryside.

Some of these are areas where subsistence farmers have long displaced animals. The slopes of Mount Elgon on Kenya's western Ugandan border are threaded with paths and trails where wildlife poses little threat. But where the risk from animals is reduced, humans can be more of a problem: check the security situation by asking around, since border areas are often sensitive. Weeks can be spent on extended treks along the inter-village trails in the Nandi and Cherangani Hills in western Kenya, which is a memorable way to meet Kenya's welcoming people, even if on a tight budget. Camping out in these populous districts is not wise: better to come to an arrangement with a villager to stay with their family or use one of the mountain huts. You won't be short of offers and you will generally get the family bed. This is a brave option too, though, and it would be insensitive and unwise to flaunt your wealth with photographic equipment or even expensive clothes. Bear in mind that medical facilities are few and communications can be poor, so falling off mountains is not advised.

The most popular area for hikers is **Mount Kenya**, where a guide is usually advisable. Mountaineers definitely need a guide: many climbs are technical and demanding. Contact the Mountain Club of Kenya ((02) 501747, Box 45741, Nairobi, or Savage Wilderness Safaris Ltd. (/FAX (02) 521590 WEB SITE www.kilimanjaro.com, Thigiri Road, Box 44827, Nairobi. If in the Mount Kenya region, Joseph Muthui ((02) 242627 FAX (02) 250734, Box 391, Naro Moro, offers friendly and flexible guide services.

Those with just a day to spare can head out of Nairobi to the **Ngong Hills**, but not alone: over the past few years it has been the spectacular setting for plenty of robberies.

Other areas are safe simply because the countryside is too inhospitable to support enough wildlife to be dangerous. Usually the problem is lack of water: most of northern Kenya is classed as desert, a rugged world of exceptional beauty and piled dried boulders where dramatic color-shifts mean even the same view constantly changes. Dotted by the red robes of nomadic hunters, trekking in the drylands takes planning, and preferably a camel. Once more, camping out here is only advisable in groups.

Some areas of Kenya can be explored on foot simply because that's the only way to travel. The forests of **Arabuko-Sokoke** near Watamu Bay on the northern coast (see ARABUKO-SOKOKE FOREST, page 276 of THE COAST) or of **Kakamega** in the west (see KAKAMEGA, page 164 of WESTERN KENYA) are threaded with narrow game trails. No danger of being eaten here: even the lithest predator would find it hard to stalk prey in the thick undergrowth. Buffaloes can make

faster progress than fleeing humans, so if you meet an angry one, climb a tree. In such forests, the greatest risk is getting lost: underneath the jungle canopy it would be easy to lose your bearings. In practice it's not such a problem, as both these forests have friendly and informative guides determined to show you around, and there's little chance of escaping their helpful attentions.

To walk amongst wildlife takes more than nerve — you'll need an armed ranger, a watchful eye and a thorough respect for Nature's killing machines. In general, animals steer well clear; although they're used to cars and safari vehicles, predators and prey alike tend to take flight at the first whiff of a human on foot. Notable exceptions include hippos and buffaloes: easily the most dangerous of all Kenya's wildlife and always to be treated with the greatest respect. If traveling with an experienced guide, the risks are small, and walking safaris are specialties of some of the most inviting private game reserves, often

OPPOSITE: Sheldrick's Falls in Shimba Hills National Park. ABOVE: A diver explores Kenya's fragile coral reef.

bordering national parks, that have set up in Kenya over recent years. Two of the best are **Sweetwaters**, reserved with Lonhro ((02) 216940 FAX (02) 216796, Box 58581, Nairobi (US$205 per double, full board); and **Lewa Downs**, bookable through Bush Homes of East Africa ((02) 350703, (02) 571661 or (02) 571592 FAX (02) 571665 E-MAIL bushhome@africaonline .co.ke WEB SITE www.bush-homes.co.ke, Box 56923, Nairobi (from US$325 per night, full board).

Many visitors, especially those who've been on different types of safaris before, find there's no better way than a walking safari to get a feel for the bush, and it is undeniable that seeing an elephant on foot is a very different experience to spotting one from the high viewpoint of a car. Especially if it's coming your way.

Sporting Spree

For the sports-inclined, Kenya offers a special welcome. On every flat patch of land, goalposts seem to have been put up for soccer matches, and rugby too is very popular. But few travelers arrive in Kenya with a whole team at their disposal, so for most visitors it's the individual activities, such as fishing, golfing, diving, mountaineering and horseback riding, that provide the sporting high points of their stay in the country.

Golfers in Kenya have the pick of some of the world's finest greens, often enlivened by crocodiles and hippos adding their own special frisson to water hazards. Nairobi has a range of golf clubs, most of which offer special guest membership rates to patrons of the city's most famous hotels. There are six high-quality 18-hole golf courses in the Nairobi area: the best is the Windsor Golf and Country Club ((02) 862300 FAX (02) 802322, 13 km (eight miles) from the city center off Garden Estate Road. Another ten 18-hole courses are within easy reach of Nairobi around the Rift Valley and the central highlands. Golfing safaris can be arranged by UTC (trips include tours and nanny services) ((02) 331960 FAX (02) 331422 WEB SITE www.unitedtour.com, Box 42196, Nairobi; or Let's Go Travel ((02) 447151 or (02) 441030 FAX (02) 447270 or (02) 441690 E-MAIL info@letsgosafari.com WEB SITE www.letsgosafari.com, Box 60342, Nairobi.

Malindi, Diani and Mombasa have good courses, while most other major towns have the facilities to play nine holes at least. In Kenya, the clubhouses are often cozy time-warp zones that retain the atmosphere of colonial days; in quiet settings, the rush of the modern world seems to pass them by. A game of golf is a great way to unwind from the excitement of life on safari. For further information, contact the Kenya Golf

Union ((02) 763898 WEB SITE www.kgu .or.ke, Box 49609, Nairobi.

Horseback riding and **horseracing** are big in Nairobi. Throughout the year, the Nairobi Racecourse on Ngong Road holds events almost every other weekend. This can be a great day out, and although it is never quite going to match the famous races of Europe or the United States for sheer scale and pageantry, it makes up for it with a cheerful and convivial atmosphere in the stands. A bar, a restaurant and the chance to place some really small bets (Ksh20 or about 30 cents is the minimum) make this an ideal way to pass a Saturday or a Sunday afternoon. Everyone says the races are fixed, but then who cares? Look in the sporting pages of the *Nation* newspaper to see if there's a race on or call the East African Jockey's Club ((02) 561002.

If you want to ride yourself, it's a great way to experience the country. Lessons and horse rental are available in Nairobi from Arifa Riding School ((02) 882937, Marula Lane, Karen, Nairobi, while the Kitengela Polo Club ((02) 882782 also offers picnic rides and polo lessons. For long-distance horseback safaris and up-country operators contact Let's Go Travel ((02) 447151 or (02) 441030 FAX (02) 447270 or (02) 441690 E-MAIL info@letsgosafari.com WEB SITE www.letsgosafari.com, Box 60342, Nairobi. One United Kingdom operator

who specializes in offbeat farmhouse and horseback safaris is Art of Travel ((0171) 783 2038 FAX (0171) 738 1893, 21 The Bakehouse, Bakery Place, 119 Altenburg Gardens, London SW11 1JQ.

Mountain biking is relatively new to Kenya, where ancient bone-shaking bicycles are the usual transportation for impoverished farm workers. It can — for the fit — be a great way to see the country, perfect for exploring the footpaths and game tracks of Kenya. A new operator opening up this field of African travel is Bike Treks ((02) 446371 FAX (02) 442439, (or reserve with Let's Go Travel, above), while more expensive bike tours are now being promoted in the north by luxury operator Cheli and Peacock ((02) 604053/4 or (02) 603090/1 FAX (02) 604050 or (02) 603066 E-MAIL chelipeacock@africaonline.co.ke WEB SITE www.chelipeacock.com, Box 39806, Nairobi.

Deep-sea fishing has been popular since Hemingway's day. All along the coast of Kenya, operators offer charter boats for fishing trips, with a new specialty of night-fishing with diving-light lures for swordfish. The north is best known for sailfish, while the south prides itself on marlin catches.

OPPOSITE TOP: Horseracing at Nairobi Racecourse, and, BOTTOM, windsurfing on Diani beach. ABOVE LEFT: Driving in the Masai Mara and, RIGHT, on track in Samburu.

North to south, every major town is home to at least one reliable operator for tag-and-release fishing; where fish are released live into the wild. In Malindi it is Kingfisher ((0123) 21168 FAX (0123) 30261, E-MAIL kingfisher@swiftmombasa.com, Box 29, Malindi. Ten kilometers (seven miles) to the south, Watamu Bay is home to Hemingways ((0122) 32624 FAX (0122) 32256 WEB SITE www.hemingways.com and Ocean Sports ((0122) 32008 FAX (0122) 32268, Box 100, Watamu. Just to the north of Mombasa, Hallmark Charters Ltd. ((011) 485680 FAX (011) 475217 is at Mtwapa Creek. Head south to Diani Beach, and Grand Slam Charters can be reserved through the Safari Beach Hotel ((0127) 2726 FAX (0127) 2357. Towards Kenya's southern border with Tanzania, Shimoni is base for Sea Adventures Ltd. FAX (011) 227675 and the famous Pemba Channel Fishing Club ((011) 313749 FAX (011) 316875.

Lakeland game fishing is also possible on Lake Victoria, where huge fish are regularly caught. Mfangano Island Camp is booked through Governors Camps ((02) 331871 FAX (02) 726427 WEB SITE www.governorscamp.com, Box 48217, Nairobi (extremely expensive, all-inclusive), or try Rusinga Island Club ((02) 574689 FAX (02) 564945 E-MAIL ras @swiftkenya.com, Box 24397, Nairobi (extremely expensive, all-inclusive).

Scuba diving attracts enthusiasts from all over the world. Diving off the Kenyan coast is notable for pelagic sightings and countless shoals of smaller fish. The Indian Ocean here has twice as many fish species as the Red Sea and rewards snorkelers and divers alike. Reputable operators, from north to south along the coast, start in Malindi, and can be reserved through the Driftwood Beach Club ((0123) 20155 FAX (0123) 30712. A good school in Watamu is Aqua Ventures ((0122) 32008 FAX (0122) 32266. In Mombasa, the top operator is Buccaneer Diving, based at the Whitesands Hotel ((011) 485926 FAX (011) 485652. At Diani, the largest operator is Dive the Crab, which can be booked through Safari Beach Hotel ((0127) 2726 FAX (0127) 2357.

To explore the spectacular waters of the southerly Kisite Marine Park, diving is operated by the Wasini Island Restaurant ((0127) 2331 FAX (0127) 3154 or Pemba Diving Ltd. ((0127) 2331 FAX (0127) 3151.

Whitewater rafting is an increasingly popular way to explore Kenya, although not many of the seven major rivers are suitable. Just one operator exploits Kenya's raftable rivers, which include the Athi, the Tana, the Muthoya, or the Ewaso Ngiro. Day excursions or longer river-based safaris out of Nairobi are offered by Savage Wilderness Safaris Ltd. (/FAX (02) 521590 WEB SITE www .kilimanjaro.com, Thigiri Road, Box 44827, Nairobi (see RIDE THE RAPIDS, page 21 in TOP SPOTS).

The Open Road

Sadly, though Kenya does have roads, few would describe them as "open." At first sight, driving in Kenya would seem to be the action of the terminally insane. I prefer to see it as an adventure. Drivers who are prepared to face the challenges will be rewarded with some of the finest views in the world, the chance to spot exotic game by the side of the road, and the unbeatable sense of satisfaction inherent in independent exploration.

There are a number of truly spectacular drives. The newly surfaced and little-used C51 from Marigat to Eldoret passes through the Tugen Hills in an endless succession of switchbacks and turns, combining ease and beauty; but many of the country's greatest drives match beautiful landscapes with quite demanding conditions. The C71 heading north to the eastern shores of Lake Turkana is an adventurous epic journey that few visitors — or even Kenyans — ever manage. Dropping down to the Masai Mara from the west or north, over the Oloolo or Mau Escarpments, provides vivid memories no amount of time can erase. The coast road breezes through the

The Talek River in the Masai Mara Reserve: a dry-season magnet for game.

lowland heat with patches of jungle and farmland, strips developed for tourism, and other communities where life goes on at the speed of the seasons. And whenever the sun gets too tempting, the sheltered waters of Kenya's Indian Ocean shore are never more than five minutes away. If you can cope with the slow belching traffic heading north out of Nairobi, the view on cresting the African Rift Valley stretches seemingly forever.

For most motorists the point of arranging their own car is to link specific outlying settlements and a chosen range of national parks. In the 1970s it was quite normal for visitors to rent a car and just explore in a huge loop. As car-rental

has become more expensive and security less certain this is a less common, but still rewarding, experience; however be ready to invest considerable time and money in the venture. An ultimate tour of the country could, with 63 days and US$20,000 dollars to spare, be structured as follows:

Days	Destination
1–2	Nairobi: museum, other sites, national park
3–4	Lake Naivasha and Hell's Gate National Park
5–7	Aberdare National Park
8–11	Mount Kenya National Park
12–13	Meru National Park

44

This would be very much a "dream ticket" ultimate safari, but could easily be divided into less ambitious sections for those with less time or money. To travel in the back country and the wilder game parks a four-wheel drive will be essential, preferably a Mitsubishi Pajero, Landrover or Toyota Landcruiser. Check with the car-rental companies listed on page 289 in TRAVELERS' TIPS.

Before you leave, make sure your vehicle is roadworthy, that it has good tires and a good spare (two spares, and extra tubes and patches if you intend to attempt East Turkana and the Chalbi Desert), a functional jack, and at least one extra jerry-can for gas. Check that your vehicle is in tip-top condition, and doesn't overheat or burn too much oil. Any troubles you may have near Nairobi will be multiplied tenfold in the desert. If your vehicle isn't equipped with a five-gallon jerry-can for radiator water, ask at gas stations — you should be able to pick up a used plastic one cheaply.

Read the sections of this book pertinent to the areas you want to visit (especially the Northern Frontier District) before venturing into them. In the desert of the Northern Frontier District, for example, gasoline is even rarer than water; it's *very important* to call ahead and reserve gas at the few places listed, if they have some.

Wherever you drive in Kenya, the journey is spiced by the beauty of the landscape and the details of everyday life (the roadside shacks and shops, colorful costumes and gentle smiling people), and game glimpsed feeding by the side of the road or racing, flustered, away from your car. Drive on. In the end, perhaps all you need to know is that you drive on the left side of the road.

Conditions are harsh in the Northern Frontier District, but the views superb.

Backpacking

Backpacking in Kenya is easy, cheap and recommended, although travelers should be ready for a completely different experience of the country than their more moneyed counterparts will find in lodges and game-parks.

Whatever the style, on a budget, the travel experience is going to be crowded. Clunky ancient buses, packed minivan *matatus*, or fast station wagon expresses hurtling between cities all have one thing in common: they're always packed to capacity and beyond. Don't carry too much luggage: often it will stay on your lap, and bulky backpacks will be a constant burden. It will be the lucky backpacker who avoids any experience of breaking down on Kenya's poor roads. When and if this happens, it is important to be flexible: if your *matatu* is clearly not about to be fixed by nightfall, flag down any passing vehicle. Whether truck or car, your chances of getting a lift are better as a backpacker than a local Kenyan, not least because you are most likely to be able to pay for the favor.

If the light is failing in a patch of country haunted by buffaloes, lions or bandits, all of whom are immediately interested in a wounded *matatu*, getting to the nearest town should be your first objective: there will be plenty of time

later to fret about your special status and the eventual fate of your fellow passengers. Generally they arrive, tired and dusty, a few hours later.

In normal circumstances hitchhiking is no longer safe between the major cities, but in very rural areas it can be the only way to travel, and is regarded as normal. All passengers are expected to pay for their rides, and you should be ready for it to take some time. I once spent eight days hitching to Lake Turkana, a distance that took me as many hours returning in a fast car. Near urban areas, transportation is so plentiful — and cheap — that few people try to hitch, and in any case it is not safe. Bear in mind that the poorest foreign backpacker will be far wealthier than most Kenyans, and will be assumed to have valuable baggage. The first car to stop might not be a Samaritan.

Accommodation in Kenya can be very cheap, in small B&Ls ("Boarding and Lodgings") that range in comfort from clean-sheeted double beds with en-suite bathrooms and gushing hot water, to small, insect-ridden sheds

with a long-drop toilet, half a candle for lighting, a rag of a towel and a bucket in case you demand a shower. Rates as low as 50 cents allow travelers on any budget to visit Kenya for extended periods, but conditions won't always be comfortable. Don't get too hopeful when you see a sign saying "Hotel": often this just means restaurant and doesn't necessarily mean they provide accommodation. Small restaurants serving local food are usually cheap and welcoming: there's a sink to wash your hands before and after eating, as cutlery is a luxury. In any case, the local staple, *ugali* (maize), is best eaten with the fingers and mashed into the rest of the meal: eaten with a fork it's completely tasteless.

Seeing Kenya's game is where backpackers might lose out. You have to choose between blowing your hard-kept budget and just giving it a miss. Park entry fees vary down from US$27 a day: enough to keep public transportation well clear. Ostrich, zebra and buffalo glimpsed from a crowded *matatu* is the most that can be expected from public transportation. Unless you strike it lucky and find someone — by hitching or starting up a conversation in a bar or hotel — who has a car and can give you a lift to a national park, the only way of ticking the "Big Five" — elephant, lion, buffalo, rhino and leopard — off your list is to reserve a quick camping safari through a budget operator (see TAKING A TOUR, page 76 of this chapter).

However, backpackers in Kenya can have the best time of all. They are more likely to meet the local people and find out about local culture first hand. Backpacker centers include Lamu Island off the northern coast, where many visitors stay for months, and the distinctly untouristy center of Maralal town to the north of Nyahururu. Don't let a shortage of funds stop your visit, as traveling on a budget will give you even more opportunity to come to know the Kenyan urban culture than tourists

OPPOSITE: Campfire cuisine tastes even better in the bush. ABOVE: Local guides are best in the remote Shaba Reserve.

cosseted in luxury lodges out of the main towns will ever get. If money is really short you can just leave the game viewing until you're older. And richer.

Living It Up

Kenya pioneered mass safaris, but it also saw the birth of the earliest luxury safaris. Now it once more has some of the classiest lodges in Africa and the most extravagant tourist opportunities.

Unfussy and, with all its luxuries, vaguely decadent, the Kenyan high life is not something you usually have to get dressed up for. Only in East Africa are the most exclusive places to stay campsites. The country's most luxurious establishments are generally the simplest, and the idea of total paradise for most Kenyans — and visitors — is to take a **private tented safari**.

They are not campsites as we know them. The tents are made from heavy canvas, are large enough to walk around and usually offer en-suite facilities. Even if the shower consists of a bucket swinging from an overhanging tree, there will be a chain of Kenyans making sure the water, heated over open fires or by solar panels, gushes hot. Dining is often under the stars, with silver service, linen tablecloths and cut glass, lit by the flickering light of hurricane lamps and the dancing shadows of a campfire. Instead of the grand buildings of the great European hotels, in Africa the magnificent landscapes and prolific game take center stage: accommodation is modest and practical, with the luxuries being the view from the wooden deck of your tent or lodge, and the sophistication provided by the company of fellow travelers and the insights of your hosts around a communal dining table.

Even amongst the lodges the trend has been relentlessly upmarket, as smaller, more luxurious properties have been developed for the overseas markets, while established properties that once catered to the very rich have succumbed to the temptations of the mid-market tour

groups. Those who can afford to do so take **private chartered flights** to get well away from the crowds.

Road travel in Kenya will knock most of the luxury out of your itinerary, and well-heeled travelers generally take to the air. There are scheduled services, of course, but there's nothing quite so handy as having your own plane: two charter companies include Boskovic Air Charters Ltd. ((02) 501219 FAX 505964, Box 45646, Nairobi, and Tropicair ((0176) 32890/1 FAX (0176) 32787 E-MAIL tropicair @kenyaonline.com, Box 161, Nanyuki: costs are (approximately) US$1.68 per mile (1.6 km) for a Cessna carrying two passengers, with a minimum of 500 miles.

Three Nairobi-based associations, between them, are responsible for marketing most of Kenya's more luxurious lodges and camps. **Mellifera** ((02) 574689, (02) 577018 or (02) 567251 FAX (02) 564945 E-MAIL Mellifera@swift kenya.com, Box 24397, Nairobi, operates central reservations for a number of lodges, including one (Loisaba) that uses a helicopter (with leather seats, eight-stack CD and air conditioning) for luxury tours of the remote northern regions. Mellifera's other partners include Cottars 1920s Camp, offering period luxury near the Masai Mara, Galdessa Camp in the wilds of Tsavo East, and Nderit Estate on the banks of Lake Naivasha.

Members of a number of Kenya's long-established East African dynasties, most of whom have grown up in the bush alongside the country's wildlife, have linked together in creating **Bush Homes of East Africa** ((02) 350703, (02) 571661 or (02) 571592 FAX (02) 571665 E-MAIL bushhome@africaonline.co.ke WEB SITE www.bush-homes.co.ke, Box 56923, Nairobi. This organization provides the opportunity for the more dynamic descendents of the old East African aristocracy to bring remote and

ABOVE: Diani Beach is a favorite with travelers and also popular with European tour operators. OVERLEAF: Buffalo drink at Mountain Lodge's waterhole on the slopes of Mount Kenya.

much-loved parts of Kenya to a wider
audience through private parks and
reserves, the best known of which is
perhaps Lewa Downs. Others include
Rekero on the eastern side of the Masai
Mara, Lokitela Farm on the slopes of
Mount Elgon, Kitich in the northern
Mathews Range and Sirita Siruwa
between Nairobi and the Tanzanian
border. The group also offers the mobile
luxury of Patrick's Camp, which follows
the dry season from Solio to Tsavo East
and Tsao West national parks. Two of
their properties bring exclusive luxury
to the coast: Tana Delta Camp and
Takaungu House, near Kilifi.

Finally, **Cheli and Peacock** ((02)
604053/4 or (02) 603090/1 FAX (02) 604050
or (02) 603066 E-MAIL chelipeacock@africa
online.co.ke WEB SITE www.chelipeacock
.com, Box 39806, Nairobi, is a long-
established agency that coordinates
a scattering of specially smooth and
sophisticated small lodges around the
country, including Elsa's Kopje in Meru
National Park, Tortilis near Amboseli and
Kiwayu on the remote northern coast.

As the luxury end of East African travel
booms, even the mainstream operators
have established — or refurbished — their
best properties to offer more sophistication
to high-spending visitors. Thus **Governors
Camps** ((02) 331871 FAX (02) 726427
WEB SITE www.governorscamp.com,
Box 48217, Nairobi, has developed Ilmoran
in the Masai Mara; the **Heritage Group**
((02) 446651 or (02) 447929 FAX (02) 446533
E-MAIL info@heritagehotels.co.ke WEB SITE
www.heritagehotels.co.ke, Box 74888,
Nairobi, has opened 10-bedded "Explorers
Camps" in the Masai Mara and at
Kipungani, on Lamu Island; while the
Conservation Corporation ((02) 441001/5
FAX (02) 746826 E-MAIL info@conscorp.co.ke
WEB SITE www.ccafrica.com, Box 74957,
Nairobi, has built Bataleur Camp
alongside its already quite luxurious
Kichwa Tembo in the Masai Mara.
All these properties are described in more
detail in the touring chapters below.

Camping in Kenya doesn't always mean
roughing it.

Family Fun

The excitement of watching the world's wildlife walk from the pages of books and onto the savanna by your safari vehicle will bring a smile to the face of any child. The sheer size of some of nature's wonders can't fail to impress, and the experience sets the groundwork for a lasting interest in wildlife and conservation in almost every child.

Perhaps strangely, Kenyan **safari operators** have been slow to tailor their arrangements to this emerging market. The first to do so was the Heritage Group ((02) 446651 or (02) 447929 FAX (02) 446533 E-MAIL info@heritagehotels.co.ke WEB SITE www.heritagehotels.co.ke, Box 74888, Nairobi, which runs a portfolio of lodges and hotels around the country, and takes considerable pride in running "Adventurers Clubs" on all their properties. These introduce children ages four to fourteen to the African world with an irresistible combination of wildlife tracking, spear-throwing sessions, bow-and-arrow or beadwork making and lizard-hunts, not to mention plenty of time in the pool. To appeal across the board, the Heritage Group has larger lodges, such as the Voyager Safari Lodge in the Masai Mara and the Voyager Mombasa Beach Resort, which offer cheerful and communal clubs with up to 40 children at a time running around on chaotic treasure hunts. At their medium-sized properties, such as the 27-tented Samburu Intrepids and the Mara Intrepids in the Masai Mara, groups are smaller and the clientele more select.

Parents love it — they often join in — and although other operators are lumbering into position to launch their own imitations, it is the Heritage Group's clubs they are likely to be copying: this is where you should look for the best childcare program for some time to come.

One thing to bear in mind is that children don't, on the whole, enjoy traveling too much or moving too often. It is better to pick a destination and stay

there rather than undertake ambitious mobile safaris, especially with long road journeys. Under the age of five or so, children probably won't appreciate some of the more wonderful sights, and might remember instead long hours spent in vehicles and in the company of strangers, and the break of their routine. Renting a car is one option, as this will give you the freedom to stop where necessary and alter plans to suit changing requirements. Bear in mind that you probably won't find a child-seat in Kenya and should bring your own. Bring too a light collapsible stroller as many hotels have long paths between rooms and public areas.

Children aged six or above are usually transformed by the experience of nature and the excitement of **camping out** and eating around a bonfire. Flat spots can occur driving along dusty roads in the middle of the day: bring plenty of things to entertain them. Excellent children's toys are on sale locally. Handcrafted from wood or wire, these can often provide hours of entertainment for the imaginative child, and hours of entertainment might actually be needed.

Parents will also want to bear in mind that, in the wild, infants of all species are generally prey. Some of the unfenced **game lodges** don't accept children simply because they don't want to see their

OPPOSITE: A swimming pool is an ideal refuge from the midday sun. ABOVE: The Thinker — an olive baboon.

guests eaten, and their minimum accepted ages can vary: some lodges aren't prepared to take children under seven, while for others, 12 is their lower limit. Check ahead with your selected lodges to see if they have any special restrictions.

Fenced lodges are generally far more accepting of small children. And for warm, loving childcare, there is no better place than Kenya. With one of the world's highest birthrates, they get plenty of practice: the majority of the population is under 15 years of age. There aren't that many facilities especially for children, though: normally they're just included in adult activities from a very early age, and for most Kenyans this generally means work.

Kenya is an exotic destination at all levels and the average child's fascination with the surroundings can be dangerous. It can take time and a consolidated effort to persuade them not to drink the water. Nairobi's **Snake Farm** might be a good early stop if children are unaware of the dangers of venomous snakes, as they will get the chance to see a selection in relative safety.

Most resort hotels have **babysitting and nanny services** that are staffed by well-trained and practiced professionals, but it is well worth considering hiring a nanny for the duration of your stay, to ensure continuity of attention and consistency of care. Rates are not too expensive. Let's Go Travel ((02) 447151 or (02) 441030 FAX (02) 447270 or (02) 441690 E-MAIL info@letsgosafari.com WEB SITE www.letsgosafari.com, Box 60342, Nairobi, should be able to assist in this.

Health is of course the major problem. To ensure clean toilet facilities, stay in mid-range hotels and lodges. Most good hotels have links with reliable and well-qualified doctors and most mainstream Western drugs are available to those who are able to pay for them, but bear in mind that in case of injury or serious illness good medical facilities are generally limited to the major cities.

For general child maintenance, you can buy all the **basics**, including sterilizer, diapers and baby food in the supermarkets of any major town, but your favorite brands might only be available — if at all — in the boutiques of the better hotels. Disposable diapers, preferred brands of baby food and motion-sickness pills should all be brought along in case they are unavailable: hats, sandals and sunscreen are also wise supplies to carry.

Malaria is a special problem. Even if young children can be persuaded to swallow malaria medicine — not always easy — it's still important to minimize their exposure to mosquitos in the morning and evening. Which means nets: not every child's favorite way to go to sleep. Risks of malaria are much lower in the cool up-country air than in the steamy climate of the coast — a fact that, with young children, might end up dictating much of your travel itinerary.

In rural areas, it's accepted to view the whole country as a playground. This indeed is what the local children do if they haven't been taken out to work the fields. But there are a few establishments set up specifically to cater to children. There are two **waterslide centers** that should be top of the list for parents: in Nairobi, Splash is next door to the Carnivore Restaurant, and in Mombasa there is Pirates on Nyali Beach, where waterslides through the day will keep children entertained, at least until 6 PM when both are turned back over to the adults. In Nairobi there are several opportunities for children to get right up close to animals, but this should not be attempted if they are young or naturally nervous: at Nairobi's **Giraffe Sanctuary** a raised platform allows kids to feed endangered Rothschild's giraffes, but children younger than eight might find the animals just a little big. Although Nairobi's **Maasai Ostrich Farm** gives a unique opportunity to get close to the world's largest birds, it is important to remember that ostriches don't hide their heads in the sand: when scared they let out a disemboweling kick which, designed for predators, can easily fillet a human.

Children love Kenya but constant supervision is essential. There are crocs out there!

In the coastal resort hotels, most of the **swimming pools** are surveyed by alert lifeguards, but don't leave children unattended, especially on the **beach**. Occasional strong currents can be a danger and the tropical waters contain unexpected hazards from hard-to-spot stonefish to fluffy-looking sea urchins.

And whatever older children may claim, discos in Kenya are rarely suitable for teenagers, or even most adults.

Cultural Kicks

Kenya has a lively theatrical scene, based in Nairobi, and the self-censorship of the 1970s started to fade in the more overtly malcontented 1990s. The best

theater is generally thought to be Nairobi's small Professional Center ((02) 225506, in Parliament Road, which puts on modern works from Africa and classics from the West — usually with fast-talking ad-libs reflecting the concerns of the local audience. It's a small theater where the audience feels directly involved, and some of their musicals are well worth catching; contact the center to find out what they're showing. The National Theater ((02) 220536, Moi Avenue, just opposite the Norfolk Hotel, also puts on good performances, with the focus clearly on African drama and Kenyan writers. Sometimes this means that you won't understand a word! Ask what's on and don't forget to ask which language will be used. More live performances are put on at the adjacent French Cultural Center ((02) 336263, Loita Avenue, and the Goethe Institute ((02) 224640, also on Loita Avenue near Uhuru Highway in the city center. Although primarily intended to present the French and German cultures (respectively) to a Kenyan audience, they also showcase Kenyan art and dance. Call for schedules.

Tracking down good art can take rather longer. Most commercial art in the city center tends to be aimed squarely at the tourist market, with an unrelenting focus on wildlife scenes: professionally executed, but too much can wear thin. To see good contemporary **Kenyan art**, check out the upper floor of the National Archives, in the old Bank of India building on Moi Avenue. The National Gallery and, of the private galleries in the town center, Gallery Watatu on Standard Street can usually be relied upon to show some works by new artists of interest, at least until they are sold.

Much of Kenya's cultural heritage is not based in theater or flat, representative paintings, but in vivid and organic **sculptures** in wood or stone. There's a tradition of copying though, and it can be hard at first sight to distinguish real originality and flair from cheaply produced products made on industrial

scale. All it takes to get your eye in is to take a look at some quality sculpture. Some can be found, as you'd expect, at Nairobi's National Museum on Museum Road, while still more is jumbled on the floor of the National Archives. African Heritage off Kenyatta Avenue is a combination shop/museum/restaurant where some of the finest handicrafts and sculptures from Kenya and Ethiopia can be found and bought. As an added attraction, live African music is played on Saturday and Sunday afternoons. The Africa Cultural Gallery on Mama Ngina Street in the Jubilee Insurance building displays some high-quality modern sculpture — often at high prices.

More of Kenya's culture is encapsulated in **dance and costume**. Once more, your first stop should be the National Museum. However, displays that are more dramatic are on offer in the capital. The Bomas of Kenya on Forest Edge Road, just past the national park main gate, offers daily displays of traditional dancing every afternoon between 2:30 PM and 4 PM. Somewhat disconcertingly, these are performed by a professional dance troupe who quickly switch among Kenya's tribal cultures, which might

maintain athletic standards of dancing but detracts from the authenticity.

A rather better experience of potted culture awaits visitors to the Bombolulu Center, just south of Nyali Bridge in Mombasa. The center also has tribal *manyattas* (reed or mud) dwellings and costumes. Other ways of experiencing local dance styles are more haphazard: many lodges persuade their local communities to show off the local dances, while travelers will find it quite easy to gatecrash local dances that take the place of television in outlying communities: just follow the noise after nightfall and find fireside hop-alongs where the music is by voice and drum, and the lyrics mainly focused on cattle.

To track down the rich musical traditions of the present day, it helps to have a Kenyan guide: it's quite hard to find live **local music venues** in Nairobi, as most turn to the more moneyed tastes of white and Asian communities. Worthwhile venues that specialize in

OPPOSITE TOP: At Nairobi's Giraffe Sanctuary these magnificent creatures eat from your hand. But in the Masai Mara, BOTTOM, it's safer to stay on the roof. ABOVE: Entertainment by Kamba dancers from the Machakos region.

and children. The warriors will be elsewhere, and cash transactions the only point at which visitors and tribes people interact. The main thing that ruins the experience for all concerned is the omnipresent camera. Taking photos and videos always causes offence and really is best avoided. If you want a good quality picture to take home, buy a postcard, rather than seeing it all through the restricting viewfinder of a cheap camera. Things get much better if you have — or can borrow — some small children for company. Young people of all races can quickly form a common bond, and the sight of a young *mzungu* is the easiest way to get young Maasai girls to break into wreathing smiles.

Shop till You Drop

First-time visitors to Kenya are likely to be overwhelmed by the onslaught of souvenir sellers. Prices start high, especially for visitors with the pallor characteristic of a new arrival, and an American accent is a real drawback in negotiations.

But persist and there are real bargains on offer. Artisanship can be high, although you'll have to expect this to be reflected in the price. It is worth paying more for something that will persist as a thing of value than buying cheaply something you'll be embarrassed to give away on your return. Whatever you're buying, knowing more about what is available and the quality to expect will help you gain the upper hand in the long and convoluted bargaining process.

Bargaining is usually necessary, apart from a few fixed-price shops and hotel boutiques. Even then it's always worth pointing out flaws or trying for a reduction. Some people find it a frustrating waste of time while the vendors invariably regard it as an endlessly interesting duel of wits. Their opening price depends on any

African music include the Ngong Hills Hotel on Ngong Road, the Makuti Park Club in Nairobi South B Shopping Center, and the nearby Peacock Inn. These regularly provide local music, with the big nights being Wednesday, Friday and Saturday. Local bands lured by foreign dollars line the hotel waterfronts along the lively Bamburi Beach to the north of Mombasa Island. In general, authentic local music is easier to find on the weekends in the less cosmopolitan provincial cities. Just ask at your hotel, but specify that it's live African music you're after (mime a guitar) or you'll get directions for the nearest disco if you're lucky, and to a brothel if you're not.

Many visitors are fascinated by the **tribal customs** and traditions of Kenya's pastoralists: the nomadic Maasai and Samburu people, who are most often seen across the countryside outside the national parks and reserves. To meet with these people, and to begin to understand thier way of living, takes care. Most of the lodges will offer visits to Maasai *manyattas*, but following such well-worn tourist trails is almost always a depressing experience of overpriced curios amongst a few shabby huts occupied by women

ABOVE: Mombasa's Jain Temple is a vibrant blast of Hindu culture. RIGHT: The colorful dress of Kenya's rural pastoralists.

number of factors, one of which will be how much money they think you have. The first secret of successful bargaining is to avoid getting bounced into making an offer higher than what you think the product is actually worth. If in doubt keep quiet, and don't let a big opening price persuade you to revise your initial estimate of value upwards. Once you've named a price you will be expected, if not to shift upwards, at least to stick to it. An offer once made cannot be retracted without causing real offence. An occasional and rather dishonorable way of getting the keenest deal can be to bargain on the basis that you're buying five — or ten — of whatever object is being discussed, and then, at the last minute, decide just to buy one.

Woodcarvings can represent exceptional value. Napkin rings, salad servers, elegant hardwood bowls and coasters, if well made, are always useful. Stylized stick sculptures, masks festooned with matted hair, and herds of miniature carved rhinos can travel less well. "Makonde statues," usually of people and with a high ebony gloss, are often just lighter wood dyed with shoe-polish; check the quality by the weight, although it is best, in general, to buy blackened lightwood — there are more souvenir vendors around than surviving ebony trees and it is illegal to carve Kenyan ebony.

Basketry is an art form in Kenya, and prices often very low indeed. Craft shops invariably have a stock of handmade place mats, fruit bowls and laundry baskets, painstakingly crafted and often using natural dyes. For more substantial products like sofas, dog kennels or carports, head out to the Racecourse Road. Sisal handbags are strong and hardwearing, but check how much they cost, imported, back home. This is essential information to the bargaining process, as often, even at their source, you'll end up paying more.

Soapstone sculpture is found in almost every Kenyan souvenir stall, and all originate from mines near the village of Tabaka near Kisii in the west of the country. Often beautifully carved and

painted, it is also very cheap, considering the hours of work that go into carving and polishing. Once more, bowls and plates are most likely to be useful, but bear in mind that soapstone is heavy: think ahead to how far you'll have to carry it.

Tribal beads characterize many goods fashioned by the Maa tribes, which include the Maasai, the Samburu and Turkana. From key rings to necklaces, these are often exceptionally beautiful and easy to carry, and provide a lifesaving income to traditional women working from their home *manyattas*. Price should depend on quality: watch carefully to make sure it does. In the same category, **shields**, **spears and tribal regalia** are more expensive if actually used rather than purpose-made for the tourist industry. These can be cheaper bought in their region of origin but if that isn't possible and you're in Nairobi on any Tuesday, check out the Maasai Market, which takes place on waste ground off Muranga Road one day a week. Quality is often very high and the prices low. Metal **bracelets** and **necklaces** are tempting buys but beware: within a few hours of use they often dye your skin with metal impurities, which lessens their beauty and usefulness considerably.

The single most underrated product available in Kenya is its **cotton fabric** — batiks and weavings produced for the highly critical local market. *Kangas*, designed for women, are sold in pairs, with one half used as a papoose for the inevitable child. In thin cotton and delicate patterns, they also generally have a proverb included in the design. Ask the vendor to translate the message. My favorite reads "Don't sleep with fleas." *Kikois* derive from the coast: generally striped, they have their origins in Islamic Lamu, are made in thicker cotton and are designed to be worn by men. Other fabrics on offer include

TOP: Watch painters at work in Nairobi's art galleries. BOTTOM: Cowrie-shell necklaces are very much part of Kenyan culture.

batiks, often designed to be stretched and hung, with prices totally dependent on the quality of workmanship and the textile used. Pay a lot for a lot.

In general, one of the best places to buy handicrafts is Nairobi, which attracts some of the best produce from all over the country. Shop at the **Central Market**, however, and expect to pay dearly for the privilege. Around a small core of vegetable sellers are poised ranks of sharp salesmen selling products usually of indifferent quality but always at premium prices. Better is the **Kariakor Market** (named after the World War I "Carrier Corps" in which many Kenyans "decided" to help the British war effort), off Racecourse Road east of the city center, where you'll be rubbing shoulders with local shoppers rather than other tourists. Or let your money go to a good cause: some of the best outlets are run by charities or have a proportion of their revenue going to a good cause. Two of these in Nairobi include the **Undugu Shop** in Woodvale Grove, Westlands, with a wide range of handicrafts benefiting several charities around Nairobi, or the **Utamaduni Crafts Center**, Bogani Road, Langata, where 18 specialist shops trade on behalf of the Kenyan Wildlife Service.

Short Breaks

Kenya might seem a long way to go for just a short time, but there are plenty of short breaks that can give a vivid feel of the country in just a few days. On a short break, there is little point in driving yourself as this is not a place to drive jet-lagged and even small distances on the ground will take longer than you expect. Both Kenya Airways ((02) 210771 or (02) 229291 FAX (02) 336252, Box 41010, Nairobi, and their subsidiary Flamingo ((02) 210771 FAX (02) 823612 fly to Kenyan airports, including Eldoret, Kisumu, Lamu and Malindi, on a daily basis from the international airport. Most domestic flights go from Wilson Airport, five kilometers (three miles) south of the city center on Langata Road: passengers

from the international airport therefore do not need to travel in to the city center to transit for their domestic flight. The largest operator here is the main regional airline, Airkenya Navigation ((02) 501421/3 FAX (02) 500845 E-MAIL info@air kenya.com WEB SITE www.airkenya.com, Box 30357, Nairobi, that flies daily to Lamu, Kiwayu, Amboseli, Nanyuki/Samburu/Lewa Downs, Mombasa and, of course, the Masai Mara, with regular services also to Malindi. For charter flights, the main operator is Boskovic Air Charters Ltd. ((02) 501219 FAX 505964, Box 45646, Nairobi.

Don't cut things too fine on the way back though: internal flights in Kenya are liable to delay and a missed international link can stop a short break being short.

If it's your first visit to Kenya and you have little time, there's really no contest. Kenya's main international attraction lies in its wildlife. As such the **Masai Mara**, the country's most game-filled national park, is the obvious choice. Fly-in safaris can quickly reach most of the main lodges, meaning that within hours of leaving your desk it is possible to be immersed in the famous migration of wildebeest. You won't be the first — or indeed the only — person with more money than time; most of the mainstream travel companies are used to arranging short breaks in the Mara and many have daily departures — by air or road — at prices far lower than you would be able to arrange independently. But be warned that even two nights in the Mara will seem rushed after six to eight hours on a poor road with the same prospect again on the way home. Charter flights and many small, dirt airstrips open up the most remote parts of Kenya as realistic destinations for increasingly busy travelers to pack the African experience into just a few days.

Most of Kenya's more expensive lodges are well used to collecting clients from the local airport and just as capable of arranging short game-spotting breaks,

Africa's giant baobab trees can live for more than 1,500 years.

YOUR CHOICE

as well as being valuable parts of longer tours. Choose one that combines several immediate activities such as riding, as well as tame — or at least reliable — game since there's not going to be time to tune in thoroughly to the wild. Although a town with an airport is ideal, most of the more expensive lodges have access to private airstrips.

A short break is probably not the best time to experiment with complicated travel arrangements within Kenya. Internal flights are subject to overbooking and schedules change. Although individual lodges are described in detail later in this book and contact details are given, in the context of a short break it is probably wise to use a major Kenyan operator accustomed to making travel arrangements on the ground such as Let's Go Travel ((02) 447151 or (02) 441030 FAX (02) 447270 or (02) 441690 E-MAIL info@letsgosafari.com WEB SITE www.letsgosafari.com, Box 60342, Nairobi, or UTC ((02) 331960 FAX (02) 331422 WEB SITE www.unitedtour.com, Box 42196, Nairobi.

If restricted to travel by car it is best not to aim too far from Nairobi. The main safari operators are well able to supply vehicles and drivers to explore, or you can rent a car of your own, but ambitious itineraries overland snarl up in heavy traffic and poor roads. Distances feel longer than they look on the map and although you will see a lot of Kenya, you

might not enjoy it. Sensible objectives for short breaks starting in Nairobi generally head north up the spectacular **Rift Valley** and include **Lake Naivasha**. Not only beautiful in itself, it is good for bird watching, spotting hippos and relaxing, and is only a two-hour drive north of Nairobi. There is a good range of accommodation options, but it's popular with city weekenders too: reserve ahead.

Lake Nakuru is a two-hour drive further north from Naivasha and contains an underrated park surrounding a flamingo-filled lake — a good place to spot game of all kinds including black rhinoceros.

Beyond the Rift Valley are the **Aberdare Mountains**, a drive of five hours north from the capital. These cloud-kissed mountains are unspoiled and little visited: partly because the roads are so bad within the park. It's easy to get stuck, which is not an excuse accepted by many airlines for missed flights. So it's safest to stay instead at the Aberdares Country Club, where the greatest danger is a low-flying golf ball; and if time permits reserve a night spotting game at The Ark. See THE ABERDARE MOUNTAINS, page 208 in CENTRAL HIGHLANDS for further details.

An alternative destination, a five-hour drive from Nairobi, is **Sweetwaters**

ABOVE: Three-horned chameleons blend in with the leaves. OPPOSITE TOP: Bird watching on Lake Naivasha. BOTTOM: Zebras in Samburu take no notice of safari vehicles.

Reserve. This private sanctuary is near Nanyuki and is home to a tame rhinoceros called Morani who likes to have his stomach scratched. The reserve also houses Kenya's largest chimp sanctuary. Night drives in search of leopards are a specialty here.

If time is really short, a matter of a few hours between connecting flights, there's the chance to spot almost all the "Big Five" — elephant, lion, buffalo, rhino and leopard — within half an hour of the airport in **Nairobi National Park**. Even a taxi driver can be persuaded to drive through, although you're likely to see a lot more from the higher position of a safari vehicle, and a qualified driver/guide, possibly linked by radio with other vehicles and park rangers, is much more likely to find you good sightings. Within hearing distance of the hum of Nairobi's traffic, the 120-sq-km (46-square-miles) of the national park contains everything from rhinoceros to cheetah: only elephants are banned as they knock over too many trees. The best way to see it is on a half-day tour: minivans and drivers are available at reasonable rates through Let's Go Travel, or with other operators such as UTC.

Fly into Mombasa's international airport and a whole range of different opportunities opens up along the coast. If time permits, it's best to make the three-hour drive to **Watamu**, for a quick dive, game fishing, or conventional water sports. Not a bad way to fill the decompressing hours, as 24 hours are needed after scuba diving before any flight. If time is really short, though, there are plenty of worthwhile dives and beaches even nearer Mombasa: **Bamburi Beach** is barely 20 minutes by car from the airport. To the south, the Likoni Ferry puts you on a good road to **Diani Beach**, an hour and a half away, which offers a waterfront array of package hotels with a good, if faintly sanitized, atmosphere.

Your beach hotel will, in any case, be surrounded by exotic plants and animals: look closely and however luxurious the facilities, there'll never be any doubt you're deep in Africa. Watamu is backed by the **Arabuko-Sokoke Forest**, in Mombasa itself, the resident hippopotamuses are just part of the attraction of the **Bamburi Quarry** Nature Trail, and at Diani Beach the beachfront hotels share their surroundings with colobus monkeys. For a short-break safari experience from a coastal base, ideal for overnight stays, head back inland from Mombasa to the **Shimba Hills Forest Lodge** or **Kwale Elephant Sanctuary**, both within two hours of Mombasa and with transportation readily arranged from Mombasa's hotels or through UTC.

OPPOSITE: Five out of Kenya's seven rivers start from the Aberdares Mountains. ABOVE: Hippos yawn through the day. RIGHT: Lamu Island is perfect for a beach break.

Festive Flings

As most of their lives are devoted to surviving through years of continuing recession, most Kenyans need quite a lot of encouragement to come out and party. The many religions of the country provide the vital spark.

For the majority **Christian** population, the biggest public celebration is Easter, with Christmas, as in the West, being a quieter, more low-key display. And it is the Christian calendar that dictates Kenya's national holidays. However, **Muslims** make up 30 percent — and rising — of the population, so their big festivals are also observed, especially on the coast. The beginning and end of Ramadan and the Muslim New Year are the cause for major celebrations, but exact dates will vary from year to year — the biggest parties happen at Eid. Maulidi, the Prophet's birthday, is celebrated most in Lamu, with processions and parties; it too shifts date every year.

Meanwhile a significant minority of **Hindus** celebrate the colorful festivals of their own religion, especially inland. Once more, the exact dates vary and predicting them even a year ahead is a matter for an astrologer familiar with the lunar calendar. Further festivals particular to specific tribal groups are also observed but rarely advertised. Ask around.

Some of the biggest festivities are entirely secular, grouped around government-run agricultural shows. These tour the provincial cities and can provide an insight into Kenya's rural way of life.

For most "Kenyan Cowboys," the endangered, hard-drinking white Africans, the last weekend in May is party time. To attend you'll need initiative and probably some camping equipment, as the precise location of festivities moves about. From the coast, they converge on Diani for an anything-goes sporting extravaganza called

"**Diani Rules**," the secret being that there are no rules. To track down this year's Diani Rules, a good starting point is the Safari Beach Hotel ((0127) 2726 FAX (0127) 2357, Box 90690, Mombasa. On the same weekend the Nairobi population decamp in their green Range-Rovers and baggy shorts to a secret location in the heart of the bush for an unique rally called the **Rhino Charge**. The aim is to cover 10 checkpoints over the course of a day while clocking up the minimum mileage: many cars don't make it, but the weekend in the bush has become a Kenyan tradition. One operator who can help you find this event, and can even arrange for you to enter if you give plenty of notice, is Rafiki Africa Ltd. ((02) 884238 FAX 710310 E-MAIL safarico @arcc.or.ke WEB SITE kilimanjaro.com/ safaris/rafiki, Box 76400, Nairobi.

Most of the small towns around Kenya tend to be quiet and low-key most nights of the week. If you are planning a night out, however, Fridays and Saturdays are often the time for serious drinking and dancing, with music continuing, a little more calmly, through Sunday.

Galloping Gourmets

East Africa is not known as a gastronomic paradise. So Kenya comes as a pleasant surprise. The best chefs are the subject of hot competition amongst Kenya's top restaurants and lodges, and standards are often extremely high. They are helped by one great factor: Kenya's range of climates that run from the snow-capped peaks of Kilimanjaro through the temperate highlands and down to the steamy tropics of the coastal belts. Great cooks can pick and choose from the finest ingredients, be they lobster, Aberdeen Angus grazing manicured fields, or humped, zebu cattle bought from pastoral herders. Meanwhile, a thriving agricultural sector produces almost every type of fruit: strawberries and apples rival the finest of Europe, while mangos and papayas are just some of the tropical specialties. Everything is locally grown, glistening fresh and tasting of rich Kenyan soil. As a result, the best restaurants and hotels are free to specialize in every type of world cuisine, working with the best ingredients.

These advantages do not apply so readily to the local cooks at traditional restaurants, whose aim is generally to provide cheap, filling dishes at minimal cost. Often the cooking equipment is limited to a saucepan and a small clay oven filled with firewood. However the local Kenyan cuisine should be a feature of every visitor's experience of the country, and can often be delicious, especially at better restaurants. The cheaper versions are likely to be a central feature for travelers on a budget.

In the mornings, the standard diet at local establishments is *mandazi*, home-cooked doughnuts washed down with a mug — or two — of hot, sweet tea. Local restaurants are often open only at lunchtime, and serve a limited menu that comprises maize (*ugali*) with beans and a tough stew made from whatever meat was available that morning, often goat,

and perhaps a plate called spinach but usually kale. *Matoke* is something of a luxury: this Ugandan specialty is made from mashed green plantains. *Githeri* is a vegetable stew with everything put in, sometimes meat. Thanks to the Asian influence, a common side-dish is chopped chapatis.

Generally Kenyan food is eaten with the hands, partly because knives and forks are a comparatively recent sophistication, but also because many of the dishes, especially *ugali*, need to be kneaded with the fingers to become at all palatable.

Almost every hotel will advertise "*Nyama Choma*," the classic Kenyan dish of roast meat, usually goat. Perhaps surprisingly in view of the primitive conditions in which they are prepared, meals are often absolutely delicious. Even the meanest shack can sometimes surprise. However most good hotels will put on Kenyan dishes, prepared to the highest standards, for their guests to experience local styles of cooking.

On the coast, the long maritime tradition has made coconut milk and the spices of Asia integral ingredients in meals that reflect the cosmopolitan influence of many cultures. The basis is invariably fish from the ocean.

LEFT: Kenya's Muslims celebrate the holy days of Islam according to the lunar calendar. ABOVE: Cooks in Kenya lack sophisticated kitchens, but the cuisine can be superb.

Meanwhile the pastoral tribes, such as the Maasai and Samburu, live entirely on blood, "milked" from the necks of their cattle, and milk — this does not, to my knowledge, figure on any international hotel's menu.

Only in the cities, Mombasa and Nairobi, will visitors to Kenya have the chance to experience a true variety of cuisines. Kenya's widespread Asian influence means that there is a wide range of — often excellent — Indian restaurants. Urban Kenya has some world-class restaurants specializing in French, Japanese, and Chinese cuisine. Tourist lodges and hotels offer a range of classic recipes and small establishments specialize in Ethiopian or West African traditional menus. If just seeing Kenya's wildlife isn't enough, restaurants such as Nairobi's Carnivore Restaurant on Langata Road, or the restaurant at the Safari Park Hotel, 14 km (nine miles) north of the city center, offer special all-you-can-eat selections where the animals of your choice are grilled and carved onto your plate. Zebra steaks hover between the flavors of cow and horse; giraffe has a gamey edge; while crocodile, despite tasting rather of lobster, invariably manages to turn my stomach with its reptilian texture.

For drink, the choice reflects an enthusiasm that leads many visitors to assume that this is Kenya's elusive national sport. Although there is a full range of soft drinks available, my favorite is Stoney, the local ginger beer. As for real beer, countless versions are produced, all tasting much the same, sold in half-liter bottles and all of about the same strength — four to five percent alcohol. Kenyans take their choice of brands very seriously, and will often refuse a drink if the label's wrong. Tusker is the market leader, White Cap favored by more mature drinkers, Export for the upwardly mobile (if you believe the advertising, which most Kenyans do), and Malt (sold in smaller bottles) for epicures. Cans of Castle Beer, from South Africa, are a relatively new

arrival, and tourist lodges and hotels will sell a range of imported beers. Sometimes, to justify high prices, they only serve imported beers. Beer in tourist lodges will be sold chilled, but most of the drinks handed through security cages in local bars will be warm. Specify *"baridi"* if you'd like your drink chilled, and hope they have a working refrigerator.

For wine, some drinkable brews are produced in the Naivasha area, but nothing that would have serious tasters reaching for their wallets. Papaya wine is an interesting experience — worth one try at least — but most good wines in Kenya have been imported from South Africa.

Most rural Kenyans have never tasted wine, and can't afford beer. They rely on *changa'a*, distilled from maize in huts and *manyattas* all over the country. Fiery and potent, newspaper stories often report drinking binges that end in sickness, blindness and death, but Kenyans sipping and stirring their homemade spirits in the privacy of their own huts insist this is an evil rumor put about the government to boost tax-paid sales. It's better though to stick to the local spirits; vodka, whiskey or rum, sold in bottles or 30-ml (one-fl-oz) sachets (called mini-packs) by small bars and shops throughout the country. Tear the mini-pack open with your teeth and mix the contents with anything that will mask the taste.

Special Interests

Kenya has a wide range of special interest tour operators. They are often focused on specific sports, in which case they are listed in SPORTING SPREE, page 40. But not everything in Kenya has to do with sport. More appropriate, perhaps, are directed at Kenya's spectacular wildlife. The following specialists cater to focused travelers.

TOP: The wildlife's on your plate at Nairobi's Carnivore Restaurant. BOTTOM: Kenya's farms provide a steady supply of fresh fruit.

BIRDWATCHERS

Kenya is a paradise for birdwatchers. A range of habitats is available: the arid north, the Rift Valley lakes, forests at Kakamega in the west and at Arabuko–Sokoke on the hothouse lowlands, swamps at Saiwa, and the different habitats of the famous national parks mean that every species of East African and European migrant bird is represented. See BRUSH UP YOUR BIRDING, page 24 in TOP SPOTS.

ELEPHANT WATCHERS

If spotting birds is just too fiddly, elephants might better fill the viewfinder of your field glasses. The professional elephant-watcher is Cynthia Moss, who has spent years in Amboseli studying these great pachyderms. As a famous elephantologist, however, she's likely to be wary of video-toting tourists.

There is someone who can help. Iain Douglass-Hamilton, one of the prime activists who persuaded CITES (Convention on the International Trade of Endangered Species) to ban the trade of ivory and thus save Kenya's elephants from extinction in the 1980s, operates Elephant Watch Safaris ((02) 242572 FAX (02) 243976 E-MAIL oria@iconnect.co .ke or olerai_town@net2000ke.com, which orchestrates close encounters with one of Africa's most fascinating animals, with prices from US$300 per person, per night, in the northern Samburu district.

LITERARY TOURS

Kenya's great literary traditions are reflected in a number of special attractions. Remember *Out of Africa*? **Isak Dinesen's** house in Nairobi has been lovingly preserved as a recreation of the pioneer years where Happy Valley was a larger-than-life world at the frontier of civilization. The modest grace of her plantation house puts the experience in perspective, and even the shortest visit will bring her novels to vivid life. Much of the film was shot in the grounds, although interior shots were taken in a studio. But the ghosts of the past are so stained in the wood that after visiting the house one question remains: how much was fiction?

Kuki Gallmann shot to fame with the best-selling *I dreamed of Africa* (now a feature film starring Kim Bassinger) and is still resident in Kenya. She used her income from the book to establish a private reserve in the Laikipia region and, at it's heart, a stunning lodge northeast of Lake Baringo called Mukutan Retreat. Three chalets in the style of African rondavels are built into the rock of Mukutan Gorge, they are run as an exclusive home-stay where Africa takes center stage. The main person doing the retreating, however, is Kuki herself, and guests she hasn't met socially are positively discouraged. It's a wonderful, but very expensive, place, and you shouldn't expect to get Kuki along with the (hugely expensive) overnight rate. Her long-awaiting follow-up book, *African Nights*, was a depressing account in which all the central characters steadily die. But hopefully your own company will be more cheerful, over dinner, as you look out over Mukutan's stunning view.

Even more important was **Joy Adamson**, whose books about Elsa the Lioness introduced Africa's wildlife to a world audience. Until then lions had been seen as little more than targets. Her writing, often filmed, changed forever the relationship between Western cultures and nature. Joy Adamson's famous house, Elasmere, set on the Naivasha Lake shore towards Kongoni Game Valley, is a pleasant and very quiet place to stay and soak up the atmosphere of a private ranch. This was where her life with lions brought Africa to millions and thrust conservation issues onto the world stage. Less a hotel experience and more like staying in a private house, the friendly staff are happiest when they find guests are familiar with Joy Adamson's life and work, and committed to conservation. Reservations can be made directly from Elasmere ((0311)

Water is the lifeline in the arid north of Kenya.

21055 FAX (0311) 21074, Box 1497, Naivasha (expensive). Much of her research, if that's the right word, with lions took place in Meru National Park, where Elsa's Kjope, run by the upmarket operator Cheli and Peacock Ltd. ((02) 604053/4 or (02) 603090/1 FAX (02) 604050 or (02) 603066 E-MAIL chelipeacock@africa online.co.ke WEB SITE www.chelipeacock .com, Box 39806, Nairobi, is set up in honor of her memory. Her last years were spent in Shaba Game Reserve, where she met her end in a dispute with a 14-year-old boy — with a knife — she had peremptorily dismissed without pay. There's a memorial here, where she was stabbed, but her original camp was taken down: only the site remains. It's an interesting place to visit because it picks out one incident seen very differently by black and white Kenyans. From one side, it was an example of savage murder. From the other it exemplified the high-handed way (usually white, usually female) conservationists sometimes treated Africa's wild animals with greater consideration than they did the people. Either way, if you want to find out more, the only lodge in Shaba is the Sarova Shaba Lodge ((02) 713333 FAX (02) 718700 E-MAIL reservations@sarova.co.ke WEB SITE www.sarova.com, Box 72493, Nairobi. For access, there are scheduled flights with Airkenya ((02) 501421/3 FAX (02) 500845 E-MAIL info@airkenya.com WEB SITE www.airkenya.com, Box 30357, Nairobi, to nearby Samburu.

Taking a Tour

Although many travelers prefer the freedom and flexibility of making their own travel arrangements, in Kenya this will rarely, if ever, save money. Kenya's tour operators are able to negotiate special rates and discounts at lodges and hotels around the countryside that cannot even be dreamed of by the individual traveler. At lodges in the

The cliffs around Lake Baringo teem with life, a paradise for birdwatchers.

Masai Mara, for instance, a tour operator will be paying just US$30 for a bed that would cost an individual six times as much. Whether for a safari or a beach break, reserving with a tour operator often works out cheaper than going it alone.

Tours of Kenya are generally structured round visits to the national parks, listed under THE GREAT OUTDOORS, page 35, and more fully described under their relevant sections in the touring chapters. Itineraries vary, though even the shortest, these days, include the Masai Mara. Because the Mara is rather out on a limb in the southwest of the country, this means there is certain to be a fair amount of traveling involved: quickly by air or laboriously overland. Overwhelming with its wildlife in the migration season (July to October) the Mara is much less impressive when it has rained and all the wildlife has dispersed. At these times it is worth looking to other, dryer regions.

Other parks can be linked sequentially: for example, Nakuru, Aberdare, Samburu and Meru; or alternatively Amboseli, Tsavo West, Tsavo East. It is worth trying to reduce your travel time when choosing your safari, as long overland journeys are expensive and tiring.

When **choosing a tour operator**, the first decision is whether to make your bookings before your arrive or when you arrive in Nairobi. There are advantages on both sides. Overseas operators will offer all the consumer protection available in your home country, and the better operators will also ensure that the itinerary you finally purchase will meet your requirements. Tour operators based in Nairobi, however, can sometimes offer more up-to-date knowledge about more adventurous itineraries and plan your trip more closely around the prevailing weather conditions. Here we list first some of the most respected operators in Kenya, some of whom also have overseas representation, before going on to mention the better of the overseas operators.

The ultimate way to travel is on an elegant **private safari**, some of which claim to recreate *Out of Africa*, while others are camping trips that are more realistically like African safaris at the turn of the last century. The most common are minibus tours that race you, at six to nine persons per vehicle, along the rattling, potholed dirt tracks from one park or reserve to the next. Tours catering to visitors with specific interests such as ornithology or photography are also available.

On a private safari, which is the most expensive of the options, you can tailor destination, itinerary, and schedule. However, once these details are established, it can be difficult to change them, particularly during the December to February high season, as the safari operator has to reserve hotels, guides and campsites and sort out other logistics. Many private safari operators have their own tented camps and gourmet cooks, and some have access to private game refuges.

Organizing a private safari requires a good rapport between the traveler and operator. And not a little money: expect to spend anything from US$300 to US$1,000 per head, per day. If you take this alternative, try to contact the operator *directly*, to minimize misunderstandings and to get a sense of his or her viewpoint and methods of operation. Discuss your wishes and the particulars involved. Since you'll be investing a sizable amount of money in your trip, take time to ensure it will meet your expectations. Allow several months for correspondence, and don't hesitate to use the telephone, although the Internet provides an increasingly useful source of up-to-date information and fast, cheap communications. Before you start, read up on the various sections in this book to decide what areas of Kenya interest you the most.

SAFARI OPERATORS IN KENYA
Among top safari operators are **Cheli and Peacock Ltd. (** (02) 604053/4 or (02) 603090/1 FAX (02) 604050 or (02) 603066 E-MAIL chelipeacock@africaonline.co.ke

In rural Kenya, life is still lived according to ancient traditions and ceremonies.

WEB SITE www.chelipeacock.com, Box 39806, Nairobi, and **Abercrombie and Kent** ((02) 334955 FAX (02) 228700, Box 59749, Nairobi, both of whom offer extreme luxury but at prices that can be a bit frightening. If packaged travel just isn't your bag and you want to try a private tented safari without breaking the bank, there are a number of local operators who offer this service. Vehicles and standards vary, however. One known and trusted local operator (well, actually it's run by an expat New Zealander, but he knows the country well) is **Chameleon Tours** (/FAX (02) 860541 or (02) 891375 E-MAIL chamtour @africaonline.co.ke WEB SITE www.chamel eonafrica.com, Box 15243, Nairobi, who can offer tented expeditions from as little as US$200 per person per day. This will get you comfort rather than luxury, but personally, I think this is more appropriate for a bush environment.

For specialist wildlife expeditions in search of gorillas in Zaire and longer private tented safaris way off the beaten track, one Kenyan operator which has received particular praise from film companies and private parties for personal service at reasonable cost is **Rafiki Africa Ltd**. ((02) 884238 FAX (02) 710310 E-MAIL safarico@arcc.or.ke WEB SITE www.kilimanjaro.com/safaris/rafiki, Box 76400, Nairobi.

These companies will provide private safaris in comfort, with knowledgeable guides for groups of any number of people, according to their own special requirements. For more generic tours, though, the bulk of Kenya's tour operators undercut these operators substantially, using minibuses with viewing hatches cut into the roofs (though they may use four-wheel drives on occasion). They usually leave Nairobi on regular schedules and offer neither flexibility nor personalized service but can provide excellent value. The better operators will guarantee that every client at least has a window-seat, though few provide enough space for everyone, simultaneously, to peer together through the rooftop hatch. Of this category,

the most reliable are: **Abercrombie & Kent** who offer both private safaris and organized tours; **United Touring Company (UTC)** ((02) 331960 FAX (02) 331422 WEB SITE www.unitedtour.com, Box 42196, Nairobi, and **SOMAK** with offices in Nairobi ((02) 535500/2/3 FAX (02) 535175, Eighth Floor, Corner House, Mama Ngina Street, Box 48495, and Mombasa ((011) 313871/2 FAX (011) 315514, Somak House, Mikindani Road, Box 90738, Mombasa. All of these also sell their safaris to international tour operators, but as these add on their markup before selling it on to you it's usually best to book directly.

Among younger, more adventurous and more impecunious travelers, camping safaris are justifiably the most popular. Safari companies spring up like desert roses after the rain, some departing the scene with equal rapidity, using trucks decked out with bench seating to up passenger numbers to achieve economically viable group size. For about US$80 per person per day, depending on the size of group and destination, these operators provide transportation, meals, tents, camp beds, and game drives or walking tours. Usually you are expected to bring your own sleeping bag, although even that can be provided at an extra cost, and usually there'll be someone to do the cooking.

Because these groups often take you into inhospitable wilderness, it's wise to rely on someone with experience and reputation. Consistently praised by their clientele are **Gametrackers Ltd**. ((02) 338927 FAX (02) 330903 E-MAIL Game @africaonline.co.ke, Box 62042, Nairobi, and **Safari Camp Services** ((02) 228936 FAX (02) 212160 WEB SITE www.kenyaweb .com/safari-camp, Box 44801, Nairobi (operators of the famed Turkana Bus). Even cheaper companies direct-sell on the streets of Nairobi. Three that have been around for long enough to acquire a veneer of respectability include **Savuka** ((02) 225108; **Kenia** ((02) 223699 FAX (02) 217671 or (02) 444572 WEB SITE www.gorp .com/kenia/; and **Come to Africa Safaris** ((02) 213186. However, these are just the

most established of a rather risky end of the industry. Providing the safari experience for as little as US$50 a day, they don't venture far from the standard trail or offer much in the way of backup, service or information, but for many young travelers they offer the only affordable way to meet Africa's wildlife. Industry insiders suspect that they can only maintain their prices by cheating the national parks out of much-needed revenue on entry fees.

One example of what can go wrong on these cheap safaris happened to me in the city of Nakuru. Our driver/guide interrupted our dinner to tell us the morning game-drive would have to be delayed. Our vehicle had broken down. He suggested that we spend the morning in town while he got the car fixed. The infamous mechanics of Nakuru had struck again. In this case our safari vehicle had been sabotaged in the hope of stopping our morning visit to the national park. Each client had prepaid park entry fees of US$27, but two of us also had night flights to catch in Nairobi.

A few hours detained by a back-street garage would mean racing direct to the airport, releasing the park entry tickets for sale on the black market. I looked at the engine. Exhaust fluid was leaking from the joint between manifold and muffler. Could be simple to fix: but with a couple of stripped threads and a few inventive mechanics it was easy to see how the job could be stretched. It was a bit difficult. I wanted him to go and fix the problem immediately while we finished our meal. But for him to do this would have gone too far to admitting the con. I insisted that we take the game drive, at least, the next morning. Even though it wasn't ideal to put up with a noisy car, it removed the motive to draw out the repair.

This wasn't the only problem I found on a recent trip investigating cheap safaris. Others included breaking down in the Masai Mara — not so funny next to five angry lions — and being abandoned by the side of the road for half a day. This

The hyena plays an essential role as scavenger of the savanna, but will kill his prey when he can.

meant that instead of providing the evening game drive, our vehicle could slip into the national park on a minor track under the cover of dusk.

In most cases, making reservations locally doesn't even save money. Kenya's cheapest safaris rely on subcontracted minivans with no history of maintenance and drivers who don't speak English and would never be featured by international tour operators. Savings evaporate as bulk reservations cut out the benefits of tracking down safaris privately. Move up a notch to the middle of the market and service improves dramatically. Even backpackers are better advised to keep off the absolute baseline: beyond a certain point economies can only be made at your expense.

When safaris go wrong, there's more than convenience at risk: in isolated national parks, untrained guides or mechanical problems with subcontracted vehicles both spell danger. International tour operators choose reputable ground operators, and if difficulties arise they are an easy target for complaints or legal action. Make reservations in Nairobi and any dispute will be resolved in a place where Africa's wildlife can really charge: a Kenyan courtroom.

To make sense of the bewildering choice available, it is often a good idea to use a local travel agent. **Let's Go Travel** ((02) 447151 or (02) 441030 FAX (02) 447270 or (02) 441690 E-MAIL info@letsgo safari.com WEB SITE www.letsgosafari .com, Box 60342, Nairobi, has been consistently recommended by travelers over the years for being knowledgeable, efficient, and helpful without being pushy. They specialize in coming up with travel plans for independent travelers and are based above the Continental Supermarket in ABC Place, Waiyaki Way, Westlands, with offices also in Karen ((02) 882505, above Karen Provision Stores, and in the City Centre ((02) 340331 FAX (02) 214713, Caxton House, Standard Street. Another reputable operator is **Express Travel** ((02) 334722 FAX (02) 334825 E-MAIL expressk@africaonline.co.ke, Standard Street, Box 40433, Nairobi.

BOOKING FROM ABROAD

Internationally, **Abercrombie & Kent** is a leading operator at the top end of the market with 30 years of experience arranging travel in Africa. A&K has offices in the United States ((708) 954-2944 US TOLL-FREE (800) 323-7308, 1520 Kensington Road, Oak Brook, Illinois 60521; in Australia ((03) 9699 9766, 90 Bridgeport Street, Albert Park, Melbourne, Victoria 3206; in the United Kingdom ((0171) 730 9600 FAX (0171) 730 9376, Sloane Square House, Holbein Place, London SW1 8NS; and in Nairobi ((02) 334995 FAX (02) 228700, Bruce House, Standard Street, Box 59749. **SOMAK Travel** has offices in the United Kingdom ((0181) 423 3000 FAX (0181) 423 7700, Harrovian Village, Bessborough Road, Harrow on the Hill, Middlesex HA1 3EX.

From the United States, leading operators include the **African Adventure Company** ((954) 781-3933 US TOLL-FREE (800) 882-WILD, 1600 Federal Highway, Pompano Beach, Florida 33062, which offers a range of African programs and safari choices. **Mountain Travel Sobek** ((510) 527-8100 US TOLL-FREE (800) 227-2384, 6420 Fairmount Avenue, El Cerrito, California 94530, specializes in hiking, rafting and adventure travel for travelers based in the United States.

Africa Travel Centers are specialist safari outlets, and have offices in the United States, Australia and New Zealand, all sister companies to the London-based Africa Travel Shop. Contact details are: in the United Kingdom ((0171) 387 1211 FAX (0171) 383 7512, 4 Medway Court, Leigh Street, London WC1H 9QX; in the United States ((908) 870-0223 FAX (908) 870-0278, 197 Wall Street, West Long Branch, New Jersey 07764; in Australia ((02) 9267 3048, Level 12, 456 Kent Street, Sydney NSW 2000; in New Zealand ((09) 520 2000, 21 Remuera Road, Box 9365, Newmarket, Auckland.

The sun sets over Lake Turkana, the Jade Sea.

Welcome to Kenya

Open savanna dotted with lions, cheetahs, antelopes, elephants and giraffes; skies the color of coal and blood as the sun sets; warriors leaning on their spears in the dry desert air as they watch their herds; grass-roof huts clustered behind thornscrub fences, the miraculous stars of clear African nights — all these images haunt ancestral memories and childhood reveries. Modern, exciting, cosmopolitan Kenya, "the pride of Africa," has incomparable parks and reserves that resurrect this vanished world. Here, with excellent accommodations at more than

to a community ranch or lesser-visited areas, where you'll share the experience with a local guide whose time-honored way of life is so very different to that of the West. The arid, thinly populated north of the country best protects, by its sheer harsh remoteness, this timeless lifestyle.

For others it is the beach that beckons: miles of sandy shoreline, protected by its offshore reef, where diving and deep-sea fishing are just some of the alternatives on offer.

And finally, there are the people. The populated centers of Nairobi, Nakuru and

reasonable prices, you can still see the earth in its pristine beauty. And because the Kenyan people have an ethic, a tribal philosophy if you will, of welcoming strangers and sharing with them, it is a uniquely warm and friendly place to travel.

There are myriad ways to explore the diversity of this country. For most visitors the main draw is the wildlife, coexisting spectacularly with ochre-painted pastoralists and their herds of cattle. To get really close to wildlife, choose a popular national park, where, although you will share the views with other minibus game vehicles, the animals themselves, no longer scared of tourists, will ignore their human audience and follow their natural pace of life. Or head off

Kisumu, sweltering on the banks of Lake Victoria, are open and friendly communities where, with a bit of caution, visitors find a warm and ready welcome.

No other destination will repay you with such lasting memories of the most diverse experiences and adventures. Whether you are traveling on public transportation and staying in basic local hotels, flying into luxury lodges in the heart of the bush, or renting your own four-wheel drive and traveling off on your own, you're assured, in Kenya, of an unforgettable travel experience.

OPPOSITE: A Samburu warrior. ABOVE: Ground transportation is the best way to get to know the wildlife.

The Country and Its People

Twenty million years ago, Kenya extended from the Congo to the Indian Ocean as a vast equatorial plain on the island continent of Africa. A carpet of thick tropical forest and woodland covered the flat and rolling plains. Animals of all stripes and colors inhabited the ground, branches and treetops, among them a variety of forest-dwelling, slender, muscular, and apelike primates we now call dryopithecines.

But Africa collided with Eurasia in the next few million years, creating the Mediterranean. This imperceptible but implacable grinding of the continents gave rise, literally, to Kenya as it is now. Over the land bridges from Africa to Eurasia crossed numerous species; the climate underwent drastic changes, and the drying habitat of the dryopithecines was invaded by the ramapithecines, whose teeth were more adapted to the harsh diet found in the woodlands and open country.

The collision of the continents, though spanning millions of years, was catastrophic in its impact: Africa was split centrally north to south by a vast, sheer fracture. The molten lava underlying the continental plates escaped from volcanoes and poured across the land, over millennia, pushing up the earth's crust more than 1,093 m (3,586 ft), even as the shifting tectonic plates pulled it apart. In 15 million or so years, it deepened what we members of the subspecies *Homo sapiens* now call the Rift Valley, and created the great volcanoes of Mount Kenya, Mount Elgon and Mount Kilimanjaro.

In the north, the Rift extended into what is now Ethiopia, creating the enormous and landlocked Lake Turkana, former source of the Nile, and often called the Jade Sea because of its marvelous green color. As the southern extension of the Rift Valley deepened, it cut off segments of earlier tropical rainforest. Its varied altitudes and climates preserved or gave rise to a diversity of ecosystems, including semiarid desert areas, grasslands, woodlands, and alpine meadows, habitats that offered new biological niches for the emerging ramapithecines. As the lava flowed and the volcanoes spread, they pushed the earth's crust down, widened the Rift Valley floor, and filled extinct craters with lakes, until the valley walls soared a vertiginous 914.4 m (3,000 ft).

FROM JUNGLE TO SAVANNA

As the valley walls rose, they cut into the clouds that, for millions of years, had carried the continent's wind drift from West to East Africa. Over long stretches of time, they blocked the rain's passage to the east, over what is now the majority of Kenya.

The lands changed in response: instead of unending tropical forest, the drier climate produced woodlands and savanna (treeless plain or a tropical grassland of seasonal rains and scattered trees). Like regiments cut off from retreat, patches of lingering tropical forest endured, preserving vegetation and animal species like those still found in West Africa, and antedating Kenya's rise from the equatorial plain. Such vestigial tropical areas, with their unusual vegetation, birds, and insects, include the Arabuko-Sokoke coastal forest south of Malindi, the Kakamega Forest north of Lake Victoria, and smaller areas along the lower reaches of the Tana River.

As the climate and vegetation altered on the East African plains, so did the animals that lived there. The drier climate, the seasonal rains, and the sparser forest gave rise to great herds of ungulates protected by the open spaces. Like many of today's apes, *ramapithecus* were omnivorous, eating leaves, stalks, berries, fruits, insects, eggs and meat. At some point, perhaps because its prey moved out to the expanding savanna, *ramapithecus* left the jungle and the woodland.

Such excursions favored upright locomotion, which, although it requires more energy per distance traveled, has many other benefits. It broadened the range of vision and freed the hands.

TELLING THE FIRST STORIES

Perhaps the thinner forest shelter in the woodland and savanna encouraged *ramapithecus* and its peers to band together; at some point they learned to feed not only themselves and their offspring but also others. Communal sharing of food developed, as did language.

The circumcision ceremony is a complicated ritual: this Samburu adolescent is preparing for the operation that will turn him into a warrior.

About three million years ago, *ramapithecus* began to walk habitually upright.
"Hunter-gatherers," Kenya's world-re-
nowned paleontologist Richard Leakey (the
son of Louis and Mary Leakey) was to call
them. These hunter-gatherers dug for roots
and berries; they harvested nuts, seeds,
shoots, edible leaves, bird and reptile eggs,
insects and fruits; they learned to hunt live
animals and feasted on dead ones when the
opportunity arose.

As the *ramapithecus* lifestyles bacame
more communal, the need developed for a
broader language — to convey such matters as the location of foodstuffs, or to argue the division of spoils or the tactics used
to achieve them. These issues all became
part of the story that enlarged the hunter-
gatherers' experience — the same way we
humans still have of sharing and building
on each other's experience.

Fossil remains of *ramapithecus* have been
found in various locations in Africa, southern Europe, and Asia. These fossils constitute three distinct hominid types (including
our direct ancestor, *Homo habilis* — able man
— and two separate australopithecines), and
have been variously estimated to be between two and five million years old. It's
possible that man's ancestors existed in Asia
and Europe during this time, but their remains have not been found, or that for climatic or other reasons, they ceased to exist
except in Africa.

HOMELAND OF OUR ANCESTORS

Through extensive archeological digs on
the shores of Kenya's Lake Turkana, in
Tanzania's Olduvai Gorge and at the junc-
ture of southern Ethiopia's Omo River with
Turkana's northern shore, the Leakeys and
other scientists have discovered tools and
fossilized bones of several different hominids. These include the complete skull of a
human ancestor who lived by Lake Turkana
a little over two million years ago, and
younger skulls of up to a million and a half
years old.

Traces of hominids and the two australopithecines from a million to a million and a

Tribal dwellings as sketched by a mid-eighteenth-
century traveler to Kenya.

half years old have been found outside Africa, but after that point, none have appeared in Africa or anywhere else except man's direct ancestor, *Homo habilis*. But, once again on the shores of Lake Turkana (at Koobi Fora) a team of paleontologists, led by Richard Leakey, later found remains of a more recent human ancestor, *Homo erectus* (standing man). Leakey's Homo erectus was a million and a half years old, predating others of its species that lived in many parts of Asia (Peking man) and Europe up to a half million years ago.

Africa, Eurasia, Asia and Europe. Their descendants painted cave interiors, fashioned sculpture, and celebrated the burial of their dead.

They improved the arts of habitation and war, literature and music, and learned to herd the ungulates they formerly stalked, farm the land, and set up property. These advances led to even greater warfare and dissension, but also to the building of cities, roads, universities, industry, and now the rockets that take them into space, far from the ancient plains of Kenya.

From *Homo erectus* evolved *Homo sapiens* (thinking man), and 50,000 years ago came modern human beings, anatomically unrecognizable from ourselves. But it was the find of *Homo erectus* skulls at Lake Turkana that proved for the first time that man's ancestor evolved in Africa.

About the time of *Homo erectus*, the shape and precision of stone tools became finer than was necessary for their immediate purpose. Anthropologists think this resulted from their growing language skills.

Through changing climates, the advance and retreat of northern glaciers, new shifts in continental drift, and the narrowing and widening of the Mediterranean Sea, *Homo erectus* and his peers went on to populate

NATURE UNPOSSESSED

"… they walked about their country without appearing to possess it … they had not aspired to recreate or change or tame the country and to bring it under their control … had accepted what God, or nature, had given them without apparently wishing to improve upon it in any significant way. If water flowed down a valley they fetched what they wanted in a large hollow gourd; they did not push it into pipes or flumes, or harass it with pumps. Consequently when they left a piece of land and abandoned their huts, the bush and vegetation grew up again and obliterated every trace of them, just as the sea at each high tide wipes out footprints and children's sand-castles, and leaves the beach once more smooth and glistening." (Elspeth Huxley, *The Flame Trees of Thika*.)

Because the ancient residents of inland Kenya built no castles, roads, or cities, few clues exist as to their recent history. Through archaeology, we know that approximately eight to nine thousand years ago, Kenya became the home of primitive hunters, probably related to the others of southern Africa. About 2000 BC, pastoral Cushitic tribes from Ethiopia moved into western Kenya in search of new grazing land. Some two thousand years ago, other pastoral and agricultural migrants settled the Rift Valley, and by AD 100, there may have been 1,400 pastoral communities living among what are now agricultural populations on both sides of the western Rift Valley.

These tribes migrated along the valley, interacting with other tribes from what are now Uganda, Ethiopia, Sudan and Tanzania. They exchanged and developed cultures that are identifiable in present-day tribes, such as the Kambas in central Kenya, the Kikuyu on the slopes of Mount Kenya, the Luo along the shores of Lake Victoria, and the Kalenjins on the high slopes of the western highlands.

When trade routes were established in the seventeenth century, the Europeans found four basic population groups: the Hamitic, Nilotic, Nilo-Hamitic and Bantu. The National Museum in Nairobi has superb ethnological displays of numerous tribes within these groups. Today, many still keep their social structure and traditions, though their lifestyles and dress have not completely escaped the influence of the West. It is not uncommon to see tribal members exchange their traditional clothes for Western garb.

The Hamitic tribes (Galla, Somali, and Rendille) came originally from the north, settling in the Tana Valley and northern Kenya between 1300 and 1500. The Nilotic people (Luo) migrated from Sudan along the Nile River to settle along the shores of Lake Victoria. According to Luo tradition, they were led to Kenya by two brothers, Adhola and Owiny. Near Mount Elgon, they quarreled and the tribe split. Adhola and his followers stayed around Mount Elgon; Owiny with his supporters settled the area south of Kisumu.

The Nilo-Hamitic tribes, which originated in Sudan, inhabit most regions of Kenya: the Turkana are found near Lake Turkana in the north, the Suk south of the lake, the Kalenjin tribes (Nandi, Kipsigis, Marakwet, Tugen, etc.) in west-central Kenya, and the Maasai in the south.

The fourth group consists of Bantu-speaking peoples who are spread throughout southern Africa. In Kenya, the Bantu tribes (Kikuyu, Meru, Embu, Chuka, Tharaka, Kamba, and other smaller tribes) live around and to the south of Mount Kenya. The Luhya

to the northwest of Lake Victoria, and the Nyika along the coast are also Bantu.

The ancestors of the coastal Bantu came to the Tana and Juba river valleys from the Taita Hills before the Galla; some Bantu tribes were probably assimilated into the Arabic coastal empire. The Bantu tribes in central Kenya did not arrive until much later. The Kikuyu, now Kenya's major tribe, may not have reached its present location until about 1800. The whites and Asians, Kenya's two newest "tribes," began to move to the interior at the end of the nineteenth century.

Remains OPPOSITE of *Homo erectus* are displayed at the archaeological site of Koobi Fora on the shores of Lake Turkana. Nairobi University, with starkly modern architecture and art ABOVE, has students from every corner of Kenya and the world.

THE COAST — A DIFFERENT HISTORY

The Kenyan coast, on the other hand, has been visited throughout history by personages familiar to students of Western and Eastern civilizations. Alexander the Great certainly sailed the Indian Ocean, but whether he reached Kenya is not known. During the first century, a Greek merchant named Diogenes (though not he who went looking for an honest man) undoubtedly spent a portion of his life here. His log, *The Periplus of the Erythraean Sea*, is one of Western civilization's earliest documented records of East Africa. It describes Kenya's coastal inhabitants as "men of the greatest stature, who are pirates ... and at each place have set up chiefs."

These coastal chiefs were probably Arab traders who had settled and intermarried among the Bantu tribes. Their communities were actively involved in trade with Arab, Indian and Indonesian merchants. They sold foodstuffs (wheat, rice, sesame oil and sugar), cloth, hardware, porcelain and glassware in exchange for ivory, rhinoceros horns, tortoise shell, palm oil and, in some areas, slaves and gold. Here, native and foreign influences merged into a new culture and a new language, Swahili, today one of Kenya's official languages (English is the other).

A century later, the Greek-Egyptian geographer and mathematician Ptolemy included Kenya, which he called Parum Litus, in his *Geography*. Despite its many errors, this work remained the authority on Africa until the sixteenth century. There is no record that Ptolemy ever visited inland Kenya, yet he documented lakes and mountains with relative accuracy.

Trade followed the rhythm of the monsoons. Numerous dhows, pushed by the northeast winds, or *kaskazi*, arrived in Kenya between November and April, departing between May and October when the *kusi*, or southeast winds, began. Coastal communities, each with its own autonomy, developed, but trade remained under Arab control until the fourteenth century.

Local builders make skillful use of natural papyrus to fashion their dwellings.

From the time of Ptolemy (second century) until the eighth century, no major changes took place in the coast except for the advent of religion. Schisms within Islam over the selection of Mohammed's successor drove religious refugees to Kenya in search of a new homeland.

These new Arab immigrants, who were neither merchants nor sailors, helped turn the Kenyan coastal settlements into sophisticated cities built from blocks of coral that were carved from the barrier reef: crisp, white architecture with narrow streets, ramparts,

numerous mosques, sultans' palaces, and urban housing with elaborate courtyards for the well-to-do. Remnants of these cities still exist at Manda, Malindi, Mombasa, Pate, Lamu and Kilifi, and are most visible today at Gedi, where the extensive ruins of an ancient city still stand.

Kenya's coastal treasures were traded in the richest kingdoms of the ancient world. India, China, Indonesia, Malaysia, Ceylon, Persia, Arabia, and the countries of the eastern Mediterranean were favored destinations for ivory, rhinoceros horns and palm oil. El Idrissi, a thirteenth-century Andalusian historian of the court of the Norman king of Sicily (a distant cousin of Richard the Lion-Hearted), claimed that iron ore exported from

Malindi was the reason for the high quality of Toledo's swords and knives.

Similarities in style, culture and language among Kenyan coastal peoples gave early voyagers the impression of a unified empire. In fact, except for brief periods, they existed independently and in relative peace, until the arrival of the Portuguese in 1498. This marked the end of the most prosperous period for coastal Kenya.

PORTUGUESE DOMINATION

During the late fifteenth century, under the reign of King John II and his son, Henry the Navigator, Portugal began a period of extensive ocean exploration aimed at breaking the Arab monopoly of the spice trade from India.

After Dias rounded the Cape of Good Hope in 1488, the Portuguese decided they had found the route to India, and began planning an extended expedition up the East African coast. With four vessels under his command, Vasco da Gama left Portugal on July 8, 1487. In November, he passed the Cape and began traveling the East African coast, whose residents soon discovered the Portuguese preached "vulgar" Christianity, and responded with reserve and hostility.

News of the Portuguese predated their ships' arrival in Mombasa on April 7, 1498; they were attacked and quickly retreated to Malindi. Da Gama's log reports that Malindi's sultan received them warmly: "For nine days we had fetes, sham fights and musical performances." Having replenished the ships' stores and acquired a navigator, they set sail with a favorable *kusi* and reached Calcutta on May 23. Three months later, Da Gama began his return voyage, making another call at Malindi.

On subsequent expeditions, the Portuguese were welcomed at Malindi but met continued open hostility in Mombasa. Cabral, who on a voyage to Kenya in 1500 accidentally sailed far enough west to claim Brazil for Portugal, sacked Mombasa before returning home.

In 1505, Portugal decided to install itself permanently in its new territory, and sent Francisco de Almeida as Viceroy of India. For reasons more strategic than commercial, it decided to capture the Arab positions along the East African coast. Mombasa was again sacked during d'Almeria's four-year struggle for control. Once victorious, the Portuguese imposed strict and often brutal rule, reserving for themselves a better part of the local resources and wealth; only friendly cities, such as Malindi, were spared. The Kenyan coast, for the first time in its history, was unified into a single empire.

It was, however, an empire that no longer enjoyed commercial supremacy, but strained from the antipathies between conqueror and conquered. The Portuguese were never able to revive the once prosperous trading cities, perhaps because they failed to provide traditionally traded commodities, or perhaps because the Kenyans ignored their European goods and culture. As a result, the coastal people shifted from a mercantile to an agricultural way of life.

The Portuguese stayed for almost three centuries. At Mombasa, they ultimately felt compelled to build Fort Jesus in 1592 to maintain control, but even this imposing Italian-designed fortress did not put an end to local hostilities.

In 1595 or 1596, the Swahili governor of Pemba was poisoned for becoming a Christian; at the beginning of the 1600s, Sultan Ahmad of Mombasa, generally considered an ally, repeatedly complained of insulting treatment by the Portuguese. His son and successor, Hassan, quarreled openly with Portuguese officials in 1614 and fled inland. Hassan's brother was then allowed to rule for four years before the Portuguese replaced him with a young nephew, Yusuf Chinguliya, whom they promptly sent off to an Augustinian priory at Goa, India, for 13 years of "education."

Upon his return to Mombasa, Yusuf renounced Christianity for his native Islam, and massacred all the Portuguese at Fort Jesus. After defeating a punitive force of 800 Portuguese sent from Goa in 1632, he demolished the fort and left Kenya for Oman. He continued naval raids on the Kenyan coast, but by 1635, the Portuguese had regained control of Mombasa and rebuilt Fort Jesus.

The Portuguese never recovered from their defeat at Fort Jesus; for the next half-century, they battled raids from Omani merchants exercising Yusuf's claim to sovereignty and anxious to regain control of the East African waters. A three-year siege of Fort Jesus brought an end to the Portuguese presence in Kenya in 1698, except for two years (1728–1730) when they briefly held Mombasa.

"You have concealed and preserved
Dreadful secrets
Unrevealed.
Nothing remains
But deathless fascination."
— Amin Kassam, *Fort Jesus*

The Portuguese departure, however, did not bring independence to the Kenyan coastal cities. The Iman of Oman appointed governors who too often quarreled among themselves; commerce continued to wane. In 1741, Mombasa's Mazrui family claimed sovereign control of the island. Opposed to any foreign domination even though it be Muslim, it began the task of unifying the political and economic structures of the coastal cities.

Some coastal cities soon tired of Mazrui domination. In 1817, Pate requested the aid

Johann Rebmann OPPOSITE, one of several proselytizing eighteenth-century missionaries who also explored the hinterland, notably Mount Kilimanjaro. ABOVE: Children at a present-day missionary school.

of the Sultan of Oman, one Seyyid Said; a resolute and aggressive young ruler who at age 15 had assassinated his regent for supposedly not acting in his best interests. Pate's request opened the way for Said to reestablish the Omani empire in East Africa. He easily gained control of Pate and the northern Kenyan cities, but failed to take Mombasa when the Mazrui allied themselves with English forces in the Indian Ocean, who were at the time trying to stop French slave traders.

With the British flag flying over Fort Jesus, Said admitted the futility of attacking

and began negotiations. In 1822 he signed an anti-slave-trafficking agreement; the English removed their protectorate from Mombasa, giving Said control over the entire Kenyan coast.

Finding East Africa more to his taste than the Omani countryside, Said moved his capital to Zanzibar in 1832, where he began an intensive, highly successful commercial development program. He transformed Zanzibar into a gigantic clove plantation and directed the planting of sesame crops on the mainland. The British remained in East Africa with their headquarters in Zanzibar, ostensibly to enforce and strengthen antislavery agreements, but actually to obtain a foothold in the prosperous new land.

On Said's death in 1856, Zanzibar and East Africa were split from Oman. His successor, Seyyid Majed, with support from the English, maintained control of the African portion of the empire, and continued both Said's policies and his close association with England. His brother, Seyyid Bharghash, took over in 1870. Under severe pressure from the English, Bharghash forbade all slave trading in East Africa, by sea or land, and prohibited the entrance of slave vessels into his territorial waters. His reign saw the beginning of the partition of East Africa and the fusion of the two separate histories of Kenya.

THE INTERIOR EXPLORED

The antislavery movement drew European attention to the great expanse of Kenyan land waiting to be claimed, and the legions of "heathen" that could be converted to Christianity. During the second half of the nineteenth century, a handful of missionaries and explorers were lured to Kenya by these challenges, and provided the first more-or-less complete geographic picture of the interior. In previous centuries, coastal Arab traders had established trade routes to Lake Victoria; these, however, did not cross Kenya, but went south of Mount Kilimanjaro through Tanzania, then up the western side of the Rift Valley. This was the general route taken by Burton, Speke, Stanley and Livingstone on various expeditions seeking the source of the Nile.

In 1846, German missionaries representing the English Lutheran Church Missionary Society settled in Rabai, about 20 km (12 miles) northwest of Mombasa. Although not truly the hinterland, Rabai was beyond the coastal belt of Muslim influence. The missionaries, Johann Krapf, Johann Rebmann and Jakob Erhardt, made several proselytizing expeditions to the interior, but did not find the residents much more interested in Christianity than had the Portuguese. From Krapf came Europe's first geographical information about Mount Kenya; Rebmann provided data on Mount Kilimanjaro. Krapf also transcribed Swahili into Roman letters, and published a Swahili dictionary, grammar, and translation of the New Testament.

In 1872, a well-armed German exploratory expedition led by Dr. Gustav Fischer came to investigate the possibility of colonizing the interior. His forces reached the Lake Naivasha region but were ambushed in Hell's Gate Gorge by *moran*, or Maasai warriors. Defeated, Fischer retreated to the coast; German colonial activities shifted south to Tanzania.

The English Royal Geographical Society funded the next major European expedition. Its president, Lord Aberdare, intrigued by the descriptions from Krapf and Rebmann, sent a young Scot, Joseph Thomson, with a small expeditionary force to find a direct route for European traders from the Kenyan coast to Lake Victoria.

Thomson left Mombasa in March 1883 with 143 men, and was soon met by Maasai warriors who arrived in the guise of a peace party. But "as the day wore on," Thomson later wrote, "matters became ominous. The warriors grew boisterous and rude. One of them tried to stab me because I pushed him away and we had to remain under arms from morn till night. On the morning of the third day, our worst fears were realized. We had been deluded and entrapped and we knew they were about to take their revenge on our small party for their failure to annihilate Fischer."

Thomson retreated hastily to Mombasa, regrouped, and began again. Choosing a more northerly route, he crossed the slopes of Mount Kenya, named the mountains to the west after his patron, Lord Aberdare, located Nyahururu Falls (for many years called Thomson's Falls), and arrived on the shores of Lake Victoria near the present-day Kenya–Uganda border. On his return, he detoured north to map Mount Elgon.

Thomson's adventures were filled with encounters with hostile Maasai, countless animals, sundry illness and injuries, witchcraft, stunning panoramas and intriguing discoveries, all of which he recorded and published on his return to England. His tales captured the imagination of Europeans looking for adventure. And the safari business was born.

Kenya's most isolated region, the north, was explored by Count Teleki von Szeck in 1887; he named Lake Rudolf (now Lake Turkana) in honor of a Hapsburg prince.

COLONIALISM

And so began what historians have termed the colonial period of Africa, when individuals at negotiating tables in Europe decided, with the stroke of a pen, the fate of the African peoples and the boundaries of present-day African countries. In 1879, it was estimated that more than 90 percent of the African continent was self-governed. By 1900, all but a tiny percentage was governed by European powers.

In 1886, England's Prime Minister, Lord Salisbury, and Germany's Chancellor, Otto von Bismarck set the present-day boundaries of Kenya and Uganda; an international commission ruled that Sultan Bharghash's holdings on the coast extended only 16 km (10 miles) inland. England then negotiated a £17,000/year lease of the Kenyan coast that remained in effect until the nation's independence, when the Sultan ceded the territory to the new Kenyan government.

The Imperial British East African Company, which was chartered in 1888, became the

OPPOSITE: An anchor outside Fort Jesus in Mombasa, one of the few reminders of Portuguese domination of the Kenyan coast. ABOVE: Some of Kenya's colorfully dressed city dwellers.

administrative and development arm of British colonialism. It purchased valuable goods from Kenya, particularly ivory, in exchange for less-valuable English goods. The enterprise collapsed in July 1895, causing a Victorian financial crash. The British government acquired the floundering company for £200,000, and the territory became officially known as British East Africa. Construction of the Uganda Railway from Mombasa to Lake Victoria began, fulfilling a Kikuyu/Maasai prophecy of an iron snake breathing fire and smoke.

Mombasa retained its position as the major port, with the remaining coastal cities losing all of their previous prosperity. A new nation built around the railroad emerged. As Sir Charles Eliot, Commissioner of British East Africa in 1903, put it, "It is not an uncommon thing for a line to open up a country but this line literally created a country."

The building of the Mombasa–Uganda Railway, so-named because it would connect Uganda with the Indian Ocean, aroused controversy in England, which had made an interest-free loan for its construction. The £5.5 million loan for this "Lunatic Line" was later written off as a gift. The saga of this railroad is well-told in Nairobi's Railway Museum, and in Charles Miller's *The Lunatic Express* and P.H. Patterson's *The Man-eaters of Tsavo*. They tell the heroic story of man's defeat of nature, of thousands of imported Indian laborers who came to build the railroad, of those who stayed permanently and of scores killed and eaten by lions.

Nairobi emerged as the administrative and business center of a country thrust into the twentieth century by the influx of Western (primarily British) settlers, entrepreneurs, developers, explorers and missionaries.

Kenya's colonial history reads very much like that of the Americas, with the appropriation of native lands, with smallpox and measles epidemics, mass slaughter of wild animals, clearing of forests for agriculture, subjugation and confinement of indigenous peoples to reserves, and massive campaigns of "depaganization."

The colonial government chose the temperate plateau between Nairobi and the Rift Valley, the best agricultural land in the country, as Crown Land. In these White Highlands, the government adopted a policy of

not selling to Asians, and an unwritten policy of assuming that no land belonged to the Kenyan tribes. Officially, if the government mistakenly sold or leased lands still occupied by an African, the European purchaser was supposed to advise the government and give up title to the land. In practice, this policy was rarely implemented.

With little or no regard for African rights, white settlers cultivated large expanses of land, using virtually free African labor to plant a variety of crops. The most profitable of these was coffee, which Africans were banned from growing. Big-game hunting and safaris came into vogue, especially after visits by Winston Churchill and Theodore Roosevelt. Although Roosevelt sought fame as a hunter, existing accounts portray him as a terrible shot and a very poor sportsman.

The great variety of African animals, principally lions, leopards, elephants, rhinos, buffaloes and antelope, as well as countless species of birds and reptiles, were slaughtered without quarter. A European community, somewhat loosely organized by the eccentric Lord Delamere, developed with all the trappings of genteel colonial life: antique furniture, European-style homes, formal dinners, polo matches, horse races, and clubs.

The easy lifestyle was briefly interrupted by World War I. Husbands left their wives in charge of plantations, or shipped them home to England, and rode off to fight the Germans in nearby Tanzania. The war in East Africa was not a major British military effort, yet it brought Tanzania under British control via a League of Nations mandate.

In the first years after the war, British veterans were lured to Kenya under the "Soldier Settlement Scheme," whereby land was given away in lotteries and sold on long-term, low-interest credit. The influx of settlers caused a labor crisis; Africans were understandably reluctant to work their own land for someone else at a tiny percentage of the return. The colonial government began to put pressure on the chiefs to direct their subjects into European employment.

Many of the old settlers returned to neglected plantations in need of both labor and money. As Elspeth Huxley describes it in *The Mottled Lizard*:

"So it was a question of starting again, more or less from the beginning, and in the meanwhile everyone had spent his capital. To balance this, the managers of the three main banks in Nairobi were in an expansive, benign and optimistic frame of mind. They conferred large overdrafts upon their customers, rather with the air of monarchs dispensing orders and stars, and details such as rates of interest and terms of repayment were considered by both parties to be almost too insignificant to be brought into the conversation at all. Happily for the banks, who

"Many other farmers were in the same boat. Some went off to hunt elephants, others to work as transport contractors or as road-gang overseers for the Government, one man to collect the skeletons of hippos on the shores of Lake Victoria, pound them up and sell the resultant bonemeal as fertilizer. Another way to turn a modest penny was to recruit labor for the sisal companies, or for some other large employer. One of our neighbors … had taken to this.

"One day he rode over to propose to [Father] that the two of them should go together

in fact charged eight percent, their liberality was rewarded by the stabilization of the rupee, which had been worth 1s. 4d., at the rate of 2s. This meant that one evening [you] went to bed owing £2,000, and woke up next morning owing £3,000; by a stroke of the pen, the banks had gained a bonus of fifty percent at the expense of everyone who had borrowed from them, which meant almost every farmer in the country.

"Because of the state everything had fallen into during the war we could not expect an income from the coffee for three or four years, and … [Father] doubted whether Mr. Playfair and the overdraft would support us, unaided, for as long as that. So he … cast about in all directions for ways of tiding things over…

to a district he knew of, hitherto neglected by other recruiters, in search of stalwart young men willing to put their thumb-marks on a contract binding them to work for six months on some distant plantation… They would get one shilling for each recruit delivered to a prospective employer."

In 1920, there were approximately 9,000 Europeans in British East Africa, most clamoring for London to give them self-rule. London responded by renaming the territory the Kenya Colony and Protectorate, for lofty Mount Kenya, and restating its policy in the Devonshire White Paper of 1923: "Primarily Kenya is an African territory, and His

Many photography shops take photos of their customers: selling film is often only a sideline.

Majesty's Government thinks it necessary definitely to record their considered opinion that the interests of the African natives must be paramount, and that if and when those interests and the interests of the immigrant races should conflict, the former should prevail ... In the administration of Kenya His Majesty's Government regard themselves as exercising a trust on behalf of the African population."

Until after World War II, to which Kenya sent many native regiments, a succession of colonial governors administered Kenya with

TOWARD INDEPENDENCE

It was from the educational system, a random assemblage of missionary establishments, that Kenya's national spirit, for the most part a story of Kikuyu dissatisfaction and resistance, sprang. The Kikuyu population was growing, yet was hemmed in by the White Highlands and the forest around Mount Kenya. Many members of the tribe went to work on European plantations; others left the land for Nairobi.

little regard to the Devonshire Paper. Julian Huxley, after a 1929 tour to evaluate education in Kenya, summed up the prevailing situation: "On top of all this variety of nature and man there impinge Western civilization and Western industrialism. Will their impact level down the variety, insisting on large-scale production to suit the needs of Europe and Big Business, reducing the proud diversity of native tribes and races to a muddy mixture, their various cultures to a single inferior copy of our own? Or shall we be able to preserve the savor of difference to fuse our culture and theirs into an autochthonous civilization, to use local differences as the basis for a natural diversity of development?"

The Country and Its People

After World War II, Harry Thuku, a Kikuyu government clerk, began organizing Kenya's first nationalist group, the Young Kikuyu Organization — for which he lost his job and was arrested and eventually banished to Kismaiya, a small town on the northern Kenyan coast. This fractured the movement, but only briefly. In 1924, the Kikuyu Central Organization (KCA) was formed, with Jomo Kenyatta as secretary.

The Africans were particularly incensed about colonial interference in tribal customs, such as female circumcision, as well as the

OPPOSITE: Musicians TOP and a gourd craftsman BOTTOM are part of a more variegated coastal lifestyle. ABOVE: Mzee Jomo Kenyatta, first president of Kenya.

misappropriation of native lands for European settlement. These and other grievances were carried to London in 1929 by Jomo Kenyatta, who remained abroad in London and Moscow for 15 years, organizing the African rights movement, studying anthropology at the London School of Economics, and publishing a study of Kikuyu life and customs, *Looking on Mount Kenya.*

London responded to Kenyatta's pleas with a series of studies and reviews. One conducted by the 1934 Kenya Land Commission found that 47.5 percent of the

regulation," to justify its actions, claiming that a copy of *Mein Kampf* had been found at KCA headquarters and that its leadership had been suspected of consorting with the Italian Consulate in Nairobi.

The ban did not stop the nationalist movement. It gave rise instead to the Kenyan African Study Union, a multi-tribal organization that became the Kenya Africa Union (KAU) six years later. On Kenyatta's return from England in 1946, he assumed leadership of this party that was to form the government of independent Kenya.

4.4 million hectares (17,000 sq miles) of the highlands reserved for European settlement were not being cultivated. Twenty-five percent lay fallow and another 20 percent was occupied by African squatters, who were allowed to stay so long as they worked part-time for the European farmer, on his terms. At that time, the coffee ban, in which the government prohibited Africans from planting coffee by requiring a license that was virtually impossible to secure, was also still in effect.

These conditions catalyzed the nationalist movement, primarily under the KCA. In 1940, the leaders of all African organizations were arrested, detained, and their groups banned. The government invoked a "defense

After World War II, there were four Kenyan communities — African, European, Asian (primarily Indian) and Arab — all demanding independent and equal representation. Even though the KAU was multi-tribal, it was primarily Kikuyu, and the Africans were divided by tribal affiliations, the Asians by religious beliefs, and the British by the differing attitudes of farmers, businessmen, educators and missionaries. Only the Arabs had a common front, but they were too few to be a major political force. Everyone, however, found fault with colonial rule; some made their viewpoints known in unorthodox ways:

"After the Legislative Council passed an ordinance requiring men of all races to carry an identity card with fingerprints, many whites erupted in fury. Until that time, only Africans had been required to carry identity cards, a measure which they intensely resented. Across the White Highlands, angry meetings were held at which the more zealous whites advocated open defiance of the new law ... At one stormy meeting in Nakuru, a member of the Legislative Council who supported the ordinance was faced with an opponent who strode up and down the gangway of the hall with two large pistols hanging from his belt, fixing a threatening eye on anyone voting against him. In the end, the administration retreated. A compromise was reached by which those who could complete a form in English and provide two photographs were not required to be fingerprinted." (Martin Meredith, *The First Dance of Freedom*.)

Others used traditional avenues in opposing unfair laws. The Kikuyu chief, Mbiyu Koinage, asked the Land Commission for the return of his lands, which had been appropriated for a European coffee farm. He was awarded about one-tenth of the acreage he claimed and ordered to comply with the coffee ban by removing the coffee bushes growing there. Koinage took the case to court and lost.

But the KAU grew stronger. Government policies were challenged by strikes that were often ruthlessly suppressed. In his 1948 annual report, the District Commissioner of Nakuru in the Rift Valley noted that there was thought to be a clandestine movement among the Kikuyu called "Mau Mau." What had caught his attention were oath-taking ceremonies that took place among the inhabitants of the Mau Escarpment. These bound individuals to political objectives such as land reform. Oath-taking ceremonies were outlawed in 1950, during a rash of ritual murders in the Rift Valley, whose victims were primarily Christian Kikuyus who had refused to take the oath.

The killings increased in 1952 and began to include outlying English farmers. Chief Koinage's son organized the Kenya Christian Association advocating peaceful change. The KAU organized a meeting, attended by more than 25,000, where leaders including Jomo Kenyatta denounced the Mau Mau movement. But the Mau Mau now had too much momentum. On October 20, 1952, England proclaimed a state of emergency. Jomo Kenyatta and 82 other nationalists were arrested. Rather than crippling the Mau Mau, this seemed to incite them.

"On March 27, 1953, they pulled the worst of their raids, the Lari Massacre, in the course of which more than 200 Africans of all ages and sexes, living in a compound whose chief was a friend of the British, were murdered and mutilated hideously. And with this horror the Mau Mau war entered a grim phase ... And as counterbalance, the whites began to direct their determination and their superior weaponry into complementary savagery: torture, subversion, and bribery of captured Kikuyu; morbid floggings at the prison camps, where African soldiers were instructed to use Mau Mau methods on suspected inmates, often supervised in these outrages by English officers; the berserker mania that seized the minds of so many 'civilized' Europeans ..." (Peter Ritner, *The Death of Africa*).

Meanwhile, Kenyatta was brought to trial, convicted of organizing the Mau Mau, and sentenced to seven years in jail in Lodwar and Lokichar. The trial was a farce — the chief witness was bribed with two years' study in an English university with all expenses paid and guaranteed government employment on his return. The magistrate received £20,000 to leave Kenya immediately after announcing his verdict.

Even though the KAU leader was no longer Kikuyu, but a Luo, Walter Odede, the government banned the organization and all native groups. It also created fenced "protected villages" where Africans were required to live, and brought in British troops to "enforce" the peace.

During this time, a new constitution, which promoted multiracial participation, was adopted. African politicians complained that democracy was impossible while hundreds of people remained jailed and political organizations banned. In 1955, the colonial government announced that regional political parties could be formed "to encourage a simple and orderly development of African political life."

The Tana River, red with erosion, seasonally greens the arid eastern plains of Kenya.

Under the new constitution, eight communally elected Africans would represent five million constituents, and 14 Europeans would represent 5,000. The Africans refused the Colonial Office's offer of six more seats; in the 1958 elections, all African candidates pledged to refuse office in a move to reject the constitution. Boycotts and protests followed. These maneuvers finally resulted in the all-party, all-race "Lancaster House Conference" in London in 1960.

From the start, the British Government, which had regained political control of the country during the Mau Mau war, made it clear that Kenya was destined to become an African country. A transitional multiracial government, tipped slightly in favor of the African majority, was endorsed, and national political parties were allowed. Two parties emerged: the Kenya African National Union (KANU), which supported a strong central government which would have its seat in Nairobi, and the Kenya African Democratic Union (KADU), which advocated a federal, decentralized government.

UHURU

When the British released Kenyatta from detention in 1961, he gained the leadership of KANU and a seat on the Legislative Council. Two and a half years of disputes between the two parties resulted in a compromise constitution which provided for considerable regional autonomy and a date for the end of colonial rule:

"Kenya regained her *Uhuru* (Freedom) from the British on December 12, 1963. A minute before midnight, lights were put out at the Nairobi stadium so that people from all over the country and the world who had gathered there for the midnight ceremony were swallowed by the darkness. In the dark, the Union Jack was quickly lowered. When next the lights came on the new Kenya flag was flying and fluttering and waving in the air. The Police band played the new National Anthem and the crowd cheered continuously when they saw the flag was black and red and green. The cheering sounded like one intense cracking of many trees, falling on the thick mud in the stadium." (Ngugi wa Thiong'o, *A Grain of Wheat*.)

Four days later Kenya was admitted to the United Nations. With a Kikuyu, Jomo Kenyatta, as president and a Luo, Oginga Odinga, as vice president, independent Kenya adopted policies to encourage foreign investment and participation in the economy while internally restructuring the government to overcome tribalism.

Since agriculture was the basis of the economy, the new government gave priority to the problems of land distribution and ownership. Within five years of independence, through a land resettlement program mainly financed by Britain, one-fifth of the Highlands reverted to African hands. During the 15 years of Kenyatta's rule, Kenya's economy flourished and social services reached a greater number of people. On the political front, the KADU merged with the KANU in 1964, making Kenya a single-party state. The KANU was challenged only briefly, when Vice-president Odinga formed the Kenya People's Union (KPU) in 1966, after he was forced to resign from the government because of his "leftist" views. Three years later, the Minister for Economic Affairs, a Luo named Tom MBoya, was assassinated by the Kikuyu and violence broke out in Kisumu, the Luo heartland: Odinga and his KPU were blamed. Using tactics learned from the colonial government, Kenyatta detained Odinga and other KPU leaders and banned the KPU.

Kenyatta remained in office until his death on August 22, 1978. He was succeeded by David Arap Moi, a Kalenjin who had become vice president when Odinga resigned in 1966.

Moi continued the basic policies of Kenyatta and remained in power after elections in 1983 and 1988, but amid growing controversy that included an amendment to the constitution that changed voting from secret ballots to voting by lining up, widely and correctly seen as a step backwards for democracy. Councilors from the country's majority Kikuyu tribe were removed from many positions of power and further constitutional changes dissolved the separation between judicial and executive areas of government. Despite this divided opposition,

OPPOSITE: Coastal Kenyans TOP have turned their mangrove swamps to a profit — poles for construction. BOTTOM: The narrow, dusty streets of old town Malindi remain the domain of hand-pulled carts and pedestrians.

intertribal violence in key areas enabled Moi to win further elections in December 1992, but many international agencies were dissatisfied with the results: aid programs were suspended and the economy suffered. For the 1997 elections, Moi changed the constitution to allow himself a further term of office, and in an atmosphere of increasing tribal unrest — especially in the Rift Valley and around Mombasa — scraped in for what is widely considered to be his final term of office. Over the last 10 years, freedom of speech has increased greatly in Kenya and

be to be significant threats to Kenya's democratic tradition.

Central to Kenya's economic survival is the creation of jobs and industries to generate foreign exchange. Tea surpassed the traditional "big money" export, coffee, in 1988, while tourism led both in foreign revenues. However, tourism is a fragile industry. Kenya's main international draw is its national parks and most visitors come to see the animals. A rash of poaching in late 1988 caused such a dramatic fall in animal numbers and such security problems in the

the voices that are heard are expressing widespread dissatisfaction with a political regime riven with corruption and cronyism. Nearly 40 years after independence, Kenya remains the most stable country in East Africa and perhaps in all of Africa. Nonetheless, it faces problems of overpopulation, unemployment and insufficient foreign exchange to buy needed imports.

To the casual traveler, tribalism is not readily apparent, except perhaps in the obvious difference in dress. But tribal problems exist and can be fanned for political ends: many political analysts feel that therein lies the greatest threat to Kenya's stability. Moi's amendments to the constitution, the basis of Kenya's independence, might also prove to

national parks that tourism suffered. Increased pressure on the government by the East African Wildlife Society and tour operators brought about more stringent anti-poaching measures. No sooner were the most pressing environmental problems brought under control than human factors started to threaten. Tribal conflict surrounding the 1997 elections and the occasional, internationally reported, incidents of violent crime brought personal security to the top of the agenda: the tourist industry all but collapsed, bringing the economy grinding to a halt and starving the Kenya Wildlife Service of funds.

Things are currently starting to turn around. The powerful political figure of Nicholas Biwott — a man who strikes fear into many Kenyans — has been put in charge of tourism, and a newly pragmatic approach to Kenya's chief foreign exchange revenue source can be detected. Entry to the national parks, once bled dry by forgery, has been computerized and is newly secure. The country still offers a warm and sincere welcome to foreign visitors, and crime, in Nairobi at least, has been brought under control. This is just as well. Without tourism Kenya's wildlife has little chance of survival.

LAY OF THE LAND

Slightly smaller than the state of Texas, but larger than France, Kenya lies on the equator and is bordered by the Indian Ocean, Somalia, Ethiopia, Sudan, Uganda and Tanzania. In a stretch of 800 km (500 miles) from east to west, the land rises from the reef-fringed sandy beaches of the Indian Ocean to the mile-high plateau of Nairobi, higher still to the lofty snow-capped summit of Mount Kenya (Africa's second-tallest mountain), then drops across the Great Rift Valley to Lake Victoria — 1,157 m (3,795 ft) above sea level. From south to north along another 800-km (500-mile) axis, the Kenyan countryside contrasts jagged, forested mountains, and lush red-soil agricultural lands with Lake Turkana and the timeless, sandy-colored dusty desert that covers more than one half of the country.

Before the formation of the Rift Valley, Kenya's climate and vegetation were probably uniformly tropical. The gigantic eruption that created the Rift also triggered dramatic climatic changes. After millions of years of evolution, Kenya's climates are now dramatically varied — semiarid, tropical, temperate, alpine and arctic. Only the visitor who wishes to climb to the peaks of Mount Kenya, Mount Elgon or Tanzania's Mount Kilimanjaro, however, need prepare for temperatures below freezing. Some day, nowhere in Kenya will warm clothing be necessary, according to United Nations Environment Program (UNEP) scientists in Nairobi. The country's overall climate is warming and its desert growing, due to the greenhouse effect.

Kenya's varied climates and vegetation are home to an endless parade of animals, ranging from miniature antelope only 25 cm (10 inches) tall to six-ton elephants. To enjoy this animal carnival to the fullest, patience is needed. Kenya has approximately 90 species of ungulates or grazing animals, along with innumerable predators and scavengers, 1,500 different birds, hundreds of aquatic and reptilian species, and countless types of insects and arachnids. With 10 percent of Kenya's land and a portion of its coastal waters devoted to the preservation and protection of flora and fauna, you are never more than a few hours from one of 48 national parks and game preserves where animals still reign supreme, and where man is only a spectator.

THE COAST

Kenya's 480 km (300 miles) of coast along the Indian Ocean is world-famous for its sand beaches lined with palm trees and backed by rocky inlets and mangrove swamps teeming with miniature aquatic life. The beaches are protected from harsh ocean waves by extensive, multicolored coral fringe and barrier reefs. These shelter hundreds of aquatic species, such as the graceful black-and-white striped Moorish idol, electric-blue striped blinny, lacy basket starfish, prickly sea urchins and spongy sea cucumbers, which are protected in the Kisite, Watamu, and Malindi Marine National Parks.

The reefs have for centuries also provided building material for coastal cities, and served as a deterrent to sharks visiting waters near bathing beaches. But there are exceptions! Those who swim on the eastern side of the reef should *always* be alert for sharks.

Inland of the beaches runs a narrow coastal plain three to twenty kilometers (two to twelve miles) wide in the south and 150 km (90 miles) wide along the Somalia border in the north. The wider northern plain was formed by Kenya's largest river, the Tana, which meanders from its source on the slopes of Mount Kenya for 1,120 km (700 miles) to empty into Ungwana (Formosa) Bay between Lamu and Malindi. Some areas of the plain are suitable for agriculture,

Cooling themselves lazily in the Mara River, hippopotamuses look more tranquil than they actually are. They kill more people than lions!

but most are dry scrub. A few stretches of thick coastal forest are protected as natural reserves.

An ever-present wind off the Indian Ocean brings relief from the average daytime temperature of 30°C (87°F). Even in the cooler summer season, night temperatures rarely fall below 20°C (68°F).

Along the coast, rainfall is frequent but of short duration, except during the April to June monsoon season. A tropical cloudburst may slow the unsuspecting visitor, but Kenyans casually proceed along their routes,

CENTRAL PLATEAU AND HIGHLANDS

The plateau beyond the coastal plain ascends gradually to the central highlands in the south, and across the Ethiopian border in the north. With only a few low valleys and monotonous but unique vegetation — flaming thorn trees, monstrous upside-down baobabs, and scrub — the plateau conveys a sense of endlessness, a place described by Elspeth Huxley as a horizonless void where "you could walk straight across to the rim of the

knowing it will soon be followed by sun and drying wind. Annual rainfall along the coast and coastal plain is 1,000 to 1,250 mm (40 to 50 inches); but even in May, the peak of the monsoon season, seven hours of sunshine is normal per day (situated on the equator, Kenya has 12 hours of daylight year-round). Tourism to the coast is affected, however, by the trade winds that turn on the shore from May to November. Hitting the northern coast in particular, these coat the beach in seaweed and prevent boats from crossing the sheltering reef. In the north, many hotels close completely over this period, and even in less affected regions, such as Mombasa and Diani in the south, few visitors will be found in these months.

world." Here in Tsavo East and Tsavo West national parks roam elephants, buffaloes, Grevy's zebra, giraffes, lions, aardvarks, impalas and antelope, including the miniature five- to six-kilogram (10- to 12-lb) dik dik, and gerenuks which stand on hind legs to feed. Guinea fowl, francolins, black-headed orioles and red-billed hornbills are only some of the birds you can expect to find.

In the northwest, the Rift Valley and Lake Turkana cross the plateau, changing the landscape. The vegetation is much the same but sparser: Kenya's growing desert. Sibiloi National Park, along the shores of Lake Turkana, protects several hundred square kilometers of Pleistocene era fossil beds and the "cradle of mankind."

The plateau is dry and hot, with average daytime temperatures of 34°C (93°F). Rainfall is minimal, between 250 to 500 mm (10 to 12.5 inches) per year; the area suffers from periodic drought. Yet the meager vegetation sustains a large variety of wildlife, including elephants, giraffes, zebra and antelope which have been pushed by human and livestock expansion from the more temperate lands.

South-central Kenya, termed the Highlands during colonial days, is split by the Great Rift Valley. High tablelands with forested volcanic mountains, savannas and a temperate climate, the Highlands have, in modern times, become a highly populated region.

Here, the savannas are interrupted by deep green valleys, narrow canyons with cascading waterfalls, and steep, rugged mountains. Although not as high as 5,895-m (19,650-ft) Mount Kilimanjaro in Tanzania, at 5,199 m or 17,085 ft, Mount Kenya is taller than Europe's highest peak, Mont Blanc. The days are pleasantly warm and the nights cool. In Mount Kenya and Aberdare national parks live many of the same animals that inhabit Tsavo, but they are joined by other animals not adapted to the arid plateau.

Mount Kenya, on the eastern side of the Rift Valley, and the Aberdare Mountains on the west capture up to 3,000 mm (120 inches) of rain per year, while the lower rich agricultural lands receive between 750 and 1,000 mm (30 to 40 inches): primarily from March to May, the "long rains," and from October to December, the "short rains." As on the coast, although a lot of rain can fall, it generally does so quickly, and in the worst season, April and May, Nairobi and the highlands still average five hours of sun per day. Climate change has made these seasons less dependable, however, and these once reliable dates have, over recent years, varied drastically.

In Nairobi and other low-lying plateau areas, temperatures are comfortable year-round at 10° to 14°C (50° to 58°F) at night and 22° to 26°C (72° to 79°F) during the day. When traveling to high altitudes the visitor will generally experience an average drop of 0.6°C (1°F) per 100 m (328 ft), descending to below freezing on Mount Kenya and the Aberdare Mountains. Evenings in the low mountains are usually brisk, with temperatures around 7°C (45°F) not unusual.

TROPICAL JUNGLE

The western slope of the Rift Valley descends to an elevation of 1,157 m (3,795 ft), where the world's second-largest freshwater lake, Victoria, covers 69,490 sq km (26,830 sq miles). With such a large surface area, Lake Victoria — its islands, papyrus beds, creeks, bays, and beaches — has created a tropical microclimate. Hippos and crocodiles inhabit the shores, as do Egyptian geese, flamingos, cormorants, blue herons, pelicans, Marabou storks and other flying species. The enter-

taining hammerkops and jacan or lily trotters go about transported on the backs of hippos.

Only here, on the surrounding hills and valleys near Kakamega, will one still find in Kenya the tropical forest of African jungle movies, with its monkeys, baboons, bush duikers, forest hogs, buffaloes, waterbucks, bongos and eagle owls. Rainfall here reaches 1,000 to 1,300 mm (40 to 50 inches) per year, and day and night temperatures are more distinct — 14° to 18°C (58° to 64°F) at night and 30° to 34°C (86° to 93°F) during the day.

OPPOSITE: The hardy acacia tortilis survives in soil scorched by drought. ABOVE: Kenya's jungles are paradises of birds, dense vegetation and waterfalls.

Nairobi
and
About

THE CAPITAL

Unless you are flying into Mombasa for a beach break, your trip to Kenya is most likely to begin in Nairobi, a bustling city whose ultramodern skyline loses some of its glitter as the buildings get increasingly shabby near street level. In fact, they tower over a sometimes daunting but always exhilarating street-life that does take some getting used to. As Nairobi is over a mile above sea level, its climate is temperate and not too drastic an adjustment for travelers arriving from colder northern climates, but it's not a city where many visitors to Kenya spend much time.

On most travel itineraries Nairobi only figures as a first-night jet-lag dispersal point, before travelers head out to the national parks. After the safari experience, they are flown back early (in case of flight delays) and frightened by tales of crime and lawlessness into hiding in hotel day-rooms until their overnight outbound flights depart. This is a real shame, because there is far more to Kenya than the wildlife experience, and Nairobi is one of the best places to explore the culture and society of East Africa's most accessible societies. Over the last few years crime levels have been brought down significantly, and those who have come to know and love Kenya will find Nairobi a civilized and inviting focus of the social, cultural and financial aspirations of most urban Kenyans.

Nairobi is today one of the most important commercial centers in East Africa, and the largest city after Johannesburg and Cairo. Its official population is currently estimated at four and a half million, and growing at three percent a year.

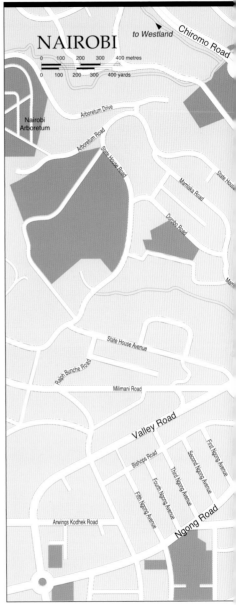

NAIROBI

to Westland

Chiromo Road

0   100   200   300   400 metres

0   100   200   300   400 yards

Arboretum Drive

Nairobi Arboretum

Arboretum Road

State House Road

Mamlaka Road

State House

Dennis Road

State House Avenue

Ralph Bunche Road

Milimani Road

Valley Road

Bishops Road

First Ngong Avenue

Second Ngong Avenue

Third Ngong Avenue

Fourth Ngong Avenue

Fifth Ngong Avenue

Arwings Kodhek Road

Ngong Road

BACKGROUND

Nairobi, "the place of cold water" in the Maa language spoken by the Maasai, was not inhabited until George Whitehouse, chief engineer for the Mombasa–Uganda railroad, decided in 1899 to make this papyrus bog his construction headquarters and the railway's principal nerve center. Almost overnight, a boom town sprang up on the "black cotton" soil that expands to a sticky, impass-

able mud when wet and contracts to a solid crust when dry.

"With its irregular lines of weather-beaten tents and faceless, barrack-like corrugated iron bungalows, Nairobi at the turn of the [twentieth] century bore a not altogether inexact resemblance to a miniature Dachau without walls. There was a main thoroughfare called Victoria Street which became a canal of thigh-deep mud whenever rain fell. A proliferation of the cramped, fetid shops

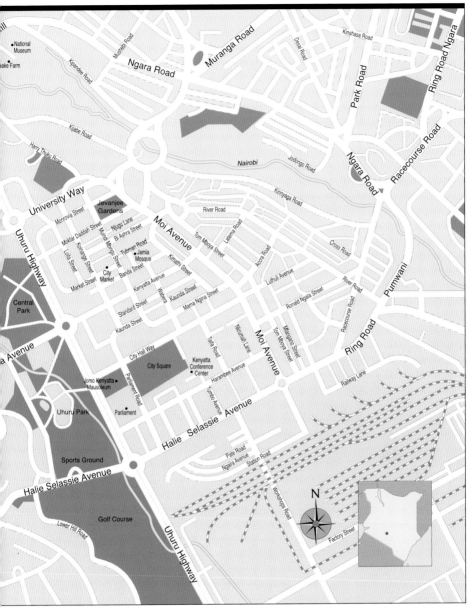

known as *dukas* pockmarked the town, and at the western end of Victoria Street sprawled [an Indian] bazaar … Other points of interest were a post office, a soda water factory and a shaky timber structure known as Wood's Hotel which doubled as a general store and which burned down several times before being abandoned as a poor insurance risk. Social life centered on a singularly uncongenial heap of wood and corrugated iron which railway officials and other British residents were pleased to call their club." Thus did Charles Miller, author of *The Lunatic Express*, a chronicle of the Mombasa–Uganda railway, describe Kenya's future capital.

The railway was finished on December 19, 1901. The British East African Company soon realized that it could not entice the Kenyans to produce enough export crops to keep the £5 million investment paying for itself. Thus began a publicity campaign to attract European settlers with offers of cheap land in return for crops that would provide freight for the new line.

The scheme was only a minor success. It brought settlers by the thousands, many of whom were more interested in getting rich quickly than working the land. Although the land was fertile, it was difficult to clear and maintain. European crops were often attacked by tropical blights and parasites.

Nonetheless, many European settlers fell in love with Kenya and stayed. Nairobi, not their homesteads, became the center of commerce and society.

And although Nairobi has evolved into an international center with a character all its own it has still retained a strong feel of a frontier city, on the edge of a wild and rugged country. The Norfolk Hotel, from which Elspeth Huxley began her journey to Thika, has been restored and enlarged, and is now an international class hotel. Another popular European watering hole in the early days, the Stanley Hotel, has been replaced by a modern structure housing the five-star New Stanley Hotel. The city is cosmopolitan, with its mosques, temples, churches and a

In 1906, the colonial offices were moved from Mombasa to this new city that now had the air of a Wild West town. Men carried guns; brawls were not infrequent. Parties were wild and uninhibited, lasting for several days until the participants staggered out of town back to their farms and ranches. Indian merchants dominated businesses, Europeans controlled the banks and administrative services, and Africans were relegated to a subservient role, a formula that has remained much unchanged to the present day. As the naturalist I.N. Dracopoli described Nairobi in 1914, it was "neither African nor European but seems to combine in one city the discomforts of two civilizations without the advantages of either."

synagogue; its international organizations such as the United Nations Environment Program, Food and Agriculture Organization and World Health Organization; its multinational businesses and foreign embassies. For most of the correspondents covering the neighboring countries of Somalia, Uganda and beyond, Nairobi is the city they call home.

Yet it has retained some of its original flavor. The Indian *dukas* have grown up into a great variety of shops throughout the city. The dust and mud still exist, and the population is still exploding faster than jobs can be created and houses constructed.

The inhabitants are warm and helpful. The city offers every modern comfort but on Kenyan terms. It is good to remember that

Nairobi is Africa and the tropics. Little happens immediately, but it happens. A phone call to Europe or the United States during business hours can go through instantly or take up to an hour. Faxes usually go through instantly, especially outside office hours in the United States or Europe, and Internet access is just starting to open up international communications. Meanwhile domestic communications remain in the dark ages. Trying to make internal telephone calls is one of Kenya's great frustrations: lines often drop out of service, ring endlessly or just don't

impression, and a disproportionate number of robberies happen in a visitor's first 24 hours. There are ways to make your transition easier. If a visa is required (regulations do change, though currently a tourist visa costs US$54 or £35), either obtain it in advance or, if at the airport, make sure you have the correct change, in dollars or sterling. Leg it quickly from the plane to get a good place in the line and to clear passport control. In the arrivals hall, collect your luggage and check it is intact (make a fuss here if it isn't, before clearing customs) and then stow any valuables

work, and the whole process becomes quite expensive without making any usable connection. Industry and commerce carry on their business in a quiet vacuum untroubled by effective or efficient communication, and to avoid ulcers it is easiest to regard this as a liberating experience. Satellite communications and cell-phones have started to improve the situation in Nairobi and the major cities and it is hoped that expanded coverage will bring effective and affordable communication to the hinterland over the coming years.

— cameras, jewelry, etc. — in relative peace and privacy. There are banks and ATM machines both before and after customs: it's best, if possible, to change money first and stow your money and papers securely. Then, and only then, are you ready to pass through into the inevitable sea of taxi touts.

To get into town, there is an office of Kenatco taxis as well as a line of taxis offering rides into the city for a fixed price, currently Ksh1,000 to most hotels. Lower prices can be negotiated with other, unmetered cabs if you're feeling up to the hassle.

AIRPORT ARRIVALS

First-time visitors to Nairobi International Airport rarely emerge with a favorable

OPPOSITE: The Parliament Building on City Square is a landmark of Kenya's *Uhuru* (Independence). ABOVE: Friday prayers outside Jamia Mosque in downtown Nairobi.

Between 6:15 AM and 8:30 PM the no. 34 bus runs into the central bus station, with tickets costing just Ksh30, but you'll probably be sharing the bus with a few professional thieves who might need discouraging by your generally alert disposition and steely resolve. Personally, and especially after an overnight flight, I find a taxi less stressful.

Once you're established at your hotel, Nairobi is all yours.

GENERAL INFORMATION

There is no official tourist information office in Nairobi — a foretaste of the help you can expect in more remote parts of the country. So you'll be relying on the, necessarily biased, advice given by commercial organizations. Fortunately, the Kenyan tradition of upright civility means the advice most travelers get is better than they deserve. A good place to start would be **Let's Go Travel (** (02) 447151 or (02) 441030 FAX (02) 447270 or (02) 441690 E-MAIL info@letsgosafari.com WEB SITE www.letsgosafari.com, Box 60342, Nairobi.

To get about, extremely battered **taxis** can be found outside most hotels and tourist attractions, but if you need to call one the leading companies are Kenatco **(** (02) 225123, (02) 338611 or (02) 230771 and, for a gray London-type taxi, Kenya Taxi Cabs Association **(** (02) 215352. Otherwise there are always plenty of taxis in most of the places you'll need them, many barely roadworthy. Arrange the fare before you set off and don't be scared to bargain: the usual rates are generally much lower than you end up paying.

A medical emergency (dial **(** 999 from any phone) would have to be an emergency indeed before checking into the under-funded public hospital, the **Kenyatta National Hospital (** (02) 726300, Arwings Kodhek Road. Better, here, to go private: two hospitals with good reputations include the **Consolata Sisters' Nazareth Hospital (** (02) 335684, Riara Ridge Road, Limuru (25 km or 18 miles outside Nairobi), or the more central **Aga Khan Hospital (** (02) 740000, Third Parklands Avenue. If you need to get to these hospitals from the bush, the **Flying Doctors Service** (Amref) **(** (02) 501280 or (02) 602492 FAX (02) 336886 and **AAR Health Services (** (02) 717375/6 are the heroes who might save your life.

Nairobi is the best place in Kenya to pick up your e-mail, with plenty of Internet cafés, generally good connection speeds and competitive rates. One chain (of three) with good connection speeds is **e-world** with branches on Haile Selassie Avenue, Moi Avenue (junction with Kimathi Street), and Barclay Plaza on Loita Street. Alternatively, try **Browse Internet Access (** (02) 251947 WEB SITE www.browseinternet.co.ke, Norwich Union House, Fourth Floor, Mama Ngina Street, opposite the Hilton and open from 7 AM to 9 PM daily.

ORIENTATION

The city center lies on both sides of Kenyatta Avenue, bounded by Uhuru Highway to the west, University Way to the north, Moi Avenue to the east, and Haile Selassie Avenue to the south. The grid of reasonably well-marked streets below the high-rise buildings is compact and enjoyable to walk around during daylight hours, but stay alert and don't carry any obvious valuables. At night taxis are preferable. The same is true all day long if you venture too far across Moi Avenue to the east. After a block or so you'll be in the densely-populated Latema/River Road area, where you'll find the city's cheapest accommodation, most upcountry bus offices and a selection of cheap, local bars. It's an area to be cautious in.

Follow Uhuru Highway northwest (its name changes to Chiromo Road) and after two miles (three kilometers) you'll reach the Westlands district. This suburb is, increasingly, the area of choice for the better bars, businesses and restaurants escaping from the seething action of the inner city. It's quite normal to spend plenty of time shuttling between the city center and Westlands by taxi, at Ksh300 or so a time.

As a newly arrived tourist, don't be surprised if you are approached frequently by young men offering their services as guides to help you find a hotel, safari operator or car rental. They can be helpful but more often are just annoying. Once you get a tan and have found your way around town, you probably won't be bothered as much.

Mosques built by Kenya's Muslim minority are among Nairobi's most graceful buildings.

If you do decide to deal with one of these young men, never follow him down alleys or to businesses that do not have offices. Even some of the Nairobi offices are nothing more than a front for services that are not readily available. There is an abundance of legitimate tour operators, car rental businesses and travel agencies, so there's no need to risk swimming with sharks.

WHAT TO SEE AND DO

The city center is mainly a place to shop, eat, meet and drink. There are some attractions in the central area but not many. It is also possible to visit **Parliament** and the **Kenyatta Conference Center**. Both are situated around City Square, set around the statue of Mzee Jomo Kenyatta and his mausoleum with an eternal flame. Parliament is open to the public, but during a session you must obtain a permit from the gatehouse on the corner of Parliament Road and Harambee Avenue to visit the public or speakers' gallery. If Parliament is not in session, the guards can usually arrange a tour of the building. When a conference is taking place or there are visiting dignitaries in town, City Square is brightly decorated with flags and drapes, but despite the bougainvilleas and manicured lawns the area is just too clean, too free of traders, to give much of a feel of Nairobi. The main reason to visit used to be to go, for a fee, to the top of the conference center for a panoramic bird's-eye view of the city but it's no longer the highest, or even the best, vantage point these days. The gleaming high-rise **ICEA Building**, on Kenyatta Avenue, with its glass-walled lift, is currently the most popular place, with a tip to the security guards in order, or less trodden are the stairs of **View Park Towers** on Loita Street, where you can even go up at night to watch the parade of mismatched headlights thread through the potholes of the city's main roads.

The **National Archives** ((02) 228959, Moi Avenue opposite the Hilton, Monday to Friday 8 AM to 4 PM, Saturday to 12:30 PM, free, are worth a visit, being the nearest the city center gets to a non-commercial art gallery/museum. Downstairs there are a great number of ethnological artifacts, refreshingly — or frustratingly — free of any organized

presentation, and on the upper gallery there is an interesting collection of historic photographs. Tourists are also steered towards the **Jamia Mosque**, near the City Market, though quite why, considering non-Muslims are not allowed in, I fail to see. At any rate, it's in all the guidebooks.

Broaden your horizons beyond the central city grid, however, and there are plenty more attractions within a short taxi range.

First visit should be the **National Museum** ((02) 742131-4 WEB SITE www.museums.org.ke, open 9:30 AM to 6 PM daily, Ksh200, located

just over two kilometers (less than a mile and a half) from the city center on Museum Hill. It provides an informative orientation to Kenya's paleontology, geology, ornithology, ethnology, history and wildlife. It also has a small gift shop whose prices may be slightly higher than some of the downtown shops, but the proceeds go to the museum, a worthy cause. Guides, who are in theory free but generally expect a tip, should be available on request. Adjacent to the museum is the **Snake Farm**, which houses an extensive collection of poisonous and non-poisonous African snakes, crocodiles, tortoises and fish. Admission is Ksh200. It is safer to see these creatures here than in the wild.

Near the railway station, at the end of the potholed Ngaira Avenue south of Haile Selassie Avenue, is the **Railway Museum**, Station Road, 8:30 AM to 5 PM daily, Ksh200. Even though it's quite close to the station I'd take a taxi here as the access road looks unsafe to me. A lot of the exhibits, a collection of period trains and carriages, are rusting gracefully in the open air. Coach No. 12, from which Superintendent C. H. Ryall was dragged and eaten by one of the man-eaters of Tsavo, is also here: look in the main museum for the picture of the lion dragging the body clear. The locomotive that was used in the filming of *Out of Africa* is also well preserved, along with a fascinating photographic display of the building of the "Lunatic Express," and a collection of memorabilia from the railway and Lake Victoria steamers.

Nairobi has several parks and green spaces. Although **Uhuru Park**, across Uhuru Highway from the city center, is not generally safe even during the day, the **Nairobi Arboretum**, five kilometers (three miles) northwest of the city center on Arboretum Road, has been restored to its former glory, and **City Park**, three and a half kilometers (just over two miles) northeast of the city center on City Park Road, is the third largest. Here, you can enjoy the tropical vegetation and bird life on foot, but even in daylight, strolls here can be insecure.

Better then to take to a car and make a first safari to **Nairobi National Park (** (02) 500627 FAX (02) 505866, Box 42076, on the outskirts of the city limits. Turn off the residential street into the any of the park gates, pay the entrance fee (steep at US$20 for adults, US$5 for children, Ksh200 for the car, although this is less than many other parks in Kenya), and suddenly you're transported to the vast open plains of Africa, fenced, but full of all the native animals. A troop of olive baboons are residents of the main gate area, but you can expect to see plenty more than these. There are ostrich, zebras, impalas, gazelles, jackals, giraffes and warthogs amongst the 80 species of large mammals present. You'll perhaps spot rhinos, cheetahs, lions, hippos and crocodiles. Within its 117 sq km (44 sq miles) it contains all the "Big Five" except the rather unmanageable

elephant. If you don't have a guide, ask the rangers at the gate, who generally have a good idea where to find the rarer animals. It is hard to describe the sudden thrill of being surrounded by such a variety of wildlife with the noise of Nairobi traffic faint in the distance. The park fills in the area between the (domestic) Wilson Airport and the main (international) Jomo Kenyatta Airport, and can be incorporated in a slow, circuitous, expensive but highly rewarding route between the two, much favored by tour operators with VIP clients.

For those with a serious interest in conservation, within the park it is possible to make an appointment to see the **David Sheldrick Wildlife Trust Elephant and Rhino Orphanage (** (02) 891996 FAX (02) 890053, 11 AM to noon, entry by donation. Here visitors come a distant second to the priorities of the animals, but this is an unusually accessible chance for the seriously interested to watch some groundbreaking conservation work. There are manned entrance gates all around the park but the main gate, off Langata Road near the Carnivore Restaurant, has a further couple of attractions. There is a café, a brand-new walking trail, and a Mini Animal Orphanage (open 8 AM to 5:30 PM daily, entrance costs US$5) where animals are looked after before being returned to the wild.

It is perfectly possible to travel round the park in a rented car, though you'll see more

OPPOSITE: The Uhuru Monument celebrates Kenya's struggle for independance. ABOVE: Modern buildings, interspersed with jacaranda, bougainvillea and palm trees, are features of urban Nairobi.

from the higher perspective of a minibus: most of the safari companies will run tours of the park for about US$50 but generally not at the optimum dawn and dusk periods. Check with **Let's Go Travel** ((02) 447151 or (02) 441030 FAX (02) 447270 or (02) 441690 E-MAIL info@letsgosafari.com WEB SITE www .letsgosafari.com, Box 60342, Nairobi, or **UTC** ((02) 331960 FAX (02) 331422 WEB SITE www .unitedtour.com, Box 42196, Nairobi, for further details.

One kilometer (half a mile) past the park's main gate are the **Bomas of Kenya** ((02)

891801 FAX (02) 891401, Forest Edge Road, with a collection of huts built in the traditional styles of the different ethnic groups. Energetic but uninspiring examples of tribal dancing are laid on for tour groups, with performances at 2:30 PM and 4 PM Monday to Friday, 3:30 PM and 5:15 PM Saturdays, Sundays and holidays, Ksh300. On weekends there's a disco after the main show.

For Isak Dinesen fans, her house in the smart suburb of **Karen**, 15 km (nine miles) south of Nairobi, has been restored and turned into the **Karen Blixen Museum** ((02) 882779, Box 40658, Nairobi, Karen Road, 9:30 AM to 6:30 PM daily, Ksh200, with a museum featuring an exhibition of her life and work amongst the original furnishings and decor. The setting for the image-forming *Out of Africa* experience is far smaller and more human than you'd expect; the grounds contain early farm machines and are well maintained. Many tour operators offer half-day tours that take in the Karen Blixen Museum and the nearby **Giraffe Sanctuary** ((02) 891658 FAX (02) 890973,

Box 15124, Koitobos Road, three kilometers (one and a half miles) off Langata Road, open 10 AM to 5:30 PM, entrance Ksh250, where each afternoon visitors can feed cattle nuts to endangered Rothschild's giraffes. It's not just their necks that are long: their tongues have nervous tourists squealing in excitement, but the sanctuary actually does sterling work in preserving this exceptionally rare and vulnerable giraffe species. There's a tea-house and, if you're feeling flush, an extremely expensive but small and exclusive hotel here.

The **Denys Finch-Hatton Memorial** in the Ngong Hills used to be one way to recapture the romantic isolation of colonial times: now the private owner charges entrance fees and the atmosphere has gone. It's better to stroll off alone, relax under the trees and let Kenya seep into your soul as it did into the young author's.

From the top of the Ngong Hills is a magnificent view, but it is not safe to go alone. In the past few years there have been several muggings and robberies here. In spite of an ever-present security force, it is suggested that you park your car at the police station at the foot of the hills and take a police escort. Single women, or even two women alone, should definitely not make the hike alone: even Kenyans don't.

A carry-over from colonial times are the races at **Nairobi Racecourse**, 10 km (six miles) northwest of town on Ngong Road, which take place one weekend out of two. Check the sports pages of the *Nation* newspaper to see if there's racing scheduled during your visit. The races are usually a lively gathering where everyone knows both horses and riders and the even the bookies seem to know the winner in advance. Admission is Ksh200 and the first race is at 2 PM. Racecourse Road, outside the grounds, is lined with traders and a is good place to hunt for folding chairs, wicker furniture and large-sized earthenware pots.

SHOPPING

In a city where there are few government-run galleries and museums, the commercial organizations step in to fill the breach. Even if you're not going to buy, some of Nairobi's shops contain the best selection of cultural arts and crafts you're likely to find in the country, although prices are often steep.

Curio and craft shops and stores are found everywhere in the city center. You can bargain in most but generally only with cash. Expect to pay near full price if you use a credit card. Before buying, shop around, because prices and quality vary greatly. To get some idea of the best quality available check out **African Heritage**, on Banda Street, a combination café/museum/shop and, on weekends, live music venue. Prices reflect quality. For possibly the worst quality and value head to the **Central Market**, where a central core of vegetables is ringed by balconies of sharp salesmen. Many visitors prefer to head out of town and buy where they know excess profits are going to a good cause: the **Undugu Shop** in Woodvale Grove, Westlands, has a wide range of handicrafts and Ethiopian antiques sold to benefit a number of charitable projects around Nairobi. An even wider range of products is available at the **Utamaduni Crafts Center** in Langata, where 18 specialist shops trade in a center opened by the Kenyan Wildlife Service. For safari clothes, try **Colpro** in Kimathi Street: it outfitted Michael Palin on the BBC *Pole to Pole* television show. Behind banked and junky tee-shirts they run a specialist outfitting department with a full range of gear that can be tailored to fit.

The **East African Wildlife Society** runs a shop on the mezzanine floor of the Hilton Building, on Mama Ngina Street and City Hall Way; proceeds help support their wildlife projects. Several artists sell their work only here. Some unusual items are produced with the American or European buyer in mind, such as hand-painted animals on handkerchiefs and scarves. The Society sell its own "impala" tie and a safari board game which makes a great present for children and adults alike. From it you can learn Kenyan geography and the names of animals in Swahili. The Society also has a selection of books on Kenya.

Books in Kenya are not expensive, and the selection is excellent. It is a good idea to bring a book or two on safari because, once in the game parks, you will generally have a couple of hours in the mid-afternoon when

reading on the verandah of your room or tent or around the swimming pool will be as energetic as you feel. There is a wealth of good literature available. There are also many coffee-table books on Kenya and its animals that you may want to take home. For children, the East African Publishing House has two beautifully illustrated legends, *The Hot Hippo* and *The Greedy Zebra*, for Ksh230. They are good for the read-aloud-ages and are written at a third-grade reading level.

For the best selection of books in Nairobi, go to the bookstore in the New Stanley Hotel,

the **Select Bookshop** on Kimathi Street, or the **Text Book Center** located in the Sarit Center, Westlands.

Near the bus station, the **open market** on Mfangano Street and Hakati Road serves the nearly 50 percent of Nairobi's population who inhabit the area bounded by Moi Avenue and the Nairobi River. The market is similar to those of country villages, and a great variety of dried beans, *ugali* (white maize meal), rice, potatoes, cabbages and the other essentials of everyday Kenyan life are sold.

Your first day in Nairobi is probably not the best for bargaining: traders here take a special pride in judging how long tourists have been in the country, and newcomers are easy prey for these astute business people. Their aim is to get you to place a value on their offerings: say a price and you're hooked,

OPPOSITE: Cotton and silk fabrics in Nairobi shops are as colorful as the butterflies and birds of the national parks and reserves. ABOVE: The temperate climate means every sort of fruit and vegetable can be found in Nairobi's markets.

so just stay quiet. After a safari or two, schedule a day in Nairobi for shopping; you'll feel much more in control and be able to enjoy the frantic excitement of the market. Then you'll be ready for the **Maasai Market**, which takes place 9 AM to 3 PM Tuesdays by the traffic circle between Muranga Road and Kijabe Road, near the Meridian Court Hotel, where you can bring down prices by trading unwanted cosmetics or tee-shirts of your own. For woven sisal and wooden furniture (for example, wooden directors chairs for about US$10 each), the best market is **Kariakor Market** (a corruption of "Carrier Corps"), between Racecourse Road and Ring Road. If traveling with children it might be worth checking out some of the soulless but stress-free shopping malls. The best are the Sarit Center, Westlands, and the Yaya Center, Arwings Kodhek Road, Hurlingham, but although the Kenyans are very proud of their malls they won't impress visitors from the West.

WHERE TO STAY

The good news is that there is no shortage of hotel rooms in Nairobi, and it is rare to have trouble finding a bed. The bad news is that it is quite easy to understand why none are in special demand. International-standard hotels generally price themselves for room only, and this is perhaps just as well: facilities in the haven of your own private space are good, including satellite television, air conditioning and mini-bar, while few offer especially exciting menus or food. Mid-range hotels seem to be feeling the effects of Nairobi's long recession, and usually give off the distinct air of investor neglect, while the cheapest hotels sometimes double as brothels. The choice here gives you some idea of what to expect.

Extremely Expensive

Of all the places in Nairobi to stay, the most expensive — and unusual — is **Giraffe Manor (** (02) 891078 FAX (02) 890949, Koitobos Road, which is part of the AFEW Giraffe Sanctuary off Langata Road. There are just a few rooms and you might find an endangered Rothschild's giraffe poking its head through your window in search of a snack.

Very Expensive

At the high end of the spectrum are the international-class hotels; rates here are for room only. The two best-known are the veteran landmarks: the **Norfolk Hotel (** (02) 216940 FAX (02) 216769 WEB SITE WWW .kenyaweb.com/lonrho-hotels/norfolk/ norfolk.html, Harry Thuku Road, Box 5851, where the rooms are okay but the food ordinary, and the equally famous **New Stanley Hotel (** (02) 333233 FAX (02) 229388 E-MAIL reservations@sarova.com, Kenyatta Avenue and Kimathi Street, Box 30680,

which costs a few dollars less. The latter has a good restaurant (closed Sunday nights) upstairs but the food at the ground floor café, where the landmark "thorn tree" that used to carry travelers' notices has been replaced with an unimpressive sapling, is ordinary. It's hard to avoid the feeling that you're paying for the history at both these places, though if I had to choose I'd go for the Stanley, as you can walk out of the front door and straight to the city center. From the Norfolk you have to pass a bit of a mugger's gauntlet, past the university, to get into town.

The **Hotel Inter-Continental (** (02) 335550 FAX (02) 210675, City Hall Way and Uhuru Highway, Box 30353, could do with a facelift.

The **Holiday Inn Mayfair Court Hotel** ((02) 740920 FAX (02) 748823, Parklands Road, Box 74957, is simply overpriced. The best of the luxury range though is currently the **Serena Hotel** ((02) 711077 FAX (02) 718012 E-MAIL cro@serena.co.ke, Nyere Road, Box 46302, which is a member of the Leading Hotels of the World and priced appropriately at US$200 for a double. These prices do not include meals.

Expensive to Mid-range

Mid-market the choices open up further. The **Hilton International** ((02) 334000 FAX (02) 339462, Watalii Street off Mama Ngina Street, Box 30624, is central and although the rooms haven't any great character they're acceptable for the price (expensive). Less expensive and just as central is the moderately priced **680 Hotel** ((02) 332680 FAX (02) 332908, Box 43436, Muindi Mbingu Street, or on the edge of the city center, the **Hotel Ambassadeur** ((02) 336803 FAX 211472, Moi Avenue, Box 30399 (mid-range).

For a bit more character head just above the center to Nairobi Hill for the graceful and welcoming **Fairview Hotel** ((02) 723211 FAX (02) 721320, Bishops Road, Box 40842 (mid-range), while nearby is the huge and rather run-down **Panafric** ((02) 713333 FAX (02) 715566 E-MAIL reservations@sarova .co.ke WEB SITE www.sarovahotels.com, Box 72493, Kenyatta Avenue (mid-range). Near the National Museum is the **Hotel Boulevard** ((02) 227567 FAX (02) 334071, Harry Thuku Road near Museum Hill, Box 42831 (mid-range), whose main advantage is the location. In the up-and-coming suburb of Westlands there are two middle-range hotels orientated towards the package market, but although tour operators get cheap rates they are definitely expensive for the individual traveler: the **Landmark** ((02) 535412-4 FAX (02) 545954, Chiromo Road, Box 40075 (expensive) is the better of the two, and is within walking distance of two of the city's best bar/restaurants.

Inexpensive

There are a few town center hotels in the Ksh1,000 to Ksh2,000 range, filled mainly — but not exclusively — with a Kenyan clientele: the friendly **Terminal Hotel** ((02) 228817,

Moktar Daddah Street, Box 66814, has now been ruined by the opening of a sedate — but surprisingly loud — bar downstairs. Sleep is impossible until the early hours. The idiosyncratic **Parkside Hotel** ((02) 333348 FAX 334681, Box 53104 (inexpensive), overlooking the Jevanjee Gardens (not safe at night), provides good value and its small "Wiseman's Bar" is quietly contained in the heart of the building.

The **Iqbal Hotel**, Latema Road, is most guidebooks' favorite amongst the "cheap" downtown Nairobi hotels in the rather dodgy River Road area (very inexpensive for a bed in dormitory, double, or triple rooms), but I can't for the life of me think why. You cannot make reservations and may even have to put your name on a waiting list for dingy rooms that are not even en-suite. It does have a useful notice board, and is handy for the infamous Green Bar, but otherwise seems to have little to recommend it. There are several other dirt-cheap lodgings in the surrounding River Road area, but it's not a good place to be looking for accommodation after dark.

Long-term visitors on a budget, such as aid workers or fledgling businesspeople, can't do much better than the **Heron Court** ((02) 720740 FAX (02) 721698 E-MAIL herco @iconnect.co.ke WEB SITE www.heronhotel .com, Milimani Road, with cheap rooms and excellent-value apartments. The downstairs bar is lively but kept well separate from the accommodation.

For the cheapest rooms, with nothing like the Green Bar or its equivalent for your neighbor, try the **Nairobi Youth Hostel** ((02) 721765, Ralph Bunche Road, Box 48661 (very inexpensive). It is an International Youth Hostel Association member.

In the suburb of Parklands, reached by the No. 107 bus, is **Mrs. Roche's Guest House**, Parklands Avenue, where you can take a bed in one of her cabins (inexpensive) or camp in the garden (very inexpensive). Mrs. Roche has been renting beds for more than 25 years and can provide you with interesting and sometimes helpful information. It is popular with overlanders on their way to or from the Cape.

The lights of the Hilton International Hotel sparkle in Nairobi's clear night air.

WHERE TO EAT

Nairobi offers a superb variety of restaurants in every price range. According to the Tourism authorities, there are over 200 different cafés, restaurants and snack bars offering a choice of more than 20 different cuisines, but there are probably twice as many as their estimate. Nairobi is one of the few places in Kenya where you'll be able to pick and choose your meals; Mombasa, on the coast, is the other.

In Nairobi, nearly every nationality is well represented, although there are few American fast-food chains. There is, however, Kenyan fast-food — fish and chips (the fish is fresh Nile perch, but the chips usually greasy), curries, sausages, kebabs and stews. These "stand-up and eat" shops are found everywhere in Nairobi; often the food is good at Ksh50 to Ksh150 per serving. Before selecting an establishment, look discreetly at what others are eating. If it looks appealing and the surroundings relatively clean, try it. Avoid salads and cold meals. Your best bet in a tropical environment is hot food, because cooking keeps bacteria to a minimum.

Be sure while you're in Nairobi to try some of its internationally renowned restaurants. A gastronomical treat is the **Carnivore** ((02) 602775, Langata Road, Nairobi. The Carnivore serves spit-roasted wild and domestic meats on an "all-you-can-eat" basis, accompanied by soup, salad, relishes, baked potato, dessert and coffee or tea for Ksh1,000. For meats, there are the standards — spare ribs, lamb, beef, chicken, and pork — and countless varieties of game — eland, hartebeest, crocodile, zebra, giraffe, Cape buffalo, warthog, ostrich or wildebeest — depending on availability. The wild meat comes from game farms in Kenya. For example, the crocodile comes from a farm on the coast that grows crocodiles for their skins. The skins are exported to Italy and Carnivore buys the meat. If you have a non-carnivore in your party, there is a good vegetarian menu or fried trout, fresh from the Carnivore's trout farm on the slopes of Mount Kenya. They also serve the best Irish coffee to be found outside San Francisco.

The Carnivore is very popular, and reservations are advisable. Lunch, from noon to 3 PM, and dinner, from 7 PM to 10:30 PM, are served daily except New Year's Day, when they close to recover from a lavish New Year's Eve bash in the adjacent Simba Saloon (see NIGHTLIFE, page 131). If you make reservations early enough, you can request a table inside around the open hearth where the meat is roasted, or outside on the terrace which is airy and cool. It is a good idea to bring a jacket or sweater in case you are seated outside. The Carnivore is a 10-minute drive from the city center. You can take a *matatu* or bus, but there's a kilometer (half-mile) walk; at night a taxi is always recommended, which shouldn't cost more than Ksh600.

Nairobi has numerous, generally excellent, Indian restaurants. Best is currently the **Minar** ((02) 330168, with three outlets, the original is on Banda Street; they serve some of the best Indian Mughlai cuisine outside India. Their closest rival is the **Haandi** ((02) 448294, Westlands' Shopping Mall. Prices reflect the quality; you can expect to pay between Ksh600 and Ksh1,000 per person for dinner. The menu is extensive and at Haandi's they are happy to prepare special orders off the menu. If you have difficulty deciding, the waiters can explain what each dish is.

A fine Japanese restaurant is the **Restaurant Akasaka Ltd.** ((02) 220299, 680 Hotel, Kenyatta Avenue, Box 47153, formal and traditional in decor and service, especially in the evenings, their lunch boxes make a perfect meal while shopping downtown. The sashimi is fresh (as is most fish in Kenya).

The **Delamere Coffee Shop** ((02) 216940 in the Norfolk Hotel on Moi Avenue has been and still is a favorite tourist hangout. Its atmosphere is relaxing, a good place to sit and watch the passersby while adjusting to the pace of Africa, but the food is pricey and disappointing.

Another popular tourist stop for coffee, tea, or buffet meal is the **Thorn Tree Café** ((02) 333233 of the New Stanley Hotel. The four-story tall thorn tree, once covered with thumb-tacked messages left by travelers, has

At Nairobi's Carnivore restaurant, wild and domestic meats are roasted in the open hearth.

been cut down, but the location, in the heart of the city, is some compensation.

There are several good Continental restaurants. Best for French food is the expensive (by Kenyan standards: Ksh1,000 to Ksh1,500 — US$15 to US$20 — for dinner) **Allan Bobbe's Bistro** ((02) 336952, Cianda House, Koinange Street, where reservations are essential and where the food is either homegrown at their private ranch or flown in fresh from the ocean off Somalia.

Drinkable wine has also started to become available in Kenya, mainly imported from

South Africa though some is produced domestically. The local vineyard, Naivasha Winery, produces an excellent white wine, but the reds and rosés are more variable.

For Kenyan food, just look through any number of steamed-up windows: special offerings include *ugali* (maize meal), roast meats, *mboga* (vegetable stew with some meat) and *pilau* (rice with meat) at very reasonable prices (Ksh100 to Ksh200). The **Chic Joint**, on Uhuru Avenue, is one good place for local food and they often have good live African music on weekends. In the city center, the **Harvest House**, Kenyatta Avenue, Nairobi, half a block from the Kipande House branch of Kenya Commercial Bank, offers an African Platter (Ksh300) with a

variety of local dishes. Alternatively, nearby **Simmers** ("the answer on a plate") ((02) 217659 FAX (02) 217632, Kenyatta Avenue, cooks local and regional specialties priced separately. In concept, both these are like a Mexican combination plate, but not in taste. If you like cornmeal or polenta and baked or refried beans, you'll enjoy Kenyan food. It is subtly spiced and hearty. Perhaps Nairobi's best Kenyan food is served at the **Utalii Hotel**, eight kilometers (five miles) out of the city center on the Thika Road. Owned and run as the practical part of the university's tourism department, it is where student chefs and waiters hone their craft with enthusiasm and skill. Tuesday lunchtime is a special Kenyan buffet, but the restaurant offers great value every day and is a favorite with Nairobi residents.

There are also moderately priced Chinese, Korean, and Ethiopian restaurants in Nairobi. All are worth a try.

NIGHTLIFE

Nairobi's nightlife does not, in general, start out lively but, unchecked, can become so. In general, it is best not to walk around at night, nor to hang about waiting for a bus. The sight of a lone *mzungu* (white person) glowing gently in the dark is an open invitation to thieves who then melt away into the shadows. Even for short distances it's wise to use one of the many taxis available. Their minimum fee is Ksh200 so bar-hopping can become expensive.

Popular bars with expatriate workers in the town center start with the **Delamere Terrace** at the Norfolk Hotel and the bistro at the New Stanley. Most of the hotels have their own bars with their particular characters: in the Hilton, for example, the **Jockey's Bar** gives an evening's free beer to anyone successfully downing a yard of ale. Unless you know the trick of twisting the yard to avoid a sudden flood of beer halfway through don't try this — you'll end up with a soaked shirt, a laughing audience and paying for the yard along with the rest of your night's drinking.

Travelers who don't mind being the only white face in a Kenyan crowd are always surprised by the welcome they receive in local bars, for security reasons often located on the first floors of city center office blocks. Try **Tanager Bar** in Rehema House, Kaunda Street, to mix with senior civil servants or **Invitation Bar**, opposite the New Stanley, for a younger crowd of office workers. The infamous **Green Bar** in the River Road area is featured in so many guidebooks it is constantly packed with hustlers and petty criminals geared up to fleece the tourist market — go prepared if at all. For a young, professional atmosphere and the chance to play several games of pool, try the **Klub House** ((02) 742149, Ojijo Road, Parklands, where there is mellow indigenous music every Wednesday and Sunday.

Later at night, when most of the local dives will be infested with at least one too many drunks, the smart money and the *mzungus* (white people) will have moved out of the city center and on to the suburbs: either to the mock-Tudor **Horseman** in Karen, or to Westlands where two bars close together form a focus. **Gypsies'** serves seafood *tapas* and drinkers spill out onto the street, while **Papa Loca** is a Tex-Mex joint with a courtyard. Depending on the crowd, both these bars are quite capable of serving through until 4 AM, but after about midnight serious party animals head on out to the **Simba Disco**, a part of the Carnivore Restaurant, which offers disco at least and usually has a DJ or live music from Wednesday to Sundays. Wednesday is rock, Thursday jazz, Friday groove, Saturday disco and the only noticeably African night is Sunday. The cover charge (after 9 PM) is Ksh150. This is a fairly standard charge for Nairobi discos. As the disco scene changes relatively quickly, it's best to ask at your hotel for other recommendations. The **Cantina Club**, on Wilson Airport Road, features African music, dancers and acrobats. Meanwhile, every night is crowded at both the **Florida nightclubs** in the city center, where you can be sure of the opportunity to meet more prostitutes than you ever knew existed. The current favorite, however, is the **Pavement** on Waiyaki Way in Westlands, where there's a pleasant café area and a nightclub where proceedings are kept relatively respectable by refusing entry to unaccompanied Kenyan women. This is where you'll find customers who at least have a serious interest in dancing.

For a more restrained but potentially even more expensive finale to the evening, Nairobi has a choice of casinos. The largest is the original **International Casino** on Chiromo Road, but this area is unsafe at night, even in a taxi: better to go the extra mile to the rather more civilized casino attached to the **Mayfair Court Hotel** in Westlands.

How to Get There

The easiest, if not the cheapest, way to travel around Kenya is by air, and this is more true than ever of Nairobi. International flights, and internal flights with Kenya Airways, use **Jomo Kenyatta International Airport** ((02) 822111 or (02) 822206, 15 km (nine miles) southeast of the center. Reconfirm all tickets and check ahead to make sure your flight is leaving when scheduled. Eight flights a day reach Mombasa and there are also flights to Malindi and Kisumu. Internal flights, Airkenya services to Somalia, Kilimanjaro, Zaire and Ethiopia, and charters use the small and friendly **Wilson Airport** ((02) 501941 FAX (02) 501944, off the Langata Road to the south of the city center. Flights from here ferret into both regional airports and obscure landing-strips in the bush. Departure tax is Ksh100.

Nairobi's **Bus Station**, wryly referred to by the locals as "Machakos Airport," is one and a half kilometers (a mile) east of the town center, though tickets are best reserved first at the company offices in the River Road area. It is a fascinating hub of human activity at the end of a working day. Drivers stand, bidding for passengers to overfill their already crowded buses. Vendors hawk food, toys, and other items to passengers through the open windows — often having to run alongside to collect money or give change as the bus pulls out. Buses are loaded with every type of cargo imaginable, all strapped helter-skelter atop, to proceed slowly and cheaply to destinations all around the country. Unfortunately there are pickpockets and thieves aplenty, and there have been numerous incidents of drugging travelers — it's not for the unwary. Of the many bus companies, **Akamba Bus** ((02) 556062, (02)340430 and

---

For more conventional meals, Nairobi has an abundance of good seafood and European-style restaurants.

(02) 221779, Lagos Road, is one of the largest and most reputable lines, especially useful for the grueling Mombasa route. Their vehicles leave either from their offices in the River Road area or from "Machakos Airport" — check which.

Matatus are quicker, marginally more expensive and, despite a poor record for safety, are a better way of covering long distances. They do not leave from a single central base: rather, they congregate informally in certain areas for each particular route. Just to confuse matters, they change rendezvous from time to time. Taxi drivers usually know where you need to be to catch a *matatu*, and will show you where to board. It is always best to start early as services to less popular destinations thin out through the day. Dawn is the best time to start such a journey.

Due, perhaps, to the shocking nature of the road to the coast there are no direct *matatus* to Mombasa. The best overland way of getting to and from the coast is by overnight train, with sleepers bookable in advance. The **Railway Station (** (02) 221211 extension 2700, at the southern end of Moi Avenue has trains leaving for Mombasa at 7 PM, and at 6 PM to Kisumu. Rail services to Moshi via Voi and Kampala are currently suspended but might resume at any time.

TO THE SOUTH

OLORGASAILIE

The prehistoric site of Olorgasailie and the pink-tinged waters of Lake Magadi in the Rift Valley (see below) can be visited as a long day-excursion or relaxing overnight trip from Nairobi (if you're willing to rough it).

In 1890, geologist John Walter Gregory discovered stone tools and other evidence of prehistoric habitation of this Rift Valley crater that probably contained a lake some 400,000 to 500,000 years ago. It was not until the 1940s, however, that the site was systematically excavated by Louis and Mary Leakey. The Leakeys concluded that the lakeshore had been inhabited by *Homo erectus* of the Acheulean culture, early men who had the same culture as those who had lived in Saint-Acheul, France, during the lower Paleolithic. A variety of tools for skinning animals, crushing bones and hunting, as well as hand axes for which this culture is best known, were unearthed and are displayed *in situ*. Despite the large concentration of tools, no human remains have been discovered. The Leakeys also found a gigantic fossilized leg of an extinct species of elephant. Your Ksh200 entrance fee includes a guided tour by a usually well-informed ranger.

Where to Stay

The only accommodations at Olorgasailie are self-service *bandas* or bunkhouses (Ksh500 per person) and a campsite (Ksh100 per person) run by the National Museum **(** (02) 742131, Box 40658, Olorgasailie, but you'll need bedding and cooking equipment. Without this it's perhaps best treated as a day trip.

How to Get There

Leave Nairobi, head south past Wilson Airport and the national park and turn left onto the C58. After 40 km (25 miles), just after the village of Oltepesi, follow the signpost to Olorgasailie and turn left to drive one and a half kilometers (one mile) to the site. Alternatively buses do occasionally leave from Nairobi bus station, usually early in the morning. It's not a busy route and it is more convenient to rent your own car or reserve a vehicle and driver from an operator such as **Let's Go Travel (** (02) 447151 or (02) 441030 FAX (02) 447270 or (02) 441690 E-MAIL info @letsgosafari.com WEB SITE www.letsgosafari .com, Box 60342, Nairobi, or **UTC (** (02) 331960 FAX (02) 331422 WEB SITE www.unitedtour .com, Box 42196, Nairobi.

LAKE MAGADI

At 600 m (2,000 ft) above sea level, Lake Magadi is one of the hottest spots in Kenya and the world's second-largest trona deposit (first is California's Salton Sea). This alkaline lake acts as a gigantic evaporating pan in which trona (a solution of sodium salts) deposits are 30 m (100 ft) deep, giving the lake its unlikely pink or green color, depending on the season. The lake is leased by the Magadi Soda Company Limited: signs by the road warn visitors to report their visit to the police station, but permission is freely given.

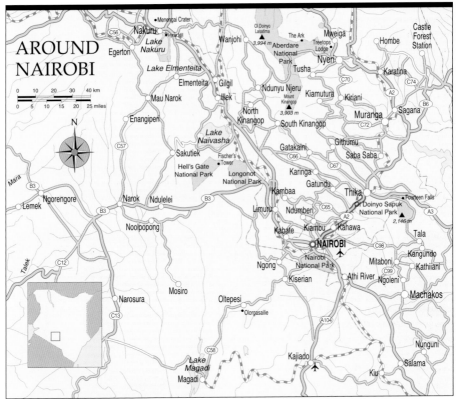

Lake Magadi once received international attention when the flamingos left their normal breeding grounds in lakes Nakuru and Baringo and laid their eggs here. The hatchlings were unable to free themselves from the sticky sodium deposits. A massive rescue operation ensued that took thousands of the stranded birds to safety. The bird life at the southern end of the lake and in the small freshwater swamps is varied enough to make the trip worthwhile for the dedicated bird watcher. This is the only place in Kenya where you are likely to see the chestnut-banded sand plover.

Geologically, the site is unique. Each year, Magadi receives less than 500 mm (20 inches) of rainfall and has an average temperature of 20°C (68°F), varying between 15°C and 41°C (59°F and 106°F). Its evaporation rate is 3,500 mm (120 inches) annually. Thus, theoretically, the lake should be dry. But it is not, and the trona deposits are growing more rapidly than they are mined.

Obviously, local rainfall is not keeping the lake alive, but rainfall from the neighboring areas of the Rift Valley drains into the lake underground. In addition, this underground seepage is being geothermally heated, which accelerates the rate at which the water can leach soda salts from the subsurface rocks. Once the hot water, already rich in soda, reaches Lake Magadi, evaporation takes place quickly, leaving solid trona crystals on the surface of the lake. Some deposits are so solid that cars can drive across them. In spite of the heat, it's fascinating to walk over these Technicolor fields on the factory causeway. The two factories operated by the Magadi Soda Company produce approximately 166,000 tons of soda ash and 40,000 tons of table salt annually.

Where to Stay

The town has, thanks to the factory, a public pool that is free to all comers. You might want to cool off here before beginning the journey back to Nairobi. Camping is possible here if you ask permission, although you're more likely to be invited to stay by a company employee. Alternatively, check in to the **Lower Guesthouse (** (0303) 33000 or (0303) 33278 (very inexpensive).

How to Get There

Leave Nairobi heading south past Wilson Airport and the national park and turn left onto the C58. After 83 km (51.5 miles) you will reach the end of the road and Lake Magadi. Alternatively, most days a bus does leave from Nairobi's bus station early in the morning. It is easier to rent your own car or reserve a vehicle and driver from an operator such as **Let's Go Travel** ((02) 447151 or (02) 441030 FAX (02) 447270 or (02) 441690 E-MAIL info@letsgosafari.com WEB SITE www .letsgosafari.com, Box 60342, Nairobi, or **UTC** ((02) 331960 FAX (02) 331422 WEB SITE www .unitedtour.com, Box 42196, Nairobi.

NORTHWEST OF NAIROBI

Because Longonot Crater, Lake Naivasha and Hell's Gate National Park are so close to Nairobi (within a two-hour drive), it is easy to speed by them in haste to get to more distant safari destinations. Each can be visited on a day trip from Nairobi, but Naivasha is a rewarding overnight stay before continuing west or returning to Nairobi.

LONGONOT NATIONAL PARK

The attractions of Longonot National Park are hiking and picnicking in the ragged volcanic crater, which takes its name from the Maasai "Oloonong'ot" meaning mountain of many spurs or steep ridges. A trail starting at the Longonot police station takes you to the rim. Like the Ngong Hills, security here has been a problem in recent years, so don't hike alone. You will be accompanied by a Kenya Wildlife Service ranger in any case. Admission to the park is US$15, with vehicles charges at Ksh500.

On reaching the rim, your response might be similar to that of Major Joseph Thomson, the first European to describe his visit here, in 1884. "The scene was of such an astounding character that I was completely fascinated, and felt under an almost irresistible impulse madly to plunge into the fearful chasm. So overpowering was this feeling that I had to withdraw myself from the side of the pit."

You can descend into the crater but the walk around the rim offers better views. It takes over two hours to make the circuit, as the path is narrow and often crumbly. You will need a sturdy pair of shoes. For those not interested in the climb, there are superb views of the crater and nearby **Suswa Crater** from the Nairobi–Naivasha road, where there are scenic overlooks (although the souvenir vendors will make it hard to enjoy in peace). Don't leave your car unlocked anywhere in Kenya, especially here.

How to Get There

To reach Longonot from Nairobi take the Naivasha Road northwest towards Limuru. After 28 km (17.5 miles) the road splits: the new Uplands Road heads on to Limuru and Lake Naivasha, while the B3 forks left.

After a further 22 km (14 miles) turn right onto the C88 signposted for Longonot. Park at the Police Station after 16 km (10 miles).

LAKE NAIVASHA

Lake Naivasha is one of the most beautiful of Kenya's Rift Valley lakes, surrounded by feathery papyrus, marshy lagoons, and grassy shores. It was the setting for M.M. Kaye's mystery, *Death in Kenya*. The story isn't great, but it describes the Naivasha area accurately.

Over the centuries, the size of the lake has fluctuated greatly. In the 1920s a Swedish geologist, Eric Nilsson, found a buffalo skeleton in sediments of a former, larger Lake Naivasha. This buffalo had a horn span of over two meters (six feet) and its teeth indicated that it fed on soft juicy foliage rather than the tougher, drier vegetation that sustains buffaloes of today. Nilsson suggested that this buffalo lived in an environment more moist than prevails at present in the Naivasha basin. Other research supports Nilsson's hypothesis; it is now generally agreed that the Rift Valley as a whole had a colder, wetter environment 10,000 to 20,000 years ago.

Early explorers such as Thomson and Fischer in the 1880s described it as a smaller

Lake Magadi has the hottest climate in Kenya and an unusual resident population of aquatic birds, including the chestnut-banded sand plover.

lake. Records from the 1890s show that during that decade it rose 15 m (50 ft) and was much larger than it is now.

Today the lake water irrigates the surrounding countryside, where much of the fresh vegetables for Nairobi's markets are grown. On the south shore is Kenya's only vineyard, and a plantation that employs approximately 4,000 people to grow flowers that are exported throughout the world. Many of the flowers in the world-famous Amsterdam market are flown there daily from Kenya, though there are mounting concerns about the amount of pesticides demanded to keep these introduced plants perfectly blooming.

From all waterfront hotels you can take a boat to **Crescent Island** (Ksh500 per person and Ksh200 entrance), a private game sanctuary, where you can walk around the island and view, at close range, zebras, waterbucks, giraffes and several species of antelope. Hippos are almost always seen and heard during the boat ride. Bird life around the lake is also abundant.

Where to Stay and Eat
Around the lake are several places to stay. In town is the excellent and fun **La Belle Inn** ((0311) 21007 FAX (0311) 21119, Moi Avenue (inexpensive, B&B). On weekends, this small hotel is often full with Kenyans up from Nairobi, and it can even be difficult to find a seat for coffee or tea. White rabbits nibble the courtyard grass and a caged python provides a touch of local color. In addition to the French fare it offers American-style milkshakes, pizza and superb panini, all served in an atmosphere 40 years adrift in time.

Most tourists, however, will opt to stay on the shores of the lake itself. Here you'll find the **Lake Naivasha Country Club** ((02) 535412-4 FAX (02) 545954, Block Hotels, Box 40075, Nairobi (expensive, full board), which is still the best place to stay, with bird walks, boat rides, and countless butterflies in the garden. On a budget, travelers might choose the famously friendly and very inexpensive **YMCA** ((0311) 30396, Box 1006, which is Spartan but a good base for hiking.

Naivasha's earlier position at the heart of the colonial plantation culture, however, means that it has a number of atmospheric home-stays that are, perhaps, the best way to recapture its timeless appeal. Sometimes these are seriously expensive. **Olerai House** (extremely expensive, all-inclusive, book through Bush Homes of East Africa ((02) 350703, (02) 571661 or (02) 571592 FAX (02) 571665 E-MAIL bushhome@africaonline.co.ke WEB SITE www.bush-homes.co.ke, Box 56923, Nairobi) is the home of Iain and Oria Douglas-Hamilton, activists involved in elephant conservation, and a maximum of 12 guests are treated to an informative and entertaining stay. **Kiangazi** ((0311) 21052 FAX (0311) 21059, Box 719, is another home-stay offering game-drives and excellent cuisine (very expensive, all-inclusive). **Loldia** ((0311) 30024, Box 199, North Moi Lake Road was originally built by Italian prisoners in World War II and still is one of the grandest buildings in the area, with horseback riding a specialty (extremely expensive, all-inclusive). For a really exclusive experience, **Mundui Estate** (extremely expensive, all-inclusive, book through Bush Homes of East Africa) is a two-bedroom cottage offering a full range of activities as well as a swimming pool, croquet and badminton court.

If you are interested in conservation, consider a stay at Joy Adamson's famous house, **Elasmere** ((0311) 21055 FAX (0311) 21074, Box 1497, Naivasha, set on the lakeshore towards Kongoni Game Valley (expensive, full board), which offers a private, home-like experience. This was where Adamson's life was spent working with lions, as immortalized in her writing, which put conservation issues onto the world stage. It prefers guests to have an interest, if not in Joy Adamson's life and work, at least in conservation.

Travelers on any sort of budget here will have to be prepared to look after themselves: bring all your own food and bedding to stay at self-catering **Eburru Guest Cottage** or **Melili Cottage** next door, both bookable through Let's Go Travel ((02) 447151 or (02) 441030 FAX (02) 447270 or (02) 441690 E-MAIL info@letsgosafari.com WEB SITE www.letsgo safari.com, Box 60342, Nairobi (inexpensive).

How to Get There
It's a two-hour drive to Naivasha although the frequent buses and *matatus* that leave

Longonot Crater towers over the Rift Valley.

Nairobi from the lower end of River Road will take rather longer. Drive northwest on Uhuru Highway, which turns into the Chiromo Road, and climb out of Nairobi on one of the country's few stretches of dual lane road — shared, unfortunately, with a lot of heavy traffic — to climb the shoulder of the Rift Valley. It's a spectacular drive.

HELL'S GATE NATIONAL PARK

Nearby is one of Kenya's unsung but most accessible national parks, Hell's Gate (entry

control the herbivore population), it is possible to hike throughout the park. During and after the rains, the road to the gorge is impassable and you will probably have to walk most of the way from the gate if you wish to see the 180-m (600-ft) cliffs, formed by Lake Naivasha's prehistoric outlet.

It is a full-day's hike, 25 km (16 miles) round trip from the park gate to the south end of **Hell's Gate Gorge**. If you don't want to hike the full distance you can usually drive at least to the head of the gorge, six kilometers (four miles) inside the gate.

US$15, children US$5, vehicle Ksh500), shaped by violent volcanic forces millions of years ago. It was here that the German explorer, Dr. Gustav Fischer, was attacked by the Maasai during his 1882 expedition. Fischer's Tower, a volcanic plug near the north entrance, identifies the approximate site of the ambush.

The park has an abundance of herbivores (zebras, impalas, gazelles, klipspringers and buffaloes), an outstanding bird population, a small Maasai population centered in several *manyattas*, and a spectacular red-cliffed gorge with a resident pair of lammergeyers (bearded vultures).

Because there are few or no predators (although lions may soon be introduced to

While hiking you will need to carry water and food; a hat and sunscreen are highly recommended.

The descent into this miniature Grand Canyon is steep at first, but becomes very pleasant as you reach the bottom of the gorge. At the south end you will see, but hear first, the steam of the **Olkaria geothermal station** that now produces much of Nairobi's electricity. Here underground water temperatures exceed 304°C (579°F), one of the world's hottest geothermal sites. Olkaria is expected to eventually supply half of Kenya's energy requirements.

Hiking in the park gives one a sense of the freedom, open space and wildlife that abounded a century ago in Kenya. It is a pleasure to travel on foot with wildlife grazing along the route. The terrain is rolling, and you need not make the trek to the gorge. Even a two-hour walk around the plains looking out on Longonot Cráter is an experience not to be forgotten. During the week there are few visitors and one can explore undisturbed. Fischer's Tower and Hell's Gate Gorge offer every level of rock-climbing difficulty. We watched several climbers scaling the east face of Fischer's Tower, while dozens of rock hyraxes sunned themselves unconcernedly below.

There are several primitive campsites in the park (US$8 per person), but you must bring your own water and food. Ask the rangers at the gate for the best locations.

How to Get There

Access to Hell's Gate National Park is usually from Naivasha: drive south around the lake on South Lake Road where two left turns lead to Elsa Gate and Olkaria Gate respectively. Alternatively, in the dry season (July to September, January to March), Hell's Gate can be reached along a rough track from the B3 Narok–Limuru Road.

FURTHER EXCURSIONS

There are other excursions northwest of Nairobi that can be done as day trips, most notably, starting early and returning late, Nakuru. But while these can be done as day trips, these are also good destinations in their own right, and are detailed in THE NORTHERN RIFT VALLEY, page 181.

EAST OF NAIROBI

The mountainous plateau to the north of Nairobi contains some of the country's wildest landscapes, finest game parks and most inviting communities. Thanks to the altitude the climate is perfect, with plenty of rain, warm days and cool nights, and it is not for nothing that the early colonists established most of their farms here, on land formerly inhabited by the Kikuyu people. Thika is the gateway town to the mist-shrouded forests of the Aberdares and the varied landscapes of snow-capped Mount Kenya, fully described in THE CENTRAL HIGHLANDS, page 203.

To the east the plateau extends to the town of Machakos, before the main road bumps off southwards Mombasa and the wonderful national parks of Amboseli and Tsavo East and West, covered in the EASTERN PLAINS, page 237.

THIKA

The journey to Thika, which took Elspeth Huxley three days to complete in an ox-drawn wagon at the turn of the century, now takes less than an hour on a four-lane freeway. The red dust is still there (though you won't be covered with it), but the papyrus and tall grasses have been replaced by government buildings, apartment complexes, a sports stadium, Kenyatta University, cattle ranches and sisal, pineapple and coffee plantations.

Thika is now a Nairobi bedroom community and manufacturing center that sprawls haphazardly on both sides of the freeway.

Where to Stay and Eat

Still in operation, the **Blue Posts Inn** ((0151) 22241, Box 43, Thika, which offers inexpensive B&B, was the first permanent business site in Thika and a gathering point for the early European settlers. Situated at the junction of the Thika and Chania river, it has attractive gardens that overlook two spectacular waterfalls and is an ideal spot to stop for lunch, coffee or tea. The restaurant is good and reasonably priced (Ksh200 to Ksh300 for a dish), and the rooms have recently been refurbished. The original structure, built in 1907 by a British captain affectionately nicknamed Major Breeches, got its name from its blue hitching post. Most of today's Blue Posts buildings were added in the 1930s and renovated in 1988.

An inexpensive alternative is the **December Hotel** ((0151) 22140, Commercial Street, but be sure to ask for a self-contained room.

How to Get There

Thika is 42 km (26 miles) from Nairobi along the busy Muranga Road. From Thika or Nairobi you can make an interesting side trip to Ol Doinyo Sapuk National Park and Fourteen Falls on the Athi River.

The dramatic landscapes of Hell's Gate National Park.

OL DOINYO SAPUK NATIONAL PARK

Ol Doinyo Sapuk ("big mountain," in Maa) or Kilima Mbogo ("buffalo mountain," in Kikuyu) rises to 2,146 m (7,043 ft) and is the major attraction of this park. It is here that the colonial owners, William Northrup McMillan and his wife Lucie, are buried.

McMillan, a Canadian, and Lucie, an American, came to Kenya in 1905. He apparently won Ol Doinyo Sapuk in a poker game at the Norfolk Hotel. The couple also owned land at Juja, Saba Saba and Ondiri; their 16,000 ha (40,000 acres) at Juja were a private game sanctuary as well as a farm. McMillan spent much of his time studying animals as well as hunting them. Lucie was an avid photographer.

After World War I, McMillan was knighted for his services in the 25th Fusiliers. He and Lucie spent most weekends at their cottage known as "Lucie's Folly" on the slopes of Ol Doinyo Sapuk. McMillan died in 1925 and was buried on the slopes of the mountain. In 1958, a year after her death, Lucie's executors began the long and tortuous proceedings to carry out her last wishes that Ol Doinyo Sapuk be given to the government as a park. There was much interference from relatives. For a long time nothing appeared to happen, though the colonial government gratefully accepted the gift of land and, with it, the stipulation that the area should be known as the McMillan Memorial Park, and that the graves should be cared for.

By 1964, illegal *shambas* or farms dotted the hillsides, and it would have been easy for the new Kenyan government to assert that the squatters needed the land. But it honored the stipulations of the will and today Ol Doinyo Sapuk is a national park.

The view, on a clear day, is superb — Nairobi and the Athi River to the south, and Mount Kenya to the north. The dirt track to the top is rough and steep, thus a four-wheel drive is advisable, particularly after heavy rains. During the period of long rains, from April to June, the road may be closed: it's best to ask in Thika or Nairobi before making the trip.

Even though walking is not permitted during periods of road closures, a climb can

sometimes be arranged with rangers at the gate for a nominal fee. Under no circumstances will a single individual be allowed to hike or climb anywhere within Ol Doinyo Sapuk National Park, due to hostile buffaloes, the predominant inhabitants of the park. If you are lucky, you can also see Sykes' monkeys or black-faced vervets. Unsubstantiated rumor has it that there are still leopards in the forest. During both the long and short rains (April to June and October to December), butterflies are abundant, as is a multitude of wildflowers. Year-round, the ravines are alive with hundreds of species of forest birds. The entrance fee, as for all this grade of national park, is US$15 per person. The park is open from 6 AM to 6 PM.

Fourteen Falls

It's a short drive from Ol Doinyo Sapuk National Park to Fourteen Falls on the Athi River. After a heavy rain, the numerous small cascades merge into a spectacular rush of water. Unfortunately, upstream overgrazing and farming have caused erosion that turns the water a murky red. The avid waterfall lover can descend to the base of the falls along a rocky and often slippery trail. The falls are surrounded by dense tropical vegetation and were used years ago as the setting for one of the many Tarzan movies. Just which one, no one seems to know. Entrance costs Ksh100 per person, with a further Ksh120 for your vehicle.

How to Get There

In your own car, is the short answer, though *matatus* do occasionally leave from the Koinange Street near the New Florida night-club in Nairobi.

Just a 40-minute drive from Nairobi, Thika is little more than a satellite of the city, and there is little reason to stay overnight here. Few tours head out this way, and it is more popular as a weekend destination for Nairobi residents with their own cars.

Fourteen Falls on the Athi River, a 40-minute drive from Nairobi.

The
Masai Mara
and the
Southwest

At dawn, a vast plain of dusty brown extends before you. The red sun inches above a jagged, distant ridge. In the stillness of breaking light, the morning breeze carries the songs of a hundred different birds and, from afar, the loud roar of a waking lion.

Suddenly, the entire brown plain before you stirs. It begins to move with the surprising quickness of an earthquake, with the thudding of many thousand hooves. In the quick-rising dust, you see that the entire plain was but one herd of wildebeest, aroused now by that lion's roar.

With the earth rumbling and roaring, the wildebeest pour past. It seems they will never end. The air grows thick with their dust and loud with their strange cries. Zebras are passing too — fat, striped, whinnying horses, thousands of them, kicking up their heels. Finally, the herds diminish. Here and there, a loner gallops nervously to catch up, glancing back over its shoulder. And you think, "Ah, the lion's coming."

But no, the ground begins to shake again. More wildebeest are thundering towards you, dashing madly about, bleating, tossing their glossy horns. Still more come, then more, until finally they thin out. Exhausted with waiting, you say, "There, that's over!" only to find you've misconstrued. This entire vast dawn shadow moving toward you across the valley is not bush, as you thought, but wildebeest — hundreds of thousands of them.

No words nor photographs can convey the Masai Mara. It and Tanzania's adjoining and even more vast Serengeti National Park are perhaps the only places left in Africa that retain a sense of the vastness of plains and its game before the coming of the white man.

The standard rule among Kenya outfitters is to save the Masai Mara for last, lest everything that would follow it seem anticlimactic. But as time gets more valuable, many visitors to Kenya see only the Masai Mara, on quick fly-in safaris. It is, without doubt, most amazing at the time of the annual migration (July to October), but even after rain the sheer density of the game here means there is always plenty to see. But the experience will depend, to a significant extent, on where you go within the national reserve, which covers 1,812 sq km (700 sq miles), or whether you stay in one of the private game ranches bordering the reserve itself, which can offer an even more private experience free of Kenya Wildlife Service regulations and sometimes (but not always) escaping the lumbering herds of predatory minivans determined to share your every sighting.

To the west the reserve is bounded by the sheer cliffs of the Oloolo Escarpment, then the little-visited highland towns of Kisii and Kericho, and finally the huge mass of Lake Victoria, most commonly reached by small plane from one of the Mara airstrips.

THE MASAI MARA

The Masai Mara is the northern extension of Tanzania's Serengeti National Park. It is far smaller than the Serengeti, with the gazetted reserve area comprising a mere four percent of the Serengeti ecosystem, and of course it is also one of the most visited parks in Africa. Paradoxically this actually makes for better game viewing. There are more tracks and the game is more habituated to the sight of vehicles. Generally, in the Masai Mara, the animals have seen so many minivans and four-wheel drives they carry on playing their role in the drama of the wild world without taking any notice of their eager audience. In the migration season (July to October) the reserve is packed with game of all kinds, but at any time of year it has the highest density of wildlife in Africa. It is possible to count off more species than you have fingers from a single viewpoint here. For sheer numbers of animals and range of species it is, by a comfortable margin, the best park in Kenya.

Until relatively recently, this land was shared among pastoralist Maasai, their cattle, and the wildlife, with occasional incursions by armed hunters. It was only gazetted in 1974, when conservationists and governments decided the needs of Africa's endangered wildlife outweighed the burgeoning Maasai people's need — or even their own — for increased grazing and land. All around the reserve you will see the red robes of warriors and the beaded figures of Maasai

Many Maasai still practice polygamy; many may have 20 or more children.

women. Inside the reserve this all changes: here it's a world of lift-top safari vehicles, pointed cameras and hosts of animals.

By road from Nairobi, the east of the park is several hours closer than the west, and for this reason is always slightly more crowded with safari vehicles, though to be honest they get everywhere. There are other reasons to make the effort to visit the west. By common consent the countryside there is more beautiful, cut through by the important — and large — Mara River, with the dramatic backdrop of the Oloolo Escarpment.

and lions, and the high, steep country in the southeast of the reserve, beautiful and more thickly forested, is an excellent habitat for lions, leopards, giraffes and most other herbivores. And the endless variety here extends to the skies. Some 53 different species of predatory birds have been identified in the Masai Mara, and 430 other bird species. It's not surprising that it is the most popular game area in Africa. Entry fees are US$27 per adult per day, US$10 per child, Ksh500 per vehicle; under a new and probably worthwhile development you'll also be

This area, known as the "Maasai Triangle," is where you'll find the largest herds of wildebeest (in Boer Dutch, literally a "wild beast," also known as gnu) and common zebras, and consequently the greatest numbers of predators. Also excellent for game watching is Musiara Swamp and the downstream area outside the Musiara gate, where cheetahs and lions are frequently sighted. The entire course of the Mara and Talek river in the reserve is a good area for elephants, giraffes, hippos, antelope, crocodiles, buffaloes, spotted hyenas, warthogs, blackbacked jackals and even the solitary leopard. This isn't to say the western area of the park has all the action, however. The Mosee Plains to the east are good for all the herbivores

charged this to visit the group ranches, owned by displaced Maasai communities or private concessionaires, that border the park. The same tickets cover both ranches and the reserve itself.

In general, the activities in the Masai Mara focus on the wildlife. There are two unusual specialties here, however, to tempt those with a well-stacked wallet. Ballooning is a local specialty (see TAKE TO THE SKIES, page 14 in TOP SPOTS) and costs US$385 per person, or there are also fishing trips — with travel by light aircraft — at Rusinga and Mfangano Island on Lake Victoria. This can be done as a daytrip (allow US$385 per person) or as a very pleasurable overnight (see page 156 for details).

WHEN TO VISIT

Although there is always something to see in the Mara, the best time to visit is during the migration. This is generally from July through October. Low season here is April and May, where rain cuts off many roads and brings high grass: it's hard to see the game, which in any case will have widely dispersed. Low season rates apply through June, however, and this can be a good time to take a gamble as in recent years the seasons have become increasingly erratic.

WHERE TO STAY

Within the park itself there are surprisingly few lodges, all controlled by a small number of major safari companies. If traveling independently they are relatively expensive; tour operators will be paying less than you, so a tour is by far the cheaper option. For this reason, if no other, many independent travelers opt to camp. There are campsites outside most of the gates. Furthest east is Sand River, which is pleasantly located but is also where Julie Ward, a British tourist was murdered in 1998, so it's hard to avoid feeling spooked. Talek Gate has a selection of camp sites, and Musiara Gate's campsite, justifiably popular, is often shared with passing lions. Oloolo Gate's campsites overlook the escarpment and, sometimes, hippos playing below.

It is important to be careful, of course. There are wild animals all around, so don't leave your tent in the middle of the night however many beers you drank before retiring. Security can be a problem, surrounded as you are by hardened communities where poverty is relentless: check with the local situation the park rangers. The reliability of camping changes from season to season in the national parks and it's always possible to become a first, unwelcome statistic. If you wish advance information and think it will help, write to the Warden, Masai Mara National Reserve, Box 60, Narok.

A wiser choice in the Mara is a tented camp or lodge, fenced or unfenced, especially if you can get package rates through a Nairobi, or international, operator. The advantage of an unfenced tented camp is that it's more open, often cooler, and the sounds of the natural world filter closely through the thin canvas of the tent wall. This is, however, a matter of taste: for some people it's an adrenalin rush, while others get no sleep at all as they darkly imagine just what might be bumping against their guy ropes and nuzzling up to their door and would infinitely prefer a fenced, stone-built lodge — an especially good idea if you're traveling with children young enough to wake up curious when a lion grunts outside. One factor that might influence your choice is whether game-drives are included or not. If you're traveling independently with your own vehicle it's better to choose a full-board lodge. Those listed as all-inclusive include game drives in their rates, which will suit those who fly in. Whether tented camps or built lodges, your options within the reserve, once again from east to west, are as follows.

Sarova Mara Camp ((0305) 2386 or (02) 713333 (reservations) FAX (02) 715566 E-MAIL reservations@sarova.co.ke, WEB SITE www.sarovahotels.com, is an expensive, full-board camp that is large but well-landscaped with comfortable, well-furnished tents. It is has the advantage of being the closest camp in the reserve to Nairobi by road. To the south is **Keekerok Lodge** ((0305) 2525 (expensive, full-board), book through Block Hotels ((02) 535412-4 FAX (02) 545954 WEB SITE block hotels.com, a rather touristy but undeniably comfortable lodge that is especially good value in some mass-market packages. There's a pleasant hippo pool with a lone hippo, overlooked by a raised bar on wooden decking.

Cross over to the east of the Talek River to the **Mara Intrepids** ((0305) 2168, reservations through Heritage ((02) 446651 or (02) 447929 FAX (02) 446533 E-MAIL info@heritage hotels.co.ke WEB SITE www.heritagehotels .co.ke, which overlooks the river, where they bait leopard daily (extremely expensive, all-inclusive). They offer especially good programs for introducing children to the wonders of the bush (leaving adults free to go on long, patient game drives). Pricey but recommended. The **Mara Serena Lodge** ((0305) 2252

From the Masai Mara's Limutu Hill, the plains seem to stretch "beyond the rim of the world." OVERLEAF: Wildebeest congregate on the banks of the Mara River.

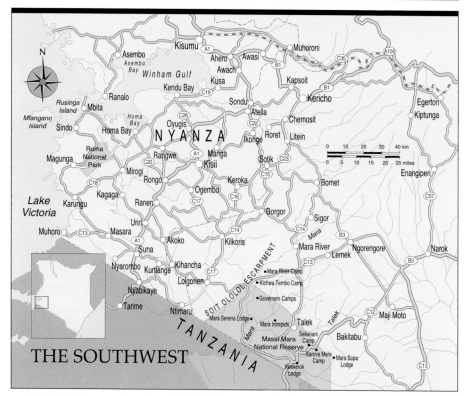

THE SOUTHWEST

or (02) 711077 (reservations) FAX (02) 718012 E-MAIL cro@serena.co.ke, Nyere Road, Box 46302, Nairobi, is a large but unobtrusive lodge set high on a ridge which has spectacular views (very expensive, full board). Most easterly of all are the Governors Camps, with three options, all extremely expensive and all-inclusive. The camps overlook a steep gorge of the Mara River. **Governors** ((0305) 2273 is the largest, **Little Governors** ((0305) 2040 somewhat smaller, while the most luxurious of all is **Il Moran**, where 10 lavishly huge tents, decorated with polished olive-wood furniture, contain every luxury including (unusually for the Mara, where water is short) huge, free-standing claw-footed baths. If, at US$740 all-inclusive, this isn't enough, a private tented camp can be rented for parties. For reservations contact **Governors Camps** ((02) 331871 FAX (02) 726427 WEB SITE www.governors camp.com, Box 48217, Nairobi. These are especially well-situated for Musiara Swamp, but as road-access is difficult most guests fly in.

Outside the unfenced reserve boundaries but in the dispersal areas of all the Mara's animals a whole new range of activities opens up, including cultural visits, game walks and night drives, free of reserve regulations. A wider choice of lodges also beckons. From east to west again, the first option is the **Mara Sopa Lodge** ((0305) 2196 or (02) 336088 (reservations) FAX (02) 223843 E-MAIL enquiries @sopalodges.com, Box 72360, Nairobi, whose pleasant *bandas* make good bases for a safari (expensive, full-board). To the north, convenient to the main Nairobi Road, is **Siana Springs Camp** ((0305) 2553, reservations through Conservation Corporation ((02) 441001/5 FAX (02) 746826 E-MAIL info@conscorp .co.ke WEB SITE www.ccafrica.com, Box 74957, Nairobi, a small and select luxury tented establishment, beautifully shaded by mature trees and with leopard and bird hides, and the very highest standards of cuisine (very expensive, full board). Further north again and **Cottars 1920's Safari Camp** ((02) 884508 FAX (02) 882234 E-MAIL Cottars@form-net.com, Box 44191, Nairobi, recreates a mythical world of grace and comfort that might have existed in the 1920s if they'd had portable fridges, solar power, and posturepedic mattresses (extremely expensive, all-inclusive).

Back on the boundaries of the Masai Mara is **Sekanani Camp** ((0305) 2454, reservations through Southern Cross Safaris ((011) 471960 FAX (011) 471257, Box 90653, Nyali, Mombasa, which consists of 15 stilted tents and is exceptionally comfortable (very expensive, full board). West and the **Mara River Camp** ((0305) 2186, reservations through Savannah Camps ((02) 331684 or (02) 335935 FAX (02) 216528 or (02) 330698 E-MAIL eaos@africa online.co.ke WEB SITE www.savannahcamps .com, 11th Floor, Fedha Towers, Standard Street, Box 48019, Nairobi, is rather less sophisticated than the other camps in this price bracket, which is not in itself such a bad thing; it is well-thought-of by serious naturalists (very expensive, all-inclusive). **Kichwa Tembo Camp** ((0305) 2465, reservations through Conservation Corporation ((02) 441001/5 FAX (02) 746826 E-MAIL info@conscorp.co.ke WEB SITE www.ccafrica.com, Box 74957, Nairobi, is another very smart establishment (very expensive, full-board) with an even smarter offshoot, **Bateleur Camp** (extremely expensive, all-inclusive), a short walk away through the woods, with period furniture, all comforts, and food and drink included. A short 15-minute drive from here is **Olonana**, run by Abercrombie & Kent ((02) 334955 FAX (02) 228700, Box 59749, Nairobi, a curiously dated but eco-friendly, well-run and integrated establishment that knows how to introduce the wildlife and cultural aspects of the area (extremely expensive, all-inclusive).

There are some more, but these are, in my opinion, the best. And if there doesn't seem to be much for travelers on a budget, I'm sorry, they'll just have to camp — or save by pre-booking a tour. Overland safaris with a couple of nights at the Keekerok or Serena should only cost US$300 or so, including park fees, game drives and meals.

HOW TO GET THERE

While the Masai Mara is impressive, the road from Nairobi is less so. Those who can afford to do so, fly. **Airkenya** ((02) 501421/3 FAX (02) 500845 E-MAIL info@airkenya.com WEB SITE www.airkenya.com, Box 30357, Nairobi, flies twice daily from Wilson Airport, taking just one and a half hours to the airstrip in the east of the reserve for US$188

round trip. The morning departure, at 10 AM, is especially useful for those flying in on an overnight flight.

The conventional route is from Nairobi. Leave the city heading towards Naivasha, but once you've dropped down the side of the Great Rift Valley turn left on the B3 for Narok, where the pavement ends. This small town has seen rather too many tourists to keep the friendly atmosphere of less visited parts of Kenya. It is, however, the last gasoline stop you'll see for a while. Continue on the B3 for 17 km (10 miles) to the Ewaso Ngiro River. At this point it is possible to turn right on the B3 and drive west towards Lemek and the west of the park, but the road can be rough, especially after rain. Only attempt this if you have a good high-clearance four-wheel drive and plenty of confidence. Otherwise keep straight on: the road is reclassified as the C12 and dirt rules for the next 60 km (37 miles) to the park gate. Newly surfaced roads mean five hours driving can get you into the heart of the Mara.

All the major tour operators run daily safaris on this route, but the road is poor and not getting better. Alternatively, it can be approached, with your own transportation, from Kisumu and Kisii, after wandering through the Kericho tea district, Ruma National Park and the coast of Lake Victoria. This allows you to drop down over the Oloolo Escarpment, with the Mara spread out before you in all its vastness — or so it seems. This route is likely to be impassable in wet weather. Take plenty of local advice. Equally, this route can be used to climb up from the Masai Mara to Kisii, Kericho and Kisumu.

KISII

Pretty, full of energy and developing rapidly, with good architecture and dynamic people, the town of Kisii is situated at an altitude of 1,700 m (5,580 ft) and is a welcome relief from the sultry humidity and ubiquitous mosquitoes of Lake Victoria. It is one of the most vital, fastest-growing commercial centers in western Kenya.

Center of the one-and-a-half-million-strong Gusii tribe, Kisii was an area of strife early in this century, when nearly a thousand tribesmen were massacred by the British. Next came massive engagements between the British and Germans during World War I, with the Gusii forced into service as British troops. Now it seems the most peaceful place in Kenya, and its people among the most hospitable.

Sixteen kilometers (10 miles) south of Kisii is the village of **Tabaka**, where most of the world's soapstone comes from. This is the source of racked soapstone candlesticks, animals, vases and bowls that fill countless shelves in all of Kenya's souvenir stalls.

agencies. One is the **Kisco Co-op**, where profits are shared with the artists — see more at their shop on the route between the quarries to the north and the village.

Almost every house in town is devoted to polishing and sanding soapstone carvings, washing the sculptures in water to soften the stone and finally waxing the finished product to give it a characteristic luster. Specialists focus on animal shapes, candlesticks or stylized sculptures, while others polish fruitbowls, either sent for immediate export or delegated for etching and painting. Once

It's hard to believe. The village is friendly and small. The mines are to the east of the village, mountainsides laid bare to the sun and crowds of workers chipping out rocks. Different areas produce soapstone of various colors. The road is filled with workers carrying sacks and bags of stone or staggering under the weight of heavy chunks. Back at the village small, family-run factories carve and polish the rocks on piecework to precise formulae. Artisans — mainly women — chisel, polish and paint, establishing a national art form for the entire country. You won't go short of shopping opportunities. It seems more ethical to sidestep capitalism and shop instead at one of the cooperatives, often set up with the help of foreign aid

racked in Nairobi shops or at Rift Valley viewpoint stalls, there are so many soapstone sculptures they start to look mundane, but at the source the level of skill, craftsmanship and sheer effort is suddenly clear. Prices are low, making this a great place to buy some lasting memories.

From Kisii you can hike up to the **Manga Ridge** (ask directions at the Kisii Hotel), or trek among the green, terraced slopes reminiscent of the Himalayan foothills. You can also drive south to **Tarime** in Tanzania or take the macadam road to **Kilkoris**; from Kilkoris, you can cross the savanna on a dirt road to **Lolgorien**, at the foot of the Oloolo Escarpment, and suddenly you're back in the land of the Maasai.

The Masai Mara and the Southwest

WHERE TO STAY

Kisii is the best base to explore the area, and there is another advantage: you can stay in the **Kisii Hotel** ((0381) 30134, Box 26, Kisii, a quaint hangover from colonial days, with spreading gardens overlooking the fields just below the hilly and potholed center of town (very inexpensive, B&B). It's a comfortable and friendly place with good food and a bar full of gregarious people most evenings.

HOW TO GET THERE

Those with their own transportation choose between the demanding route up the Oloolo Escarpment from the Masai Mara and two routes to Kisii from Kisumu: fastest is to stick to the A1 heading south towards Tanzania. However, it is well worth the detour to take the tarmac C19 that runs along the coast of Lake Victoria, and then link back with the A1 by taking the 20 km (14 miles) dirt road to Oyugis. It's a spectacular drive and doesn't take much longer. From Homa Bay, it's 45 km (28 miles) of poor but passable tarmac to Kisii.

By public transportation, frequent *matatus* make the three-hour journey from Kisumu. Two bus companies link Kisii with Nairobi three times a day; reserve tickets a day in advance. The trip takes nine hours.

KERICHO

If you were asked the color of tea, you'd probably say brown or black. Once you've seen Kericho, tea will always mean green. For as far as you can see around the town of Kericho, tea plantations carpet the rolling hills. From a distance, the chest-high bushes look soft and cushy. Up close, they are brittle and sharp. Pickers wear oilskin aprons and protective sheaths on their picking fingers.

On any given day, you can usually see a crew (mostly women with male supervisors) working the fields. They move methodically across bright green rows to pick the thumbnail-sized leaves, returning every two weeks to each row. On a good day, a worker can pick up to 70 kg (150 lb) at Ksh3 per kilogram (Ksh1.34 per pound). The baskets can hold

between seven and twelve kilograms of tea and it takes about an hour and a half to fill it. A Luo woman who picked tea for nine years told us that some days were better than others. "After several hours of picking, your fingers always get sore and eventually they are covered with calluses. It is hard work, but a relatively secure job with a wage that is determined by how hard you work." The almost daily rainfall in Kericho has made it the tea capital of Kenya. Over the past years, tea has steadily grown as an industry, surpassing earnings from coffee.

Because most of the inhabitants of the area live and work on the tea plantations, the town of Kericho is mainly a shopping, and not a trading, center. Stores in town cater to the needs of the estate owners and managers as most plantation workers rarely come to town. Nonetheless, the town is one of the tidiest in Kenya and has a beautifully maintained central square.

The area also offers good trout fishing, particularly during the drier months (November to March). The **Itare** and **Kipteget rivers**, each about an hour's drive from town,

OPPOSITE: Lions in the Masai Mara National Reserve have come to accept man and his vehicles as part of everyday life. ABOVE: Tea has replaced coffee as Kenya's largest export crop.

The Masai Mara and the Southwest

have the best fishing and scenery. They run through the dense rainforest on the western edge of the Mau Escarpment, which has numerous butterflies, birds and wild orchids. Closer to town is the **Mara River** and a short walk from the Tea Hotel is the **Kimugu River**. The Upper and Lower Saosa Dams also offer good fishing, particularly in the evenings. Arrangements for fishing can be made through the Kericho Tea Hotel.

If you don't have time to visit Kericho, but still want to see a tea plantation, there are several near Nairobi. **Mitchell's Kiambethu Tea Farm** ((0154) 50756 gives guided tours on prior arrangement, at a cost of Ksh1,100. They prefer groups to individuals. If you would like some help arranging it, **Let's Go Travel** ((02) 447151 or (02) 441030 FAX (02) 447270 or (02) 441690 E-MAIL info @letsgosafari.com WEB SITE www.letsgosafari .com, Box 60342, Nairobi, are the best people to find a group you can join.

WHERE TO STAY AND EAT

Before or after visiting the fields, you can stop for a cup of tea or a meal at the **Kericho Tea Hotel** ((0361) 30004 FAX (02) 20576, Box 75, Kericho (mid-range, B&B). The pink, Spanish-style hotel was built in 1952 by the then-owner of the surrounding tea plantations, Brooke Bond. It now belongs to African Tours and Hotels. The hotel has an excellent restaurant and well-maintained rooms.

Less expensive and in a rather better (riverside) setting is the **Kericho Lodge and Fish Resort** ((0381) 20035, Box 25, Kericho (inexpensive, B&B). The **TAS Lodge** (no phone) on the Moi Highway in Kericho is the backpacker option and allows camping in its gardens.

HOW TO GET THERE

Kericho is an hour and a half by road and 83 km (52 miles) from Kisumu: travel east along the B1, which continues to Nakuru, Naivasha and Nairobi. From Kisii take the C23, which skirts the Mau Escarpment for a spectacular 115 km (72 miles). By public transportation, frequent *matatus* link Kericho with Kisumu and Nakuru, with plentiful connections on to Nairobi. Overland access from the Masai Mara is possible with a good four-wheel drive if the weather is dry; a beautiful route through the rolling, terraced hills of the Nyanza district.

RUMA NATIONAL PARK

Formerly known as Lambwe Valley Game Reserve, Ruma has 194 sq km (75 sq miles) of rolling savanna mixed with trees and brush. It is set between the lakeside **Gwasi Hills** and the sheer **Kaniamua Escarpment**. Hot, humid and boggy during the rains, it is nonetheless one of the best places in Kenya to see several rare species such as the magnificent, scimitar-horned roan antelope; the huge, curve-horned Jackson's hartebeest; and the diminutive, graceful oribi. You may also see Rothschild's giraffes and the occasional leopard and cheetah.

The park's bird life is spectacular and includes species not likely to be seen elsewhere, such as the barefaced go-away bird, the blue-cheeked bee-eater, the Hartlaub's marsh widow-bird, the yellow-fronted tinkerbird and the African mustached warbler. Despite the battering roads, Ruma is not to be missed.

WHERE TO STAY

The nearest town to Ruma National Park is Homa Bay. Although it suffers from humidity and insects, it offers a good place to stay in the **Homa Bay Hotel** ((02) 229751 or (02) 330820 FAX (02) 227815, Box 42013, Nairobi (US$75 for a double, B&B), which is the best point from which to start exploration of the relatively unknown Ruma National Park.

HOW TO GET THERE

Part of the reason for Ruma's unspoiled status is that it is almost impossible to reach without your own transportation. With a vehicle, the easiest access is from Kisumu, from where the road takes you 104 km (65 miles) southward through the low hills behind the lake, past Mount Homa, which rises over 600 m (nearly 2,000 ft) above the shore in prime hiking country (with a guide). Alternatively, Homa Bay is 59 km (37 miles) from Kisii on good (when dry) dirt roads.

LAKE VICTORIA

The source of the White Nile, Lake Victoria covers 69,490 sq km (26,830 sq miles). It is Africa's largest, and the world's second largest, freshwater lake, and its waters travel some 3,700 km (2,300 miles) to the Mediterranean Sea. It is a huge body of water, the size of Ireland. Most of the time it is blue and tranquil, but it must be treated with respect, as it can change mood suddenly, blowing up into sudden, choppy storms. Lake Victoria would be ideal for swimming, and indeed has plenty of beautiful beaches, but bear in mind that, like most slow-moving or stationary fresh water in Kenya, it is a source of bilharzia, a sickness derived from minuscule flukes that live in snails and bore into the skin to multiply. It is not advised to go bathing. The flukes take a few minutes to burrow through the skin, so dry any freshwater splashes promptly. All this blue water is not completely wasted, however. Kenyans make the most of the lake's opportunities for sport fishing.

This isn't just a white man's sport. Lake Victoria also supplies a major portion of Kenya's protein. In fact, over 90 percent of Kenya's fish catch is freshwater; despite the country's long coast, only 10 percent of the catch is from the ocean. Lake Victoria produces much of this freshwater supply, although its resources have lately been reduced by the replacement of the original tilapia species, highly favored by the local Luo peoples, with the less-preferred Nile perch that, it was hoped, would reduce the mosquito population that causes the humid lakefront region to be so unhealthy.

It took four attempts by fishery biologists and the United States Agency for International Development (AID) before the more expensive perch adapted to the lake in the 1950s, but the introduction of Nile perch, like most experiments with nature, has proved a damaging ecological time-bomb. Current reports indicate that the larger perch have started to prey on the smaller perch, raising the intriguing distant possibility that, at some date in the far future, self-predation will go to its logical conclusion and there will

just be one huge Nile perch in the middle of the lake. In fact, the lake is not deep enough, being little more than 100 m (330 ft) at its deepest. The success of this experiment also spelled disaster for the resident cichlid species, and hit the staple lake-fish, tilapia, which was almost wiped out.

In addition to being favored by the local restaurateurs, the tilapia is a fascinating fish, raising its young in its mouth. The male first clears a nest on the sandy lake bottom and attracts a female, who lays her eggs there; he fertilizes them and she then gathers the

eggs into her mouth and incubates them. She is unable to eat during this entire period. After the fry hatch, the mother guards them for the first 10 days or so, gathering them back into her mouth at any sign of danger and then ejecting them by swimming backward and blowing.

Although it is still possible to fish for tilapia — locals use a simple stick with a hook coated with algae to catch a steady stream of fish usually small enough to return to the water — most visitors to the lake attempt to catch the much larger Nile perch, and generally don't do too badly. The fish grow up to 250 kg (550 lbs) and few visitors return disappointed from a fishing venture.

Traditional Luo basket fishing on Lake Victoria.

RUSINGA ISLAND

Rusinga offers a visit to the birthplace and mausoleum of Tom Mboya, the brilliant young civil rights activist and pro-Western Luo politician gunned down, apparently by Jomo Kenyatta's assassins, in Nairobi in 1969. Mboya was so beloved in Kenya that he stood in the way of an arranged transfer of power from Kenyatta to Daniel Arap Moi, and was accordingly eliminated. His life, accomplishments and burial on Rusinga are recounted in Grace Ogot's *The Island of Tears*, required reading for anyone interested in Kenya or women's literature.

"To Kenyans," Ogot says, "Mboya was one of the greatest men who had ever been born by a woman. To the world beyond the seas, he was a symbol of stability, unity and peace. To the Lake Region people he was a warrior and a hero … He appeared to have been blessed by God of the mighty waters, so that he made blades of grass grow where there was nothing before. He had introduced the ferry which could carry people and vehicles … He had given the island adequate schools, good hospitals and roads. He had encouraged the islanders to adopt modern methods of farming. In ordinary conversation, people would say, 'Oh, it is as miraculous as Mboya's ferry,' or 'It is so big, like Mboya's school' …"

Rusinga Island was also the site of a major find in human prehistory, that of a *Proconsul africanus* skull discovered by Dr. Mary Leakey in 1948. An apelike primate estimated to have lived about 25 million years ago, *Proconsul africanus* may have been a direct ancestor of man, and is similar to two other *Proconsuls* considered likely to have led to the development of the chimpanzee and gorilla.

Most people's reasons for visiting Rusinga are far less cerebral. It currently holds the record for the largest Nile perch fished here, and there are also the full range of water sports on what is effectively an inland coastal resort.

Where to Stay

Rusinga Island Club ((02) 574689 FAX (02) 564945 E-MAIL Mellifera@swiftkenya.com, Box 24397, Nairobi, is the smart place to stay (extremely expensive for full board including

all excursions); otherwise there are a couple of small, friendly lodges in Mbita costing a hundredth of the price. Try **Patroba Okgeno Lodge** (0385) 22184, Box 315 (inexpensive).

How to Get There

Rusinga is connected to the mainland by a causeway, even though this is not shown on many maps, and can be reached in an hour by car from Homa Bay, itself two hours' drive from Kisumu. There are occasional lake ferries from Kisumu and along the lakeshore, but these take significantly longer if the hyacinth rafts allow them to leave at all. Most visitors here arrive by light airplane from the Masai Mara: book this through **Mellifera** ((02) 574689, (02) 577018 or (02) 567251 FAX (02) 564945 E-MAIL Mellifera@swiftkenya.com, Box 24397, Nairobi.

MFANGANO ISLAND

Rusinga might be linked to it by causeway, but Mfangano is definitely an island. There's no electricity, piped water or motor vehicles, and life proceeds at the slow pace of a drifting fishnet. Few visitors make it here, apart from day-trippers flying in to fish in the lake, which all adds to its appeal. In the hills an hour's hike above the fishing village of Ukula there are ancient, undated sites of rock art, and the atmosphere on the island is relaxed and friendly — perfect for hiking.

There's only one place to stay, at the **Mfangano Island Lodge** (extremely expensive, all-inclusive), book through Governors Camps ((02) 331871 FAX (02) 726427 WEB SITE www.governorscamp.com, Box 48217, Nairobi, with atmospheric rondavels decorated in local style. It offers excellent food, as well as the chance to sip sundowners while fishing for tilapia from the lodge's pontoon as the glassy lake-waters are dyed myriad colors by the setting sun … irresistible. Backpackers can stay with locals.

Access is almost always by light aircraft from the Masai Mara, as Mfangano Island Lodge is owned by the same company as Governors Camps or, for backpackers, by motorized floating *matatu* from Mbita on the mainland.

Early settlers brought nineteenth-century technology to Kenya.

The Masai Mara and the Southwest

Western Kenya

The hot, wet west of Kenya doesn't see too many visitors. It's a populous, fertile region where just a few, small reserves hang on in face of population pressures and the need for agricultural land. For those whose interests in Kenya extend beyond the wildlife, however, it is a treasure-trove. A world away from the Muslim coast, far removed from the Kikuyu heartlands of the center and remote from the warring rivalries of the arid north, western Kenya is where you'll find the exhilarating mix of tribal cultures forging ahead into a new Africa. Here unspoiled villages

northern California Coast Range, or of coming down to the Caspian from the Caucasus. It is a sense of the infinity of both land and sea.

The land is green and everywhere cultivated; the water is flat, reflecting the sky, and free of man except when a small boat cuts across it. Above Kisumu, a white Coptic church is set against the slope as if transported from the Cyclades.

The sprawling city of Kisumu has, like Mombasa, a maritime atmosphere due to its former eminence as a major port on Lake Victoria. The upper part of the city contains

languorously rot in the tropical heat and life proceeds at the pace of growing plants. There are tea plantations and coffee farms, lively markets and the great, sea-like waters of Lake Victoria itself. Take time out to tread the path less trodden in western Kenya.

KISUMU

The capital of Western Kenya is best approached by road. Suddenly, you break through the last of the foothills above Kisumu, and Lake Victoria, resplendent, blue and expansive, lies before you. It feels very much the same as dropping down to the Mediterranean from the French or Italian Alps or the Costa del Sol, of reaching the Pacific from the

many large colonial buildings and residences, set amid more recent shanties and modern structures, on well-shaded wide streets leading down to the port.

At the main traffic circle coming into town you'll find the market and bus station, noisy and teeming with people. Overloaded buses seem to leave every moment for the ends of the earth while black-belching *matatus* are jammed like sardine cans, the squeezed faces of passengers stacked against the dirty windows; other riders hang out the half-shut doors or cling desperately by fingertip to the roof rims and windows, their feet dangling over the speeding pavement.

Kisumu's passenger ferries connect Kenya's major towns and islands on Lake Victoria.

In the days of the East African Community, when Kenya, Tanzania and Uganda were loosely united in a common market and transportation scheme, the port of Kisumu boomed with shipping to and from Kampala in Uganda and Musoma and Mwanza in Tanzania. Since 1977, each nation has become responsible for its own transport networks and the port's business has declined. Yet the town itself is busy, and a walk through its jammed, colorful streets, with their traces of Victorian gingerbread and colonial prosperity, is well worth an hour or two.

It was at Kisumu that the final spike of the "lunatic line to nowhere," the Uganda Railway, was driven on December 19, 1901. It had taken more than five years to build, covered a distance of 920 km (570 miles), cost £5,500,000 and employed a total of 31,983 people, many of whom perished from man-eating lions, accidents, tribal warfare and disease.

Kisumu was called Port Florence in honor of Florence Preston, a woman of great endurance who accompanied her husband, Ronald, the line's railhead engineer, the entire length of the railway from Mombasa to Lake Victoria. It was she who drove the final spike on that last day.

The town was not considered unduly attractive in its early years. One historian, Charles Miller, described it as the least desirable place to be posted in the British Empire, "a pesthouse, conspicuously vulnerable to malaria, dysentery, blackwater fever and a broad range of other tropical scourges. During construction of the railway, an epidemic of sleeping sickness swept the town and took nearly five hundred African lives. For some years, bubonic plague was endemic in Kisumu."

Those days are long gone. Today, Kisumu, though still packed and hot, is an enjoyable stop, especially if one wishes to take a boat across Lake Victoria or continue on southward to Ruma National Park (see page 154). Although Lake Victoria had long served as a transit and shipping zone for Arab slave traders (the lake's indigenous sailboat is rigged with the same lateen sail as the Arab coastal dhow), it was only after the opening of the Uganda Railway that Kisumu acquired commercial status. It soon became the largest Kenyan community on the lake. Despite the failure of the East African Community, Kisumu now has a thriving fish industry, a sugar refinery, marine workshops and flour, textile and cotton mills, threatened only by the rafts of hyacinth that might look pretty but are in imminent danger of stifling all life on the lake.

The **British Council Library** ((035) 45004, at the top of Oginga Odinga, has a selection of books and periodicals. The new **Kisumu Museum** ((035) 40804 E-MAIL kisumuse@arcc .or.ke, on the Nairobi road east of town, is worth a visit, with ethnographic exhibits and more animals than some zoos. The **Kisumu Park**, with orphan leopards and monkeys pacing in cages and an expanse of unspoiled lakefront, is safe-ish for walking as far as the Sunset Hotel, but not, as friendly park wardens are quick to point out, any further.

WHERE TO STAY

Kisumu is an ideal base for exploring western Kenya. The city has two luxury alternatives: the **Imperial Hotel** ((035) 41470 FAX (035) 40345, Box 1866, Kisumu, located on Jomo Kenyatta Highway near Oginga Odinga Road (Ksh3,900 for a double with bed and breakfast), which also offers suites and long-let apartments; and the **Sunset Hotel** ((0345) 41100, Box 215, Kisumu (US$72 for a double with bed and breakfast), located just south of the city center, bookable through ATH ((02) 336858, Box 30471, Nairobi. Get up to the roof for the best view of Lake Victoria and, when the wind's onshore, the vast rafts of hyacinth engulfing the port. Less expensive but still good is the **New Victoria Hotel** ((035) 21067, Box 276, Kisumu, on Gor Mihia Street; doubles with balconies overlooking the city center and lake cost Ksh900 with bed and breakfast. Cheapest is the **Western Lodge** ((035) 42586, Box 276, Kisumu, on Kendu Lane, at Ksh500, bed only.

HOW TO GET THERE

Kenya Airways ((02) 210771 or (02) 229291 FAX (02) 336252 flies once or twice a day between Kisumu and Nairobi. Flight time is one hour, the cost is US$80 one way. Note that in Nairobi, they do not fly from Wilson

Airport but use the International Terminal. Their office in Kisumu ☎ (0345) 44055 FAX (0345) 43339 is on Oginga Odinga Street. Buses and *matatus* leave morning and evening for the six- to eight-hour journey to Nairobi. Trains leave daily for Nairobi at 6 PM, arriving the next morning at 7 AM, although the service can be suspended for long periods, especially during the rainy seasons. Reservations are essential for first- (Ksh2,200) and second- (Ksh1,800) class travel. Kisumu Railway Station is at the lakeside end of New Station Road, and the booking office is open 8 AM to noon and 2 PM to 4 PM.

LAKE VICTORIA TRANSPORTATION

Lake ferries link small towns and islands along the coast to the port, as well as to Mwanza in Tanzania.

Although Kisumu's Port has, over recent years, often been completely clogged with hyacinth, recent breakthroughs using imported weevils to break up the rafts of floating weeds should, if all goes well, open up lake transportation once more. It's not easy, however, to find the passenger port — turn left about midway off Oginga Odinga Road before you get to the Caltex depot and cross to a dilapidated freight yard where you can ask employees for directions to the steamer booking office. There, at a very reasonable price, you should be able to buy a round-trip ticket to any one of several lake communities in Kenya.

Kendu Bay, Kuwur, Asembo Bay and Homa Bay are the main ferry destinations on Lake Victoria, and often there is no way to return to Kisumu until the next day. Similarly, you can leave on Tuesday for Homa Bay, returning Wednesday, or can depart Wednesday and Friday for the port of Mbita (on Rusinga Island) and Mfangano Island, again returning the following day. It's a local boat so fares should vary around the low shilling level. It is possible to get across here to Uganda, although this involves lengthy negotiations with both the immigration department and the skipper of the cargo ferry. The crossing will take 12 hours or more. Be warned that this isn't always a tranquil cruise. The lake can seem placid, then turn rough suddenly.

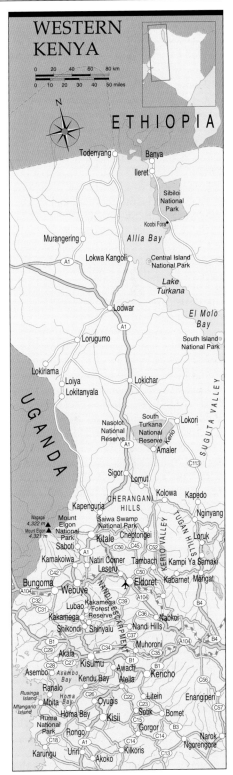

NORTH OF KISUMU

Much of the area between Mount Elgon and Lake Victoria is rolling hills, steep escarpments and narrow valleys. The entire area was once thick tropical rainforest. Kenya's burgeoning population and extensive logging have reduced the original forest to a few scattered remnants, which the government has recently tried to protect by gazetting as forest reserves.

One of the most important of these — well, about the only one that still exists — is the world-famous Kakamega Forest Reserve, located just east of the town of the same name.

KAKAMEGA

Conservationists in Kenya are now attempting to change the status of the Kakamega Forest to a national park, but at present it is just a reserve — and the entry fee is just Ksh100. Unfortunately, this won't pay for any environmental protection measures — well, to be honest not enough visitors make it here anyway — and human encroachment continues apace. The forest, all that remains of the equatorial jungle that once stretched from the Atlantic through the Zaire basin, may not survive for much longer. Kakamega is similar to the equatorial rainforests of West Africa but drier. As a result, much flora and fauna are found in Kakamega Forest that exist nowhere else in Kenya, or probably the world. At least 350 bird species have been identified in the 100 sq km (39 sq miles) that remain of the original forest, including turacos, parrots, trogons, barbets and woodpeckers, honeyguides, greenbuls and crowned hawk eagles.

Whereas the typical North American or European temperate zone forest may contain an average of eight to ten tree species per hectare, equatorial rainforests like Kakamega often have 100 to 150 different tree species per hectare. This amazing diversity of vegetation supports an equal variety of animals; over 40 percent of the mammals in the Kakamega Forest live in the trees, and some amphibians, insects and reptiles never descend to the ground. More than half the mammals inhabiting Kakamega are nocturnal, sleeping during the day in tree hollows or high in the branches.

The proposed Kakamega Forest National Park will provide at least temporary protection to the undamaged part of the forest. This is the portion lying northeast of the town of Kakamega, including nearly half the watershed of the Isiukhu River. However, even if the park is approved, the pressures on the forest are so overwhelming that it will probably not last long as a viable habitat for the rare species still remaining there.

Kakamega's problems are similar to those threatening all the parks, reserves and wildlife of Kenya: logging (both authorized and illegal); firewood collection, which kills young trees; cutting of saplings for household and agricultural use; livestock grazing; and game poaching. The root cause of all these is population growth. Kenya not only has the world's highest birth rate, desertification is expanding and further areas are made unsafe by politically motivated tribal unrest. This means that most of the population settle in areas such as Kakamega and use up its resources.

The flowering plants of Kakamega bloom most colorfully after the long rains, from July to September, when the forest's butterflies are at their peak. From various points in the forest, the hiker can see the grassland, **Nandi Plateau**, escarpments to the east, and the **Kisere Forest** to the north. The major tree species include ebony, podocarp, teak, mukumari (*Cordia africana*) — favored by bees — and seven species of fig including the "strangler fig." The latter is a huge, broad-canopied tree found in most hardwood forests in Kenya, from Lake Victoria to the Matthews Range and the coast. It usually propagates when its fruit is eaten by birds or monkeys, whose droppings may be excreted on the branch of another tree species. The seed then grows, sending down long tendrils to the earth for nutrients and water. Over a period of years, these tendrils multiply, thicken and join, until the fig completely encompasses its host tree, killing it and growing above and around it, to achieve the great height and wide crown often seen in Kakamega.

Specially worth noting in Kakamega Forest are the red-tailed, Sykes' and colobus monkeys, giant forest squirrels up to 65 cm (26 inches) in length and flying squirrels that can glide up to 19 m (60 ft) from tree to tree, the ant-eating tree pangolin, the giant fruit bat, the potto, bushbabies, the rare leopard and more common wild forest hogs, baboons (near the Buyango Hill road), and the occasional duiker that has escaped poaching.

The forest was once home to elephants (exterminated by white hunters before World War I), Cape buffaloes, Uganda kobs (a small,

If bitten, pressure bandages are the only approved method of treatment before medical advice is sought: try to kill the snake for identification. To our knowledge, however, no tourist has expired from snakebite in Kenya for many years.

The Gaboon viper, like its similarly-patterned cousin, the puff adder, which is more common in open country and closer to the coast, is viviparous, bearing its young alive. It may give birth to 80 offspring at a time, all of which, in true snake fashion, are on their own from the moment of birth.

reddish, thickset antelope with ringed horns) and the Defassa waterbuck, all of which are now gone.

Still present, though the tourist is unlikely to see them, are snakes. They include at least five highly poisonous cobras and mambas, and the delightful Gaboon viper, Africa's biggest poisonous snake, which can grow to over two meters (six feet five) and weighs up to 11 kg (25 lbs). Its fangs are over five centimeters (two inches) long. Although its bite is fatal to humans, the Gaboon viper is not usually aggressive unless cornered or annoyed. The tourist who keeps to the trails in Kakamega, and is willing to tread heavily (and carry a big stick), need generally not fear an unscheduled demise by snakebite.

Where to Stay
The **Kakamega Forest Rest House** is famous among ornithologists, naturalists and just plain tourists for self-help rooms in a rotting wooden building set amid a dense grove of trees (US$2 per person); some space is available for camping and if I had a tent I'd use it here. Space is limited, so it's best to make reservations first with the Kakamega Forest Ranger (no phone), Box 88, Kakamega. In any case, accommodation is basic at best. Four kilometers (three miles) to the east is **Rondo Retreat Center (** (0331) 30268 FAX (0331) 20145, ᶜ/₀ Trinity Fellowship, Box 2153,

Tranquil Lake Elementeita, another lake where flamingos breed, remains the private domain of the Delamere family.

Kakamega, a restored saw-miller's house where *The Kitchen Toto* was filmed (expensive). Very elegant but no alcohol. For urban comforts you'll need to stay in Kakamega town at the **Golf Hotel** ((02) 229751 or (02) 330820 FAX (02) 227815, Box 42013, Nairobi (mid-range, B&B). It has handsome large rooms overlooking elegant lawns pecked by vultures, a swimming pool and cheerful staff.

How to Get There

Kakamega town is 50 km (31 miles) north of Kisumu on the main A1 road heading north

station set among subsistence farms and a recently clear-cut pine forest. If using public transportation, take a *matatu* heading towards Webuye, but you'll have to walk the last stretch from the main road. Going south, you drive 10 km (six miles) toward Shikondi and turn left (east) on to a dirt road at the sign "Forest Rest House" (the sign may be missing, however). Drive the 13 km (eight miles) through the village of Shinyalu, past the reserve boundary and the Isicheno Forest Station and turn left for the last few hundred meters to the Forest

to Lodwar. By public transportation the most frequent *matatus* run from Webuye and Kisumu.

Finding the forest from the town can appear confusing unless you realize that there are two access points into the forest, both, in their way, worth visiting. Thus equally valid directions can send you in opposite directions. With your own vehicle, drive from Kakamega either south toward Kisumu or north toward Webuye. Going north, you pass Lubao and turn right (east) some 16 km (10 miles) from Kakamega, just before the road to Kambiri, at the sign reading "Ministry of Tourism and Wildlife." From there, it's two and a quarter kilometers (nearly one and a half miles) to a forest

Rest House. By public transportation ask for the daily *matatu* traveling between Kakamega town and Eldoret via Shinyalu village and Kapsabet. Ask to be dropped at Isecheno, 10 minutes' walk from the Forest Rest House. At either forest station, it's possible to hire a guide.

South of Kakamega you may see men pushing bicycles laden with large burlap sacks — these are 90-kg (200-lb) bags of maize kernels being transported all the way to Kisumu. Depending where the man began, this may be a distance of 60 km (37 miles) or more, nearly all of it up and down steep hills. For this he receives, if the maize is good, about as much as tourists pay for a quick meal at a lodge.

ELDORET

Above the western edge of the Rift Valley, the countryside levels out on the 2,100-m (7,000-ft) elevation **Uasin Gishu Plateau**. Here are large wheat and cattle spreads intermingled with cedar, fir and pine plantations, reminding one of the American Midwest.

It's hard to imagine this area as the early colonists described it — a veritable paradise filled with animals that had never been hunted. None are to be seen today.

During the Boer War, the area was settled by Afrikaners and in 1912 Eldoret became a town when J.C. Shaw opened a branch of the Standard Bank of South Africa. In *The Mottled Lizard*, Elspeth Huxley describes the event. "[He] had arrived in an oxcart with a too heavy safe which he had pushed out at the back onto a wagon track that traversed the bare, brown plateau. As it was heavy to move, a mud hut had been build round it with two rooms, one for the safe and one for Mr. Shaw. The town then consisted of a few little stores and was called Sixty-four, after the survey number on which it stood. Sixty-four served a sparse community of Afrikaners who had arrived together — men, women, children, babies, predikants and household goods — from Bethel in the Transvaal, and trekked in their semi-covered wagons up roadless, forested escarpment to a promised land."

Today Eldoret is an ideal village. Very much a Moi area, it has had a great deal of investment and, rather to its bemused surprise, has an international airport. So far, however, the only international flights persuaded to land are those on the so-called "slave run" taking workers to Saudi Arabia. It is a center of industry (fabric and leather) and commerce. On the west edge of the shopping district is a small city park, one of the few found outside Nairobi, the state hospital is better than average and there is a private hospital as well, the Uasin Gishu Hospital ((0321) 32720.

Where to Stay and Eat

Whether because it is a commercial center for a large agricultural community or because of its many businessmen trying, over a few cocktails, to find some hometown angle to interest Moi, Eldoret has an abundance of hotels. The best is the **Sirikwa Hotel** ((02) 336858, Box 30741, Nairobi, with a restaurant, bar, and swimming pool (mid-range, B&B). The best of the budget accommodations are the **Kabathaya Hotel and Lodging** ((0321) 22160, Box 832, Eldoret (very inexpensive) and the **New Wagon Wheel** ((0321) 32271 (inexpensive), which does allow camping in the garden.

How to Get There

The international airport ((0321) 61299 is served four time a week by **Kenya Airways** ((02) 210771 or (02) 229291 FAX (02) 336252, Box 41010, Nairobi, flying from Nairobi via Kisumu. Eldoret is on a main freight highway between Kenya and Uganda, with heavy truck traffic and as a result a disintegrating road surface. From Nairobi allow four hours for the journey of 312 km (195 miles). *Matatus* leave from the Nyamakima Bar on Duruma Road in Nairobi, and Akamba buses leave from "Machakos Airport." If heading north the situation is worse: the 70 km (43 miles) between Eldoret and Kitale is dreadful and things don't improve until after Kitale, where most of the trucks turn off for Uganda.

KITALE

Kitale is a pleasant town with a wide tree-lined main street, a large produce market and the **National Museum of Western Kenya**. This small museum has a limited wildlife and ethnology section featuring the Maasai, Turkana, Pokot and Luo tribes. On the grounds are a Turkana village and an agricultural demonstration of "terraced" land to supplement the interior displays on soil conservation; a nature trail leads through a miniature rainforest, a remnant of pre-colonial days. There is also a reasonably priced and usually well-stocked craft shop featuring local wares. Although there's not enough of interest here to plan a lengthy stay, a night here might be inevitable if heading up to Mount Elgon National Park, Saiwa Swamp, or to break the drive to Lodwar and the western shores of Lake Turkana.

The giant groundsel *(Senecio)* grow to 10 m (33 ft) on the highest slopes of Mounts Kenya and Elgon and the Aberdares.

Where to Stay and Eat

There are a number of good mid-range and very inexpensive places to stay in Kitale. The most expensive is the **Kitale Club** ((0325) 20030, Box 30, one kilometer (three-fourths of a mile) on the Eldoret road, an old club that once served as a camp for slaves being marched to export (mid-range). Perhaps this is why the atmosphere isn't that welcoming. Better are the **Lantern** (/FAX 30360, Box 4566, Kenyatta Street, where some rooms have balconies looking out over the town (inexpensive), or the **Alakara Hotel** ((0325) 20395, Box 1984, Kenyatta Street, next to the Post Office (inexpensive). On a real budget the **Mount Loima Lodge** ((0325) 31929, Box 1517, near the market, is adequate (very inexpensive). Those with their own transportation, however, are better off traveling north to take advantage of superb accommodation at Saiwa Swamp (see page 172) or east to Mount Elgon National Park (see page 170).

How to Get There

Kitale is served by several bus companies, of whom the best is Akamba ((0325) 31732. Coming up from Nairobi, book through their River Road office. Seats can be reserved for the return journey, but they only run two buses a day so it is usually a matter of clambering onboard whichever bus looks fullest; Eldoret Express has more departures.

Matatus leave Nairobi for Kitale from the Nyamakima Bar, Duruma Road, every day. Returning, they go every morning to Nairobi (six hours), to Lodwar near Lake Turkana (five hours) and to Kisumu via Kakamega (two hours).

MOUNT ELGON

The massive, cloud-cloaked slopes of Mount Elgon offer a refreshing relief from the hotter parts of Kenya. Mount Elgon, only 877 m (2,877 ft) shorter than Mount Kenya, is far bulkier. In the local language, Maa, the mountain is known as Ol Doinyo Ilgoon, "Breast Mountain," and it massively straddles the Ugandan border. The first European to climb to the top was Frederick Jackson, in 1890.

The highest peak on the rocky crater, Wagagai, at 4,322 m (14,178 ft), is actually in Uganda outside the national park. You may have great trouble getting a guide to take you there, or find yourself on the wrong side of the border without a reentry visa. The Mountain Club of Kenya does not recommend climbing this peak because of the potential border problems and the occasional presence of hostile, armed Ugandan rebels. Recommended instead are short hikes within the park itself, paying the daily fee of US$10 (adult) or US$5 (child), or freely outside the park limits.

Mount Elgon National Park is a hiking and camping paradise that is seldom visited by travellers. Wildlife is plentiful, and there are specified hiking trails to the major caves, along **Elephant Platform**, or to 4,038-m (13,248-ft) **Koitoboss Peak**, the highest of Mount Elgon's peaks in Kenya.

The hiking is especially good because the driving is singularly bad. You will often be denied admission unless you have a four-wheel drive. Indeed, it is doubtful that you could be able to get as far as the gate if you didn't have four-wheel drive. I once met an American family in Kisumu whose rental car could not, even during a dry spell, tackle the steep climb to the Kitum or Elephant Caves, once one of the major attractions in the park.

Along the eastern slope of Mount Elgon is a series of enormous caverns — **Kitum**, **Mkingeny**, and **Chipmyalil Caves**. During colonial times they were inhabited by Maasai and thought to be manmade. Descriptions of them by the explorer Joseph Thomson supposedly inspired the English writer, H. Rider Haggard, to site part of his famed novel *She* in the El Goni caves.

It is now, however, the accepted theory that the caves were dug over the millennia by elephants in search of salt. And there is certainly enough elephant dung on their floors to support this theory. When I visited, I wondered how the elephants could have moved some of the gigantic boulders that littered the floor. This mystery was explained by Mike Clifton, the naturalist at The Ark (see THE ABERDARE MOUNTAINS, page 208). They were deposited there during an earthquake, which coincidentally was filmed.

"A film crew had obtained a permit to set up lights in Kitum Cave to film the elephants at night," Mike said. "On one particular night, while elephants were present and film rolling, the cave ceiling began to fall. The footage was spectacular, with the giant animals fleeing to avoid the shower of rock."

"However, during the next week the director had his film confiscated and his research visa revoked. He was accused of having set off explosives in the cave. Luckily, he was able to prove from seismographic data at the university that there had indeed been an earthquake whose shock waves, not explosives, had caused the rock shower. The footage was recovered and used as part of a television documentary on elephants."

hiking. If they see no problem, the trail starts at the end of the "drivable" track to the northern boundary of the park, and should take from two to three hours. From the peak, a trail leads to the left across glacial moraines down into the crater and the Suam warm springs for a relaxing bath. This walk can be done in a day, but get an early start in order to be out of the park or back to your campsite by the 6:30 PM curfew.

The forests of Mount Elgon are among the most impressive in Kenya, with giant podos (podocarpus), junipers and Elgon

These caves were also the setting for the movie *Quest for Fire*. However, without doubt the caves' biggest claim to international fame was as the suspected epicenter for the Ebola virus — immortalized in the film *The Hot Zone*. Despite several spacesuited research expeditions by American scientific teams, no connection was ever proven. Hard-hit hoteliers blame the international media for yet another scare story. Nonetheless, the caves are eerie, and you'd be wise to bring a flashlight and extra batteries if you wish to explore. Thousands of bats of several species darken the sky as they flock into the dust.

If you want to go to **Koitoboss Peak**, check with the rangers at the entrance of Elgon National Park as to the dangers of

olive trees, the largest variety of olive in East Africa. Some reach heights of 25 m (80 ft). Flowers are abundant in the forest and moorlands at all times of the year, but they are at their peak in June and July, when you can also find several varieties of terrestrial and epiphytic orchids.

The park's animals are extensive but well-hidden. They include the Sykes', brazza and colobus monkeys, olive baboons, civets, genets, the rare golden cat, giant forest hogs, bush pigs, duikers, sunis and bushbucks. Leopards are fairly common but difficult to see, and usually not dangerous. Buffaloes are frequent up to at least 3,000 m (10,000 ft), and

The Mount Elgon Lodge was once a rancher's idyllic estate.

should be treated with extreme caution. Elephants are rare due to poaching, and the black rhino is gone.

Where to Stay

You can either camp in the park or stay at **Mount Elgon Lodge** ((02) 229751 or (02) 330820 FAX (02) 227815, Box 42013, Nairobi (expensive, full board). The lodge is two kilometers (just over a mile) before the Chorlin Gate. Formerly a colonial estate, the lodge has several elegant spacious rooms with large bay windows in the manor house, and double cottages on grounds with sculptured shrubs and formal glades. Alternatively, **Lokitela Farm** (book through Bush Homes of East Africa ((02) 350703, (02) 571661 or (02) 571592 FAX (02) 571665 E-MAIL bushhome @africaonline.co.ke WEB SITE www.bush-homes.co.ke, Box 56923, Nairobi) is a working farm on the slopes of Mount Elgon with a full range of activities and excursions (extremely expensive, all-inclusive).

Days on Mount Elgon are warm, but, like Mount Kenya and the Aberdares, the nights are chilly, near-freezing at the higher campsites. Even when staying in lodges, a sweater and/or jacket will be useful, particularly if there are no logs blazing the dining room's massive two-meter (six-foot) fireplace.

Let's Go Travel ((02) 447151 or (02) 441030 FAX (02) 447270 or (02) 441690 E-MAIL info @letsgosafari.com WEB SITE www.letsgo safari.com, Box 60342, Nairobi, keeps a list of private estates on Mount Elgon which take visitors on an occasional and usually expensive basis; otherwise there are several grassy campsites in the park (US$2 per person), all with running water. **Kapkuru Campground**, 500 m (550 yards) from Chorlin Gate, is at the lowest elevation and would be the best place to stop unless you have plenty of warm clothes and heavy sleeping bags. If you are planning to camp at Mount Elgon, be sure to buy provisions in Kitale. The best way to see Mount Elgon is to camp and hike.

How to Get There

It's not just the security situation nor the limited accommodation that restricts the popularity of Mount Elgon National Park. It's also hard to reach. A four-wheel-drive vehicle is recommended year-round. The best access is through the Chorlin Gate, 27 km (17 miles) from Kitale, via Endebess Road (watch the signs carefully and ask directions if in doubt). It will take the better part of an hour to cover this distance. The road is paved for the first 19 km (12 miles) west from Kitale to the village of Enderbess, which is as far as you'll get by *matatu* — or indeed, saloon car. The rest of the distance to Chorlin Gate is rough — if hitching don't expect more than a couple of vehicles to pass each day.

SAIWA SWAMP NATIONAL PARK

Just north of Kitale is the 26-sq-km (10-sq-mile) Saiwa Swamp National Park, entry US$15 per adult, US$5 per child, created to protect the rare and endangered semi-aquatic sitatunga antelope. First classified by Speke, the sitatunga have highly specialized, splayed and elongated hooves that allow them to spread their weight over a greater area than a normal hoof would permit. They are thus able to move about the swamp, semi-submerged. They swim well and are reputed to submerge, leaving only their nostrils showing, when threatened.

Several tree blinds have been constructed along the western edge of the swamp to provide viewing. As usual, late afternoon and early morning are the best times for watching these normally shy and increasingly rare creatures, but their semi-aquatic lifestyle makes them hard to see. The swamp has also become the home for the white-bearded brazza monkey, and colobus and vervet monkeys, which can be spotted at almost any time of the day. And even if the sitatunga are being shy, there are plenty of bushbucks to keep your interest.

Bird watchers should enjoy the turacos, cuckoos, kingfishers, hornbills and crowned cranes. Following the rains, you will get the extra bonus of innumerable butterflies and mountain orchids. And on very rare occasions, when pushing the dusk curfew, you may find a potto. Perhaps best of all, vehicles can't drive in the swamp so viewing is all on foot.

At any time of the year, the swamp is cool and a wool sweater will be welcome. Also

A rocky outcrop on Mount Elgon.

bring film with a fast ISO (1,000 to 1,600 ISO) rating if you plan to take photos, as there is not much light in the swamp of the sitatunga.

Where to Stay

There is primitive camping (US$2 per person) near the park entrance, with running water, and a *banda* (inexpensive), but this is a bit basic. Better by far to drive six kilometers (just under four miles) to the north to **Sirikwa Safaris Guesthouse and Campsite** ((0325) 20061, Box 332, Kitale, signposted, where the Barnley family offer B&B (expensive to mid-range), camping and *bandas*, as well as guides for hiking and bird watching. This place is one of Kenya's undiscovered secrets and well worth a detour and some time and, most unusually in Kenya, it combines very expensive and comfortable accommodation with more basic accommodation for travelers with less money.

How to Get There

Saiwa Swamp is 18 km (11 miles) north of Kitale off the Lodwar road, while the Barnley's house is six kilometers further on, signposted on the right. There are *matatus* for the determined, leaving from Kitale, but you might well have to pay the fare for the full journey to Lokichar, if not Lodwar. For security reasons, these long-distance *matatus* travel in convoy, leaving at 6 AM and noon.

NORTH FROM KITALE

North of Kitale, banditry and cattle-rustling have caused plenty of security incidents. At time of writing, driving here was only in convoy, but as a result of this there had been no incidents for the last few months. The road has deteriorated too, and only trucks can negotiate the tarmac — cars use the hard shoulder, and even that's slow going. Plenty of time to enjoy the view of the savannas of Trans-Nzoia and along the western and northern slopes of the Cherangani Hills but, in convoy, the only chance to stop is when a vehicle breaks down. After Kapenguria, the last gas before Lodwar, the scenery changes from open rolling hills to steep, forested mountains as you climb Marich Pass. On a clear day to the northwest, you can see jagged, unusually shaped mountains, the

tallest of which is 3,068-m (10,066-ft) Mount Kadam, beyond the Uganda border.

Descending the pass, the road follows the Moran River, clear and fast-running over large granitic boulders. Emerging from the Cherangani Hills, you again look down into the Rift Valley with its extinct volcanoes of varying sizes. To the northwest is 3,325-m (10,910-ft) **Sigogowa** or **Mtelo Mountain**, the Pokot sacred mountain and one of the sources of the Turkwell River. The Pokot bury their dead on the mountain with their heads facing the summit. It used to be possible to hike to the top of Sigogowa, but this is no longer considered safe. Should things change the easiest climb is from the village of **Sigor**, the major Pokot market center, on the north side of Marich Pass.

As you continue north toward the Jade Sea, the scenery becomes less and less varied, more alien. Familiar vegetation begins to disappear as the land becomes more and more arid.

As you go north tall thorn trees dry to sparser, squatter thornscrub to golden grasses and doum palms. And the soils change as well. The traditional African red fades to coral, then pastel pink, and finally to sandy white. The few clouds are like puffballs; dust devils swirl about the barren volcanic hills and across dry river beds where women and children dig for water. There are the familiar livestock — goats, sheep, and cows — but now there are also camels, blending into the sandy scenery. Hares, squirrels, gazelles, sunis and jackals are the major, though scarce, wildlife.

LOKICHAR

The only settlement of any size along the route is Lokichar, where a local mission has organized an excellent Turkana crafts cooperative (which is closed on Sundays). The shop is well stocked with baskets and mats, Turkana bead necklaces and bracelets, wrist and finger knives, carvings, bowls and beaded goat skin aprons. The variety is great, the quality good, the prices fair. There is no middleman taking a cut, so I recommend that you not bargain too ruthlessly here. The proprietor told us that it took a week to make a basket that I purchased for

Ksh40. It is hard to offer less. There's nowhere here to stay, however, and no very good reason to tarry.

Lokichar and Lodwar have the unfortunate history of being sites of Kenyatta's detention by the English during the Mau Mau Rebellion. Even today with a paved road they seem remote and it is easy to imagine how alien they must have seemed to Kenyatta, with no electricity or guaranteed source of water after the lushness of Kikuyuland. Certainly the lack of green was a great deprivation to one so unjustly detained.

LODWAR

Lodwar's inauspicious history began in 1933 when a Pakistani trader, Shah Mohammed, arrived with his donkey on the banks of the seasonal Turkwell River. He eventually built a permanent trading center which today is the last stop on the road to Sudan. It now has a 24-hour gas station, and is supported by aid agencies heading north to work in Sudan and smuggled goods coming the other way. Optimistic talk of oil in the region has evaporated and hustlers are especially determined to milk every possible shilling out of the few tourists who brave the drive up from the south. Watch out for these. Most foreigners here are heading for Lake Turkana and there are countless "guides" offering to help. Few of them have been so far, and are totally panicked when they are hired for the trip. Many travelers head for the lake, lured by tales of mythical ferries and dreamtime lodges, only to end up having to sleep in the bush. Sometimes they are then robbed. When they report to the police the reaction is "How could you be so stupid." Hard to say. Perhaps it is the dry, dusty desert that induced some sort of dissociation from reality — and normal caution. For Kenyans it's a hardship posting: teachers, civil servants and soldiers all dread being sent here.

The town blends old and new. On its outskirts are traditional Turkana straw domed-huts. In town, radios blare from concrete buildings. There are a few *hotelis* and restaurants, and large missionary complexes competing for members, one offering "Salvation Music."

Where to Stay and Eat

This is one place where having a fan is recommended. Air conditioning would be better, but at the time of writing, in a hot dusty town that could really do with some, there isn't any. The best place to stay is the politically very correct **Nawoitorong Guest House** ((0393) 21208 FAX (0393) 21572 E-MAIL edfrh @imul.com, Bow 192, Lodwar, run by Turkana women as part of an educational co-operative (very inexpensive). You can spend a bit more at the **Lodwar Club** ((0393) 21252, Box 123, Lodwar, but it's a bit rundown (inexpensive). Both these places are to the east of the town center. In town, the **Turkwel Lodge** ((0393) 21201, Box 14, Lodwar, though it can be noisy, especially at weekends (very inexpensive, B&B). *Matatus* drop their fares at the **Salama Hotel** (no phone), which has basic inexpensive rooms and one of the best restaurants in town, though no alcohol or smoking is permitted.

How to Get There

With difficulty. Lodwar is beyond the reach of bus services, but not far enough for scheduled flights which, depending entirely on aid workers, fly further north. With your own car it is 355 km (222 miles) north of Kitale. It's no closer by *matatu* and it doesn't feel it either, although at least, because they have to travel in armed convoy, at least don't stop too often to pick up fares.

TURKANA'S WESTERN SHORE

Of the two settlements on the western shores of Lake Turkana, Ferguson's Gulf (of which the local village is called Kalokol) and Eliye Springs, neither has many facilities of any sort. Whichever you choose, be ready for an experience of unreality and strangeness. The air is dry, the sun so intense that all color fades. But then there are minute variations in the landscape — bleached sand, golden grasses, sapphire sky and jade lake. Occasionally there is a dash of green, but only in the first week following the rains in October and November or April and May. They dry all too quickly.

The sun rises red to announce each new day as hippopotamuses return to the coolness of the lake. Young Turkana begin their march to the sea to fill sundry containers with the brackish water. Some pause for a quick, playful swim, always aware they share the water with crocodiles. Sacred ibis patrol the shore, cormorants bob for fish and Egyptian geese float silently.

Later the young men arrive with nets which they lay from their raft-like boats to trap Nile perch. Mothers bring their infants to bathe. Children chase and scream along the shore. Some make a game out of washing clothes, stamping on them in their wash buckets as if they were mashing grapes.

For the young, school has been added to this rhythm. Most learn the standard Kenyan curriculum in a thatch hut among the dunes; those whose parents can afford it go to the boarding school in Lokwa Kangoli. What changes education will make in their age-old lifestyle in this dry, fragile environment cannot be foretold.

Their survival is constantly being threatened. The waters of Lake Turkana recede and return, mocking any attempts to build harbors or fish-canning plants funded by overseas aid agencies. Onshore, growing

The shore is a hub of measured activity: graceful human figures gliding on shimmering sand, a herd of sheep and goats browsing the tan, gilded grass, a white, glinting scatter of shorebirds. Northward, the land leaves a blank horizon, where the Jade Sea extends forever carrying your eye off the edge of the globe straight into space in which this earth floats like a tiny speck in a more infinite sea.

As sunset approaches, a glow creeps across the sky like a giant jacaranda dropping its purple snow, and people move gracefully, loads atop their heads, back to their dune dwellings. All is silent except for the snorts of hippos as they leave the water to graze along the shore until the sun rises red again.

African desertification and global climate change are certainly contributing to a long-term change.

Fish have proved the lifeline. In an increasingly competitive market, fish from Lake Turkana are now transported south for sale in the markets around Lake Victoria.

Unlike most national parks and reserves, Turkana's shores can be explored on foot. Although there are plenty of crocodiles, they are generally scared of man and don't appear to be a problem. Trailing gangs of small children are more of a problem, and will make life unbearable for hot, sweaty backpackers traveling on foot. Distances, around the shrinking lake, are huge and the climate unforgiving. Early morning and late afternoon are still the best times because the midday sun is unmercifully hot. Along the shore you can find giant Nile perch skeletons, which I first took to be crocodile bones; and some of the many children who will try to accompany you on your expeditions will offer to sell you croc teeth — the Crocodile Dundees of Africa. They will also pose for a photographic fee, request T-shirts and give you their addresses if you wish to strike up a friendship. If you want to see crocodile bones ask one of the children to show you the way.

Admittedly there is not a great variety of destinations or sights to see, but the ephemeral quality of the environment weaves its spell.

Where to Stay and Eat
Eliye Springs used to have *bandas* and a lodge, but this is now only a primitive campsite. Water is usually available, but before making the rough 42-km (26-mile) drive, check in Lodwar if anyone knows the latest status of the place. In any event make sure you have enough water for at least one day. The site is usually deserted and tranquil. You will, however, probably be visited by local children once the nearby village becomes aware of your presence. Very few visitors make it here.

Ferguson's Gulf does, in the village of Kalokol, have a few basic huts that will take in visitors. There is also the remains of a luxury lodge: the **Lake Turkana Fishing Lodge** (no phone now) which still serves warm drinks and has rotting *bandas* (inexpensive). The only halfway reasonable place to stay in the area at all is **Lebolo Lodge** (contact through Bush Homes of East Africa ((02) 350703, (02) 571661 or (02) 571592 FAX (02) 571665 E-MAIL bushhome@africaonline.co.ke WEB SITE www.bush-homes.co.ke, Box 56923, Nairobi), which is set in an idyllic lakeside oasis between Eliye Springs and Ferguson's Gulf (very expensive). This is run by long-time Turkana veteran Halewijn Scheuermann and guests here benefit not just from his effective and reliable trucks and boats, but also from his unparalleled local knowledge.

How to Get There
To reach the western shore of Lake Turkana, you continue 24 km (15 miles) north of Lodwar before choosing a lakeside destination — turn right on a dirt road for the 48 km (30 mile) trip to Eliye Springs or stick to the *murram* for the 42 km (26 mile) journey to Ferguson's Gulf. Only Ferguson's Gulf is regularly served by *matatu*: there's one most days, and the trip takes about an hour. Travelers are dropped off at the village of Kalokol and left to walk to the lakeshore past endless Turkana settlements. Harried by local Turkana kids, this can take two hours. Most visitors find their two-litre water bottle lasts them outbound, but there's nowhere to buy another for the long, hot, walk back. Many travelers arrive here looking for a ferry across the lake but there isn't one. Don't sleep out here waiting for onward transportation because this won't eventuate and you will probably get robbed.

CENTRAL ISLAND NATIONAL PARK

One excursion from Ferguson's Gulf is a half-day trip to Central Island National Park. The problem here is finding a boat that will do it, and the park fee of US$15 per adult and US$5 per child will be the least of your prob-

OPPOSITE AND ABOVE: Turkana's El Molo tribe, which subsists principally on fish, is not averse to eating crocodile.

lems. At time of writing, the only person able to organize reliable transportation was the manager of Lebolo Lodge (see above).

Approximately 20 km (12 miles) southeast of Ferguson's Gulf, this island sanctuary is the most concentrated breeding ground for crocodiles in Africa. The five-square-kilometer (two-square-mile) island is three connected volcanic cones, two of which contain fresh water lakes. The island shores are black lava sand and rock, and the vegetation thorny, bleached scrub.

The southern and smallest cone, a five- to ten-minute hike from the shore, is the domain of the crocodiles, a turquoise rimmed lake with an iridescent, almost algal verdancy of brilliant scrub. From the rim above you can see crocodiles cruising like immense sunken logs, only the knobs of their eyes showing. If you are in Kenya during April and May, this crater can be "the" place to be, and not just to get away from the rain. It's hatching season and the crater is alive with squeaks and yelps of the young, who will spend their first year here before heading out to the Jade Sea. Some, however, spend their entire lives in the crater.

A morning trip is usually the best for viewing the reptiles, while the afternoon excursions frequently include a trip to the northern cauldron and its pink flamingos standing one-legged along the shore. As there are supposedly no crocs here, I once climbed down the steep dusty trail to the water's edge. Scorpions leapt from a trailside boulder as I descended. The flamingos rose and circled to the far side of the lake, which is larger than it appears from above. Butterflies rode the updrafts. I walked across the hard, cracked mud where scorpions nest. Further on, flat pinnacles of calcified mud rose above the water, where you can walk as if they were stepping stones. The water's edge is thick with algae and almost too hot to touch. Across the lake the flamingos can appear like a pink ribbon edging the brown pleated crater wall.

Central Island has more than its share of shorebirds, a few hippos and a resident lizard population. I saw several lava-colored reptiles over a meter (a yard) long. As I left,

The barren shorelines of Lake Turkana, the Jade Sea.

four hippos decided they'd had enough of the tourists for the day and blocked the route of the boat. Making light of what could have been a nasty situation, one of our French companions for the trip joked that the hippos only wanted to have their photos taken and to give us their address. And what's more they didn't ask for Ksh20!

If you are on a tight budget, you can sometimes find a local fisherman who'll take you to Central Island for about Ksh500 per boat and hope the park ranger isn't around. If you go this route make sure the boat is seaworthy and has plenty of fuel, and that the crew is experienced. Turkana's weather can change suddenly and winds can quickly whip up meter-tall waves.

For a trip to the island, wear sturdy shoes: sandals just won't make it. Bring a hat, sun screen and water. The island is hot by 10 AM and remains so until dusk.

ACROSS THE LAKE

The third and most exciting of opportunities is a two or three day trip across the lake to **Sibiloi National Park** and a visit to **Koobi Fora** (see page 200). Other than flying to Sibiloi, this is the most comfortable, relaxing way to get there, and crossing Lake Turkana is exhilarating, unless of course you are prone to seasickness. The crossing is not something that can be easily achieved on the spur of the moment: it's not a trip to make in an unreliable boat and in any case you will need to be sure there is a vehicle — with gasoline — at Allia Bay. Plans for the journey must be made in advance: **Let's Go Travel** ((02) 447151 or (02) 441030 FAX (02) 447270 or (02) 441690 E-MAIL info@letsgo safari.com WEB SITE www.letsgosafari.com, Box 60342, Nairobi, can help with charter flights, though for boat transport from Ferguson's Gulf you'll need **Bush Homes of East Africa** ((02) 350703, 571661, 571592 FAX (02) 571665 E-MAIL bushhome@africaon line.co.ke WEB SITE www.bush-homes.co.ke, Box 56923, Nairobi.

From Ferguson's Gulf it takes about three hours to make the crossing to Allia Bay or Koobi Fora. Time of departure depends on the weather; usually the water calms in the afternoon.

At Allia Bay, a guide with a four-wheel drive meets any arrivals and takes them to the *bandas*, prepares any meals (if you've brought food — otherwise you'll starve) and provides transportation to archaeological digs and on game drives. There's no guarantee they'll have gas, however, so bring your own.

For this trip you will have to be self-sufficient. Apart from sturdy shoes, hat, sun screen, wind breaker and a change or two of clothes, don't forget food, fuel and water.

Lake Turkana does exert a spell, and many visitors try to include it into their visit to Kenya. However they often expect to be able to include it into a round-trip journey taking in both western and eastern shores. This rarely works. Few if any boats seem to make grueling crossing between Ferguson's Gulf to Loyangalani where there is, in any case, no reliable transportation south. A speedboat will take at least six hours to do the journey, and if you go with local fishermen you're looking at an adventure that will take a week or so. Those wishing to "close the circle," therefore, will be disappointed. It is worth the trip as there is something captivating about the hot, dusty frontier atmosphere of the northern towns, but you should bear in mind that neither side of the lake is especially secure, and armed cattle-rustlers and bandits travel with far more freedom than motorbound visitors. Check locally for the current security situation.

The only way back from Ferguson's Gulf is the way you came. There's a certain pleasure in this expedition into the arid north, however. On your return colors are one by one added to the previously monochrome landscape until you are once again into the verdant greens of the Marich Pass. It probably didn't seem quite so green or cool on your northward journey.

An El Molo, fishing from his *ambach* raft, pulls in a crocodile.

The Northern Rift Valley

The East African Rift Valley is supposedly large enough to be seen with the naked eye from the moon, and it runs over 8,000 km (4,960 miles) from Ethiopia on the Red Sea to Mozambique on the southern Indian Ocean. Formed some 20 to 40 million years ago by faulting and warping, continuing still as the tectonic plates floating on the earth's crust pull apart, the Great Rift contains seven lakes in Kenya (Magadi, Naivasha, Elmenteita, Nakuru, Bogoria, Baringo, and Turkana) and is liberally punctured with both recent and ancient volcanic craters. Of these lakes, Magadi and Naivasha are featured in the NAIROBI AND AROUND chapter, on pages 132 and 135 respectively. This chapter will detail the Great Rift lakes of Nakuru, Bogoria and Baringo, the town of Nyahururu, the Laikipia district up to Maralal, as well as the route up to Lake Turkana's eastern shore. The road systems and communications make this a logical way to proceed.

LAKE NAKURU

Lake Nakuru, one of the most beautiful of the Rift Valley lakes, can be visited in a long day trip from Nairobi or an overnight stopover on safari going north or west. The perimeter is protected as a national park, though it is a little manicured and enclosed, and if Menengai Crater and Hyrax Hill Archaeological Site are included then there's enough to keep a visitor busy for two days or more.

Alkaline Lake Nakuru was first mapped by Major Thomson, as was the nearby, smaller **Lake Elmenteita**, which is privately owned by the descendants of Lord Delamere. Lake Nakuru completely evaporated during a dry period from 1939 to 1940, but filled up again during the mid-1940s. By the end of the 1950s it was dry again, and dust devils whipped up and scattered white soda sediments over nearby farm fields. The dust often traveled 64 km (40 miles) away, threatening the productivity of the agricultural lands. The lake refilled in the 1960s and has remained wet ever since.

The lake is world-famous as the feeding ground of both lesser and greater flamingos, which can be distinguished by size and the color of their bill. The lesser flamingo has a deep carmine-red bill, the greater a pink one with black tip. The lesser also has a deeper pink plumage, but unless both species are present, it is difficult to use this as a basis for identification.

Lake Nakuru and a wide strip of shoreline were made a national park in the 1960s and entry is US$27, US$10 for children. It was estimated then that there were, at times, more than a million flamingos on the lake. Ornithologist Roger Tory Peterson described it as "the most fabulous bird spectacle in the world." The concentration of flamingos fluctuates greatly, depending on which of the soda Rift Valley lakes (Magadi, Elmenteita, Bogoria, Turkana or Nakuru) has the best food supply, but even when food is more abundant elsewhere, there are sizable flocks of flamingos on Lake Nakuru.

A species of alkaline-tolerant fish, tilapia, was introduced into the lake in the 1970s, and the number of resident white pelicans has since increased substantially. On the southern and northeastern shores are blinds and viewing platforms from which you can watch the pelicans and flamingos.

Besides the more than 400 species of birds that can be seen in the park there are hippos, reedbucks, waterbucks, bushbucks and, recently introduced, Rothschild's giraffes and black rhinoceros — which are now fenced and under tight security since the poaching of the white rhinoceros in Meru National Park in 1988. Between the lake and the cliffs in the west, large pythons inhabit the dense woodland, and can often be seen crossing the roads or dangling from trees.

MENENGAI CRATER

The 11-km-wide (seven-mile) Menengai Crater is one of the largest in the world. Although you get the best view of it from the Nyahururu–Nakuru road, the easiest access is from Nakuru. When the first European settlers arrived, they found the crater and the surrounding area surprisingly void of inhabitants. Later archaeological finds, however, indicate that the area had been inhabited since prehistoric times.

OPPOSITE AND FOLLOWING PAGES: Once a single tribe, the Samburu and Maasai maintain many original dances and traditions.

Legends about the Menengai volcano, whose name in Maa means "corpse," may account for the lack of nineteenth-century inhabitants. Several tell of scouting and raiding parties venturing into the crater never to be seen again. One story relates how the now-extinct Ilaikipiak tribe celebrated their victory over the neighboring Ilpurko by throwing themselves to death in the Menengai. They supposedly gathered at the edge of the crater, gorged themselves on looted meat, and finally called upon God to witness their mass suicide, as there was nothing left for them to live for since they had defeated everyone worthy of their prowess. Another version claims that the Ilpurko pushed hundreds of Ilaikipiak warriors over the crater rim. Today, there is a satellite tracking station on the rim, although the bush-covered lava floor 500 m (1,600 ft) below is still relatively uninhabited.

The crest of the crater is about eight kilometers (five and a half miles) from Nakuru; follow Menengai Road to Crater Climb. There is a path from the signed, but now defunct, "Campsite and Picnic Area," past the satellite tracking station to a lookout tower. Only on a clear day will you be able to see the opposite wall of the crater. Hiking to the crater is best done with a guide, for reasons of security.

HYRAX HILL

Six kilometers (four miles) east of Nakuru is Hyrax Hill, one of three archaeological sites managed by the National Museum (Koobi

Fora and Olorgasailie are the others). It is open to the public at Ksh200 per person. Here, in 1926, Louis Leakey discovered utensils and bones, some dating from the Neolithic period. Mary Leakey's excavations during 1937 and 1938 uncovered dwellings, a fort, livestock enclosures, a burial mound and a great variety of bones, utensils, obsidian fragments and pottery remnants.

Most of the site has been dated to the late Kenyan Iron Age (the fifteenth and sixteenth centuries AD), but one burial ground is Neolithic. A large stone slab that once sealed it has been removed to display the bones of Stone Age inhabitants. In another site to the north, 19 more Neolithic graves were discovered in an Iron Age burial site. It is interesting to note that in the Neolithic graves, women were buried with their tools, while men were buried alone. This might indicate that even then African women did the bulk of the physical labor — they certainly do today.

There is a small museum housing the finds from the dig and you can walk along the rocks to see the dwellings and burial mounds. An excellent guide, which will help you identify the sites, is on sale in the museum and your entry includes a guided tour by the museum's curator. The site is a bumpy two kilometers (one and a half miles) off the main Nairobi road.

WHERE TO STAY AND EAT

Accommodation is available in the park or in Nakuru town just north of the main gate. Within the park are **Sarova Lion Hill** ((02) 713333 FAX (02) 715566 E-MAIL reservations @sarova.co.ke, Box 72493, Nairobi (expensive, full board); **Lake Nakuru Lodge** ((02) 226778, Box 561, Nairobi (expensive, full board); and camping facilities (US$15 per person), most with running water, but you are warned not to leave anything valuable at your campsite.

The best of the town lodgings is the rather soulless **Midlands Hotel** ((037) 212125, Box 908, Nakuru (inexpensive), or the central **Waterbuck Hotel** ((037) 215672 FAX (037) 214163, Box 3227, Nakuru (inexpensive). As Kenya's fourth largest city, Nakuru also has a great variety of *hotelis* (which can mean anything from the most basic food-hut to a

modest hotel), some small restaurants and even a couple of discos, but the town itself has little charm and what character it has is not very prepossessing.

HOW TO GET THERE

Nakuru is three to four hours' drive from Nairobi, an hour and a half beyond Naivasha on the A104 Uplands Road. The lake is 158 km (99 miles) northwest of Nairobi. Motorists should watch out for Nakuru's mechanics: they're famous for staging or faking mechanical breakdowns and then dragging out repairs. A steady stream of buses and *matatus* link Nakuru with Nairobi.

LAKE BOGORIA NATIONAL RESERVE

Some 30 km (19 miles) south of Lake Baringo, as the ruddy duck flies, is Lake Bogoria, a national reserve. This small equatorial lake has geysers and hot springs. There are relatively few good vantage points, but its topaz and green water is strikingly beautiful.

The Maasai know the lake as Mbatibat, the Tugen as Makwaria, and before independence the maps called it Lake Hannington, named for the Bishop of Uganda, who was supposedly the first European to see it. Though history is somewhat vague on the subject, it has been accepted that in 1885 James Hannington, en route to his missionary post in Uganda, sighted the lake from a point, now called **Hannington's Lookout**, northwest of Nyahururu near Chepkererat, and not easily accessible. Hot and thirsty, Hannington's party climbed down the steep wall of the Rift only to discover the water was saline. His luck did not improve: upon arrival in Uganda he was murdered by the Bagandas as he tried to cross the White Nile.

In 1902, the English adventurer / chronicler, Sir Harry Johnston, wrote that a forest of large trees in the center was slowly dying, and speculated that there must have been recent geological activity or an overflow from Lake Baringo. However, nothing supports these theories, and local traditions claim that the lake had always been here, with or without the dying forest.

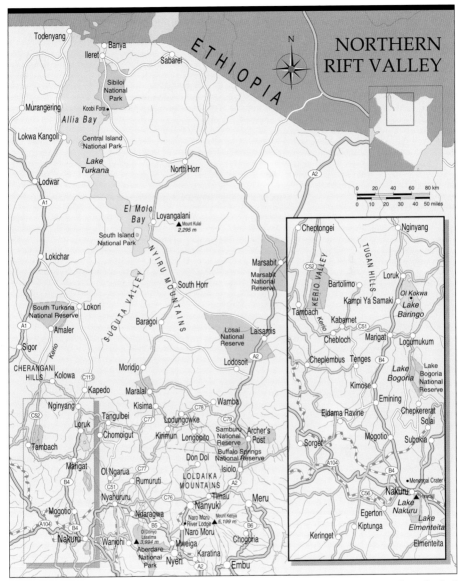

Sir Harry also noted a large population of flamingos and photographed their nests. Today you can occasionally see some of these giant, pink birds, but they no longer nest in Bogoria's mud.

Along Lake Bogoria's western shore is a bed of hot springs and blowholes that infrequently erupt two and a half to three meters (eight to ten feet) into the air and constantly emit a pungent sulfur smell. These geothermal phenomena are intriguing, but also dangerously hot. Often the surrounding crust cannot support much weight and recently

a visitor fell through the crust and was boiled to death.

Lake Bogoria National Reserve entry fees are US$15 per adult and US$5 for children.

WHERE TO STAY

The **Lake Bogoria Hotel** (/FAX (037) 40748, Box 208, Menengai West, is three kilometers (two miles) north of Loboi Gate, making use of the hot springs for one of its swimming pools, but it is overpriced and strangely dull (expensive). However there are several campsites. The best, and well worth the trip for a relaxing day in the water, is **Fig Tree Campground**, book through the warden ((037) 40746, Box 64, Marigat (US$2 per person, paid at the reserve gate). The campground is on the banks of a crystal clear, drinkable spring which flows into several natural whirlpools.

HOW TO GET THERE

Access to this little-visited reserve leaves much to be desired. No public transportation

400 species of birds. It has an average depth of only eight meters (25 ft) and its three islands (Gibraltar, Teddy Bear and Ol Kokwa) are breeding grounds for the statuesque one-and-a-half-meter (five-foot) Goliath heron, the largest of the heron species.

The area is home to many communities of Njemps, one of three Maa-speaking tribes in Kenya. The others are the Maasai in the south and Samburu in the north. They are unusual in that they have broken the pastoralist's traditional taboo of not eating fish, and live on a mixed diet of fish

reaches it, and you need a four-wheel drive unless the weather has been particularly dry. The road from Nakuru is not recommended. It is easier, and, in the end, quicker, to approach Lake Bogoria from Lake Baringo, 30 km (19 miles) to the north.

LAKE BARINGO

Lake Baringo is a good stopover site to break the long drive across the Rift Valley, or for a two-day trip from Nairobi. Because it is now accessible by paved road from Nairobi, it has become a popular Kenyan weekend destination. This brown saline lake is the most northern of Kenya's six small Rift Valley lakes and is home of hippos, crocodiles and over

and goat meat. Their one-man boats are made from ambach trees, which grow around the lake. Like those used by the Turkana, these raft-like craft float semi-submerged, giving the occupant the appearance of sitting atop the water. Most of the inhabitants of the Lake Baringo area are from one of two Kalenjin tribes, the Pokot and the Tugen. President Moi is Tugen, which may explain the high quality of the roads in this area. They are primarily pastoralists and the land around the lake is severely overgrazed and eroded as a result. If you visit the lake after a rain, the water will have a distinct red tone, while during the dry season (July to September, January to March) it appears browner.

The surrounding countryside is arid, red-soiled and sparsely vegetated with several types of the omnipresent thorn trees and candelabra euphorbias. Termite castles of every size and shape abound. After the rainy seasons, the hillsides are dotted with bright pink but poisonous desert roses.

The shores are a mixture of sand and marsh, which provides some cover and shade for the resident hippos. Many visitors swim and water ski in the lake, which is supposed to be free of bilharzia.

I have seen no crocodiles in Baringo, and a few people swimming round the dock at Ol Kokwa Island. By all local accounts there have been more problems with hippos than crocs. Only the month before I arrived, one boat was attacked and another smashed by angry hippopotamuses. Because the lake is shallow, these aquatic giants can be found anywhere, not just along the shores. Apparently the sound of boat motors particularly annoys them; they are also known to kill people for getting between them and the water, which is their traditional refuge when they feel under threat. If you want to swim, the less-accessible Lake Bogoria (see above) or the swimming pools at Lake Baringo's two lodges might be safer and considerably more relaxing.

WHERE TO STAY

Accommodation options at Lake Baringo are varied. There are a couple of *hotelis* in Kampi Ya Samaki, the only town on the lake, but head out to the waterfront and **Betty Roberts's Campsite** ((0328) 51403 (between 10 AM and noon), Box 1051, Nakuru, with *bandas* for Ksh500 per person or campsites for Ksh400, is one of the nicest campgrounds in Kenya; with running water and showers, and no extra charge for grazing hippos at night.

Next to Betty Roberts's is the luxurious **Lake Baringo Lodge** ((02) 540780 FAX (02) 543810 E-MAIL blockreservations@net2000ke .com, Box 40075, Nairobi, which has very comfortable doubles for US$126 with full board. This is also a good place to eat while staying at Betty's. Because of the influx of weekend travelers, the lodge has a Ksh100 entrance fee for visitors to their bar, gardens, swimming pool and hippo-viewing pier. It

is often waived. As an added attraction, they offer guided bird-watching walks with 400 species to spot.

Just north of town is the dock where boats leave for Ol Kokwa Island. **Island Camp** (make reservations with Let's Go Travel ((02) 447151 or (02) 441030 FAX (02) 447270 or (02) 441690 E-MAIL info@letsgo safari.com WEB SITE www.letsgosafari.com, Box 60342, Nairobi) is a luxurious and peaceful tented camp with double tents for US$200 full board. If you have a day to spend at the lake the island is probably the

most interesting way to spend it; the boat ride costs Ksh600 round trip. You can walk on the island, which is inhabited by thousands of birds, a few waterbuck, and several hundred Njemps and their livestock.

HOW TO GET THERE

The instructions I was given to get to Lake Baringo on my first visit were "Leave Nairobi on the Naivasha Road and at the second roundabout go right," and the directions were spot on. It was more than two hours

OPPOSITE: Remnants of a prehistoric dwelling on the slopes of Hyrax Hill, one of several archaeological sites open to the public. ABOVE: Leafy Lake Baringo Lodge is popular with weekend visitors to the lake.

before I hit the first roundabout (traffic circle) at Naivasha and another hour and a half to the second at Nakuru. Overall, the drive takes about five hours, with the road starting off laden with trucks and buses but improving steadily all the way. By public transportation, frequent buses and *matatus* service Nakuru from Nairobi and other towns, and it is reasonably easy to arrange onward travel to Marigat. From there transportation is likely to become infrequent for the last 21 km (13 miles); carry plenty of water.

NORTH AND WEST FROM LAKE BARINGO

Going north from Lake Baringo is not currently recommended. Although there are two alternative routes that take you through equally beautiful though different terrain, the area is at the heart of some of Kenya's worst tribal conflict. Take advice locally and see if the situation has calmed. Look forward to some difficult driving conditions in any case: the situation does not encourage road maintenance.

There is a choice of routes heading west. The more difficult route heads north from Baringo through Loruk and Nginyang, then crosses the Kerio Valley and River to Tot at the foot of the Elgeyo Escarpment and swings north to Sigor, where it picks up the new section of A1 that goes north to Lake Turkana and Sudan. North of Tot a second dirt track can be taken roughly following the Kerio River through the South Turkana National Reserve and meeting another dirt track from Baringo and Kapedo, then meeting the A1 finally in Lokichar. The latter is a four-wheel-drive adventure through barren hill and desert scrub, crossing the northern end of the magnificent, desolate Suguta Valley, one of the hottest — and the most dangerous — places on earth. During the rains and for several weeks after (or possibly months depending on the scheduling of road crews) these roads are impassable. Even during the dry seasons (July to September, January to March) this route can be dangerous and should only be attempted if you are fully contained (food, water, camping gear, etc.) and have a full tank of gas and at least two full jerrycans.

Timewise it is just as quick to take the longer paved route, a 20-minute drive south from Lake Baringo to Marigat and then west. This is itself a beautiful drive and along some of the best roads in the country, a butter-smooth ribbon of little-used pavement, dotted with local farmers selling wild honey, formerly the route of the East African Rally through President Moi's hometown of Kabarnet to Eldoret. The route begins at Marigat, 19 km (12 miles) south of Lake Baringo. From Marigat, the road climbs steeply into the Tugen or Ilkamasya Hills, offering magnificent vistas of Lake Baringo and, from one upper point, Lake Bogoria, as well as numerous volcanic craters, reminders of the turbulent eruptions that have pockmarked the land over millions of years. The high country, only a little less arid than the lake valley floor, is predictably covered with thorn scrub, but where possible the Tugen have terraced the slopes to grow maize.

Perched atop the Tugen Hills, **Kabarnet** overlooks the lush Kerio Valley. As the administrative center for the Baringo District, the town has complete shopping facilities, a multitude of government buildings and the recently constructed **Kabarnet Hotel** ((02) 336858, Box 109, Kabarnet (inexpensive, B&B).

The **Kerio Valley**, with some of Kenya's richest agricultural land, is a welcome relief after the browns and reds of the lakes. (If you are traveling this section in reverse — Eldoret to Marigat — you probably won't be so impressed with the lush greens or the variety of crops.)

Approaching the western slope of the Kerio Valley, the Tambach or Elgeyo Escarpment, you can't help but wonder how the road will ever get to the top of these sheer, wooded cliffs. But it does in 15 km (nine miles) of twisting, hairpin turns that are a challenge to negotiate in any vehicle. Imagine what these must have been like before they were paved!

About halfway up the escarpment, just past the village of Tambach, you get a full view of **Torok Falls**. If you want to walk to them you will have to do it from Tambach, where you can usually find a guide who will gladly show you the way or accompany you for Ksh30 and provide some local history as well.

The Northern Rift Valley

NYAHURURU

Leaving Mombasa on March 15, 1883, Joseph Thomson led a ragtag group of 113 "vagabond" porters and other African coastal sailors on what was to be the grandest safari of them all, the first to cross Maasailand and reach the shores of the fabled lake which would be called Victoria, passing by the cascades now called Nyahururu, which in honor of himself he named Thomson's Falls.

Already a famed naturalist and explorer at the age of 24, Thomson was engaged by the Royal Geographical Society to discover if a practicable route existed across Maasailand to Lake Victoria and Uganda. He was soon intercepted by Maasai north of Kilimanjaro, an advance guard of the same *morans* (warriors) who had ambushed Gustav Fischer's party at Hell's Gate the year before. Thomson was forced to retreat to Taveta and then to make a 323-km (200-mile) dash all the way back to Mombasa in just six days.

Rather than give up, he recruited more men and joined an Arab ivory and slave trading caravan as far as Kilimanjaro. From there the Maasai harassed him all the way through the Satima mountains, which he renamed the Aberdares after the president of the Royal Geographical Society. He finally convinced the Maasai he was a wizard by removing, then replacing, a false front tooth and offering to do the same to a warrior's nose, by using a battery to shock them, and by making a magical potion of fizzy Eno fruit salts. After an abortive attempt to reach the top of Mount Kenya, he was forced once more to retreat from the banks of the Ewaso Ngiro by threats of a Maasai attack.

With great relief he passed out of Maasai country, reaching the shores of Lake Victoria on Christmas day, from there traveling north to Mount Elgon, where he visited the Elephant Caves. On the last day of 1883, while hunting for his New Year's dinner, he shot a buffalo which vengefully gored him and tossed him over its shoulder, and which then was killed by one of his men as it prepared to give him the *coup de grace*. Badly injured, Thomson was carried on a litter back to

Meal time for a gerenuk who knows the freshest nibbles are higher up.

Naivasha, where he contracted dysentery and lingered for two months on the edge of death as the Maasai continued to threaten on a daily basis. He finally regained sufficient health to return to Mombasa on May 24, 1884, having traveled 4,839 km (3,000 miles) in 14 months, where he opened a direct route for the first time to Lake Victoria, and completed one of the most difficult and courageous feats of African exploration.

Thomson's Falls, named after this adventurer, are where the Ewaso Narok River pours roiling and brown over a stony ledge into its narrow, forested chasm, perpetual mist rising from the clash of water and rock, rainbows cloaking the green, chilled slopes. An array of souvenir kiosks mars the view of the falls, however, and a quartet of painted "native dancers" may waylay you in an attempt to sell a photo opportunity.

More interestingly, there is a path along the edge of the falls, and a trail you can take to the bottom. However, it is slippery and quite dangerous in places, and it's easy to lose your way; tourists have also been robbed here, thus it's best to check at the hotel desk on trail conditions and safety, and to engage a guide if necessary. At the desk they'll also tell you where to pick up a trail that crosses the river on the bridge above the falls and descends the other side, crossing again lower down and returning to Nyahururu — it's a beautiful walk that takes you into the wall of rainbow and cloud amid the canyon.

WHERE TO STAY

A few minutes walk from the falls, **Thomson's Falls Lodge** ((0365) 22006 FAX (0365) 32170, Box 38, Nyahururu, offers double cottages comfortably overlooking the Thomson's Falls, with grassy campground behind (midrange B&B). Built in the 1930s, the hotel is a relic of colonial times, but has borne the change with considerable grace. The rooms are spacious and very clean with carefully-laid fireplaces, the food ample and good, and the staff friendly. At 2,375 m (7,800 ft) above sea level, Nyahururu can be cold at night, but the hotel bar usually has a roaring fire, and is a cheerful place to strike up a conversation, far more lively than the average sedate game lodge.

The town of Nyahururu itself has a number of small *hotelis*, including the inexpensive **Baron Hotel** ((0365) 32056, Box 423, Nyahuru.

HOW TO GET THERE

Nyahururu is 198 km (124 miles) north of Nairobi, a two- to three-hour drive by *matatu* or your own vehicle. The town itself has little to detain the visitor and Thomson's Falls themselves (and the Thomson's Falls Lodge) are four kilometers (three miles) from the town, which is either a steady and not unpleasant walk or a quick ride by taxi.

EASTERN LAIKIPIA

The Laikipia Plateau covers an ill-defined area the size of Wales, spreading across Kenya to the north of Nyahururu, and west above the Aberdares and Mount Kenya. After World War I, much of the land was handed over to western settlers as ranches or farms, but since then cattle rustling, droughts and occasional tribal conflicts have reduced the population considerably. It is not a national park, but contains within its region some of the best game-viewing available. Protected from the outside world by, among other things, really appalling roads, this is home to four of the world's most important rhino sanctuaries and the "big five" (rhino, elephant, lion, leopard and buffalo) are often seen here. That the experience is also shared with cultural contacts with the resident tribespeople, settlers and ranchers adds a depth to a visit here that is invariably missed, or diluted, in the animal-only national parks.

The scenery varies from the edge of the Great Rift Valley to (when it's clear), the snow-drifted peaks of Mount Kenya, encompassing rivers and waterholes, plains and grasslands. In recent years a new initiative has linked together the descendants of the original, imported and imposed settlers, private ranchers, subsistence farmers and roaming pastoralists to form the Laikipia Wildlife Forum, uniting the community to

The Ewaso Ngiro flows from the slopes of the Aberdare Mountains through arid Samburu country and dries up in the vast Lorian Swamp.

resolve the inevitable conflicts. While it's not the most accessible nor secure area of the country, it is one of the most interesting, and there are a number of characterful establishments that offer very different insights into their particular environments free of any park regulations or entry fees.

WHERE TO STAY

Although charter flights to Laikipia often, for reasons of economy, leave from Nanyuki Airport, for purposes of clarity the lodges

described here are those in the east, best accessed by the C77 as it heads north from Nyahururu. Those in western Laikipia, normally accessed by road via Nanyuki, are covered in the CENTRAL HIGHLANDS, page 212. Budget travelers can skip this section completely: there's nothing below the extremely expensive category here.

The experience depends on where you stay, and even if money is no object, time and the distance between the ranches here will mean you have to choose.

Most easterly is the extremely expensive, all-inclusive **Mukutan Retreat (** (02) 520799 FAX (02) 521220 E-MAIL mukutan@africa online.co.ke WEB SITE www.mukutan.com, Box 45593, Nairobi, owned by Kuki Gallmann,

the Italian-born author of *I Dreamed of Africa*, who lives nearby. Her famous bestseller has now been made into a film starring Kim Basinger. Her second book, which was a long time coming, failed to wow the critics as it is a rather depressing tale in which everyone seems to die. Still, the first book allowed her to set up a huge private reserve in memory of her dead husband and son. At its heart, Mukutan, with just three guest dwellings — generally let to only one party at a time — and sweeping, open views, is certainly stunning and a wonderful place to stay. Allow five hours from Nairobi by car: travel to Nyahururu and continue left on the C77, before turning left on the C51. Most guests here, already paying handsomely for their accommodation, find it more convenient to fly to the nearby airstrip.

Stay on the C77, through Rumuruti and you'll first reach **Mugie Ranch** where there are two accommodation options in a working ranch with plenty of game — lion, Jackson's hartebeest (only found in Laikipia) and all the other dry-country animals of northern Kenya — coexisting with camels, cows and other cattle. There is **Cheli and Peacock's Laikipia Camp (** (02) 604053/4 or (02) 603090/1 FAX (02) 604050 or (02) 603066 E-MAIL chelipeacock@africaonline.co.ke WEB SITE www.chelipeacock.com, Box 39806, Nairobi, a luxury mobile camp that brings guests close to moving predators (extremely expensive, all-inclusive), or the more settled home of **Mutamaiyu House (** (02) 882521 FAX (02) 882728 E-MAIL Bonham.luke@swift kenya.com, Box 24133, Nairobi, a delightful settlers house, atmospherically furnished with antiques (extremely expensive, all-inclusive). The house is run by Anthony and Marie Dodds, who are especially welcoming guides to the area. If you want an introduction to the Pokot, Samburu, Kikuyu and Ndorobo tribesmen, this is a comfortable place to start, and game drives, of course, are included.

Further north and it's more luxury again at **Loisaba (** (02) 574689, (02) 577018 or (02) 567251 FAX (02) 564945 E-MAIL Mellifera@swift kenya.com WEB SITE www.loisaba.com, Box 24397, Nairobi, a very luxurious lodge set on a 150 sq km (58 sq mile) private game reserve (extremely expensive, all-inclusive).

Highlights here include "star beds," in which you sleep under the stars but can wheel the bed back in at the first sign (very rare, up here) of rain. The lodge has a helicopter that flies up the remote Suguta Valley.

North again, Ol Malo (book through Bush Homes of East Africa ((02) 571661 FAX (02) 571665 E-MAIL bushhome@africaonline.co.ke, Box 56923, Nairobi) is run by Kenya legends Colin and Rocky Francombe (extremely expensive, all-inclusive). This is probably the most luxurious of all the lodges in the area, and there's always the chance of seeing an exceptionally rare black leopard, which occasionally has come to drink at the waterhole below the guest buildings.

North again, set on a cliff overlooking the Ewaso Ngiro River, is the **Sabuk Lodge** ((02) 891065 FAX (02) 890266 E-MAIL glen.ewaso @swiftkenya.com, Box 15094, Nairobi, write to Simon Evans, Box 243, Gilgil, Kenya; or make reservations with Let's Go Travel ((02) 447151 or (02) 441030 FAX (02) 447270 or (02) 441690 E-MAIL info@letsgosafari.com WEB SITE www.letsgosafari.com, Box 60342, Nairobi (extremely expensive, all-inclusive). This is also the base for the Ewaso River Camel Hike. Run by Simon Evans, member of a local ranching family, the camel hike allows you to travel on foot and on camel — no experience is required — through the lovely ranchlands and semiarid brush of the upper Ewaso Ngiro; all the way, if you wish, to Samburu National Reserve. Costs for a camel safari are a little higher than a standard full-board park lodge, but include food, camels, mattresses, mosquito nets, laundry and all the bush lore you can ingest. You need to bring your sleeping bag, a good pair of boots and standard safari hiking gear. For more information, see EXPERIENCE A CAMEL SAFARI, page 18 in TOP SPOTS.

MARALAL

Whether traveling independently from Wamba or, more probably, emerging dustily from a *matatu* at the end of its line, Maralal is an atmospheric and relatively secure outpost of civilization, and a good place to relax casually with the local Samburu people. It has two gas stations in a part of the world where one is a lifeline; it also has a range of accommodation and even a small natural reserve to call its own. This mountain town, in its windswept cleft of hills, cedar forest on both slopes imparting a perfumed, resiny flavor to the cool, thin air, is on the edge of civilization. There's electricity, shops, a thriving market, and a throng of souvenir sellers guaranteed to make you wish you were back in the desert. There is a fancy police post with a spanking new flag and new government buildings overlooking an imposing traffic circle, from which sign-less, potholed dirt roads unravel in all directions, one leading by chance to the town itself. The main street, with clapboard verandahs and trees not so much lining the streets as growing in it, has a Wild West feel. Cattle and at least one ostrich wander from shop to shop; Samburu tribesmen are driven in from the bush by tribal conflict, and barefooted gangs of children run around cheerfully. Three bars offer warm (and sometimes cold) beer, and there are a number of surprisingly good restaurants to be found.

If you've missed purchasing Samburu trinkets so far, Maralal's a good place to catch up: trouble in the Rift Valley has brought scores of refugees in from the country and they're having to sell their heirlooms. There are two-piece, wooden-handled, steel-shafted spears made by local blacksmiths for the tourist trade, and the wicked foot-long double-bladed knives known as *simis* or *lalem*, central to every Samburu warrior's health and longevity.

The true *simis*, those the *morans* carry, are cut down from large machetes made in England — look for the brand-name of the machete, such as "Giraffe" or "Birmingham," and the words "Made in England," which are stamped into the steel just above the hilt, and which are carefully conserved when the machete is ground down into a *simi*. The tourist-grade *simis* are made of brighter, lighter Kenyan steel, and will not keep an edge; in either case make sure the goatskin sheath of your *simi* is not split along the edge, or it can give you a nasty cut. The going rate for *simis* is Ksh450 to Ksh600 depending on size and condition; a good spear can cost up to Ksh1,000.

Thomson's Falls.

WHERE TO STAY

Most of the better places to stay here are a serious hike out of town — not something to try after dark in an area where elephants and buffaloes are often found. The **Maralal Safari Lodge** ((02) 211124 FAX (02) 211125, Box 15020, Nairobi, about four kilometers (two and a half miles) south of town, is the best place to stay, even though it is often, rather depressingly, empty (expensive). Their 24 comfortable cedar cabins with fireplaces, a cozy bar and lounge and large dining room all overlook a salt lick and water hole of the Maralal Game Sanctuary, with grazing zebras, buffaloes, impalas, gazelles and elands. Guides from the lodge will take you on a game walk through the surrounding refuge;

early in the mornings both birds and beasts are generally abundant. There used to be a leopard as well but apparently an Italian guest shot it some time ago.

If the Maralal Safari Lodge doesn't fit your budget or lifestyle, **Yare Safaris Ltd.** (/FAX (02) 214099 E-MAIL travelkenya@iconnect.co.ke, Box 63006, Nairobi, three kilometers (two miles) south of town, is a clean and quite classy campground with *bandas* and bunkhouses just to the east of the main road south of town (very inexpensive to inexpensive). There is a range of accommodation to suit all budgets and a campsite used by overland trucks. There's a well-stocked bar, a restaurant, a fake Samburu *manyatta*, and extensive campsites with a beautiful panorama of the surrounding cedar-clad hills. The lodge

commonly pulling out at around lunchtime, packed to the gills. The 146 km (91 miles) trip through the Laikipia region and beyond takes three hours if everything goes well, which it often doesn't as most of the route is dirt and punctures are frequent. In your own vehicle it is possible to reach Maralal from Nairobi, a distance of 344 km (215 miles), in a mere five hours.

NORTH TO LAKE TURKANA

For many adventurous travelers, Maralal is the last vestige of comfort on the way north to the eastern shores of Lake Turkana, but bear in mind that the security situation in this part of Kenya is uncertain. Check for up-to-date information on recent bandit attacks and tribal tensions. There's no public transportation — though those with a couple of weeks to spare can hitch — and you'll need your own vehicle, enough gasoline and drinking water, and some stamina. The 210-km (130-mile) trip from Maralal to Loyangalani will take six hours if you're lucky. The small town of Baragoi can usually be relied on for pancakes at least, and there is a simple but comfortable hotel (I've forgotten the name but you can't miss it, very inexpensive), while South Horr will only provide food if you buy some meat and share it with someone who cooks it. Here you can hire a guide to explore the **Nyiru Mountains** and forest all the way to the **Tum Valley**, which offers superb views on Lake Turkana and the desolate expanse of **Suguta Valley**. This area is home to **Desert Rose Camel Safaris ((02) 228936 FAX (02) 212160, Box 44801, Nairobi, perhaps the best-informed and equipped camel safari operators, who have a new lodge built overlooking the river (see EXPERIENCE A CAMEL SAFARI, page 18 in TOP SPOTS). Otherwise, continue on along the shores of Lake Turkana and to the fishing village of **Loyangalani**.

LAKE TURKANA

Lake Turkana has a majestic splendor all its own. Like its name, it seems jade, then turquoise gray as clouds mask the sun, silver

itself can be rowdy and lively or cavernously empty, depending which safari trucks, if any, are in town, apart from it's annual high-spot, the **Maralal Camel Derby** (see RACE TO VICTORY, page 27 in TOP SPOTS). Yare also organizes camel safaris, accompanied by Samburu *morans*, at unbeatable prices starting at US$500 for a week all-inclusive. This is one of the cheapest places in Kenya to try this reliably. Alternatively, small *hotelis* in town have basic accommodation at very inexpensive prices, starting at a mere US$1 for the **Midpoint Hotel**.

HOW TO GET THERE

Maralal is the end of the line for *matatus*: they leave from Nyahururu, with the last one

Vervet monkeys await nightfall in the forked branches of a doum palm.

at dawn and deep red at dusk; placid as a pond or wild and wind-tossed as the sea, so elementally vast that its far shore seems to fall beyond the horizon, and the curvature of the earth is visible in its limitless north–south expanse.

Four million years ago it appears Turkana, still by far the largest of the Rift Valley lakes, was a huge freshwater lake four times its present size of 7,200 sq km (2,800 sq miles). By two million years ago, sediments deposited from the Omo River and tectonic shifts had diminished the lake to a wide-based

Similar French and Italian dam building on the Turkwell and Kerio Rivers will undoubtedly lessen their peak flows and thus their contribution to the lake.

At the same time, explosive population growth among pastoral tribes, due to improved healthcare without the requisite increase in family planning services, has vastly increased livestock herds and led to catastrophic overgrazing of the parched uplands surrounding the Rift. The consequent denuding of vegetation and soil erosion has altered the climate, reducing or changing rainfall,

system of rivers, channels, and marshes, which may have drained eastward into the Indian Ocean. Since then it has expanded and contracted in the wide low bed of the Rift, has become increasingly saline (average pH is now 9.2), and no longer has an outlet other than evaporation.

The water lost by Turkana to evaporation now generally exceeds inflow from the Omo River and from the meager seasonal rainfall carried by the Turkwell and Kerio Rivers. Today about 435 km (270 miles) long by an average of 30 km (19 miles) wide, the lake is shrinking again, due perhaps to climatic fluctuation, but also to manmade changes. Foreign-aid irrigation projects in southern Ethiopia have decreased the Omo's flow.

and further diminished the lake. All of this strikes home as you look out over Turkana's beaches to its present shores, particularly at Loyangalani.

Bathed by onshore breezes in the palm trees, Loyangalani is a nice place to recover from the rigors of East Turkana. To the east, the imposing ridges of **Mount Kulal**, 2,295 m (7,530 ft), are climbable for those not tired of adventure, and are reputed to offer an inspiring panorama of the lake, the Ethiopian escarpment and out into the **Chalbi Desert**. It's possible to swim in the lake here with only minimal fear of hippos and crocodiles (however, one local told me that a British crocodile researcher was recently devoured here).

As always around Lake Turkana, flocks of children will follow you wherever you go, speaking good English, asking to be photographed for a fee or to sell some trinket. The local population is diverse, comprising remnants of the El Molos, considered the most ancient of Turkana's inhabitants, who live principally on fish, hippo steaks when they can get them and occasionally crocodile meat. They have largely merged into the overpowering Turkana and Samburu peoples, and their language is now considered lost. The remaining 400 or so of

the tribe live on **El Molo Bay**, fifteen minutes' drive north of Loyangalani. For a fee you can visit the village; most visitors find the experience depressingly commercial.

The Turkana and Samburu are more evident, having learned how to fish from the El Molo. Their herds can be seen watering at the lake edge. If the weather is calm, from Loyangalani you can rent a boat for an hour's ride to fascinating **South Island National Park**, a withered volcanic core surprisingly rich with crocodiles and bird life. Birds are not lacking along the entire east shore of Turkana, with flamingos, pelicans, ibis, cormorants and avocets being common.

The waters of Turkana have long been famous for their fish, including a world record

Nile perch (which can exceed 150 kg or 330 lb), tilapia, golden perch and the fierce tiger fish, which can weigh up to eight kilograms (18 lb) and fights like a trout when hooked.

Where to Stay and Eat

Lodging is Loyangalani's only disappointment. The **El Molo Lodge** is now almost derelict, though you might be able to camp there, and the once luxurious **Oasis Lodge**, which you can reserve through Bunson Travel ((02) 221992 FAX (02) 214120, Box 45456, Nairobi (expensive), is really not worth it and no longer has working vehicles or boats of its own — a sure sign, in this part of the world, that it is on its way out. The budget option, at around Ksh500, is cheap but not luxurious: **Mama Shanga's** consists of a few concrete sheds with a padlocked long-drop outside toilet as the only sanitary facilities. Outside the major lodges there are a few basic restaurants — most of which are better than the expensive fare at the Oasis Lodge. My favorite has a sign written on the wall "we give you the best service no matter how long it takes."

How to Get There

There is no public transportation to Loyangalani and even *matatus* stop at Maralal. Those prepared to undergo a participation-camping expedition, with up to 18 young tourists and aid workers traveling together in a truck, can get there on either the Turkana Bus operated by **Safari Camp Services** ((02) 228936 or (02) 330130 FAX (02) 212160 E-MAIL Safaricamp@form-net.com, Box 44801, Nairobi, or its main rival, **Gametrackers** ((02) 338927 or (02) 330903 E-MAIL Game@africaonline .co.ke, Box 62042, Nairobi. With your own transportation, it's a relatively easy three-hour drive from Nairobi to Nyahururu, but soon after this the pavement ends and it takes a rather slower three hours on dirt road to Maralal. From there the road deteriorates markedly and if you complete the last 220 km (137 miles) in less than a further six hours you'll be doing well. Bear in mind that there's no gasoline further north than Maralal unless you call ahead to make sure that there

Crocodiles are found at Turkana and many of Kenya's other lakes and rivers. They are both dangerous and swift.

is some waiting for you at Loyangalani. This might not be possible, so make sure you have some jerrycans. There is an airstrip at Loyangalani if you have the budget for it (allow about US$1,200 for a charter) but then, unless the Oasis Lodge can borrow a vehicle, you'll be stuck.

THE FAR NORTH

If you wish to visit the blazing moonscape of Sibiloi National Park and its fascinating archaeological and paleontological sites, you

will need your own rugged vehicle, a touching confidence in the local fishing boats and their engines or, better still, access to a small plane. To get there you either cross the lake from Kalakol (see page 179) or drive via North Horr to Allia Bay on Lake Turkana, south of Richard Leakey's digs at Koobi Fora, contained within the Sibiloi National Park. On a slope overlooking the lake a weird assortment of ochre, brown and yellow pillars lie like a broken temple among the gray commiphora brush and tawny grass — petrified vestiges of a once-great tropical forest.

At Allia Bay you can hire a guide (essential if you wish to explore Sibiloi National Park), and drive past the park offices

then two hours north to the peninsula of Koobi Fora, where there's a small museum containing some recent finds. Although it's best to have asked permission in Nairobi (at the National Museum) before visiting Koobi Fora, the resident archaeologists are friendly and if you manifest a reasonable knowledge of and interest in their excavations may offer a quick tour. As well, there are *in situ* fossil elephant, tortoise and crocodile exhibits in the nearby uplands at **Bura Hasuma Hill**.

SIBILOI NATIONAL PARK

Sibiloi National Park is both fascinating and different from any other site in Kenya; considering the terrain and climate, a quite diverse wildlife community exists. It was originally a haven for elephants (the Koobi Fora museum displays a one-and-a-half-million-year-old example), but white hunters shot these out before the World War II. The park's relatively common large animals include the tiang race of topi, common and Grevy's zebras, reticulated giraffes, Grant's gazelles, gerenuks, dik diks, golden jackals, lions, hyenas, a few leopards, a surprising number of cheetahs, many crocodiles and some hippos near the lake.

Many of the fossils that have pushed back the dawn of human history millions of years have been found near Koobi Fora (the name derives from the local Gabbra tribe's word for the commiphora bush common to the area). Building on discoveries made by his parents, Louis and Mary Leakey, at Olduvai Gorge and other locations in Tanzania, Richard Leakey came to the east shore of Lake Turkana because its wind- and water-eroded barrens seemed to offer unusually clear incisions into the sedimentary rocks, which bear, like the piled pages of a manuscript, the decodable history of our human past.

Since 1968, Leakey, his wife Meave, and other scientists have made a series of breathtaking finds at over 200 East Turkana sites including, in 1972, the skull of a *Homo habilis* over two million years old, and now considered to be our direct ancestor. Enough information has been gleaned from the over 6,000 fossil specimens in Sibiloi to form a coherent picture of the development of a gatherer-hunter society as it evolved to language and tool making, as its brains enlarged and, stressed by changing climates and competition, it expanded and diversified until it came to consider itself apart from other animals and favored with dominion over the earth.

In all, the sedimentary deposits of East Turkana have yielded nearly 200 different hominid specimens, including several skulls and other major skeletal sections. Earliest discoveries (three and a half to four million

sive) and something to eat if you bring it. Even in the busy months of July and August, when American archaeologists move in, the *bandas* are generally empty and there's no need to book ahead. However booking is done through the National Musuems of Kenya ((02) 742161 FAX (02) 741424 E-MAIL nmk@africaonline.co.ke, Box 40658, Nairobi, who'll let you pay in advance if you weaken. Without your own transportation, you'll have to rent the resident Landrover (if working and gassed up) at Ksh50,000 per day to get around.

years old) appear to be of *Australopithecus afarensis*, the earliest recognized hominid. More recent specimens comprise three major hominid groups (*Australopithecus robustus, Australopithecus africanus,* and the *Homo* lineage which led to today's humans); all appear to have lived during the same one-million year period, with *Homo erectus* evolving from the earlier *Homo habilis* about one and a half million years ago.

Entry fees to the park are US$27 per person per day.

How to Get There

Overland, the route is via North Horr, then turning to drive the 130 km or 81 miles (three to four hours) to Allia Bay. The best way though, by far, is by air. Contact Fuf Aviation ((02) 505541. The other way to get there is by boat from Ferguson's Gulf, detailed under WESTERN KENYA, page 179.

Where to Stay and Eat

At Allia Bay there is a small campground, some basic but comfortable *bandas* (inexpen-

OPPOSITE: One of nature's stranger creations, giraffes can make loving parents. ABOVE: Flocks of lesser flamingo pink the lakes of the Rift Valley.

The Central Highlands

Kenya's central highlands contain, in many ways, the best of the country. There are some of the finest parks, such as Aberdare, Mount Kenya and Meru, great national reserves such as Samburu, Buffalo Springs and Shaba, and, of course, the snow-capped brooding bulk of Mount Kenya. Interspersed with this are a host of upcountry towns where all the vibrant urban life of Kenya exists in a gentle climate, warm through the daylight hours and fresh at night. It's the foodbasket of the country and the cultural homeland of the most populous, successful and dynamic tribe, the Kikuyu.

KIKUYULAND

The freeway ends abruptly a short distance north of Thika, as you travel toward the dwelling place of the Kikuyu god, Mount Kenya. This is Kikuyuland, home of Kenya's largest tribe and its first president, Mzee Jomo Kenyatta.

The countryside is cloaked with an infinite number of green tones on terraced hillsides where corn, beans, peas, bananas, coffee, and tea are grown. After the rains in October and November, the flame trees dot the hillsides with orange. A month later, the jacarandas bloom, casting an otherworldly purple glow across the fields.

The land is always a hub of female activity. Brightly dressed women, with infants and toddlers in tow, fetch water, weed and harvest crops, gather and carry firewood, wash clothes in the rivers and ponds, and do whatever is necessary to manage their households. The more affluent women, with babies tied on their backs, have the luxury of going about their journeys with an umbrella to shade them and their offspring. Older children tend cattle, goats and sheep that graze in wooded strips between fields or along the roadside.

MURANGA

Muranga is chiefly important as the last major city before you need to decide between three roads heading north. Those that split to go around Mount Kenya do so further north, but at Muranga a turning heads off to Nyeri and the Aberdare Forest. There are,

however, one or two things to see here and it is worth a quick stop. Formerly Fort Hall, Muranga is still the district headquarters, with modern administrative buildings and the **Church of St. James and All Martyrs**. In the church is a mural of the life of Christ as an African, designed by the Tanzanian artist Elimo Njau. It was consecrated in 1955 by the Archbishop of Canterbury as a memorial to the Kikuyu victims of the Mau Mau Rebellion.

At the turn of the century, Muranga was little more than a military outpost administered by officers of the King's African Rifles. Many of the commanders spent their time shooting animals and leading occasional punitive expeditions to settle intertribal disputes or settlers' problems with their Kenyan workers. Justice was frequently expedient rather than fair.

You can find accommodation at Muranga, if necessary, although it will be basic. One of the best central hotels is the **Rwathia Bar** ((0156) 22527, Market Street (very inexpensive). With your own transportation there are better options out of town on the main A2 highway: the **Muranga Mukawa & Lodges** ((0165) 22542, Box 207, Uhuru Highway (inexpensive), and **Muranga Tourist Lodge** ((0156) 22120, Box 52, Uhuru Highway, in the direction of Thika (inexpensive).

To get to Muranga, catch a *matatu* from Accra Road in Nairobi heading to Embu (or Karatina, or Nyeri) as they all stop off here, and ask to be let off. The town is 87 km (55 miles) from Nairobi on the A2.

KARATINA

North of Muranga, turn left for the market town of Karatina, a popular stop for tour vans going to Aberdare and Mount Kenya national parks. There are a few stalls selling tourist items, but inside the concrete-walled open market all is local business — fresh fruits and vegetables, dried beans of every color and size, rice, *ugali*, houseware and soap. It is worth stopping just to see the cabbages as large as basketballs. Woman vendors pass the time weaving baskets and the ever-popular Kenyan bags. If you want to buy cattle,

Vervet monkeys look sweet but watch out: they are skilled at stealing your lunch.

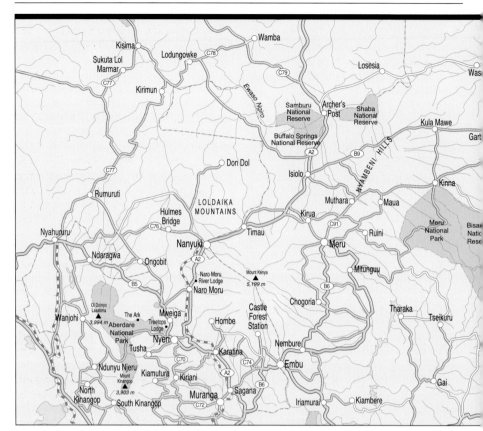

as one does, here you will find the largest selection in the country.

In the market's southeast corner, women treadle sewing machines to repair torn garments or sew new ones to the buyer's specifications. The best market days are Tuesdays, Thursdays and Saturdays. Usually, no one objects to your taking an overall picture of the market, but be sure to ask if you want to photograph a single individual or a small group.

Good and inexpensive accommodation can be found in the **Karatina Tourist Lodge** ((0171) 71522 FAX (0171) 72520, Private Bag, Karatina (inexpensive). The smartest option in the area is 30 km (19 miles) out of town (the turning is signposted off the road towards Nairobi), and this is the **Mountain Lodge** (/FAX (0171) 30785, Box 123, Kiganjo, reservations through Serena Hotel ((02) 711077 FAX (02) 718012 E-MAIL cro@serena .co.ke, Nyere Road, Box 46302, Nairobi, which is one of the best of Kenya's treetop hotels, with great views over a busy floodlit

waterhole (very expensive). At the other end of the scale, the very inexpensive **Three-in-One Hotel** ((0171) 72316, Box 768, will put up travelers on a budget.

Karatina is 41 km (26 miles) from Muranga but otherwise is easiest reached from the town of Nyeri, 27 km (17 miles) distant, within easy taxi or *matatu* distance.

Twenty kilometers (12 miles) north of Karatina, the road splits. The left branch leads west to Nyeri and Aberdare National Park, the other north to Mount Kenya.

NYERI

The main town in the area is Nyeri, formerly a market center for European-expat highlands farmers, now a busy commercial and industrial center and the dropping-off point for Aberdare National Park. Its cemetery attracts visitors to the graves of the famous author and hunter of man-eaters, Jim Corbett, and of the founder of the Boy Scouts, Lord Baden-Powell, who spent the last years of

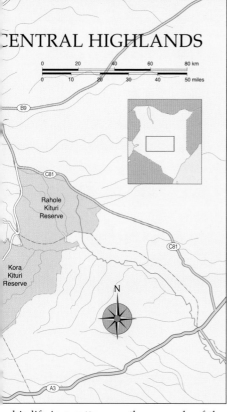

CENTRAL HIGHLANDS

| 0 | 20 | 40 | 60 | 80 km |
| 0 | 10 | 20 | 30 | 40 | 50 miles |

B9

C81

Rahole
Kituri
Reserve

C81

Kora
Kituri
Reserve

N

A3

In the town itself, the best hotel, just sliding in below the package market, is the **Greenhills Hotel (** (0171) 4233, Bishop Gatimu Road, Box 313, Nyeri, although it can be noisy on Wednesdays, Fridays and Saturdays because of its packed disco (inexpensive). Backpackers might prefer the pleasures of the **Thingira Guest House (** (0171) 4769, Box 221, located off Kenyatta Road (very inexpensive).

Most accommodation aimed at the overseas market, however, is out of town, and is therefore suitable for people with their own cars or on organized packages. Leading these is the **Aberdare Country Club (** (02) 216940 FAX (02) 216796, Box 58581, Nairobi, 10 km (seven miles) north of Nyeri in Mweiga (very expensive). This is an elegant establishment, but it suffered a considerable knock when a British tourist was killed by robbers within the hotel grounds seven years ago. The rooms, many of them recently built, are large and well furnished and the grounds, looking out on Mount Kenya, are alive with colorful flowers and shrubs, and flocks of peacocks. There is an aviary, a nine-hole golf course, tennis courts and a swimming pool; the trout fishing is reputedly excellent in the section of the river on the grounds. Not only do they operate the nighttime treetop game viewing at The Ark, but the Aberdere is also a good contact point for two of the area's other great attractions: **Solio Ranch (** (02) 763638, Box 2, Naro Moru, or **(** (0171) 420157 FAX (017) 55235, entry fee Ksh1,600, an important rhinocerous breeding center where Kenya's rhino population was saved from extinction, and **Sangare Ranch**, a luxury tented camp (reservations through Savannah Camps and Lodges **(** (02) 331684 or (02) 335935 FAX (02) 216528 or (02) 330698 E-MAIL eaos@africaonline.co.ke WEB SITE www.savannahcamps.com, 11th Floor, Fedha Towers, Standard Street, Box 48019, Nairobi, very expensive). The rival to the Aberdare Country Club is the **Outspan Hotel (** (02) 540780 FAX (02) 543810 E-MAIL blockreservations@net2000ke.com, Box 40075, Nairobi, opposite the CalTec Garage on the Nyeri Road, Nyeri (very expensive). Just as the Aberdare Country Club operates The Ark for nights spent game-viewing, the Outspan operates Treetops.

his life in a cottage on the grounds of the nearby Outspan Hotel, and who once said, "Nearer to Nyeri, nearer to heaven."

At the time of independence, the government purchased all lands around Nyeri still in the hands of European farmers, then divided and distributed it by drawing lots among the Kikuyus. These farms are some of the most prosperous in Kenya, harvesting up to four crops of maize per year. However, with the park nearby, farming has not always been easy. Elephants frequently devastate the crops and volunteer fundraisers are still frantically raising funds to build a boundary ditch and electric fence around the park to keep humans and elephants apart, restricting these giant pachyderms to a limited migratory right-of-way. During migration, a herd of elephants will push a younger elephant through the electric fence, and the rangers must then radio farmers along the route to Mount Kenya to have them open their gates so the elephants can pass.

The Central Highlands

THE ABERDARE MOUNTAINS

The mountains of the Aberdares, not often visited by travelers, contain some of Kenya's most wonderful forest, interspersed with open moorlands and stretches of savannah. The lowland areas were once settled by Europeans — it is from here the myth of "Happy Valley" was propagated, though there are not many signs now of those halcyon days.

ABERDARE NATIONAL PARK

Established in 1950, the Aberdare National Park (entry US$27, children US$10) covers 590 sq km (230 sq miles), mostly at altitudes greater than 3,000 m (10,000 ft). To the local Kikuyus, these mountains had always been the Nyandaraus, but in 1884, Major Thomson renamed them after Lord Aberdare, president of the Royal Geographical Society that funded his expedition, and the name has stuck.

Because of its high altitude, the park has chilly weather — high rainfall and almost freezing night temperatures — and some of Kenya's most unusual vegetation; bamboo forest and open moorland with tussock grass and giant heath. Year-round, a four-wheel-drive vehicle is recommended; sometimes, even this may not get you through the park's black cotton soil, as the roads wind along the sides of steep, wooded valleys and across the moors. There seems to be little maintenance of any kind and roads are often closed. Even on the open roads it is easy to get stuck — not a very happy situation when, as can happen, you get stuck beside a pride of lions who show no intention of moving.

The road to **Chania Falls** is usually passable, even for two-wheel drives, and the walk down to the base of the falls is like a fairytale with rolling mist, giant lianas, Spanish moss and innumerable flowering plants and trees. Above the falls, the **Chania River** has superb brown trout fishing. Arrangements for trout fishing in the Gura, Karuru, or Chania river should be made through the park rangers.

From the peaks of **Ol Doinyo Lasatima**, 3,994 m (13,125 ft), and **Mount Kinangop**,

Kenyan women caring for their large families.

3,903 m (12,810 ft), are beautiful views of the Rift Valley and Mount Kenya, but these may be shrouded with mist after early morning.

Wildlife is abundant but often difficult to see. Along the roadside are many places where elephants have dug into the soil with their tusks in search of salt. Buffaloes, baboons and impalas are the easiest to find. Lion sightings are becoming more frequent and the Aberdare lions, most of whom have been transported in from ranches, are known to be very aggressive and have attacked tourists. Don't hike to the falls alone.

Leopards, including the rare black panther (a melanistic leopard), are found near the Wanderis Gate, but it's a good idea to ask the rangers where they were last sighted. A game driver from the Aberdare Country Club tells the story of a young couple whom he was taking on a private game drive en route to their overnight stay at The Ark. The driver came upon the elusive black panther on the road while the couple were having an argument. Ignoring the panther, they refused to let the driver stop, insisting that they be taken immediately to their rooms. The guide, irate that they did not understand the rare opportunity they had missed, was even more upset that he had not been able to watch the panther himself.

It's worth bearing in mind that the experience at both The Ark and Treetops, involving frequent wake-up calls and activities through the night, can often leave you feeling short of sleep and rather washed out. It's as well to schedule a restful day afterwards, perhaps back at the Aberdare Country Club. For an overnight stay in the Aberdares, you'll want to bring film of 1,000-ISO or higher. Warm clothes can be useful too: year-round night temperatures are near 3°C (40°F). Long pants, wool sweater and windproof jacket are a must, and even then you'll probably feel cold if you stay outside during the night.

Four species of sunbirds and 200 other bird species inhabit the park. Whether you can identify the birds or not, their songs, color and activity are a delight. The best time for viewing Aberdare's wildlife is during first light.

Where to Stay
The only full-service hotel accommodations in the park are **The Ark** ((02) 216940 FAX (02) 216796, Box 58581, Nairobi (very expensive, full board), or at the slightly less pricey **Treetops** ((02) 540780 FAX (02) 543810 E-MAIL blockreservations@net2000ke.com, Box 40075, Nairobi (very expensive, full board). For more on both of these see TRY OUT A TREETOP LODGE, page 15 in TOP SPOTS. Because of the difficulty in negotiating the roads, visitors who come to view animals, not the falls and mountains, stay at one of these two forest night-viewing lodges. Being older, **Treetops** is better known to tourists, but is far less frequented by lions and leopards than The Ark since its surrounding forest has disappeared into firewood and *shamba* construction, some of which can be seen from the lodge in daylight. By all accounts, the Treetops experience is good, but you are paying for the prestige of staying in the place where Queen Elizabeth became queen (her father died while she was viewing the animals), rather than for the accommodations (tiny bedrooms with paper-thin walls and a bathroom down the hall). **The Ark** is generally thought to be better, offering

ABOVE: Kenyan women do most of the heavy household labor, planting crops, carrying firewood and water. RIGHT: The spectacular Gura Falls in Aberdare National Park.

some of the most exciting game watching in Kenya, even if this is under floodlights of animals artificially attracted by salt licks. Neither allows children under seven, though the management has been known to bend the rules with the understanding that your child must be well-behaved and quiet (this rule applies to all guests regardless of age, rank or nationality). Another plus for The Ark is a no-smoking viewing lounge, which is very much appreciated when the outside temperatures drop.

Reservations are a must for The Ark and Treetops; both can provide transportation to and from Nairobi if you don't have your own (at US$75 round-trip) and in any case insist on providing transportation from the Aberdare Country Club or the Outspan Hotel respectively. You may also camp or rent the self-service *bandas* or bunkhouses at the **Aberdare Fishing Lodge** ((0171) 55024, c/o Warden, Aberdare National Park, Mweiga, near the Kiandongoro Gate. The rate is US$15 per person for bunkhouse accommodation, US$10 per person for camping. Bring your own bedding, food, and cooking utensils. Perhaps the best option, if driving yourself or in a party, is to stay at **Tusk Camp**: for Ksh5,000 up to eight people can camp in the wilds of the park. Reserve through Let's Go Travel ((02) 447151 or (02) 441030 FAX (02) 447270 or (02) 441690 E-MAIL info@letsgo safari.com WEB SITE www.letsgosafari.com, Box 60342, Nairobi.

How to Get There

Private vehicles are not allowed to make their own way to either Treetops or The Ark, so most guests arrive on packages from Nairobi. Guests with their own vehicles leave them at the Outspan Hotel or the Aberdare Country Club respectively and are then shuttled into their treetop lodge. It is, of course, possible to drive through the park — with skill, nerve and a four-wheel drive; there are park gates west and north of Nyeri. *Matatus* run from Nairobi to Nyeri but not the two minor roads that turn off for the south of the park. For the central and northern regions the road onwards from Nyeri to Nyahururu, which is served by *matatu*, passes close (within five kilometers or three miles) to the Aberdare Country Club, even closer to Solio

Ranch, and within two kilometers (one and a half miles) of Rhino Gate into the north of the park, but you won't get far into the park on foot before being eaten. You need your own transportion to explore much up here.

NANYUKI

An important air base and training center for, among others, the British Army, Nanyuki is well-positioned as a base to explore the northern flanks of Mount Kenya as well as being a good place to organize charter flights or four-wheel-drive expeditions off into the wilds of eastern Laikipia. Just across the equator, it started life as a basic collection of *dukas* serving the surrounding farms, and did not develop until the railway arrived in the 1920s. Now that the trains no longer run the town has lost some of its optimism, and although there are some charming shops reminiscent of the colonial days — including the "Settlers Store," in operation since 1938, the United Stores, and the Modern Sanitary Stores — there's not a great deal to see here. Worse, the ongoing presence of British soldiers has done little to improve the image of *mzungus* (white people) here. One ray of light, should you need one, is that there is a good private hospital: the Nanyuki Cottage Hospital ((0176) 22684.

WHERE TO STAY AND EAT

Staying in town is only recommended for those who don't have their own transportation, need to be at the airport early, or are interested in exploring the nightlife — of which there is plenty. The best place to stay is the **Sportsman's Arms** ((0176) 32347/8 FAX (0176) 22895, Box 3, Nanyuki, has a certain period charm though this might be hard to identify if they're hosting a loud disco — especially likely at weekends (inexpensive, B&B). The **Nanyuki River Lodge** ((0176) 32523, Box 101, Nanyuki, is best geared up for Mount Kenya climbs and has more facilities, but, once again, can get noisy (mid-range). Quieter is the **Nanyuki Guest House** ((0176) 22822, Box 211, Meru, just along the Nyahururu road (inexpensive).

As is often the case in Kenya, the best accommodation is a way out of town. Eight kilometers (five miles) to the southeast, the **Mount Kenya Safari Club** ((0176) 22960 FAX (0176) 22754, Box 35, Nanyuki, reservations made through Lonrho ((02) 216940 FAX (02) 216796, Box 58581, Nairobi, was founded by actor William Holden and still maintains some traces of Hollywood glamour (very expensive, all-inclusive). The resort offers horseback riding, golf and fishing, and has an animal orphanage in addition to being surrounded by animals in the private Mount Kenya Game Ranch … all good fun.

walks (separately charged). **Ol Pejeta Ranch** ((0176) 23414, Box 763, Nanyuki, book through Lonrho (see above) which is a six-roomed luxury lodge, colonial down to stuffed trophies on the wall and super-rich clients in the leather furniture (extremely expensive, full board).

HOW TO GET THERE

Nanyuki Airport benefits from its military significance, and has regular flights to and from the Masai Mara with **Airkenya** (US$173)

Northeast of Nanyuki and you are fringing into the west of the **Laikipia** area (see page 193), with its characteristically expensive, but rewarding, private reserves. **Sweetwaters Game Reserve** is where the most famous resident is a tame rhino, called Moran, who trails around guests like a large primeval dog, and a chimpanzee sanctuary for chimps orphaned in their Uganda and Zaire homelands. This reserve contains two establishments once owned by arms dealer Adnan Kashoggi but taken over, in exchange for unpaid debts, by Lonrho. **Sweetwaters Tented Camp** (/FAX (0176) 32409, Box 763 Nanyuki, book through Lonrho (see above) is a well-run tented camp (very expensive, full board), with night drives and game

((02) 501421/3 FAX (02) 500845 E-MAIL info @airkenya.com WEB SITE www.airkenya.com, Box 30357, Nairobi. It is also the base for **Tropicair** ((0176) 32890/1 FAX (0176) 32787 E-MAIL tropicair@kenyaonline.com, Box 161, Nanyuki, a good charter company run by well-respected Kenyan Jamie Roberts, and able to reach most of the luxury lodges in the Laikipia area in less than half an hour. As charter costs are (approximately) US$1.68 per mile (1.6 km) for a Cessna carrying two passengers, this puts Nanyuki firmly on the map for reasonably well-heeled, but not profligate, travelers.

The Aberdare Country Club has magnificent facilities and food.

By road, Nanyuki is 200 km (125 miles) north of Nairobi, 97 km (61 miles) east of Nyahururu, and 90 km (56 miles) west of Meru. All these towns are linked by regular *matatus*, though the C76 to Nyahururu is dirt and bad dirt at that. Be ready for a long slow journey.

MOUNT KENYA

One of the best things you can do in Kenya is to take a trek around or, even better, an ascent of, Africa's second-tallest peak, Mount

Kenya. Named by the various tribes as Ol Doinyo Ebor, Ndur Kegnia, or Kima ja Kegina, it is at 5,199 m (17,057 ft), taller than Mont Blanc, the Matterhorn, the Rockies, the Sierras and most of the peaks of the Himalayas and Caucasus.

Composed of a huge volcanic base and plug whose outer mantle and crater have eroded away, Mount Kenya has three main peaks and a series of subsidiary cones scattered about its crest. The first European, and perhaps even the first person, to reach the mountain's top was the British geographer H. H. Mackinder, on September 13, 1899. He named the taller two peaks **Batian**, 5,199 m (17,052 ft), and **Nelion**, 5,188 m (17,017 ft), in honor of two famed Maasai medicine men.

The third and lower peak, **Lenana**, is 4,985 m (16,361 ft).

During the early era of human history, six to three million years ago, when our ancestors were wandering the shores of Lake Turkana and probably the foothills of Mount Kenya, the mountain was even taller, estimated by geologists to be over 7,000 m (23,000 ft). Since then, the mountain's mass has caused it to sink into the earth's crust, and the combined effects of glaciation, wind and weather erosion have further lowered its peaks.

Both Batian and Nelion are glaciated spires set in a gleaming array of snow-clad cirques and arêtes, like the Matterhorn and many of the Himalayan peaks. They are the province of skilled mountaineers only, with a variety of routes from Grade IV and above, depending on the time of year, and should *never* be attempted without the requisite experience, equipment and guides. Lenana, however, is far more rounded, slightly lower, and beloved by Kenyans because it is accessible to hikers who are fit and reasonably conditioned to altitude.

CLIMBING LENANA

Climbing Lenana is one of the peak experiences of a lifetime — a view of all Kenya awaits you on the top, and if you're lucky enough to reach Lenana at dawn, after a short climb from a hut below, the sunrise across the vast plains and hills of Africa will stay with you all your life.

Mount Kenya is visible from afar, its peaks usually covered with clouds by noon, but often glitteringly free in early morning or just before sunset. Explorer Joseph Thomson was one of the first Europeans to see the mountain, on his epochal safari from Mombasa to Lake Victoria in 1883:

"Suddenly there was a break in the clouds far up in the sky, and the next moment a dazzling white pinnacle caught the last rays of the sun, and shone with a beauty, marvelous, spirit-like, and divine, cut off, as it apparently was, by immeasurable distance from all connection with the gross earth."

Thomson did not reach the mountain itself, having been threatened with extermination by Maasai while encamped on the

Ewaso Ngiro River 24 km (15 miles) away, and forced to flee westward toward Lake Victoria. Today, the locals are more welcoming, and a variety of options are available for those who wish to hike or drive to Mount Kenya's lovely lower slopes or ascend Lenana Peak.

The Naro Moru Route

There are four main routes up Lenana. The most direct and popular, though perhaps less scenic, is the Naro Moru Route. Its advantage is that you can stay a night at the 62211, Box 27, Nyeri, at Ksh400 per night, which is a good place to meet up with other climbers if you want to team up.

First stocked with trout in 1910, the **Naro Moru River** stays clear most of the year, except during and just after the rains. Good fishing for browns and rainbows is also available in the nearby **Burguret** and **Nanyuki** river, although overgrazing, logging, and intensive farming have led to increased turbidity and sedimentation of spawning beds, diminished minimum flows and reduced fish habitat.

marvelous **Naro Moru River Lodge (** (0176) 62212 FAX (0176) 62211, Box 18, Naro Moru (reservations are also available through Alliance **(** (02) 443357/8, 448000 FAX (02) 448507 E-MAIL alliance@africaonline.co.ke WEB SITE www.alliancehotels.com, Box 49839, Nairobi). Its lovely cedar cabins are spaced among giant podocarp trees, green lawns and gardens along the south bank of the Naro Moru River (inexpensive to expensive). It also offers a bunkhouse and an exposed campsite. It has excellent cuisine, a very friendly staff, more birds on the grounds than you can count, and great fishing for rainbow trout literally at your doorstep. Alternatively there are cheap *hotelis* in Naro Moru village, including a **Youth Hostel (** (0176) 62412 FAX (0176)

You can rent fly tackle at the Naro Moru River Lodge, as well as all the gear you'll need for a hike around the mountain and up to Lenana Peak. The lodge offers everything from hiking boots (it's better, of course, to bring your own) to backpacks and even climbing hardware. It will also arrange porters if you wish, and organize your stays in upper mountain huts depending on your pace and aspirations. Steven Wahome, a member of Kenya's 1989 Mount Everest team, is the manager of the lodge's climbing office, so needless to say you're in very good hands.

OPPOSITE: Lionesses can be tender with their cubs, yet are skillful hunters when they get hungry ABOVE.

To reach Naro Moru, follow the road north through Thika, Muranga, Karatina and Nyeri. If you've come from Aberdare National Park, you can return to Nyeri or take the back road shown on the map to the town of Naro Moru. An intersection just north of the town of Naro Moru leads either two kilometers (one and a quarter miles) west to the Naro Moru River Lodge or 17 km (11 miles) east to the **Mount Kenya National Park (** (0171) 21575, Box 69, Naro Moru (US$15 per day adults, US$5 children, Ksh200 per vehicle) and the start of the Naro Moru route

to Lenana Peak. This first 17 km (11 miles) takes you through gradually ascending farmlands and scattered forest over ancient lava flows, then into towering conifer forest with vast clear-cuts where potatoes have been planted between the new seedlings. During the rainy seasons, this section of the road may be impassable due to the huge ruts gouged into it by trucks bringing down harvested potatoes. Usually, you cannot drive beyond the park gate at 2,400 m (7,874 ft); however, if the road's good, you can take your vehicle all the way to the **Meteorological Station** at 3,050 m (10,000 ft).

In any case, it's a beautiful walk from the park gate up to the Meteorological Station, as the conifers give way to hardwoods, then

thick bamboo forest with magnificent vistas over thickly vegetated, mist-shrouded valleys. Once common throughout much of Kenya, the hardwood forests diminished as tectonic movement raised the earth's crust and split the Rift Valley, decreasing rainfall in much of East Africa. They are now found in isolated areas such as lower **Mounts Kenya** and **Elgon**, in the **Aberdares** and the **Mau Escarpment**. This mixture of hardwoods begins at about 1,800 m (5,600 ft) on Mount Kenya, shifts to bamboo and then moorland and heath at 3,200 m (10,500 ft), with the hardwoods more dominant on the south and east slopes due to the prevalence of rain-bearing winds.

Buffaloes are common on the road all the way from the park gate to well beyond the Meteorological Station, and may be dangerous, particularly if they are solitary. If you're hiking, don't get too close: they are very bad-tempered, and old males are especially likely to charge. They're much faster than they look and a lot faster than you. If you encounter them on the trail, try throwing rocks to chase them into the bush; if that doesn't work or if they move toward you, climb a tree as the locals do — and stay up until the coast is completely clear, which can take all day. Similarly, avoid hiking off the main road unless you have a local guide and he's willing to go first; buffaloes have a habit of exploding out of the bamboo thickets and trampling the unwary wanderer.

The Meteorological Station has a campsite and self-help *bandas* with cooking facilities and mattresses but no food. Bushbucks, Sykes' and colobus monkeys, giant forest hogs, eagles and, of course, buffaloes are common near the station, and leopards not infrequent in the boggy meadow below the *bandas*. If you arrive before noon, it's possible to ascend further to **Mackinder's Camp** the same day. But the altitude can suddenly become a problem if you're not acclimated; it's usually better to spend an afternoon hiking up to treeline (3,200 m or 10,500 ft) and enjoying the view. In the afternoons, the weather frequently turns rainy and visibility

OPPOSITE: Marabou storks confer in the branches of a thorntree. ABOVE: Mount Kenya, considered the home of God by many Kenyan tribes, is Africa's second-tallest mountain.

drops; the trail to Mackinder's Camp has a section known as the "Vertical Bog" which is best left alone in the rain.

From the station, you break out above treeline in less than an hour, slog up through the bog past the rain gauge and Picnic Rocks in another hour, and soon cross the Northern Naro Moru River, coming upon a marvelous view up and down narrow **Teleki Valley**, the imposing snow-covered peaks glittering above you. Since the station, the vegetation has changed from bamboo and hardwood forest, to stunted trees, to heather

covered glaciers a deep pink and little whips of violet hovering above its icy pinnacles. The black rock-faces, tooth-edged crags, all the weight and massive solidity of those twin towering peaks, Batian and Nelion … was transmuted into something as light, as airy and ethereal as a phantom ship riding upon a fleecy ocean …

"The night was cold, our single fly-sheets scarcely broke a chilly wind, damp rose from the ground to penetrate our blankets. So clear was the sky that the Milky Way looked like a plume of spray thrown across it by the

and tussock-grass moorlands, with giant yellow-flowered groundsel (*Senecio*) and giant lobelia standing up to 10 m (33 ft) tall.

While not luxurious, the concrete and rock bunkhouse of Mackinder's Camp will seem more than welcoming. If the clouds have not descended, there is a fine view of the peaks; from the ridge above camp it's possible to climb northward to **Two Hut Tarn** and other small lakes. Sunset on the peaks is beautiful beyond description, but Elspeth Huxley, in 1919, comes closest:

"The land stretched it seemed forever into a setting sun that had inflamed the whole sky with purple, crimson and gold. And then the peak emerged from its sheath of cloud, incredibly sharp and delicate, its snow-

bursting of some colossal breaker and held there in myriad frozen droplets. Above us, the peak loomed silently in darkness. Rocks were black as tarn water, grass a misty gray, mysterious shapes waited on the fringe of our vision, and we seemed to be afloat on some motionless vessel high above all the oceans of the world."

Alternative Routes up Mount Kenya

Three other routes up the mountain deserve special mention. The **Chogoria Route** from the eastern side is the most scenic and strenuous of all the ascents, more popular now the road on the east side of the mountain has been paved to the roadhead at 3,200 m, or 10,500 ft. Above this point, there are some spectacular views of the incised **Gorges Valley** and **Lake Michaelson**, a "trough lake" dug by glaciation. To reach this route, turn off the Embu–Meru highway north of Chuka at the sign for **Meru Mount Kenya Lodge**. Don't be confused by the grand title: it's less a lodge than a set of huts, self-service *bandas* (inexpensive) but no food or beverages, and a good campsite (very inexpensive); reserve through Let's Go Travel ((02) 447151 or (02) 441030 FAX (02) 447270 or (02) 441690 E-MAIL info@letsgosafari.com WEB SITE www.letsgo safari.com, Box 60342, Nairobi. The lodge is

thick rainforest and fabulous moorlands with long views of the peaks. Noted for its wildlife, Sirimon begins 13 km (eight miles) east of Nanyuki before the bridge crossing the **Sirimon River** and Timau. Leaving the highway, drive 10 km (six miles) through open farmland to the national park gate at 2,440 m (8,000 ft), then another nine kilometers (over five and a half miles) to the roadhead at 3,200 m (10,500 ft), where you'll find a campsite.

From the roadhead, it can take a day to climb the Barrow to **Liki North Hut** at

30 km (19 miles) from the highway but it is possible to hike an hour further up to **Urumandi Hut** at 3,060 m (10,050 ft), for a (very inexpensive) bunk bed.

There are magnificent rainforests and bamboo jungle on the way up to Urumandi, and from there it's an exhilarating four- to six-hour hike to **Minto's Hut**, spectacularly set into a bowl of three small tarns. You can stay in the hut or camp, again leaving early (3 AM) if possible. It's a two-and-a-half- to four-hour hike from Minto's to Lenana Peak, with a long scramble over slippery scree, which at this altitude can be more than exhausting.

Alternatively, the **Sirimon Track** is the longest and driest route, much of it through

4,000 m (13,123 ft). If you're in very good condition, you might like to continue on around the wall above Mackinder Valley. This route leads past **Shipton's Caves** at 4,150 m (13,615 ft) — an emergency shelter — and then straight up to **Kami Hut** at 4,425 m (14,518 ft). After Kami, it's possible to circle eastward below Batian across **Simba Col** and pick up the Chogoria route up Lenana. It's also possible to climb Lenana from this side, but this is inadvisable, as the scree makes for significant danger, particularly in the dark if you're trying to reach the peak by sunrise.

OPPOSITE: Mount Kenya's Nelion Peak rewards fit climbers. Much of the route up the mountain passes through montane forest ABOVE.

Finally, a fourth approach is via the **Burguret Trail**, from the **Mountain Rock Hotel (** (0176) 62625 FAX (0176) 62051, Box 333, Nanyuki, eight kilometers (five miles) north of Naro Moru on the Nanyuki road, where there is a very inexpensive campground, mid-range *bandas*, and a restaurant. As at Naro Moru, you can get guides and can drive to 3,000 m (9,840 ft), then follow the **Burguret River** to the Highland Castle Camp at 4,000 m (13,120 ft), and ending at **Two Tarn Hut**, from where a three-hour scramble will take you to the top of Lenana.

Mount Kenya by one route and descend by another, such as Burguret Trail and Sirimon Track, which makes an easy circle. If you can, try to spend a day or two on the high peaks, as the huts are very inexpensive and the views majestically different from each side. Remember that no food or beverages are available, so bring plenty.

If you're thinking of climbing Lenana Peak or just want to hike some of the lower trails of Mount Kenya, it's best to pick up a copy of the excellent *Mount Kenya Map and Guide* by Andrew Wielochowski and Mark

Mountain Practicalities

The scree, or talus, at the top of Lenana, particularly when wet or icy, is difficult for the average hiker. Originally formed by the freeze-thaw weathering of the mountain's glaciated upper slopes, it is loose enough in some areas to take a great deal of high-altitude energy just to get through. Thus if you're not experienced in mountain trekking and scree climbing, consider hiring a guide, who will make your trip a lot more relaxed and see that you don't miss things that are easy to pass by. From about Ksh1,000 per day, it's an inexpensive way to double your pleasure and minimize potential danger.

Another option, if you're not pressed for time and love the mountains, is to ascend

Savage. It is available at most lodges round the mountain and sometimes in Nairobi. The **Mountain Club of Kenya (** (02) 501747, Box 45741, Nairobi, has built and manages many of the huts on the mountain, and has extensive information and guidebooks. Call or find out more at its clubhouse at Wilson Airport, Nairobi, where it holds public meetings every Tuesday at 8 PM.

Guided hikes can be arranged through the following contacts. For the Naro Moru Route, contact **Naro Moru River Lodge (** (0176) 62212, Box 18, Naro Moru. To head up the Sirimon and Burguret Routes get in touch with **Tropical Ice Ltd. (** (02) 740811, Box 57341, Nairobi, who operate from Mountain Rock Hotel. The operators who specialize in the Chogoria Route are **Savage Wilderness Safaris** incorporating **East African Mountain Guides** (/FAX (02) 521590 WEB SITE www.kilimanjaro.com, Thigiri Road, Box 44827, Nairobi. If you want to try technical climbing on the peaks (ice and rock to Grade VI), you have a choice of operators. Call Steven Wahome at Naro Moru River Lodge, Tropical Ice Ltd., or Savage Wilderness Safaris incorporating East African Mountain Guides. For hiking and climbing all routes, try **Joseph Muthui** ((02) 242627 FAX (02) 250734, Box, Naro Moro, a previous member of the mountain rescue team, who is famously patient and good-humored, and charges a very reasonable price.

One final point. If you are hiking independently, the park fees you pay on the way in will estimate how long you plan to stay within the park. Overstay and search parties will be organized. It is especially important, even if you don't overstay, to register with the park authorities when you leave the park, as you are likely to be pursued for expensive search costs.

WHERE TO STAY

Where you decide to stay will partly depend on which route you choose and the lodges and campsites are listed above. If, on the other hand, you want to just have a gentle stroll around the area but haven't the slightest intention of climbing any mountains whatsoever, a good place to stay is the once very smart but now merely comfortable **Mount Kenya Safari Club**, operated by Lonhro ((02) 216940 FAX (02) 216796, Box 58581, Nairobi (very expensive); just before Nanyuki turn right and thread up the mountain for six kilometers (four miles) (see also under NANYUKI, page 213).

HOW TO GET THERE

Most of the routes up Mount Kenya approach it from the western flanks. Leave Nairobi on the Thika road heading north and continue to Karatina, turning right just before Nyeri (signposted Naro Moru River Lodge and Samburu Lodge), and continue on towards Nanyuki. The drive will take about four hours but it can take longer: the road surface is bad, especially in the latter stages. Public transportation will take longer and unless you start very early (leaving by five or six in the morning) will probably involve a change of *matatu* at Karatina and Nyeri. Alternatively, perhaps because it is Kenya's air force center, Nanyuki (see page 213) is well served by air. **Airkenya** ((02) 501421/3 FAX (02) 500845 E-MAIL info@airkenya.com WEB SITE www.airkenya.com, Box 30357, Nairobi, flies every day between Nairobi and Nanyuki, with round-trip tickets costing US$136, and even have a daily service between Nanyuki and the Masai Mara costing US$173 one-way.

For the Chogoria Route, on the mountain's eastern flank, turn right at Sagana or Muranga for Embu and continue towards Meru. At the village of Chogoria turn left for the 16 km (10 miles) of rough track to the self-service Meru Mount Kenya Lodge. Take your own food and bedding. On the eastern slopes of Mount Kenya check locally about the current security situation as this area is at the heart of Kenya's production of *miraa*, the fairly intoxicating drug made of the leaves and stems of a bushy plant common to the Meru area; and drugs and safety rarely go together.

NORTH OF MOUNT KENYA

North of Mount Kenya there are two main wildlife areas that are rated highly by visitors: the popular and groundbreaking private conservancy of Lewa Downs and the very rewarding Samburu National Reserve, with its neighbors, Shaba and Buffalo Springs reserves. North of these and the land dries up and the population density falls away.

The residents in this area are Samburu pastoralists, tall nomads tending their cattle, following a timeless and traditional way of life, and sharing many aspects — including language and appearance — with the Maasai to the south. There are nature reserves further north — most notably Losai and Marsabit — but generally the wildlife coexists with humanity here, in a wild and lawless area where anything can happen. Before traveling on from Samburu National Reserve, carefully check with the authorities

Large farms on the plains surrounding Mount Kenya produce much of the country's wheat.

on the security situation and make sure you are equipped to cope with any mechanical or medical emergency. Up in this part of Kenya public transportation is all but non-existent and north of Archer's Post the only person who will get you out of trouble is you. The road as far as Isiolo is generally regarded as safe but there have been some problems (bandits attacking tourists) between Isiolo and Samburu National Reserve (though the park itself is safe). North and east of here the security situation is dire, and travel is not recommended.

This is a commercial venture as well: entry to the reserve is US$35 for adults and US$20 for children.

Where to Stay

There are three places to stay here, none of which are very inexpensive. All are bookable through Bush Homes of East Africa ((02) 350703, (02) 571661 or (02) 571592 FAX (02) 571665 E-MAIL bushhome@africaonline.co.ke WEB SITE www.bush-homes.co.ke, Box 56923, Nairobi. The most exclusive is in **Wilderness Trails** (extremely expensive, all-inclusive),

LEWA DOWNS

The Lewa Downs Conservation Center is one of Kenya's most successful blends of conservation, traditional ranching and tourism projects, encompassing an L-shaped patch of land 60 km (37.5 miles) northeast of Nanyuki that was originally set up by Anna Merz, who is well-known for taming orphan rhinos. Well into her eighties, she has since retired to South Africa, but her brand of patriarchal conservationism lives on. There are protected, fenced-in rhinos and there is also a small swamp where a few endangered sitatunga can be found. With daily air links to Nairobi and a fast turnover of visitors, it's a slick and successful wildlife experience.

with three cottages, full luxury cuisine and game-drives included. Step down to **Lewa Tented Camp** (extremely expensive), formerly Lerai Tented Camp, which is sited within the rhino sanctuary itself. The third option here is at Samburu-run **Il Ngwesi Lodge** (very expensive, all-inclusive), which involves the local community directly in its management. Comforts are reduced, with even the shower-water brought up from underground wells by camel, but the lodge remains in the international price range. Good and authentic camel-rides and walking expeditions help, though charging US$20 to visit the local *manyattas* does seem a touch excessive, given how much most guests are already paying into the local community coffers. Following the success of

Il Ngwesi, a new community project has opened to the north, **Tassia** (extremely expensive), book through Let's Go Travel ((02) 447151 or (02) 441030 FAX (02) 447270 or (02) 441690 E-MAIL info@letsgosafari.com WEB SITE www.letsgosafari.com, Box 60342, Nairobi, which is generally self-catering with exclusive use of the whole camp for two to twelve people, but bring your own drinks. There is a standby rate within a week of the booking date, so it might be worth a call at the last minute.

How to Get There

Lewa Downs is normally reached on the daily flights from Wilson Airport with **Airkenya** ((02) 501421/3 FAX (02) 500845 E-MAIL info@airkenya.com WEB SITE www.air kenya.com, Box 30357, Nairobi, priced at US$120 one-way. It can also be reached from the Nanyuki–Isiolo road: the turning is signposted clearly if you're in your own car. Travelers using public transportation will find the game reserve too far from the main road for this option to provide a practicable access, but in any case the overnight fees will scare off any backpacker using *matatus*. Lewa Downs Conservation Center is only 20 km (12.5 miles) south of Isiolo.

NORTH TO ISIOLO AND SAMBURU

On the northern flanks of Mount Kenya, the road from Nanyuki, skirting Mount Kenya to the west, meets that from Meru curving round the eastern flanks, and a turning heads north. On either side are magnificent views: the purple slopes and peaks of the Loldaika Mountains to the west, and the soaring Nyambeni Hills, where most of the country's slightly narcotic *miraa* is grown, to the east. It's not insecure here, at the moment, but it's on the edge: check locally to make sure there aren't too many bandits around before attempting this drive alone. The provincial capital of Isiolo is 30 km (22 miles) to the north of Mount Kenya's ring-road.

ISIOLO

The first thing most visitors to Isiolo remark is its Somali influence. Many veterans were settled here after World War I, and there is also a substantial immigrant population from Kenya's troubled neighbor, making it Kenya's largest Somali city. But there are also plenty of Kenyan tribes represented in this town, which has a strong and irrepressible frontier feel. It's worth spending a little time in Isiolo, for the town is a striking clash of southern and northern desert cultures, with an overflow of the more sultry Meru temperament and a strong Somali influence.

The town itself is reasonably secure, thanks perhaps to three military training colleges and a tank regiment. The general area, however, is not.

If you're heading north, which is not currently recommended, bear in mind that Isiolo is the last sure place to buy gasoline until Moyale, some 525 km (325 miles) to the north, at the Ethiopian border; even on a very grand safari, you may not be traveling that far. Marsabit, a mere 275 km (170 miles) north from Isiolo, may have gasoline at the rundown **Marsabit Lodge** ((02) 229751 or (02) 330820, but don't depend on it unless you've called one of these Nairobi numbers to reserve some.

Isiolo's most famous blacksmith, one Mumin Hassan, who should be well beyond retirement age, known locally as "Ayatollah Khomeini," has almost single-handedly created a thriving industry in daggers, Somali swords, *kols* or curved knives, and other such instruments of mayhem, which he and his flock of sons cheerfully sell to tourists, Samburu warriors and *shiftas* (Somali bandits) alike. Usually, he can be found sitting beneath a spreading euphorbia tree, unfinished dagger in hand.

Isiolo is also a regional center for packing and trading *miraa*, a fairly intoxicating drug. The *miraa* arrives by truckloads early each morning, to be sorted and bound by Isiolo women into bundles of a kilo each (called *kilos*) for resale. Chewed by many northern Kenyans and Somalis, *miraa* is reputed to have a slow, amphetamine-like effect. Although not illegal, it appears to lead to outrageous fantasies and occasionally, when combined with alcohol, to violence, particularly when imbibers have their swords in their belts. Like "uppers" in the

Young leopards are among the most appealing of Kenya's cats.

United States, it is a favorite of long-distance truckers, another reason why the tourist is best advised not to drive in Kenya at night.

Where to Stay

There are several cheap inns for the intrepid traveler. The **Bomen Tourist Class Hotel** ((0165) 2389 FAX (0165) 2225, Box 67, Isiolo, at the end of the alley opposite the new white Barclay's Bank, is the newest and best in town (inexpensive). However the **Mocharo Lodge** ((0165) 2385, Box 106, Isiolo, is much better value and has safe parking (very inexpensive). A luxury alternative 20 km (12.5 miles) south of Isiolo on the Nanyuki Road is **Lewa Downs**, reserve through through Bush Homes of East Africa ((02) 350703, (02) 571661 or (02) 571592 FAX (02) 571665 E-MAIL bushhome@africaonline.co.ke WEB SITE www.bush-homes.co.ke, Box 56923, Nairobi, see above (very expensive).

How to Get There

Isiolo is 285 km (178 miles) north of Nairobi. Traditionally, the preferred route is to the west of Mount Kenya via Nyeri and Nanyuki, though the newly paved road on Mount Kenya's eastern flank makes the route via Meru rather quicker. Early-morning buses and *matatus* link Isiolo with Nairobi, although if you miss the last one (sometimes even 6 AM is too late!) you might face a long hopping journey. Frequent *matatus* link Isiolo with Nanyuki, a center for air travel with occasional *matatu* links west to Nyahururu.

EAST FROM ISIOLO

The fascinating, if barren, area from Isiolo through **Wajir** to the Somali border is only recommended for those with plenty of time who enjoy incinerating desert temperatures and abysmal roads. It is also very insecure and travel here is by convoy only.

If this is the adventure for you, take the **Garba Tula–Mado Gashi** road east from Isiolo, being as usual sure that you have sufficient gas and water reserves, plenty of spare tires and tubes, and food. The countryside is flat, blistering hot and sandy all the way to **Habaswein** at the headwaters of the **Lorian Swamp**, with occasional mirages

or the lone figures of Somali and Borana nomads breaking the isolation of the desert. From Habaswein east, you're in the **North Eastern Province**, Kenya's least populated, and the most remote from central rule in Nairobi.

Again, don't believe any map that shows gasoline at Habaswein (it can be found, occasionally, at Wajir — call ahead to the **Wajir Administrative Center offices** ((0136) 21112, though they may say there is some when there isn't). It's a long 260 km (160 miles) from Isiolo to Habaswein, another 70 km (44 miles) to Wajir, with its single-story white houses, mosque, Foreign Legion-type fortress, cheap hotels (none particularly recommended) and places to eat, and all the camels you can count.

From Wajir, it's another searing 190 km (120 miles) to **El Wak**, with its own fort, camels and *miraa* traders. Beyond it, the road is potholed but paved the remaining 225 km (140 miles) across the **Sardindida Plain** to **Mandera** on the Somali border. Another way to reach this godforsaken patch of the world is on the sandy, flat road from Meru National Park up to Wajir through Garba Tula, via the park's gate beyond Leopard Rock. It's a lawless, frontier land, contested by Somali tribesmen and the older settlers of Borana and Samburu. Cattle thieving is common, with occasional bloody shoot-outs between AK47-toting Somalis and local police if the latter can't get away fast enough. The best advice is to steer clear.

SAMBURU COUNTRY

Although there are plenty of Samburu to the west, around the towns of Maralal and the northern desert regions, Isiolo regards itself as the gateway to Samburu country. These slender, handsome people are known for their quiet friendliness and simple, grave demeanor. They are closely related to the Maasai, from whom they separated in tribal disputes some centuries ago during the migration southward from Sudan and Ethiopia. In the Maa language, which both tribes share, "samburu" means butterfly — the Maasai say because the Samburu fled the tribe, the Samburu say because they flutter around and don't stay put.

Like the Maasai, the Samburu are principally nomadic, wandering their vast, often arid territory in search of grazing for their herds of cattle, sheep and goats. They live on the meat of their sheep and goats, on berries, tubers and wild fruits, and on cow and goat milk, often mixed with blood taken from a vein in the necks of their cattle.

Young Samburu men and women are permitted to have relations, the man providing his lover with necklaces as proof of his affection. The young women are then betrothed to older men, circumcised on the day

Samburu wives and daughters do the majority of the physical work around the *manyatta*, but their word is respected and often outweighs their husbands'.

From the *manyatta*, young Samburu *morans* wander with their herds for days, often months, in search of grazing. They are colorfully dressed in blazing red cloaks, their faces and chests dyed ocher, their *simis* — short, lethal swords made of cut-down machetes — at their waists, their razor-sharp spears always in their grasp. The weapons are not for show. Not infrequently, *morans*

of their marriage, and, thereafter, not supposed to continue relations with the younger men. The young men are circumcised at roughly the same age, but cannot marry until much older, long after they become warriors (*morans*), according to an intricate age-set system that provides multiple brides for older, prosperous men who are or will become the elders (*mzee*) of the tribe.

The Samburu settlement, or *manyatta*, is most often a kraal of several mud, wattle and thatch huts, surrounded by a thorn enclosure in which the herds are kept at night for protection from four- and two-legged predators. Family ties are strong, as are the oral traditions of legends and laws that enliven the fireside. Like most women in Kenya, the

find themselves attacked by *shiftas* (Somali bandits), better-armed and ruthless. No Samburu who sets out to wander the Northern Frontier District with his herds can be assured of returning. When forage in one area is spent, the *manyatta* may be moved also, depending on the season.

The terrain north of Isiolo town contains some of Kenya's finest game parks and most beautiful scenery. Less than 30 km (19 miles) north of Isiolo are the linked areas of Samburu, Buffalo Springs and Shaba National Reserves. They cover a total area of some 430 sq km (170 sq miles). Samburu is the

The common zebra, with stripes across its underbelly, populates the open plains of central and southern Kenya.

most famous, an expanse of semiarid, often volcanic prairies and hills, divided from Buffalo Hills to the south by the serpentine, crocodile-infested Ewaso Ngiro River. It's a good place to spot leopards, for the simple reason that both the Samburu Lodge and the Samburu Serena Lodge bait the most elusive of all the big cats with dangling game.

Although the three reserves can impose their own daily fees even if you are just passing from one to another, or even in transit, this rarely happens. The US$27 per adult and child/student rate of US$5 is averaged across the reserves, with each sharing the revenue of shared tickets. Game-drives commonly traverse from Samburu Reserve into Buffalo Springs, depending on wildlife movements, whereas Shaba is a significant 40-minute drive away by road. There have also been some incidents of robbery both on the road from Isiolo to Samburu and at the public campsites here. Caution is recommended. In the off-season between April and July, most of the luxury lodges here drop their rates by as much as half to fill empty tents and *bandas*.

BUFFALO SPRINGS NATIONAL RESERVE

In many ways, Buffalo Springs, adjacent to Samburu National Reserve, is the most beautiful of the three reserves. Its springs and stream of the same name, with their volcanic pools and black-rock water chutes flanked with tall grass and doum palms, should not be missed. The graceful doum palm often reaches 20 m (66 ft) in height, towering over other riverine trees. It is the only palm species whose trunk and boughs divide into branches, making it instantly recognizable. Baboons and elephants eat its orange-brown fruit, and its leaves are used by people for weaving baskets and mats, so extensively that in many areas the tree no longer exists. Its broad-spreading, V-branched canopies are good places to look for black-faced vervet and Sykes' monkeys.

Both Buffalo Springs and Samburu are excellent areas for reticulated giraffes, the unusual beisa oryx with its lovely straight, long horns and gleaming black-and-white coat, impalas, blue-legged Somali ostriches, waterbucks, Grant's gazelles, dik diks, duikers, warthogs, olive baboons, lions and spotted and striped hyenas. Grevy's zebras, the desert race with large, rounded and fringed ears and narrow stripes that don't meet under the belly, are common in all three reserves. Also frequently seen are gerenuks, the long-necked antelopes that graze like giraffes on the upper branches of thorn trees, and are fittingly named *swara twiga* (antelope giraffe) in Swahili.

Elephants are rare, having been poached by Somalis and, occasionally, Samburu during their annual migrations from the reserves towards Marsabit and the northern plains. But if you're lucky you can see hunting dogs and occasionally cheetahs and leopards along the waterways or in the rocky, inaccessible hills. The cone-like hanging nests of weavers are visible everywhere in the acacias, their gregarious chatter a constant background sound, especially in the mornings.

Where to Stay

The last lodge here, just outside the reserve, is the **Samburu Serena Lodge** ((02) 711077 FAX (02) 718012 E–MAIL cro@serena.co.ke, Nyere Road, Box 46302, Nairobi, which is well-run and comfortable (expensive).

Campsites line the river in the Buffalo Springs Reserve. Now the spate of robberies in the 1980s and 1990s seems to have been stemmed, their use, once more, is generally recommended; at Ksh825 per person on top of the US$27 reserve entry fee. Their sites are even more attractive than those at neighboring Samburu Reserve are. Check at the gate on the current security situation.

The lodge is less than two hours' drive north of Nanyuki, and less than one north of Isiolo along the A2.

SAMBURU NATIONAL RESERVE

From Buffalo Springs, you cross Ewaso Ngiro River on a good bridge, often crowded with baboons, into Samburu. The higher hills at the south end of Samburu Reserve offer lovely views of the Ewaso Ngiro, and the hills and plains of Buffalo Reserve beyond. On the nearer side of the river, the land is dry and thornbush becomes the common vegetation in the barren, sandy soil. The Ewaso Ngiro begins some 300 km (186 miles) to the southwest, on the 4,000-m (13,000-ft) slopes of Ol Doinyo Lasatima in the Aberdares. It has no outlet, disappearing into the vast Lorian Swamp another 300 km (186 miles) downstream of Samburu.

Where to Stay

The most expensive place to stay in Samburu Reserve is the small and exclusive **Larsen's Tented Camp** ((02) 540780 FAX (02) 543810 E-MAIL blockreservations@net2000ke.com, Box 40075, Nairobi (very expensive). Seventeen tents here overlook the river but there are no children's rates, nor indeed children under seven because they're not permitted,

Alternatively, it is possible to camp for just Ksh825 per person downriver from the bridge and the park entrance (accept the offer of an armed guard). Many of the campsites are in superb riverside locations, but are not easy for incomers to find or reserve: most will be taken by established mobile camping operators, for their clients.

SHABA NATIONAL RESERVE

To reach the unvisited and fabulous Shaba National Reserve, you must drive three

and the atmosphere is, perhaps, rather self-consciously superior. The food is good though. The **Samburu Intrepids** ((02) 446651 or 447929 FAX (02) 446533 E-MAIL info@heritagehotels .co.ke WEB SITE www.heritagehotels.co.ke, Box 74888 Nairobi, is noticeably cheaper and, for families, has (like all the Intrepids) an excellent "explorers club" for children (expensive). With 27 luxury tents, it's not too much bigger either and is a very good option.

The nearby **Samburu Lodge** ((02) 540780 FAX (02) 543810 E-MAIL blockreservations @net2000ke.com, Box 40075, Nairobi, where gasoline is available, is the original camp in the area, and still has the best setting, on a bend in the Ewaso Ngiro River, although it is currently rather run-down (expensive).

kilometers (two miles) south from Archer's Post and turn east at the sign for the Sarova Shaba Lodge. From this turnoff, it's about six kilometers (four miles) of rough road to **Natorbe Gate**, the entrance to the reserve. From the gate, a series of roads branch east and south through an arid, volcanic expanse of rugged hills and sharp valleys.

The reserve extends for nearly 30 km (19 miles) along the south bank of the Ewaso Ngiro, with vulture nesting areas visible across the river on the **Bodich Cliffs**, and monkeys frolicking in doum palms along the water.

Back-country tented lodges, such as Larson's in Samburu National Reserve, offer the ultimate in luxury.

In central Shaba, a marsh feeds a seasonal tributary of the Ewaso Ngiro. This is a favorite locale for foraging antelope and their predators, including leopards, cheetahs and lions. It was at Shaba that a resentful ex-employee murdered Joy Adamson in 1980 as she was completing a study of leopards and cheetahs. It is possible to camp where her settlement once stood (sadly, it was never preserved) and there are still plenty of lions about.

Shaba takes its name from a 1,620-m-tall (5,318-ft) volcanic cone just to the south, which has overflowed areas of the reserve with yet-unvegetated black lava. If you feel unusually adventurous, and your four-wheel drive is in good condition, ask the rangers at Natorbe Gate for a guide to accompany you on the narrow track that descends 30 km (19 miles) along the Ewaso Ngiro beyond the reserve, heading eastward to beautiful **Shanriki Falls**. Shanriki Falls are very often referred to as "Penny Falls," after one of Joy Adamson's lions.

Shaba National Reserve is one of Kenya's most beautiful reserves, but visitors are kept at bay by the unforgiving roads of battered lava and the fact that the game, though plentiful, is painfully shy. Photographers here tend to get plenty of pictures of distant, disappearing tails. But for those who like having the bush to yourself, Shaba is an ideal place to visit.

Where to Stay

Excellent camping is available in Shaba, as the *shiftas* (bandits) that put the park off-limits are now kept at bay by a rugged team of well-armed wardens (Ksh825, once more, per person, on top of the US$27 reserve entry fee). To be safe, check with the rangers first at Natorbe Gate. Fortunately there is a lodge here: the **Sarova Shaba Lodge** ((02) 713333 FAX (02) 718700 E-MAIL reservations@sarova .co.ke WEB SITE www.sarova.com, Box 72493, Nairobi, which is a large establishment looking older than its 11 years but offering unpretentious, reasonably-priced accommodation in 85 suites, all with the luxury of full-length baths (expensive, full board). Somewhat isolated, they are also able to offer extras, such as game walks, that are not, strictly speaking, permitted here.

HOW TO GET THERE

Access to Samburu, Buffalo Springs and Shaba are generally by daily scheduled flight from Nairobi by **Airkenya** (US$120 one-way) ((02) 501421/3 FAX (02) 500845 E-MAIL info @airkenya.com WEB SITE www.airkenya.com, Box 30357, Nairobi. It's a seven-hour drive from Nairobi, but public transportation dries up around Isiolo, leaving travelers 31 km (20 miles) short of the three reserves.

NORTHERN FRONTIER DISTRICT

Driving north from Archer's Post you truly enter the Northern Frontier District: lawless, vast, sun-parched and visionary. This area is currently unsafe, however, and is unlikely to become safe in the lifetime of this book, thanks to heavily-armed gangs of *shiftas* (bandits across from Somalia) and warring tribesmen. Before you, dominating the endless stony steppe, is sheer, towering Ol Doinyo Sabachi, a huge table mountain (*inselberg*) which many of the Samburu people consider the home of *Ngai*, God. If you're really determined to travel this road, you will be taken in a convoy of trucks. The only real reasons to do so is to cross over into Ethiopia or, less ambitiously, to visit Marsabit and the Marsabit National Park.

MARSABIT AND ITS NATIONAL PARK

Inselbergs (from the German for "island mountain") are not uncommon in the plains country of Kenya. Like mesas in the American southwest, they are formed of harder or less-jointed rock that withstands erosion better than the surrounding peneplain. Sabachi is certainly one of Africa's most imposing, often cloud-covered, thickly wooded on its lower slopes and atop its broad plateau, whose springs, marshes and grassy meadows are used by the Samburu for grazing in the dry seasons (July to September, January to March). Few travelers appreciate the view too much, as they are concentrating on surviving the endless corrugations on the road. Marsabit's volcanic

Salt deposits among volcanic rock in Shaba are harvested by desert tribes.

mass rises into the fleecy clouds like Shangri-La amid the desert, its coolness paradise after the molten desert. Permanently green thanks to its sudden elevation, it is a colorful place of Rendile and Borana tribesmen, as well as Ethiopian and Somali refugees. There's a bank and a few basic places to stay, the better of which is the run-down **Kenya Lodge and Hotel** ((0183) 2221, Box 176, Marsabit (very inexpensive). Since the lodge in the park closed, this is your best option — there are too many animals in the park to camp there.

A visit to the park, however, is a must. Watered by the mist and clouds of air blown east from Lake Turkana, the volcanic cones of Marsabit contain important remnants of Kenya's upland forest, its often-immense trees cloaked in *usnea* lichens and gray-bearded mosses, its flora and fauna of exceptional beauty and diversity. The country's longest-tusked elephants have traditionally come from Marsabit Mountain, the most famous being Ahmed, who died in 1974 and is now on display, life-sized in fiberglass, at the National Museum in Nairobi (a humorous account of Ahmed's demise and subsequent enthronement is contained in Patrick Marnham's *Fantastic Invasion*).

Although Ahmed enjoyed the protection of President Kenyatta, the president's last wife, Mama Ngina, was more mercenary in her concern for elephants, having by most accounts directed Kenya's largest poaching ring, with the result that nearly all of Ahmed's peers have vanished from Marsabit, their tusks sold via South Africa to the ivory merchants of Japan, China and Taiwan, and the park is seriously encroached. Curiously enough, Mama Ngina's brother followed as Kenya's Minister of Tourism and Wildlife, thus becoming responsible for the safety and well-being of those few pachyderms that escaped his sister's ministrations.

Many other superb animals remain, however, in the 2,100-sq-km (811-sq-miles) Marsabit National Park, including greater and lesser kudus, reticulated giraffes, spotted and striped hyenas, caracals, serval cats, leopards, lions, beisa oryx and the unusual petersi Grant's gazelles, with its near-parallel horns. What's more, the place is an ornithologist's fantasy, its microclimates shifting from cloud forest to blasting desert, the home of 52 different birds of prey. Grebes, herons, spur-wing geese, ducks, teal and pintail can be found around Lake Paradise itself, with the rare lammergeyers (bearded vultures) nesting on the precipitous cliffs of **Gof Bongole**, and many more rare species found in the black lava desert surrounding the park.

Six kilometers (three and three quarter miles) from the town of Marsabit, off the main road from Isiolo, are the **Ulanula** or **Singing Wells**, more looked for than found: ask a local to show you where they are. In the dry season (July to September, January to March) the local Borana herdsmen form human chains to hand up buckets of water from the well's muddy depths, singing when the mood strikes (or for benefit of tourists, when recompense is offered).

How to Get there

There are no *matatus* or other forms of public transportation traveling overland up to Marsabit, and the only way is in your own four-wheel-drive car, traveling in convoy for safety, along a truly awful corrugated track 242 km (150 miles) up from Archer's Post at the northern boundary of Samburu National Reserve. The only sensible way of getting there is by air charter: contact **Fuf Aviation** ((02) 505541 or **Sarman Aviation** ((02) 606416. With either company the cost is likely to be around US$1,200, depending on how long you intend to stay; without your own transportation on arrival, however, you might not want to stay too long.

WEST FROM SAMBURU

If the security situation is suitable, it is possible to drive west to Wamba. Take enough fuel, as the next provisions are in Maralal. There are two remote and atmospheric camps here. **Sarara** ((02) 501853 FAX (02) 608487 E-MAIL acacia@swiftkenya.com WEB SITE www.africatravelreview.com, Acacia Trails, Box 30907, Nairobi, is a community ranch run by the Samburu people and a real chance to get close to the local community and make a (serious) contribution to their finances (extremely expensive). There is also the even more remote luxury of **Kitich Camp**, reserve through Bush Homes of East Africa ((02) 350703, (02) 571661 or (02) 571592 FAX (02) 571665 E-MAIL bushhome@africaonline.co.ke WEB SITE www.bush-homes.co.ke, Box 56923, Nairobi (very expensive). Camp consists of six luxurious en-suite walk-in tents, each for two people, with individual bathrooms and copious bucket showers filled each morning with hot water from the large wood-fed boiler near the kitchen tent.

The spacious dining tent and the guest tents each look out from groves of shady fig trees onto a magnificent small valley with

baggage transported by horses. This is a pleasure for those who've flown in, but even more for those who've drive up: it's a chance to get out of the car. The nearest town is Wamba, which has a good mission hospital — accustomed to snakebites and bullet wounds — which can, in this part of the country, be useful.

How to Get There
Kitich is an eight-hour drive from Nairobi, traveling north on the A2 to Isiolo, through the Buffalo Springs (paying an entry fee) and

the shimmering Ngeng River in its center and the rugged ridges of the Matthews Range rising abruptly on the far side. On the opposite slopes grow 800-year-old cycads, a prehistoric species of palm which is the most primitive extant seed-bearing plant, and some of the largest podocarp and cedar in Kenya. Other plants include six species of hibiscus, crotons, whose bright flowers produce a very sweet honey, and combretum. The valley boasts a population of butterflies unique in the world, with new species still being found, and is a major stopover for European migratory birds.

From Kitich, accompanied hikes through the Matthews Range can last from a day up to eight-day expeditions with food, tents and

forking left for Wamba. Alternatively, travel north to Naivasha, bear left to Nyahururu and complete the second half of the drive on *murram* roads, turning right before, but near Maralal for Wamba. The fact that there are two routes raises the interesting possibility of a short circuit lasting anything from four days to a week. If you don't relish the eight-hour drive from Nairobi, it's possible to fly directly to Wamba and have someone from Kitich pick you up there. There is no regular overland transportation along the C78 that links Isiolo with Maralal so the trip may take many days if hitching. Wamba itself is five kilometers (three miles) off the

As the sun sets on Lake Turkana the sound of drums come alive in the local settlements.

main road and Kitich 40 km (25 miles) further still. This doesn't mean it's impossible, quite, but it will be an adventure. You should be prepared to do some fairly serious walking and to be ready for days on end waiting for a lift.

EAST OF MOUNT KENYA: ELSA'S COUNTRY

Mount Kenya's eastern flanks, traversed by a newly resurfaced road, guide the main road around towards the town of Meru, the Nyambeni Hills and Meru National Park itself, where the film of Joy Adamson's tale of Elsa the lioness awoke the world to the beauty and romance of African wildlife. Traveling north from Nairobi, the first town you'll come to after bearing right at Muranga is the small settlement of Embu. There seems no very good reason to stay here, but if required the **Izaac Walton Inn** ((0161) 20128/9 FAX (0161) 30135, Box 1, on the Meru Road, is a pleasant enough place to settle into a laid-back, vaguely colonial atmosphere (inexpensive to mid-range). Most people, however, put their foot on the throttle to make the most of the new and, if in a *matatu*, frighteningly fast road that heads across the ravine-ridden eastern slopes of Mount Kenya to the town of Meru. Halfway you'll pass **Chogoria**, starting point for one of the best routes to climb Mount Kenya (see CLIMBING LENANA, page 214).

MERU

The town of Meru is a major hub for transportation in all directions, with buses, matatus and even planes rattling off in every direction, traveling to Uganda, Somalia, Ethiopia and beyond. There's a reason for this, and the reason is *miraa*. This green shrub is chewed all over East Africa, stretching time and reducing appetites, and this is where it grows. It's a mild narcotic and something of an acquired taste (I find it quite resistible), but you'll see how much passion it arouses in the Kenyans whenever you board a *matatu* leaving Meru, loaded with bunches of *miraa*. Your rate of progress is slowed to a crawl as it is sold, bunch by bunch, to people standing by the side of the road.

The town itself is pleasantly sited on the northeastern slopes of Mount Kenya, and is the administrative and commercial center of the district of the same name. The town doesn't see many Western visitors but is all the better for that. The Bantu-speaking Meru tribe, related to both the Kikuyu and the Embu people to the south, are thriving and populous, and the **Meru Museum** ((0164) 20482, 9 AM to 6 PM daily, Ksh200, is a good place to find out more. Housed in the oldest building in town, it has ethnographic displays, a collection of medicinal herbs (including *miraa*, of course) and a well-preserved homestead. The market is large, and it's interesting to see the *miraa*-trading area on Moi Avenue.

Where to Stay and Eat

The best place to stay in town, by a comfortable margin, is the **Pig and Whistle** ((0164) 31411, 20574, Box 3160, Meru (inexpensive). It has been in operation since World War I, and various renovations have done little to drag it into the present day. The cabins, either in concrete or wood, are well-equipped (for Meru) and the creaky wooden bar is a delight. Meal prices are reasonable and the food is delicious and ample. More modern is the **Meru County Hotel** ((0164) 20342 FAX (0164) 31264, Box 1386, Meru (inexpensive). There are plenty of restaurants serving African food, probably best at the Meru County Hotel but with plenty of other establishments such as the **Ivory Springs Café**. Just follow your nose.

How to Get There

There is a choice of routes to Meru from Nairobi (290 km or 181 miles), both via Muranga but then passing either side of Mount Kenya. It is faster to come via Embu (since the mountainside road was repaired), but the road through Karatina and Nanyuki can give more pretexts to stop along the way. Allow six hours or so — more in the wet season (April to June, October to early December). Isiolo is 57 km (36 miles) distant. Thanks to its pivotal role in the production of *miraa* Meru is served by plenty of buses and *matatus* (and unscheduled flights), but are often very full when they leave and none are sympathetic to overladen backpackers.

Unless, of course, their backpacks are full of *miraa*, which would be a novelty.

MERU NATIONAL PARK

Meru National Park, 85 km (53 miles) beyond Meru town, is on few itineraries following many years of poor security and the closure of all park accommodation. Now, however, it is gradually opening up again, with the arrival of a new luxury lodge and increased security.

It is one of the most beautiful of all Kenya's parks. Stretching out before you are the golden, rolling plains where Joy Adamson released the lioness Elsa. The park is the locale of the book and later the movie, *Born Free*. The park, 1,812 sq km (700 sq miles), descends in a series of plateaus from the 1,000-m (3,000-ft) Nyambeni foothills southeast across savanna and open woodland to less than 300 m (1,000 ft) on the banks of the Tana and Rojewero river.

Meru contains a variety of ecosystems, from near-desert savanna to tropical marshes and riparian zones, even rainforest (the **Ngaia Forest**). Occasional rugged, reddish-yellow rocky outcrops thrust up from the plateau amid combretum and commiphora scrub, grassland and acacia trees. A series of sizable waterways, including the **Murera**,

Rojewero, **Tana**, **Kiolu** and **Ura** Rivers, flow southeast across the plateau, providing water for wildlife and riparian forest zones of towering fig and tamarind trees, and raphia and doum palms. The northwest section of the park has numerous large marshes packed with wildlife such as **Bwatherongi**, **Mughwango**, and **Mururi Swamp**, all accessible by the park's excellent road system.

Sizable animal populations inhabit the park — lions, elephants, buffaloes, both common and Grevy's zebras (although you'll probably see only the common), reticulated giraffes, Somali ostriches, waterbucks, leopards, impalas, Grant's gazelles, beisa oryx, olive baboons, aardwolves, Sykes' and patas monkeys, cheetahs, caracals, wildcats, serval cats, hippopotamuses and crocodiles, as well as countless birds. Until November 1988, its major attraction was five very tame white rhinos. They were slaughtered by Somali poachers with automatic weapons who opened fire on the rhinos and nearby rangers, who immediately took cover.

The incident created an international outcry; security at the park tightened, but the poachers, of course, were never found. A major result of the ensuing security crackdown was the closure of several remote campsites. This incident has tainted the park's fame, but rhinos or no rhinos, Meru remains one of Kenya's, and the world's, best parks.

Lions often rest during the day on outcrops and termite mounds on the savannah.

Meru offers superb views of Mount Kenya in the early morning and late afternoon, when the clouds usually clear. It has a well-designed road network and the intersections of the park roads are numbered — note them in your head as you pass and it's less likely you'll get turned around. Also, in the rare event that you can procure a map of Meru, these markers are shown.

During and after the rains, when forage and water are easily available, Meru's wildlife is generally more dispersed, but in the dry seasons (July to September, January to

There is a nearly endless series of short and long game drives you can take in Meru, alternating riverine roads with open savanna ones. **Elsa's Camp** on the Ura River is near its junction with the Tana, in the southeast corner of the park. From here, it's less than an hour's drive along the north bank of the Tana to dazzling **Adamson's Falls**, where you will often find hippos and a profusion of birds including the loud Pel's fishing owl. Be sure to check with park rangers as to the status of the road before departing on these itineraries; take a guide if they so advise.

March), it tends to congregate near the rivers, swamps, and ponds, when the marsh in front of the now-closed Meru Mulika Lodge is visited regularly by elephants, buffaloes, impalas, baboons, ostriches and waterbucks.

The northeastern section of the park has the most varied vegetation — magnificent stands of doum palms and whistling thorns. You may not see a lot of game here, but you will often find monkeys and baboons shaking the fruits from the palms. Germination of the doum palm is facilitated by passage through the bowels of an elephant, thus, where you see these palms, it's likely there once were (and may still be) elephants.

Accessible from Meru are the **Bisanadi**, **North Kitui**, **Rahole** and **Kora National Reserves**, all semi-desert except along the banks of the Tana, which they adjoin. The barren, sweeping landscapes and the birds in these areas make the long excursions memorable, but you are also rewarded with excellent undisturbed game viewing.

Before you attempt trips into any of these reserves, however, be *sure* to check with the park rangers on dangers and restrictions. Ever since the rhinos were poached, it has been impossible to make the trip without a ranger/guide. Don't let it disturb you if he climbs into your vehicle armed with an Enfield .303 or a German G-3 automatic rifle. Traveling with tourists offers the rangers a chance to patrol, but he's also there for your security; there are few maps and numerous chances to get lost, and the 6:30 PM curfew is strictly enforced in Meru. Chances are he can point out scores of animals you'd miss alone.

Meru boasts over 300 species of birds. They are everywhere and of all colors of the rainbow. Meter-tall (three-foot) kori bustards often patrol the entrance to the lodge, iridescent superb and Hildebrant's starlings flash about everywhere, and there are four species of honeyguides in residence. Guinea fowl

and francolin are abundant enough to be annoying as they scurry ahead of your vehicle, refusing to give way. They do give way, but not until the very last millisecond, quite unlike the large land tortoise who simply pulled in his head and legs as I approached.

Where to Stay

By far the best place to stay in Meru is **Elsa's Kjope**, run by the upmarket operator Cheli and Peacock Ltd. ((02) 604053/4 or (02) 603090/1 FAX (02) 604050 or (02) 603066 E-MAIL chelipeacock@africaonline.co.ke WEB SITE www.chelipeacock.com, Box 39806, Nairobi, which offers game packages of day and night game-drives, guided walks and fine, Italian-influenced cuisine (very

expensive, all-inclusive). Since the Meru Mulika Lodge closed, the only other accommodation is at designated primitive campsites for US$2 per person, and that *must* be arranged first at the gate or the park headquarters. In consolation, Meru offers some of the best game viewing for travelers allergic to the sight of other vehicles.

How to Get There

To reach the park from Meru, follow the signs in the center of town, taking the macadam highway 30 km (19 miles) northeast (it has marvelous views opening northward on the Nyambeni Hills). Turn right on a dirt road just before the town of Maua (the highway soon turns to dirt also); there is usually no sign to indicate the turn and you may have to ask. This dirt road, which can be difficult during the rainy season, descends 55 km (34 miles) through former forest now jammed with small farms (*shambas*), and lined from time to time with tiny shops (*dukas*).

The parade of women heavily laden with firewood and water containers, of children herding livestock and of men promenading while chewing *miraa*, the local drug, is endless. As recently as 1970, this entire region between Meru National Park and the highway was solid forest, wild and filled with animals. Now, every inch is under cultivation, eroding or being overgrazed — a lesson in the earth's crying need for population control. At the park boundaries such development stops abruptly.

ONWARDS FROM MERU

From Meru, there is an enticing-looking road heading northeast toward Wajir and the Somalia border. Minor routes, on the map, head down toward Garissa. All these roads are lousy: fiendish in the rainy season and blistering when it's hot. Worse, there are just too many bandits and too many guns to make it worth attempting. Think about trying it, fine, but then think again and leave the locals to their local feuds.

OPPOSITE: Once common nearly everywhere in Kenya, elephants have been reduced by ivory poaching to remnant, threatened populations in a few national parks. ABOVE: Most Kenyan tourist hotel rooms are spacious and comfortable, as here in Samburu.

The Eastern Plains

Long before the Masai Mara stole the wild-life show, white hunters in Kenya went to Tsavo on the great Eastern Plains to find, and then shoot, the wildlife. When these early colonists hung up their guns, indig-enous hunters took over: in the trackless bush, poachers ran riot, and throughout much of the 1980s, the broad savannahs of Tsavo East National Park were turned into a battleground.

These days things are much improved. Elephant populations, worst hit by the poachers, are recovering, and areas once off-limits to tourists are now open again. Tsavo East National Park, north of the main Nairobi–Mombasa road, now offers many miles of untouched wilderness, and Tsavo West National Park, south of the main road, has areas of spectacular beauty. The volca-nic Chyulu Hills, barely crossed by navigable roads, are havens for wildlife dispersing from the national parks through the rainy season, and valuable grazing lands for the cattle of the indigenous Maasai people. Meanwhile, to the west, the small oasis of Amboseli con-tinues to attract huge herds of elephant, all backed by the stunning peak of snow-capped Kilimanjaro.

At the heart of all this is the scattered, unimpressive town of Voi.

VOI

The only settlement of any size on the main Nairobi–Mombasa road is Voi, a simple town that sports several ATM cash machines, a few gas stations and some bars and inexpensive hotels. It is mainly significant as a jumping-off point for the nearby reserves of Tsavo East and Tsavo West.

WHERE TO STAY AND EAT

Although most travelers pass through here on their way to the game lodges in the park, there are places to stay in Voi and it is pos-sible to have quite a good time here. The best place is the **Tsavo Park Hotel** ((0147) 30050 FAX (0147) 30285, Box 244, Voi, with surpris-ing sophistication for such an isolated spot and a good restaurant serving Western staples (inexpensive). On a budget, another good lodging is **Ghana Guest House** ((0147)

2503, Box 492, Voi, quietly run by a woman's co-operative (very inexpensive). Wednesday, Friday and Saturday are disco nights at the Tsavorite Club, in a converted sports hall near the market.

MAN-EATER COUNTRY

" …the lions had a range of some eight miles on either side of Tsavo to work upon; and as their tactics seemed to be to break into a different camp each night, it was most dif-ficult to forestall them. They almost appeared, too, to have an extraordinary and uncanny faculty of finding out our plans beforehand, so that no matter in how likely or how tempt-ing a spot we lay in wait for them, they in-variably avoided that particular place and seized their victim for the night from some other camp. Hunting them by day, moreover, in such a dense wilderness as surrounded us, was an exceedingly tiring and really fool-hardy undertaking."

So does Colonel J.H. Patterson describe, in his *The Man-eaters of Tsavo*, some of the difficulties he faced when sent by the Brit-ish Foreign Office in 1898 to direct a section of the Mombasa–Uganda Railway, where the depredations of two ravenous man-eating lions brought work to a standstill. After months of hunting them, during which time they killed numerous workers, Patterson describes being stalked by one lion:

"I again kept as still as I could, though absolutely trembling with excitement; and in a short while I heard the lion begin to creep stealthily towards me. I could barely make out his form as he crouched among the whitish undergrowth … I took careful aim and pulled the trigger. The sound of the shot was at once followed by a most terrific roar, and then I could hear him leaping about in all directions …"

Patterson was finally able to kill another man-eater and capture a brazen third that had entered a railway carriage and killed and carried off one of the line's engineers. Hid-den away in Nairobi's Railway Museum there's a photo of the lion doing just that. But man-eating lions have remained part of the lore and mystique of Tsavo.

The distinctive markings of the reticulated giraffes, are specially adapted to blend with its habitat.

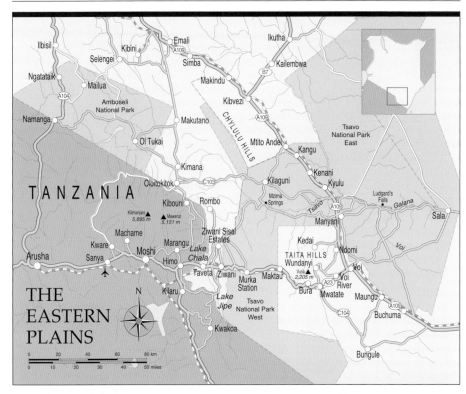

Now the biggest park in Kenya, and at 20,807 sq km (8,000 sq miles) one of the largest in the world, Tsavo National Park is an international wildlife and environmental treasure chest. It contains a variety of habitats, geologic/soil types, animals, birds and plants, and offers excellent camping, lodges and other accommodation.

Divided by the Nairobi–Mombasa road and railway into Tsavo West (7,000 sq km or 2,700 sq miles) and Tsavo East (more than 13,000 sq km or 5,000 sq miles), the park is a change from nearby Amboseli. Confusingly, although the two parks are named after their east/west location, in fact they are more defined along a north/south axis: Tsavo East spreads north from the main road, while Tsavo West occupies a C-shaped swathe to the south of the main road.

Tsavo West is hillier, greener and much more vegetated than its northern neighbor, but also has more tourists. For isolation, head instead out into the wilderness areas of Tsavo East. Each has its advantages.

TSAVO EAST

Tsavo East is vast even by African standards. It is the legendary Kenyan wilderness, with limitless vistas across its gray-brown scrub, dotted with baobab trees, to impossibly distant table mountains. Entry fees to the park are US$23 per adult and US$8 per child.

Of its 13,000 sq km (5,000 sq miles), nearly two-thirds (the area north of the Galana River) has spent the last decades off-limits to tourists. This was in part to allow the park to recover from the droughts of the 1970s and the even more devastating poaching wars of the 1980s. Now the area is, once more, opening up to wealthier visitors through walking safaris and mobile tented camps, though movements are still restricted in this area, and you're likely to be assigned, and charged for, a ranger.

South of the Galana River there are no such restrictions and there's more than enough to keep any wanderer occupied for months. The easiest place to start is the main (but not surfaced) C103 road from Manyani Gate, west of Voi, following the south bank of the Galana, with its numerous offshoots up tributary ravines. If you wish, you can take this road all the way to the coast city of Malindi. A highlight of Tsavo East is the imposing **Mudanda Rock**, a flat-topped *inselberg* of Promethean proportions some 13 km (eight miles) south of Manyani Gate. It has a water hole that draws wildlife from miles around, except at the height of the dry seasons (July to September, January to March). Just south of Mudanda Rock, you can turn northeast down the bank of the seasonal Mbololo River, and in 29 km (18 miles) pick up the Galana River road again.

The joining of the Tsavo and the Athi River, which descends all the way from Nairobi, forms the Galana River. It drops from the high plateau country into a narrow canyon at **Lugard's Falls**, named for the adventurer, soldier and antislavery activist Lord Frederick Lugard, who stopped here in 1890 on his way to becoming the proconsul of Uganda. (Surely, the courageous Lord Lugard deserves greater commemoration than this brown, turgid cascade, with its complement of crocodiles basking below.)

From Lugard's Falls, it's an easy half-day drive down the Galana River to Sala Gate. From there, another three hours down the south bank of the Sabaki River brings you to a whole other world in Malindi.

If you've come from Mombasa, Tsavo West or the Taita Hills, the normal place to enter Tsavo East is by the park headquarters at **Voi Gate**. From here, it's a quick drive to several lodges or past the **Kandari Swamp** (which, disastrously, dries out in times of drought) down the north bank of the Voi River. Some 34 km (21 miles) from the Voi Gate is **Aruba Dam**. During the early dry seasons (July to September, January to March), when there's little water to be found in the area, the dam provides a strong draw for wildlife. Here, you have excellent chances of seeing gazelles, impalas, buffaloes, greater kudus, Defassa waterbucks and associated predators.

From the dam, you can follow roads back up to the Galana River or descend further on the Voi, depending on the season. Although Tsavo East is much drier than Tsavo West, its roads can become boggy in the rains and sandblasted ruts in the dry seasons, so proceed with caution.

Foreplay is an intricate part of lion courtship.

Where to Stay

In Tsavo East, there are excellent places to stay, and it's worthwhile spending a day or two wandering this largely unvisited park. Seasonal, between the months of June to November, is **Patrick's Camps**, a mobile tented camp that spends the rest of the year in Solio. Patrick's gets guests closest to the bush through night drives, fly camps and bush breakfasts (extremely expensive, all-inclusive). Reserve through Bush Homes of East Africa ((02) 350703, (02) 571661 or (02) 571592 FAX (02) 571665 E-MAIL bushhome

most expensive, is **Galdessa Camp** E-MAIL www.galdessa.com, reserve through Mellifera ((02) 574689, (02) 577018 or (02) 567251 FAX (02) 564945 E-MAIL Mellifera@swiftkenya.com, Box 24397, Nairobi, on the southern side of the Galana River west of Lugard's Falls (extremely expensive, all-inclusive). Bush breakfasts here are a specialty, followed by walking safaris and fishing on the river. Downstream, and down-market, but much better value, is **Epiya Chapeyu** ((02) 749796 FAX (02) 750990 E-MAIL bigi@formnet.com, Box 14653, Nairobi, which has 20 tents, fairly

@africaonline.co.ke WEB SITE www.bush-homes.co.ke, Box 56923, Nairobi. Otherwise, the most northerly lodge, accessed through Mtito Andei Gate, nearest to Nairobi, in the restricted area, is **Tsavo Safari Camp** ((02) 227136 FAX (02) 219982 E-MAIL ksc@africa online.co.ke, Box 30139, Nairobi, located 24 km (15 miles) northeast of Mtito Andei Gate on the east bank of the Athi River (expensive, full board). It offers guided tours into the off-limits zone of Tsavo East. It is necessary here to make a reservation, or the guards at the parking lot won't let you cross the river (by boat) to the lodge on the far bank.

Through the western Manyani Gate there are two lodges on the southern banks of the Galana River. Perhaps the best, certainly the

close together, and a relaxed and welcoming, Italian atmosphere (expensive, full board).

Enter the park through Voi Gate, by the park headquarters, and the **Voi Safari Lodge** ((02) 336858 FAX (02) 218109, Box 30471, Nairobi, is nearby (expensive, full board). It is justifiably famous for its endless panorama across the dry savannah and two water holes that entice a multitude of beasts. This is also where Tsavo East's most popular campsite, which also has a few basic *bandas*, is found. Guests here share the place with Daphne Sheldrick's orphaned elephants, now grown up. If you're not careful, you might end up sharing your food as well. These elephants have no fear of man, which is potentially a very dangerous situation: watch out.

Follow the seasonal Voi River and you'll reach Aruba Dam, where there is currently a **campsite** and plans for a lodge. Either way it's worth a visit for its game. Follow the river to **Satao Camp**, reserve through Southern Cross Safaris ((011) 471960 FAX (011) 471257, Box 90653, Nyali, Mombasa, a luxury tented camp built on a (seasonal) island (expensive, full board). It is in the heart of the park and, if coming from Mombasa, is better reached from Buchuma Gate.

Entering the park along the dirt C103 road from Malindi, one of the first places to stay

Airkenya flights into Tsavo are currently suspended, and charter flights (try Boskovic Air Charters Ltd. ((02) 501219 FAX 505964, Box 45646, Nairobi) are now the quickest way. Tsavo East has airstrips at Lugard's Falls, Aruba Dam and Satao Camp. In your own vehicle, the first park gate coming from the capital is at Mtito Andei (literally meaning "the place of the vultures"), 236 km (147 miles) from Nairobi, 249 km (156 miles) from Mombasa, or, further east, at Voi, 334 km (208 miles) from Nairobi and 151 km (94 miles) from Mombasa, where the park

is far downstream, just outside the park boundaries on the coast side by Sala Gate. **Tsavo Buffalo Camp** ((0147) 2547 FAX (0123) 30715 E-MAIL coralkey@africaonline.co.ke, Box 556 Malindi, is the cheapest option without camping and easiest to reach from the coast but you'll need your own vehicle for game drives (mid-range). Nearby is **Kulalu Camp**, reserve through Hemingways ((0122) 32624 FAX (0122) 32256 Box 267, Watamu, or **Ocean Sports** ((0122) 32008 FAX (0122) 32266, Box 100, Watamu, much favored by bird-shooting Kenyans (mid-range).

How to Get There

Access to the lodges in the huge expanses of Tsavo East depends on their specific location.

headquarters are found. Both Voi and Mtito Andei are served by *matatus* but there is no public transportation into the park itself.

TAITA HILLS

Sitting somewhat strangely between Tsavo East and Tsavo West are the Taita Hills. Set against the broad plains, they rise steep and forested, punctuated with crashing creeks and waterfalls. It was from their tallest peak, Vuria, at 2,209 m (7,247 ft), that the missionary Rebmann saw Kilimanjaro's white spire in 1848, the first European to do so.

The wild landscapes OPPOSITE of Tsavo East and are home to exotic plants such as this toothbrush plant ABOVE.

The hills are home to the friendly Taita people, of whom the explorer Thomson spoke fondly. Their settlements are centered on the bustling hill town of Wundanyi and the terraced slopes between Voi and the Tanzania border. To reach the Taita Hills, leave Tsavo West by the Maktau Gate and drive toward Voi. The area between Maktau and the town of Bura was the site in World War I of intensive fighting between the British and German troops. The latter, under the command of Colonel Von Lettow-Vorbeck, were trying to cut the Mombasa–Uganda Railway.

Maktau or west all the way to Lake Jipe. Check with the people in Bungule first as to road conditions, and whether the gate's open. From Bungule, you can also attempt the drive across to **Mackinnon Road** on the Mombasa–Nairobi highway — again, ask first about road conditions.

Where to Stay

The best, but not the cheapest, place to stay here is in a private reserve known as the Taita Hills (but in fact on the less dramatic lowlands) and operated by the Hilton Group.

If you're in an adventurous mood, or like military history, there's a rough road (often impassable in the rains) leading southeast from the next town, **Mwatate**, across the arid flatlands, called "durststeppe" (thirst plains) by the German troops. This leads to the sheer escarpments of **Kasigau Mountain**, 1,641 m (5,384 ft), where blistering battles were fought between the Germans and British for control of the region's only water sources.

Providing your vehicle is in good shape and you have plenty of gas, you can turn west at **Bungule**, the town at the foot of Kasigau Mountain, to reenter Tsavo West by the Kasigau Gate. This takes you into some of the finest, and emptiest, terrain in the park, with the possibility of swinging north up to

Entry is US$24 per person, which is included for guests of the **Taita Hills Safari Lodge** (very expensive, full board), just outside the reserve. There are two more places to stay in this price bracket. The **Salt Lick Lodge** (very expensive, full board), in the south of the reserve, is the one that always appears in the photographs — stilted tents on a wide, game-strewn plain — while the **Hilton Safari Camp** (very expensive, full board) is probably the nicest, with no electricity (but no children under seven either). All three can be booked through **Hilton Kenya (** (02) 334000 FAX 339462, Box 30624, Nairobi. This is the only place in Kenya apart from the Masai Mara where it is possible to go ballooning: it's cheaper too, at US$250 per person;

reserve through Hilton. On a budget, and to see the people rather than the animals, there's basic but clean accommodation just outside the small town of Wundanyi at the **Hills View Lodge** ((0148) 2417, Box 1262, Wundanyi (inexpensive); market days are Tuesday and Friday.

How to Get There

The most common way to reach the Taita Hills is from Mombasa. The road is paved all the way, and the drive takes just three hours. Nairobi is just too far — and the road too poor

visitors than its neighbor across the main road. The landscape of Tsavo West is everywhere spectacular, with wide valleys, rivers, ridges and peaks. The most famous of Tsavo West's sites is **Mzima Springs**, where rainfall collected in the porous volcanic rock springs forth at the rate of 225 million liters (50 million gallons) a day, more than 10 million liters (over two and a half million gallons) an hour, into a pool and stream full of crocodiles and hippopotamuses. Here, you can walk along an interpretive trail and even descend to a partially submerged lookout to

— to make this a sensible option from visitors based inland. The turning to Taita Hills is at Voi, 140 km (87.5 miles) from Mombasa and 300 km (187 miles) from Nairobi, where the A23 forks west towards Mwatate and the two Hilton lodges are 55 km (34 miles) on. This road continues on to Moshi and then Arusha. This means it is possible to get here by public transportation: change *matatus* at Voi for one heading to Taveta, Kenya's border town with Tanzania, but then there's no transportation into the game reserve.

TSAVO WEST

More accessible, and with more accommodation options, Tsavo West receives more

watch the animals swim by. Schools of fat barbel inspect the tourists from the far side of the glass. Unfortunately, some three-quarters of Mzima's flow has been diverted by pipeline to Mombasa, to serve as the city's water supply. This has reduced its downstream flows and aquatic life. Despite this, the springs remain a miracle of nature, a green outpost of tamarind, wild date, raphia palms and wild figs amid Tsavo's dry expanse.

An adventurous itinerary from Mzima is to follow the south bank of the **Tsavo River** east on the dirt track, winding in and out of the many luggas draining from the south. This is *definitely* four-wheel-drive country, and may

The lava fields of Tsavo West stretch to the distant mountains.

be impassable even then. It's best attempted with two vehicles (hopefully one can go for help when the other's incapacitated), and has proved fatal to unprepared tourists in the past. It's well worth the effort, but *not* for the faint of heart, or the inexperienced.

Less dangerous, but also four-wheel drive only, is the track along the river's north bank, 35 km (22 miles) from the Ngulia intersection (number 18) to Tsavo gate. The cardinal rule in any backcountry wandering is: *do not leave your vehicle*. If you do, you can become prey to various carnivores, lions in

of Tsavo's carrying capacity. After they had eaten all the grass and shrubs, the elephants tore down the trees to get at the bark and softer top branches. In the process, they fundamentally altered the vegetation of Tsavo West and turned Tsavo East from a forested savanna into desert and plains.

With vegetation depleted, drought followed. The elephants died by the thousands. As they began to recover, the poachers came to finish off those left. There are few elephants remaining in Tsavo now, but since the Kenyan government enforced proclamations to hunt

particular, alarm or irritate a passing herbivore (buffaloes and hippos kill more people in Kenya than lions do), or what's most likely, succumb to heat and dehydration. Unless you're positive no one will be looking for you, and that there's no way another vehicle will pass (overflights of most parks are common), stay in your car. *Always* let someone know (a park ranger or lodge personnel) before attempting any backcountry driving.

Only 20 years ago, Tsavo was host to the largest herds of elephants still left in Africa — with counts of up to 20,000 at a time. People who have seen them speak of elephants covering the entire surface of the land as far as the eye could see. But such a concentration led rapidly to a degradation

down poachers (including those with government ties), numbers are now recovering.

The outlook for the black rhino is bleaker. Thirty years ago, there were up to 9,000 in Tsavo alone; now there are none in Tsavo and probably fewer than 500 in Kenya. Only by massive international fund-raising efforts are numbers slowly starting to creep upwards.

To the north, Tsavo West extends up to the **Chyulu Hills**: steep volcanic hills that bump parallel to the main road, dividing the dispersion areas of Tsavo and Amboseli. The road from Tsavo West passes over lava beds so new that not a blade of grass has grown. To the north, the most recent cones stand naked and black. One, named Shetani ("devil" in Swahili), is thought to have erupted most recently 200 years ago; a trail of several kilometers winds around the flow but the lava has folded into many caves that shelter leopard, so check with the rangers at Kilaguni Gate before hiking.

Tsavo West's southern extent borders with Tanzania around the shores of Lake Jipe. Lake Jipe appears to have been visited by ancient Greek mariners whose belief that it was a source of the Nile was quoted by Ptolemy. Ptolemy's map of Africa, completed in the second century, was used well into the 1500s. Just north of the lake are the extensive sisal

Where to Stay

A number of excellent lodges in Tsavo West have, over recent years, suffered rather from the long-term consequences of drought and then poaching. The most expensive is **Finch Hattons (** (02) 604321 FAX (02) 604323 E-MAIL finchattons@iconnect.co.ke, Box 2443, Nairobi, with luxurious tents set around a hippo-filled spring (very expensive, full board). Service and cuisine is very smooth here, with crystal glass and silver.

Less formal is the **Voyager Safari Camp** (it used to be called Ziwani Tented Camp)

plantations begun by the eccentric and brilliant Captain Ewart Grogan, an incredibly wealthy timber exporter who in 1898 walked 7,250 km (4,500 miles) from Capetown to Cairo (supposedly for a fiancée he then decided not to marry), and later posted a mining claim on the city of Nairobi. Amid the sisal is **Grogan's Castle**, the huge, rambling, disorganized mansion that he built in the 1930s.

As pretty as Lake Jipe but less commercialized is **Lake Chala**. It straddles the Tanzania border 10 minutes north of **Taveta**. Follow the dirt road east of Taveta northward until you see a small hill: this is a crater, with Lake Chala inside it. Descend with care, there are crocodiles in the lake. Entry fees to the park are US$23 per adult and US$8 per child.

E-MAIL info@heritagehotels.co.ke WEB SITE www.heritagehotels.co.ke, Box 74888, Nairobi, to the west of the reserve (very expensive, full board). With just 20 comfortable tents and under the management of the very professional Heritage group this is a good place to stay, and because it is outside the park boundaries, it can offer walks and other activities. In the heart of the park, and surrounded by all its exuberant small animals, is **Kilaguni Serena Safari Lodge (** (02) 710511 FAX (02) 718103, Box 48690, Nairobi (very expensive, full board). Overlooking two busy waterholes, there's always some-

OPPOSITE: The magnificent views of Tsavo West are easily accessed. ABOVE: Mother lions are gentle with their cubs and ferocious in their defense.

thing to look at here. Even if it's out of your budget it's a good place to stop for lunch. East towards the Ngulia Rhino Sanctuary, **Ngulia Safari Lodge** ((0147) 2698, Box 42, Mtito Andei, is famous among ornithologists for the migrating birds from Russia and western Europe that stream by in autumn (expensive, full board). The lodge also offers self-catering *bandas* (inexpensive). The **Lake Jipe Lodge** ((02) 227623, Box 31097, Nairobi, on the shore of the lake is becoming run down, but does offer dhow trips on the lake (expensive).

Keep a fire going during the night to keep the more aggressive of predators at a distance, and be sure to leave nothing in your tent during the day, lest it fall prey to baboons or other primates.

There are excellent self-help *bandas* at **Ngulia** and **Kitani Safari Camps** (inexpensive, bring your own beverages and food), operated by Let's Go Travel ((02) 447151 or (02) 441030 FAX (02) 447270 or (02) 441690 E-MAIL info@letsgosafari.com WEB SITE www .letsgosafari.com, Box 60342, Nairobi, but these may be full in peak season.

If you've brought a tent, Tsavo is a great place to use it, even if just to store your gear: nothing can beat the millions of sharp, bright stars visible in Tsavo's clear night sky. There are good campsites in the park, as well as very inexpensive self-help *bandas*. One of the best is located just west of the **Chyulu Gate** (US$12 per person, payable at the gate). There are thatched verandahs to place a tent under or next to, along with fireplaces, running water, showers and toilets. You can also camp at the **Mtito Andei** and **Tsavo Gates**, not far from the Nairobi–Mombasa highway; at **Ziwani**, where there are more self-help *bandas*; and at **Lake Jipe** on the Tanzania frontier, with its astounding views of Kilimanjaro and Tanzania's Pare Mountains.

How to Get There

Tsavo West is on the main road between Nairobi and Mombasa, although it is rather nearer Mombasa and the coast. From Nairobi take the A109; how long the journey will take depends on the state of the road. Once the trip used to take six hours, but it has been known to take twice as long. The nearest gate to Nairobi is at Mtito Andei. From here it is 40 km (25 miles) to Mzima Springs. Tsavo Gate is 48 km (30 miles) closer to Mombasa, and a main access point for visitors from the coast. If traveling by public transportation, get off at Mtito Andei and pray for a lift with another tourist vehicle.

Looking like a desert outpost, Salt Lick Lodge provides a viewing platform for Kenya's wildlife.

Chyulu Hills

Now protected as a national park, the southern foothills of the Chyulus contain a couple of worthwhile establishments for the well-heeled, both run as Maasai community ranches. **Ol Donyo Wuas** ((02) 882521 FAX (02) 882728 E-MAIL Bonham.luke@swifkenya.com, Box 24133, Nairobi, is a small lodge run by Kenya legend Richard Bonham in partnership with the local Maasai (extremely expensive, all-inclusive). Stunning rooms make the most of views of Kilimanjaro, and even the toilets look directly out over the plains. Horse-riding is a specialty here, but access isn't: most guests fly in on private chartered planes, often Richard's own.

AMBOSELI

It's not just the animals that attract visitors to Amboseli National Park, but also magical Kilimanjaro, the largest mountain in Africa at 5,895 m (19,340 ft). Hemingway immortalized it in his *Snows of Kilimanjaro,* later filmed in Amboseli. When the border was being drawn between German Tanzania and British Kenya, Queen Victoria put a kink in the line to give the mountain, sight unseen, to her cousin, Emperor of Germany. As amusing as this story is, it reflects the callousness of the nineteenth-century partitioning of Africa, where all it took was the stroke of a pen to divide one country from another, and brother from brother.

Though Kilimanjaro seems so close from Amboseli's flat open plains, its peak is almost 50 km (31 miles) away, across the Tanzanian border, making it a major expedition for the Kenyan tourist. On your own, this means an extra visa for Tanzania, a re-entry visa for Kenya, road tax in Tanzania (approximately US$60), and US$20 (in United States currency only) per person for entry into the Kilimanjaro National Park. It may be wiser to return to Tanzania as a separate destination. If your aim is just to climb Kilimanjaro, bear in mind that Mount Kenya offers easier climbing to a higher altitude, without needing climbing gear, expertise and pre-planning, while taking the "Coca-Cola Route" up Kili is little more than a trudge. If you are dead set on visiting

Mount Kilimanjaro, Let's Go Travel can arrange a tour and help you with the visas.

For many who visit Amboseli, the mountain can be as elusive as its wildlife, but the early riser is usually rewarded with an unobscured view of Uhuru Peak, the summit, and Mawenzi, 5,151 m (16,900 ft). During the day, clouds usually play hide and seek about one or both peaks. Sometimes they become so thick you are unaware of the mountain's presence. If you have arrived on a cloudy afternoon, look to the south early the next morning. The mountain is so huge it is incredible how it can completely disappear.

Even without Kilimanjaro, Amboseli, just a four-hour drive from Nairobi, has much to offer. It has a unique ecosystem and variety of game. There are five different wildlife habitats — the seasonal lake bed of Lake Amboseli, swamps and marshes with a few sulfur springs, open plains, yellow-barked acacia woodlands, and lava rock thornbush country. It's not huge, at 392 sq ķm (151 sq miles), and a couple of days are enough to cover most of the paths.

Amboseli is probably the best place to watch elephants in Kenya; if you'd like to learn more about them, *Elephant Memories* by Cynthia Moss, an American scientist who has studied them in Amboseli since 1972, is the best book available.

In recent years, poaching has driven many elephants into Amboseli, where Moss's research project has followed their lives and where, perhaps, the presence of many scientists and observers has provided a slight protection. Nonetheless, the poaching continues. *Elephant Memories* chronicles one example: "Torn Ear was just reaching for a small succulent herb that was nestled in amongst the grass when a quick movement to her left caught her eye. She whirled toward the movement and there were two men only 30 yards away. Without hesitation she put her head down and charged toward them. She did not even hear the explosion before the bullet ripped through the light airy bone of her forehead and penetrated deep into her brain. She was dead by the time she fell forward onto her head and tusks and skidded along the ground for several feet from the momentum of her charge. Her son was hit next, first in the shoulder, which made him scream with pain and rage, and then through his side into his heart … The men turned and began to run but let off one volley of shots, missing most of the elephants but catching Tina in the chest with a shot that went into her right lung … it took seven shots in her head and neck and shoulders before Wendy fell and died.

"Teresia took them to the far side of Meshanani, a small hill up on the ridge above the lake. There was some protection here, and Tina could go no farther. The blood pouring from her mouth was bright red and her sides were heaving for breath. The other elephants

Every tourist who visits the game parks of Kenya is helping to protect the elephants by manifesting his or her interest in Africa's wildlife. In addition, we can all help by refusing ever to purchase any item made of ivory, even if it's sold as an "antique," by adding our support to the East African Wildlife Society, the World Wildlife Fund and other conservation groups, and by joining in international efforts to discourage ivory smuggling which is almost entirely organized by Japan, Taiwan, Hong Kong and China.

crowded around, reaching for her. Her knees started to buckle and she began to go down, but Teresia got on one side of her and Trista on the other and they both leaned in and held her up. Soon, however, she had no strength and she slipped beneath them and fell onto her side. More blood gushed from her mouth and with a shudder she died.

"Teresia and Trista became frantic and knelt down and tried to lift her up. They worked their tusks under her back and under her head. At one point they succeeded in lifting her into a sitting position but her body flopped back down. Her family tried everything to rouse her, kicking and tusking her, and Tallulah even went off and collected a trunkful of grass and tried to stuff it into her mouth …"

Despite the continuing threat of poachers, the elephants of Amboseli have become accustomed to tourist vehicles, and they generally will not flee if you wish to sit and watch them as they go about their daily routine — showers, dust baths, around 16 to 18 hours of grazing and playful bouts of rock or stick throwing.

You can also expect to see waterbucks, Maasai giraffes, buffaloes, Coke's hartebeests, common zebras, elands, gazelles and impalas. Cheetah and lion sightings are almost sure bets.

Entry to Amboseli is US$27, children US$10 and vehicles are charged at Ksh200.

Zebras, like domestic horses, are playful and generally unafraid to block the road.

Where to Stay

Among the better lodges in the park are: **Amboseli Serena Lodge (** (02) 710511 FAX (02) 718103, Box 48690, Nairobi (very expensive, full board), and **Tortilis Camp (** (02) 748307/27 FAX (0154) 22553 or (02) 740721 E-MAIL cheli peacock@africaonline.co.ke WEB SITE www .chelipeacock.com, Box 39806, Nairobi (extremely expensive, all-inclusive). Less good than they used to be are **Amboseli Lodge** and **Kilimanjaro Safari Lodge** both **(** (02) 227136

At Namanga, a pretty town 75 km (47 miles) west of Amboseli on the border with Tanzania, is the **River Hotel (** (02) 330775, Box 4, Namanga, a very scenic array of cottages under shady acacias with a good restaurant serving Kenyan cuisine. The rate is Ksh1,500 bed and breakfast for doubles. Camping is also available at Ksh150 per person. Also in Namanga are a couple of cheaper *hotelis*. Since Namanga lies on the direct route south from Nairobi to Amboseli, it can make a nice stop for lunch, or for the night if you're taking your time or started late.

FAX (02) 219982, Box 30193, Nairobi (expensive, full board). Near Lemito Gate is the slightly dilapidated **Kilimanjaro Buffalo Lodge (** (02) 227136 FAX (02) 219982, Box 72630, Oloitokitok (expensive, full board). **Ol Tukai Lodge (** (02) 540780 FAX (02) 543810 E-MAIL blockreservations@net2000ke.com, Box 40075, Nairobi (expensive, full board), near Cynthia Moss's elephant research station, is better.

South of Serena Lodge is a **campground** run by the Maasai (Ksh600 per person). Sites are flat, dry and well-spaced, usually with water but few amenities. The wildlife is so tame that elephants and giraffes often pass through. Most campers leave a large fire burning upon retiring. Because of the nearby marshes, mosquito netting is a must.

The Eastern Plains

How to Get There

From Nairobi, join the lines of heavy traffic heading southeast on the Mombasa Road. Turn right 25 km (16 miles) out of town, onto the A104 towards Arusha. At Namanga, 165 km (103 miles) south, turn left onto the C103 for the final 75 km (47 miles) to Amboseli on dirt road. By public transportation it is easy to get to Namanga but hard thereafter. Hitching will be your only option. The quickest way to get to Amboseli is with Airkenya , which flies at 7:30 AM daily from Wilson Airport (US$88).

LEFT: Mount Kilimanjaro's snow-capped peak. ABOVE: Kilimanjaro Lodge in Amboseli.

The Coast

Throughout time, Kenya's coast has had a separate, but connected, history to the inland cultures. This remains somewhat true today. For tourists, there's a great difference between a coastal resort and a game park lodge.

Coastal development has primarily catered to those who wish to relax in the sun, dine well and be entertained at night. Most Kenyan coastal resorts are like those at Miami Beach or the Caribbean, with the major difference being that they generally cost less. However they also offer the opportunity to explore Kenya, whether the inland world of

The Indian Ocean offers some of the best snorkeling and diving in the world. The water is calm and crystal clear during the dry months, and the marine life is astounding. Because there are relatively few motorized coastal fishing boats (one deep-sea fisherman estimates that there are fewer than 300 for the entire 480-km/300-mile coast and fewer than 20 north of Kilifi), fish here can reach enormous sizes.

In the marine parks at Malindi, Watamu Bay and Shimoni, the coral reefs grow relatively undisturbed with resident populations

game and parks or the coastal life of weekend discos and local restaurants.

Typical coastal development is based on large hotels catering for sun 'n' sand visitors. Luckily, there are exceptions: notably the areas of Watamu Bay, Lamu, and Shimoni.

As the coastal resorts have been developed mainly for and by the European market, there is a preference for employees speaking Italian, German and English. Unlike the practice in other parts of Kenya, Swahili is the first, and often the only, language spoken at home. Beach-boys concentrate on the main resort strips north and south of Mombasa; travel further, or stay in any area for length of time, and you are rarely bothered.

of fish so numerous and colorful as to defy description. Outside the parks, however, the coastal coral reefs have been abused, and fishing keeps the shoal size down. At low tide, you can walk along the beaches and find pools that often contain small fish and a variety of crustaceans. You can also watch the fishermen setting nets from the shore or dhows. In recent years, the spear gun has been introduced. Many a young fisherman, weaned from his canoe carved from a mango tree by offers of nets from the West, has now progressed to goggles, snorkel and spear-gun to earn his livelihood.

OPPOSITE: Traditional Arab dhows still ply the coast of Kenya. ABOVE: The old and the new blend in Mombasa's skyline.

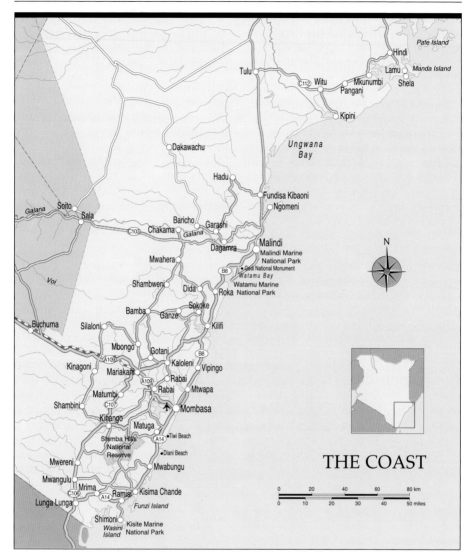

THE COAST

| 0 | 20 | 40 | 60 | 80 km |
| 0 | 10 | 20 | 30 | 40 | 50 miles |

Except at river inlets and bays, the ocean bottom slopes gently out to wide fringing and barrier reefs. There are three main reefs, starting with the sheltering onshore reef, often exposed at low tide and heading out to three kilometers (two miles) offshore, a fertile home to the ocean's big fish some 30 m (100 ft) below sea level. Occasional small atolls, such as at Shimoni, complete the wide variety of habitats that make Kenya's coast the marine treasure-trove of East Africa. The water near the shore is heated to surprisingly high temperatures. Average monthly temperatures for offshore surface waters vary from 25°C (77°F) in the fall to 29°C (84°F) in

the spring; at low tide, it's possible to find shallow pools over 35°C (95°F). Even at high tide, the coastal water is warm and it's possible to swim for hours without getting cold. As the sun sets and beaches become shaded, it's often warmer in the water than out, although the coastal breeze is more likely to cool than chill.

Kenya's coastal beaches are of the finest white sand. During and after the northeast trade winds, called the *kaskazi* (December to April), they are swept clean by an offshore current and virtually no debris is present. Unfortunately, a change of direction, precipitation and current during and after the southeast trade winds or *kusi* (May to November) brings seaweed to shore. This is the coast's low season and bargain hotel prices can be negotiated, especially in the north around Watamu, while further north still, in Lamu and Kiwayu, most hotels close completely. The seas run high and there is daily rain. Many of the deep-sea fishermen take their boats out of the water, but in any case they are unable to ride the reef out to the open sea. Further south, around Diani, Mombasa and Shimoni, the weather is less severe and beach surf breaks from July onwards are fine.

High season on the coast is December through mid-February. Rain is infrequent, the water is calm, snorkeling is excellent, the fish are numerous, and there is usually enough wind to make windsurfing exciting. Even if you are not interested in sailing, the breeze will be welcome, because without it, the heat and humidity can be exhausting.

The pace of life along the coast is slow. "Coasties" are famously more laid-back than their "upcountry" brothers. For these Islamic believers, life is tranquilly easy. Traditionally, there has been an abundance of fish for the taking, bananas, coconuts, mangoes and papayas grow wild, and small garden plots supply plentiful vitamins for a family's sustenance. No wonder it's hard to find labor to work in the tourist industry.

In dress and architecture, the Arab influence, dating from as early as the sixth century, is undeniable, particularly in the ancient towns of Lamu, Malindi and Old Mombasa. The elegance of the thirteenth through fifteenth centuries, the height of coastal Kenya's power and affluence, has disappeared, but in the ruins of Gedi and the island of Lamu, you can still capture a glimpse of the past.

Reminders of the period of Portuguese domination during the sixteenth and seventeenth centuries are Mombasa's Fort Jesus and a small chapel and monument in Malindi. This period created much disruption but left little mark on the daily life of the native Kenyans. Although Catholicism endured in the Portuguese colonies of the New World, it never really took hold in Muslim coastal Kenya, and once the Portuguese left, so did their influence.

As in earlier times, the coast today is separated into individual spheres of influence. There is Mombasa with its northern resort strips, linking into a nightlife center but with beaches that recede at low tide to the distant horizon. To the south are the self-sufficient resorts of Tiwi and Diani. For the independent traveler the best areas are further afield The first place of interest is quietly charming Kilifi, then Watamu Bay for deep-sea fishing and the offshore marine park, then the nightlife resort of Malindi with its Italian restaurants and casinos. A short air hop reaches Kenya's northern coast, the Swahili island of Lamu, and a mangrove coast leading up to the exclusive hideaways of Kiwayu.

Head south from Mombasa over the Likoni Ferry to Tiwi and Diani Beaches, and further south towards Tanzania to Shimoni, with the offshore Wasini Island and the marine park of Kisite.

The road between Malindi and Shimoni is paved and in relatively good condition — one roadside stop is proudly called the "New Surface" café. This link makes it easy to reach the different marine parks, ruins, coastal forests, wildlife areas and old towns that line Kenya's shore. The road to Malindi is also good, but from there north to Lamu and Pate becomes a bit of a challenge. Unpaved, and often impassable during the rains, even in good weather it is an endurance test and best circumvented by a short air hop.

MOMBASA

Mombasa is Kenya's second largest city and its only deepwater port. In many ways, it is the country's lifeline to the world. Once a scarcely developed island in a mangrove-lined bay with dhows in the harbor, today Mombasa is crowded and busy with container berths at Kilindini ("place of deep water") on the west side of the island. The surrounding mainland sprawls with industrial development and suburbs.

There are no bathing beaches on Mombasa Island, so you may choose not to stay here, but the Old Town and Fort Jesus will make one- or two-day trips worthwhile.

Mombasa appears on Ptolemy's map as Tonika, and was probably the most sophisticated and largest of the coastal city-states in Kenya in the early days. It resisted Portuguese domination in the fifteenth and sixteenth centuries and was looted and burned by them on four separate occasions. As a result, only a few archaeological remains of its early glory have been found. It is interesting to note that Mombasa's population in 1500 was estimated at 10,000, roughly the same as medieval London. Fort Jesus remains a reminder of the eventual Portuguese victory that cost the lives of every native of Mombasa who had not fled the island, and ultimately every Portuguese stationed there.

After the Portuguese came a period of Omani control that was scarcely more peaceful, as the governing Mazuri family and the Sultan were constantly at odds. These differences led directly to reluctant British involvement in Kenya when Mombasa became a protectorate.

From the end of the nineteenth century until 1906, Mombasa boomed. Government buildings were erected and affluent Indian merchants constructed large two- and three-story houses along the main roads. Most of the Old Town dates from this period. In 1906, the government headquarters moved to Nairobi, but Mombasa still remained Kenya's major commercial and industrial center until after World War I. Though still a major industrial center today, Mombasa has lost its former splendor.

GENERAL INFORMATION

Grandly surveyed by the much-photographed arch of twin tusks, Mombasa's business center is along Moi Avenue, which splits in the east into Nkrumah and Makarada Roads, and this is where you'll find the police station, most travel agents, banks, airlines and banks. To the east, nearest the coast, are the most interesting areas: the brooding bulk of Fort Jesus, and the Old Town. This is best explored on foot, with an early start to avoid the sultry heat of a tropical midday.

Unusually for Kenya, there is a **Tourist Information Office** ((011) 225428 FAX (011) 228208 E-MAIL mcta@africaonline.co.ke, Box 99596, in Moi Avenue near the tusks, which is open 8 AM to noon and 2 PM to

4:30 PM Monday to Friday, and 8 AM to noon Saturday. The staff are, however, more enthusiastic than effective as they suffer a characteristic shortage of printed material.

Taxis, generally can be found at all the sites of tourist interest, but **Kenatco** ((011) 227503 offers a fixed-price, 24-hour alternative. In case of medical problems **Panddya Memorial Hospital** ((011) 314140, Dedan Kimathi Avenue, has an ambulance service and full medical facilities. Out of hours, this is where you'll have to go to buy medicaments, though **Yudah Pharmaceuticals** ((011) 316028, Duruma

Road, is open from 9 AM to 10 PM Monday to Friday, and until 8 PM on Saturday. If you're heading out to the bush, temporary coverage can be arranged with **Africa Air Rescue** (AAR) ((011) 312405, Harbour House, Moi Avenue. If you need to check your e-mail there are a couple of cybercafés, with more opening daily. Try the **Online Café** ((011) 220008, Yusuf Ali Mansion, Moi Avenue, open 8 AM to 7 PM weekdays, or **Clicks Netcafe** ((011) 221579, Superior House, Makarada Road, open 8 AM to 6 PM.

WHAT TO SEE AND DO

Mombasa is built on an island. A causeway heads inland — and to the airport — while the relatively new Nyali Bridge heads off to link up the northern resorts of Nyali, Bamburi and beyond. Access to the south and Diani Beach is by the endlessly shuttling Likoni Ferry. Don't try to save money by swimming across as sharks are plentiful and have very urban appetites.

Old Town

The streets of Mombasa's Old Town are narrow and not designed for automobiles. They are just wide enough for a camel or a donkey with panniers to pass, or for the hand carts (*mkototnei* or *hamaili*) still used in the area today.

Although most of the buildings date no earlier than the early 1900s, they often stand on older foundations, and show strong Arab influence. The Fort Jesus gift shop sells an excellent historical guide, *The Old Town Mombasa*, which gives a history of the town and details for a self-guided walking tour. With it, you can trace the lines where the Portuguese built a wall to separate the "Cidade dos Portugusos" (Portuguese City) and the "Cidade dos Moros" (Moorish or Swahili City). But nothing remains of the wall that was said to be one and a half meters (five feet) wide with several towers and three gates.

The Old Town has numerous mosques, each built by different groups of Muslims arriving at various times in Kenya. There are many colorful buildings with intricate grillwork, a few with fretted balconies. The carved wooden doors described by Portuguese chroniclers have long ago disappeared, many lost when the Portuguese burned the city, but the stone *baraga* seats are still found flanking the doors of many Old Town houses. Examples of carved doors can be seen in Fort Jesus; the best surviving examples grace homes in Lamu, further north on the coast.

Mombasa also boasts Kenya's first public library, as well as an open-air pavilion, Jubilee Hall, built to commemorate Queen Victoria's diamond jubilee in 1897. There's also Government Square, a hub of colonial activity in the 1890s. Glen's Building was named for a dog called Glen owned by a government official, Sir Ali bin Salim. The dog appears in many photos of Sir bin Salim taken at state functions.

Fort Jesus

Fort Jesus, a national historical monument, is a testimony to the determination of the Portuguese to control the coast of Kenya, and to the tenacity of Mombasa's inhabitants in retaining their identity and culture. Once inside (entry fee is Ksh350 per person), you are isolated from everyday Mombasa, just as the Portuguese were. The fortress is not unlike medieval castles along the Mediterranean.

The fort is very well maintained. Several major buildings and the ramparts looking toward the sea are restored. In one barracks

room, drawings of ships, churches, and figures in armor have been uncovered, revealing the longing of many Portuguese sailors for a more familiar home. There are the foundations of a chapel, a storeroom, and dwellings or shops against the inland wall. Fort Jesus is impressive, and although it might lack some of the charm and romance of European fortresses it catches the nervous isolation of Europe's first settlers, the Portuguese sailors charged with maintaining a precarious toehold on the East African shore, where threats came from both land and sea.

OPPOSITE: The strong influence of Islam on the coast results in many mosques. ABOVE: Fort Jesus in Mombasa: "Nothing remains but deathless fascination."

There are several carved doors in the fortress, not original, but hung for display. Also preserved are chambers with carved beams and inlaid inscriptions that were decorated by the Omani after they defeated the Portuguese in the eighteenth century. These rooms are reminiscent of the splendor of the Moorish castles of Spain, a few with traces of poetry similar to that which embellishes the Alhambra.

A museum in the main courtyard houses "treasures" from the wreck of the *Santo Antonio de Tanna*, which sank in Mombasa Harbor in 1697. The museum also has an extensive display of pottery recovered along the coast. Some of these are over 1,000 years old, from as far away as China. The pottery finds are keyed to the ancient settlements and ruins along the coast. This is a good place to begin if you plan to tour the coastal ruins. It also has a small collection of Swahili artifacts from Old Town Mombasa.

The fort has a gift shop selling reasonably priced craft items and an excellent selection of books on Mombasa and the coast. Proceeds from the shop help support restoration and maintenance of the site. You can tour the fort by yourself, as it is adequately marked, or you can hire a guide. The guides are very well-informed and can usually give their tour in Swahili, Italian, German or English.

SHOPPING

Mombasa is a rather more restful place to look for handicrafts and fabrics than Nairobi, with a relaxed, tropical heat calming the bargaining process and a provincial moderation muting some of the opening prices. Thanks to its long tradition of coastal trading it is also important for fabrics, all neatly contained in a single, specialized street, Biashara Road, where *kangas* are the specialty, brightly-colored textiles with proverbs (generally in Swahili) making the cloth more memorable. The main tourist shopping area is along Moi Avenue, from the Tusks to Digo Road, and gets more hassle as you go along. A good place to visit first is Haria's Gift Shop on Moi Avenue (near the tusks), which gives a good idea of the "correct" prices.

WHERE TO STAY

Most people staying here cross Nyali Bridge to the north and choose one of the many resort hotels that line the coast. These are listed later on under THE SOUTH COAST, page 267, and under NORTH OF MOMBASA, page 271.

There are those, however, who prefer to stay in the city itself, even though water supplies are erratic and, in the wet season (April to June, October to early December), what water there is needs to be purified. Perhaps because Mombasa Island lacks a beach, recent years have seen many of the city center hotels deteriorate if not close down completely. The remaining establishments are good value. The **Lotus Hotel** ((011) 313207 FAX (011) 220673, Box 90193, Mvita and Cathedral Road, is probably the best but is often full (inexpensive, B&B). The **Royal Court Hotel** ((011) 223379 FAX (011) 312398, Box 41247, Haile Selassie Road, is centrally located, but avoid the single rooms, which are oppressively small (mid-range, B&B).

For less expensive rooms, there's the decaying charm of the **New Palm Hotel** ((011) 311756, Nkruma Road (inexpensive, B&B). The **YWCA** is on the junction of Kaunda and Kiamba Avenues: good in that it takes both men and women, bad in that it caters mainly to stays of a month or longer.

If you want to stay at the ocean for a week or so, you might consider renting a house or cottage. Prices range from Ksh750 per day for one bedroom to Ksh10,000 per day for a villa. **Let's Go Travel** ((02) 447151 or (02)

441030 FAX (02) 447270 or (02) 441690 E-MAIL info@letsgosafari.com WEB SITE www.letsgo safari.com, Box 60342, Nairobi, can make advance reservations or help with immediate reservations. Reservations are rarely necessary except during December, January and August. Travel agents in Mombasa usually have listings of houses available up and down the coast. You can also ask residents when you find an area where you'd like to stay. The houses are generally sparsely furnished, but come with cook and housekeeper. Though the cook and housekeeper get a wage

from the owner or manager, it's customary to leave Ksh500 for each of them for each week you're there.

Both north and south of Mombasa are numerous coastal resorts. Each hotel at least tries to have its own appeal, and the quality and type of food varies. Most are relatively modern, have standard resort accommodations and quote prices in United States dollars or sterling. To head south along the coast from Mombasa Island means using the Likoni ferry, which makes the southern resorts feel pleasantly isolated from the bustle of city life, and the beaches are better than

OPPOSITE: Even in Fort Jesus the Portuguese were never safe. ABOVE: Mombasa's sun sets to the distant call of countless muezzins.

those an equivalent distance from town to the north. Accommodation options in these resorts are listed below.

WHERE TO EAT

Even if you don't stay in town, Old Town Mombasa is one of the best places in Kenya to experience the local cuisine. An excellent stop for lunch after visiting Fort Jesus is **Surya Restaurant** on Nyeri Street, Mombasa's best Ethiopian restaurant. The wood-paneled front room has plastic tablecloths and is aimed at the local market. Behind is a large, shaded courtyard with traditional furniture and rather smarter style. Whenever you eat at local restaurants wash your hands in the sink provided or in the jug and bowl brought to you as not to do so is considered very rude. And as in all Muslim societies, eat only with your right hand. Food is served on a base of *ngara*, a flat Ethiopian bread that also serves as knife and fork. Mounds of spiced meats and vegetables are designed to be picked at and shared, with costs in the range of Ksh200 per person. The Surya is open for lunch and dinner.

A few doors up is Mombasa's best Swahili restaurant, **Recoda**, but it opens only for dinner. If you're early enough you can sit outside at sidewalk tables and watch the inhabitants go about their evening routine. There is no menu: the waiters will explain what has been prepared for the day, usually mild curry-flavored stews, fish cooked in coconut milk and *pilau* (spiced rice with meat). Desserts include iced, pureed papaya with slices of orange, mango and banana, or chilled, pureed avocado with milk and spices. Prices, once again, in the region of Ksh200 per person. Don't expect a wine list — or even a beer — at these two restaurants, but they will provide cutlery if you ask. They're both worth visiting for the excellently prepared and quite unique food, and I'm still trying to work out which I prefer.

HOW TO GET THERE

The main road from Nairobi, the A109, links Mombasa with Nairobi, 485 km (303 miles) away. Several buses leave Nairobi every day for Mombasa, but although the road is being repaired, a journey that once took as little as six hours now can often take twice as long. Don't complain too much: not so long ago it could easily have taken 20 hours or more. The best service is with **The Connection** ((011) 221361, Vogue Travel, Jubilee Insurance Building, Moi Avenue, Ksh1,000. There are other bus companies charging half as much, such as **Akamba** ((011) 316770, Jomo Kenyatta Avenue, Mombasa.

An overnight train links the two cities and takes 12 hours. Reservations are essential for traveling first or second class; two or three days in advance are generally enough to secure a berth. Without a reservation you'll end up traveling on the benches in third. Reservations can be made in person at Nairobi Station, one and a half kilometers (one mile) from the city center on Station Road, or at Mombasa Station, on Haile Selassie Avenue. Rather less securely, reservations are apparently taken by telephone — Nairobi ((02) 221211, Mombasa ((011) 312221 — or perhaps are easiest through a travel agent such as **Let's Go Travel** ((02) 447151 or (02) 441030 FAX (02) 447270 or (02) 441690 E-MAIL info@letsgosafari.com WEB SITE www.letsgosafari.com, Box 60342, Nairobi.

Alternatively, many visitors arrive at Mombasa's Moi International Airport, which is on the mainland 10 km (six and a half miles) from the city. Although there are no scheduled flights from Europe into Mombasa there are plenty of direct charter arrivals. Domestically, **Kenya Airways** ((02) 210771 or (02) 229291 FAX (02) 336252, Box 41010, Nairobi, and ((011) 221251 FAX (011) 313815, Box 99302, Mombasa, flies five times every day from Nairobi International Airport for US$80. **Airkenya** ((011) 229777/229106 FAX (011) 224063, TSS Nkrumah Road, Mombasa, with an office at the airport ((011) 433982 FAX (011) 435235 E-MAIL info@airkenya .com, WEB SITE www.airkenya.com, Box 84700, Mombasa, also runs up to six flights a day from Nairobi's Wilson Airport, with one-way tickets costing Ksh5,385. The flights take an hour and a half. Airkenya also has flights up to Malindi, Lamu and Kiwayu. There's also a very useful daily flight provided from Mombasa to the Masai Mara operated by **Blue Bird Aviation** ((02) 602338 FAX (02) 602337, Box 62045, Nairobi.

Fixed-fare taxis head from the airport to the major resorts, while those going on safari will usually leave directly from the airport.

AROUND MOMBASA

Around Mombasa, there are several sites to lure you from the beach, or to occupy your time if you've overdone the sun. All these can be easily reached from Mombasa's satellite resorts in Diani to the south, or the northern resort areas.

could worship. Near the north-facing wall of the mosque are several tombs, one of which has an interesting inscription, which translated reads: "Every soul shall taste death. You will simply be paid your wages in full on the Day of Resurrection. He who is removed from the fire and made to enter heaven, it is he who has won the victory. The earthly life is only delusion."

Entrance fee to Jumba is Ksh200; you can buy a guidebook to the site at the entrance. The ruins are smaller and less intricately planned than Gedi to the north, but after a

JUMBA LA MTWANA NATIONAL MONUMENT

A short drive north along the coastal highway, just past Mtwapa Bridge, is **Jumba la Mtwana National Monument**, ruins of a fourteenth-century town. Situated right on the beach, the town, whose Swahili name means "Mansion of the Slaves," gives one the impression that at its peak Jumba was much more in the mainstream of coastal commerce, with nearby Mtwapa Creek as a safe anchorage. The site is dotted with the giant-trunked baobabs, some of which could have existed when Jumba was inhabited.

The most interesting of the ruins is the mosque by the sea. According to archaeologists, it has a separate room in which women

wander around you can stroll onto the beach, which has a stand of aerial rooted pines, the mangroves of the pine family.

BAMBURI NATURE TRAIL

Closer to town is Bamburi Nature Trail (open daily, Ksh500 per person), the most zoo-like park you'll find in Kenya. There are somewhat tame hippos called Sally, Potti and Cleopatra, aldabra tortoises, crocodiles, a tilapia aquaculture project that produces over 30 tons of fish per year, pelicans, crowned cranes, antelopes, and a family of serval cats. An attached restaurant called

The coastal mangrove swamps are a dense haven for bird life.

Whispering Pines is good for lunch. Set amongst the casuarina trees it provides a welcome breath of the bush experience at a cost of about Ksh400 per person. Thursdays to Saturday the restaurant stays open for evening meals.

The nature trail is a rehabilitated quarry owned by the Bamburi Cement Factory, which moves its operation north and west as its mining techniques dictate. The quarry revegetation began in 1971 with the planting of hardy casuarina trees from Australia. Now a dense forest of whistling pines has taken

To get the most of a trip to the reserve, consider staying a night. If you're equipped (food, cooking equipment and mosquito nets), there are the superb **Shimba Hills Self-Service Bandas** (US$10 per person) overlooking a steep, thickly-vegetated ravine where the air is cool and refreshingly dry. The view east is magnificent and the sunrise across the Indian Ocean is beyond description.

Alternatively, **Shimba Hills Lodge (** (02) 540780 FAX (02) 543810 E-MAIL blockreservations @net2000ke.com, Box 40075, Nairobi (expensive, half board), is a night-viewing lodge built

hold and the ground below is starting to recover its fertility.

SHIMBA HILLS NATIONAL RESERVE

Even if your primary interest is the beach and the sun, you shouldn't pass up an opportunity to explore at least one of Kenya's game parks and see the animals. Easily accessible from the coastal highway is Shimba Hills National Reserve. Wildlife here is not as abundant as in Amboseli or the Masai Mara, but you can often see the rare sable antelope. With luck, you can find genets, elephants and civet cats and, occasionally, leopards. Entry fees are US$20 per person per day, US$5 per child, and Ksh500 per vehicle.

along the same lines as Treetops (see THE ABERDARE MOUNTAINS, page 208) but with infinitely more style and charm. Children under seven are not permitted. Shimba Hills is a good coastal version, a sturdy and comfortable tree-house in the heart of dense jungle. If Shimba is the only wildlife reserve you will visit, by all means stay at the lodge for a night. Elephants occasionally visit the waterhole and bushbabies are attracted to the activities. Shimba Hills National Reserve is the only place where you'll find the rare sable antelope, which can be seen along with other game on the morning or the evening game drives.

The lodge overlooks an emerald glade of dense coastal rainforest with giant cycads. In the early morning and late afternoon, you can sometimes see a leopard; giant monitor lizards are numerous. Animals are now well used to whispering visitors in their domain. There have been sightings of elephants at night, but these are rare at present.

Nearby — but just outside Shimba Hills National Park — is the **Mwalugange Elephant Sanctuary** (US$10 entry), a community-based project to protect a large population of elephants marooned by encroaching human development and preserve their migratory routes. Accommodation here is at **Travelers Mwalugange Elephant Camp** ((0127) 51202 E-MAIL travellershtl@swift mombasa.com, Box 87649, Mombasa (very expensive). Reservations can also be made through **Traveler's Beach Hotel** ((011) 485121 FAX 485678, Box 87649, Mombasa.

How to Get There

Shimba Hills is 30 km (19 miles) southwest of Mombasa, and even nearer Diani Beach Resort, while the access road to Mwalugange, just to the northwest of the reserve, is slightly more demanding. Although it is an easy drive in your own vehicle, it is easier and usually cheaper to buy a package to Shimba from one of Mombasa's travel agents.

RABAI

A 45-minute drive west of Mombasa (towards Nairobi, turning north at Mazeras on C-107) is Rabai, site of Krapf and Rebmann's mission. It was from here that they left on their separate expeditions, which led to the mapping of Mounts Kenya and Kilimanjaro. The ruins of Krapf's house can be seen; Rebmann's is still occupied. The people of Rabai will be glad to show you around.

Krapf departed on several expeditions from this mission at Rabai. He became the first white man to cross the Tsavo River, to explore the Yatta Plateau in what is now Tsavo East National Park, and to locate Mount Kenya. Local tribesmen had described the mountain as taller than Mount Kilimanjaro, which no one had climbed because of "the intense cold and the white matter which rolled down with great noise" — a reference to the snow avalanches that now, with world climate change, no longer occur on Mount Kenya.

THE SOUTH COAST

Heading south from Mombasa means using the Likoni Ferry, which shuttles cars and flooding pedestrians across 400 m (a quarter of a mile) of water to the mainland and the southern strip of the B8 coast road. This tends to give the southern resort areas a more timeless, relaxing atmosphere even though, as the crow flies, they are quite close to the city. The beaches tend to be better than those an equivalent distance north of Mombasa, with the ocean — and the fringing coral reef — nearer to land.

Thread straight through the suburb of Likoni, scene of some of the worst disturbances in the 1997 elections and still with an uneasy atmosphere. This quickly fades. Although some hotels have been built on the shore here as Likoni Beach merges into Shelley Beach — it's not especially recommended: the sea goes a long way out at low tide and it's prone to seaweed. If you do want to stay here, try the **Anglican Church of Kenya Guest House (ACK)** ((011) 451619, Box 96170, Mombasa, which is good value, and convenient for public transportation although a bit of a walk from the beach (inexpensive, B&B).

TIWI BEACH

It's better to carry on south: after 20 km (12.5 miles) two turns to the left head off into the small, cottagey atmosphere of Tiwi Beach, four kilometers (two and a half miles) from the B8 coastal road. Traditionally this area is popular with Kenya residents and backpackers who shudder alike every time they see the enormous Traveler's Beach Hotel that has been built on the coast and stay instead in a range of smaller chalet-type developments. Few *matatus* mean that visitors without a car will find most of Tiwi's beach lodges feel quite isolated; access is by taxi or rental car and the pleasures quiet, beach-based ones. One of the best is **Tiwi Sea Castles** ((0127) 51220 FAX (0127) 51222, Box 96599, Likoni (inexpensive, B&B), while another is **Sand Island Beach Cottages**

Craftsman sculpts attractive tropical hardwoods for tourists.

((0127) 51233 FAX (0127) 51201 E-MAIL hat field@form-net.com, Box 5516, Diani, which is closed May and June (mid-range, B&B). Both conform to the general pattern of lodges here, which is to have self-contained cottages, ideal for families, where guests stay for weeks — or months. The liveliest bar is at **Twiga Lodge** ((0127) 51267, Box 96005, Mombasa, which also has rooms (but not very good ones).

DIANI BEACH

Ten kilometers (six miles) further south at the small town of Ukunda a left turn leads down to the resort of Diani, the most developed stretch of Kenya's coast. There's even a **Tourist Office** (0127) 2227 FAX (0127) 2156, Box 702, Ukunda, behind the Agip Gas Station, 8 AM to 1 PM, 2 PM to 5 PM Monday to Friday. There's a taxi rank here as well.

Treating where the road from Ukunda meets the coast road as point zero, the resort spreads out to north and south. Generally, the southern direction is better, passing most of the major hotels, a couple of small shopping centers and most of the best restaurants and nightclubs before becoming, once more, unspoiled. There's more forest squeezing between the vacation-style resorts, and colobus monkeys swing around. One kilometer (less than a mile) north of point zero is the small **Diani Beach Hospital** ((0127) 2435/6, beside the Diani Complex shopping center.

What to See and Do
The classic Diani activities are scuba diving on the fringing reef or game fishing out in deeper waters. For game fishing, **Grand Slam Charters** are endlessly helpful and accommodating, while the best dive operator is **Dive the Crab**. Both are bookable through **Safari Beach Hotel** ((0127) 2726 FAX (0127) 2357, Box 90690, Mombasa. Day-trips from Diani head down to Kenya's deep south for the very best diving: Shimoni, the offshore island of Wasini, and the Marine National Park of Kisite. At a cost of US$80 (US$85 if you're being picked up from the northern resorts) these excursions include a sail by dhow out to the best snorkeling area and an after-swim feast of crab and seafood

that renders most people comatose. Fortunately wicker beds are laid out under trees. Reserve through **Kisite Dhow Tours** ((0127) 2331 FAX (0127) 3154, Box 281, Ukunda. There are plenty of other dhow operators offering day-trips. Amongst the best are **Kimazini Funzi Dhow Safaris** ((0127) 3182, Diani Beach Shopping Centre, who tour Funzi Creek, visit local schools and have lunch on a desert island; and **Funzi Island Lazy Lagoon** ((011) 225546 FAX (011) 316458, Box 90246, Bodo Village, with a range of tours, including bird- and croc-watching. All pick up guests from their lodges. Away from the water, Leisure Lodge, north of the junction, has an 18-hole golf course. Jadini Forest breaks out between developments to the south, providing a refuge for countless colobus monkeys.

Where to Stay
Most of the hotels here depend on European tour operators for their business: walk-in rates, for room only unless otherwise stated, are steep and trade discounts are huge. Generally, therefore, it is cheaper to buy a package vacation from home. There are exceptions: most notably a small Seychellois restaurant called **Boko Boko** (/FAX (0127) 2344 (inexpensive) at the northern tip of the resort road, opposite Neptune Village Hotel; they have four en-suite guest rooms available. This represents exceptional value here. The German-run **Diani Beachalets** ((0127) 2180, Box 26 Ukunda, is a well-run place with a range of accommodation options to suit all budgets (very inexpensive to inexpensive), and is quietly set south of the main Warandale Cottages.

Otherwise it's back to international-standard luxury. Four kilometers (three miles) south of point zero is the sophisticated but welcoming **Safari Beach Hotel** ((0127) 2726 FAX (0127) 2357, Box 90690, Mombasa (very expensive), possibly the best, closely followed by its two neighboring sister hotels, **Jadini Beach Hotel** (expensive) and **Africana Sea Lodge** (expensive). Three kilometers (two miles) north of point zero is the good-value **Southern Palms Beach Resort** ((0127) 3721 FAX (0127) 3381, Box 365, Ukunda (expensive). For families, especially, the all-inclusive option can be attractive. There are a few all-inclusives here but the best — and the best value — is **Papillon Hotel (** (0127) 2627 FAX (0127) 2216 E-MAIL onearth@africa online.co.ke, Box 83058, Ukunda (expensive, full board), formerly known as Lagoon Reef, five and a half kilometers (three and a half miles) south of point zero. Traditionally the cheapest beachfront hotel is **Nomad (** (0127) 2155 FAX (0127) 2391, Box 1, Ukunda (mid-range but negotiable), four and a half kilometers (three miles) south. Perhaps it's too cheap, as Nomad totters along, seemingly on the verge of bankruptcy, holding out

clubs, but it is worth getting out occasionally, and the best nightlife clusters about three kilometers (two miles) south of point zero: it's here you'll find **Ali Baba's Restaurant**, perhaps the most atmospheric eatery on the East African coast, set deep underground in limestone caverns. For evening drinking, the Kenyan watering-hole next door is the **Forty Thieves Bar** where "YMCA" echoes from disco speakers over the sea. For a more Kenyan experience cross the road to the open-air **Bushbaby** night club, or the rather more hardcore **Shakatak** next door. Alter-

against any attempt by its snooty neighbors to drag it upmarket.

To the south of Diani is the luxurious, but ecologically very unsound, **Chale Paradise Island (** (011) 222502 E-MAIL islands@africa online.co.ke, Box 12396, Mombasa (expensive). Well, it was a nice island until they built this resort all over it. Further south again, just short of Shimoni, is Funzi Island, connected to the mainland at low tide, where **Funzi Island Club (** (0127) 2044, Box 1108, Ukunda (expensive), is a really exclusive tented camp set amongst the mangrove. Total paradise.

Where to Eat

Generally, guests look to their own resort hotels for a choice of restaurants and night

natively, take a *matatu* or drive to the town of Ukunda on the main coast road: for instance, at the (unlicensed) **Happy Moment** café, it's a struggle to spend more than US$2 on a meal.

HOW TO GET THERE

Take the Likoni Ferry from Digo Road, Mombasa and follow the A14 coast road, which stays near, but not in sight of, the ocean, and the beaches are clearly-marked turnings to the left. Tiwi comes first, 20 km (12.5 miles) and two turnings south of Likoni. The Diani turning is another 10 km (six miles) further

Tiwi Beach is a favorite with backpackers and ideal for a longer stay.

south, at the town of Ukunda. Turn left and drive three kilometers (two miles) to a strip of tarmac that runs along the back of the beach developments. Turn right for most of the hotels and restaurants. Drive carefully here: there are ladders to let the colobus monkeys cross the road but they still sometimes use the road, and have very little traffic sense.

Diani is easy to get to by public transportation. Buses and *matatus* leave from the Likoni Ferry throughout the day and take about 30 minutes. Many buses and *matatus* go directly to the beach, although it might be necessary to disembark at Ukunda if your bus is heading to Tanzania. If heading for Tiwi Beach, taxis lurk around the turning and offer the only alternative to a long hot walk to the coast.

SHIMONI

Shimoni is a low-key coastal resort catering primarily to deep-sea fishermen, but it offers excellent snorkeling in Kisite Marine National Park, subterranean caves, and Wasini Island to explore.

Kisite Marine National Park is one of Kenya's three offshore reserves where fishing and collecting shells and coral are strictly forbidden. Because of this, the underwater spectacle is unrivaled. You can snorkel anywhere off Shimoni or Wasini Island, as the sea is calm and clear. The best viewing, however, is around Kisite Island. There are organized trips from the hotels along Diani Beach or reserve directly with **Kisite Dhow Tours (** (0127) 2331 FAX (0127) 3154 Box 281, Ukunda.

The cost — US$80 per person including transfers — includes a sailing-dhow crossing to the island, snorkeling equipment rental, and a lavish banquet lunch after which most people collapse on rattan beds spread around under shady trees. Alternatively, walk to the small and friendly Wasini Village. The Kisite National Park has probably the best snorkeling in Kenya and qualified divers can also rent scuba equipment.

The town of Shimoni takes its name from the Swahili *shimo*, meaning caves, which refers to a series of underground coral grottoes. A path from the Shimoni jetty leads to

a ladder entrance. Bats now inhabit the caves, but legends claim that they were once used for storing slaves or were the secret refuge of the locals against Maasai raids. They evoke thoughts of pirate ships and hidden treasures among the nooks and crannies that some claim extend for 20 km (12 miles). The adventurous should bring a flashlight although the area around the entrance is well-lit by sunlight filtering through holes like the one through which you descend.

WASINI ISLAND

A short boat ride offshore from Shimoni is Wasini Island, a small scrub-covered atoll. It measures five kilometers by one kilometer (about three and a half miles by two-thirds of a mile) and is home for a few fishermen. There are no cars; it is a bit like living adrift on the sea. You can wander around the island, explore a raised dead coral garden alive with birds and butterflies instead of fish, swim and snorkel off the beach in front of the village, and discover the ruins of an Arab-African town around which the present village is built. The **Wasini Island Restaurant** caters to snorkeling groups during the day although it closes for the months of May and June.

WHERE TO STAY

Shimoni Reef Lodge ((011) 471771 FAX (011) 473249 WEB SITE www.africa-direct. com, c/o Reef Hotel, Box 82234, Mombasa, caters mainly to keen scuba divers (mid-range), while the **Pemba Channel Fishing Club** ((011) 3132749 FAX (011) 316875, Box 86952, Mombasa, is a club (in the British sense) for serious deep-sea fishermen (very expensive, half board). They do, however, open their doors to nonmembers who share their fishing interests.

If you'd prefer to stay on Wasini Island itself it is always possible to stay at **Mpunguti Guest House**, where rooms cost Ksh1,000 per double, bed and breakfast, or it is possible to camp for Ksh200 per person. Negotiate hard with a boatman for a dhow ride across to the island: how much they charge depends on how much money they think you have; Ksh800 would be a reasonable price.

HOW TO GET THERE

To get to the south coast from Mombasa, drive to the end of the Digo Road and down the ramp to the Likoni Ferry. Two boats shuttle across the water and it's rare to wait more than 20 minutes. Pay at the office before driving on board if in a vehicle; the charge is Ksh25. Pedestrians travel free. *Matatus* and buses wait on the other side. Kenya Bus Service buses leave every 20 minutes or so. For Shimoni, a couple of buses and *matatus* each day go directly; otherwise take anything heading for Lunga Lunga on the Tanzanian border and get off 32 km (20 miles) early at the Shimoni turning. You'll then have to hitchhike the last stretch.

If driving your own vehicle, the A14 coast road stays near, but not in sight of, the ocean, and the beaches are clearly marked turnoffs to the left. The Shimoni turn is 70 km (44 miles) south of Likoni. Then a *murram* road takes you the final 14 km (nine miles) to the tip of the peninsula.

NORTH OF MOMBASA

To the north of Mombasa the new Nyali Bridge has brought the northern beaches within easy reach of the city and given the hotels a rather busier feel. The beaches aren't great, but it has settled into the liveliest place on Kenya's coast, as a chain or bars and clubs break up the chain of resort hotels, whose entertainment tends to the cheesy, along the beach. Easy access to Mombasa keep it lively, while foreign exchange means the resorts of Bamburi, Nyali and Shanzu suck all the best bands and entertainers out of the city. There are water sports here, of course, generally run by the resort hotels and aimed at their packaged clientele, but plenty of people get away without bothering themselves with too much daylight.

There is no real center to the three beach suburbs, spreading out along the Indian Ocean coast: rather there's a line of hotels along the waterfront catering to foreign tourists, while the indigenous population has largely moved to the inland side of the main road.

There's no resentment, though. Kenyans are not likely to spend much time tanning on the beach and are generally happy to let visiting *mzungus* (white people) pay huge prices for being near a sea which, for bathing purposes, is outclassed by their hotel swimming pools. The beach itself shelves gently, and for much of low tide the water is well out of range.

WHAT TO SEE AND DO

The leading attraction here is Bamburi Nature Trail, see page 205, and Rabai, see page 267. There is also **Mamba Village** ((011) 472709 FAX (011) 472281 E-MAIL mamba@africa

online.co.ke, Box 857223, Mombasa, Links Road, 8 AM to 6 PM daily, Ksh500 adults, Ksh250 children, which is the largest crocodile farm in Kenya. It has camel and horse riding, a tropical garden and a disco, as well as the chance to try a croc-burger. The **Marine Aquarium**, 9 AM to 6:30 PM daily, Ksh250 adults, Ksh150 children, is right next door and includes a snake farm and horses that can be rented for rides.

WHERE TO STAY

Prices here are seasonal, and there are bargains to be had after the peak months of

The coast has been built over millions of years by coral growth.

December to February. There are more than 30 large hotels along this stretch of coast, and so there's little point trying to be exhaustive here, especially as the package-orientated establishments offer such big discounts to tour operators that walk-in travelers are actively discriminated against.

The first place you reach leaving Mombasa Island, and which rather breaks this rule, offers probably the best value on the entire coast: the newly-built but strangely empty **Orchid Bay Hotel** ((011) 473238 FAX (011) 471365, Nyali Road (inexpensive, B&B). Perhaps prices will go up when it gets better established but it is rather a beach resort without a beach. The most comfortable place here, staying well clear of the package market, is perhaps **Tamarind Village** ((011) 474600 FAX (011) 473073 E-MAIL tvlmsa@africaonline .co.ke WEB SITE www.tamarind.co.ke, Box 95805, Mombasa (very expensive), with one- to three-bedded apartments overlooking the harbor. Attached to the city's best restaurant, at least you can be sure of a good breakfast.

The longest-established, and perhaps the best hotel for holidaymakers is **Nyali Beach Hotel** ((011) 471567 FAX (011) 471987, Box 1874, Mombasa (expensive, half board), which is a family-friendly place with a good range of water sports. Rather cheaper is the **Traveler's Beach Hotel** ((011) 485121 FAX (011) 485678, Box 87649, Mombasa (expensive, half board). Somewhat more expensive, but with a notable "Adventurer's Club" for children, is **Voyager Beach Resort** ((02) 446651 or (02) 447929 FAX (02) 446533 E-MAIL info@heritage hotels.co.ke WEB SITE www.heritagehotels .co.ke, Box 74888 Nairobi (very expensive, half board), which is large but cheerful. One of the largest hotels in this area, and certainly with the longest beach frontage, is the very smart **Whitesands** ((02) 713333 FAX (02) 715566, E-MAIL reservations@sarova.co.ke WEB SITE www.sarovahotels.com, Box 72493, Kenyatta Avenue, Nairobi (very expensive, half board).

Step away from the package market and there are some places for travelers who prefer non-packaged, self-contained accommodation, even if they can sometimes be overshadowed by the nearby resorts. Top of the league is **Bamburi Chalets** ((011) 485706 FAX (011)

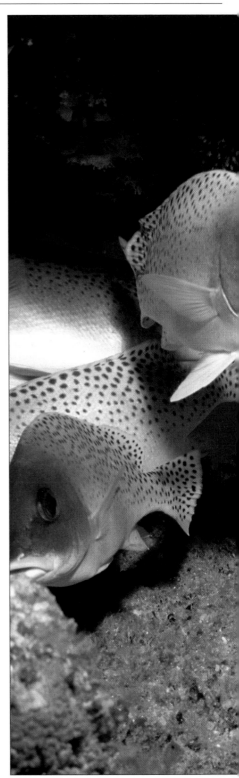

Rainbow reef shelters a myriad of tropical fish.

485594, Box 84114, Mombasa (expensive, per cottage), sleeping six self-catering, with the less expensive **Baharini Chalets** ((011) 487382 FAX (011) 486302, Bamburi Beach, Box 90371, Mombasa (inexpensive), which has a popular (and in Kenya this isn't always such a good thing) bar. For basic, inexpensive rooms, try **Mombasa Safari Inn** ((011) 485094, opposite the Mombasa Continental Resort in Shanzu, Box 87452, Mombasa (very inexpensive). On a real budget, head away from the tempting ocean waters and go inland and go indigenous: **Monique Hotel** ((011) 474231, Box 97263, Mombasa (very inexpensive, B&B), won't break any budget and includes breakfast.

Most hotel rates in the Mombasa region are negotiable. If you're arriving in the high season and want to reserve in advance, try one of the hotels listed above directly, but you might find better value by asking your travel agent to help — tour operators have often negotiated the keenest rates. Even in December, January and August, you should, in the current climate, be able to pick and choose where you want to stay. Charter airlines from Europe and Canada often include several nights at coastal hotels for the price of a round-trip ticket (see TRAVELERS' TIPS, page 291). This option gives you the security of a place to stay on arrival and time to decide how and where you are spending the remainder of your vacation.

WHERE TO EAT

In the early evening, **Mtwapa Marina Pub** at the northern limits of Mombasa's northern resort sprawl is a good place to watch the sun go down over a beer or three. Meals are available, but for food there are other places to go. Most of the resort hotels have their own specialty restaurants, of which the better ones are **Sher-e-Punjab** at the Travelers Beach Hotel, and the grills at the **Mombasa Safari Inn**, opposite Mombasa Continental Resort. One of Mombasa's best restaurants, with international prices, is the **Tamarind Restaurant** ((011) 471747, overlooking Mombasa's Old Port. It's expensive — but well worth it — and there's a top-floor casino to try to recoup the service charge. Reservations are usually needed. **Splendid**

View Café ((011) 314763, near the Planet shopping center, doesn't actually have any such thing, but the Indian cuisine is very good for less than Ksh1,000 per person.

NIGHTLIFE

For nightlife, there are a number of options along the waterfront, and in many ways it is easiest just to walk up the beach and see which bands are playing, where. To make a start **Beach Corner** at the Baharina Chalets, Shanzu Beach, is a bit of a pick-up joint, with the **Cha Cha Bar** rather calmer. Later on, **Tembo Disco**, just north from the Bamburi Nature Trail, and the **Bora Bora Club** at Ocean View shopping Plaza, offer some of the best music and lighting on the coast.

HOW TO GET THERE

From Mombasa, any number of *matatus* head along the main coast road. Taxis also ply the route, and it doesn't take long to get used to the pricing structure: it's rather less than the fixed fares quoted by Kenatco. Driving yourself, the route, across the Nyali Bridge and following the main road, is umistakable.

THE NORTH COAST

North of Mombasa and the Nyali, Bamburi, and Shanzu hotel strip, there is little development. Most of the coastal land up to Kilifi is the privately owned Vipingo Sisal Estate, one of the largest sisal estates and Kenya's most impressive. The sharp-pointed sisal plants in neatly lined rows cover the landscape in an endless sea of dark sage-green.

Sisal's succulent leaves, which can grow up to one and a half meters (five feet) have sharp spikes at the tips, and when not "in bloom" sisal is easily mistaken for pineapple. (Pineapples are grown at the coast and they are the best I have eaten anywhere, even better than the famed Hawaiian ones.) The bloom of the sisal plant is a three- to six-meter-tall (10- to 18-ft) rigid stalk that bears yellow flowers. A coarse, yellow-white fiber is obtained from a process of crushing and beating the succulent leaves. These dry one- to two-meter-long (three- to six-foot) fibers are then used to make twine and rope for nets, hammocks and carpets. Sisal was one of Kenya's major exports until lighter synthetic fibers elbowed it out of the world market. Nonetheless, Vipingo is still in operation and a major employer on Kenya's north coast.

The monotony of the sisal rows is broken frequently by huge, light-gray, almost silvery, baobabs. These trees are without leaves for most of the year, bearing leaves only after periods of heavy rain. Most Africans consider the baobab a sacred tree. They can live up to 2,000 years, and at Vipingo, when one eventually dies, it is removed.

The baobab looks like a normal tree until it is about four and a half meters (15 ft) tall. Then its trunk begins to swell and continues to swell throughout its life. Some trees reach a diameter of six meters (20 ft) and the trees look somewhat absurd with trunks almost as broad as they are tall.

There are several local legends as to why the baobab looks the way it does. One suggests that the baobab was once the most beautiful tree in Africa, but it was also very proud and boasted too much. As punishment, God turned it upside down, making its beautiful foliage its roots. Another claims that the first baobab refused to stay planted in one place. It wandered the countryside causing trouble. When God caught it, he planted it upside down as punishment.

The baobab's green nuts can be used to make flour and the leaves and fruit-pulp are a Kenyan cure for fever. Inside its thin bark, the trunk is soft and pithy, storing a great amount of moisture. During periods of drought, elephants rip the baobabs apart and extract the water.

KILIFI

Kilifi is the first town north of Mombasa with any tourist amenities. Originally dependent on trading with traffic waiting for the ferry, a 1991 bridge has left it rather without purpose. But as the locals say, it's "a bit cool." It has several *hotelis* in town, a motel, and two coastal resorts. When the Portuguese arrived on the Kenyan coast, Kilifi was known as Mnarani and was centered on the south bank of Kilifi Creek. Ruins of the town are situated on a high cliff above the creek and include a pillar tomb and mosques. There is little

mention of this establishment in Portuguese or Arab writings of the times, and one theory is that the settlement was solely a slave trading center, not mercantile and agricultural like Mombasa, Malindi, Lamu and Pate.

The best hotel around here is **Kilifi Beach Resort (** (0125) 22264 FAX (0125) 22258 WEB SITE www.clubsinternational.com, Box 537, Kilifi, six and a half kilometers (four miles) north (expensive, half board). The **Mnarani Club (** (0125) 22320 FAX (0125) 22200, Box 1008, Kilifi, used to be run by Clubs International (expensive, all-inclusive), but at time

of going to press might have been changing to a good-value, room-only hotel. On a budget, behind the Agip station on the highway going north is the **Mkwajoni Motel and Restaurant (** (0125) 22474, Box 171, Kilifi (very inexpensive, B&B). It has clean rooms with mosquito nets, but be warned: the rooms surround a disco that operates Wednesdays, Fridays and Saturdays. On these nights the similarly priced **Dhows Inn (** (0125) 22028, south of the bridge, is a quieter bet. North of the cashew plantation are grazing lands, a coconut grove or two, and the start of the Arabuko-Sokoke Forest, a designated UNESCO Biosphere Reserve.

Lantern-sailed outriggers along the coast.

WATAMU BAY AND WATAMU MARINE NATIONAL PARK

Watamu Bay is the prime destination for this part of the coast, a quiet community sandwiched between two UNESCO Biosphere Reserves: the forest (Arabuko-Sokoke) inland and the marine park offshore. Watamu Marine National Park has superb snorkeling, or "goggling" as it is locally called. As at Shimoni in the south, fishing of any kind is forbidden in the park and the variety of fish, coral and anemones is phenomenal.

Sometimes, a thousand or more gregarious and colorful fish may surround a swimmer. Among the common species are butterfly fish, angelfish, golden trevally, cardinal fish, hawkfish, white-breasted sturgeons, blue-lined snappers, rock cod (groupers) and jewelfish. The rock cod can grow to several hundred kilograms in weight, and hide under coral outcrops; most of the others are very small, from one to ten centimeters (one-half to four inches) in length.

Low tide is the best time for snorkeling because the sea water filters the sunlight, and the red end of the spectrum disappears after the first one to two meters (three to six feet) of depth, depending on water clarity. Thus the reef will appear much more colorful at low tide as there is less water covering it.

The local hotels all have boats to take you to the reef and along the coast for Ksh300 to Ksh450 per person, although the park entrance fee is also US$5 per person per day. The park extends the length of the ocean in front of the hotels, and you won't be charged an entrance to swim as long as you're not using a mask and snorkel. If you want fins, ask at the dive centers at **Hemingways** or **Ocean Sports** (see WHERE TO STAY, below). To protect the reef none of the standard snorkeling operators include fins: they argue you'll see more without them. Some of the largest fish are near shore, hiding under the moored boats in an area known to the early settlers as "The Larder." For scuba diving, the best operator is **Aqua Ventures** ((0122) 32008 FAX (0122) 32266, next to Ocean Sports.

At the south end of Watamu Bay is another drowned river valley, **Mida Creek**. It is lined with low-lying mangrove swamps and mud flats. A boat tour of Mida Creek is a pleasant way to spend a morning or afternoon and it can be combined with snorkeling stops in the marine park.

Late April, just before migration, is the best time to watch the birds in Mida Creek. The more expensive hotels in Watamu run boats daily to the marine park and Mida Creek, and have boats that can take you deep-sea fishing. Their catch includes blue and black marlin, sailfish, shark, bonito and tuna. Kenya is at the forefront of East Africa's tag-and-release program though it has to be said that many fish caught die of shock and exhaustion. If you're tempted to give game fishing a try, see GAME FISHING, page 22 in TOP SPOTS, and SPORTING SPREE, page 40 in YOUR CHOICE.

ARABUKO–SOKOKE FOREST

To fill your time away from the beach in the Watamu Bay area, you will find the Arabuko-Sokoke Forest, the largest surviving lowland jungle in Kenya. It has stands of hardwoods and rubber trees and the borders of the forest, thanks to its Biosphere listing, seem relatively secure. You can hike along the many dirt tracks and logging roads and will see birds, butterflies and, if you are lucky, the Zanzibar or Aders' duiker, a 35-cm (14-inch) antelope, or the forest's two unique species, the Scopps owl and the elephant shrew (which rattles, occasionally, across your path like a very large rat).

GEDI NATIONAL MONUMENT

Gedi National Monument is the most extensive of the ruins on the Kenyan coast. It comprises the remains of a city constructed in the late thirteenth- or fourteenth-century that was at its peak in the middle of the fifteenth century and was abandoned in the early seventeenth century. Its history is somewhat a mystery. No one is certain exactly when it was founded and by whom. Unlike most of the Arab-African towns, it did not have a harbor and was possibly not a major commercial or political power. Nonetheless, the quantity and quality of porcelain discovered here indicate that its inhabitants were prosperous. The city had a palace that covered about a tenth of a hectare (a quarter of an acre), houses with sunken courtyards, numerous mosques, ornate pilaster tombs, and inner and outer protective walls.

Archaeologists suspect that only a few of the buildings were still occupied in the sixteenth century. By the end of the seventeenth century, Gedi was empty. The writings of the Portuguese from this period shed no light on the history of this mysterious city.

In the seventeenth century, the invading Galla from Somalia either massacred or chased away the inhabitants of all the Arab-

take a dislike to visitors and toss fruits and nuts on the unsuspecting. Recently a new visitors center has been built to formalize what has been learned of this lost coastal culture, replacing the small museum that used to display some of the artifacts uncovered during the excavations between 1939 and 1958. You can purchase a booklet at the entrance that guides you through the town and along the walls, though Abdallah, the manager of the visitors center, is the best local guide, and really brings the site to life. The **Gedi Museum** ((0123) 32065 is open daily.

African cities between Juba River in present-day Somalia and Mtwapa, 24 km (15 miles) north of Mombasa. Gedi was probably no exception. In the second half of the nineteenth century, the Galla were in turn attacked by Somalis and Maasai and lost control over the northern coastal area. The site of Gedi was never reoccupied or rebuilt, but a nearby town, also named Gedi, has been built. There is a school, a few shops, and numerous homes and small farms.

A national historic site, Gedi has been partially excavated and the grounds are well maintained. A tall coastal forest that has grown up around and in the site all but dwarfs this 18-ha (45-acre) town. It is now home for vervet monkeys who frequently

The Ksh200 admission also gets you into the neighboring butterfly project (see below).

KIPEPEO BUTTERFLY PROJECT

One of the few good things to result from the Rio Conference on climate change, the Kipepeo Butterfly Project has started to reap benefits for local farmers living on the border of the Arabuko-Sokoke Forest. At least eight farmers, working from makeshift frames on the edge of the forest, are breeding butterflies for export to Europe. At the heart of this project is a butterfly center by the Gedi Ruins, where the pupae, often more

Watamu Bay Marine Park protects some of the best coral on the coast.

beautiful than any jewel, are packed in cotton-wool for the journey to the West. This has brought US$50,000 to the local economy, in an area that already contains at least 260 butterfly species, fluttering through the dense trees of the forest in vivid bursts of color.

WHERE TO STAY

There are three main resorts in Watamu. **Turtle Bay** ((0122) 32003 FAX (0122) 32268, Box 10, Watamu, is an all-inclusive hotel popular with tourists from Europe (very expensive, all-inclusive). **Hemingways** ((0122) 32624 FAX (0122) 32256 WEB SITE www.hemingways.com, Box 267, Watamu, is a luxury hotel catering mainly — but not exclusively — to big-game fishermen (very expensive, half board). Local Kenyans tend to walk a few meters up the beach for the family-owned **Ocean Sports** ((0122) 32008 FAX (0122) 32266 E-MAIL oceansps@africa online.co.ke, Box 100, Watamu (mid-range, half board), with lunch as a supplement. However, in the heat of the coast, half-board is adequate, with afternoon tea with fresh homemade scones instead of lunch. During May and June, admittedly when seaweed cloaks the beach and the boats are unable to cross the offshore reef, Ocean Sports reduces its rates dramatically. As it should. It's called "Open Shorts" locally, but for the ageing Kenya Cowboys who droop on the bar at this time of year this seems little more than wishful thinking. More sensibly Hemingways closes completely through May.

Unless you've very keen on a hotel atmosphere, by far the best place to stay is **Baraka House** ((0122) 32250 E-MAIL tara@baraka house.co.uk WEB SITE www.barakahouse .co.uk, Box 402, Plot 24B, Mida Creek Road, Watamu (very expensive), a superbly comfortable beach property that can be rented as a whole. With three luxury en-suite rooms this can be very good value for groups, though it can be a bit expensive for singles or couples.

On a budget, look to Watamu village, a 30-minute walk up the beach and across a headland from Watamu Bay but a world apart, culturally. The (very inexpensive) **Dante Hotel** ((0122) 32083, next to **Happy Nights Disco**, doesn't offer breakfast, while opposite, **Veronica** ((0122) 32243 (very inexpensive), does. Whichever, Happy Nights Disco is a blast on weekends.

HOW TO GET THERE

It takes just over an hour to get to Watamu from Mombasa. Leave Mombasa on the B8 coast road and after 90 km (56 miles) turn right at Gedi Village. Pass Gedi National Monument and drive four kilometers (three miles) to the beach. By public transportation, take a bus or *matatu* heading for Malindi, and get off 24 km (15 miles) early at Gedi village. Further *matatus* will reach Watamu village. Alternatively it is possible to fly to Malindi with Airkanya's daily service and take a taxi back to Watamu; the cost to cover the 24 km (15 miles) should not be much more than Ksh1,000.

MALINDI

Malindi was the city-state that in the fourteenth century sent a Kenyan giraffe to China, gift of the Sultan of Malindi to the Chinese emperor, which was transported by one of China's most renowned navigators, the Ming Dynasty's Admiral Zheng He. The gift probably served a twofold mission. First, it attempted to prove to the isolationist emperor that the lands beyond China did have something to offer. Secondly, the Sultan wished to establish direct trade with the Chinese fleets that had, since the sixth century, sailed only as far as India or Arabia to purchase slaves and other East African goods. Malindi also welcomed and entertained Vasco da Gama on his visits to the Kenyan coast, but has since lost some of its previous charm to tourism: a rapid boom in Italian development ended in a bust from which it will take years to recover and silt has affected both its marine park and beaches. The old town is a mishmash of Arab-style buildings, few of which are older than 1900, and boom buildings from the 1930s, while to the north are the rather grander reminders of the 1990s boom.

Most of Malindi's old buildings went to ruin after its ruling family moved to Mombasa in the sixteenth century. When the Portuguese captured Mombasa, they installed Malindi's royal family as titular head of the coastal communities.

Without a ruling family, Malindi's power and prosperity declined. The port no longer attracted merchant vessels and Malindi became a ghost town. Gone are the inlaid doors described by the early Portuguese visitors. Tourism in the past 25 years revitalized the town, and left it hanging. During the peak of the high season (December and January, and, later on, in August), the town is flushed with tourists, mostly German and Italian, while at other times bars and hotels stand empty. The high tide of this seasonal invasion still leaves a **Tourist Information Office (** (0123) 20747

WHERE TO STAY

The smartest option here is the newest: the **Woburn Residence Club (** (0123) 30073 FAX (0123) 31183 WEB SITE www.woburnrc .com, Box 33, Malindi (expensive), seven minutes' walk from town by the Galana Hospital, with as many comforts as you could happily throw a stick at and accommodation mainly in apartments and suites. It's owner-run and small enough to remain intimate and friendly.

FAX (0123) 30429, Utali Parade, Harambee Road, Box 421, Malindi, 8 AM to 4:30 PM Monday to Friday. There are taxis everywhere, but you can also call **Baobab Taxis (** (0123) 30499. If you need medical treatment urgently, **Galana Hospital (** (0123) 2083, Lamu Road, is the best. For e-mail try **Bit House** in the Malindi Complex shopping center.

Located at the mouth of the Sabaki River, Malindi's bay often turns red due to seasonal runoff from upstream overgrazed land. This makes Watamu Bay a better choice for divers keen to spot the coral, though most dive schools are prepared to travel for good reefs. The coral in the **Malindi Marine National Park** suffered lasting damage from the El Nino floods in the 1990s and has not yet recovered.

The main resort hotels, all rather less expensive booked overseas as a package, are set well back from the beach. The **Driftwood Beach Club (** (0123) 20155 FAX 214120, Box 63, Malindi (mid-range), is the nearest refuge, for Kenya Cowboys who fail to get into Ocean Sports in nearby Watamu, or for the all-inclusive beach experience there is **Lawfords (** (0127) 3081 FAX (0127) 3439, Box 37, Ukunda. But the best of these big international package places is the most southerly: the **Eden Roc (** (0123) 20480 FAX (0123) 203333, Box 350, Malindi (expensive), also with some fan-cooled rooms (mid-range), is great for families and not too smart — perfect for the rather

Ruins of the thirteenth- to fifteenth-century Arab city of Gedi.

scruffy charms of the town. Though a recent change of management has dragged it nearer the twenty-first century, it's still two and a half kilometers (one and a half miles) south on the "British" side of the city center. For something a little different, the **Kobokoni Riding Centre** ((0123) 21273 FAX (0123) 21030, Box 857, Malindi (expensive), north of town, offers an beachfront atmosphere for horsey romantics.

On a budget, in Malindi town there are several small hotels, the best of which, though sandwiched between a bus station and a mosque, is **Ozi's Bed and Breakfast** ((0123)

fly from Nairobi's International Airport to Malindi. They have a Malindi office at ((0123) 20237, Box 634, Malindi. **Airkenya** ((02) 501421/3 FAX (02) 500845 E-MAIL info @airkenya.com WEB SITE www.airkenya.com, Box 30357, Nairobi; ((011) 229777 FAX (011) 224063, Nkrumah Road, Mombasa; or ((0123) 30808 FAX (0123) 21229, Box 548, Malindi, fly here too — and on up the coast — from Mombasa and also link Malindi with Nairobi. The fare between Malindi and Mombasa with Airkenya is a very reasonable Ksh2,000, and from Nairobi (via Mombasa), Ksh5,385. If

20218, Seafront Road, Box 60, Malindi (very inexpensive, B&B), although its position between mosque and bus station might make for a restless night. If driving, the **Starlight Hotel** ((0123) 30424 FAX (0123) 21225, Box 194, Mama Ngina Street, near the market, has secure parking (very inexpensive).

you're depending on this flight to catch an international connection, reconfirm often as overbooking does happen. Frequent buses and *matatus* link Mombasa with Malindi but traveling north to Lamu overland is not currently recommended, even though convoys of *matatus* occasionally make the trip.

HOW TO GET THERE

Malindi is two hours by car from Mombasa along the coast road. It can also be reached by air from Nairobi or Mombasa: the flight from Mombasa offers a spectacular half-hour overview of the fringing coral reef of the shore. **Kenya Airways** ((02) 210771 or (02) 229291 FAX (02) 336252, Box 41010, Nairobi,

THE LAMU ARCHIPELAGO

North of Malindi, when the paved road ends, you enter a no-man's-land that Somali bandits (*shiftas*) rule. The landscape is flat with marshy green and arid brown stretches. During the rainy season, the route north is impassable in any vehicle; bus service is often interrupted for weeks. Even in the dry season, *shiftas* make the route unsafe. Visitors wanting to go further north to Lamu usually fly from Malindi, Mombasa or Nairobi.

There are daily flights from Malindi and Mombasa, and if you are in a hurry you can tour Lamu in a day, flying up in the morning and returning the same night. But that's not really long enough. Lamu is the most exotic site on the Kenyan coast, a mini-Katmandu-by-the-sea, that appeals particularly to long-staying backpackers, lone travelers and the occasional honeymoon couple.

religious refugees from the Arabian or Persians regions of the Caliphate.

These refugees, like those who migrated to Malindi and Mombasa, became the religious, political and economic force in the area. They assimilated parts of the native population and culture. Lamu and the nearby islands of Manda and Pate were part of the Portuguese Indian Ocean empire. The Portuguese constructed a fort on Pate, but apparently never had a large force on Lamu or Manda. From the number of old buildings still standing, it seems reasonable to

From the airport a dhow takes new arrivals from the mainland to Lamu; the slow approach to the toytown buildings of the old city center transports you back to the nineteenth century. There is one automobile, belonging to the District Commissioner, but it's a rarely used status symbol. Electricity has only just arrived. Donkeys and dhows are the only transportation, and mostly both are wind-powered. The pace of life is accordingly slow.

Archaeologists and historians have established that the island has been inhabited since about AD 1200, though the towns of Lamu and Shela on Lamu Island did not exist until the fourteenth to fifteenth century. The founders of Lamu and Shela were most likely

assume that the inhabitants did not openly oppose the Portuguese, but maintained their cultural and religious identities without aggravating their rulers. There are reports of the Portuguese executing one of Lamu's sheiks for collaboration with the Turks in the late sixteenth century — a minor punishment when you consider the massive slaughter and pillage the Portuguese inflicted on Mombasa.

Lamu became prosperous in the seventeenth century when Pate's harbor began to silt in. It reached its peak of affluence in the eighteenth century. From the ancient poetry of the region and a few western accounts,

A luxury restaurant in Malindi. Malindi and Lamu are the most interesting places to stay on the coast.

historian J. de V. Allen has reconstructed life on the island then:

"Rich men clad in fine silks and turbans moved about surrounded by crowds of retainers, young men who competed, both individually and collectively in personal display, in witty exchanges, in composing poetry and epigrams and also in ceremonial sword-dances. There was a constant buzz of activity, with business being transacted in the streets and coffeehouses, workmen and slaves building or refurbishing houses, heavily-laden sailing boats entering or leaving

"Warfare, when it occurred, was an occasion for impassioned speeches, the wholesale distribution of invulnerability charms, and menacing processions accompanied by the beating of many gongs." (J. de V. Allen, *Lamu Town*.)

Lamu, Pate and Manda aligned themselves with Oman and later Zanzibar, when Seyyid Said moved his court there, and thus traded regularly with European and American merchants. There was a period of German occupation in the late nineteenth century, but by then, the islands' prosperity

the harbor, and great men coming and going on the eternal safaris which are still so much an integral part of Swahili life.

"Music was provided for the master of the house when he returned home, also massage and baths (both hot and cold) and couches strewn with jasmine. While the women, probably already in seclusion for much of their lives, lived for the weddings and other occasions when they could congregate to dance their own dances and compete with each other in poetry and song, and concentrated meanwhile on enjoying life as much as they could without exciting their husband's suspicions. The art of enjoying harem life is one in which Lamu women have become, over the centuries, very skilled.

was already in decline. Pate's harbor was completely silted in, Manda never had a good deepwater harbor, and Lamu's could not accommodate the new steamships.

LAMU

Lamu is an amalgam of twelfth- through eighteenth-century buildings in Arab style, with its traditional town plan still intact. Streets are narrow and have the dual purpose of providing shade and producing a slight wind tunnel effect. There are over 20 mosques, the oldest, Pwami, dating from 1370.

ABOVE: Dhows are still used for daily transport on this island without cars. OPPOSITE: A few coastal artisans still construct dhows by hand, as on Lamu.

Lamu's ornately carved wooden doors, wall niches and plaster detailing generate the greatest interest, being close to hypnotic in their intricacy. Most of them are distinctly Arabic, but some include universal motifs often found in Celtic, Phoenician and Roman designs.

Daily life takes place out of doors; artisans work on their doorsteps, businessmen meet on verandas, children play anywhere and everywhere. Although the absence of cars is certainly a factor in this style of life, this has been the rhythm here for centuries.

The **museum** at Lamu is one of the best in Africa. Housed in a classic open-centered building, the museum has a room depicting a Swahili wedding. It also features excellent displays on coastal maritime culture, a collection of ivory and brass *siwas* (ceremonial horns), and exhibits of daily life of the Swahili and the non-Swahili peoples of the nearby mainland. Here, you can buy J. de V. Allen's guide, *Lamu Town*, which gives a detailed history of the area and an excellent description of the historic buildings in the town and the island.

Women still live in relative seclusion, though this is beginning to change. The people of Lamu are social and convivial, most of them sharing common ancestors and history.

Processions occur frequently. The most common are the *ziara*, or visits to the graves of holy men. There are festivals for weddings, betrothals, and funerals.

Annually, on the last Thursday in Rabai al-Awal, the week-long festival of **Maulidi** begins (currently in the summer and moving back through the year, according to the lunar calendar). Lamu is then overcrowded as pilgrims come from all over Kenya, Tanzania, Uganda and Arab countries as well. The island is alive with traditional dance, song and open-air religious ceremonies.

Lamu is the most populous island in the archipelago. The long white beaches are a 40-minute walk from Lamu town (or a 50Ksh dhow ride), near Shela village. Walk far enough and many will be deserted; but don't sunbathe nude or topless as someone will appear and take offense.

The reefs offshore offer good snorkeling, but only from November through February; at other times visibility is a problem. Windsurfing and deep-sea fishing are always available. When the wind is up, you can also body surf — the only place apart from a few dangerous locations further south where this is possible in Kenya.

If you have an extra day (or two) to spend in the area, it is worth visiting **Pate**. There are plenty of dhows providing ferry service; departure times depend on the time and weather. There are no hotels or restaurants on the island, but residents meet the ferry boats offering rooms and meals. You can spend only a day, but make sure your dhow or another is going back in the evening. In any case, it is best to bring your own food and water. Around the island (on foot), there are the modern villages of Kizingitini, Bajumwali, and Nyabogi, which have a few carved doors, and the ancient towns of Pate, Siyu and Faza.

runs the best bar in town (there are only about five) on its rooftop terrace. For both, contact **Romantic Hotels** (/FAX (0121) 33107, Box 4, Lamu. The small hotels in town are more in keeping with the mood of the city: **Casuarina Guest Lodge** ((0121) 33123, Box 12, Lamu (very inexpensive, B&B, with bargaining), is one good example that rejects commission-paid touts. Hoteliers — and their friends — make finding a hotel on your own a significant challenge. Usually there is too much help, and bargaining is expected.

WHERE TO STAY

The best tourist-class hotel on Lamu is located a 40-minute walk — rather quicker by dhow — from town, but it is right on the edge of the town's nearest beach. The very comfortable **Peponi Hotel** ((0121) 33154 FAX (0121) 33029 Box 24, Lamu (very expensive, full board), is closed annually from April 15 to July 1 but is still the best place to eat and sleep on the island.

In the town of Lamu itself, the two smartest places are owned by the same organization. On paper the best is their **Lamu Palace** (mid-range), though **Petleys** (inexpensive, room only), despite recent refurbishments, is more atmospheric and still

HOW TO GET THERE

Part of the reason Lamu has retained its special character is that access to it has always been far from easy. Not only is the road north of Malindi in extremely poor condition, and generally becomes impassable at the onset of the rains, but the entire route is plagued by *shiftas* (bandits).

Occasionally, convoys of buses and trucks make it through this hazardous route, but for most visitors access to Lamu is by air, with reasonably regular flights from

OPPOSITE: Lamu's population LEFT reflects the influence and immigration of northern Arab traders and RIGHT most women go modestly veiled. ABOVE: Sunset falls over a timeless sailing dhow.

Nairobi and Mombasa, and less regular flights from Malindi, on **Airkenya (** (02) 501421/3 FAX (02) 500845 E-MAIL info@air kenya.com WEB SITE www.airkenya.com, Box 30357, Nairobi; or **(** (011) 229777 FAX (011) 224063, Nkrumah Road, Mombasa; or **(** (0123) 30808 FAX (0123) 21229, Box 548, Malindi; or **(** (0121) 33445 FAX (0121) 33063, Box 376, Lamu. The fare to fly from Malindi to Lamu is US$7 one way. It is possible to charter a dhow from Malindi to Kiwayu, but allow a few days for the journey, at least. Take plenty of water.

extremely expensive, all-inclusive **Kiwayu Safari Village (** (02) 503030 FAX (02) 503149 WEB SITE www.kiwayu.com — Kiwayu Safari Village can also be booked in Nairobi through Cheli and Peacock **(** (02) 604053/4 or (02) 603090/1 FAX (02) 604050 or (02) 603066 E-MAIL chelipeacock@africaonline.co.ke WEB SITE www.chelipeacock.com, Box 39806, Nairobi.

Just offshore on Kiwayu Island, the generally very busy **Munira Camp (** (02) 512543 FAX (02) 512213 E-MAIL bigblue@africaonline .co.le, Box 40088, Nairobi, is the rather less

KIWAYU

Isolated in the far northeast of Kenya are two final outposts of luxury, accessible only by air and offering the sort of comforts only huge amounts of money can buy. By all accounts, it's worth it.

The emphasis here is on leisure, with most guests relaxing thoroughly and fast. Even so, Kiwayu is surrounded by one of the country's least-visited nature reserves and within a few kilometers are the "hanging gardens" growing from the great baobab trees of Kitangani.

Kiwayu is primarily a beach destination though, with the smartest of its small handful of tourist resorts being the luxurious, if

sophisticated alternative favored by Kenyan nationals (very expensive, all-inclusive).

Finally, there's an Italian-run luxury lodge called the **Blue Safari Club (** (02) 890184 FAX (02) 890096 WEB SITE www.blue safariclub.com (extremely expensive, all-inclusive). Access is generally by air, using **Airkenya** from Mombasa via Malindi and Lamu (US$150 one-way), although it might be possible to arrange (long) transfers by speedboat from Peponi's in Lamu, or a very long (think overnight) trip in a local dhow.

ABOVE: Dhows are a major means of transportation among the islands of the Lamu archipelago.
OPPOSITE: Lamu's shady, colorful open market.

Travelers' Tips

GETTING THERE

Finding a reasonably priced ticket to Kenya takes time and a fair amount of persistence.

FROM THE UNITED STATES AND CANADA

No flights fly direct, non-stop to Kenya from North America, and a change of plane and airline will be needed, usually in Europe. Depending on departure point, length of stay and season, the APEX fare will be around US$2,500 to US$3,500. KLM's code-share link with Northwest Airlines and Kenya Airways make them amongst the most frequent fliers, with a comprehensive range of departures across the United States. Routing through the United Kingdom can give the best rates: operators in London have access to consolidated fares and special rates with safari companies and beach resorts. Student travel companies such as STA or Council Travel offer low fares. Refer to advertisements in the travel sections of major newspapers for more specialists — book by credit card for added security.

FROM EUROPE

Your options are greatest from Europe. Prices and restrictions vary. There are direct flights from London, Paris, Amsterdam, Brussels, Copenhagen, Frankfurt, Madrid, Moscow, Athens, Rome and Zurich on regularly scheduled airlines: British Airways, Air France, Sabena, SAS, Lufthansa, Iberia, Aeroflot, Olympic Airways, Alitalia and Swissair, respectively. Some fly daily, but most once or twice weekly. Kenya Airways, now a code-share partner with KLM, flies from Paris, London, Amsterdam, Zurich, Athens, Frankfurt, Rome and Cairo on a daily basis. APEX fares are the most reasonable you can get with these airlines, and from the United Kingdom these can cost as little as US$600 round trip, even with scheduled airlines. Some companies will restrict your length of stay and flexibility to change travel dates at this price so check conditions before you part with your money.

For cheaper fares, often on the regularly scheduled flights, you should contact a travel agent who is familiar with the charter and consolidator scene. In the United Kingdom, one of the best is **Flightbookers** ((0171) 7572444 FAX (0171) 7572200 WEB SITE www .flightbookers.net, 177-178 Tottenham Court Road, London W1P OLX, with further branches around the United Kingdom.

FROM AUSTRALASIA

There are no direct flights or to Kenya. A stopover is inevitable. Most direct is via Mauritius using Air Mauritius' weekly flights from Perth: a code-share arrangement with Ansett opens this route up to New Zealand and Australian cities. Perth is lucky again with flights to Nairobi and Harare. Kenya's substantial Asian population ensures plenty of flights from India, so good linkages exist from from Australia via various cities in Asia, especially Bombay. Good services are also supplied by Middle Eastern Airlines, including Gulf Air and Emirates. Flying via the United States is not only much longer but also raises the problems already faced by Americans trying to get to Africa, but Kenya can be fitted into round-the-world itineraries. Specialist operators include **Africa Travel Centre** ((02) 9267 3048, Level 12, 456 Kent Street, Sydney NSW 2000, and in New Zealand ((09) 520 2000, 21 Remuera Road, Box 9365, Newmarket, Auckland.

ARRIVING (AND LEAVING)

VISAS

To the despair of tour operators and hoteliers, visa requirements do change regularly. When things are going well the government will try to introduce substantial visa charges, to be waived when things are going badly. Visas are required for all visitors except citizens of some British Commonwealth countries and several other countries with which Kenya has reciprocal agreements, namely Denmark, Ethiopia, Germany, Finland, San Marino, Spain, Sweden, Turkey and Uruguay. However at time of going to press all United Kingdom and United States citizens

The first view of Nairobi is from the air as your plane comes in to land.

needed visas, at a cost of £35 sterling or US$57 per person. Citizens of Australia, Nigeria and Sri Lanka also need visas. Although any currency will be accepted, credit cards are not.

These requirements are subject to change and should be checked with Kenya government offices abroad or a travel agency before departure. If visas are required, best get them before leaving home: airport lines can be long and the requirement that the visas must be bought with a hard currency mean that lines move slowly. Standard tourist visas

or a valid certificate of loss, leaving Kenya can suddenly get bumpy.

The import of fruit, plants, seeds, or animals is prohibited. Your dog or cat may accompany you, for which you must submit a health certificate to the same office as for your visa to obtain an entry permit. However, dogs are not allowed in national parks and reserves.

If you have any ivory articles (jewelry), make sure you can prove in which country the ivory was purchased by means of a receipt, or else it will probably be confiscated.

are valid for 30 days and for one entry. Passports must be current for six months from your date of entry into Kenya.

CUSTOMS ALLOWANCES

Travelers over 16 years of age may import duty-free up to 200 cigarettes or 50 cigars of 250 grams (eight and three quarter ounces) of tobacco, one liter of alcoholic beverage and a quarter-liter of perfume. Personal effects, including unexposed film, cameras and accessories, may be temporarily imported duty-free, but laptop computers and other valuables may well be listed in your passport so they can be checked off when you depart. Without the same laptops or cameras,

Avoid any hassles and leave ivory objects at home.

Firearms and ammunition require a permit issued by the Central Firearms Bureau, Box 30263, Nairobi. In view of the recent crackdown on poachers, these permits are difficult to acquire.

Export of ivory, rhinoceros horns, game skins, game trophies and all other anatomical relics of wildlife is strictly forbidden, as is export of live animals, birds and reptiles, except by licensed dealers.

AIRPORT TAX

To leave Kenya, it is necessary to pay an airport exit tax of US$20 (in United States currency *only*). Officially, this should be integrated into the cost of the ticket, but this hasn't always worked. If you didn't pay this with your ticket make sure you have US$20 spare when you get to the departure gate: changing money at the airport can be time-consuming and it's not unknown for harassed tourists to be tricked into changing more than they wanted to at a very poor rate. The need for all currency transactions to be noted in your currency declaration is no longer generally required.

EMBASSIES AND CONSULATES

As a rule of thumb, allow six weeks to get your visa from one of the Kenya diplomatic missions listed below, or from the British consulate if Kenya has no diplomatic representation in your country. When time is tight, advise the appropriate mission so it can speed your application. Kenyan embassies and consulates abroad include the following:

Australia ((02) 6247 4788, 33 Ainslie Avenue, Box 1990, Canberra.

Austria ((01) 633242, Rotenturmstrasse 22, 1010 Vienna.

Belgium ((02) 230 3065, Avenue Joyeuse Entrée 1-5, Brussels.

Canada ((613) 563 1773, Gillia Building, Suite 600, 415 Laurier Avenue East, West Ottawa, Ontario.

Egypt ((02) 704 455, 20 Boulos Hanna Street, Box 362, Dokki, Cairo.

France ((01) 4553 3500, 3 Rue Cimarosa, 75116 Paris.

Germany ((0228) 356041, Villichgasse 17, 5300 Bonn 2.

Italy ((06) 578 1192/808 2718, CP 10755, 0014 Rome.

Japan ((03) 479 4006, No. 20-24 Nishi-Azobu 3-Chome, Minato-Ku, Tokyo.

Netherlands ((70) 350 4215, Konninginnegracht 102, The Hague.

New Zealand — No representation: apply to the Australian consulate.

Sweden ((08) 218 300, Birger Jarlsgatan 37, 2tr 11145, Stockholm.

Uganda ((041) 231 861, 60 Kira Road, Box 5220, Kampala.

United Arab Emirates ((02) 366300, Box 3854, Abu Dhabi.

United Kingdom ((020) 7636 2371, 45 Portland Place, London W1N 4AS.

United States — Embassy ((202) 387 6101, 2249 R Street NW, Washington, DC 20008; Consulate ((212) 421 4740, 866 United Nations Plaza, Room 486, New York, NY 10017; ((310) 274 6635, 9150 Wilshire Boulevard, Suite 160, Beverley Hills, CA 90212.

Foreign embassies and consulates in Kenya iclude the following:

United States Embassy ((02) 537800 FAX (02) 537810 E-MAIL usis@usis.africaonline.co.ke, WEB SITE usembassy.state.gov/nairobi, Barclays Plaza, Loita Street, Box 30143, Nairobi.

Australian High Commission ((02) 445034/9 FAX (02) 444718, Riverside Drive, Box 39351, Nairobi.

British High Commission ((02) 714699 FAX (02) 719082, E-MAIL bhcinfo@iconnect.co.ke, Box 30465, Nairobi.

Canadian High Commission ((02) 214804 FAX (02) 226987, Comcraft House, Haile Selassie Avenue, Box 30481, Nairobi.

French Embassy ((02) 339978 FAX (02) 339421, Ninth Floor, Barclays Plaza, Loita Street, Box 41784, Nairobi.

German Embassy ((02) 712527/8 FAX (02) 714886, Eighth Floor, Williamson House, 4 Ngong Avenue, Box 30180, Nairobi.

South African Embassy ((02) 215616/8 FAX (02) 223687, 17th Floor, Lonrho House, Standard Street, Box 42441, Nairobi.

New Zealand Consulate ((02) 722467 FAX (02) 722566, Minet ICDC Insurance, Third Floor, Minet House, Nyere Road, Box 47383, Nairobi.

TOURIST INFORMATION

This is where Kenya really hasn't got its act together. Even the Kenyan tourist office in Britain has been closed recently, and in Kenya itself you'll be relying, apart from a few under-funded bureaux on the coast, on the impartiality of those who work within the tourist industry and, often, on the kindness of strangers.

Fortunately, in Kenya strangers can be very kind indeed.

A ballon flight can be relaxing way to visit Kenya's national parks Here balloonists appreciate an alfresco champagne breakfast after an early-morning trip.

TRAVEL AGENTS

If you're going on your own, you may want to make reservations ahead of time. **Let's Go Travel** ((02) 447151 or (02) 441030 FAX (02) 447270 or (02) 441690 E-MAIL info@letsgo safari.com WEB SITE www.letsgosafari.com, Box 60342, Nairobi, will do this for you and answer most questions you may have about road and travel condition. In all our wanderings through Kenya, Let's Go Travel has consistently received good reports from its clientele. Efficient and informative without being pushy, they provide useful help to all classes of traveler, although it has to be said that there are other agencies in Kenya that are just as helpful.

GETTING AROUND

BY BUS

Buses of all sizes and shapes, and communal taxis or *matatus* go virtually everywhere in Kenya, except through most national parks and reserves. Prices are minimal, depending on owner and operator, but are usually below Ksh5 per kilometer (half-mile). They are famously crowded but somehow, there's always enough room — just barely. This hasn't changed the fact that drivers are more concerned with speed than safety. Schedules are often erratic; drivers will rarely leave without an overfull load. Nonetheless, they will get you to your destination, and can run into some exciting adventures along the way. *Matatus* and buses are cheap. Hitchhiking is not generally recommended, and is most unwise near cities — the only exception might be in very rural areas where it is the only way to get around.

BY TAXI

In Nairobi and Mombasa, there are taxi services at reasonable prices. The cabs have no meters so always agree the price to your destination before getting in. Bargain or ask a different driver if you think the price too steep.

The minimum rate is generally Ksh200: don't accept higher minimums. Even in Nairobi Ksh300 should get you a long way, and even the international airport shouldn't be more than Ksh1,000. In general, taxis are usually around when needed, but they rarely cruise, and only in Nairobi and Mombasa are there dial-up taxis. If you're unsure about your return ride, book a taxi ahead.

BY TRAIN

The Mombasa–Uganda Railway, now Kenya Railways, provides nightly service between Mombasa and Nairobi, and Nairobi and Kisumu. The night trip to or from Mombasa to Nairobi is particularly recommended. With a private compartment and an excellent railroad meal, it feels a bit like the old Orient Express, or the still-marvelous trip on the Trans-Siberian Railway from Moscow to Vladivostok.

To reserve a seat on the train, you generally must make arrangements at the train station in Nairobi, Mombasa, or Kisumu, where you may be told no first-class tickets are available. If so, buy a second-class one and visit a nearby travel agency, where they may be able to upgrade your ticket to first class for a nominal fee. If this arrangement strikes you as peculiar, try going to a travel agency first. A word of caution: the travel agency may send you to the train station …

BY CAR

Car Rental
It's possible to rent both two- and four-wheel-drive vehicles in Nairobi and Mombasa; occasionally it's possible also to rent four-wheel drives (with or without drivers) at some hotels and lodges.

If you plan to drive only during the dry season (July to September, January to March) and avoid the Northern Frontier District, Mount Elgon, Tsavo East, Lamu and all the other areas off the main tourist circuit, you may be able to get by with a two-wheel-drive car. However heavy-duty tires are almost essential for occasional potholes that afflict even the best roads, let alone the collapsing surfaces of the worst.

Buses and *matatus* are Kenya's major form of transportation.

To ensure full freedom of travel, and to get into the backcountry (or to get practically *anywhere* during or after the rains), choose a four-wheel drive. Many of the roads in Kenya are so bad in the rainy season even a helicopter could get stuck in them. By sub-Saharan African standard they're not bad, but by any other they're dreadful.

There are special problems with renting cars in Kenya. First is cost. Bad roads are part of the reason why car rental is expensive, and this factor also means checking over the car for mechanical soundness is very important before driving off on an ambitious safari. There are also traps in the small print for the unwary. First is that cheap rates hide expensive charges per kilometer, often starting to click up your bill from the moment you edge out of the parking space. Rates rarely include CDW (Collision Damage Waiver), TP (Theft Protection) or tax at 17 percent. Even experienced travelers can be caught by insurance excess: some companies charge clients up to US$10,000 in the case of any accident, and that is when they've paid the CDW excess. Our best recommendation, in terms of vehicle reliability, price, and overall helpfulness, is **Central Rent-a-Car** ((02) 222888 FAX (02) 339666, Standard Street, Box 4939, Nairobi, while other reputable operators — with offices in Nairobi and Mombasa — include **Avis** ((02) 334317 FAX (02) 215421, Box 49795, Nairobi, and **Hertz** ((02) 214456 FAX (02) 216871, Box 42196, Nairobi. Central has more than competitive rates on both two- and four-wheel-drive vehicles, and their cars are clean, well-maintained, and reliable.

The second question is: what type of vehicle? The best four-wheel drive is probably a Landrover, followed closely by Mitsubishi Pajero and Toyota Landcruiser. Slightly cheaper — to buy or rent — is the Isuzu Trooper. I chose it after test-driving a number of similar vehicles and found I liked it most: it was comfortable yet rugged, roomy and solid but economical on gas. Due to its longer wheelbase, its ride is much smoother than the shorter Suzuki Sierra, which seemed also potentially hazardous and top-heavy. As experienced four-wheel drivers, we know the importance of freewheeling hubs that can be disengaged when two-wheel traction is insufficient.

If there are only two of you, it might be worth considering the four-seat model of the Suzuki Sierra (the two-seat version with a back bench being unstable on the road). The ride in the Sierra is a lot bouncier than the Trooper's, which becomes more and more important as you log more kilometers. If you're not going far, the Sierra may be fine. A compromise would be the Diahatzu Feroza, rather bigger and heavier than the Suzuki but still economical to rent: try Avis.

In any case, no matter what vehicle you choose, be sure it has sufficient seatbelts for each person traveling. Accidents are common in Kenya, and acceptable hospital facilities invariably distant.

Driving in Kenya

By Western standards, the roads in Kenya are poor. Even the best-surfaced ones have sudden jarring potholes, and the worst tarmac often entails a laborious, snaking slalom which leads some drivers to take to new tracks on either side. Many roads are still *murram*, or surfaced with local clay. If not regularly maintained these turn into rutted and unforgiving channels and however well prepared, any rain will transform the surface into mud more slippery than ice. This is even more of a problem if the surface is deeply rutted: the effect on the car is to make it, as the locals say, "dance." At any point roads can be blocked by trucks or cars that break down or simply get bogged.

Traffic is heavy, with slow trucks crawling up the steeper hills. Constant passing in the face of oncoming traffic can be wearing. Driving at night is not recommended, as other vehicles often drive without lights, and if they have them, rarely turn down the high beams. Blind corners are littered with unlit broken-down trucks, and a growing incidence of banditry and car-jacking make daylight hours the safest option. At any given time, some of the roads in the country will be unsafe due to cattle rustling or tribal disputes. The only way of finding out where it is safe to travel is to ask locally and place your trust in the answer.

Each Easter the East African Safari Rally takes place on public roads, and for much of March it seems that half the population is practicing speed-driving, often in heavy rain. Long distances irresistibly increase speed: watch out for speed bumps, often unmarked, which are frequent hazards near every school and settlement. Sometimes they are mere rumble strips, but often very serious mounds of tarmac that can bump the unwary driver hard against the roof and cause loss of control. Off the beaten track, road bumps are less of a problem than finding gasoline; sometimes it's necessary to phone ahead and ensure supplies are available at key lodges on your route. In any event, keep the tank well topped up, as it is easy to run dry in Kenya. Street signs are limited, and even major junctions are frequently unmarked. It's not even easy to get an accurate map, as the authorities regard these as classified information and seem to believe the average visitor is planning an invasion rather than a vacation.

Put off? Good. Because only the brave should head out behind the wheel of their own car. That said, the freedom of having your own vehicle can transform your experience, and a self-driver in Kenya is also rewarded with a considerable sense of achievement. All Kenya's roads have aspects of beauty. However, for the driver, appreciation of this is often glimpsed only in snatched glances from upcoming hazards on the way ahead. Roads subject to heavy traffic are usually the worst. The main road artery between Nairobi and Mombasa, for instance, is a bore: bad surface and slow trucks mean the view palls even for passengers. Many of the same trucks continue through towards Uganda and Africa's interior, taking their toll on routes across the Rift Valley, but better views compensate. Main roads not used by heavy traffic, dead-ending up towards Lake Baringo, Eldoret and Kitale are usually far better, and are considerably helped if their local MP is well-connected. At their best these roads can have light traffic and the only hazards are occasional potholes and stray animals.

Minor roads can deteriorate quickly over the wet season (April to June, October to early December), and their condition depends whether they have been graded. The little-used western route down from Kericho into the Masai Mara is one of the country's most scenic, but the dreadful *murram* surface

means that pleasure is tinged with concern: will you make it? In the wet season the answer is often no, although a little maintenance would make a great difference. The only way of finding out if this has taken place is to ask locally. The situation can change from mile to mile as well as year to year, but improvement is rare.

The condition of the vehicle is all-important. It is not always easy to find competent mechanics up-country, and there are plenty of situations where your life depends on the car's correct mechanical function. In general,

the driver is responsible for minor repairs that become necessary along the way, and just to complicate matters there are unscrupulous mechanics — especially around Kenya's third city, Nakuru — who specialize in tricking motorists into shelling out substantial amounts of money on unnecessary repairs. The favorite trick is to pour oil under your car when it's parked and then persuade you to visit their local garage. Don't let anyone take a wrench to your rented car without checking first with your rental agency. Travelers visiting Nakuru with a car and driver are faced with the same problem: often the driver will disappear for half an hour and come back with a mechanical fault. Nine times out of ten, your vehicle has been sabotaged. Understand that this will have happened often to most rental cars, and a quick glance underneath the hood will often make any competent mechanic blanche. Parts that should have been bolted will have been welded and mechanical parts thought

Checking the "Lunatic Line" in Tsavo.

essential in other countries will, inexplicably, be missing. When repairs are needed they are unlikely to be straightforward.

A further special hazard is the risk of carjacking. This is when armed thieves ambush your car while you wait for the gate to be opened in a private residence, or foolishly stray into the wrong part of town and then stop at a traffic light. The problem gets worse after dark. Asian drivers are often beaten up, while whites are generally treated with a weird civility, though as with all situations where there's a scared man — or some-

Courtesy on the road takes a slightly different form in Kenya. Whereas elsewhere flashing brights means "Go ahead," in Kenya it is more likely to mean "I am going ahead — keep clear" and often it just means "hello." Although in principle cattle, bicycles, ox-carts and pedestrians should get out of the way of trucks and cars, in practice frequent use of the horn serves as a useful reminder to people who might have forgotten that they are sharing the road with faster vehicles, and constant beeping that would seem rude and assertive in the West is perfectly acceptable

times woman — pointing a gun at your head there is a big element of risk.

There is no way to reliably avoid this risk, though knowing your way around clearly helps. Some vehicles are fitted with Cartrack, a vehicle-tracing transmitter that allows the local organizers, who employ their own policemen, to chase down and track stolen vehicles and, effectively, steal them back. This is a good safety aid, if fitted. Check perhaps with Cartrack ((02) 712780 FAX (02) 713010 directly.

The best map of the country for motorists is Freytag and Berndt's 1:1,500,000, which also includes reasonable city-maps of Mombasa and Nairobi as well as a useful 1:700,000 inset of the Kenyan coast.

in Kenya. Although it might seem harsh, it is no longer recommended to stop for broken-down vehicles or hitchhikers waving desperately by the side of the road: there have been too many cases of ambush or hijack.

In case of breakdown, pile branches or trees 50 m (50 yards) downstream on the road. It's a local equivalent to a warning triangle and will alert oncoming traffic, which might or might not have functioning lights. Get flat tires repaired as soon as possible: there are plenty of cheap puncture repair places (agree on the price first) in every village and, perhaps for this very reason, punctures seem to be far more common here than in any developed country. You never know when your next puncture might happen. Keep the doors locked when driving through cities, and be ready to step on the gas if approached. In the event of an accident involving a pedestrian or casualty, it is recommended to drive to the nearest police station rather than stopping to assist. Emotions can run high and the situation can spiral out of control to no one's benefit. It is wise to sacrifice common humanity and play things safe.

It is usual, when parking in towns or cities, to pay a small parking fee to private security guards or official parking boys: they will also, to a considerable extent, look after your car and its contents. A 20-Ksh note is useful here: motorists should make sure they keep a reasonable supply of these small blue notes, worth about 30 cents, as the alternative might be to part with a larger note, encouraging inflation as well as increasing the cost of traveling.

Finally, vehicles drive on the left side of the road.

Rules of the Road

1. DON'T DRIVE ALONE. Be sure to travel with at least one other person in your car. Several tourists who've rented cars recently for solitary wandering in Kenya have turned up dead.

2. DON'T DRIVE AT NIGHT. Kenyan roads are narrow, often in poor condition and can be singularly lacking in guard rails, center lines and other safeguards. Some of the vehicles coming the other way may be without lights or in dreadful mechanical shape ("Brakes? What brakes?"); large trucks often break down (particularly on hills) and are not infrequently left on the road in the dark with no hazard lights or other indication (the normal breakdown alert is to spread branches along the roadside).

3. DON'T GET OUT OF YOUR VEHICLE IN THE PARKS AND RESERVES unless it's allowed at the specific place where you are. Lions have attacked tourists, but buffaloes, hippos, crocodiles and even elephants are more dangerous. Alternatively, take advantage of the many wonderful places where it's safe to walk around. If you have any doubt, check with rangers, lodge personnel or local folk.

4. DON'T CAMP JUST ANYWHERE. Many of the parks and reserves have reliable campsites at minimal cost, and the rangers can keep you up-to-date on the best places. But camping at non-designated areas can lead to trouble, from both people and animals. Particularly in the Northern Frontier District, be careful where you camp.

5. NEVER LEAVE THINGS IN YOUR TENT, particularly food. Lock them in your car. Baboons will tear a tent apart for a box of cookies; elephants will crush it for a cabbage; as friendly and honest as the Kenyans are, there are still a few who'll rip you off (particularly on the coast or in the cities). Crime in rural areas is minimal but in the cities stay alert: crime rates are approaching American levels.

6. IF YOU'RE A WOMAN, you can expect few male hassles, but keep alert. I've met single women hitching the Northern Frontier who've had nothing but fun, and lots of women driving (two to a car). But, especially in Nairobi and on the coast, take no chances.

7. IF YOU BREAK DOWN in the middle of nowhere, or run into any other kind of trouble, you'll probably be overwhelmed with help. Kenyans are unusually kind and sympathetic, and have a national ethic of peace and assisting others. Their tribal philosophies, often summarized as "African socialism," in most cases require treating a stranger almost as family. But follow your instincts — if somebody makes you uptight, act accordingly. Breaking down at night in any major city represents real danger. Try to avoid any such situation.

ACCOMMODATION

While the rates at some of the upcountry resorts and game lodges might look horrendous, bear in mind that they usually include all meals (there is, in any case, rarely anywhere else you can eat), all game activities and the services of a skilled and knowledgeable guide.

Trying to arrange your own safari and book lodges on arrival might be more satisfying but is unlikely to save you money. The "milk run" safaris that link a few game parks together in a quick package are particularly competitive and the major operators will have negotiated better deals than you will be able to privately.

Shoe-shine boys in Nairobi.

Moderately priced "Kenyan" hotels used mainly by locals but also used by expatriates and, occasionally, tourists, can usually be relied upon to provide perfectly adequate accommodation; although most bars in these hotels will probably tend to double as informal brothels, the pressure is rarely severe. Every major town will have one or more hotels that used to be grand in colonial times and are still open for business, charmingly starting to become rundown. Rates priced in Kenya shillings are almost always lower than those rated in dollars and often you'll find a great atmosphere: such places are almost always family-run. A double, with a good dinner and breakfast, at a "Kenyan" hotel, can run as low as US$30 for a comfortable, clean room with a private toilet and bath. Places quoted in Kenya shillings are invariably looking more to a resident market and are invariably cheaper. The service is more offhand, the food more African. Prices take a quantum leap in those establishments aimed at the overseas visitor, which will generally quote their rates in dollars.

For the purposes of this book accommodation costs have been calculated on two sharing, per night, and are B&B (bed and breakfast) unless otherwise stated. Half-board comes with breakfast and dinner included. Full-board indicates all meals are provided. All-inclusive means that extra services, such as game drives, alcoholic drinks, or water sports, are included in the rate. At the top end of the Kenyan travel market some serious charges are imposed, and the "Extremely Expensive" is a new category all of my own of which I am very proud. Perhaps, however, I just suffer from the poverty characteristic of the guidebook writer.

The price bands used in this book, in United States dollars, are, for a double room:

Very Inexpensive	under $10
Inexpensive	$11 to $50
Mid-range	$51 to $100
Expensive	$101 to $200
Very Expensive	$201 to $400
Extremely Expensive	over $400

Young elephants usually stay with their mothers for seven to ten years or more, females often forming a two- or three-generational matriarchal clan.

Tented Accommodation

In general, tented camps in Kenya are just as comfortable — and expensive — as stone-built lodges. If taking your own tent, it should be roomy enough to move about in and close securely at the bottom and doors, with reliable mosquito screens.

You can rent tents and some camping equipment from **Atul's** ((02) 228064 FAX (02) 225935, Biashara Street, Box 43202, Nairobi.

Those who are willing to rough it can find board and lodging at very inexpensive rates in campsites in most national parks, charging from US$1 a night upwards. More usefully still, often having a tent will open up rarely-visited regions where the lack of accommodation means you'll have the place to yourself.

Don't, however, fly-camp. The remote area sare just those where the forces of law and order are spread most thinly, populated areas are always much less safe at night, and wild enclaves might harbor animals to whom a human in a tent is just a well-wrapped tasty morsel.

EATING OUT

Regular readers of the *Traveler's Companion* series might notice the comprehensive WHERE TO EAT sections in many of the smaller towns and settlements featured in these pages are strangely missing. There is a good reason for this. While there is a choice of restaurants in the larger cities and in tourist areas, in most Kenyan towns you will be most likely to find your hotel is the only place that can be relied on to provide food. There is little tradition of eating out amongst rural Kenyans, and if you do find a restaurant its quality will probably depend on what has died and how recently. The WHERE TO EAT section has been included where justified.

BASICS

ELECTRICITY

Electricity is 220–240 volt, 50 cycles and most of the smarter establishments use three-prong plugs as found in the United Kingdom. Less ambitious establishments also use two-pin plugs with round connectors. It is useful to carry adapters for many kinds of outlets, which can be purchased at most hardware stores in Nairobi. The larger hotels will have adapters, as well as separate outlets, for 110–120 volt razors, but often these will not provide full power. In remote areas electricity is generally provided by generators, which operate only during specific hours each day. Even in urban areas, however, electrical power cannot be guaranteed. Don't rely on electrical appliances like curling irons, hairdryers, etc. This will also have the effect of keeping your luggage light.

TIME

Local time is three hours ahead of Greenwich Mean Time; Kenya does not have daylight savings time. During winter, it is two hours ahead of continental Europe (only one hour during summer) and eight hours ahead of New York (seven hours in summer).

WEIGHTS AND MEASURES

Weights and measures in Kenya are metric. Distances are measured in meters (just more

OPPOSITE: The world's fastest land animal, the cheetah, runs down his prey in short sprints. ABOVE: Two of the black rhinos to be seen in Kenya's game reserves.

than a yard) and kilometers, as are speed signs. Multiply by 1.6 to convert kilometers to (approximate) miles: one kilometer is five-eighths of a mile. Fuel is sold in liters, (4.5 liters = 1 Imperial gallon, while 3.8 litres = 1 US gallon), and beer is usually sold in 500-ml bottles, which are just more than a pint. Vegetables are sold in kilograms, with one pound equal to 4.5 kg. Temperatures, generally, are expressed in Celsius.

PUBLIC HOLIDAYS

Public holidays follow the Christian calendar, with New Year's Day, Good Friday and Easter Monday, Christmas Day and Boxing Day. June 1 is Madaraka Day, celebrating the granting of self-government; October 10 is Moi Day (with crowds paid to celebrate this one at the moment); October 20 is Kenyatta Day and December 12 is Independence Day.

CURRENCY

The unit of currency is the Kenya shilling (Ksh), divided into 100 cents. Notes are in denominations of 500, 200, 100, 50, 20, and Ksh10. The blue Ksh20 note is sometimes called a "Kenya pound" and is a useful tip for services both small and large. Coins are 5, 10, and 50 cents and 1 Ksh. At the time of publication, **exchange rates** were US$1 for Ksh78.75 and 1 euro for Ksh66.52.

Any amount of foreign cash or travelers' checks may be brought into the country, and the old currency declaration forms, made ridiculous by the ATM's all around the country, are no longer important. The black market in currency has also ceased to exist, and you should not be tempted to change on the streets. Changing money in banks can be interminably slow, but will give you better rates than you'll get in your hotel.

Banks are open from 9 AM to 3 PM, Monday to Friday and most from 9 AM to 11 AM on Saturdays. All transactions, whether the bank is empty or full, seem to take 20 minutes and involve plenty of forms. Licensed exchange bureaux and hotel cashiers generally stay open longer, give a marginally worse exchange rate, but do the transaction quickly. ATM machines give the best rate of all with cash advances on Visa and Master

Card if you have a PIN number. They are found in all major towns but sometimes run out of money or break down: look for branches of Barclays. There are machines throughout Nairobi as well as Nyeri, Meru, Kitale, Nakuru, Diani, Kisumu, Kisii, Embu, Thika, Nyahururu, Kakamega, Naivasha, Limuru, Mombasa, Bungoma, Nanyuki, Eldoret, Kericho and Malindi. Travelers' checks are useful for carrying substantial amounts in relative safety.

Banks at the Mombasa and Nairobi airports are supposedly open 24 hours.

Your Visa, Mastercard, American Express and Diners Club cards will be accepted by many hotels and shops.

Many national parks, hotels and services catering to the tourist market quote their prices in United States dollars. Those that quote in Kenya shillings are looking more to a resident market and are invariably cheaper. The service is more offhand and the feel more African. Those quoting in dollars are slicker and sometimes lack the Kenyan feeling. I have kept this distinction by quoting prices as the service providers quote them.

ETIQUETTE

Etiquette, in Kenya, is usually relaxed. On the generally Muslim coast, topless bathing on public beaches is needlessly provocative and should be avoided. It is easy too to run foul of political sensibilities. Never tear up a Kenyan banknote (though some may, literally, fall apart on you) as this is seen as a deep insult to the country. Don't take photographs of the president, his palace, or the national flag, and you can get into trouble if you pull your camera out at airports and near police stations. If you suddenly find your car pushed off a Nairobi street by a flood of motorcycle outriders, pull off completely, get out of your car, and stand respectfully. In due course President Moi will pass.

HEALTH

It's strongly recommended that you talk with your own physician when planning a Kenyan vacation. At present, the only certificate required is for yellow fever for travelers from endemic areas. However, it is recommended that visitors take anti-malaria medication; beginning 10 days before they leave and continuing until three weeks after their return. Ask your doctor for advice.

It is generally stated that tap-water in Nairobi and other cities is potable, although our experience does not always bear this out. If you're susceptible to stomach upsets, it's wise to treat all water supplies, and to ask before drinking the water in lodges and hotels. Peel your fresh fruits and vegetables, or wash them with potable water. Avoid uncooked foods from sidewalk stands. Even with these precautions, you may get a mild attack of dysentery or the "runs." If you are struck with a serious case of dysentery, the best medication is available in pharmacies under the name of Gabboral, which has replaced Flagyl, but many doctors think that wiping out the stomach's natural gut flora with high doses of antibiotic is the worst thing to do with an upset stomach. Personally, I find the old Caribbean favorite of a teaspoonful of Angostura Bitters mixed with five times as much Coca-Cola invariably settles things down. There are numerous pharmacies with well-qualified staffs to help in the event you do become ill, but they may not have familiar brand names. If you use medication regularly, bring it with you.

Nairobi and Mombasa have modern, well-equipped hospitals, capable of dealing with any emergency, but even smaller towns usually have reliable clinics. Health insurance is strongly recommended: get it before you leave home and make sure it covers you for travel in Africa. If you are planning to spend a lot of time in the bush, it would be wise to make sure evacuation by Flying Doctor is covered.

AIDS is in Kenya, is heterosexual and widespread. If you need an injection, make sure it's a new needle, or bring your own, and in the event of needing a blood transfusion (which is to be avoided if possible) try to contact your embassy: often they have lists of healthy donors.

Make sure your tetanus vaccination is up to date to avoid this inoculation in the event of a bad cut. In general, avoid any inoculation. Do not swim in fresh water. As in most

of Africa, still fresh water is infested with bilharzia, a parasite that enters the body and causes a general deterioration in health. Treatment is usually effective and straightforward, but there can be complications. Note that flowing water is generally clear of bilharzia, so whitewater rafting is fine, but still water is dangerous, ruling out swimming in Lake Victoria. Take local advice before taking any quick dip.

Remember that Kenya straddles the equator and the sun is directly overhead for longer periods of time than most of us are used to.

Sunstroke and sunburn are dangers. If you're sensitive to the sun, consult your doctor or pharmacist about the best sunscreen to use. Even if you have never burned, use sunscreen during your first days of exposure and avoid prolonged exposure during the middle of the day. For children, a T-shirt while swimming is always a good precaution. This is highly recommended also when snorkeling, because time passes quickly and reflection from the ocean surface magnifies the effect of the sun. Children should always use sunscreen, which should be reapplied regularly.

A member of Kenya's northern desert anti-poaching unit. The government has adopted a shoot-to-kill policy in a last-ditch attempt to save its remaining elephants.

Bring a sun hat or invest in one on arrival, and use it. Sunstroke's nausea and dizziness can ruin several days of your visit.

The altitude at Nairobi and the highlands can also cause discomfort to some travelers in the form of drowsiness and passing dizziness. Such mild symptoms usually pass in a couple of days once you've become acclimated to the thinner air, but travelers attempting to climb Kenya's mountains should take the risk seriously and take time to acclimatize. Altitude sickness can kill. Headaches or trouble breathing mean it is time

Make use of these services rather than leaving money, passports, or travelers' checks in your room. In Nairobi, Mombasa and other cities, don't wear jewelry on the streets or walk after dark — especially past bush areas where muggers can lurk. Strangely, street crime is worst on weekends, when you're dealing with students: they're much brighter than the down-and-outs (known as "Parking Boys") whose ambitions usually extend only as far as snatching necklaces and watches. In taxis, don't rest your arm on the window if you're wearing an expensive watch, as it

to lose altitude fast, even if someone has to carry you, until the symptoms disappear. Then spend a day acclimatizing before continuing your climb.

may well be torn free. Car-jacking is an increasing problem in Nairobi and Mombasa, but seems confined to certain suburbs. Stick to the main roads and try to avoid driving at night and you should be safe.

SECURITY

Opportunistic crime is increasingly common, especially in the cities. In rural areas the temptation can overwhelm — and penalties are harsh if they are caught. It is unfair to tempt — often very poor — locals by leaving out goods they could not possibly buy. Never leave cameras, handbags and other valuables unattended or visible in your locked vehicle, even in the bush. Most hotels and lodges have safes where you can leave your valuables.

ANIMAL WATCHING

For the wildlife observer, a pair of binoculars and the Collins *A Field Guide to the Natural Parks of East Africa*, *A Field Guide to the Birds of East Africa*, and *A Field Guide to the Butterflies of Africa*, all by J. A. Williams, are essential. At all the parks and reserves, wardens are more than happy to explain what species you can expect to see, where and when to find them, and the "rules of the game."

In general, the "rules of the game" are speed limits of 30 km/h (19 mph), confinement to vehicles except in specifically designated areas, and, of course, no shooting except with a camera. Travel after dark and before dawn (6:30 PM to 6 AM) is strictly forbidden and enforced. There may be variations from one park or reserve to another, so it's best to check the regulations each time you pay an entrance fee. No matter how cute, friendly, docile, cuddly or harmless animals may seem, they are all wild and are potentially dangerous. Young animals invariably

the arid regions a little more green than usual, the dangers of sunstroke and sunburn somewhat reduced, and the ocean as refreshing as ever. Particularly now the climate in Kenya is less predictable, there is a lot to be said for off-season travel. Accommodation is easier to find and the staff have more time to spend with you individually explaining the countryside and its attractions. May is probably the exception: many hotels and lodges close for refurbishment and roads during rainy seasons are even more dreadful than usual.

have parents who might kill you for disturbing their offspring.

WHEN TO GO

Being on the equator, the Kenyan "season" is anytime, with the winter months (December through February) and the school holidays (July and August) the busiest. During these times, it's advisable to make arrangements ahead of time for safaris and coastal accommodations.

During the rainy seasons (April to June, October to early December), you can frequently get reduced rates on hotels, but many safari outfitters do not operate then due to impassable roads. The animals are still there,

WHAT TO BRING

Year-round, you will need to bring lightweight comfortable clothing, which is preferable wash-and-wear. Away from the coast, most of Kenya is well above sea level, which makes the climate perfect: warm in the day and pleasant at night. Dress is casual throughout the country. For footwear, again the key is comfort. Canvas or running shoes are ideal, and only the more adventurous travelers — those attempting the peaks of Mounts Kenya or Elgon, or those taking a camel safari or a

OPPOSITE: Twenty-seven tons of ivory, confiscated from poachers, go up in smoke. ABOVE: Until recently Kenya's anti-poaching unit was equipped with ancient Enfield rifles.

walking tour of the parks or reserves — will need hiking boots. Locally made boots and shoes are good and inexpensive, but it's better to come with broken-in, supple shoes. Sandals are only suitable for wearing in town and on the beach, and not suitable for walking in the bush.

Whether your plans include an overnight in the mountain lodges or not, bring a warm sweater and light waterproof jacket as the high altitude means that evenings can be cool and, beyond the occasional open fire, heating is unlikely. A good combination is a polar fleece pullover and a windbreaker or K-way. In the bush, long pants are preferable to shorts, and shirts with long sleeves that can be rolled down to protect you against the sun and insects are recommended. Your clothes will get covered with the ever-present red dust of Kenya, so make sure they are all washable. Laundry is done almost every night in safari camps and lodges, or you can wash it out yourself and it's usually dry by morning. Of course, don't forget a swimsuit.

If you have made arrangements for a safari, your outfitter will provide you with a list of things to bring. Follow their advice, as they are professionals with years of experience in making Kenya vacations as comfortable as possible for visitors.

Don't forget to pack a flashlight, spare batteries and binoculars. Sunscreen and a hat are necessities for everyone. You may want to wait and buy your hat in Nairobi, where there is a wide choice, and if time permits you can get an entire safari outfit made-to-measure.

PHOTOGRAPHY

Since the game-hunting ban in 1977, most legal "shooting" of wildlife has been done with cameras. Print film is readily available throughout the country, especially in Nairobi, but slide film isn't. Processing can be quick but the quality variable.

A 35-mm camera, with a telephoto lens of at least 300 mm is ideal, and films of varying speeds are recommended: 400 ISO for dusk, sunrise, and dense vegetation; 64 and 200 ISO for midday on the savanna, and 1,000 ISO or higher for night shooting in

lodges like The Ark and Treetops (see THE ABERDARE MOUNTAINS, page 208). If you are using a APS (advanced photo system) camera, be warned that film supply and film processing may not be readily available in some places.

But don't weigh yourself down with a lot of bulky and new equipment. If photography will be a major part of your Kenyan vacation, ask the advice of a professional at your local camera store. Then decide which combination of camera, lenses and film fits your style of shooting best. It might be better to use familiar equipment even if it's a fixed lens or compact camera than to waste precious time trying to operate an unfamiliar camera. The animals won't wait for you to change lenses and focus. You will miss not only the shot, but also the enjoyment of observing the animals.

On the other hand, a lion or giraffe who seems close at hand will end up shrunken and distant in a normal 50-mm SLR or compact camera slide or print — so if you have the means and a bit of experience, a telephoto lens (at least 200 mm) is a real advantage. The most important thing, however, is to have fun: if you're too hung up on getting a picture of whatever strange beast stands before you, you'll miss the opportunity of seeing it in a relaxed, enjoyable fashion.

Be sure to keep your film as cool and dry as possible; never expose film canisters or camera to prolonged heat or direct sunlight, as on the dashboard or rear ledge of your car. The best time to take pictures is early morning or late afternoon — the light's best and the animals more abundant. Always pay attention to your light meter reading. If your subject's in the shade, get your reading from him, not from a sunlit area.

Always ask permission before you take pictures of anyone. Many Kenyans are afraid of cameras; there is a widespread feeling in Kenya that being photographed robs the subject of his or her soul or of a future life — and perhaps they're right. Others are willing to take the chance for a posing fee. Always agree on the fee before you shoot. Usually, a few shillings will do, but occasionally you'll encounter someone, typically a Maasai, who'll demand outrageous fees. Negotiate or walk away.

COMMUNICATIONS

POST

Mail service from Kenya is good, taking three to six days to reach Europe or the United States. And the stamps are beautiful! Main post offices in Nairobi are open from 8 AM to 6 PM, others from 8:30 AM to noon, and 2 PM to 4 PM; some up-country post offices are open only in the morning. More expensive hotels and lodges sell stamps for postcards and letters.

TELEPHONES

With the Kenya telephone service, you can direct-dial domestic and international numbers, but in general the telephone system is expensive and inefficient. Telephones are provided in some hotel rooms, but be aware that hotels can and do add hefty surcharges to an already large bill. Often charges are made — and high ones — for calls even if they don't go through, so even unsuccessful attempts to send faxes can result in an expensive bill. It is more practical to make your international calls from the post office. Even from a post office or private phone, long-distance calls in Kenya are very expensive as well as being unreliable. Don't chat too long.

TELEGRAMS, TELEX AND INTERNET

Telegrams can be sent by phone through the operator. Telex and fax facilities are available at many post offices or private businesses, providing direct dialing to most major international cities on a 24-hour basis. Internet bureaus are just starting to become available in the business centers of the larger hotels and small offices in Nairobi, but they are invariably expensive: they usually charge in dollars for the time you're on the machine, as well as to send or receive e-mails. Increasing numbers of Internet cafés now grace the streets of Nairobi and Mombasa, often with very low costs — as little as Ksh3 per minute.

At the moment, Internet cafés haven't spread beyond the towns of Mombasa and Nairobi. In a country where the telephone system is so bad, however, commercial establishments are increasingly switching to e-mail for their business communications. In upcountry areas your hotel might let you borrow their computer, or let you use your own through the telephone system, but the connection speeds are just too slow to make even e-mail effective and recreational surfing is impractical. Just to make it worse, long-distance calls (to the hubs in Nairobi or Mombasa) are very expensive.

SWAHILI

Swahili is the *lingua franca* of Kenya, and English the language of business and commerce. English is taught in schools all over the country, so you can usually make yourself understood everywhere.

Nonetheless, whenever you travel, it is always appreciated when you attempt the native language. Swahili is one of the easiest languages to learn. The pronunciation is entirely phonetic, and the grammar need not worry a beginner. For the vowels, A is pronounced as in *father*, E as the *a* in *day*, I as the *e* in *see*, O as in *go*, and U as the *o* in *do*. The consonants are generally pronounced as in English. If people ask — and they will — if you speak Swahili, *"kidogo sana"* — meaning "very little" — is less abrupt than "no."

SOME BASIC EXPRESSIONS AND VOCABULARY

Politeness and Introductions
hello   *jambo*
good-bye   *kwaheri*
good morning   *habari ya asubuhi*
good afternoon   *habari ya mchana*
good evening   *habari ya jioni*
how are you?   *habari?*
I am well (I am very well)   *mzui (mzui sana)*
please   *tafadhali*
thank you (very much)   *asante (sana)*
what is your name?   *jina lako mani*
my name is …   *jina langu ni …*
excuse me   *samahani*
I am sorry   *pole*
yes   *ndiyo*
no   *hapana*

Places and People

hotel (or occasionally just foodhut)   *hoteli*
room   *chumba*
bed   *kitanda*
police   *polici*
hospital   *hospitali*
street   *barabara*
airport   *uwanja wa ndege*
river   *mto*
mountain   *mulima*
where?   *wapi?*
where is the hotel?   *hoteli iko wapi?*
what?   *nini?*
Mrs.   *bibi*
Mr.   *bwana*
Miss   *bi*
who?   *nani?*
I, me   *mimi*
you (singular)   *wewe*
he, she   *yeye*
we   *sisi*
you (plural)   *ninyi*
they   *wao*
woman   *mwanamke*
man   *mwamamume*
child   *mtoto*
mother   *mama*
father   *baba*
daughter   *binti*
son   *mwana*
wife   *mke*
husband   *mume*
friend   *rafiki*

Food

food   *chakula*
coffee   *kahawa*
tea   *chai*
beer   *tembo* or *pombe*; *Tusker*, the name of the leading brand, is usually good enough.
ice   *barafu*
meat   *nyama*
chicken   *kuku*
fish   *samaki*
bread   *mkate*
rice   *wali*
butter   *siagi*
sugar   *sukari*
vegetables   *mbogo*
fruit   *matunda*
water   *maji*
milk   *mazima*
salt   *chumvi*

pepper   *pilipili*
dessert   *tamutamu*

Common Kenyan Dishes

githeri   beans and maize
irio   peas and other vegetables with maize
matoke   steamed bananas
mkate mayui   a flour and egg mixture
mrere   cooked green vegetables
muhogo ya kuchoma   roasted cassava with chilies and lemon
nyama ya kuchoma   roasted meat
samosa   Kenyan sandwich
sukuma wiki   boiled spinach (or kale)
ugali   maize meal

Numbers

half   *nusu*
one   *moja*
two   *mbili*
three   *tatu*
four   *ine*
five   *tano*
six   *sita*
seven   *saba*
eight   *nane*
nine   *tisa*
ten   *kumi*
eleven   *kumi na moja*
twelve   *kumi na mbili*
twenty   *ishirini*
twenty-one   *ishirini na moja*
thirty   *thelathini*
forty   *arobaini*
fifty   *hamsini*
sixty   *sitini*
seventy   *sabani*
eighty   *themanini*
ninety   *tisini*
hundred   *mia*
one hundred   *mia moja*
two hundred   *mia mbili*
thousand   *elfu*

Adjectives and Adverbs

good   *mzuri*
bad   *mbaya*
cold   *baridi*
hot   *moto*
now   *sasa*
quickly   *haraka*
slowly   *pole-pole*
big   *kubwa*

small *kidogo*
more, another *ingine*
much, more *mwingi*
that *yule*
this *huyu*
sweet *tamu*
cheap *rahisi*
expensive *ghali*

Directions

right *kulia*
left *kushoto*
turn (right) *geuka (kulia)*
go straight *enda moja kwa moja*
where are you going? *una kwenda wapi?*

Time

now *sasa*
today *leo*
tomorrow *kesho*
yesterday *yana*
morning *asubuhi*
afternoon *alarsiri*
evening *jioni*
nighttime *usiku*
daytime *mehana*
day *siku*
week *wiki*
month *mwezi*
year *mwaka*
Sunday *Jumapili*
Monday *Jamatatu*
Tuesday *Jumanne*
Wednesday *Jumatano*
Thursday *Alhamisi*
Friday *I jumaa*
Saturday *Jumamosi*

Shopping

money *fedha*
cent *senti*
how much? *ngapi?*
how much does this cost? *inagharimu pesa ngapi?*
that's expensive *wawezakupunguz*
shop *duka*
cigarettes *sigareti*
newspaper *gazeti*
clothes *nguo*
shoes *viatu*

Recommended Web Sites

Kenya has been slow to get online, though the dreadful general state of its telecommunications have helped a late surge. The most relevant newsgroups for Kenya are rec.travel.africa and soc.culture.kenya. The following sites might be of interest.

Kenya News www.kenyanews.com, updated every weekday, is a worthy source of up-to-date information about events and news stories in Kenya. It's a great introduction to the issues in the country and a good way to stay in touch after your visit. Kenya's leading national paper online, **The East African Standard** www.eastandard.net, carries all the stories, and is searchable too.

Africaonline's Kenya Site www.africaonline.co.ke has a good range of general information about Kenya, and **Kenyaweb** www.kenyaweb.com is especially comprehensive, with a virtual Nairobi tour of what's on. **Kenyalogy** www.kenyalogy.com offers interesting information about the country and its national parks, with pictures; also in Spanish.

The Kamusi project's **Swahili Online Dictionary** www.yale.edu/swahili/concerns itself with Kenya's widest-used language. Don't waste your visit shopping for souvenirs: you can buy them all at **Curios200** www.curios2000.com and contribute to the homeless by doing so.

Friends of Arabuko-Sokoke Forest www.watamu.net tells you all you need to know about the forest and the village of Watamu, online. **Kenya Birds** www.kenyabirds.co.uk is a wonderful and very detailed site showing what birds are found, where. A must for birders.

Trying to link conservation initiatives nationwide is **African Websites** www.africanconservation.com/kenya.html, while the **East Africa Wildlife Society** www.eawildlife.org is the official site of this worthy conservation movement, who also publish the influential *Swara* Magazine.

Three Routes Scuba Diving Guide www.3routes.com/scuba/africa/keny/index.html provides up-to-date links to Kenya's main diving operators, not necessarily those whose contact details are in the text of this book.

The Kenya Embassy in Washington DC has a cosular services site, **The Kenya Embassy** www.kenyaembassy.com, which is good place to find out the current situation regarding frequently changeable visa requirements.

To keep abreast of new cybercafés across Kenya, try **Net Café Guide** www.netcafe guide.com/africa.htm

Recommended Reading

Literature relevant to Kenya tends to concentrate on three main aspects of the country. The drama and glamor of exploration and the colonial years inspired some of the most famous books, often made into films, while the spectacular and intriguing natural history of the country has provided the base material for many glossy coffee-table books, a number of autobiographies where the animals play leading roles and a few more scientific tomes, and the African experience, with all its tribal complexity, has left relatively few literary traces. In all these categories, market forces have done little to ensure the immortality of the written word, and many of the best titles are now out of print. Kenya is one place where time spent in second-hand bookshops or searching web sites such as www.abe.com are likely to be especially rewarding.

For literature from the colonial era, some titles have been kept in the public eye by the later attentions of the movie industry. Thus *Out of Africa* by Karen Blixen (first published 1937 under the penname of Isak Dinesen), a tale of a Dutch settler's relationship with a colonial settler, is still the best-known tale of a Nairobi where hunting was a way of life. The material for the film of the same name, however, drew more on the biography of the author, *Isak Dinesen: the Life of a Storyteller*, by Judith Thurman (Picador, first published 1984) which is rather more revealing and honest. Perhaps the books — and later films — that did most to put wildlife conservation on the world's agenda were written by Joy Adamson, including *Born Free, Living Free*, and *Forever Free* (first published 1960, 1961, 1962 respectively; now published as a trilogy by Pan), which relate to the author's time living amongst lions. Ernest Hemingway did his bit to immortalize Kenya, with books such as *The Green Hills of Africa* (1935) and *The Snows of Kilimanjaro* (1948). Elspeth Huxley's books *The Flame Trees of Thika* (1959) and *Nine Faces of Kenya* (1991) provide a more autobiographical background. For a more informed overview of Kenya's early years there's still not much that can match Alan Moorhead's seminal tale of Burton, Speke and the race to find the source of the Nile, *The White Nile* (1901), which will have most readers booking their air ticket the next day for an exploration of their own.

When it comes to wildlife the keen reader is spoiled for choice. *Elephant Memories* by Cynthia Moss (1988) is a fascinating account of her observations — still continuing — of the elephants of Amboseli, while the same elephants also provide the material for Joyce Poole's *Coming of Age with Elephants* (1996). *Gorillas in the Mist* by Diane Fossey (1983) shifts the action just over the border into Uganda, but is still an insight into one of the world's most important conservationists.

For those with any interest in the natural world a good field-guide to Kenya's wildlife will be a great investment, both to aid identification in the field and as a souvenir of your visit. Some of the best are published by Collins, and written by John Williams, whose three titles cover the birds, butterflies, and national parks of East Africa. *The Field Guide to the Larger Mammals of Africa* by Chris and Tilde Stuart (1998) is a useful guide to have aboard your safari vehicle, as is the comprehensive *Field Guide to the Birds of Kenya and Northern Tanzania* by Zimmerman, Turner and Pearson (1999).

For an African perspective on Kenya, a good place to start is Jomo Kenyatta's *Facing Mount Kenya: the Tribal Life of Kenya* (1962), whose important reflections on the country he helped guide through independence are interesting from a political and anthropological point of view. One important but deceptively cheerful contemporary Kenyan writer is Meja Mwangi, whose titles include *The Cockroach Dance*, (1979) *Going Down River Road* (1976, now unfortunately out of print) and *The Return of Shaka* (1989 — generally available). Rather luckier with his publishers (Heinemann) is the altogether more serious Wa Thiong'o Ngugi, whose titles *I will Marry When I Want* (1982), *A Grain of Wheat*,

(1967) and *Devil on the Cross* (1982) are still in print, alongside *Decolonising the Mind: the Politics of Language in African Literature* (1986).

When it comes to conventional travel books, some of the best include Dervla Murphy's *The Ukwimi Road* (1994), an account of her cycle ride from Nairobi to Zimbabwe, while Shiva Naipaul's *North of South* (1980) is a readable and often very funny account of the country. *No Picnic on Mount Kenya* (1999) by Felice Benuzzi is essential reading for anyone intending to climb Kenya's highest mountain.

Photo Credits

STORM STANLEY PHOTO AGENCY —
Karl Ammann: Front cover, pages 19 *top*, 20 *right*, 66, 200.
Allan Binks: pages 3, 17 *bottom*, 35, 36-37, 40 *top*, 43, 46, 50-51, 52-53, 57, 58 *bottom*, 67 *top and bottom*, 71, 75, 76-77, 83, 191, 219, 231, 263, 284 *right*, 285.
Rick Edwards: ARPS: pages 23, 32-33, 34, 47, 66, 80, 201, 215, 244-245, 306.
Nicolas Granier: pages 41 *left*, 69 *top*, 214, 242.
Douglas Granier: pages 20 *left*, 27.
Thierry Greener: pages 63 *top*, 103, 125, 138.
Frants Harmann: pages 12 *bottom*, 26, 44-45, 65, 73 *bottom*, 112, 120, 143, 262.
Storm Stanley: pages 38, 40 *bottom*, 54, 61, 63 *bottom*, 69 *bottom*, 142, 218, 246, 282.
Ian Vincent: pages 48-49, 253.
Duncan Willetts (Camerapix): pages 13, 22-23, 39, 59, 68, 70, 73 *top*, 79, 122, 211, 252, 277.

JACK BARKER: Pages 21, 27, 30 *left and right*, 58 *top*, 60, 257, 260, 269.
NIK WHEELER: Back cover, pages 4, 5 *left*, 6 *right*, 81, 85, 110, 143, 144, 148-149, 152, 184-185, 213, 229, 236–237, 240, 279, 283, 287, 292, 305, 307.
PEGGY AND MICHAEL BOND: Pages 92–93, 186–187, 227, 223.

All other pictures: CAMERAPIX — Mohamed Amin and Duncan Willetts.

Quick Reference A–Z Guide
to Places and Topics of Interest